PISA

Grade Expectations

HOW MARKS AND EDUCATION POLICIES SHAPE STUDENTS' AMBITIONS

Please cite this publication as:
OECD (2012), *Grade Expectations: How Marks and Education Policies Shape Students' Ambitions*, PISA, OECD Publishing.
http://dx.doi.org/10.1787/9789264187528-en

ISBN 978-92-64-18750-4 (print)
ISBN 978-92-64-18752-8 (PDF)

Photo credits:
Getty Images © Ariel Skelley
Getty Images © Geostock
Getty Images © Jack Hollingsworth
Stocklib Image Bank © Yuri Arcurs

Corrigenda to OECD publications may be found on line at: *www.oecd.org/publishing/corrigenda*.

Foreword

The expansion of the knowledge-based economy and technological progress has created a large market of highly paid jobs for individuals who are highly skilled. Moreover, in much of the industrialised world, the demand for highly-skilled individuals is rising faster than supply, as mirrored in rising wage premia on university-level qualifications. Leveraging the talent of all individuals, whatever their social background, must therefore be an important goal for educators and policy makers alike.

This PISA report provides a first systematic attempt to examine the performance of students in school jointly with the expectations they have for their own educational future. First of all, the range of educational expectations which the report reveals is striking: in Korea, four out of five 15-year-olds expect to graduate from university, while in Latvia it is just one out of four. Second, given the changes in skill requirements in most labour-markets, and the rapidly rising number of university graduates, the educational expectations of students in school have remained surprisingly stable. Third, while, overall, performance on PISA tends to be associated with educational expectations, the data show that not all 15-year-olds with advanced knowledge and skills aspire to high levels of further education and not all 15-year-olds who aspire to a university degree possess the knowledge and skills needed to pursue such pathways successfully. Such mismatches between expectations and actual abilities can result not just in personal disappointments but also incur important economic and social costs.

While performance in school is an important factor shaping students educational expectations, there are worrying signs that other contextual factors interfere with this relationship. In most countries and economies, boys and socio-economically disadvantaged students tend to hold far less ambitious expectations than girls and socio-economically advantaged students who perform just as well.

The findings of this report have far-reaching implications. Students who hold ambitious – yet realistic – expectations about their educational prospects are more likely to put effort into their learning and make better use of the educational opportunities available to them to achieve their goals. Therefore educational expectations, in part, become self-fulfilling prophecies. Education systems need to strike a careful balance between promoting ambitious expectations among students – because the labour-market demand for high-level skills is surging and will probably continue to grow in the future – while not neglecting those students who aim for a smooth transition from upper secondary school into the labour market. School systems also need clearly marked occupational pathways and high-quality information, guidance and support so that they understand the demands of the labour market and have the kinds of skills that employers need.

Since many 15-year-old students have only limited understanding of their underlying skills and potential to succeed in higher education and in the labour market, school marks are an important source of information for students about their potential success in subsequent education. Not least, in many countries and economies, marks directly determine the educational opportunities available to students and thus contribute to students' eventual educational attainment and labour market prospects because, in many countries, student marks help to determine access to higher education.

Perhaps the most crucial finding of the report is that socio-economically advantaged students and girls are more likely to receive better marks from their teachers, even when compared to socio-economically disadvantaged students or boys who perform equally well in PISA and report similar attitudes and behaviours. What this suggests is that teachers give higher-than-expected marks to girls and socio-economically advantaged students, possibly because they tend to reward, on top of performance and the set of attitudes and behaviours that are measured by PISA, other attitudes and behaviours that girls and advantaged students are most likely to adopt. Whatever the reason, inequalities in marking practices may lead to inequalities in educational expectations, and, later, to inequalities in educational attainment and labour-market outcomes, thus perpetuating social disparities and reducing opportunities for upward mobility, especially among disadvantaged boys.

Teachers can use marking practices to positively influence their students' educational trajectories. For example, teachers can develop in-class assessments throughout the year that clearly explore student mastery of different sets of skills; and they should mark such assessments on the basis of proficiency in those specific skills, including both cognitive and non-cognitive skills. Teachers and schools can best serve their students if they use marking practices that are objective and criterion-based, whereby teachers give marks to students according to absolute levels of mastery rather than according to students' performance relative to their peers. They should also accompany quantitative marks with in-depth qualitative evaluations that explore students' progress, strengths and weaknesses, giving students the tools to develop the skills that matter for eventual success in further education and beyond.

School systems can encourage effective marking practices and align them with broader assessment policies. Because marks may ensue such important consequences, effective marking practices can promote the kinds of classroom dynamics that enhance learning. School systems can also evaluate how school marks fit with their broader assessment policies. Given that practically all

schools use marks to evaluate students, marks should be an important part of the general policy regarding assessment. An integrated policy of assessment that covers student marks and standardised assessments will highlight the different forms of assessment and the complementary nature of, for example, standardised assessments and criterion-based assessments conducted at the school level. An integrated assessment and marking policy will also give teachers more clarity on what attitudes, behaviours and mastery of skills should be rewarded through marks, and will allow students to have clearer and more specific information about their standing in the learning process and what steps they should take to enhance their learning experience. School systems should thus promote research that provides a complete picture of the assessments used in their school system, their purpose, and what schools, teachers and students are doing with this information.

Last but not least, many education systems need to address inequalities in performance that are reflected in inequalities in educational expectations. Where such inequalities are prevalent, opportunities for social mobility are limited, and societies lose potentially valuable workers to an intergenerational cycle of deprivation and low expectations. The findings from this report show that teachers reward proficiency, but they also suggest that teachers reward a large set of measureable and immeasurable student characteristics. While some of these characteristics undoubtedly promote educational success and thus, by rewarding them, teachers provide an extra set of useful information to students, other characteristics may have little to do with students' chances of completing a university degree or of excelling in the labour market. As such, inequalities in marking practices may unduly restrict the opportunities some students have to acquire high-level skills and competencies and overcome social inequality.

This report was prepared at the OECD Directorate for Education with the support of the countries and economies participating in PISA. The publication was drafted by Marilyn Achiron, Francesca Borgonovi and Guillermo Montt. Elizabeth Del Bourgo, Juliet Evans and Elisabeth Villoutreix provided editorial and administrative input for the report. Peter Vogelpoel did the typesetting and layout. Ildikó Balázsi, Michelle Bras Roth, Kwok-cheung Cheung, Poon Chew Leng, Ji Min Cho, Inge De Meyer, Ana Ferreira, María Antonieta Gutierrez, Steve May, Júlia Miklovičová, Laura Palmerio, Rachel Perkins, Ursula Schwanter, Anabela Serrão, Mojca Straus, Maree Telford, Sue Thompson and Susan Wee provided valuable input at various stages of the report. William Carbonaro, University of Notre Dame, provided critical insight. The development of the report was steered by the PISA Governing Board, which is chaired by Lorna Bertrand (United Kingdom).

The report is published on the responsibility of the Secretary-General of the OECD.

Lorna Bertrand
Chair of the PISA Governing Board

Barbara Ischinger
Director for Education, OECD

Table of Contents

BOXES

FIGURES

TABLES

Executive Summary

The expansion of the knowledge-based economy and technological progress has created a large market of highly paid jobs for individuals who are highly skilled. Individuals who attend university receive substantial economic payoffs and societies also benefit from a highly skilled workforce.

Enrolment in tertiary education has increased dramatically in the past decades: 50% or more of university-age young adults are enrolled in higher education. However, many students still do not enrol in tertiary education nor expect to complete a university degree. The fact that not all students are willing and able to attend university creates a challenge for education systems. While it is important to promote high educational expectations among students to maximise the economic opportunities available in a knowledge-based economy, it is equally important to leverage expectations and ensure that students form realistic expectations. Mismatches between expectations and actual abilities can result in economic and social costs.

Countries, and regions within countries, vary in the percentage of students who expect to complete a university degree.

In 2009, students in 21 of the 75 countries and economies that participated in the Programme for International Student Assessment (PISA) were asked about their expected educational attainment. In nine countries, over 50% of 15-year-old students expected to complete a university degree; in Korea, four out of five students expected to graduate from university. In Latvia, by contrast, one out of four students expected to graduate from university, while in Austria, Belgium (Flemish Community), Macao-China and Slovenia less than 40% did. Expectations of completing university remained relatively stable between 2003 and 2009, but Austria, Iceland, Mexico, New Zealand and Poland recorded a statistically significant increase in students' expectations of completing a university degree. These expectations did not change between 2003 and 2009 in Australia, Belgium (Flemish Community), Ireland, Korea, Latvia, Portugal and the Slovak Republic, and declined in Hungary, Italy, Hong Kong-China and Macao-China.

Students who expect to complete a university degree show significantly better performance in mathematics and reading when compared to students who do not expect to earn such a degree. However, in many countries and economies, expectations of graduating from university do not match students' performance or their education and labour-market prospects.

The difference in reading performance between students who expect to complete a university degree and those who do not is most pronounced in Australia, Austria, Belgium (Flemish Community), Croatia, Hungary and the Slovak Republic. This difference is smaller – yet still marked – in Hong Kong-China and Macao-China. While performance is closely associated with educational expectations, sizeable proportions of students hold misaligned expectations. For example, the percentage of low-performing students who expect to complete a university degree is relatively high in Australia, Ireland, Korea, Mexico, New Zealand, Singapore and Trinidad and Tobago, even though these students are less likely to enrol in higher education and complete a university degree. In contrast, a large proportion of high-performing students in Austria, Iceland, Italy and the Slovak Republic expect to finish their educational careers in upper secondary school, implying a potential loss of valuable talent to the economy and society.

Engagement with school can help to promote expectations of completing a university degree among high-performing students; it can also lead to better performance among low-performing students that, in turn, can result in a better alignment between expectations and ability.

School systems with a high percentage of low-performing students who expect to complete a university education face the challenge of improving student performance to the extent that all students who expect to pursue a university education have a good chance of completing a university degree. These school systems can capitalise on students' motivation and their intention to continue on to higher education by improving students' engagement with school, which, in turn, can lead to better performance. School systems with a comparatively large proportion of high-performing students who expect to complete, at most, an upper secondary degree should provide opportunities for these students to raise their expectations so as to avoid a potential loss of talent for the economy and society. This can also be accomplished by promoting these students' engagement with school and by ensuring that any selection into different education programmes, such as academic or vocational, is based on merit.

Systems that separate students into different types of schools provide for more realistic expectations if differentiation is based on merit; but they may create mismatched expectations or reinforce social inequalities if differentiation favours some groups over others.

Education systems that separate students into different types of schools create explicit paths that shape students' expectations of further education. In almost all of the subset of countries and economies that differentiate programmes according to their academic or non-academic orientation, students in academic programmes are significantly more likely to expect to complete a university degree. Countries that do not use differentiation have a higher percentage of students who expect to complete a university degree; and expectations grow at a faster pace than in countries that stratify their educational paths.

Many students expect to complete, at most, an upper secondary degree; and the proportion of these students is highest in countries with large shares of students who are enrolled in vocationally oriented programmes.

On average, across participating countries and economies, one out of every four students expects to complete his or her studies at the upper secondary level and, presumably, enter the labour force upon graduation. This proportion is highest in Austria, Croatia, Italy and the Slovak Republic and is lowest in Korea and Singapore. Three of the four countries with the highest proportion of students expecting to finish their educational careers upon acquiring an upper secondary degree are characterised by early differentiation of students into academically and non-academically oriented programmes, and have a comparatively large proportion of students in non-academic programmes. Upper secondary education should equip students who expect to end their schooling at that level with the skills needed for a successful transition to the labour market and civic life.

In most countries and economies, performance is only one of the factors that determine expectations: on average, girls and socio-economically advantaged students tend to hold more ambitious expectations than boys and socio-economically disadvantaged students who perform just as well.

In all countries and economies that were considered, students from disadvantaged backgrounds were less likely than their more advantaged peers to expect to complete a university degree. On average, a large fraction of socio-economic inequalities in expectations can be explained by socio-economic inequalities in performance: disadvantaged students tend to show poorer performance in reading and mathematics than their more advantaged peers. Yet in Croatia, Hungary, Iceland, Korea and Serbia, advantaged students who have the same reading and mathematics scores as disadvantaged students are over four times more likely to expect to complete a university degree than disadvantaged students. On the contrary, disadvantaged students are more likely than advantaged students to expect to complete their schooling with an upper secondary degree in all countries and economies, even after adjusting for PISA reading and mathematics scores.

In all participating countries and economies, marks are positively related to reading performance in PISA. Teachers also reward other attitudes and behaviours, such as students' approaches to learning and their reading practices.

Teachers use grades not only to provide feedback and identify whether students have mastered a set of skills, but also to communicate expectations and foster motivation in their students. Students in 18 countries and economies were asked to report what mark (grade) they received in their language-of-assessment course. Countries with specific criteria associated with each mark (e.g. "fail", "satisfactory", "good", "very good", "excellent") tend to differentiate students better than countries where a continuum of marks is possible. Although countries vary considerably in terms of their marking schemes and policies, students who score higher in the PISA reading assessment also tend to be rewarded with good marks in their language courses. This relationship is most pronounced in Hungary, Latvia, Poland and the Slovak Republic.

Teachers also generally reward attitudes, behaviours and habits that directly benefit performance: in practically all countries and economies, and particularly in Poland and the Slovak Republic, students who are able to identify effective summarising and understanding and remembering strategies also report receiving higher marks. Similarly, in seven countries and economies there is a moderate to strong relationship between students' enjoyment of reading and the marks they receive; this relationship is particularly strong in Croatia, Hungary, Latvia, Poland and Serbia.

Girls and socio-economically advantaged students are more likely to receive better marks, even when compared to boys and socio-economically disadvantaged students who perform equally well in reading and have similar attitudes and behaviours.

Girls are more likely to receive better marks than boys in most countries and economies, even when they have similar reading performance and learning habits. The exceptions to this trend are Iceland, Portugal (lower secondary), Singapore and Trinidad and Tobago, while girls are especially more likely to receive higher marks in Poland and the Slovak Republic. When comparing students of similar performance, habits and attitudes, students from socio-economically disadvantaged backgrounds are more likely to receive lower marks in most countries and economies, with the exceptions of Belgium (Flemish Community) and Croatia. This relationship is strongest in Iceland.

In many countries and economies, the marks students receive depend on the school they attend.

In nine countries and economies, students who attend higher-achieving schools receive lower marks when compared to students with similar performance and learning habits who attend poorer-performing schools. In Austria, Poland and Portugal (upper secondary), students are particularly likely to be graded in comparison to their peers. In Italy and Portugal (lower secondary), students in private schools tend to have better-than-expected marks; in Italy, such difference is substantial in quantitative terms. In Austria, Croatia and Latvia, selective schools tend to deflate grades relative to performance, possibly because of normative grading practices. For similar reasons, in at least six countries and economies, there is evidence of grade inflation in schools that cater to a relatively disadvantaged student population.

Students with higher marks are more likely to expect to complete a university degree.

Marks are positively related to the expectation of completing a university degree in all participating countries and economies, even after accounting for differences in performance in reading and mathematics and in the programme a student attends. On average across these countries, students who receive marks that are one standard deviation above the national mean are as likely to expect to earn a university degree as students who have a 40 score-point performance advantage in the PISA mathematics and reading assessments. In this context, marks may have particularly long-lasting consequences for some students, as students may interpret marks as being the best guide when choosing their path beyond school. As a result, for example, marks alone help to explain more than 25% of the relationship between expectations and gender among boys and girls who perform equally well in similar programmes.

Introduction

This introduction describes the Programme for International Student Assessment (PISA), the Educational Career questionnaire that was distributed among students with the 2009 PISA survey, and how they can be used to study students' educational career expectations and the behaviours rewarded by school systems through school marks.

OVERVIEW

Based on the wealth of information that is available in the optional PISA 2009 Educational Career questionnaire (ECQ), this report focuses on two aspects of students' educational experience that could shape how well they do at school, how much effort they put into their studies, and what lies ahead of them once compulsory education is over: educational expectations and school marks (grades).

Most countries have recorded sharp increases in average educational attainment – so much so that while, at the beginning of the 20th century, university attendance was a reality for less than 1% of the university-age population around the world, by 2010 around 20% of this age group attended tertiary education. Among OECD countries the expansion of higher education has been more pervasive still: in many OECD countries, 50% or more of university-age young adults are enrolled in higher education (OECD, 2011; Schofer and Meyer, 2005).

This report identifies students who expect to complete a university degree and discusses these expectations in light of the likelihood of attaining one. The report also explores the gender and socio-economic inequalities that may exist in educational expectations. Although having a university degree is a common way of gaining access to high-skilled occupations, many students do not enter post-secondary education. Many do not even expect to continue on to tertiary education; rather, they expect to enter the labour market after completing secondary school. This report focuses on this group of students as well, highlighting the need for school systems to provide these students with the skills needed to ease their transition onto the labour market and adult life. The students' own expectations, as well as those of their parents and peers, are key in determining whether they decide to work hard in their studies. Moreover, expectations to pursue university predict whether these students will apply for university admission and, ultimately, whether they will attend and graduate from university (Campbell, 1983; Carbonaro, 2005; Carbonaro, Ellison and Covay, 2011).

This report also focuses on a second aspect of students' educational experience: school marks. School marks are an important source of information for students about their progress and standing within the school, their abilities, and whether they have the potential to succeed in further education. Marks are also the primary reward system teachers use to guide and motivate students to perform, behave well, and have positive attitudes towards learning and habits that are conducive to learning. Marks are, however, sometimes imperfect sources of information for students, as they are prone to contextual effects, such as differences in school characteristics, and, as results from this report show, tend to favour girls and students from socio-economically advantaged backgrounds.

Acknowledging that students form their expectations based on their aspirations and the information they have on the likelihood of realising them, the final section of this report links expectations and marks. Many studies link student achievement as measured by standardised test scores with student aspirations and expectations. A study of school marks makes a stronger connection between those expectations and the incentives and information the students themselves have, and underscores the potentially long-term importance of the information captured by marks. It also highlights the challenges teachers and schools face in motivating students through the use of marks while communicating realistic expectations about their prospects.

INTRODUCTION TO PISA AND THE EDUCATIONAL CAREER QUESTIONNAIRE

The Programme for International Student Assessment (PISA), conducted by the Organisation for Economic Co-operation and Development (OECD), offers an opportunity to study patterns of educational expectations and school marks across many countries and economies. The assessment examines how well 15-year-old students are able to use the knowledge and skills they have acquired to solve standardised tasks in reading, mathematics and science as they approach the end of secondary school. It also collects contextual information about the students, their families and their schools, as well as a host of information gathered directly from parents. The PISA surveys and assessments are specifically designed and tested to ensure comparability across countries and economies.

In 2009, the PISA assessment focused on reading and gathered a rich set of information on factors potentially related to performance in this domain. Some 75 countries and economies and more than 500 000 students participated in PISA 2009. In addition to the student and school questionnaires that are distributed in every country and economy that participates in PISA, in 2009, PISA offered three optional questionnaires. Countries and economies could voluntarily disseminate a questionnaire on students' educational careers, a questionnaire on access and use of information technology, and/or a questionnaire that students could take home that would be completed by their parents. The ECQ seeks information on: students' continuity and mobility in primary and lower secondary schooling, attendance in out-of-school lessons, the marks students receive in the test language course, and their expectations of future educational attainment.[1]

Twenty-one countries and economies distributed the ECQ: 14 OECD countries (Australia, Austria, Belgium,[2] Hungary, Iceland, Ireland, Italy, Korea, Mexico, New Zealand, Poland, Portugal, the Slovak Republic and Slovenia) and seven partner countries and economies (Croatia, Hong Kong-China, Latvia, Macao-China, Serbia, Singapore and Trinidad and Tobago). Australia, Hong Kong-China, Korea and Slovenia did not include the question on school marks and are thus excluded from the analyses that involve marks. Portugal has different systems across ISCED levels, so results for Portugal are separated in analyses that involve marks. In 2009, Italy and Mexico

sampled a large population of students to have a sample that is representative at the regional level, so regional results for Italy and Mexico are also presented in the tables.

Because only 21 countries and economies provided information on students' expectations and 17 on student marks, the results in this report cannot be easily generalised to other countries in the OECD area or to countries and economies that did not distribute the ECQ. Caution must be taken when using the results for this limited set of countries and economies to draw conclusions regarding student expectations and school marks in other countries and economies.

The report highlights country/economy-level results and comparisons as well as within-country differences across Italian and Mexican regions. Regional results are included, whenever possible, to paint a more accurate picture of the factors that shape student outcomes and how individual teacher- and system-wide education policies promote better skills acquisition and expectations of further education. In many countries, labour markets follow region-specific or state-specific patterns, and Italy and Mexico are two such cases. Educational expectations in these countries, therefore, not only reflect the academic performance of students and what happens in schools, but also students' perceptions of the demand for skills and career opportunities that are available in their local/regional labour market. Moreover, in these countries, state and regional educational authorities play an important role in determining how schools are organised and how nationwide policies are implemented, for example with respect to marking schemes. As a result, region- and state-specific results can be of greater use for these countries in their efforts to help students make the most of their potential.

Notes

1. The Educational Career questionnaire for PISA 2009 is available in Annex A and can be downloaded at: *http://pisa2009.acer.edu.au/downloads.php.*

2. The French and German-speaking Communities of Belgium administered the Educational Career questionnaire, but chose to withdraw their data from this report because some features of their secondary and tertiary education systems could not be adequately reflected in the analysis.

References

Campbell, R. (1983), "Status Attainment Research: End of the Beginning or Beginning of the End?", *Sociology of Education,* Vol. 56, No. 1, pp. 47-62.

Carbonaro, W. (2005), "Tracking, Students' Effort, and Academic Achievement", *Sociology of Education,* Vol. 78, No. 1, pp. 27-49.

Carbonaro, W., **B.J. Ellison** and **E. Covay** (2011), "Gender Inequalities in the College Pipeline", *Social Science Research,* Vol. 40, No. 1, pp. 120-135.

OECD (2011), *Education at a Glance 2011: OECD Indicators*, OECD Publishing.

Schofer, E. and **J. Meyer** (2005), "The Worldwide Expansion of Higher Education in the Twentieth Century", *American Sociological Review,* Vol. 70, No. 6, pp. 898-920.

1

What Do Students Expect to Do After Upper Secondary School?

This chapter identifies the factors that shape 15-year-old students' expectations of further education, including academic performance, the structural particularities of the education system, gender and socio-economic background. It also compares students' expectations across countries and economies, and by the type of education programme in which students are enrolled. The problems associated with a misalignment between expectations and actual performance are discussed, as are students' expectations of social mobility.

Students' expectations of further education not only reflect academic success and students' skills, but also creates the conditions that promote academic excellence and skills acquisition. In particular, students who expect to complete a university degree are more likely to choose more demanding courses and invest greater effort in school than students who expect to complete their studies with lower qualifications. Similarly, students who hold high expectations are more likely than those who do not to complement their school work by engaging in academically oriented activities during their free time. Students' expectations function, in part, as self-fulfilling prophecies, as the effort students invest to meet their expectations pays off. When comparing students of similar socio-economic backgrounds and academic achievement, students who expect to graduate from university are more likely to complete these degrees than their peers who do not hold such high expectations (Campbell, 1983; Carbonaro et al., 2011; Morgan, 2005; Perna, 2000; Sewell et al., 2003).

While students' expectations and aspirations are closely linked, they are conceptually distinct. Aspirations of further education represent an upper limit of what students perceive will be their future, given that they reflect the educational level students *would like* to attain, regardless of their ability to do so and of any institutional, social and economic constraints they may face (Hanson, 1994; Saha, 1997). Expectations, on the other hand, reflect more realistic assessments of students' future opportunities because they take into account students' self-perceptions of their underlying abilities and potential, as well as the actual circumstances in which they operate (Goyette, 2008). Thus, even though all students may aspire to attain a university degree, not all will expect to receive that degree because expectations consider the likelihood of earning it.

Academic performance is intrinsically linked with expectations of further education: students who are proficient feel confident that they will be able to succeed in further academic studies. At the same time, students who expect to complete a university degree are more likely to put greater effort in their studies and be confident that they can master material while at school. As a result, they become more academically proficient.

Although this may be the general trend, the findings in this report indicate that not all high-performing students hold equally ambitious expectations; and that some low-performing students may have higher expectations than their better-performing peers. Most important, this report finds that institutional, social and economic constraints as well as education policies may help shape students' expectations of further education. For example, high-performing students who have positive relations with their teachers and positive attitudes towards school are especially likely to expect to pursue further studies and complete a university degree.

Other factors that shape students' expectations include people close to the student, such as peers, family members and teachers, past academic achievement, the degree of selectivity of tertiary education institutions, the direct financial and opportunity costs of attending tertiary education, access to credit or other forms of financial resources, the returns associated with different educational choices and the rigidity of the education system, which may restrict access to some educational opportunities to only those students who have followed a particular path through their education. The variety of these factors helps to explain how and why the expectations of 15-year-old students vary so considerably both within and across countries (Buchmann and Dalton, 2002; Mateju et al., 2007; Sewell et al., 2003).

A study of students' expectations reveals patterns in students' decision making and in their eventual participation, or non-participation, in higher education (Morgan, 2005). The link between expectations and student performance helps policy makers to formulate policy and direct resources not only towards developing skills but also towards providing information and incentives so that the stock of potential skills is fully realised and effectively used. Countries where large proportions of poorly performing students hold high expectations should capitalise on the willingness of students to improve their skills; and education systems should consequently ensure that these students leave upper secondary school with the tools to benefit from opportunities to enrol in higher education. On the other hand, countries with large proportions of high-performing students who do not expect to complete a university degree could suffer a loss of talent and should thus ensure, through their education policies, that these students are offered help in exploiting their skills. This help can be in the form of in-school information campaigns on education and career opportunities and of promoting the development of students' non-cognitive skills, motivation and attitudes towards learning (Hanson, 1994).

If expectations help to motivate students to invest more in learning, a study of inequalities in expectations is also a study of the inequalities underlying the motivations to learn and achieve. The results from this report can thus be used to develop measures to reduce inequalities in educational opportunities related to gender and socio-economic background before they become actual inequalities in performance and achievement.

Education systems not only have a duty to provide learning opportunities to all students, promote civic values, disseminate a common knowledge base, and help students to fulfil their full potential, they also play a crucial role in channelling skills and talent into the labour market and helping young people make the transition from adolescence into adulthood. By effectively managing students' education and career aspirations and expectations through the institutional, social and economic conditions that shape them, education systems can ensure that students' skills and interests find a suitable match in the economy. School systems must strike a careful balance between creating high expectations to motivate students and meet the demands of an economy that needs an increasingly skilled workforce and ensuring that students have the skills and competencies required to fulfil such expectations. Better matches between students' expectations and their ability to meet them will reduce the social and personal costs associated with unfulfilled expectations, whether those of low-performing students who expect to complete a university degree or those of talented students who do not expect to do so (Baird et al., 2008; Kerckhoff, 1976). Education systems can also promote social mobility and greater gender equality, although teachers, school principals and educators are often so concentrated on the core aim of helping students to learn, that they may forget their equally important task of helping students to develop a fair assessment of their future opportunities.

Performance is only one of many factors that shape students' expectations. Cross-national research has identified some characteristics of education systems that motivate students so that they hold high expectations about their futures or that tamp those expectations (Kerckhoff, 1995).

The most effective way through which education systems can influence student expectations is by creating structural mechanisms that make it easy or difficult for students to pursue different education pathways. Education systems can also channel expectations by providing information on the different opportunities available and the expected labour-market consequences of choosing a particular pathway. Mateju (2007), Buchmann and Dalton (2002) and Kerckhoff (1995; 2000), for example, illustrate how education systems that provide clear "institutional information" to students about their prospects in further education succeed in creating more realistic aspirations and expectations, and ensure that there is a solid link between students' performance and their expectations of further education. An example of institutional information is the separation of students into different educational institutions or different classes through tracking or streaming policies. In these cases, students' paths through education are clearly determined by the type of institution or class to which students were allocated, largely on the basis of their academic record. The literature on the subject suggests that students in stratified systems are more likely to have concrete information about the opportunities available to them and are much more likely to hold realistic expectations about their futures in education because the opportunities available to students follow the type of track, stream or ability group to which students are allocated.

Other forms of institutional information that education systems may provide to students to help them form realistic expectations are standardised tests and assessments that base their scales on students' likelihood of being able to advance along different educational paths. Although these forms of institutional information reduce the influence of peers, parents, teachers and background in forming expectations, inequalities in expectations may remain if access to this information and placement in different tracks vary by background characteristics (Buchmann and Dalton, 2002; Buchmann and Park, 2009; McDaniel, 2010; Morgan, 2005; Useem, 1992). Results from this report show that tracking or streaming, as a form of information, is a strong predictor of student expectations. This is not the case, however, for standardised testing.

School systems should ensure that all students are ready and able to make the most of their skills when they finish compulsory schooling. They can do so by creating conditions so that students develop expectations that are high enough to maintain student motivation to learn, but that are also realistic enough so that students avoid pursuing careers that are not aligned with their abilities. Similarly, school systems should allow talent to flourish, so that the highest-achieving students consider university-level education as a viable opportunity. Promoting expectations should be a two-step process: first, ensure that students are academically ready to pursue high-level education careers; then, once students are university-ready, strive to raise their expectations. School systems should also provide attractive and viable alternative pathways for those students who, as a result of their academic potential or their interests, prefer to end their educational careers after finishing upper secondary school (see Box 1.1 for the definitions of university and upper secondary educational expectations used in this report).

EDUCATIONAL EXPECTATIONS ACROSS COUNTRIES AND ECONOMIES

Enrolment in tertiary education increased dramatically during the 20th century. In 1900, fewer than 1% of university-age people around the world were enrolled in higher education; by 2010 around 20% of people in that age group were enrolled, and many industrialised countries have enrolment rates above 50% (OECD, 2011a; Schofer and Meyer, 2005). Furthermore, a tertiary degree has become an important antecedent for access to prestigious occupations and high social status. The expansion of the knowledge-based economy and technological progress have created a large market of highly paid jobs for those individuals who have the required high levels of skills (Arum and Roksa, 2011; Autor et al., 2003; Brand and Xie, 2010; Labaree, 1997; Rosenbaum and Kariya, 1989; Torche, 2010). Yet although enrolment in tertiary education has increased dramatically, many students still do not enrol in tertiary education nor expect to complete a university degree; instead, they expect to enter the labour force after finishing their upper secondary studies. This group of students benefits the most when their schools give them the tools to smooth their transition into the labour market.

For students to access the benefits of a tertiary education, they must first aspire to attain such a degree and, more important, expect one. Yet these benefits are by no means assured: social prestige is not accessible to all, and an economy cannot function only on the basis of high-skilled jobs. An economy may waste valuable resources in overeducating its population or in educating those who are less likely to obtain a university degree because it is training its people for an economy that is not ready or able to receive them (Collins, 1979). Conversely, many students expect to finish their education in upper secondary school, and an education system may lose talent if high-performing students are not encouraged to continue their education after completing compulsory education (Hanson, 1994).

This section analyses the distribution of expectations across the 21 countries and economies that implemented the PISA 2009 Educational Career questionnaire (ECQ) to evaluate whether student expectations are aligned with their academic potential and explore whether, within countries and economies, those students who expect to complete a university degree are those most likely to do so. The analyses developed in the following sections shed new light on whether some school systems fail to mobilise their full human potential, whether some students hold expectations that do not match their academic performance, as measured by their scores in standardised assessments, and whether disparities in expectations may prevent or promote social mobility and equity in the labour market. They also identify those students who expect to enter the labour force upon finishing their upper secondary schooling.

More concretely, the following sections answer the question: which students expect to earn a university degree and which students do *not* hold that expectation? To answer this question, students' academic characteristics, including their proficiency in reading and mathematics and their current educational standing, as well as background characteristics, such as gender and socio-economic status, are considered. This report acknowledges that information is crucial for students to form realistic expectations and recognises that schools and education systems play a key role in providing students with accurate information about their choices.

From the perspective of the education system, the report asks: are those who expect to attend university more likely to be accepted into and enrol in higher education and eventually graduate? By comparing the distribution of expectations across education systems, this chapter examines policies that can improve the likelihood that students hold realistic expectations about their futures in education. Results suggest that all countries examined report some misalignment between students' expectations and the opportunities available to them, although the degree of that misalignment varies widely.

Box 1.1 What are university and upper secondary school expectations?

This report focuses on students' expectations to complete a university degree and their expectations to end their formal schooling after completing upper secondary school. The terms "university" and "upper secondary school" are used to refer to the more formal and internationally comparable International Standard Classification of Education (ISCED) of ISCED level 5A or 6 and ISCED level 3 A/B/C, respectively (OECD, 1999).

ISCED level 5A programmes are tertiary education programmes (normally requiring the successful completion of ISCED level 3A, 3B or 4) that have a cumulative theoretical duration of at least four years, are theory- or research-based, and provide access to high-skilled professions. ISCED level 6 programmes are devoted to advanced study and original research and lead to the award of an advanced research classification. In this report, the completion of ISCED level 5A or 6 are referred to as completing a "university degree".

This report also focuses on students who expect to finish their educational careers after the completion of ISCED level 3 (of type A, B or C). ISCED level 3 degrees correspond to upper secondary education, and entrance into this level typically requires some nine years of full-time education, beginning with primary education (ISCED level 1), and the successful completion of lower secondary education (ISCED level 2). In this report, the completion of ISCED level 3 is referred to as completing an "upper secondary degree". Because students are asked to report on the education level they expect to complete, in certain countries completing ISCED 3 may be achieved by completing upper secondary school or by passing free examinations without school-attendance requirements.

Annex A provides the questionnaire about expectations that was disseminated among students. Each country that distributed the Educational Career questionnaire replaced each ISCED category with the local name of the level. For ISCED 5A or 6, for example, Mexico used "Licenciatura, Maestría o Doctorado" and Singapore used "University education and beyond".

Source: OECD (1999).

Expectations of completing a university degree

Individuals receive substantial economic benefits from attending university. On average, individuals who hold university degrees have better prospects in the labour market than their less-educated peers. They command higher wages and are less likely to suffer from unemployment, particularly long-term unemployment. Students reported on their expectations in the middle of the 2008 financial and economic crisis. At that time, unemployment rates in OECD countries increased dramatically among those with no higher that an upper secondary education, while the risk of unemployment was comparatively low among those with a university degree. In addition, university-educated individuals could expect to earn over 50% more than individuals with only an upper secondary education (OECD, 2011a).

Higher education not only benefits those individuals who attend, but also society more widely (Rosenbaum and Kariya, 1989). This is why, in many countries, public funds and incentives have been put in place to promote participation in tertiary education. In 2009, the European Commission estimated that towards 2020, job creation will be concentrated in the service sector, with losses expected in the manufacturing and primary sectors. The proportion of jobs requiring high levels of education should rise from about a quarter of all available jobs to about one-third, an increase that will be matched by a sharp decline in the share of jobs requiring low levels of education. Projections highlight the importance of ensuring that students are willing and able to attend university so that the growing demand for high-level skills can be met (Commission of the European Communities, 2009).

Although the proportion of university graduates has increased considerably over the past few decades and is bound to increase further in the coming decades, not all students are willing and able to enter tertiary education. Education systems must strike a careful balance between encouraging students to have high expectations for themselves, to maintain their motivation to strive for excellence, and being realistic about the likelihood that individual students will fulfil those expectations. Most important, school systems must ensure that those students who hold high expectations are "university-ready", to minimise costs associated with remedial education and failure to complete a degree. In the United States, for example, at least 30% of students who enter higher education must take remedial courses so that they can continue to pursue a university education (Bettinger and Long, 2009; Wiley et al., 2010). Also, systems must ensure that there are attractive pathways into the labour market for students who do not expect to continue in education after finishing their upper secondary degrees.

In 2009, students in 21 PISA-participating countries and economies were asked whether they expected to complete a university degree. University degrees include liberal arts and professional degrees, but not degrees from technical or vocational tertiary education institutions.[1] These expectations can be compared over time as students who took part in the PISA 2003 survey were asked similar questions.

Countries and economies, and regions within countries, vary in the percentage of students who expect to complete a university degree. Whereas in Latvia relatively few – one in four – 15-year-old students expect to complete a university degree, in Korea the great majority of students – four out of five – expect to do so. Of the 21 countries and economies that distributed the ECQ in 2009, in 9 of them over 50% of 15-year-old students expected to complete a university degree. These expectations are highest in Korea (81%) and exceed 60% in Australia, Singapore and Trinidad and Tobago. They are lowest in Latvia (25%) and lower than 40% in Austria, Belgium (Flemish Community), Macao-China and Slovenia (Figure 1.1). Since 2003, Austria, Iceland, Mexico, New Zealand and Poland have recorded a statistically significant increase in student expectations of completing a university degree.[2] The growth is especially strong in New Zealand and Poland (14 and 11 percentage points, respectively), and statistically significant, but smaller in size (less than 10 percentage points) in Austria, Iceland and Mexico (Figure 1.2). Students' expectations of completing a university degree did not change in Australia, Belgium (Flemish Community), Ireland, Korea, Latvia, Portugal and the Slovak Republic, and have declined in Hong Kong-China, Hungary, Italy and Macao-China.

▪ Figure 1.1 ▪

Percentage of students who expect to complete a university degree

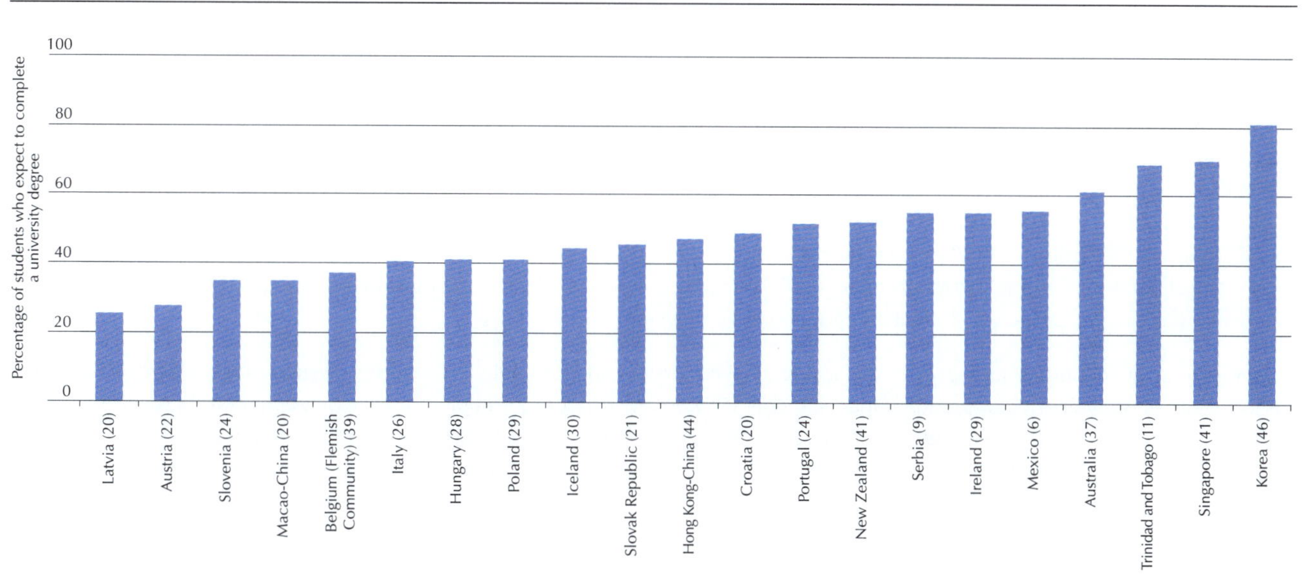

Note: The number indicated between brackets is the percentage of students performing at or above proficiency Level 4 in reading literacy.
Countries are sorted in ascending order of the percentage of students expecting to complete a university degree.
Source: Table B1.1.
StatLink http://dx.doi.org/10.1787/888932733279

▪ Figure 1.2 ▪

Change in the percentage of students who expect to complete a university degree between 2003 and 2009

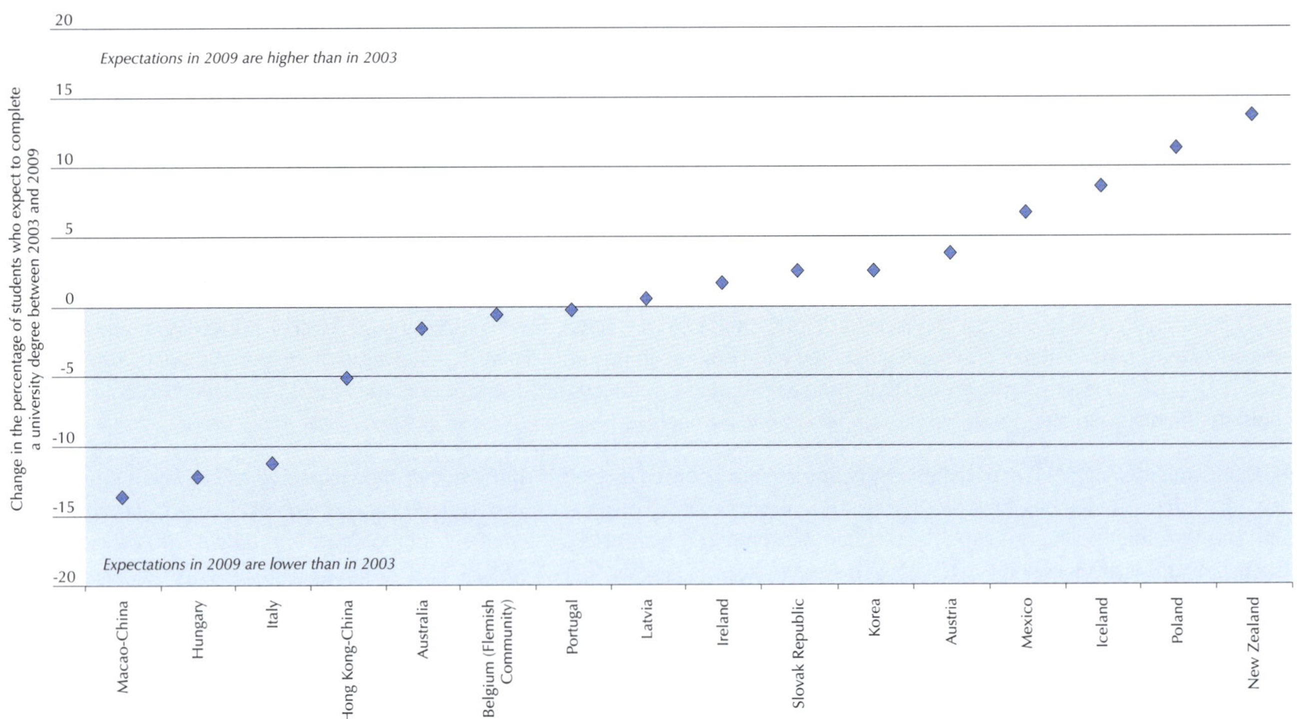

Countries are sorted in ascending order of the change in the percentage of students expecting to complete a university degree between 2003 and 2009.
Source: Table B1.1.
StatLink http://dx.doi.org/10.1787/888932733298

The percentage of students who expect to complete a university degree must be interpreted in the context of who these students are. Ideally, these should be the students who are most likely to fulfil this expectation, so that students who are highly proficient expect to attain a university education and not end their schooling at a lower level. The next sections contextualise expectations of further education and illustrate the strong association between students' expectations and their academic performance. They also identify countries and economies in which sizeable proportions of students expect to complete a university degree despite poor performance in school, and countries and economies where sizeable proportions of high-achieving students do not expect to complete a university degree. By doing so, the report aims to identify some policy levers countries can use to ensure that all students' skills are developed and used effectively.

University expectations by reading performance

Because of the selective nature of tertiary education and its academic demands, students with higher academic achievement in lower and upper secondary school are more likely to gain access to, enrol in and later succeed in higher education; in other words, "university-ready" students are those most likely to succeed in higher education (Carbonaro et al., 2011; Hanson, 1994; OECD, 2010a; Sewell et al., 2003). School systems looking to improve the alignment of their students' expectations and the likelihood of meeting those expectations should make sure that students who expect to complete university have the skills that are required to do so. Equally, school systems should promote high expectations among high-performing students to reduce the loss of talent that can result when highly proficient students do not complete university.

In general, in all countries and economies, students who expect to complete a university degree show significantly better performance in mathematics and reading than students who do not expect to complete such a degree. The difference in reading performance is most pronounced – greater than 90 points – in Australia, Austria, Belgium (Flemish Community), Croatia, Hungary and the Slovak Republic. This difference is smaller – yet still marked and corresponding to more than 50 score points in the reading assessment – in Hong Kong-China and Macao-China (Table B1.2).[3]

In all countries and economies that offer both ISCED A and ISCED B/C programmes to 15-year-old students, differences in performance between the students who do and do not expect a university degree capture the differences between ISCED A and ISCED B/C students. In most countries and economies, the differences in performance between those who do and do not expect a university degree are attenuated within ISCED programme categories (Table B1.2).

In Austria, Belgium (Flemish Community), Croatia and Hungary, among students in ISCED B/C programmes there is no significant difference in performance between the students who expect a university degree and those who do not. Although these are countries where few ISCED B/C students expect to attend university, this signals that the information provided by academic performance does not influence the expectations of students in B/C type programmes and that students in these programmes take other elements into account when setting their expectations. Other school-related factors that may influence students' expectations of attending university include the information they receive in school regarding their performance, such as school marks (these issues are discussed in further detail in Chapter 3).

However, in many countries and economies, a large proportion of poor-performing students expects to complete a university degree. PISA classifies student performance according to several proficiency levels, based on the complexity of the tasks they are able to complete in reading, mathematics and science. Students who expect to complete a university degree should be able to perform complex tasks; students unable to perform more than the baseline tasks would probably find it difficult to succeed in university (for a description of the competencies related to each proficiency level, see Box 1.2).

In the context of this report, low-performing students are students who score at or below PISA proficiency Level 2 in reading and mathematics. Level 2 is the level at which students begin to demonstrate literacy in reading or mathematics. Countries vary in the proportion of students who do not have this baseline proficiency. Because of their poorer performance, these students have a lower-than-average likelihood of entering university and ultimately succeeding in it, compared to students who perform at higher proficiency levels. Countries and economies that have a sizeable proportion of low-performing students who, nonetheless, hold high expectations, may incur high economic and social costs as these students try to follow a very difficult path for which they are not adequately equipped. More important, the economy and society pay a high price if a significant percentage of students enters university but fails to earn a degree or learn new skills. Employers in such countries may be unable to find the vocational or technical skills needed for jobs that do not require university-level qualifications.

Conversely, students who perform at PISA proficiency Level 4 or above in reading or mathematics can handle complex literacy tasks and will have comparatively less difficulty in succeeding in university. Countries and economies vary in the proportion of students who can handle the kinds of complex tasks that are commonly part of a university education (Figure 1.3).

▪ Figure 1.3 ▪

Percentage of students at or below PISA proficiency Level 2 and students at or above PISA proficiency Level 4 in reading literacy

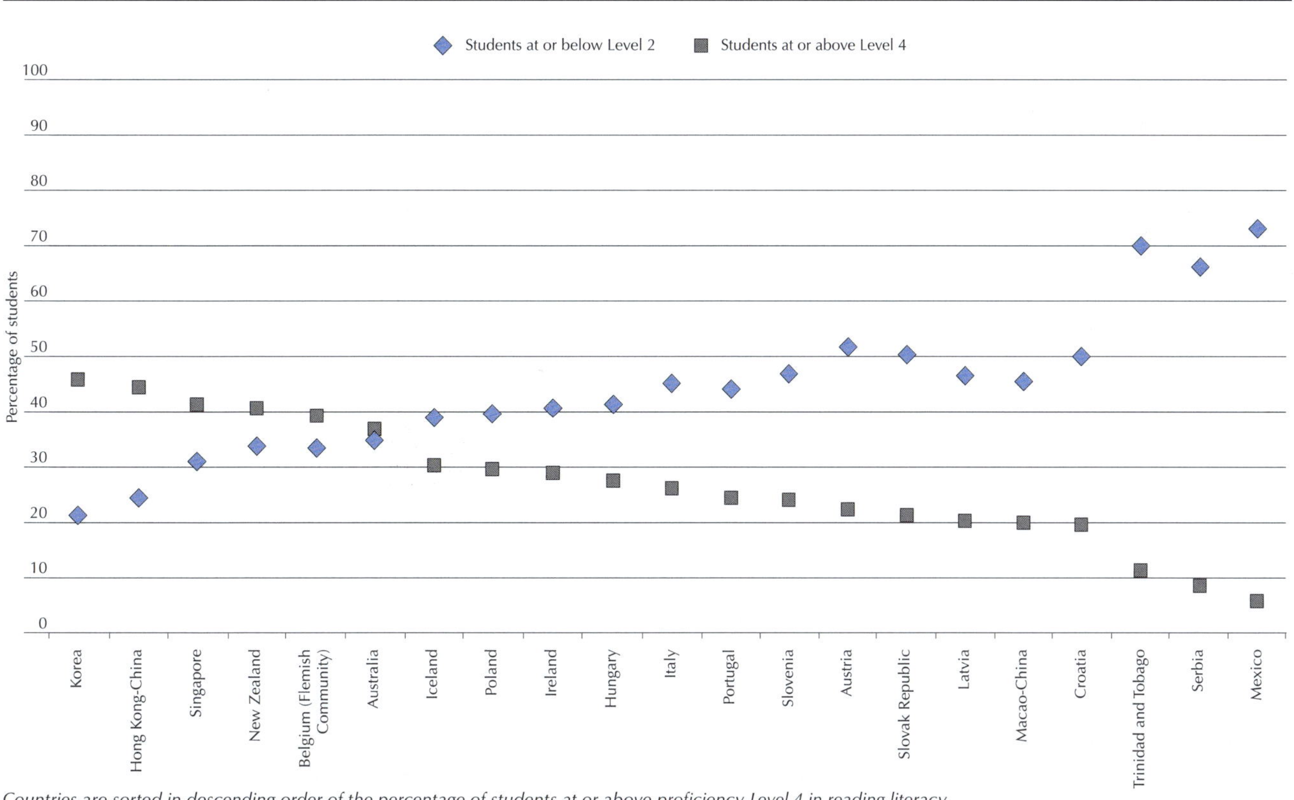

Countries are sorted in descending order of the percentage of students at or above proficiency Level 4 in reading literacy.
Source: Table B1.4.
StatLink http://dx.doi.org/10.1787/888932733317

Box 1.2 Proficiency levels in the PISA 2009 reading assessment

PISA provides an overall reading literacy scale which has a mean of 500 and a standard deviation of 100 for OECD countries in 2000. To help in interpreting what students' scores mean in substantive terms, the scale is divided into proficiency levels, and descriptions are generated based on the skills and knowledge required to complete the tasks at each level. In 2009, seven levels of reading proficiency were generated: Level 1b is the lowest described level, then Level 1a, Level 2, Level 3 and so on up to Level 6, which describes readers at the highest level identified by PISA.

Level 2 – Baseline proficiency level

Students proficient at Level 2 on the reading literacy scale are capable of tasks such as locating information that meets several conditions, making comparisons or contrasts around a single feature, working out what a well-defined part of a text means, even when the information is not prominent, and making connections between the text and personal experience. Some tasks at this level require students to locate one or more pieces of information which may need to be inferred and may need to meet several conditions. Others require recognising the main idea in a text, understanding relationships, or construing meaning within a limited part of the text when the information is not prominent and the reader must make low-level inferences. Tasks at this level may involve comparisons or contrasts based on a single feature in the text. Typical reflective tasks at this level require students to make a comparison or several connections between the text and outside knowledge, by drawing on personal experience and attitudes. Level 2 can be considered a baseline level of proficiency at which students begin to demonstrate the reading literacy competencies that will enable them to participate effectively and productively in life.

Across OECD countries, more than four in five students (81%) are proficient at Level 2 or higher.

Level 4 – Good level of proficiency

Students proficient at Level 4 on the reading literacy scale are capable of difficult reading tasks, such as locating embedded information, construing meaning from nuances of language, and critically evaluating a text. Tasks at this level that involve retrieving information require students to locate and organise several pieces of embedded information; some tasks require interpreting the meaning of nuances of language in a section of text by taking into account the text as a whole. Other interpretative tasks require understanding and applying categories in an unfamiliar context. Reflective tasks at this level require readers to use formal or public knowledge to hypothesise about or critically evaluate a text. Readers must demonstrate an accurate understanding of long or complex texts whose content or form may be unfamiliar.

Across OECD countries, 28% of PISA 2009 students are proficient at Level 4 or higher.

For more detailed definitions of PISA proficiency levels, see OECD (2010), *PISA 2009 Results: What Students Know and Can Do (Volume I),* PISA, OECD Publishing, pp. 49-53.

Source: OECD (2010b).

The percentage of low-performing students who expect to complete a university degree is relatively high in Australia, Ireland, Korea, Mexico, Serbia, Singapore and Trinidad and Tobago. In Korea, for example, 52% of students who performed at or below proficiency Level 2 in the PISA 2009 reading assessment expect to complete a university degree. In Mexico and Singapore, around 45%, and in Trinidad and Tobago as much as 60%, of low-performing students expect to complete a university degree. In Australia and Ireland, around one in three students who perform poorly expects to earn a university degree (Figure 1.4).

Another sign of misaligned expectations are high-performing students who do not expect to complete a university degree. These students are likely to succeed in completing earning this degree and their low expectations may result in a loss of talent for an economy (Hanson, 1994; OECD, 2012a). These are students who perform at or above proficiency Level 4 in the PISA 2009 reading assessment but do not expect to continue their education after finishing upper secondary education. This group is relatively large in Austria, Hong Kong-China, Iceland and Italy where more than 10% of students who perform at above proficiency Level 4 do not expect to continue in schooling after graduating from upper secondary education. As will be discussed below, Austria has a school system that differentiates students at an early age in academic or vocational programmes in secondary education. In Austria, high-performing students with low expectations may be enrolled in ISCED B/C programmes and thus dissuaded from completing a university degree. For high-performing students with low expectations who are enrolled in ISCED A programmes at the secondary level, such as those in Iceland and Italy, their low expectations may be the result of a lack of information about their own potential, or they may have vocational interests that lead them away from a university degree. This kind of loss of talent is relatively rare in Croatia, Korea, Mexico, Poland, Serbia, Singapore, Slovenia and Trinidad and Tobago, where fewer than 5% of students who perform at proficiency Level 4 do not expect to continue on to post-secondary education.

▪ Figure 1.4 ▪

Percentage of low-performing students who expect to complete a university degree and percentage of high-performing students who expect to complete at most an upper secondary level degree

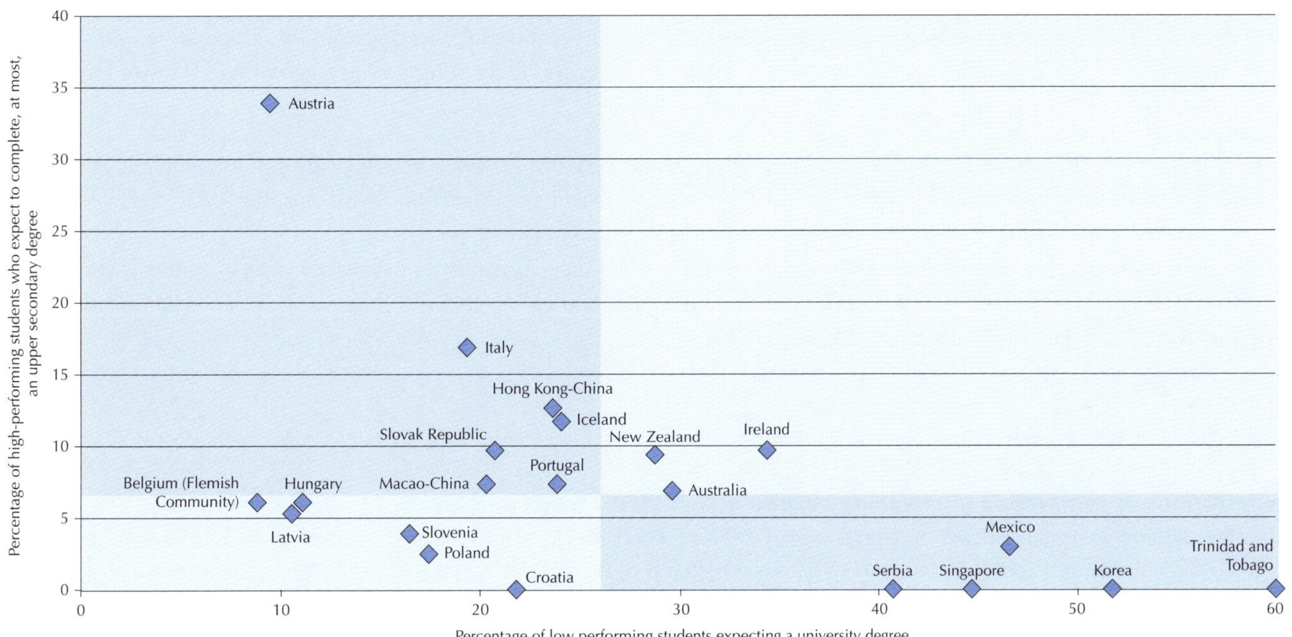

Notes: High-performing students are those at or above proficiency Level 4 in reading performance.
Low-performing students are those at or below proficiency Level 2 in reading performance.
Lines dividing the quadrants are the country/economy averages.
Estimates for Croatia, Korea, Serbia, Singapore and Trinidad and Tobago are not distinguishable from zero.
Source: Table B1.4.
StatLink http://dx.doi.org/10.1787/888932733336

Combining the percentage of low-performing students who expect to complete a university degree and the percentage of high-performing students who do not expect to do so can be used as an indicator of the overall level of misalignment between students' expectations and abilities in a country or economy. Belgium (Flemish Community), Hungary and Latvia have the lowest levels of misalignment. In these countries, fewer than 20% of low- and high-performing students hold expectations of further education that do not match their reading and mathematics skills.

The different quadrants in Figure 1.4 highlight different policy challenges for countries and economies. School systems with a high percentage of low-performing students who expect to complete a university education (lower right quadrant) need to improve student performance among low-performing ambitious students so that all students who expect to pursue a university education have a good chance of succeeding at that level of education. These are the school systems of Korea, Mexico, Serbia, Singapore and Trinidad and Tobago. They should capitalise on students' motivation and their intention to continue on to higher education. In most countries and economies, student engagement is a good predictor of whether low-performing students can improve their reading performance. Similarly, higher expectations among poor performers, which are implicit when these students follow an academically-oriented curriculum, are also related to improvements in performance (Table B1.6). Thus, countries that seek to capitalise on their students' high expectations can do so by promoting students' engagement with school; and schools can encourage higher expectations among their students by providing them with more demanding and academically oriented courses.

School systems with a comparatively large proportion of high-performing students who expect to complete, at most, an upper secondary degree (upper left quadrant) should provide opportunities for these students to raise their expectations. These countries include, most notably, Austria and Italy, where more than 30% and 15% of high-performing students, respectively, expect to finish their education at upper secondary school. These school systems can promote higher expectations among their high-performing students by improving these students' engagement with school and ensuring that placement in academic or vocational programmes is based on merit (Table B1.7). Promoting higher expectations among high-performing students is particularly important considering that it is these students who are most likely to succeed in higher education (Box 1.3).

Box 1.3 **How PISA students do ten years after the assessment**

Canada is one of the few countries that implemented a longitudinal follow-up among students who participated in PISA in 2000. Canadian data can therefore be used to examine the education and labour-market outcomes of students performing at different proficiency levels in PISA 2000. The most striking result is that students who performed at high levels when they were 15 were substantially more likely to enter and graduate from university than students who performed at lower levels in the PISA test.

Results from the Canadian follow-ups of the PISA 2000 student cohort also reveal how educational attainment is strongly associated with improvements in reading proficiency. Participation in some form of formal post-secondary education is consistently and substantially related to improvements in reading skills between the ages of 15 and 24. Because Canada is an education system that is highly flexible and allows students to enter university after they have had work experience, students who may be poor performers at age 15 but have the motivation and will to improve their skills can enter university and improve their skills later on in their lives (OECD, 2012b).

Source: OECD (2012b).

Expectations of completing a university degree across ISCED types and levels

Education systems are organised and structured around different criteria that generally match the society's values, ideals and traditions. One key feature that distinguishes education systems is whether they separate students at an early age into vocational or academic schools, or whether they have a comprehensive approach to education in which all students receive similar instruction, at least until they are 15 years old (*PISA 2009 Results: What Makes a School Successful* [OECD, 2010c] includes a comprehensive discussion of the rationale and modes of differentiation across school systems; see, in particular, Chapter 3). The countries and economies that distributed the ECQ in 2009 can be classified into three groups, defined according to the kinds of differentiation policies they adopt. In Austria, Belgium, Hungary, Singapore, the Slovak Republic and Trinidad and Tobago, differentiation into different types of schools occurs before students are 13 years old. Differentiation occurs between the ages of 13 and 15 in Croatia, Italy, Korea and Slovenia. The remaining set of countries and economies, which includes Australia, Hong Kong-China, Iceland, Ireland, Latvia, Macao-China, Mexico, New Zealand, Poland and Portugal, has a more comprehensive approach to education, whereby they do not differentiate students across different programmes, or do so at age 15 or later (see Table IV.3.2a in OECD, 2010c).

Education systems that separate students into different types of programmes generally create explicit paths that lead students to specific education outcomes. In these systems, students who attend academically-oriented schools receive an education that aims to prepare them for university. Students in vocational schools, on the other hand, not only do not receive such an education, but their secondary school degree may not allow them to continue their studies into higher education, either because this transition is not legally possible or because it is difficult and discouraged in practice. Tracking or streaming systems give students a strong, reliable and credible signal about their expected paths through education and their career prospects, strongly influencing their expectations and aspirations. In fact, differentiation is the most important school-level factor influencing student expectations. In education systems that separate students into different types of schools, students' expectations are more realistic than in systems that have a comprehensive approach to schooling at the primary and lower secondary levels (Buchmann and Dalton, 2002; Buchmann and Park, 2009; Kerckhoff, 2000; Mateju et al., 2007; McDaniel, 2010; Rosenbaum, 2001; Turner, 1960).

On average, countries that do not use differentiation have a higher percentage of students who expect to complete a university degree, and expectations have grown at a faster pace than in countries that stream students onto different pathways through education (Figure 1.5). After accounting for long-term trends in enrolment, the overall level of expectations is almost 8 percentage points lower in countries that stream students before the age of 13 and 3 percentage points lower in countries that differentiate students before the age of 15, when compared to countries with more comprehensive approaches to schooling. Similarly, in countries that differentiate students before the age of 13, expectations have risen at a slower rate (around 7 percentage points between 2003 and 2009), as have expectations in education systems that separate students before the age of 15 (by around 9 percentage points), than in countries with comprehensive systems.[4] Similarly, education systems that use differentiation also have, on average, lower graduation rates from ISCED 5A programmes.

In almost all of the subset of countries and economies that differentiate programmes according to their academic or non-academic orientation, either within or between schools (that is, school systems in which at least 8% of students are in ISCED A or ISCED B/C-type programmes[5]), students in academic programmes are significantly more likely to expect to complete a university degree. This difference is most marked in Croatia, where there is a 57 percentage-point difference between the expectations of earning a

▪ Figure 1.5 ▪

Average percentage of students who expect to complete a university degree in school systems with and without horizontal differentiation

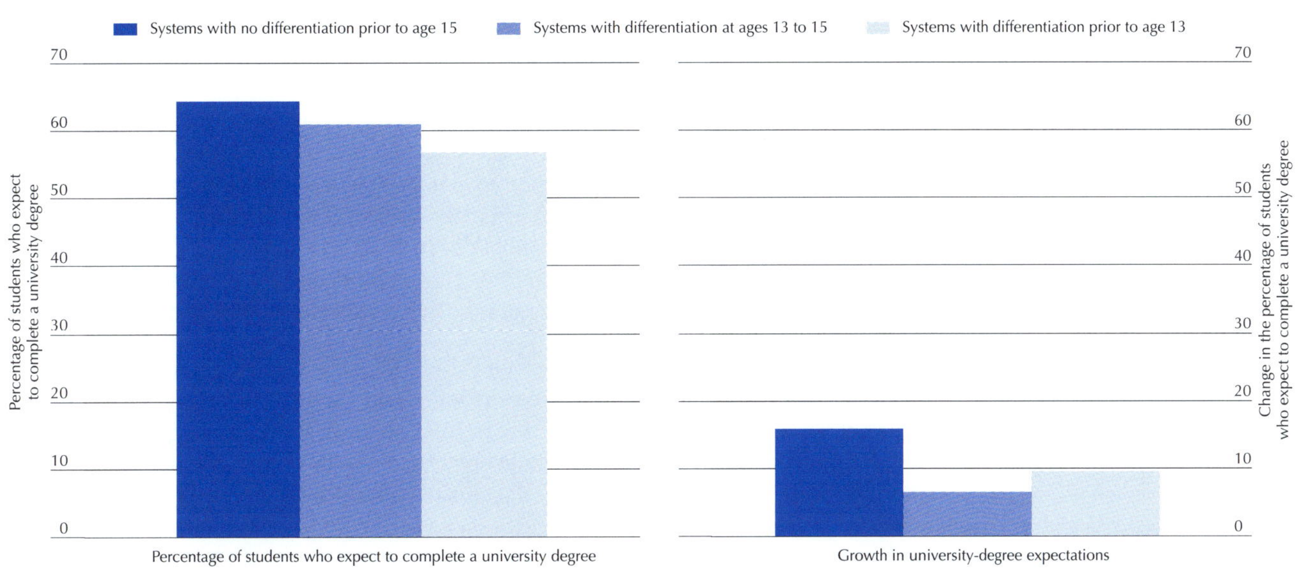

Note: Predicted values are estimated from an OLS regression at the school-system level predicting the percentage of students who expect to complete a university degree and the change in this expectation between 2003 and 2009, and controlling for changes in gross enrolment ratios from 1980 to 2009 and dummy indicators for Korea and Latvia.
Source: Table B1.5.
StatLink http://dx.doi.org/10.1787/888932733355

▪ Figure 1.6 ▪

Percentage of students in ISCED A and ISCED B/C programmes who expect to complete a university degree

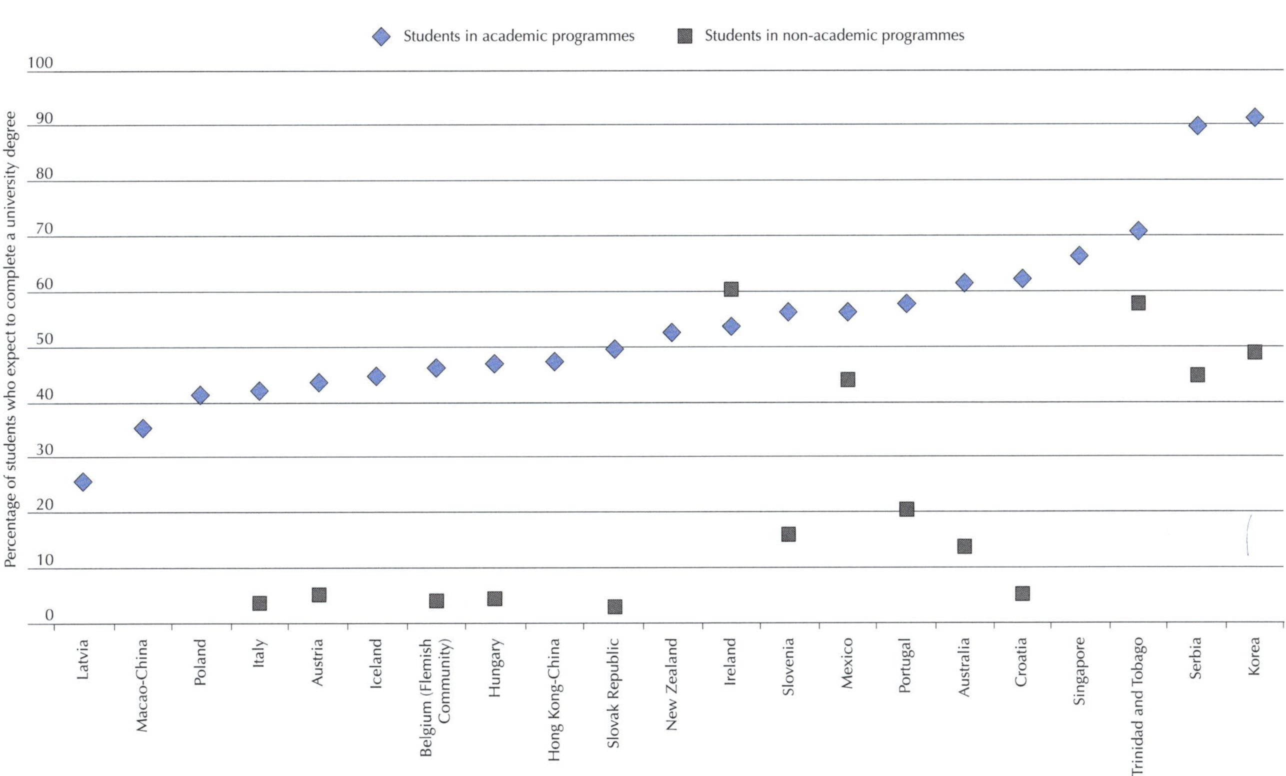

Note: Latvia, Macao-China, Poland, Iceland, Hong Kong-China, New Zealand and Singapore either do not offer non-academic programmes or have too small a sample in these programmes to provide reliable estimates.
Countries are sorted in ascending order of the percentage of students in academic programmes expecting to complete a university degree.
Source: Table B1.1.
StatLink http://dx.doi.org/10.1787/888932733374

university degree among students in academic and non-academic programmes. The difference is also significant in Belgium (Flemish Community), Hungary, Korea, Serbia and the Slovak Republic, at 40 percentage points or more. In these countries, students who attend non-academically oriented programmes tend to realise the difficulty of entering university and adjust their expectations accordingly. In Trinidad and Tobago, the difference between the expectations of students in different programmes is less pronounced, at 13 percentage points. In Ireland, students in ISCED B/C-type programmes are *more* likely to expect to complete a university degree (Figure 1.6).

For students attending non-academic programmes, a university degree may be a difficult goal to reach because of the nature of their academic training or because there are structural impediments to doing so. These students are thus particularly likely to face the potential frustration – and financial cost – of not achieving this goal. Expectations of completing university among students in these programmes are highest in Ireland, Korea, Serbia and Trinidad and Tobago, where more than 40% of students in non-academic programmes expect to complete a university degree. Considering the total number of students who hold expectations that would be hard to meet (those students in non-academic programmes who expect to earn a university degree), over a third of all students in Serbia and more than 10% of all students in Ireland and Korea have expectations that are structurally difficult for them to meet.

By contrast, in Austria, Belgium (Flemish Community), Croatia, Hungary and the Slovak Republic, fewer than 5% of students in non-academically oriented programmes expect to complete a university degree. In these countries, being in this type of programme dissuades students from holding high expectations about completing a university degree. Although these systems provide for more realistic expectations, if differentiation into various programmes is not based entirely on merit, these systems may lead to a loss in talent (e.g. academically able students who attend these programmes are discouraged from pursuing a university degree, even though they might be able to complete one, given their academic performance) or reinforce social inequalities if separating students favours some groups over others (Buchmann and Dalton, 2002).

Fifteen-year-old students who are in lower or upper secondary schools, may have different expectations about their future. In most countries and economies that distributed the Educational Career questionnaire, students in upper secondary schools are more likely to expect to complete a university degree. This may be the case because upper secondary education may not be mandatory in some systems, so students interested in pursuing further education have already been selected at that level. Also, lower secondary education may have a greater proportion of students who have repeated a grade because of low performance and a larger share of students from socio-economically disadvantaged backgrounds who are, in turn, less likely to graduate from university and so have adjusted their expectations accordingly. A third explanation for the difference in expectations by ISCED level is that upper secondary students are closer to the time they graduate and are more likely to see the benefits of a university education (Table B1.1).

Expectations of ending formal education at the upper secondary level

When examining students' expectations of further education, the focus is generally on whether students expect to attend and complete university because tertiary education offers a pathway to upward social mobility and greater earnings. However, in many countries, a majority of students do not expect to attain a university education, and the choices and opportunities available to these students – whether to continue on to vocationally oriented post-secondary programmes (ISCED 4 and 5B programmes), drop out before completing upper secondary education, or finish their formal education with an upper secondary degree, will shape not only their individual futures but also the type of workforce countries will be able to tap in the coming decades.

These students are known as *the forgotten half,* largely because scholars and policy makers have paid scant attention to them (Rosenbaum, 2001). This section focuses on these students because their needs are different than those of students who expect to continue their education and training in institutions of higher education. The former group expects to enter the labour market sooner, and thus requires schools to provide them with the skills that better prepare them to enter the labour market and adulthood.

Students who expect to finish their formal schooling at the end of upper secondary school generally plan to enter the labour market immediately afterwards. Although most school systems are committed to expanding access to tertiary education, education systems must not forget the large number of students who do not expect to avail themselves of that access. These students still must acquire the skills needed for a smooth transition into the labour market. For most countries, this remains a challenge: unemployment rates are high among persons with at most an upper secondary degree, and they are especially high among 15-24 year-olds. The unemployment rate among adults in OECD countries rose to 7% in 2011; but among workers aged 15-25, the unemployment rate was 17% (OECD, 2011a; OECD, 2011b). As the demand for high-skilled workers increases, meeting this challenge becomes ever more important (Box 1.4).

Countries have various strategies for ensuring a smooth transition into the labour market for students who expect to finish their formal education in upper secondary school. Germany and Japan, for example, encourage and promote linkages between schools and businesses while maintaining incentives for students to perform well. In the United States, on the other hand, schools are not expected to establish close ties with industry and potential employers (Rosenbaum and Kariya, 1989; Rosenbaum et al., 1990; Rosenbaum, 2001; Shavit and Müller, 1998). Because students are encouraged to expect to complete a university degree, policies

Box 1.4 **The NEET challenge (Not in Employment, Education or Training)**

The traditional indicators for labour-market participation are frequently criticised for their limited relevance to young people. Basic unemployment and employment statistics do not accurately capture the situation of young people because many students are classified as being out of the labour force. Many young people who do not study are also not captured by official unemployment statistics as they may choose not to enter the labour force and not look for a job because they are engaged in irregular employment or in domestic unpaid work, or because they are inactive. Since the number of young people who are not in education, employment or training is large in many countries, new measures have been developed to assess the size of this group, the challenges these young people face, their labour-market prospects, and life outcomes more generally. A young person is considered as not in education, employment or training (NEET) if he or she has left the school system and is neither employed nor in continuing education.

Skills score of young people, by participation in education and work

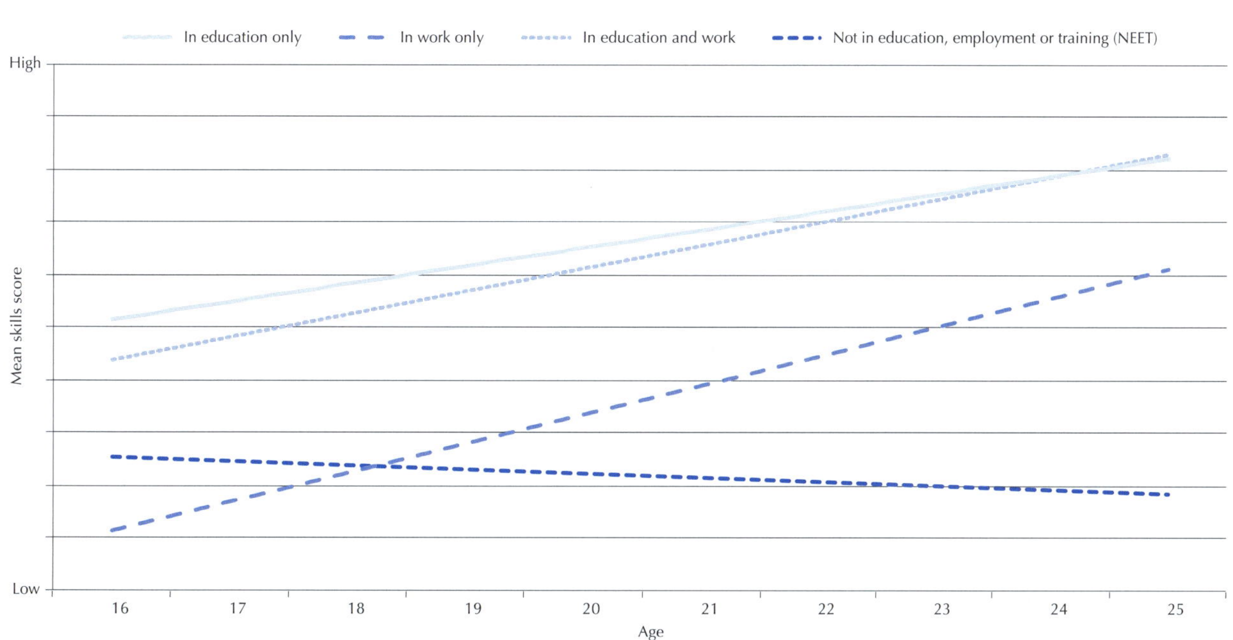

Note: This figure is based on results of the OECD Survey of Adult Skills field trial, a product of the Programme for the International Assessment of Adult Competencies (PIAAC). It is not based on representative samples and is therefore only illustrative.
Source: Figure 1.3 in OECD (2012), *Better Skills, Better Jobs, Better Lives: A Strategic Approach to Skills Policies*, OECD Publishing.
StatLink http://dx.doi.org/10.1787/888932733659

In 2009, the latest year for which data for this indicator are available, an average of 12% of young people in OECD countries were NEET. Denmark, Iceland, Luxembourg, the Netherlands and Norway had the lowest NEET rates in 2009 (between 5% and 7%), while the share of young NEETs was the highest in Turkey and Israel, at 37% and 31%, respectively. Among NEET youth, two in three were outside the labour market either because they had been unemployed for more than a year or because they were inactive and were not seeking employment.

On average in OECD countries, the NEET rate among 15-24 year-olds in 2009 also differs markedly by socio-demographic characteristics. Young women have a higher NEET rate than young men (14% and 12%, respectively), while the NEET rate for teenagers is less than half that of young adults (8% and 18%, respectively), partly because education is compulsory at least until the age of 16 on average across OECD countries. A lack of qualifications implies a much higher risk of being NEET (34%). In 2009, Turkey recorded the highest NEET rates among young people without an upper secondary education, and one of the highest rates among young people with upper secondary qualifications.

A smoother transition from school to the workplace or higher education, and resulting lower NEET rates, are found in countries that differentiate their school systems (Eurofound, 2012).

Sources: Eurofound (2012); OECD (2010d); OECD (2012a).

Box 1.4 **The NEET challenge (Not in Employment, Education or Training)** *(continued)*

Not in Education, Employment or Training (NEET) rates, by labour-force status

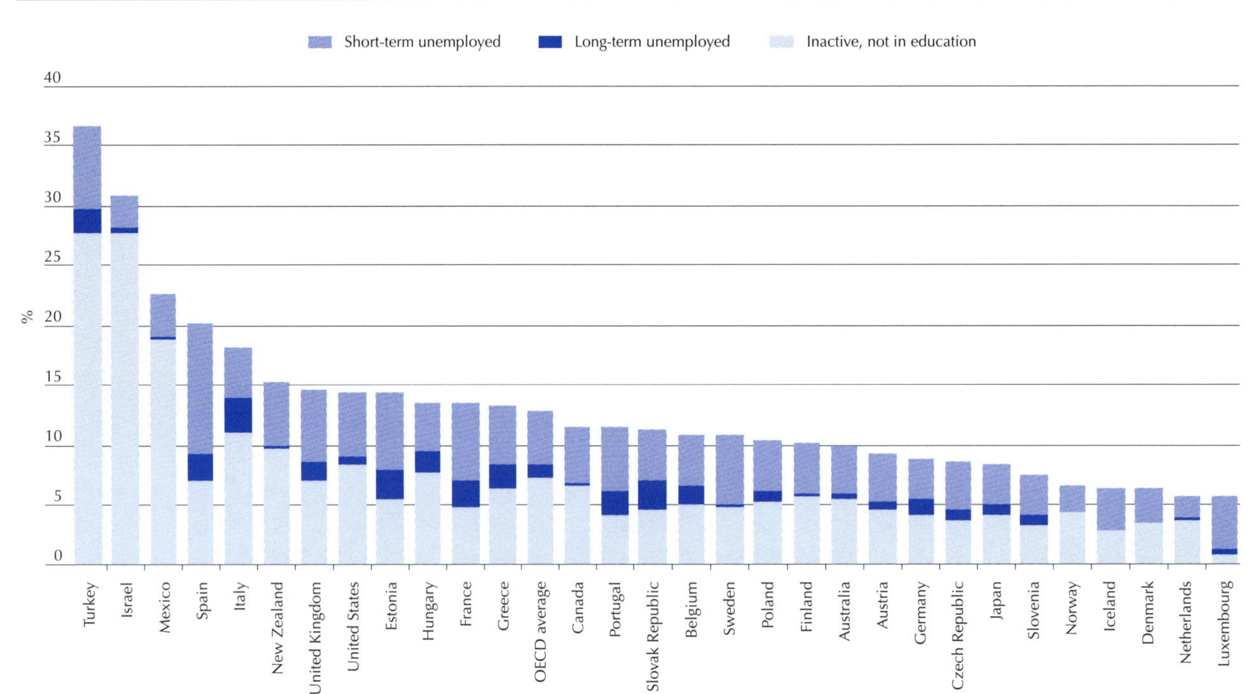

Note: NEET rates for each country are expressed as a percentage over youth population aged 15-24. Data for 2009. Countries are sorted in descending order by the total NEET rate.
Source: OECD Education Database, data for 2009.
StatLink http://dx.doi.org/10.1787/888932733678

Not in Education, Employment or Training (NEET) rates, by demographic status and educational attainment

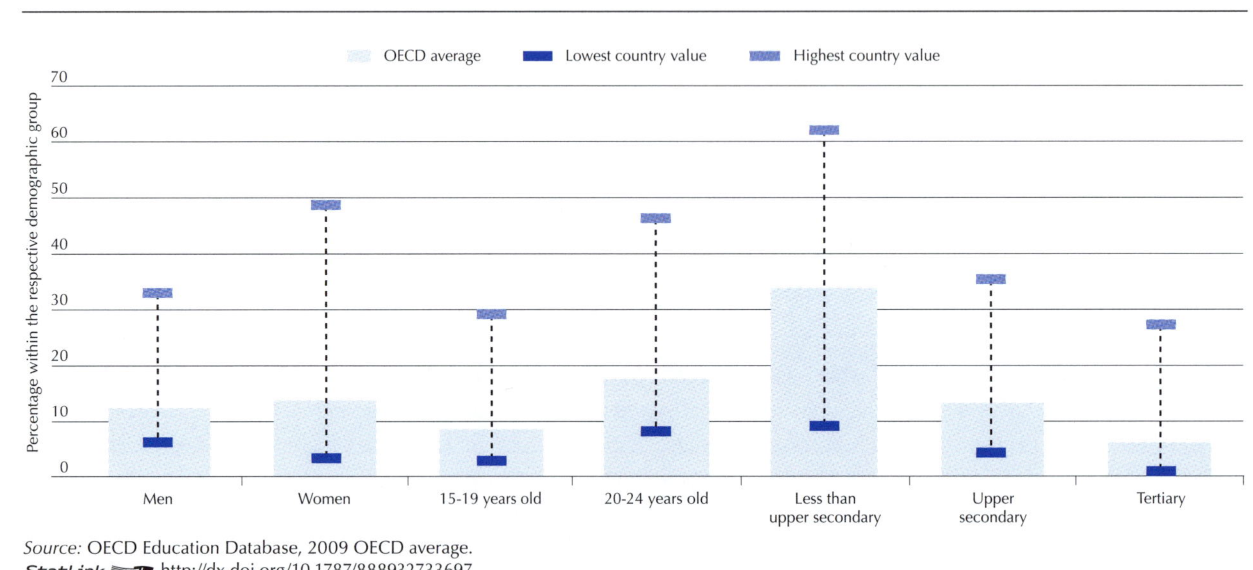

Source: OECD Education Database, 2009 OECD average.
StatLink http://dx.doi.org/10.1787/888932733697

that would ease the transition from education into the labour market at the upper secondary level may have the undesired effect of lowering students' expectations, especially among minorities and students from disadvantaged backgrounds. In this sense, Australia offers an interesting example as it has developed attractive vocational education and training (VET) programmes in the context of a comprehensive education system and maintains a high proportion of top performers (Box 1.5). Also, Finland and Denmark actively promote on-the-job training programmes (OECD, 2010d; OECD, 2010e).

Box 1.5 **Vocational education and training systems**

Vocational education and training (VET) can play a central role in preparing young people for work, developing the skills of adults, and responding to labour-market needs. Despite this role, VET has been often neglected and marginalised in policy discussions, usually overshadowed by the increasing emphasis on general academic education and the role of schools in preparing students for university education. It has also often been perceived by both students and the general public as having a "second class" status behind academically oriented programmes. As a result, comparative policy analysis is underveloped, and there are very limited data available, especially data that can be reliably compared across countries.

Increasingly, however, countries are recognising that good initial vocational education and training can make a major contribution to economic competitiveness. Many of the unskilled jobs that existed in OECD countries a generation ago are fast disappearing, either because they have been replaced by technology or because OECD countries cannot compete with less-developed countries on labour costs. Instead, OECD countries need to compete on the quality of goods and services they provide. That requires a well-skilled labour force with a range of mid-level trade, technical and professional skills alongside those high-level skills associated with a university education. More often than not, those skills are delivered through vocational programmes. At the same time, VET systems face major challenges. Vocational programmes for young people, often rooted in educational institutions, tend to develop their own dynamic, and can be too separated from the fast-changing world of modern economies.

The OECD reviews *Learning for Jobs* (2010e) and *Better Skills, Better Jobs, Better Lives* (2012a) aim to capture how the gap between learning and jobs can be closed and illustrate promising examples of countries and institutions that have been able to make initial vocational education and training for young people respond better to labour-market requirements. These publications offer concrete advice on policy reforms that enable students who only expect to complete upper secondary education to be well-prepared to enter the labour market, remain employable and continue to acquire skills throughout their lives.

VET could better help meet labour-market demands by:

- providing a mix of programmes that reflect both students' preferences and employers' needs through apprenticeship systems;
- sharing the costs among government, employers and individual students, according to the benefits obtained by each actor organising or taking part in taking part in VET beyond secondary level; cost-sharing would create incentives and motivation for both employers and individual students to make the most of participation in VET;
- engaging employers and unions in curriculum development and ensuring that the skills taught correspond to those needed in the workplace; and
- providing young people with the foundation skills to support occupational mobility and lifelong learning, and with the specific skills that meet employers' immediate needs.

For further country-specific information and a more extensive review of vocational education and training, see *www.oecd.org/edu/learningforjobs*.

Sources: OECD (2010e); OECD (2012a).

On average across the countries and economies that distributed the ECQ, one of every four students expects to complete his or her studies at the upper secondary level and, presumably, enter the labour force upon graduation. This proportion is highest in Austria, at 53%, and is also high in the Slovak Republic (40%), Italy (39%) and Croatia (34%). Students' expectations of ending their education at the upper secondary level are lowest in Singapore (2%) and Korea (5%) (Figure 1.7).

▪ Figure 1.7 ▪

Percentage of students who expect to end their educational careers at the upper secondary level

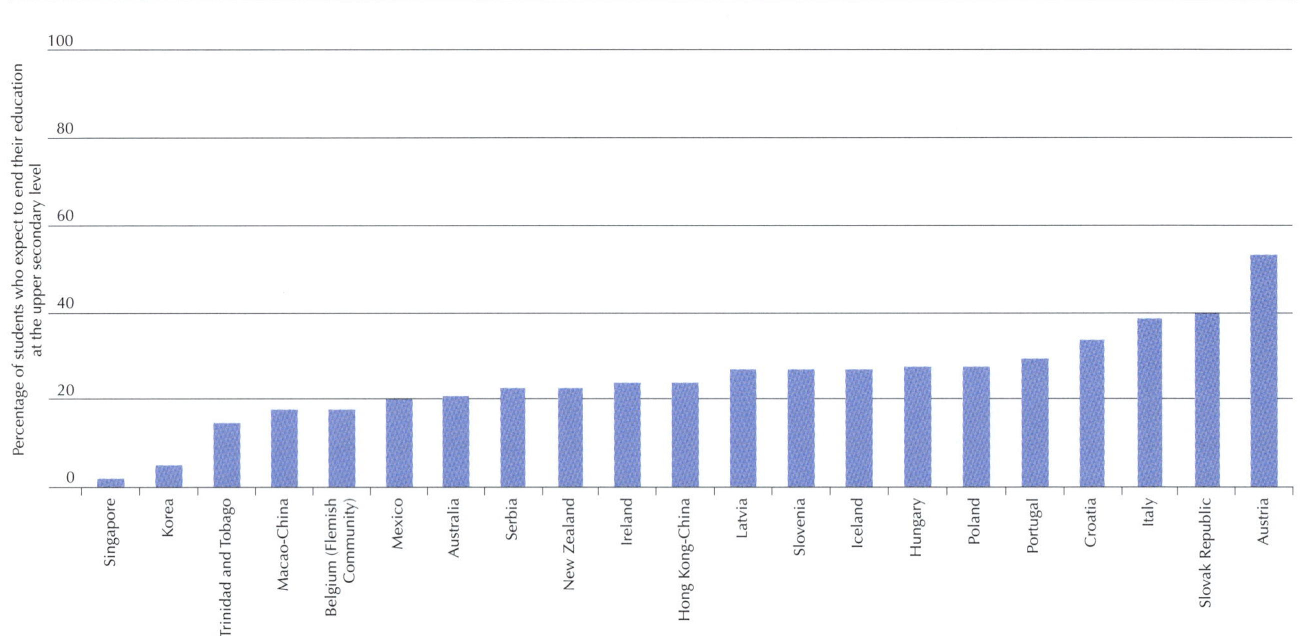

Countries are sorted in ascending order of the percentage of students expecting to end their educational careers at the upper secondary level.
Source: Table B1.8.
StatLink http://dx.doi.org/10.1787/888932733393

Of the four countries with the highest proportion of students expecting to finish their formal education upon acquiring an upper secondary degree, Austria, Croatia and the Slovak Republic are characterised by early differentiation of students into ISCED B/C and ISCED A-type programmes and by having a comparatively large proportion of students in ISCED B/C programmes. In fact, education systems that separate students into different ISCED programmes are more likely to have a larger number of students who expect an upper secondary degree as their highest qualification (Table B1.5).

The percentage of students who expect, at most, an upper secondary degree has increased significantly since 2003 in Australia, Hungary, Ireland, Italy, Portugal and the Slovak Republic. This increase is moderate in most of these countries; only in Hungary and Ireland was the increase larger than five percentage points. In most of these education systems, the increase in the percentage of students expecting to complete, at most, an upper secondary education is coupled with an increase or no significant change in expectations of completing university. Such is the case in Austria, Ireland, Portugal and the Slovak Republic, where the increase in expectations of ending formal education at the upper secondary level comes as a result of a reduction in the percentage of students who do not expect to attain an upper secondary degree (i.e. drop out). In Hungary and Italy, the increase in expectations of attaining an upper secondary degree is coupled with a decrease in expectations of attending university, signalling that many students who, in 2003, would have expected to graduate from university may have lowered their expectations of attaining only an upper secondary degree.

Between 2003 and 2009, the percentage of students expecting to end their education in upper secondary school decreased significantly in Hong Kong-China, Iceland, Macao-China, Mexico and New Zealand. In Iceland, Mexico and New Zealand, this decrease is mirrored by an increase in the proportion of students expecting to graduate from university – that is, a smaller proportion of students expect to drop out before finishing upper secondary school or a smaller proportion of students choose to pursue vocationally oriented post-secondary degrees (see Boxes 1.6 and 1.7 describing the percentage of students who expect to pursue vocational degrees and to drop out of school). Macao-China is an interesting case. This Asian economy showed a simultaneous decrease in the percentage of students expecting to complete a university degree and in the percentage of those expecting to complete an upper secondary degree, at most – both at a similar rate to the observed fall in enrolment rates between 2003 and 2009 (Tables B1.1, B1.8 and B1.16).

Box 1.6 **Students who expect to pursue vocational post-secondary studies**

Students who do not expect to complete a university degree may opt to continue their education in the form of vocational or technical post-secondary education (ISCED levels 5B or 4). The development of these skills is crucial for the well-being of an economy, as these workers sustain high-skill and technology-intensive industries. Many students in the countries and economies that distributed the Educational Career questionnaire expect to follow these educational paths, particularly in Latvia (44%), the Flemish Community of Belgium (44%), Macao-China (37%) and Slovenia (36%).

Percentage of students who expect to complete a vocational or technical post-secondary degree

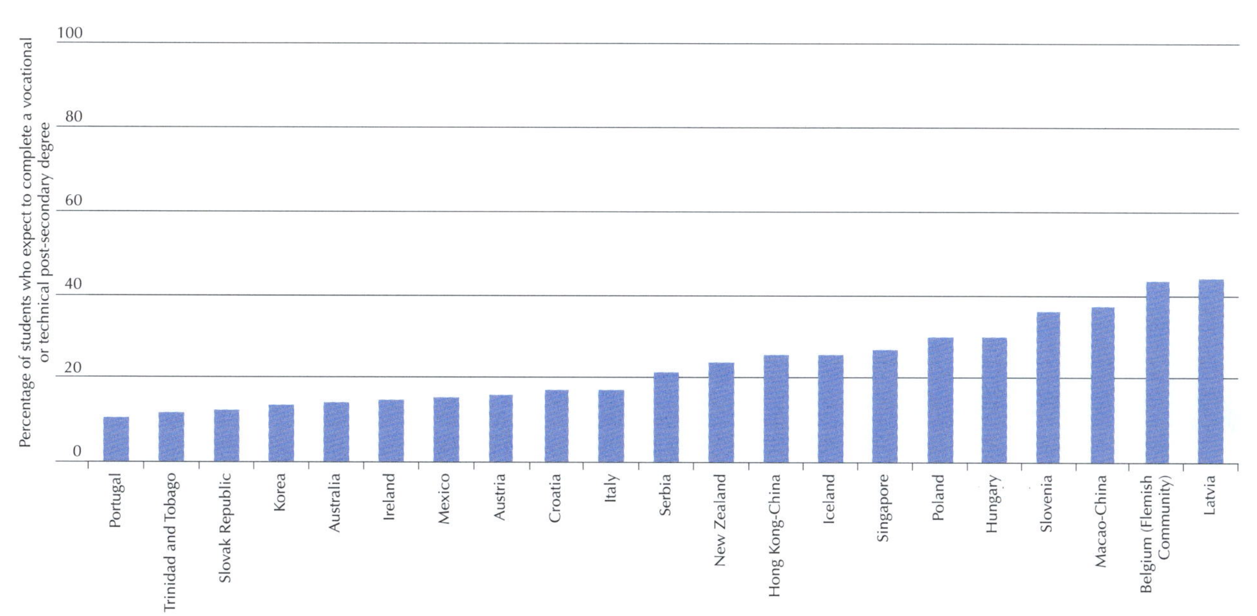

Note: Vocational or technical post-secondary degrees are ISCED Level 4 or ISCED Level 5B degrees.
Countries are sorted in ascending order of the percentage of students expecting to complete a vocational or technical post-secondary degree.
Source: Table B1.9.
StatLink http://dx.doi.org/10.1787/888932733716

Expectations of ending formal education at the upper secondary level, by ISCED programme and level

Just as ISCED B/C programmes may not offer a smooth transition into ISCED 5A programmes, as discussed earlier, ISCED A-type programmes in lower and upper secondary schools may not ease the transition into the labour market for those students who expect to finish their education at the upper secondary level. In lower and upper secondary levels, academically oriented programmes (ISCED A) provide a path towards continuing education in university. The skills set acquired by these students may not be aligned with what is required by employers looking for workers with an upper secondary degree. By contrast, students in ISCED B/C-type programmes in lower and upper secondary schools will be, at least in theory, better prepared to enter the labour market with the set of skills that is needed by employers.

As expected, in practically all countries with more than 8% of students in ISCED B/C-type programmes, these students are more likely than students in ISCED A-type programmes to expect to finish their formal schooling at the upper secondary level. This difference is the greatest – and mirrors the patterns observed for university expectations by ISCED programme – in Croatia (51 percentage points), Hungary (38 percentage points) and Slovenia (33 percentage points).

One signal of misaligned expectations is the percentage of students in ISCED A-type programmes who expect to finish their formal schooling at the upper secondary level. This percentage exceeds 25% in Austria (46%), the Slovak Republic (37%), Poland (28%) and Portugal (26%). This misalignment is particularly noticeable in Austria and the Slovak Republic because these two countries have a relatively large proportion of students in ISCED B/C-type programmes. Students in academic programmes may be considerably less prepared than their peers in non-academic programmes to enter and successfully navigate through the labour market immediately after finishing upper secondary school. By contrast, fewer than 3% of ISCED A-type students in Korea and Serbia expect to end their schooling at the upper secondary level, while 10% of students in Slovenia expect to do so. In these countries, students may determine the usefulness of finishing formal schooling at the upper secondary level based on the ISCED programme they attend.

Box 1.7 **Students who expect to end their education before completing upper secondary schooling**

Although the majority of students expects to earn a university degree or end their formal education after finishing upper secondary school, students may also opt to end their education without an upper secondary degree and without a post-secondary degree. Students who fail to finish upper secondary school are less likely to find jobs; and if they do, those jobs are likely to be precarious and low-paid. Students who drop out of education with only basic qualifications may increase the cost to the economy and society in that they are usually less productive, and they are also more likely to have health problems, engage in criminal activity, and become dependent on welfare and other publicly funded social programmes (Belfield and Levin, 2007; Rumberger, 2011). Students who fail to finish upper secondary education have different profiles requiring different approaches to keep them in school or encourage them to return to school. Dropouts tend to be students who have difficulty keeping up academically or who have behaviour problems. The latter group needs a kind of support that often is beyond the current reach of schools (Marcotte, 2012).

Across the countries and economies that implemented the Educational Career questionnaire, 3.4% of students, on average, expect to end their formal education *without* an upper secondary degree. This percentage is especially high in Macao-China (9%), Mexico (9%) and Portugal (8%) and comparatively low, at less than 2%, in Belgium (Flemish Community), Croatia, Hungary, Korea, New Zealand, Poland, Serbia and Singapore.

Percentage of students who do not expect to complete an upper secondary degree

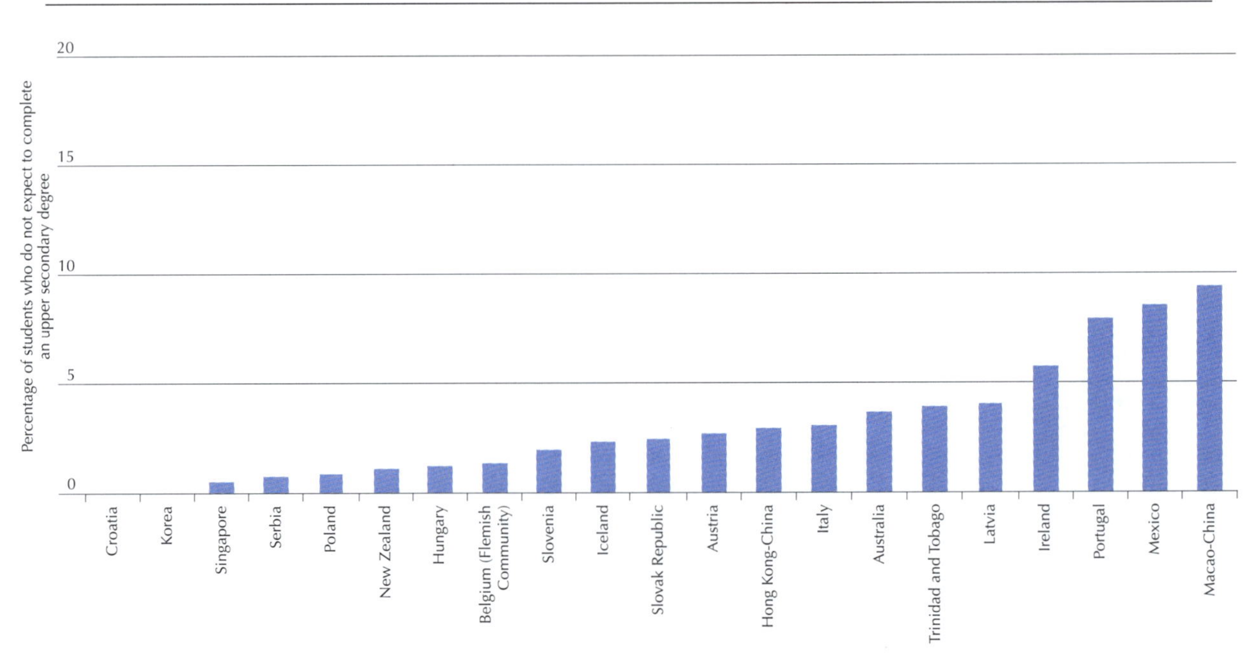

Countries are sorted in ascending order of the percentage of students expecting not to complete an upper secondary degree.
Source: Table B1.9.
StatLink http://dx.doi.org/10.1787/888932733735

Sources: Belfield and Levin (2007); Marcotte (2012); Rumberger (2011).

INEQUALITIES IN EXPECTATIONS

Educational expectations are one of the first signals of eventual educational attainment and occupational status. Students who do not expect to attain a university education, for example, are less likely to take the necessary steps to attend university and are also less likely to put forth the effort to succeed (Carbonaro et al., 2011). This section explores whether boys and girls hold similar expectations about their future educational attainment, and whether students from socio-economically disadvantaged backgrounds face barriers that lower their expectations. If so, these may contribute to disparities in actual attainment and, ultimately, in fewer opportunities for social mobility (Buchmann and Dalton, 2002).

Expectations may differ between student groups because not all students have the same opportunities to acquire skills and achieve their full potential while at school. Some education systems may have a perfect match between students' abilities and their expectations of future education, but may be highly unequal systems because students' opportunities to become proficient are determined, to a large extent, by their family's resources and background. For example, countries that sort students into different programmes – academically oriented and vocational – at an early age may reinforce inequalities in performance because the sorting may reflect students' social background rather than their underlying abilities. Moreover, students from socio-economically advantaged households have greater opportunities to learn outside of school and are therefore greatly over-represented in those academic tracks that are most likely to provide more and better opportunities to pursue university-level degrees. Inequalities in opportunities to learn (resulting, for example, from sorting into ISCED programmes) translate into inequalities in school performance that, in turn, lead to inequalities in expectations. While these expectations may be realistic, they are based on little more than the luck of the draw at birth if inequalities in sorting persist (Buchmann and Park, 2009; Kristen and Granato, 2007).

Findings in this report suggest that inequalities in expectations are present in practically all countries and economies that distributed the ECQ. In most school systems performance is only one of the factors that determine inequalities in expectations. Disadvantaged students hold lower expectations of further education even when they perform as well as students from advantaged backgrounds. This suggests that the limits to expectations of further education and social mobility may be set even more solidly than those related to educational achievement. Education systems that produce unequal expectations among students are complicit in building barriers to class and social mobility that span through generations. If inequality of expectations is related to inequalities of opportunities to learn, then countries may dismantle obstacles to upward mobility by offering disadvantaged students more and better opportunities to learn before any performance-based differentiation takes place.

Yet inequalities in expectations may persist even after accounting for students' opportunities to learn and their performance in mathematics and reading. In these cases, policies that provide equal opportunities to learn may not be enough to overcome the barriers to social and class mobility. Chapter 4 describes ways in which education systems may facilitate greater equality in expectations and ultimately establish solid foundations for greater equality in the labour market and beyond.

Inequalities in expectations by socio-economic status

In all countries and economies that implemented the ECQ, students from disadvantaged backgrounds are less likely than their more advantaged peers to expect to complete a university degree. Students in the bottom third of the *PISA index of economic, social and cultural status* are, on average, 37 percentage points less likely to expect to complete a university degree than students in the top third of this scale. This difference is over 20 percentage points in every country and economy; it is largest in Hungary (at over 50 points) and smallest in Trinidad and Tobago (at 22 points).

Socio-economically advantaged students tend to perform better than their disadvantaged peers in all countries and economies (OECD, 2010f). After accounting for these differences, however, both groups of students should hold similar expectations, as they may have similar chances of succeeding in tertiary education. On average, around 40% of the difference in the odds of expecting to complete a university degree between advantaged and disadvantaged students is explained by the fact that disadvantaged students tend to show poorer reading and mathematics performance. In New Zealand and Trinidad and Tobago the difference in university expectations to complete a university degree as related to socio-economic status is the smallest – yet still statistically significant – after accounting for students' mathematics and reading performance. In these two countries, advantaged students are between 1.8 and 2.3 times more likely to expect to complete a university degree than a disadvantaged student with the same mathematics and reading scores (Figure 1.8).

In most countries, however, there are still important differences in expectations related to socio-economic status even among students who perform equally well: students in the bottom third of the *PISA index of economic, social and cultural status* are significantly less likely to expect to complete a university degree than similarly performing students in the top third of the socio-economic status scale. In Croatia, Hungary, Iceland, Korea and Serbia, advantaged students who have the same reading and mathematics scores as disadvantaged students are over four times more likely to expect to complete a university degree than disadvantaged students. In Belgium (Flemish Community), Hungary, Portugal and the Slovak Republic, performance plays a particularly important role in shaping inequalities in university expectations related to socio-economic background. In these countries, students' mathematics and reading performance explains over half of the odds difference between advantaged and disadvantaged students in the likelihood that these groups would expect to complete a university degree.

The reverse is true when comparing students who expect to finish their educational careers after graduating from upper secondary school. Students in the bottom third of the *PISA index of economic, social and cultural status* – disadvantaged students – are more likely than students in the top third – advantaged students – to expect that their upper secondary degree will be their highest educational qualification. Although these differences are less pronounced than those related to university expectations, reading and mathematics performance also play a large role in shaping the inequality in these expectations. However, performance tells only part of the story.

Differences in expectations between students who have similar performance levels but who come from either advantaged or disadvantaged backgrounds is highest in Korea, Latvia, Poland, Serbia and Slovenia. In all these countries socio-economically advantaged students are four times less likely to expect to end their education after completing upper secondary school than disadvantaged students who perform equally well (Figure 1.8).

▪ Figure 1.8 ▪

Socio-economic differences in expectations of completing a university and upper secondary degree, before and after adjusting for students' reading and mathematics performance

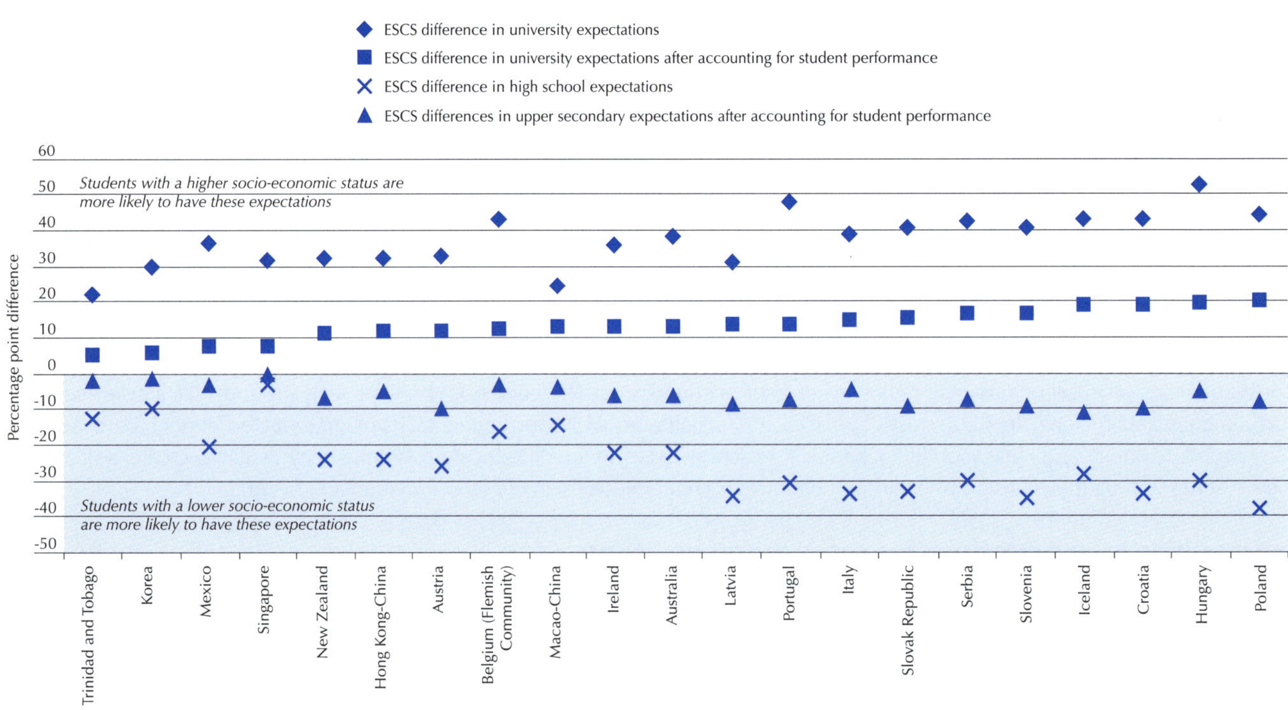

Note: ESCS differences depict differences in expectations between students with a high or low *PISA index of economic, social and cultural status* (ESCS) as defined by students who are in the top and bottom third of their country's distribution of socio-economic status.
Countries are sorted in ascending order of the difference in the percentage of students expecting a university degree by the PISA index of economic, social and cultural status *after adjusting for students' mathematics and reading performance.*
Source: Tables B1.10 and B1.11.
StatLink http://dx.doi.org/10.1787/888932733412

The fact that differences in expectations related to socio-economic status remain after accounting for reading and mathematics performance signals that other factors influence students' expectations. The parents, peers and teachers of more advantaged students tend to have higher expectations for those students, which, in turn, shapes the students' own expectations (Buchmann and Dalton, 2002; Campbell, 1983; Sewell et al., 2003). According to the literature, another key factor is differentiation into vocational or academic programmes. As socio-economic status partly determines sorting into these programmes, disadvantaged students may be denied the possibility of expecting to, and eventually succeeding in, completing a university degree (Buchmann and Park, 2009; Mateju et al., 2007; Useem, 1992). Other kinds of information, which will be discussed in Chapters 2 and 3, also influence students' expectations. In the United States, for example, as a result of their social background, students tend to adopt certain expectations early on in their lives and adapt these expectations to changes in the information they receive about their career prospects (Andrew and Hauser, 2012; Morgan, 2005). This information includes the school marks students receive. As developed in Chapter 2, disadvantaged students are also more likely than their advantaged peers to receive lower marks, even after accounting for performance, learning habits and engagement with school.

Inequalities in expectations by gender

Women today are attaining higher levels of education than men. As of 2009 and on average across the OECD, women show higher entry rates into both tertiary-type A and B programmes and higher graduation rates from these programmes (OECD, 2011a). By 2003, girls held equal or higher expectations of educational attainment in all OECD countries that participated in PISA 2003, with the exception of Japan. In fact, in 19 OECD countries, girls held expectations of significantly higher educational attainment than boys (McDaniel, 2010). In 2006, in almost all OECD countries girls expected to attain higher occupational status than boys in careers that require a post-secondary education (OECD, 2012c).

In 2009 among the countries that implemented the ECQ, an equal or greater number of girls than boys expected to complete a university degree. In 17 countries and economies, girls have higher expectations than boys; only in Austria, Belgium (Flemish Community), Hong Kong-China and Korea do girls and boys have similar odds of expecting to complete a university degree. The difference between girls' and boys' expectations of earning a university degree is highest in Poland and Trinidad and Tobago, where girls are more than twice as likely as boys to expect to complete a university degree. In these two countries, girls are over 18 percentage points more likely than boys to expect to complete a university degree.

In all countries and economies that participated in PISA 2009, girls do better than boys in reading; and in most countries and economies, they do not perform as well as boys in mathematics (OECD, 2010b). In Latvia, Macao-China and Slovenia, girls' better performance explains their higher expectations of further education, while in the remaining countries, even among boys and girls who perform equally well in reading and mathematics, girls are more likely than boys to expect to complete a university degree. In 16 countries and economies, a larger proportion of girls than boys who perform equally well expect to attain a university degree. In Mexico, Poland, Portugal, Serbia and Trinidad and Tobago, girls are at least twice as likely as boys with similar test scores to expect to complete a university degree, after accounting for their differences in performance.

Boys are significantly more likely to expect to end their formal education after completing their upper secondary degree in all but two countries: Austria and Singapore. In Iceland, Ireland, New Zealand and Slovenia, the greater likelihood that boys expect to end their formal education after completing upper secondary school is related to boys' poorer performance in reading and/or mathematics. The gender gap in expectations remains in 15 countries and economies even after comparing boys and girls who perform similarly. This means that boys are more likely than girls to expect to end their formal education in upper secondary school, even if they do just as well as girls on the PISA assessment (Figure 1.9).

▪ Figure 1.9 ▪

Gender differences in expectations of completing a university and upper secondary degree, before and after adjusting for student reading and mathematics performance

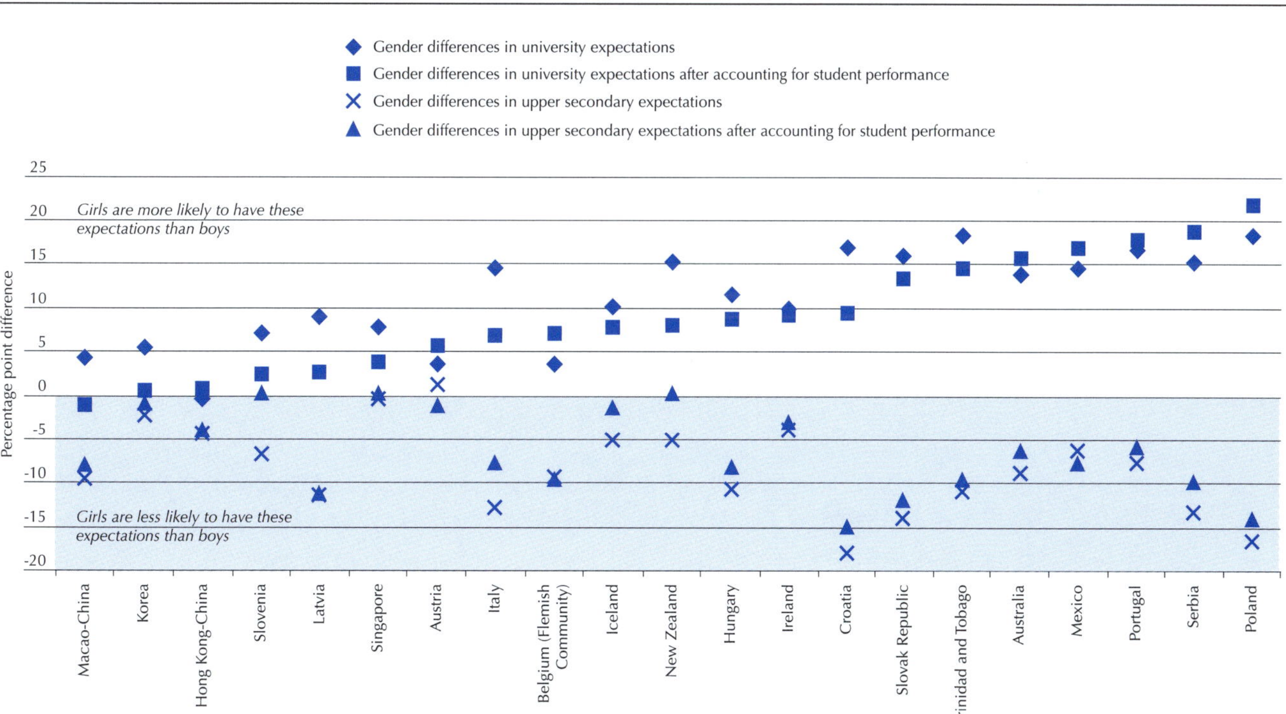

Countries are sorted in ascending order of the gender difference in the percentage of students expecting a university degree after adjusting for students' reading and mathematics performance.
Source: Table B1.12 and B1.13.
StatLink http://dx.doi.org/10.1787/888932733431

HOW GRADUATION AND ENROLMENT RATES ARE REFLECTED IN THE EXPECTATIONS OF 15-YEAR-OLDS

Student expectations of completing a university degree serve as an indication of the pressure the system of higher education will face in the future when compared to actual graduation rates. Countries and economies where more students expect to complete university than actually do so can expect high levels of competition in access to university because demand for higher education may eventually surpass supply. Because of the mismatch between the expected demand and the supply for university education, these countries and economies may need to consider alternatives for the large number of students who will not be able to earn a university degree even if they expect to.

As discussed earlier, countries, and regions within countries, vary in the percentage of students who expect to complete a university degree. Whereas in Latvia relatively few – one in four – students expect to complete a university degree, in Korea the great majority of students – four out of five – expect to do so. Of the 21 countries and economies that distributed the ECQ in 2009, in nine of them over 50% of 15-year-old students expected to complete a university degree. These expectations are highest in Korea (81%) and exceed 60% in Australia, Singapore and Trinidad and Tobago. They are lowest in Latvia (25%) and lower than 40% in Austria, Belgium (Flemish Community), Macao-China and Slovenia.

Cross-country variations in students' expectations are not strongly related to actual graduation rates. *Education at a Glance 2011* (OECD, 2011a) provides figures on university graduation rates for 14 of the 21 countries that disseminated in the ECQ.[6] Among these, the correlation between the percentage of 15-year-old students who expect to complete a university degree and the actual graduation rates is 0.37. The mismatch between expectations and graduation rates is especially large (over 10 percentage points higher expectations than graduation rates) in the Flemish Community of Belgium, Korea, Mexico and Portugal, signalling inflated expectations. In Korea and Mexico, the difference between the percentage of students who expect to complete a university degree and the percentage who do is 36 percentage points; in other words, at least one out of three students will not fulfil his or her educational expectations if graduation rates remain relatively stable.

This misalignment between expectations and actual attainment takes various forms. In Mexico, for example, some students who expected to graduate from university will not do so; in Korea, some of the students who expected to graduate from university will

▪ Figure 1.10 ▪

Percentage of students who expect to complete a university degree and university graduation rates

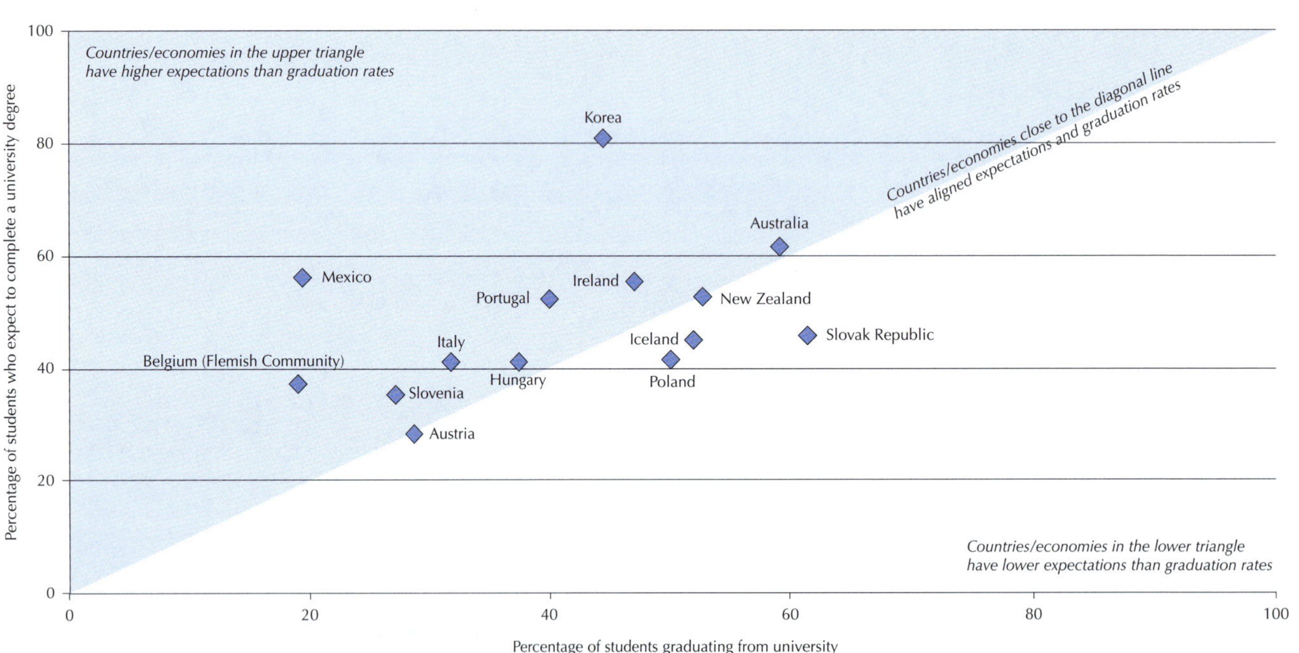

Notes: Percentage of students graduating from university as reported in Table A3.3, OECD (2011), *Education at a Glance 2011: OECD Indicators*, OECD Publishing.
Data on the percentage of students graduating from university is not available for Croatia, Hong Kong-China, Latvia, Macao-China, Serbia, Singapore and Trinidad and Tobago.
Graduation rates for Belgium (Flemish Community) represent graduation rates for Belgium as a whole.
Source: Table B1.14.
StatLink http://dx.doi.org/10.1787/888932733450

enter ISCED level 5B programmes instead.[7, 8] The misalignment of expectations of completing a university degree is also apparent in the Flemish Community of Belgium. It is less marked than that seen in Korea, but follows a similar pattern: many students who expect to complete this degree will most likely continue their education in ISCED level 5B programmes. In fact, in Belgium, a greater number of students graduate from these programmes than from ISCED level 5A programmes (Figure 1.10 and Table B1.14).

In contrast, student expectations of completing a university degree are *lower* than the actual graduation rates in Iceland, Poland and the Slovak Republic. In the Slovak Republic, for example, student expectations of completing a university degree are 16 percentage points lower than the actual graduation rates; in Poland, the difference is 9 percentage points. In these two countries, the mismatch between expectations and graduation rates points to a potential loss of talent as students who expect to complete a university degree may not be working as hard as they could be in school given the potentially low levels of competition to enter university. Student expectations of completing university closely match the actual graduation rates in Australia, Austria, Hungary and New Zealand, signalling that in these countries there is a lower likelihood of misaligned expectations (see Box 1.8 for the importance of matching the supply and the demand of skills).

Box 1.8 **Matching the demand for and the supply of skills**

Some workers are not well-matched with their current jobs: some are capable of handling more complex tasks and their skills are underused, while others lack the skills needed for their jobs. Although skills mismatch is difficult to measure, available indicators suggest that these two phenomena are widespread. Of course, such indicators need to be interpreted in context. For example, in low-skills equilibrium, people's skills are matched to their jobs, but at a very low level. And, as explained below, skills that are not used in an individual's current job may be used elsewhere, in other contexts, to the benefit of society as a whole.

The incidence of skills mismatch varies across groups of workers. Based on preliminary data from the OECD Survey of Adult Skills field trial, a product of the Programme for the International Assessment of Adult Competencies (PIAAC), a relatively high percentage of knowledge-economy workers are considered to have a "high-skills match", meaning that they have high literacy skills and that they use those skills at work. This group also shows a lower incidence of "low-skills match", meaning that fewer of these workers have low literacy skills that they use at work. In contrast, a relatively high percentage of non-knowledge-economy workers are considered to have a "low-skills match", meaning that they have low literacy skills and use those skills at work. A high proportion of these workers have high literacy skills, but they use those skills infrequently at work ("skills surplus"). Far fewer non-knowledge-economy workers enjoy a "high-skills match" as compared with those who work in the knowledge economy.

The mismatch between workers' skills and their tasks at work can also adversely affect economic and social outcomes. Over-skilling, or the under-use of skills, in specific jobs in the short to medium term can be a problem because it may lead to skills loss and a waste of the resources that were used to acquire those skills. Workers whose skills are under-used in their current jobs earn less than workers who are well-matched to their jobs and are often less satisfied at work. This situation tends to generate more employee turnover, which is likely to affect a firm's productivity. Under-skilling is also likely to affect productivity and, as with skills shortages, slow the rate at which more efficient technologies and approaches to work can be adopted. While there is evidence of skills imbalances, it is difficult to interpret for policy purposes primarily because of the complexity of the underlying causes. What is known suggests that there is scope for public policy interventions.

Source: OECD (2012a).

PERSPECTIVES ON SOCIAL MOBILITY

Students' expectations are an indication of their eventual educational attainment and occupational status; when compared with their parents' educational attainment, they also signal students' expectations of social mobility. Students who expect to attain a higher level of education than their parents expect upward mobility; students who expect to attain a lower level of education than their parents expect downward mobility.

In most countries and economies, more students expect upward mobility than downward mobility. On average across the countries that implemented the ECQ, 30% of students whose parents did not complete a university degree expect to complete one (upward mobility) and 8% of students whose parents do hold a university degree do not expect to complete one (downward mobility). Only in Belgium (Flemish Community), Iceland and Latvia is the percentage of students who expect upward mobility similar to or lower than the level of students expecting downward mobility. In Latvia, there is a higher percentage of students who expect to attain a lower educational level than their parents did. Expectations of upward mobility are especially prevalent in Hong Kong-China, Korea, Mexico, Portugal, Serbia, Singapore and Trinidad and Tobago, where more than a third of students whose parents do not hold a university degree expect to complete such a degree themselves (Figure 1.11).

▪ Figure 1.11 ▪

Percentage of students who expect upward or downward mobility

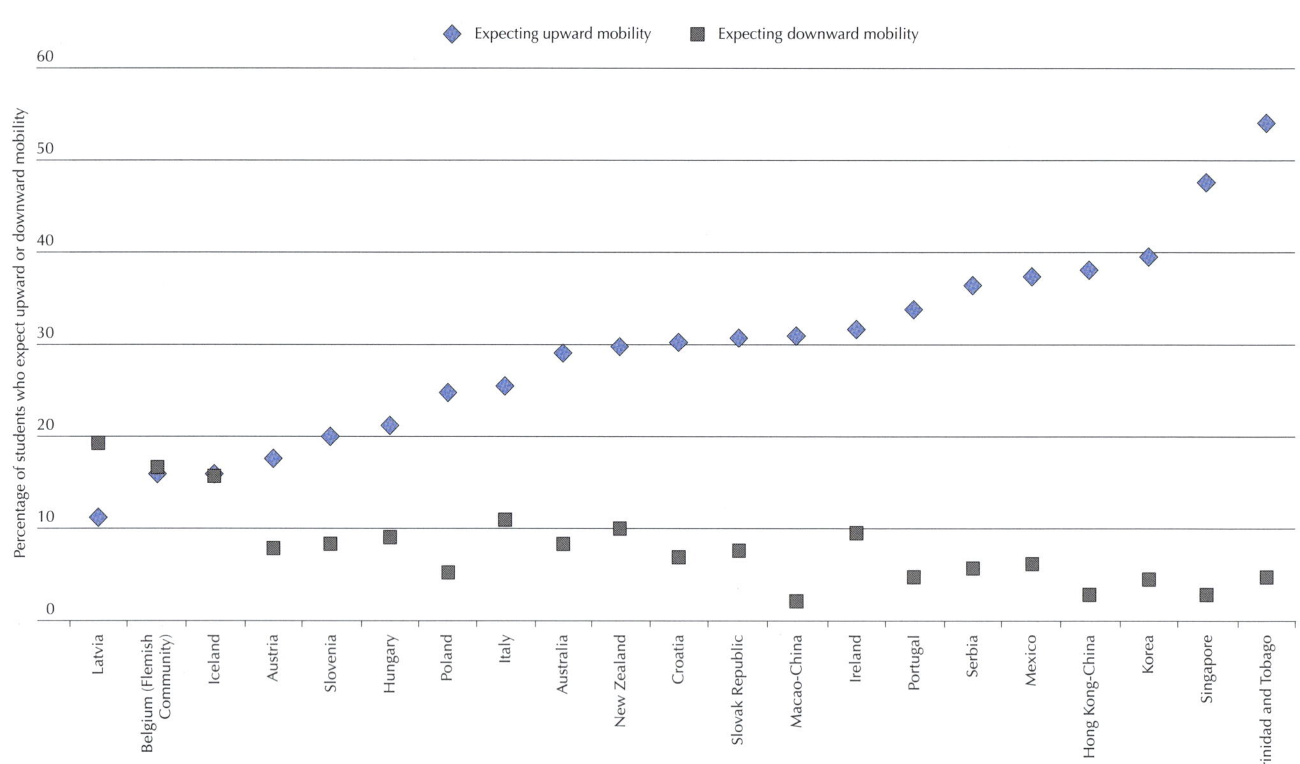

Note: Students expecting upward mobility are students who expect to complete a university degree and whose parents did not complete this degree. Students expecting downward mobility are students who do not expect to complete a university degree and at least one of whose parents did complete that degree.
Countries are sorted in ascending order of the percentage of students expecting upward mobility.
Source: Table B1.15.
StatLink http://dx.doi.org/10.1787/888932733469

The literature on social mobility distinguishes between structural mobility and exchange mobility. Structural mobility refers to improvements in intergenerational mobility that result from changes in the structure of available opportunities. Structural mobility leads to improvements in intergenerational mobility when, for example, there is a rapid expansion of tertiary education and one generation has more opportunities to improve its educational attainment than the previous generation did. Exchange mobility (circulation mobility or social fluidity), by contrast, refers to the extent to which parents' status determines the next generation's opportunities to acquire social status (Hout, 2004).

If expectations of social mobility are aligned to a system's opportunity structure, they should be higher in countries that have expanded access to tertiary education (because of the increase in opportunities for structural mobility) and in countries that have a weaker relationship between students' socio-economic status and their performance (because of the opportunities for exchange mobility).

Among the countries that participated in the ECQ, students' expectations of social mobility are only weakly related to the structure of opportunities available to them. Specifically, there is only a weak correlation between the increase in enrolment rates between 2003 and 2009 and the change in enrolments in higher education during that period (correlation coefficient of 0.16). Countries with the greatest expansion in tertiary education are not necessarily those with the highest levels of expectations of upward mobility. Similarly, there is a weak relationship between expectations of social mobility and the degree of socio-economic equity in student performance (exchange mobility). Countries with higher equity in performance tend to be those with a higher proportion of students who expect upward mobility; but the correlation is moderate (the correlation coefficient, at the country level, between the proportion of variance in reading performance explained by students' socio-economic background and the percentage of students expecting upward mobility is -0.20) (Figures 1.12 and 1.13).

Studies on social stratification that analyse trends in observed rates of educational mobility find that they have barely changed during the 20th century (Pfeffer, 2008; Shavit and Blossfeld, 1993). Yet although observed mobility has remained constant, in nine countries and economies there was an increase in expectations of upward mobility between 2003 and 2009. This increase was

▪ Figure 1.12 ▪

Relationship between students' expectations of upward mobility and change in enrolment in tertiary education

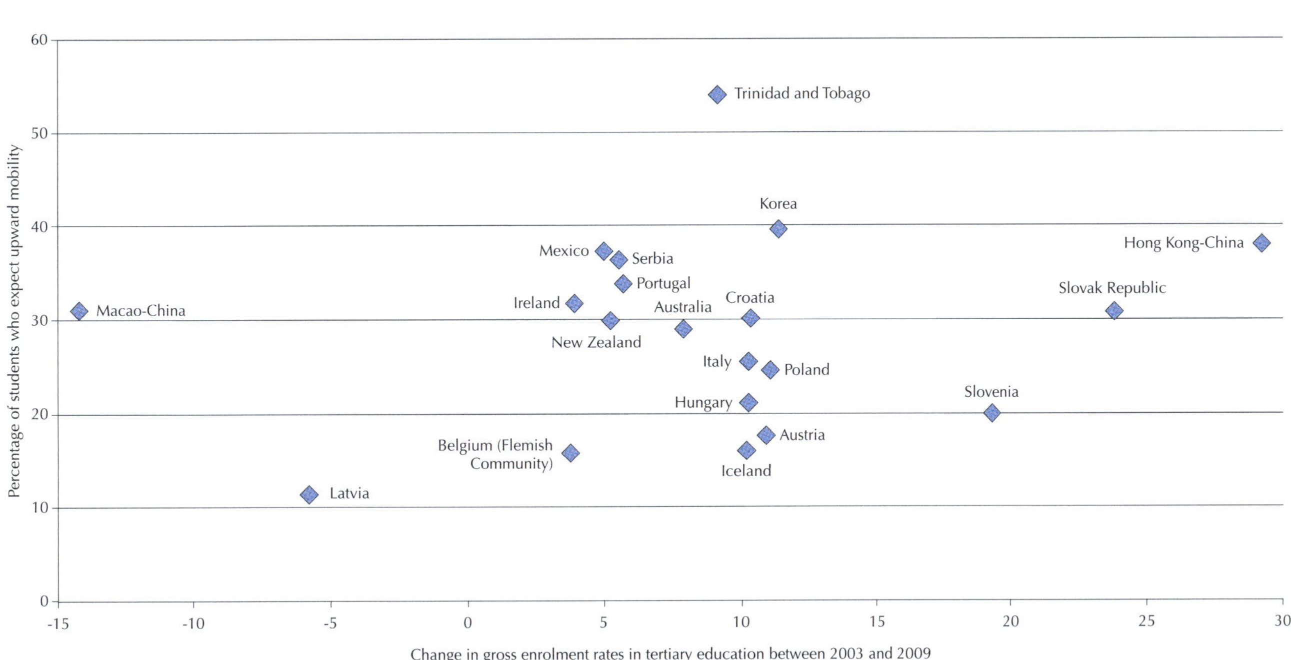

Notes: Students expecting upward mobility are students who expect to complete a university degree and whose parents did not complete this degree.
Change in enrolment rates for Belgium (Flemish Community) represent data for Belgium as a whole.
Source: Table B1.14 and Table B1.15.
StatLink http://dx.doi.org/10.1787/888932733488

▪ Figure 1.13 ▪

Relationship between students' expectations of upward mobility and equity in reading performance

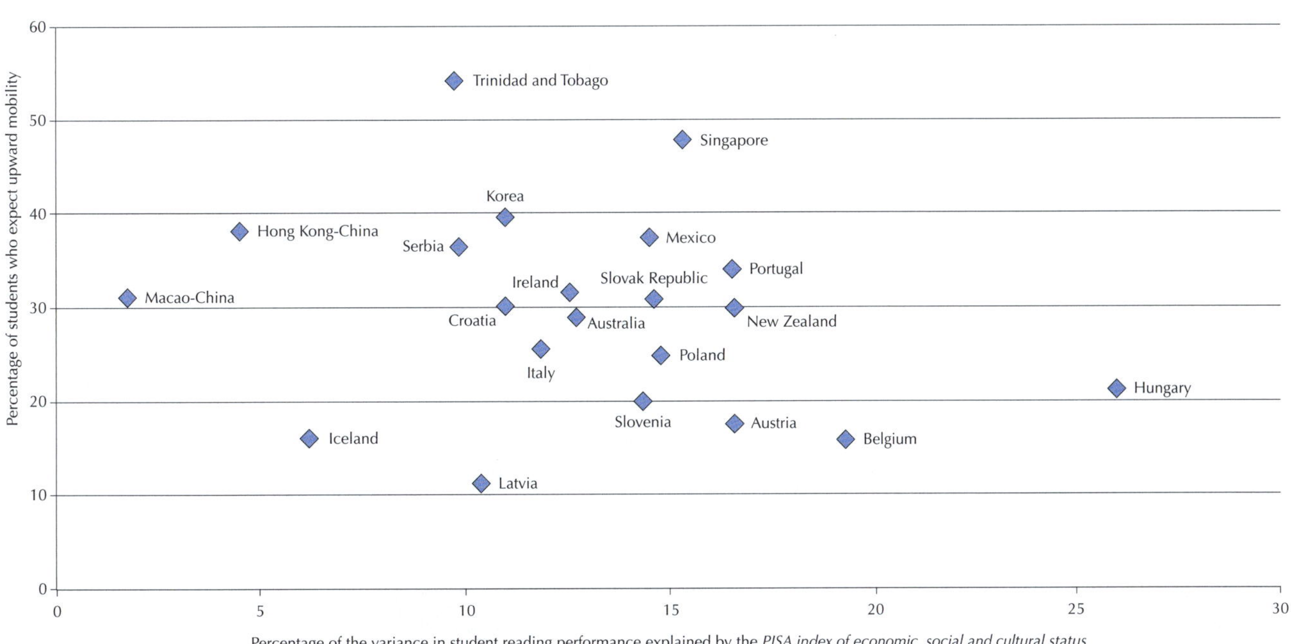

Note: Students who expect upward mobility are students who expect to complete a university degree and whose parents did not complete this degree.
Source: Table B1.15 and Table II.1.2 in OECD (2010), *PISA 2009 Results: Overcoming Social Background (Volume II)*, PISA, OECD Publishing.
StatLink http://dx.doi.org/10.1787/888932733507

greatest in Austria, Mexico, New Zealand and Poland, with an increase of more than seven percentage points. Expectations of upward social mobility have decreased significantly in Macao-China (by 13 percentage points) and in Hong Kong-China, Hungary and Korea.

Consistent with the general trend towards greater expectations of upward mobility, expectations of downward mobility decreased in 10 countries and economies between 2003 and 2009. Only in two countries – Hungary and Korea – did expectations of downward mobility increase in a statistically significant way; but the magnitude of this change is at or below two percentage points. The greatest decrease in expectations of downward mobility is observed in Austria and Latvia, where there was more than a 20 percentage-point reduction in expectations of downward mobility (Table B1.15).

CONCLUSION

In most countries and economies, a sizeable proportion of high-performing students does not expect to continue on to upper secondary education, signalling a potential loss of talent for the education system and the labour market. These students lack the motivation or the interest to pursue university-level education. Conversely, there is also a sizeable proportion of low-performing students who expect to complete a university degree. These students lack the skills that are necessary to complete university level studies and are therefore unlikely to be able to fulfil their expectations. This may prove costly, both in financial and social terms, as these students will most likely be frustrated by not meeting their goals. School systems should strive to ensure that all students expecting to enter – and eventually to graduate – from university, will have the ability to do so. School systems should also provide sufficient incentives and information for those students who are unable or unwilling to upgrade their skills so that they can develop more realistic expectations about their future but they should also ensure that attractive alternatives are available to these students once they complete upper secondary schooling.

In all countries and economies some high-performing students do not expect to complete university degrees and some low-performing students do. Students in countries that offer different education programmes to their students – vocationally or academically-oriented programmes – tend to hold expectations that more closely reflect their abilities and possibilities. This is because education systems that stream students into different programmes also create clear education pathways and linkages between education levels and the workplace, allowing students in academic programmes to continue on to university, and students in vocational programmes to find work, because of linkages between schools and employers. Yet countries that provide these clear signals about students' futures in education are also those that show a more unequal distribution of expectations, because sorting students into different educational programmes is often related to students' background characteristics.

Countries and economies benefit from fostering realistic expectations among their students in several ways: educating a population that is likely to succeed in higher education is more efficient; students who hold realistic expectations are less likely to feel frustrated; and holding realistic expectations reduces the likelihood that high-performing students will not expect to complete a university degree and thus let their talent go to waste.

Countries and economies that use differentiation – and thus promote more realistic student expectations – should strive to disconnect sorting students into different programmes from students' background characteristics. This can be done by delaying selection and providing compensatory opportunities to disadvantaged students early on, thus allowing students who enter primary school with an academic disadvantage to catch up and compete on a level playing field with other students when differentiation occurs. Countries that adopt a comprehensive approach to schooling, offering all students a similar curriculum, should strive to provide students with more accurate and reliable information about students' further eductation and suggest pathways that smooth the transition to the labour market for students who choose this avenue.

Education systems should also not forget that a large number of students do *not* expect to attend university, much less complete a university degree. Education systems should give this "forgotten half" of students the tools and information they need to enter and navigate through the labour market after they leave upper secondary education. These education systems should also strive to create linkages between employers and schools to ease the transition to work for students who end their formal education after upper secondary school – and who are thus most likely to be unemployed. These linkages can help motivate students to work hard in school, regardless of their expectations, because they provide real employment opportunities for those students who do not intend to continue their education. These education systems should strive to promote on-the-job training, and offer incentives for employers to recruit and train young workers (OECD, 2010d).

The findings discussed in this chapter also indicate considerable disparities in expectations related to gender, performance and socio-economic background. Boys and socio-economically disadvantaged students are less likely than girls and advantaged students to expect to complete a university degree. They are also more likely to expect to complete their formal education at the upper secondary level and not obtain further qualifications. Performance differences, and the resulting sorting of students into different educational tracks or into different ability groupings, explain part of the observed differences in expectations related to gender and socio-economic status. The persistence of such inequalities after mathematics and reading performance is considered suggests that the limits to expectations and social mobility may be more solidly set than those related to educational performance. These expectations are determined by a wider array of social, cultural and economic factors that may reinforce inequality, even after accounting for academic performance. Students' expectations of further education are an initial signal of eventual educational attainment, which, in turn, has important consequences not only for their entry into and success in the labour market, but also for their health, social participation and general well-being.

Notes

1. Students are asked to respond to the question: "Which of the following do you expect to complete?" with answer categories ranging from ISCED level 2 to ISCED level 6. To enable cross-country comparisons, each national version of the questionnaire uses the country-specific denomination of each ISCED level. For the purposes of this report, ISCED level 5A or 6 degrees are considered university degrees. Because of their technical/vocational orientation, this report does not consider ISCED 5B degrees as university degrees. In PISA 2003 and PISA 2009 the qualifications "engineer and licentiate" were coded as ISCED 5B programmes; therefore students expecting to complete these qualifications were not counted as those who expect to complete "university". However, in the UNESCO/OECD/EUROSTAT (UOE) joint data collection system, these qualifications are counted as ISCED 5A. This difference in coding means that the proportion of students who expect to complete university as calculated by PISA is lower than the corresponding proportion calculated using the UOE classification. For countries such as Poland, where large numbers of students expect to attain these qualifications, the difference in results between the two methods of coding can be pronounced.
2. As Croatia, Serbia, Singapore, Slovenia and Trinidad and Tobago did not participate in the PISA 2003 cycle, there is no possibility of evaluating trends in their students' expectations.
3. Analyses that focus on the difference in mathematics performance between students who expect to complete a university degree and those who do not show similar results as those presented for reading performance (see Table B1.3).
4. Due to the relatively small number of countries in the analyses, these estimates are not statistically significant. Furthermore, due to their relatively high and low expectations, Korea and Latvia exert a disproportionate influence on the estimates. As such, the regression analyses for these results include dummy variables for Korea and Latvia (see Table B1.5).
5. In order of the percentage of students attending ISCED B/C-type programmes, the countries and economies with at least 8% of students in these programmes are: Serbia, Slovenia, Austria, Ireland, Korea, Croatia, Belgium (Flemish Community), Portugal, Hungary, Trinidad and Tobago and the Slovak Republic.
6. Of the 21 countries and economies that implemented the Educational Career questionnaire, *Education at a Glance 2011* does not provide information on 2009 graduation rates for Croatia, Hong Kong-China, Latvia, Macao-China, Serbia, Singapore and Trinidad and Tobago (OECD, 2011a).
7. After adding the graduation figures for ISCED 5A and ISCED 5B programmes, the total ISCED 5A and 5B graduation rates for Korea are roughly equal to the level of student expectations to complete a university degree. The Educational Career questionnaire and tertiary education graduation rates reported by *Education at a Glance 2011* (OECD 2011a), however, distinguish clearly from ISCED 5A and 5B programmes, and in this report "university expectations" do not include ISCED 5B programmes.
8. As there is a ten-year gap between the expectations of 15-year-old students as recorded in the PISA 2009 study and the graduation rates reported in *Education at a Glance 2011* (OECD, 2011a), it is possible that graduation rates in these countries will grow to meet the demands of their highly ambitious youth.

References

Andrew, M. and **R. Hauser** (2012), "Adoption? Adaptation? Evaluating the Formation of Educational Expectations", *Social Forces,* Vol. 90, No. 2, pp. 497-520.

Arum, R. and **J. Roksa** (2011), *Academically Adrift: Limited Learning on College Campuses,* University of Chicago Press, Chicago, Illinois.

Autor, D., F. Levy and **R. Murnane** (2003), "The Skill Content of Recent Technological Change: An Empricial Exploration", *Quarterly Journal of Economics,* Vol. 118, No. 4, pp. 1279-1334.

Baird, C., S. Burge and **J. Reynolds** (2008), "Absurdly Ambitious? Teenagers' Expectations for the Future and the Realities of Social Structure", *Sociology Compass,* Vol. 2/3, pp. 944-962.

Belfield, C. and **H. Levin** (eds.) (2007), *The Price We Pay: Economic and Social Consequences of Inadequate Education,* Brookings Institution, Washington, DC.

Bettinger, E. and **B. Long** (2009), "Addressing the Needs of Underprepared Students in Higher Education: Does College Remediation Work?", *Journal of Human Resources,* Vol. 44, No. 3, pp. 736-771.

Brand, J.E. and **Y. Xie** (2010), "Who Benefits Most from College? Evidence for Negative Selection in Heterogeneous Economic Returns to Higher Education", *American Sociological Review,* Vol. 75, No. 2, pp. 273-302.

Buchmann, C. and **B. Dalton** (2002), "Interpersonal Influences and Educational Aspirations in 12 Countries: The Importance of Institutional Context", *Sociology of Education,* Vol. 75, No. 2, pp. 99-122.

Buchmann, C. and **H. Park** (2009), "Stratification and the Formation of Expectations in Highly Differentiated Educational Systems", *Research in Social Stratification and Mobility,* Vol. 27, No. 4, pp. 245-267.

Campbell, R. (1983), "Status Attainment Research: End of the Beginning or Beginning of the End?", *Sociology of Education,* Vol. 56, No. 1, pp. 47-62.

Carbonaro, W., **B. Ellison** and **E. Covay** (2011), "Gender Inequalities in the College Pipeline", *Social Science Research,* Vol. 40, No. 1, pp. 120-135.

Collins, R. (1979), *The Credential Society: an Historical Sociology of Education and Stratification,* Academic Press, New York, New York.

Commission of the European Communities (2009), *New Skills for New Jobs: Anticipating and Matching Labour Market and Skills Needs,* COM(2008) 868 Final.

Eurofound (2012), *NEETs – Young People Not in Employment, Education or Training: Characteristics, Costs and Policy Responses in Europe,* Publications Office of the European Union, Luxembourg.

Goyette, K. (2008), "College for Some to College for All: Social Background, Occupational Expectations, and Educational Expectations over Time", *Social Science Research,* Vol. 37, No. 2, pp. 461-484.

Hanson, S. (1994), "Lost Talent: Unrealized Educational Aspirations and Expectations among U.S. Youths", *Sociology of Education,* Vol. 67, No. 3, pp. 159-183.

Hout, M. (2004), "How Inequality May Affect Intergenerational Mobility" in *Social Inequality,* ed. K. Neckerman, Russell Sage Foundation, New York, New York.

Kerckhoff, A. (1976), "The Status Attainment Process: Socialization or Allocation", *Social Forces,* Vol. 55, No. 2, pp. 368-381.

Kerckhoff, A. (1995), "Institutional Arrangements and Stratification Processes in Industrial Societies", *Annual Review of Sociology,* Vol. 21, pp. 323-347.

Kerckhoff, A. (2000), "Transition from School to Work in Comparative Perspective" in M. Hallinan (ed.) *The Handbook of the Sociology of Education,* Kluwer Academic/Plenum Publishers, New York, New York.

Kristen, C. and **N. Granato** (2007), "The Educational Attainment of the Second Generation in Germany", *Ethnicities,* Vol. 7, No. 3, pp. 343-366.

Labaree, D. (1997), "Public Goods, Private Goods: The American Struggle over Educational Goals", *American Educational Research Journal,* Vol. 34, No. 1, pp. 39-81.

Marcotte, J. (2012), "Breaking Down the Forgotten Half: Exploratory Profiles of Youths in Quebec's Adult Education Centers", *Educational Researcher,* Vol. 41, No. 6, pp. 191-200.

Mateju, P., et al. (2007), "The Determination of College Expectations in OECD Countries: The Role of Individual and Structural Factors ", *Czech Sociological Review,* Vol. 43, No. 6, pp. 1121-1148.

McDaniel, A. (2010), "Cross-National Gender Gaps in Educational Expectations: The Influence of National-Level Gender Ideology and Educational Systems", *Comparative Education Review,* Vol. 54, No. 1, pp. 27-50.

Morgan, S. (2005), *On the Edge of Commitment: Educational Attainment and Race in the United States,* Stanford University Press, Stanford, California.

OECD (1999), *Classifying educational programmes: Manual for ISCED-97 implementation in OECD countries,* OECD Publishing.

OECD (2010a), *Pathways to Success: How Knowledge and Skills at Age 15 Shape Future Lives in Canada,* PISA, OECD Publishing.

OECD (2010b), *PISA 2009 Results: What Students Know and Can Do, Student Performance in Reading, Mathematics and Science (Volume I),* PISA, OECD Publishing.

OECD (2010c), *PISA 2009 Results: What Makes a School Successful? Resources, Policies and Practices (Volume IV),* PISA, OECD Publishing.

OECD (2010d), *Off to a Good Start? Jobs for Youth,* OECD Publishing.

OECD (2010e), *Learning for Jobs, OECD Reviews of Vocational Education and Training,* OECD Publishing.

OECD (2010f), *PISA 2009 Results: Overcoming Social Background – Equity in Learning Opportunities and Outcomes (Volume II),* PISA, OECD Publishing.

OECD (2011a), *Education at a Glance 2011: OECD Indicators,* OECD Publishing.

OECD (2011b), *Employment Outlook 2011,* OECD Publishing.

OECD (2012a), *Better Skills, Better Jobs, Better Lives: A Strategic Approach to Skills Policies,* OECD Publishing.

OECD (2012b), *Learning Beyond Fifteen: Ten Years after PISA,* PISA, OECD Publishing.

OECD (2012c), "What Kinds of Careers do Boys and Girls Expect for Themselves?", *PISA in Focus,* No. 14, OECD Publishing.

Perna, L. (2000), "Differences in the Decision to Attend College among African Americans, Hispanics, and Whites", *The Journal of Higher Education,* Vol. 71, No. 2, pp. 117-141.

Pfeffer, F. (2008), "Persistent Inequality in Educational Attainment and its Institutional Context", *European Sociological Review,* Vol. 24, No. 5, pp. 543-565.

Rosenbaum, J. (2001), *Beyond College for All: Career Paths for the Forgotten Half,* Russell Sage Foundation, New York, New York.

Rosenbaum, J. and **T. Kariya** (1989), "From High School to Work: Market and Institutional Mechanisms in Japan", *American Journal of Sociology,* Vol. 94, No. 6, pp. 1334-1365.

Rosenbaum, J., et al. (1990), "Market and Network Theories of the Transition from High School to Work: Their Applications to Industrialized Societies", *American Sociological Review,* Vol. 16, No. 6, pp. 263-299.

Rumberger, R. (2011), *Dropping Out: Why Students Drop Out of High School and What Can Be Done About It,* Harvard University Press, Cambridge, Massachusetts.

Saha, L. (1997), "Aspirations and Expectations of Students" in L. Saha (ed.), *International Encyclopedia of the Sociology of Education,* Pergamon Press, Oxford, pp. 512-517.

Schofer, E. and **J. Meyer** (2005), "The Worldwide Expansion of Higher Education in the Twentieth Century", *American Sociological Review,* Vol. 70, No. 6, pp. 898-920.

Sewell, W., et al. (2003), "As We Age: A Review of the Wisconsin Longitudinal Study, 1957-2001", *Research in Social Stratification and Mobility,* Vol. 20, pp. 3-111.

Shavit, Y. and **H. Blossfeld** (1993), *Persistent Inequality : Changing Educational Attainment in Thirteen Countries,* Westview Press, Boulder, Colorado.

Shavit, Y. and **W. Müller** (1998), *From School to Work: A Comparative Study of Educational Qualifications and Occupational Destinations,* Oxford University Press, Oxford.

Torche, F. (2010), "Is a College Degree still the Great Equalizer? Intergenerational Mobility across Levels of Schooling in the United States", *American Journal of Sociology,* Vol. 117, No. 3, pp. 763-807.

Turner, R. (1960), "Sponsored and Contest Mobility and the School-System", *American Sociological Review,* Vol. 25, No. 6, pp. 855-867.

Useem, E. (1992), "Middle Schools and Math Groups – Parents Involvement in Children's Placement", *Sociology of Education,* Vol. 65, No. 4, pp. 263-279.

Wiley, A., J. Wyatt and **W. Camara** (2010), *The Development of a Multidimensional College Readiness Index,* College Board, New York, New York.

2

What Behaviours Do Teachers Reward?

This chapter examines the uses and significance of school marks. It discusses the kinds of behaviours, habits and attitudes that teachers reward with better marks, some of which may be unrelated to student learning. It also explores differences in how countries and economies distribute marks and suggests ways of improving the effectiveness of school marks.

Within the classroom, one of the most important levers teachers have to guide the behaviour of students is marks/grades. Marks serve three main instructional purposes: they provide formative feedback to students, they provide teachers with feedback for instructional planning, and they certify that students have mastered skills considered relevant by the teacher or school (Carey and Carifio, 2012). Such is the recognised importance of in-class assessments that, in PISA, practically all students attend schools that assess students' work or progress through teacher-developed tests and/or assignments that the students return. In almost all countries and economies over 95% of students are assessed this way (see Table IV.3.10 in OECD, 2010). Through marks, teachers signal what kinds of attitudes and behaviours they reward, and signal what they believe is important for student success. In general, teachers reward achievement – students' mastery of skills and knowledge, as measured by standardised tests. Yet the relationship between marks and test scores is not perfect, and this difference is related to the behaviours and attitudes that teachers reward (Brookhart, 1993; McMillan et al., 2002).

While teachers use marks as a diagnostic tool, they also use them to communicate expectations and foster motivation in their students (Stiggins and Conklin, 1992), because students react to the incentives marks represent by modifying their behaviour (Bonesrønning, 1999). Marks as a mode of communication and a source of incentives influence student interest in school and the subject matter, self-efficacy, motivation, and future performance (Brookhart, 2009; Docan, 2006; Guskey, 2004). Used effectively and correctly, marks can motivate students to put forth more effort and change their behaviours and attitudes in a direction that is beneficial to students and learning. Marks can, however, discourage and disengage students when they are inconsistent with student models of motivation (Covington, 1984; Kohn, 1993).

In the context of the importance and pervasiveness of marks, this chapter answers the following questions: what kinds of behaviours, habits and attitudes do teachers reward with better marks? Do certain teachers, schools and countries/economies offer rewards for attitudes that are unrelated to student learning? Do countries and economies differ in the way they distribute marks and reward student behaviour? And, can more efficient grading patterns be identified among school systems?

Generally, teachers can be categorised according to the way in which they use marks to promote students' learning. While some teachers subscribe to the "keeping things moving" approach, others follow a "developmental" approach to marking (Kelly, 2008). Teachers who adopt the "keeping things moving" approach reward in-class co-operation and penalise disruptiveness and disciplinary problems. These teachers reward behaviours that are not necessarily directly related to future achievement, but that help to keep instruction moving smoothly (Stiggins and Conklin, 1992). Teachers who adopt the "developmental" approach, on the other hand, use marks to foster student engagement. These teachers focus on cultivating interest, concentration and effort, because they believe that student engagement is a necessary precondition for learning (Fredricks et al., 2004). These teachers seek to motivate what they believe are key student competencies that will help students become better learners inside and outside the classroom. They emphasise fairness and are sensitive to how students will react to the marks they receive so as to promote self-esteem and future engagement (Brookhart, 1993). Another incentive that motivates the way teachers determine marks is the pressure to align their teaching and their marks to the contents and results of external standardised assessments, where these are implemented and have high stakes for students, teachers and/or schools.

Marks vary according to the incentives teachers want to put in place for their students. The meaning and purpose of marks thus vary with respect to the objectives and nature of assessments. Assessments, however, should not be a synonym of marks. Assessments are the gathering of information for the purpose of making instructional or career-path decisions, and the information from assessments does not always need to be transmitted to students; not all assessments need to produce marks. Whenever assessments are graded, marks should provide clear and useful information for the purpose of enhancing learning. The criteria used in marking and the behaviours or content that is being evaluated in them should be clear to students so that the information that is contained in marks is interpretable and useful for students and teachers to improve learning (Guskey and Bailey, 2001; Marzano, 2000; O'Connor, 2002; O'Connor, 2009; Tomlinson, 2005).

Empirical research examining teachers' marking tendencies and how students react to the marks they receive generally focuses on a specific country. PISA is unique in that it allows for a comparison of how marks are distributed across countries and economies. PISA can also provide information on the proportion of schools that motivate behaviours that are conducive to learning. A careful study of marks is of utmost importance because student marks – insofar as they convey information not only about academic abilities but also about students' non-cognitive skills (e.g. engagement, approaches to learning, attitudes towards challenges, etc.) and students' rank within the class – are one of students' most important sources of information about their potential to succeed in further educational endeavours and in the labour market later on. In fact, while marks reflect, in part, students' skills and mastery of content, their power to predict students' future educational and social outcomes is stronger than the effect of academic achievement alone. For example, students' marks, net of achievement, predict educational plans, course-taking patterns, eventual achievement and earnings nine years after graduation (Kelly, 2008; Rosenbaum, 2001).

Students who take the PISA test – and similar tests – are undergoing an assessment of the skills and competencies that they have accumulated over the years. Most students are not familiar with such objective performance measures, however, and in most

countries such standardised tests only occur at the end of specific academic cycles. This means that while educators and policy makers are prompted to improve the efficiency and equity of their own school or of entire educations systems by the school's/system's performance in standardised tests, student motivation is stimulated by a different set of incentives altogether. Marks represent the most concrete form of information students have about their abilities and potential. A careful assessment of grading practices in different education systems reveals the type of incentives that are put in place to facilitate the learning process where most learning takes place.

This chapter uses data from the PISA Educational Career questionnaire (ECQ). The questionnaire was optional for countries participating in the PISA 2009 assessment. Students in 17 countries and economies were asked, among other things, to report what mark (grade) they received in their language-of-assessment class. This chapter identifies the attitudes and behaviours that are most strongly related to marks, with a special focus on those habits, attitudes and behaviours that are not necessarily conducive to improving cognitive skills, such as those associated with students' educational context and background.[1]

Because countries differ in the way in which they instruct their teachers to mark students and in the scales used to distribute marks, this chapter also offers a thorough look at the different schemes countries have developed to determine and distribute marks to students. Countries vary remarkably in the scales teachers use to mark students; but in all countries considered, teachers reward similar attitudes and behaviours. For example, students who perform well in standardised tests like PISA are more likely to receive better marks, indicating that teachers reward, first and foremost, skills and mastery of the types of knowledge of in-class content that standardised tests measure. In many school systems, teachers reward behaviours that promote learning, such as engagement with reading and control strategies. Yet in many school systems, attitudes, values and behaviours unrelated to learning are also rewarded with higher marks. In these systems teachers often mark on a curve and/or use a marking system that favours students with particular background characteristics.

HOW COUNTRIES GRADE THEIR STUDENTS: MARKS IN PISA

Very few countries share the same grading schemes. Notwithstanding the fact that PISA did not compile information on the content that is marked and the standards that are applied in grading students, Figure 2.1 highlights the different grading schemes adopted by teachers in the countries and economies participating in this study. The education systems in Austria, Hungary and Serbia use a scale from 1 to 5 while those in Croatia, Poland and the Slovak Republic use a scale from 1 to 6. The education systems in Iceland, Italy and Latvia mark from 1 to 10, and the Flemish Community of Belgium, Ireland, Singapore and Trinidad and Tobago use a scale from 1 to 100. In Portugal, students in ISCED level 2 programmes receive marks on a scale from 1 to 5 while students in ISCED level 3 programmes receive marks on a scale from 1 to 20. In most countries and economies, higher values on the scale are indicative of better evaluations. However, in Austria and the Slovak Republic, a value of 1 indicates the better evaluation. In all these countries, the scales are discrete, that is, students do not report receiving marks with decimal places.

▪ Figure 2.1 ▪

Marking schemes across countries and economies

Failing mark	Marking range					Schools or regions have different marking systems
	1 to 5	1 to 6	1 to 10	1 to 20	1 to 100	
Many possible values	Portugal ISCED 2		Iceland, Italy, Latvia	Portugal ISCED 3	Belgium (Flemish Community), Ireland, Singapore, Trinidad and Tobago	Macao-China, Mexico, New Zealand
One value	Austria, Hungary, Serbia	Croatia, Poland, the Slovak Republic				

StatLink http://dx.doi.org/10.1787/888932733526

Some countries and economies have important internal variation in the schemes teachers and schools use to mark their students. Certain schools within countries or certain teachers within schools may use one scheme while other schools and teachers use other schemes. This is the case for Macao-China, Mexico and New Zealand. Many 15-year-old students in grade 11 in New Zealand, for example, receive marks of "Not Achieved," "Achieved," "Merit," or "Excellence" that are consistent with work towards the national certificate of achievement. However, students attending lower grades, or following specific programmes (e.g. International Baccaleaurate) or in schools that choose other marking systems may receive their marks as a percentage or on another scale. In Macao-China's schools, teachers are completely autonomous in the way they choose to assess and mark their students. In Mexico, education levels have different marking schemes. As a result, Macao-China, Mexico and New Zealand asked PISA 2009 students not about the specific mark they received in the past year, but to report whether the student received a mark that placed him/her a) below the passing mark or b) at or above the passing mark.

Different education systems establish different criteria for communicating to students that they have failed the class or the assessment. In some countries, the marking scheme allows for only one possible failing value, meaning that students who fail do not know how

far they are from meeting the passing criteria. This is the case in Austria, Croatia, Hungary, Poland, Serbia and the Slovak Republic, for example. The remaining values on the marking scale reflect the quality of the passing assignment as, for example, "sufficient", "good", "very good" and "excellent".

Other countries establish the passing mark somewhere in the middle of the scale, allowing for marks to communicate how far students are from the minimum passing criteria. The Flemish Community of Belgium, Italy and Singapore, for example, establish the cut-off point in the distribution at the 50% range of the marking scale. In Ireland, the grading scale ranges from 0 to 100, but only scores below 40 are considered unsatisfactory or failing.[2] Research that evaluates the efficacy of marking schemes to motivate students to put forth more effort suggest that using extremely low values fails to motivate students to improve, especially when a student receives a minimum mark at the beginning of the school year. Moreover, students receiving an unusually low mark may have a hard time recovering to pass the course, because a low mark skews the mark average and undermines motivation. This is particularly the case for scales that allow failing marks drop far below the passing mark (Carey and Carifio, 2012; Guskey, 2004; Reeves, 2004).

Considering the different marks school systems use to identify failing students, more than 30% of students in ISCED level 2 programmes in Portugal receive failing marks, a percentage that is consistent with the large number of students who report repeating a grade (OECD, 2010). Percentages of students receiving failing marks are also high in Italy, Macao-China, New Zealand and Singapore, where at least 10% of students reported having received a failing mark in their language-of-assessment course. Receiving failing marks is comparatively uncommon in Austria, Belgium (Flemish Community), Croatia, Hungary, Iceland, Ireland, Latvia, Poland, Serbia and the Slovak Republic, where fewer than 5% of students receive failing marks (Figure 2.2). As described above, most of the school systems that have a small percentage of students receiving failing marks in their language-of-assessment courses have only one value to identify failing, but a more detailed scale to identify passing results.

▪ Figure 2.2 ▪

Percentage of students with failing marks in their language-of-assessment course

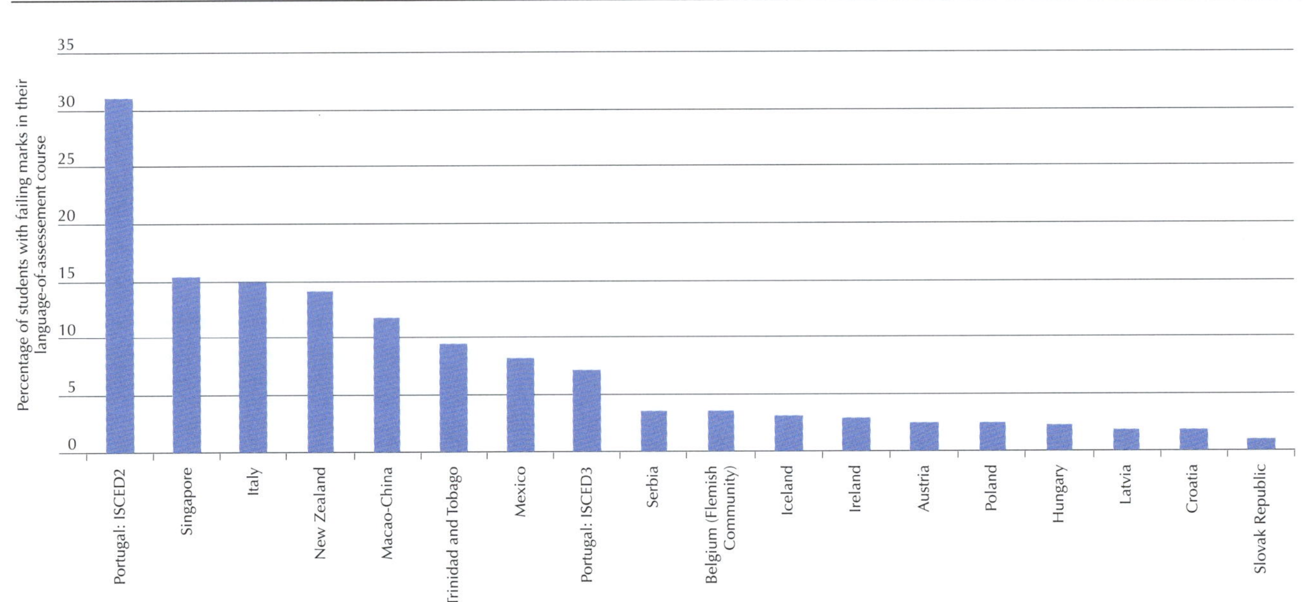

Countries are sorted in descending order of the percentage of students with failing marks in their language-of-assessment courses.
Source: Table B2.2.
StatLink http://dx.doi.org/10.1787/888932733545

Although school systems vary in the detail with which they describe failing marks, all school systems distinguish passing students in at least four categories (signalling achievement that is "sufficient", "good", "very good" or "excellent") or on a continuous scale. Figure 2.3 presents the distribution of marks for only those students who received a passing mark and presents that distribution on a scale that ranges from 50 (equivalent to the minimum passing mark) to 100 (equivalent to the maximum mark).[3] At least 5% of students receive the maximum mark in Austria, Hungary, Serbia and the Slovak Republic, but highest marks are comparatively uncommon and reserved for a smaller percentage of students in the remaining school systems. Highest marks are especially uncommon in Italy, Latvia, Portugal (ISCED 2) and Singapore. In these school systems the highest scoring five percentage of students receive marks that are equivalent to 75% of the maximum passing mark or equivalent to the midpoint of the passing scale.

The average mark received by passing students is close to the midway point of the possible passing values (75% in Figure 2.3) in Austria, Hungary, Iceland, Ireland and Serbia. It is more common, however, that the average passing mark is below this midpoint, signalling that in many countries and economies, the distribution of marks among students who pass their language-of-assessment course is skewed away from the top marks. The average mark in these participating countries is 70% of the plausible range for passing marks. Average marks are in the bottom part of the marking range in Italy, Latvia, Portugal (ISCED 2) and Singapore. Only in the Slovak Republic is the average student more likely to receive a mark that is closest to the top of the marking scale (Figure 2.3).

▪ Figure 2.3 ▪

Distribution of marks received by students who passed their language-of-assessment course

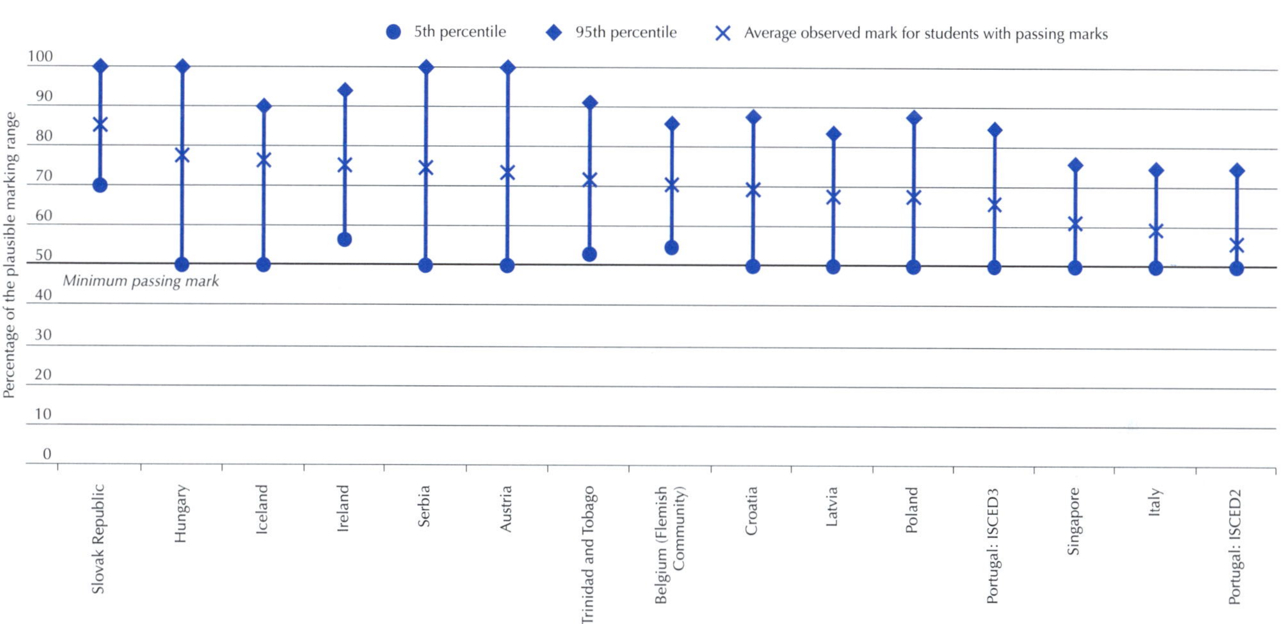

Note: Macao-China, Mexico and New Zealand are omitted from this figure because they measured student marks as pass/fail as their marking systems differ by region and/or school.
For comparison purposes, only passing marks are considered; the lowest passing mark is set at 50 and the highest possible mark at 100.
Countries are sorted in descending order of the average passing mark.
Source: Table B2.1 and B2.2.
StatLink http://dx.doi.org/10.1787/888932733564

Across participating countries and economies with sufficient data to evaluate distributions, the standard deviation in passing marks is 12% of the plausible range. The distribution of marks is more compressed in Singapore, where the standard deviation in marks represents around 8% of the plausible range in passing marks. By contrast, the spread in marks is greatest in Austria, Hungary and Serbia, all of which have a marking scheme that identifies only four, but clearly distinct, categories of passing marks. Marking schemes that allow for a more subtle distinction between students by offering a wider range of values in which to place students (e.g. Belgium [Flemish Community], Ireland and Trinidad and Tobago), do not necessarily capitalise on the opportunity to better discriminate between students. In these countries and economies, the marks students receive are more concentrated than those received by students who are in school systems where only few values are used; but those few values are used effectively to capture important differences in the performance of passing students (e.g. by distinguishing passing achievement as "sufficient", "good", "very good" or "excellent") (Table B2.2).

As will be discussed later, overall marks within a country, and especially the variation of these marks, need to be interpreted carefully. Marks reflect not only students' mastery of the courses' content, but also students' behaviours and attitudes toward learning and school, and their relative position with respect to their peers in the class or school. In this regard, as marks sometimes have a normative component (students' marks also convey information about their relative position in the school or class), and the skills relevant to define mastery of content varies across different programmes, variation in marks among education levels and schools and the meaning of marks have to be interpreted in the context of how students are distributed across grades, schools and programmes in a particular country. The section "Towards a model of marks" develops these ideas in evaluating how different student and school attributes influence the marks students receive in their language courses.

Box 2.1 **Standard-Based Assessment, reforming marking schemes and practices in Korea**

In December 2011, the Korean Ministry of Education, Science and Technology (MEST) announced the "Plans to Improve the Secondary School Academic Affairs Management" to meet the demands for creativity and character required in a global, knowledge-based society. A key feature of the plan is a change in the assessment and in-class grading system within Korean schools, known as the Standard-Based Assessment. Prior to this new academic performance assessment method, Korea's grading practices remained largely normative: assessments and marks were aimed to rank students to see who has achieved more. As a result of the new plan, grading practices have shifted to become criterion-based to evaluate whether, and to what extent, individual students achieved the national curriculum standards developed for each subject. Students in local schools throughout the country are now marked in a uniform five-category scale (with values A, B, C, D and E) that is easily recognisable and understood in Korea and an international setting.

The objectives of the new grading practices involved in the Standard-Based Assessment are multi-fold. It is consistent with the implementation of the 2009 revision of the curriculum that focuses more on creativity and character education. It expands the departmentalised classroom setting and helps create a customised educational environment that considers students' achievement levels. It also seeks to relieve students from the stress of intense competition with their classroom and school peers, provide students with more reliable information about their aptitude and career plans when choosing school subjects and improve schools' ability to select students based on their potential, talent and personal situation.

The Standard-based Assessment was introduced for all subjects in lower secondary schools and specialised subject in upper secondary schools in 2012. In 2014 it will be expanded to general subjects in upper secondary schools as well. This change is not free from complications as it changes a long-held tradition of grading and marking. The Korean government plans to strengthen teacher training on the development and implementation of the new framework to provide for a smooth transition. Parents and students will be informed of the backgrounds and goals of the plan to help them understand the new information conveyed by marks.

BEHAVIOURS REWARDED BY MARKS

Through school marks, teachers can reward different sets of student habits, attitudes and behaviours. These include, first and foremost, achievement, or the mastery of the skills and knowledge that students are expected to acquire by the time they reach agreed developmental and academic milestones. In the context of language courses, this includes abilities measured by the PISA reading assessment (e.g. the ability to extract relevant information from texts) as well as the ability to write extended texts, respond to poetry, and interpret different media, among others. Yet teachers may also reward students' engagement and the use of particular types of learning strategies that may be beneficial for students' future learning and overall well-being. Teachers may also reward behaviours and attitudes that are not directly related to learning per se, but that may determine the pace of instruction and classroom dynamics, or may be unrelated to what happens in school altogether.

This section explores the relationship between marks and student achievement, learning strategies, engagement, attitudes, relationship to teachers, and other attributes that are considered unrelated to learning. PISA does not have explicit data on what criteria teachers use to assign marks; it is thus impossible to have direct information as to which abilities, attitudes and behaviours are consciously rewarded by teachers. Nonetheless, statistical analyses can illuminate which behaviours and attitudes are best related to marks and indirectly identify which are being rewarded by teachers.

In all countries and economies that distributed the ECQ, marks are positively related to reading performance in PISA: students who score higher in the PISA reading assessment also tend to be rewarded with good marks in their language courses. In other words, in all countries and economies teachers tend to reward mastery of skills and knowledge and the ability to apply language to everyday situations, including through in-class assessments. This relationship is most pronounced in Hungary, Latvia, Poland and the Slovak Republic, where the correlation between marks and reading performance is greater than 0.5. The relationship between marks and reading performance is less strong, yet moderate, in the remaining countries (Figure 2.4). As will be discussed later, a more moderate relationship between marks and PISA reading scores may signal that marks are used to distinguish students *within* a school rather than across the whole student population.

Students' approaches to learning and learning strategies are also related to the marks they receive. In practically all countries and economies, students who are able to identify effective summarising and understanding and remembering strategies also have higher marks, indicating that teachers in most education systems reward the use of effective learning strategies. This is particularly the case in Hungary, Poland and the Slovak Republic, where the relationship between marks and the use of these strategies is the strongest.

Yet this is not the case in all education systems. In Singapore and Trinidad and Tobago, the relationship is comparatively weak (Table B2.3). For all countries and economies, these relationships remain stable after accounting for students' reading performance (Table B2.4).

▪ Figure 2.4 ▪
Correlation between the marks students received in their language-of-assessment course and their PISA reading score

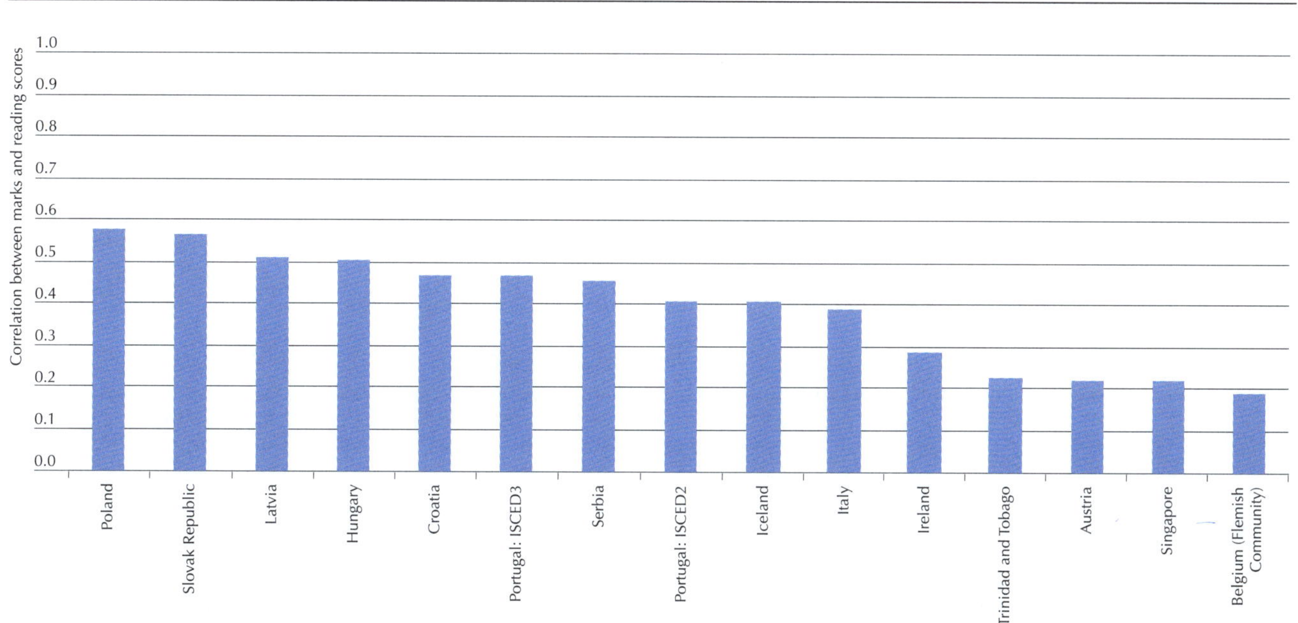

Note: Macao-China, Mexico and New Zealand are omitted from this figure because they measured student marks as pass/fail as their marking systems differ by region and/or school.
Countries are sorted in descending order of the percentage of students with failing marks in their language courses.
Source: Table B2.3.
StatLink http://dx.doi.org/10.1787/888932733583

Consistent with the "developmental" approach to teaching and assessment in language-of-assessment courses, teachers reward those students who enjoy reading with high marks. In seven countries and economies there is a moderate to strong relationship between students' enjoyment of reading and the marks they receive. The relationship is particularly strong in Croatia, Hungary, Latvia, Poland and Serbia. Teachers are comparatively less keen to give high marks to students who have good attitudes towards school. In all the countries and economies that participated in this study, the correlation between the index of attitudes towards school and student marks is lower than the correlation between the enjoyment of reading and student marks (Table B2.3). These results remain broadly stable after accounting for reading performance, with the exception of Iceland (Table B2.4).

Although there is a positive relationship in all countries and economies, the correlation between student-teacher relations and student marks is relatively weak. Teachers with a "keeping things moving" approach are more likely to reward these attitudes, as good relationships with the teacher keep the pace of instruction going; yet these rewards provide little direct benefit to developing students' learning potential. The correlation is weak (lower than 0.1) in Croatia, Serbia, Singapore and Trinidad and Tobago. Teachers reward good relationships the most in Hungary, Iceland and Portugal (ISCED 3), yet at very moderate levels (Table B2.3).

The correlation analysis suggests that, in general across participating countries and economies, teachers reward attitudes, behaviours and habits that directly benefit performance. This general trend, however, may mask a sizeable proportion of teachers and schools that reward attitudes, habits and behaviours that may be less beneficial for students' educational careers. For example, while teachers generally reward better reading performance with higher marks across all countries and economies that distributed the ECQ, on average, around 3% of schools have a significantly *negative* correlation between students' reading performance and the marks they receive in their language course. In the Flemish Community of Belgium, Hungary, Ireland and Portugal ISCED 2, more than 5% of schools show a negative relationship between marks and reading performance. There are practically no schools in Iceland, Poland, Serbia and the Slovak Republic where there is a negative relationship between marks and performance (Table B2.5).

With respect to the relationship between marks and both approaches to learning and metacognition strategies, in the Flemish Community of Belgium, more than 25% of schools show a negative relationship between marks and students' identification of metacognitive strategies and positive approaches to learning, while in Austria and Hungary, over 25% of schools show a negative

relationship with four of the five metacognitive strategies and approaches to learning that were evaluated in PISA. By contrast, a large proportion of schools in Latvia, Poland and Portugal show a positive relationship between beneficial metacognitive strategies and approaches to learning and student marks. In this latter set of countries, marks tend to be aligned with those non-cognitive attributes that are best related to student learning (Table B2.5 and B2.6).

TOWARDS A MODEL OF MARKS

School marks provide a strong signal to students about what behaviours, habits and attitudes are rewarded and which are discouraged. Ideally, marks should be positively related to academic performance and to habits that foster student learning, including positive approaches to learning, positive metacognitive strategies, and engagement with reading and school. Yet after accounting for these behaviours and habits – which, in most education systems, are positively associated with marks – other contexts and student characteristics may also be related to student marks.

In many countries, marks have important consequences for students' future educational and occupational prospects as they influence access to higher education and motivate in-school behaviour. Therefore, if teachers systematically favour, for example, socio-economically advantaged students, this inequality in grading practices may contribute to broader social disparities and reduce upward social mobility. On the other hand, marks may promote social mobility if teachers reward disadvantaged students or students from an immigrant background or those from particular social or academic contexts.

Across the countries and economies that distributed the ECQ, about a quarter of the variation in student marks is accounted for by students' performance, learning habits, engagement, background characteristics and contextual factors.[4] These factors explain a particularly large share of the variation in student marks in Latvia, Poland and the Slovak Republic, where more than a third of the variation in marks is accounted for by these characteristics (Table B2.7).

After accounting for student background characteristics, students' reading performance and learning habits remain strongly associated with the marks students receive. Reading performance is significantly associated with better marks in all countries and economies, and especially so in Latvia, Poland, Portugal (ISCED 3) and the Slovak Republic. Attitudes, habits and behaviours related to engagement and learning habits are are associated with better marks, even after accounting for students' performance. These are attitudes and behaviours that promote student learning not only in the classroom but throughout life. The use of control strategies is positively and significantly associated with better marks in 14 countries and economies. Similarly, in 16 countries and economies, especially Serbia, positive attitudes towards reading, as measured by the index of enjoyment of reading, are positively and significantly associated with better marks, after accounting for all other factors. In 13 countries and economies, students who believe that student-teacher relations in their schools are good are also more likely to receive better marks.

After taking into account students' learning habits and behaviours, some student background characteristics appear to be strongly related to marks. This indicates that, in classrooms, teachers reward attitudes and behaviours that are not directly measured in PISA but that are associated with students' background. Girls are more likely to receive better marks than boys in 13 countries and economies, even when they have similar reading performance and learning habits. The exceptions to this trend are Iceland, Portugal (ISCED 2), Singapore and Trinidad and Tobago, where girls and boys obtain similar marks when they have similar performances, attitudes and learning habits. Girls are especially more likely to receive higher marks in Poland and the Slovak Republic. Similarly, students from socio-economically disadvantaged backgrounds are more likely to receive lower marks in 15 countries and economies, with the exception of the Flemish Community of Belgium and Croatia. The association between marks and socio-economic background is strongest in Poland. After accounting for socio-economic status, performance and attitudes towards learning and school, only in Singapore do students with an immigrant background tend to receive lower marks, while in Austria, the Flemish Community of Belgium and Singapore, students who speak another language at home, but are similar in performance and attitudes to their peers, tend to receive lower marks.

The relationship between contextual factors and marks is another potential source of inequality, as students attending certain types of schools will receive lower (or higher) marks depending not on their own performance, effort and engagement, but on factors that are beyond a student's control. Students who attend higher-achieving schools tend to have lower academic self-concepts and receive lower marks (Espenshade et al., 2005; Kelly, 2008; Marsh and Hau, 2003; Marsh et al., 2008). Within the context of PISA 2009, in the majority of countries and economies, students who attend higher-achieving schools receive *lower* marks when compared to students with similar performance and learning habits who attend poorer-performing schools. In these countries and economies, marks are used *normatively*, meaning that students are evaluated in the context of their peers' achievement. This is particularly important because students are not distributed equally across different levels, programmes and school types, and this distribution influences the marks they receive. Thus, comparisons of the distribution of marks across school systems are, in part, determined by the distribution of students across grades, programmes and school types.

The reference group to which the student is compared when marks are used normatively may be the classroom or school. This type of grading is discouraged as it fosters competition that may be detrimental to students' learning (see Boxes 2.1 and 2.2). In this regard, teachers and schools may be inclined to use marks in alignment with their expectations of how students will perform in standardised, criterion-referenced examinations, so that marks are completely disassociated from students' relative position in the classroom, and are, instead, aligned with criteria defined at the national or regional level. Aligning marks with external criteria can, however, discourage low-performing students if their performance is below these benchmarks, or discourage high-performing students whose performance is far above these benchmarks. The alternative favoured by experts in the field lies at neither end: marks should be concise and clear in their scope and reflect students' achievement of clear pre-established and content-specific criteria. Teachers should thus target assessments to challenge and motivate students to learn, providing them with the information they need to enhance learning, without discouraging them.

Normative marking practices are especially notable in Austria, Poland and Portugal (ISCED 3), where students with similar performance receive marks that are almost one standard deviation lower than those in schools that perform 100 score points higher on the PISA reading assessment. In these countries, students receive marks in comparison to their peers, that is, marks measure relative performance rather than absolute performance. Students tend to be graded based on the distribution of performance within the school, so that, had they attended a poorer-performing school and maintained their performance levels, they would have obtained substantially better marks. In these education systems, and for individual students, marks are less of an indicator of their individual performance and their potential to succeed in their educational careers than an indicator of their relative standing within the school. Research on effective marking practices strongly advises *against* normative grading as it creates incentives for unhealthy competition among students and reduces the motivation to excel. The alternative is to use criterion-referenced marking, where marks reflect students' achievement in well-specified, fair and valid indicators (Guskey and Bailey, 2001; Marzano, 2000; O'Connor, 2002; Tomlinson, 2005) (Table B2.7).

GRADE INFLATION

Do teachers in all schools within a country give marks to students in a similar way? Or are teachers who teach in certain types of schools more likely to give students higher marks, not because of their actual performance but because of other factors? Do teachers in schools that benchmark student achievement with standardised tests give marks that better reflect student performance?

Grade inflation occurs when marks are systematically higher than the sets of acquired skills and abilities that they are measuring would normally merit. Under the assumption that a standardised assessment, such as PISA, provides an unbiased appraisal of the actual level of students' competencies, grade inflation can also be quantified by determining the width of the gap between marks and performance in the PISA test between groups of students.[5]

While anecdotal evidence on grade inflation abounds, studies on grade inflation in secondary schools are scarce. The existing evidence signals that grade inflation is common and that, at least in the United States, it has been increasing since the 1990s (Woodruff and Ziomek, 2004; Zirkel, 1999). Grade inflation may be problematic because in those schools where teachers systematically inflate marks, students receive inaccurate information about their performance and their potential educational careers, and high marks do not distinguish between what is excellent and what is merely good.

In PISA, grade inflation at the school level can be detected by observing the types of schools in which teachers systematically give higher marks to their students, after accounting for performance and other factors that predict successful educational careers. Teachers in certain types of schools may be more apt to inflating marks. Selective and private schools, and those schools that face stronger pressure from parents, may feel coerced into giving students higher marks because they must maintain an image of success for their stakeholders. Schools that do not administer standardised tests may be more likely to give marks to students using benchmarks that are unrelated to national or regional standards. However, as discussed below, there is no evidence to support the notion that grade inflation is pervasive across the countries that distributed the ECQ.

In this context, grade inflation is determined here by measuring whether, when predicting the marks students should receive, based on their reading performance in the PISA assessment, their metacognitive strategies, their approaches to learning, their attitudes towards reading, and school and student socio-economic status, the difference between the observed and the predicted mark is positive. Schools that have a systematic positive residual are schools that inflate marks.[6] Grade inflation is most common in Austria, Italy, Poland and the Slovak Republic, where one out of eight students attends a school that give marks well above what would be predicted by students' performance, attitudes and behaviours (Table B2.8).

PISA results do not provide evidence of pervasive grade inflation related to the type of school a student attends. In Italy, Portugal (ISCED 2) and Trinidad and Tobago, students in private schools tend to have better-than-expected marks, but this is not true in the other participating countries and economies. Furthermore, only in Italy is the magnitude of grade inflation in private schools quantitatively substantial. In Austria, Croatia and Latvia, selective schools tend to deflate marks relative to performance, possibly because of normative marking practices. Schools that, according to the school principal, are under constant pressure from parents to set high academic standards and have students meet them, and schools that use standardised tests are not systematically more likely to award higher-than-expected marks than schools where parents are less vocal and schools where the use of standardised tests is not common practice.

In a minority of countries and economies, there is evidence of grade inflation in schools that cater to a relatively disadvantaged student population. In these countries and economies, students in socio-economically disadvantaged schools tend to receive better marks than they would have had they attended more advantaged schools, given their reading performance and learning habits and behaviours, and even when students' own socio-economic status is considered when predicting marks. This is most likely due to normative marking practices rather than grade inflation. The exception to this trend is Singapore, where schools that cater to a socio-economically advantaged student body tend to give higher marks after taking into account students' reading performance and their attitudes and behaviours towards learning and school. In most countries, school attributes are not strongly related to grade inflation, indicating that grade inflation is not a pervasive phenomenon (Table B2.8).

CONCLUSION

In PISA, practically all students attend schools that assess students' work or progress through teacher-developed tests and/or assignments that the students return. In almost all countries and economies over 95% of students are assessed this way (see Table IV.3.10 in OECD, 2010). It is thus widely believed that the assessment of students' work in schools provides meaningful information to students. The marks students receive from these assessments are a constant source of information for students, and their parents, about their own achievement, progress in school and, more broadly, their alignment with the schools' expected values, attitudes and behaviours.

The marks students receive vary across countries and economies. Some countries do not differentiate among failing students, so these students do not know how far below the minimum satisfactory criteria they are; other schools allow students to receive marks that go far below the minimum criteria. The literature on the subject suggests that more efficient marking systems do not allow failing marks to fall too far below the minimum satisfactory mark. If the minimum possible mark is too far below the satisfactory mark, students who receive an unusually low mark may have a difficult time recovering from it in order to pass the course – even if they put in the effort and learn throughout the year. Moreover, students receiving a minimum mark at the beginning of the year may become discouraged and disengaged – precisely the opposite reaction that marks are intended to provoke (Brookhart, 2009; Guskey, 2004; Reeves, 2004). Some educators and researchers have sparked debate ("the minimum grading controversy") by proposing that minimum marks should be established, particularly in school systems that allow the lowest mark to go far below the minimum passing mark. Opponents of minimum marks argue that setting them would promote grade inflation and automatic promotion into higher grades without meeting the academic standards; but research on this issue suggest that minimum marks do neither (Carey and Carifio, 2012).

For those students who do receive passing marks, some school systems differentiate between distinct categories, while others use a relatively continuous scale to locate their students' progress. Results from this analysis suggest that the choice of marking scheme has implications on the degree to which marks can differentiate students who have met the criteria satisfactorily. Although counterintuitive, school systems that attribute a fixed set of four or five clearly distinct marks (e.g. "satisfactory", "good", "very good" and "excellent") describe performance differences among their students more clearly than school systems with relatively continuous marks for passing students (e.g. values ranging from 10 to 20). This is most likely due to the fact that the distinction among qualitatively different categories allows teachers to describe their students more accurately. When the scale is continuous, teachers may interpret different parts of the scale as representing different mastery levels and will tend to restrict themselves to marking around the midpoint, as they may be reluctant to give very high or very low marks (see Box 2.2 for further details on effective marking practices).

Countries and economies use different scales and are some countries are more strict than others with respect to the likelihood of students achieving the highest possible marks. Yet in all countries and economies, the marks students receive in their language-of-assessment courses are positively related to students' reading performance: in all countries and economies, higher reading proficiency is rewarded with better marks. But the information marks convey extends to other attitudes and behaviours. Marks constitute an important lever that teachers and schools can use to motivate students to work towards higher performance, but also towards deeper engagement and more effective attitudes towards learning. In many countries and economies that disseminated the ECQ, students with better control strategies are rewarded with better marks, even after accounting for their reading performance. Similarly, students who are more engaged – those who enjoy reading more – are more likely to obtain higher marks, even when comparing students of similar performance. Thus, teachers and schools reward student attitudes and behaviours that promote learning, in addition to rewarding learning, in and of itself.

Teachers also reward students who believe that student-teacher relations in the school are good, even after accounting for student performance, and may reward attitudes and behaviours that are not directly related to student performance and successful educational careers but that promote a calm learning environment that allows teachers to "keep things moving".

Similarly, in many countries and economies, marks tend to be higher for girls and socio-economically advantaged students, and are also sensitive to the academic context of the school, even after accounting for individual students' performance, attitudes and behaviours towards learning. The fact that marks are sensitive to factors that are unrelated to students' performance, engagement and learning habits signals that teachers may reward aspects that they feel are important but are not measured directly by PISA and that are strongly related to students' backgrounds. Teachers may also reward behaviours that are valued in the labour market and in other social environments. As marks constitute one of the most reliable and consistent indicators of students' own performance and potential, systematic inequalities in the allocation of marks may contribute to systematic inequalities in educational expectations, as discussed in the following chapter. Box 2.1 on Korea's initiative to reform marks earlier on this chapter signals the potential changes a reform to marking systems may bring to a school system if aligned to a wider reform project.

This chapter has highlighted how countries and economies that distributed the ECQ use marks. As will be shown in the following chapter and as underlined by the academic literature on the subject, marks may constitute an important source of information for students about their future prospects in education. This and the following chapter do not, however, provide information on how teachers and students use marks and the information conveyed by marks. In effect, this chapter works under the assumption that marks are most beneficial when they convey useful information to students; but as important as the usefulness and legitimacy of the information conveyed by marks is how students and teachers actually use marks. Box 2.2 develops this point inasmuch as effective marking practices depend not only on the clarity and usefulness of the information conveyed by marks, but on the assumption that this information is used for the purpose of enhancing and improving learning. At the system level, assessments and how marks are used should be consistent with the broader policies on student assessment.

Box 2.2 **Effective marking practices**

What are effective marking (grading) practices? Ideally, they should communicate clear, useful information *for the purpose of enhancing learning*. As such, marks should motivate students to put forth more effort, to identify their strengths and encourage them to work on their weaknesses. In general, marks should provide accurate, specific and timely feedback. They should be a final judgment about a student's achievement. Marks should be clear and concise in their scope. They should be based on clearly-specified criteria (criterion-based), measuring student achievement against a set of clear, pre-established and content-specific goals. Students should not be evaluated relative to their peers (normative grading, or grading on a curve), as normative grading spawns unhealthy competition and diminishes motivation (Marzano, 2000; O'Connor, 2007; Reeves, 2008).

Moreover, marks should not be a synonym for assessment – the gathering of information about students' achievement for the purpose of making instructional or career-path decisions. The evidence used to gather marks should be valid, measuring what they are intended to measure and not other factors (e.g. neat hand-writing, good behaviour, or pace of work in assessments that measure reading comprehension). The instrument to evaluate student achievement should reduce measurement error as much as possible, such that the task directions are clear and the "test" is aligned with its goals. Marks should reflect achievement; and if they are to reflect behaviour, behaviour and achievement should be reported separately, with an emphasis on intrinsic motivation. In fact, once achievement and behaviour are explicitly decoupled from marks, both achievement and behaviour tend to improve (Guskey and Bailey, 2001; Marzano, 2000; O'Connor, 2002; O'Connor, 2009; Tomlinson, 2005).

Many common grading practices have been labelled as detrimental to student learning. Considering that one of the goals of grading is to motivate students to learn, using marks as punishment, such as using the minimum mark as punishment for late or missing work, is strongly discouraged. The use of an average of all the marks given during the semester or school year should be evaluated, inasmuch it presumes that learning at the beginning of the term is equally important as learning at the end of the semester. Students should be evaluated with respect to their understanding at the end of the semester. Yet the use of a one-and-only evaluation (a final test, essay or research project) reduces student motivation to work throughout the entire semester (Guskey, 2004; Reeves, 2004; Reeves, 2008).

Because these effective grading practices may be hard to achieve, some researchers argue that the only effective grading practice is replacing marks by a individualised narrative assessment for each student. Eliminating the traditional notion of marks is a necessary, but not sufficient, step to promote deep thinking and engagement in learning. Marks, they contend, diminish students' interest in learning, create a preference for the easiest possible task, and reduce the quality of students' thinking. Schools can promote better learning environments by eliminating marks gradually and, if final grades are required, arrange for collaborative grading, where students mark themselves at the end of the year upon the evaluation of a portfolio and negotiate this mark with the teacher who has the final say (Kohn, 2011). The elimination of marks requires a gradual process and teachers' willingness and ability to adopt a change in incentives, behaviours and dynamics in the classroom.

Sources: Guskey and Bailey (2001); Guskey (2004); Kohn (2011); Marzano (2000); O'Connor (2002); O'Connor (2007); O'Connor (2009); Reeves (2004); Reeves (2008); Tomlinson (2005).

Notes

1. Among all PISA countries and economies, 21 countries implemented the optional Educational Career questionnaire. Of these countries and economies, Australia, Hong Kong-China, Korea and Slovenia chose not to include the question that asked students about their marks. The results in this chapter correspond to the 17 countries and economies that did include this question. Different marking systems exist in Portugal (in ISCED level 2 programmes marks range from 1 to 5, and in ISCED level 3 programmes marks range from 1 to 20), so results for Portugal are disaggregated by ISCED level to accommodate the different marking schemes.

2. In Ireland, teachers often assign letter grades rather than points on a 0-100 point scale to students. These letter grades are then converted to the 0-100 point scale (e.g. A = 85-100, B = 70-84, C = 55-69, D = 40-54, E = 25-39, etc.).

3. These analyses exclude Macao-China, Mexico and New Zealand because they asked students about whether they received a passing or failing mark and not the specific mark. It is thus impossible for analyses to infer the distribution of passing marks in these school systems. This exclusion and the conversion of the data are necessary to render comparable information that is specific to each school system.

4. These results are based on a regression model predicting students' marks in their language courses, considering their reading performance, learning habits and strategies, engagement in reading and school, student-teacher relations, student background characteristics, and school contextual factors. For education systems that use a pass/fail marking scheme, a logistic regression predicting whether students received a passing mark is used instead.

5. Grade inflation is typically understood as the increase in grades over time with no corresponding change in the underlying abilities that these marks measure. PISA does not have information on student marks to evaluate the change in marks over time compared with the change in test scores over time. However, grade inflation is a comparison between two groups – students at one moment in time compared with students at another moment in time. This report uses the comparison of groups implicit in grade inflation to identify the phenomenon by comparing residuals cross groups. This alternative approach to grade inflation is not inflation with respect to the past, but with respect to another theoretically relevant group.

6. Schools that have an average residual greater than 0.5 in a regression predicting student marks over reading scores, metacognitive strategies, approaches to learning, attitudes towards reading and school, and student socio-economic status, are considered schools that inflate grades.

References

Bonesrønning, H. (1999), "The Variation in Teachers' Grading Practices: Causes and Consequences", *Economics of Education Review,* No. 89, pp. 89-105.

Brookhart, S. (1993), "Teachers' Grading Practices: Meaning and Values", *Journal of Educational Measurement,* Vol. 30, No. 2, pp. 123-142.

Brookhart, S. (2009), *Grading,* Merrill, New York, New York.

Carey, T. and **J. Carifio** (2012), "The Minimum Grading Controversy: Results of a Quantitative Study of Seven Years of Grading from an Urban High School", *Educational Researcher,* Vol. 41, No. 6, pp. 201-208.

Covington, M. (1984), "The Self-Worth Theory of Achievement Motivation: Findings and Implications", *The Elementary School Journal,* Vol. 85, No. 1, pp. 4-20.

Docan, T. (2006), "Positive and Negative Incentives in the Classroom: An Analysis of Grading Systems and Student Motivation", *Journal of Scholarship of Teaching and Learning,* Vol. 6, No. 2, pp. 21-40.

Espenshade, T., **L. Hale** and **C. Chung** (2005), "The Frog Pond Revisited: High School Academic Context, Class Rank, and Elite College Admission", *Sociology of Education,* Vol. 78, No. 4, pp. 269-293.

Fredricks, J., **P. Blumenfeld** and **A. Paris** (2004), "School Engagement: Potential of the Concept, State of the Evidence", *Review of Educational Research,* Vol. 74, No. 1, pp. 59-109.

Guskey, T. (2004), "Zero Alternatives", *Principal Leadership: High School Edition,* Vol. 5, No. 2, pp. 49-53.

Guskey, T. and **J. Bailey** (2001), *Developing Grading and Reporting Systems for Student Learning,* Corwin, Thousand Oaks, California.

Kelly, S. (2008), "What Types of Students' Efforts Are Rewarded with High Marks?", *Sociology of Education,* Vol. 81, No. 1, pp. 32-52.

Kohn, A. (1993), *Punished by Rewards: The Trouble with Gold Stars, Incentive Plans, A's, Praise and other Bribes,* Houghton Mifflin Co., Boston, Massachussets.

Kohn, A. (2011), "The Case against Grades", *Educational Leadership,* Vol. 69, No. 3, pp. 28-33.

Marsh, H. and **K. Hau** (2003), "Big Fish Little Pond Effect on Academic Self-Concept: A Crosscultural (26 Country) Test of the Negative Effects of Academically Selective Schools", *American Psychologist,* Vol. 58, No. 5, pp. 364-376.

Marsh, H., et al. (2008), "The Big-Fish-Little-Pond-Effect Stands up to Critical Scrutiny: Implications for Theory, Methodology, and Future Research", *Educational Psychology Review,* Vol. 20, No. 3, pp. 319-350.

Marzano, R. (2000), *Transforming Classroom Grading,* Association for Supervision and Curriculum Development, Alexandria, Virginia.

McMillan, J., **S. Myran** and **D. Workman** (2002), "Elementary Teachers' Classroom Assessment and Grading Practices", *The Journal of Educational Research,* Vol. 95, No. 4, pp. 203-213.

O'Connor, K. (2002), *How to Grade for Learning: Linking Grades to Standards,* Skylight, Arlington Heights, Illinois.

O'Connor, K. (2007), *A Repair Kit for Grading: 15 Fixes for Broken Grades,* Educational Testing Service, Portland, Oregon.

O'Connor, K. (2009), "Reforming Grading Practices in Secondary Schools", *Principal's Research Review,* Vol. 4, No. 1, pp. 1-7.

OECD (2010), *PISA 2009 Results: What Makes a School Successful? Resources, Policies and Practices (Volume IV),* PISA, OECD Publishing.

Reeves, D. (2004), "The Case Against Zero", *Phi Delta Kappan,* Vol. 86, No. 4, pp. 324-325.

Reeves, D. (2008), "Effective Grading Practices", *Teaching Students to Think,* Vol. 65, No. 5, pp. 85-87.

Rosenbaum, J. (2001), *Beyond College for All: Career Paths for the Forgotten Half,* Russell Sage Foundation, New York, New York.

Stiggins, R. and **N. Conklin** (1992), *In Teachers' Hands: Investigating the Practices of Classroom Assessment,* State University of New York Press, Albany, New York.

Tomlinson, C. (2005), "Grading and Differentiation: Paradox or Good Practice", *Theory into Practice,* Vol. 44, No. 3, pp. 262-269.

Woodruff, D. and **R. Ziomek** (2004), *High School Grade Inflation from 1991 to 2003,* ACT Research Report Series 2004-4.

Zirkel, P. (1999), "Grade Inflation: A Leadership Opportunity for Schools of Education", *Teachers College Record,* Vol. 101, No. 2, pp. 247-260.

3

What is the Relationship Between Marks and Educational Expectations?

Do students' school marks shape their expectations about their future? This chapter examines the relationship between school marks and students' expectations of completing a university education. It also discusses how marks can reduce – or reinforce – inequalities in those expectations between socio-economically advantaged and disadvantaged students, and between girls and boys.

This chapter combines the results developed in Chapters 1 and 2 to assess whether marks provide useful information to students beyond the limits of the classroom and school. It evaluates the assumption that marks are a consistent and reliable source of information for students regarding their own abilities and the likelihood that they expect to attend and succeed in university. It also evaluates the extent to which inequalities in expectations, as discussed in Chapter 1, are mediated by inequalities in marks, as examined in Chapter 2. If, as the first analysis suggests, marks help to define students' educational expectations and reduce inequality, marks should be regarded as a key element in students' educational experience that shape students' choices about their education and, ultimately, their occupation.

Because the analyses that are presented in this chapter combine information on students' marks and educational expectations, the sample of countries and economies differs slightly from the sample discussed in Chapter 1. Due to different marking systems within a country, this chapter's analysis of expectations distinguishes between students in Portugal's ISCED 2 and ISCED 3 programmes. Also, as Australia, Hong Kong-China, Korea and Slovenia did not include the question on student marks in the Educational Career questionnaire (ECQ), these countries are omitted from the following analyses and discussions.

MARKS PREDICT EDUCATIONAL EXPECTATIONS

Chapter 1 highlights that students who perform better are more likely to hold higher expectations. Students tend to realise, in all countries and economies, that academic achievement is a determinant of success in higher education and form their expectations accordingly. However, students do not know their actual underlying skills and performance level. While they know what problems they can solve and how much effort they need to invest to learn new material, they lack a standardised metric to compare themselves with others and infer their likelihood to attend and succeed at university. Or do they? Do students use marks to form their opinions about their future?

Marks are a consistent, accessible and easy-to-interpret source of information about students' own achievement, habits and attitudes. Research has highlighted that marks are significantly related to long-term student outcomes, such as university completion and earnings, inasmuch as they convey information about students' non-cognitive skills, after accounting for test scores. Yet the fact that a relationship between marks and long-term outcomes exists does not necessarily mean that students will use the information marks convey when forming their expectations. In fact, employers tend to dismiss marks as subjective and consider them to be unlikely to provide much relevant information about workers' prospects (Rosenbaum, 2001). Little is known about whether students use marks as a relevant source of information when they form their educational and career expectations, even though in recent years some have suggested that marks be included as a key component in the analysis of student expectations (Buchmann and Dalton, 2002; Buchmann and Park, 2009; Park, 2008; McDaniel, 2010). In the United States, for example, students form their expectations early on in their lives and only adapt them to only large changes in their grade point averages (Andrew and Hauser, 2012).

Marks are an important source of information on which students may rely to evaluate their success in school and their potential in higher education. Yet, not all teachers assign marks using the same criteria. While some assign marks on the basis of absolute knowledge, attitudes and behaviours, others tend to reward students' relative position within the class or the school and attitudes and behaviours that have less bearing on students' future success. Hence, while marks represent a readily available source of information, at times they can be unreliable predictors of students' potential success at university and beyond. This is particularly true when marks reflect students' *relative* position within the school (as observed when teachers and schools use normative grading practices) rather than their *absolute* level of performance and likelihood of succeeding in their educational careers.

After accounting for performance in reading and mathematics as well as the ISCED programme a student attends (sources of standardised and structural information related to success in obtaining a university degree), students with higher marks are more likely to expect to complete a university degree. Beyond any standardised measure of performance and structural paths that enable access to and success in university, students still rely on their marks to form their expectations. Marks are positively related to the expectation of completing a university degree in all countries and economies that distributed the ECQ: students who receive higher marks have higher expectations. The magnitude of this relationship is such that students who receive marks that are one standard deviation above the national mean are, on average, as likely to expect a university degree as are students who score 34 points higher in the PISA mathematics and reading assessments.

The relationship between marks and expectations is especially strong in Hungary, Poland, Portugal, Serbia, Singapore and the Slovak Republic. Students with marks that are one standard deviation above the mean are more likely to expect to complete a university degree than students who score 50 points higher in mathematics and reading (roughly one half of a standard deviation in mathematics and reading performance). In Poland, for example, students who receive marks that are one standard deviation higher are as likely to expect to complete a university degree as students who score 84 points higher in the mathematics and reading assessments. For students in Serbia, the influence of marks that are one standard deviation higher is equivalent to the influence of 61 score points in the PISA mathematics and reading assessments when forming expectations of future education (Figure 3.1).

In countries where marks are strongly related to student expectations, marks may have particularly long-lasting consequences for students and may result in inequities in access to higher education if they are related to student background or school context. For example, as discussed in Chapter 2, in Poland, student marks are strongly related to gender, socio-economic status and contextual effects: boys, socio-economically disadvantaged students and students who attend high-performing schools are more likely to receive lower marks and therefore may be less likely to expect to complete a university degree, even if their performance in reading and mathematics is equal to that of girls or students attending poorer-performing schools.

In Austria, the Flemish Community of Belgium and Trinidad and Tobago, marks have a weaker relationship with educational expectations, after accounting for performance and ISCED programmes (Figure 3.1). These are school systems that differentiate students at an early age and, in this context, the characteristics of schools may provide additional information to students about their likelihood of succeeding in university.

▪ Figure 3.1 ▪

Relationship between marks and expectations of completing a university degree, after accounting for students' academic characteristics

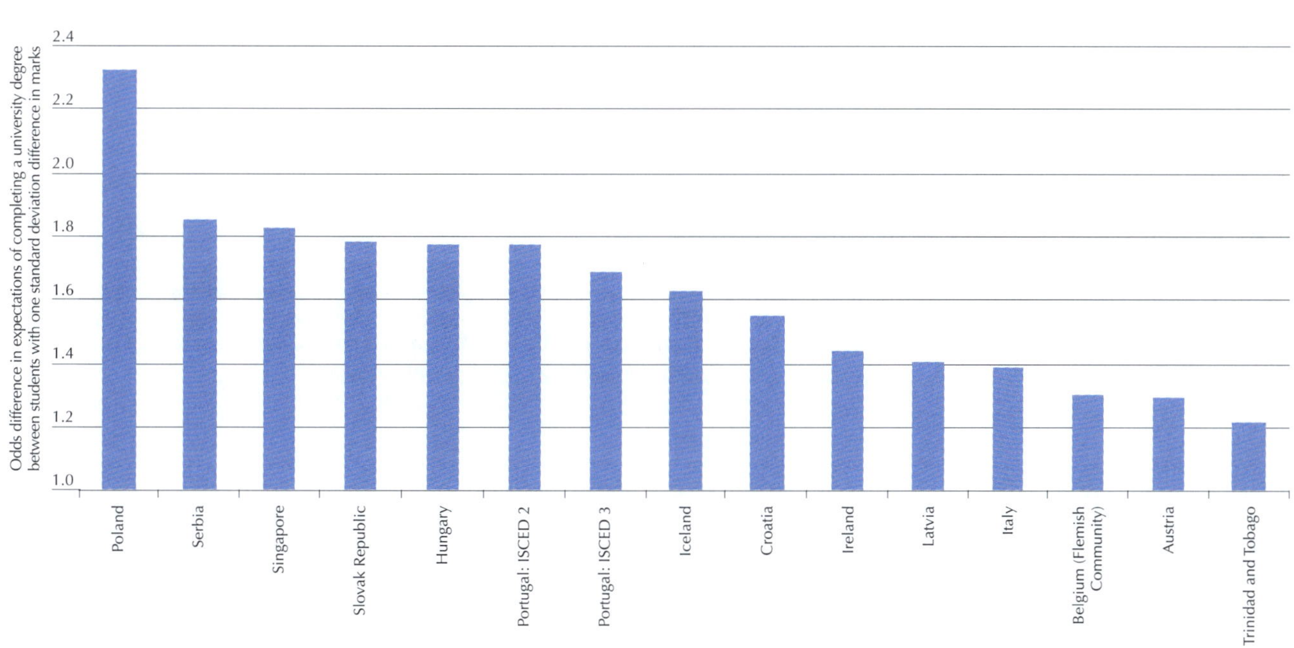

Note: Estimates correspond to the coefficient associated to marks in a logistic regression predicting whether students expect to complete a university degree. Marks are standardised at the country level so coefficients must be interpreted as the difference in the odds of expecting a university degree between students who have a one standard deviation difference in their marks. The logistic regression also includes students' scores in PISA reading and mathematics assessments as well as their programme orientation (academic or non-academic).
Countries are sorted in descending order of the size of the relationship between marks and university expectations.
Source: Table B3.1 (estimates from the tables have been converted from log-odds to odds).
StatLink http://dx.doi.org/10.1787/888932733602

Marks remain an important influence on students' formation of educational expectations even after accounting for the school's academic context and students' background (see Table B3.1 and Table B3.3). In all countries and economies, marks are positively and significantly associated with students' expectation of completing a university degree, even after accounting for students' performance and backgrounds, as discussed in Chapter 1.

These analyses stress the importance of marks not only for motivating student attitudes and behaviours within the school, but for forming students' educational expectations. Students who receive higher marks are more likely to believe that they have the potential to succeed in completing a university degree; and teachers and schools thus have a responsibility to transmit reliable information to students about their potential to succeed in further education. This responsibility comes with a challenge: to provide reliable information about students' potential that helps to build realistic expectations, while at the same time maintaining students' motivation to learn in school, since students with higher expectations may have more motivation to put forth the effort into school work to meet those expectations. The burden of this challenge falls not only on teachers who award marks and design in-class assessments, but on education systems as a whole, as the value of different levels of educational attainment is meaningful only if

desirable employment and further educational opportunities are available to students at all performance levels and all attainment levels. School systems must also ensure that marking practices are consistent with broader assessment policies.

MARKS CAN REDUCE INEQUALITIES IN EDUCATIONAL EXPECTATIONS

Chapter 1 explored inequalities in educational expectations and finds that girls and socio-economically advantaged students are more likely than boys and socio-economically disadvantaged students to expect to complete a university degree. These inequalities in educational expectations remain when comparing girls and boys (and advantaged and disadvantaged students) who perform at the same level in reading and mathematics and who have the same attitudes towards learning and learning habits. One potential explanation for this is that students are generally unaware of their actual levels of skills as measured by a standardised assessment, such as PISA, and consequently, about their potential to enter and succeed in higher education. Marks are perhaps a more accessible source of information about students' performance and potential success in university and thus have more influence as students form their expectations.

In parallel, the results from Chapter 2 also highlighted that girls and advantaged students are more likely to receive higher marks, even after accounting for reading and mathematics performance. Since marks provide students with information that can influence their expectations, do inequalities in marks explain gender and socio-economic inequalities in expectations? These analyses are particularly important because marks are perhaps the primary source of information students have about their achievement and potential to complete a university degree. Greater equality in the awarding of marks may promote greater equality in students' expectations and, ultimately, in educational attainment if the structural features of access to and graduation from university are more equal too.

Gender differences in marks and expectations

In all countries and economies, and net of immigrant background, the language spoken at home, and socio-economic status, girls are more likely than boys to expect to complete a university degree, before accounting for their marks and mathematics or reading performance. In Poland, girls are at least 2.5 times more likely than boys to expect to complete a university degree (Figure 3.2).

▪ Figure 3.2 ▪

Change in the gender-related odds difference in expectations of completing a university degree, after accounting for students' academic characteristics

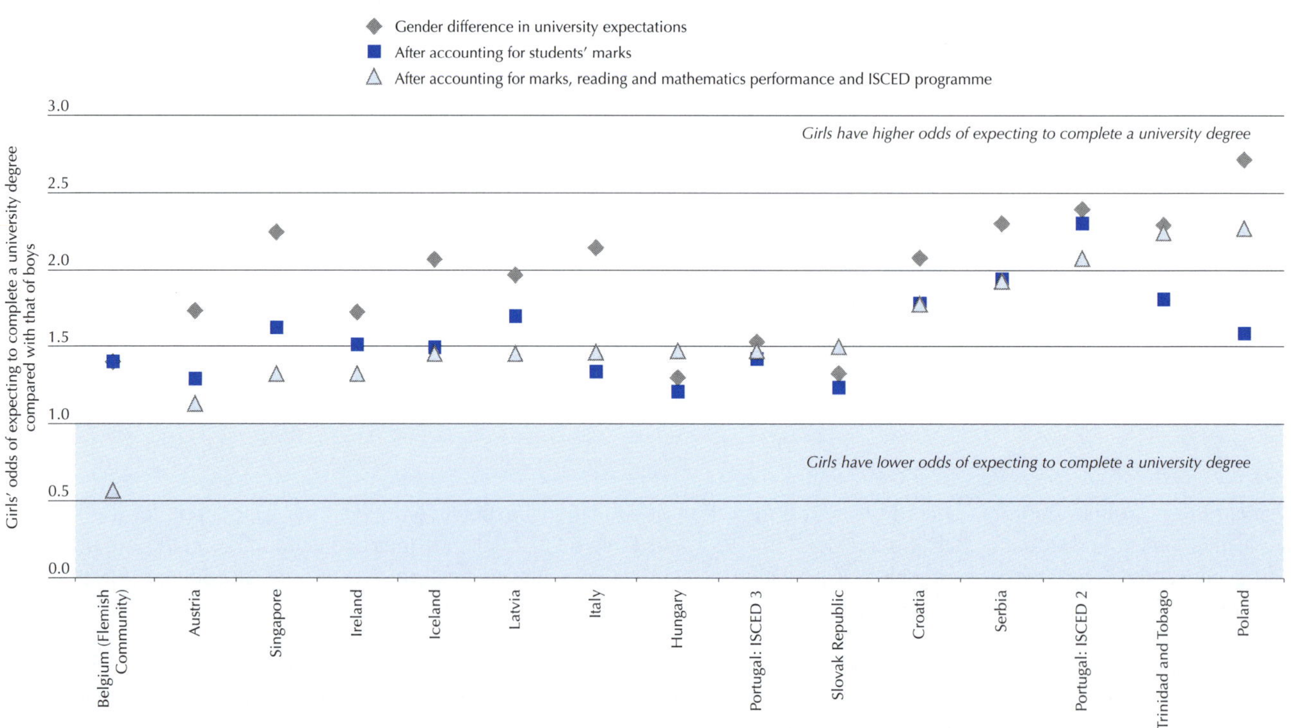

Note: Estimates correspond to the coefficient associated to being female in a logistic regression predicting whether students expect to complete a university degree. Coefficients must be interpreted as the difference in the odds of expecting a university degree between girls and boys. All models include controls for students' socio-economic status, immigrant background and language spoken at home.
Countries sorted in ascending order of girls' odds of expecting a university degree after accounting for marks, reading and mathematics performance and ISCED programme with respect to that of boys.
Source: Tables B3.5, B3.7 and B3.8 (estimates from the tables have been converted from log-odds to odds).
StatLink http://dx.doi.org/10.1787/888932733621

As discussed earlier, these differences are related to the differences in performance between boys and girls. In all PISA countries and economies, girls outperform boys in reading; and in many countries and economies, boys outperform girls in mathematics (OECD, 2010a). In Latvia and Singapore, gender differences in expectations reflect gender differences in performance and ISCED programme: after accounting for reading and mathematics performance as well as ISCED programme, the gender difference in expecting to complete a university degree is no longer statistically significant (Figure 3.2). Although in the large majority of countries and economies gender differences in expectations persist after accounting for performance and ISCED programme, in Croatia, Iceland and Italy, a large part of the gender differences in expectations is explained by performance and ISCED programme. In these countries, performance and ISCED programmes account for at least a third of the gender differences in expectations.

After accounting for ISCED programme and reading and mathematics performance, the different marks boys and girls receive explains a large part of the gender differences in expectations to complete a university degree. Yet marks also convey information that students consider relevant. On average across countries and economies where differences were statistically significant, marks help to explain 17% of the strength of the relationship between expectations and gender among boys and girls who performed equally well and were in similar ISCED programmes. In Croatia, Hungary, Poland and the Slovak Republic, marks explain more than a quarter of the gender differences in expectations that remain after accounting for performance, suggesting that differences in marks explain at least some of the differences between boys' and girls' expectations to complete a university degree (Figure 3.2).

Socio-economic differences in marks and expectations

In all countries and economies, socio-economically advantaged students are more likely to expect to complete a university degree. This difference is especially pronounced in Austria, Hungary and Poland, where advantaged students (those with a score on the *PISA index of economic, social and cultural status* that is one unit higher than the OECD average) are at least three times more likely to expect to complete a university degree than a student whose socio-economic status is equal to that of the OECD average. This difference reflects the fact that socio-economically advantaged students in all countries and economies are more likely to perform better (OECD, 2010b). In fact, after accounting for students' reading and mathematics performance, around 30% of the difference in expectations related to students' socio-economic status is accounted for by the differences in performance related to socio-economic background and ISCED programmes. In Austria, Hungary and the Slovak Republic, around 40% of the difference in university expectations related to socio-economic status are explained by differences in performance that are related to socio-economic background.

The remaining differences in students' expectations of completing a university degree that are related to socio-economic status are not substantially explained by differences in the marks that advantaged and disadvantaged students receive. After accounting for performance in reading and mathematics, school marks account for a small part of the inequality in expectations related to socio-economic status. The remaining differences are still statistically significant in practically all countries and economies. They are particularly large in Croatia, Hungary, Iceland, Poland and Serbia, where a one-unit increase on the *PISA index of economic, social and cultural background* is seen to at least double the likelihood that a student will expect to complete a university degree. These remaining differences could be due to the influence of peers, parents and teachers who assume that students from advantaged backgrounds will have higher expectations; differences in access to curricula (academic or vocational) related to socio-economic background; or to the perception, held by disadvantaged students, that they are less likely to have access to and succeed in university, even if they have similar marks and performance levels, and follow the same academic curriculum as their advantaged peers (Tables B3.5, B3.6, B3.7 and B3.8) (Andrew and Hauser, 2012; Buchmann and Dalton, 2002; Buchmann and Park, 2009; Morgan, 2005).

CONCLUSION

Students' expectations of attending and completing university depend on their aspirations and the information they have regarding their ability to succeed in higher education. As discussed in Chapter 1, a student's actual level of skills – as measured by the PISA assessment – is highly related to that student's educational expectations: better-performing students are more likely to believe they will complete a university degree while poorly-performing students are more likely to believe that they will complete their formal education at the secondary level. Similarly, students in ISCED A-type programmes are more likely to expect to complete a university degree.

Yet students also rely on another source of information, perhaps one that is more readily available to them: school marks. In all the countries and economies that disseminated the ECQ in the PISA 2009 cycle and were asked about the marks they receive, students with higher marks were more likely to expect to graduate from university than students with lower marks. Marks are relevant in predicting students' expectations of graduating from university, even after accounting for student performance and ISCED programme. This means that students rely on the information about their performance that they receive in school to form their long-term expectations; and they should: research shows that marks are related to students' long-term outcomes, like earnings and university completion (Rosenbaum, 2001). Students do well to take this information into account. Teachers and schools would do well to understand that marks are more than an appraisal of skills and knowledge acquired; they provide information to the student about what is valued not only in school but in life in general.

References

Andrew, M. and **R. Hauser** (2012), "Adoption? Adaptation? Evaluating the Formation of Educational Expectations", *Social Forces,* Vol. 90, No. 2, pp. 497-520.

Buchmann, C. and **B. Dalton** (2002), "Interpersonal Influences and Educational Aspirations in 12 Countries: The Importance of Institutional Context", *Sociology of Education,* Vol. 75, No. 2, pp. pp. 99-122.

Buchmann, C. and **H. Park** (2009), "Stratification and the Formation of Expectations in Highly Differentiated Educational Systems", *Research in Social Stratification and Mobility,* Vol. 27, No. 4, pp. 245-267.

Park, H. (2008), "The Varied Educational Effects of Parent-Child Communication: A Comparative Study of Fourteen Countries", *Comparative Education Review,* Vol. 52, No. 2, pp. 219-243.

McDaniel, A. (2010), "Cross-National Gender Gaps in Educational Expectations: The Influence of National-Level Gender Ideology and Educational Systems", *Comparative Education Review,* Vol. 54, No. 1, pp. 27-50.

Morgan, S. (2005), *On the Edge of Commitment: Educational Attainment and Race in the United States,* Stanford University Press, Stanford, California.

OECD (2010a), *PISA 2009 Results: What Students Know and Can Do, Student Performance in Reading, Mathematics and Science (Volume I)*, PISA, OECD Publishing.

OECD (2010b), *PISA 2009 Results: Overcoming Social Background – Equity in Learning Opportunities and Outcomes (Volume II)*, PISA, OECD Publishing.

Rosenbaum, J. (2001), *Beyond College for All: Career Paths for the Forgotten Half,* Russell Sage Foundation, New York, New York.

4

Policy Recommendations

This concluding chapter recommends measures teachers and school systems can take to ensure that students' expectations of their future are well-aligned with their prospects, including by encouraging teachers to use grading practices that are objective and criterion-based, working with employers to create a smooth transition from upper secondary school into the labour market, and establishing well-defined paths to enter university.

Students who hold ambitious – yet realistic – expectations about their educational prospects are more likely to put effort into their learning and make a better use of the educational opportunities available to them to achieve their goals. Therefore educational expectations, in part, become self-fulfilling prophecies. When comparing students who have similar levels of skills and competencies and attitudes and behaviours, those who expect to graduate from university are more likely than those who do not hold such expectations of eventually obtaining a university degree. Countries and economies vary widely in the extent to which their students expect to graduate from university: in nine of the 21 participating countries and economies, over 50% of 15-year-old students expect to complete a university degree. In Korea, as many as four out of five students expect to do so. Between 2003 and 2009, many of the countries and economies that distributed the Educational Career questionnaire (ECQ) saw a substantial increase in the proportion of 15-year-olds who expect to obtain a university degree. This increase was particularly strong in New Zealand and Poland. Educational expectations generally reflect students' skills and abilities: on average, better-performing students are more likely to expect to obtain a university degree than poorly performing students. However, countries vary widely in whether students' skills match their expectations.

In many of the countries and economies examined in this report, academic performance is strongly associated with the expectation of graduating from university. Across all countries and economies, some students – notably socio-economically disadvantaged students and students with an immigrant background – have lower levels of proficiency. Inequalities in academic performance may therefore automatically translate into disparities in educational expectations. Girls and advantaged students are more likely than their peers to expect to complete a university degree. However, in all participating countries and economies, academic performance is only one of the factors that contribute to inequalities in expectations. Boys and socio-economically disadvantaged students are less likely than their peers to expect to graduate from university, even when they perform at the same level as their peers. To the extent that such inequalities in expectations constitute a barrier to eventual enrolment and graduation, they pose a serious challenge for countries because of the loss of human capital and skills potential they represent.

Many students who are highly proficient do not expect to graduate from university, while many low-achieving students expect to do so. Highly proficient students who do not expect to graduate from university may signify a loss of talent to the economy and society because these students' full potential may be unrealised if they end their educational training upon finishing upper secondary education. Countries with a high proportion of high-performing students who do not expect to continue onto higher education should promote higher expectations among these students through higher levels of engagement with school and meritocratic sorting into curricular programmes.

By contrast, many countries and economies have a high proportion of low-performing students who expect to complete a university degree, in circumstances where their academic skills pose a difficult challenge for these students to fulfil their expectations. While promoting expectations of completing university is important because it may help to motivate students to put forth the effort to learn in school, school systems should capitalise on these students' motivation towards learning to create the foundational skills to allow them to succeed in university. Countries and economies should thus provide the opportunities for these students to succeed through rigorous academic training and promoting engagement with school, both of which are factors associated with improvements in performance among low-performing students.

Expectations are important because they shape students' educational careers. School systems can promote the expectation of completing university and help create the pool of skilled workers needed to meet the growing demand for high-level skills. The education sector also needs to cater to the educational needs of the sizeable group of students who expect to complete their studies at the upper secondary level. This group of students needs an upper secondary education that facilitates a smooth transition into the workplace. Education systems also need to address inequalities in performance that are reflected in inequalities in educational expectations. In these cases, opportunities for social mobility are limited, and the economy can lose potentially valuable workers to an intergenerational cycle of deprivation and low expectations.

In many countries, university expectations do not match actual graduation rates and this mismatch may signal the pressures that higher education systems will face in meeting the demands for higher education. Most countries still must determine how to promote ambitious, yet realistic, expectations so that students reap the benefits of education and there is a good match between the supply of and the demand for the kinds of skills the economy needs to thrive. A good balance also means that only those students who will be able to meet the demands of a university education enrol in university. Nowadays many countries have completion rates that are much lower than enrolment rates (OECD, 2011) and such "brain drain" is costly: since these individuals do not work, they do not pay taxes, and providing university education is expensive. Completion rates are unlikely to reach 100%; in fact, a certain degree of incompletion is desirable inasmuch as it allows for students to change to different programmes if they need to. However, over-educating students – having more students who graduate from university than the economy can absorb – is also expensive, as workers quickly loose the skills they do not use (Desjardins and Warnke, 2012).

Managing educational expectations is a key challenge for education systems that has important consequences for economic growth, labour-market efficiency and the welfare state. In recent decades there has been a rapid surge in the number of university graduates; in some countries, like Korea, this increase has been faster and more dramatic than in others (OECD, 2011). The increase in university graduates is, in part, the education sector's answer to the growing demand for high-level skills, such as expert thinking and the ability to solve problems for which there is no rule-based solution (Autor et al., 2003). The increase in the supply of highly educated workers has also spurred growth in new value-added areas of the economy. These are independent agents of economic growth and not simply conditions in which growth occurs. Although it is difficult to forecast what skills will be needed in the labour markets of the future, it is most likely that the service sector will continue to absorb an increasingly high share of workers with the skills set that only a university education can provide (Figure 4.1). However, to be able to thrive, modern economies need a balanced set of skills, and not all students have the potential and willingness to complete a university degree or want to enter occupations that require a university education.

▪ Figure 4.1 ▪

Trends in routine and non-routine tasks in occupations in the United States, 1960 to 2002

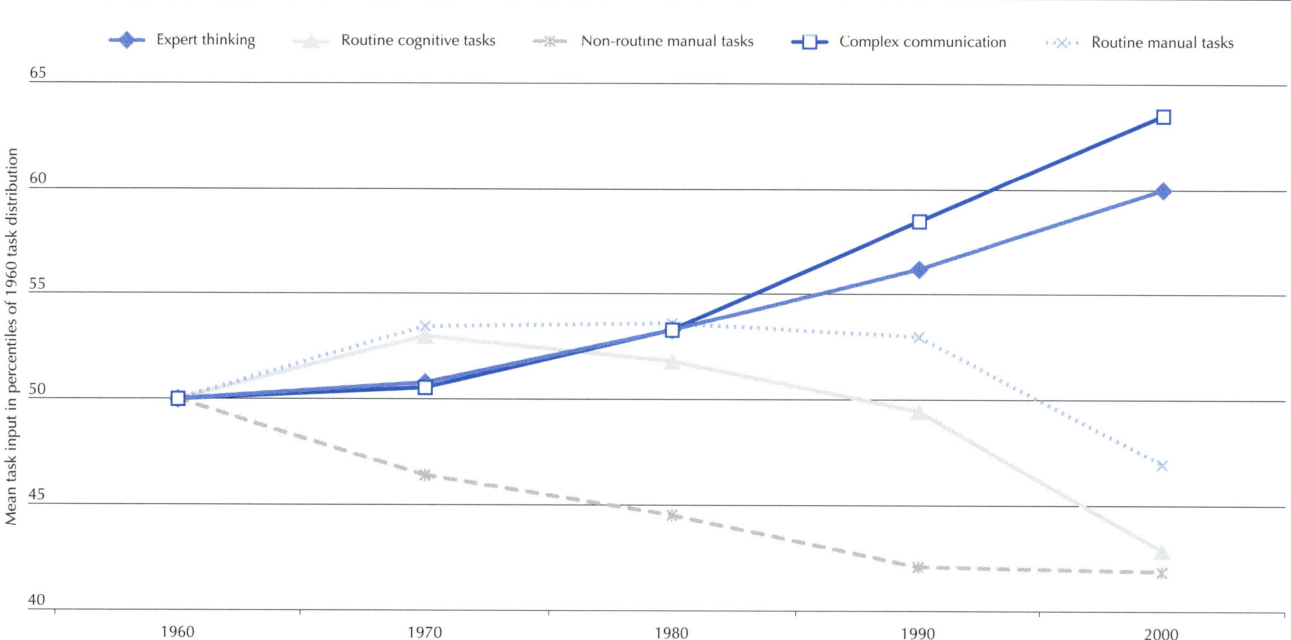

Source: Based on Autor, Levy and Murnane (2003), "The Skill Content of Recent Technological Change: An Empirical Exploration", *The Quarterly Journal of Economics*, Vol. 118, No. 4, pp. 1279-1334.
StatLink http://dx.doi.org/10.1787/888932733640

The set of skills students master by the time they complete their compulsory education influences the choices they make about whether they will leave the formal education sector, enter the labour market or continue their studies to pursue a university degree. One of the ways in which academic excellence influences the educational choices of students is by steering students' educational expectations. Yet, academic performance is only one of the factors that shape such expectations. Many countries now recognise, through PISA results, that the acquisition of foundation skills is crucial for their populations to remain competitive in a global economy (OECD, 2012). The fact that many countries saw major improvements in the skills and competencies of their average 15-year-olds between 2000 and 2009 shows that educational reforms can positively influence the outcomes and prospects of their students. This report illustrates, however, that many countries still face a significant challenge in aligning educational expectations with the opportunities available in the education system and the labour market.

One component that shapes students' educational expectations is school marks. Countries can steer students into different educational and occupational paths, but they can also use marks and grades to determine students' educational choices because marks are the primary relevant source of information for students about their success in school and their potential for success in further education. Just as countries vary markedly in how they structure students' educational careers to enter specific occupational paths (as in Austria and Germany) or remain flexible and offer the possibility of returning to formal education at any point (as in Canada and the United States), education systems vary in the way they give marks. For example, some education systems have different marking systems across schools, regions or school levels (e.g. Macao-China, Mexico and New Zealand); in others, teachers use common scales – for example, from 1 to 5 in Austria, Hungary and Serbia; from 1 to 6 in Croatia, Poland and the Slovak Republic; from 1 to 10 in Iceland, Italy and Latvia; from 1 to 100 in the Flemish Community of Belgium, Ireland, Singapore and Trinidad and Tobago, or from 1 to 20 in Portugal (ISCED level 3 programmes). Countries and economies also vary in what they determine to be a passing mark, in how marks are distributed, and in what is rewarded by marks. Most important, countries with a discreet distribution of passing marks, whereby each

value is associated with clear criteria and no mid-points are allowed (e.g. "satisfactory", "good", "very good", "excellent") have more nuanced differentiations among students, because teachers and schools do not concentrate their marks on only one part of the scale.

Since many 15-year-old students have only limited understanding of their underlying skills and potential to succeed in higher education and in the labour market, marks indirectly determine the educational opportunities that students expect to pursue. In fact, school marks are an important source of information for students about their potential success in a university environment, and students use this information to form their educational and career expectations. Moreover, in many countries and economies, marks directly determine the educational opportunities available to students and thus contribute to students' eventual educational attainment and labour market prospects because, in many countries, student marks help to determine access to higher education.

In all participating countries and economies, teachers tend to reward academic proficiency and other behaviours that are positively related to students' engagement with school and study habits. These generally promote student learning and intrinsic motivations to learn. Student engagement, attitudes towards learning, and use of learning strategies may also contribute to students' future learning, labour-market performance and overall well-being. This report also suggests that teachers give higher-than-expected marks to girls and socio-economically advantaged students, possibly because they tend to reward, on top of performance and the set of attitudes and behaviours that are measured by PISA, other attitudes and behaviours that girls and advantaged students are most likely to adopt. Whatever the reason, inequalities in marking practices may lead to inequalities in educational expectations, and, later, to inequalities in educational attainment and labour-market outcomes, thus perpetuating social disparities and reducing opportunities for upward mobility, especially among disadvantaged boys.

The report also shows that grading practices matter, as students use marks to shape their educational expectations. However, the report also suggests that teachers reward different sets of factors through marks which, in some cases, have little to do with students' mastery of skills or attitudes and behaviours that foster learning.

What can teachers do? Teachers can use grading practices to positively influence their students' educational trajectories. For example, teachers can develop in-class assessments throughout the year that clearly explore student mastery of different sets of skills; and they should mark such assessments on the basis of proficiency in those specific skills, including both cognitive and non-cognitive skills. Teachers and schools can best serve their students if they use grading practices that are objective and criterion-based, whereby students are graded according to absolute levels of mastery rather than according to students' performance relative to their peers. They should also accompany quantitative grades with in-depth qualitative evaluations that explore students' progress, strengths and weaknesses, giving students the tools to develop the skills that matter for eventual success in further education and beyond.

What can school systems do? They can encourage effective grading practices and align them with broader assessment policies. Because marks may have important consequences for students and provide incentives that guide student behaviours and attitudes towards school and learning, effective grading practices may promote the kinds of classroom dynamics that enhance learning. School systems can also evaluate how school marks fit with their broader assessment policies. Given that practically all schools use marks to evaluate students, marks should be an important part of the general policy regarding assessment. An integrated policy of assessment that covers student marks and standardised assessments will highlight the different forms of assessment and the complementary nature of, for example, standardised assessments and criterion-based assessments conducted at the school level. An integrated assessment and marking policy will also give teachers more clarity on what attitudes, behaviours and mastery of skills should be rewarded through marks, and will allow students to have clearer and more specific information about their standing in the learning process and what steps they should take to enhance their learning experience. School systems should thus promote research that provides a complete picture of the assessments used in their school system, their purpose, and what schools, teachers and students are doing with this information.

The report also emphasises that in some education systems, for example, in Austria, Italy, Poland and the Slovak Republic, teachers in some schools tend to inflate grades; but grade inflation is not a pervasive phenomenon and it does not affect some types of schools more than others. Only in Italy is grade inflation in private schools pervasive and warrants attention. On the other hand, in the majority of countries and economies that participated in the study, students tend to be graded according to the performance of their peers. In these countries, students who attend high-achieving schools receive marks that are lower than the marks they would have received had they attended poorer-performing schools. The literature clearly recommends that marks should be *criterion-referenced* and not *norm-referenced* because comparing students to others in the class promotes unhealthy competition and is shown to reduce motivation for all students (Guskey and Bailey, 2001; Tomlinson, 2005).

Overall, this report identifies a clear dilemma for teachers and educators: while marks should evaluate the knowledge and skills that students have mastered, marks influence not only the educational opportunities available to students but their educational expectations and aspirations as well. The report indicates that teachers reward proficiency, but they also reward a large set of measureable and unmeasurable (at least in the context of PISA) student characteristics. While some of these characteristics undoubtedly promote educational success and thus, by rewarding them, teachers provide an extra set of useful information to students, other characteristics may have little to do with students' chances of completing a university degree or of excelling in the labour market. As such, inequalities in grading practices may unduly restrict the opportunities some students have to acquire high-level skills and competencies and overcome social inequality.

Findings indicate that university enrolment and graduation rates are surging and today's 15-year-olds are even more likely than previous cohorts to expect to obtain a university degree. At the same time, the labour-market's demand for university graduates has increased markedly, and while many countries are rapidly improving the set of skills their students have mastered by age 15 (OECD, 2010), the average student attending university tomorrow will have a different, and in most cases, poorer set of skills than the average student who attended university a decade ago. The "democratisation of university education" that results from the expansion in university enrolments means that teaching in universities will have to adapt to more diverse student populations attending higher education as primary and secondary school educators are already doing.

The report identifies the need for education systems to strike a careful balance between promoting ambitious expectations among students – because the labour-market demand for high-level skills is surging and will probably continue to grow in the future – and recognising that the "forgotten half" of students who do not expect to complete a university education. For these students, education systems should do more to create a smooth transition from upper secondary school into the labour market by developing clearly marked occupational pathways and providing information, guidance and support so that these students understand the demands of the labour market, particularly the local labour market, and have accumulated the kinds of skills that local employers need. Schools and education systems can create relationships with employers to facilitate students' transitions and employers can gain from the better information schools have about their students to be able to choose workers with less uncertainty.

Finally, while some students benefit from education systems that allow for flexible entrance into university and multiple transitions between higher education and the labour market, other students take this as an opportunity to have a second chance in the future and refrain from putting forth the effort in school and making the choices that would enable them to flourish in the labour market. Setting up well defined structural paths to enter university may lower students' educational expectations and may prevent some students from fulfilling their potential – such as those students who develop the passion and motivation to attend university and acquire high-level skills only when they are older or in vocationally oriented programmes. However, creating these structural paths may help to better align students' expectations with their cognitive and non-cognitive skill sets and with opportunities in the labour-market, and facilitate the match between employers and prospective employees.

References

Autor, D., **F. Levy** and **R. Murnane** (2003), "The Skill Content of Recent Technological Change: An Empricial Exploration", *Quarterly Journal of Economics,* Vol. 118, No. 4, pp. 1279-1334.

Desjardins, R. and **A. Warnke** (2012), "Ageing and Skills: A Review and Analysis of Skill Gain and Skill Loss over the Lifespan and over Time", *OECD Education Working Papers,* No. 72, OECD Publishing.

Guskey, T. and **J. Bailey** (2001), *Developing Grading and Reporting Systems for Student Learning,* Corwin, Thousand Oaks, California.

OECD (2010), *PISA 2009 Results: Learning Trends: Changes in Student Performance since 2000 (Volume V)*, PISA, OECD Publishing.

OECD (2011), *Education at a Glance 2011: OECD Indicators,* OECD Publishing.

OECD (2012), *Better Skills, Better Jobs, Better Lives: A Strategic Approach to Skills Policies,* OECD Publishing.

Tomlinson, C. (2005), "Grading and Differentiation: Paradox or Good Practice", *Theory into Practice,* Vol. 44, No. 3, pp. 262-269.

Annex A

THE EDUCATIONAL CAREER QUESTIONNAIRE

In this <section> you are being asked about different aspects of your experience at school. There are no "right" or "wrong" answers.

Your answers should be the ones that are "right" for you. You may ask for help if you do not understand something or are not sure how to answer a question.

Your answers will be combined with others to make totals and averages in which no individual can be identified. All your answers will be kept confidential.

Q1 Did you ever miss two or more consecutive months of <ISCED 1>?

(Please tick only one box.)

No, never	☐
Yes, once	☐
Yes, twice or more	☐

Q2 Did you ever miss two or more consecutive months of <ISCED 2>

(Please tick only one box)

No, never	☐
Yes, once	☐
Yes, twice or more	☐

Q3 Did you change schools when you were attending <ISCED 1>?

(Please tick only one box)

No, I attended all of <ISCED 1> at the same school	☐
Yes, I changed schools once	☐
Yes, I changed schools twice or more	☐

Q4 Did you change schools when you were attending <ISCED 2>?

(Please tick only one box.)

No, I attended all of <ISCED 2> at the same school	☐
Yes, I changed schools once	☐
Yes, I changed schools twice or more	☐

Q5 Which of the following do you expect to complete?

(Please tick as many as apply)

a) <ISCED level 2>	☐
b) <ISCED level 3B or C>	☐
c) <ISCED level 3A>	☐
d) <ISCED level 4>	☐
e) <ISCED level 5B>	☐
f) <ISCED level 5A or 6>	☐

Q6 Have you attended the following <out-of-school-time> lessons during <ISCED 1>?

*These are lessons **in subjects that you learned at school during <ISCED 1>**, on which you spend extra time learning outside of normal school hours. The lessons might have been held at your <ISCED 1> school, at your home or somewhere else.*

(Please tick only one box in each row)

	Yes	*No*
a) <Enrichment lessons> in <test language>	☐	☐
b) <Remedial lessons> in <test language>	☐	☐
c) <Private tutoring> on a <one-to-one> basis in <test language> and/or other subjects	☐	☐

Q7 In your last school report, what was your mark in <test language>? [1]

______

Note

1. Countries and economies that do not have a unique marking scale could choose to include the following version of question Q7: "In your last school report, how did your mark in <test language> compare with your pass mark?" Two response options were offered: *1)* "at or above pass mark" and *2)* "below the pass mark". In PISA 2009, Macao-China, Mexico and New Zealand included this alternative question instead of question Q7 in their respective Educational Career questionnaire.

Annex B

DATA TABLES ON EDUCATIONAL EXPECTATIONS AND MARKS

[Part 1/2]

Table B1.1 Percentage of students who expect to complete a university degree, by ISCED type and ISCED level programme

	Percentage of students who expect to complete a university degree													
	All students		Academic programme		Non-academic programme		Lower secondary		Upper secondary		All students, 2003		Change between 2003 and 2009	
	%	S.E.	%	S.E.	%	S.E.	%	S.E.	%	S.E.	%	S.E.	Diff.	S.E.
Countries and economies														
Australia	61.2	(0.82)	61.6	(0.84)	13.8	(3.74)	61.1	(0.84)	62.5	(1.68)	62.8	(0.80)	-1.6	(1.20)
Austria	28.1	(0.95)	43.7	(1.43)	5.4	(0.79)	11.6	(3.06)	28.8	(0.95)	24.3	(1.29)	3.8	(1.52)
Belgium (Flemish Community)	37.1	(1.03)	46.1	(1.18)	4.2	(1.04)	17.1	(3.85)	37.7	(1.06)	37.6	(1.19)	-0.5	(1.47)
Hong Kong-China	47.2	(1.04)	47.2	(1.04)	a	a	42.7	(1.47)	49.5	(1.28)	52.3	(1.43)	-5.1	(1.82)
Croatia	49.1	(1.21)	62.2	(1.26)	5.2	(0.71)	c	c	49.2	(1.22)	m	m	m	m
Hungary	41.1	(1.46)	46.8	(1.71)	4.5	(0.77)	7.3	(2.04)	44.9	(1.61)	53.2	(1.36)	-12.2	(1.96)
Ireland	55.2	(1.07)	53.5	(1.18)	60.2	(2.04)	54.0	(1.26)	57.2	(1.54)	53.5	(1.07)	1.7	(1.51)
Iceland	44.7	(0.77)	44.7	(0.77)	a	a	44.1	(0.78)	79.5	(4.73)	36.1	(0.79)	8.6	(1.15)
Italy	40.9	(0.60)	42.2	(0.60)	3.6	(0.70)	15.4	(3.52)	41.2	(0.60)	52.1	(1.20)	-11.2	(1.38)
Korea	80.9	(1.23)	91.1	(0.71)	48.8	(3.85)	83.4	(2.98)	80.8	(1.27)	78.3	(0.96)	2.5	(1.56)
Latvia	25.4	(1.18)	25.6	(1.17)	c	c	25.0	(1.15)	41.3	(6.73)	24.9	(1.53)	0.6	(2.04)
Macao-China	35.2	(0.59)	35.4	(0.58)	c	c	27.3	(0.71)	47.2	(1.01)	48.9	(1.54)	-13.6	(1.59)
Mexico	55.8	(0.75)	56.4	(0.78)	43.9	(2.43)	42.2	(1.37)	66.1	(0.64)	49.1	(1.50)	6.7	(1.69)
New Zealand	52.5	(0.78)	52.5	(0.78)	a	a	39.3	(2.68)	53.3	(0.79)	38.8	(0.92)	13.7	(1.31)
Poland	41.5	(1.03)	41.4	(1.03)	c	c	41.0	(1.02)	c	c	30.1	(0.98)	11.3	(1.35)
Portugal	52.0	(1.57)	57.8	(1.76)	20.4	(4.88)	26.4	(1.46)	71.5	(1.28)	52.2	(1.38)	-0.2	(2.03)
Singapore	70.1	(0.59)	66.4	(3.29)	a	a	66.4	(3.29)	70.3	(0.60)	m	m	m	m
Serbia	55.1	(1.32)	89.6	(0.93)	44.5	(1.55)	12.4	(4.76)	56.0	(1.33)	m	m	m	m
Slovak Republic	45.5	(0.97)	49.5	(1.03)	3.0	(0.93)	36.1	(1.48)	51.3	(1.26)	43.0	(1.34)	2.5	(1.64)
Slovenia	35.1	(0.73)	56.4	(1.43)	15.9	(0.73)	15.2	(4.93)	35.8	(0.68)	m	m	m	m
Trinidad and Tobago	69.4	(0.74)	71.0	(0.79)	57.8	(2.25)	57.3	(1.37)	75.5	(0.90)	m	m	m	m
Regions														
Italy: Abruzzo	44.3	(2.19)	44.5	(2.20)	c	c	c	c	45.1	(2.23)	m	m	m	m
Italy: Basilicata	45.7	(1.59)	45.7	(1.59)	m	m	45.7	(1.59)	m	m	m	m	m	m
Italy: Bolzano	23.4	(0.89)	31.0	(1.17)	4.3	(0.67)	c	c	24.0	(0.89)	m	m	m	m
Italy: Calabria	46.2	(2.37)	46.2	(2.37)	m	m	c	c	46.4	(2.38)	m	m	m	m
Italy: Campania	43.0	(2.75)	43.0	(2.75)	m	m	c	c	43.4	(2.71)	m	m	m	m
Italy: Emilia Romagna	40.2	(2.04)	42.1	(2.28)	c	c	40.2	(2.04)	m	m	m	m	m	m
Italy: Friuli Venezia Giulia	39.5	(2.02)	40.1	(2.08)	c	c	c	c	40.4	(2.04)	m	m	m	m
Italy: Lazio	48.6	(1.98)	49.5	(2.00)	c	c	c	c	48.6	(1.99)	m	m	m	m
Italy: Liguria	39.7	(2.69)	40.9	(2.63)	c	c	c	c	39.8	(2.66)	m	m	m	m
Italy: Lombardia	38.0	(2.08)	40.7	(2.18)	2.0	(1.72)	c	c	38.6	(1.94)	m	m	m	m
Italy: Marche	37.2	(1.77)	37.2	(1.77)	m	m	c	c	37.4	(1.77)	m	m	m	m
Italy: Molise	43.4	(1.41)	43.5	(1.41)	c	c	c	c	43.9	(1.35)	m	m	m	m
Italy: Piemonte	37.3	(2.21)	39.2	(2.11)	c	c	c	c	38.2	(2.29)	m	m	m	m
Italy: Puglia	41.3	(2.39)	41.3	(2.39)	m	m	41.3	(2.39)	m	m	m	m	m	m
Italy: Sardegna	43.2	(2.32)	43.2	(2.32)	m	m	c	c	44.0	(2.32)	m	m	m	m
Italy: Sicilia	42.2	(2.09)	42.3	(2.09)	c	c	c	c	43.1	(2.12)	m	m	m	m
Italy: Toscana	40.5	(1.45)	40.5	(1.45)	m	m	c	c	39.9	(1.45)	m	m	m	m
Italy: Trento	35.3	(1.20)	44.4	(1.64)	2.9	(0.95)	c	c	35.3	(1.21)	m	m	m	m
Italy: Umbria	42.1	(1.57)	42.7	(1.60)	c	c	c	c	42.4	(1.48)	m	m	m	m
Italy: Valle d'Aosta	35.1	(1.58)	36.5	(1.62)	c	c	c	c	35.4	(1.59)	m	m	m	m
Italy: Veneto	34.7	(2.00)	38.7	(2.19)	2.8	(0.52)	c	c	35.2	(2.01)	m	m	m	m
Mexico: Aguascalientes	56.4	(2.53)	58.1	(2.47)	c	c	37.3	(3.52)	60.8	(3.06)	m	m	m	m
Mexico: Baja California	51.6	(2.42)	51.4	(2.35)	c	c	35.0	(2.84)	70.4	(2.32)	m	m	m	m
Mexico: Baja California Sur	58.2	(3.18)	58.4	(3.35)	c	c	44.7	(6.38)	67.5	(1.72)	m	m	m	m
Mexico: Campeche	60.7	(2.57)	61.2	(2.57)	c	c	48.8	(4.06)	72.6	(2.98)	m	m	m	m
Mexico: Chihuahua	65.5	(2.73)	66.3	(3.02)	c	c	47.2	(5.94)	71.9	(2.88)	m	m	m	m
Mexico: Colima	62.3	(2.30)	62.4	(2.33)	c	c	53.1	(5.20)	72.2	(2.10)	m	m	m	m
Mexico: Coahuila	55.8	(2.89)	56.3	(3.04)	49.4	(10.69)	41.6	(5.41)	65.8	(2.82)	m	m	m	m
Mexico: Chiapas	52.4	(2.70)	52.4	(2.74)	c	c	39.6	(4.26)	65.3	(2.92)	m	m	m	m
Mexico: Distrito Federal	71.1	(2.05)	72.8	(2.21)	c	c	63.1	(5.21)	76.3	(2.22)	m	m	m	m
Mexico: Durango	52.8	(2.34)	53.3	(2.48)	c	c	30.3	(4.84)	62.3	(1.79)	m	m	m	m
Mexico: Guerrero	46.1	(3.23)	45.9	(3.28)	c	c	30.5	(2.73)	70.9	(3.49)	m	m	m	m
Mexico: Guanajuato	44.6	(2.46)	44.9	(2.57)	c	c	30.3	(2.68)	58.7	(3.32)	m	m	m	m
Mexico: Hidalgo	57.2	(3.03)	57.9	(3.04)	c	c	29.5	(4.38)	65.5	(3.19)	m	m	m	m
Mexico: Jalisco	58.5	(1.86)	59.4	(1.92)	c	c	48.6	(2.41)	66.0	(2.86)	m	m	m	m
Mexico: Michoacán	54.1	(2.09)	56.0	(1.92)	c	c	40.6	(5.29)	60.9	(2.96)	m	m	m	m
Mexico: Morelos	54.2	(3.22)	55.6	(3.17)	c	c	47.9	(5.50)	60.4	(3.21)	m	m	m	m
Mexico: Mexico	57.9	(2.56)	59.6	(2.70)	c	c	37.2	(5.25)	66.9	(1.90)	m	m	m	m
Mexico: Nayarit	57.8	(1.60)	57.5	(1.64)	c	c	50.8	(3.12)	63.1	(2.00)	m	m	m	m
Mexico: Nuevo León	56.3	(5.72)	58.7	(5.84)	20.5	(2.52)	38.3	(8.74)	64.7	(5.51)	m	m	m	m
Mexico: Oaxaca	53.3	(4.55)	53.1	(4.67)	c	c	40.1	(9.04)	66.2	(2.65)	m	m	m	m
Mexico: Puebla	60.0	(3.50)	60.2	(3.59)	c	c	50.2	(9.47)	65.4	(2.95)	m	m	m	m
Mexico: Quintana Roo	54.4	(3.44)	54.2	(3.63)	c	c	46.9	(5.50)	66.2	(2.24)	m	m	m	m
Mexico: Querétaro	52.6	(4.14)	52.7	(4.20)	c	c	35.5	(4.82)	70.9	(2.28)	m	m	m	m
Mexico: Sinaloa	58.1	(2.18)	57.9	(2.27)	c	c	48.3	(4.36)	67.2	(1.73)	m	m	m	m
Mexico: San Luis Potosí	42.2	(3.12)	42.6	(3.20)	c	c	33.2	(3.76)	56.1	(2.71)	m	m	m	m
Mexico: Sonora	56.6	(2.28)	57.5	(2.59)	c	c	46.3	(2.38)	68.5	(2.26)	m	m	m	m
Mexico: Tamaulipas	54.1	(3.03)	54.3	(3.15)	c	c	43.9	(5.34)	64.5	(2.63)	m	m	m	m
Mexico: Tabasco	47.9	(2.21)	48.3	(2.14)	c	c	37.7	(2.78)	55.9	(2.42)	m	m	m	m
Mexico: Tlaxcala	52.8	(2.99)	53.0	(3.08)	c	c	44.7	(6.02)	59.9	(1.73)	m	m	m	m
Mexico: Veracruz	50.9	(3.12)	51.2	(3.18)	c	c	41.4	(4.35)	62.8	(3.15)	m	m	m	m
Mexico: Yucatán	52.7	(2.66)	52.4	(2.69)	c	c	33.7	(3.50)	70.0	(2.34)	m	m	m	m
Mexico: Zacatecas	48.7	(2.19)	48.9	(2.21)	c	c	29.9	(2.65)	56.0	(2.79)	m	m	m	m

1. Data from OECD (2010), *PISA 2009 Results: What Makes a School Successful? (Volume IV)*, PISA, OECD Publishing, Table IV.3.2a.
2. Data for Belgium (Flemish Community) is unavailable; data for Belgium as a whole presented instead.

StatLink http://dx.doi.org/10.1787/888932733754

[Part 2/2]

Table B1.1 Percentage of students who expect to complete a university degree, by ISCED type and ISCED level programme

	Number of programmes for 15-year-olds[1, 2]	Additional years of selection into these programmes before 15[1, 2]	15-year-old students in an academic programme		15-year-old students in a non-academic programme		15-year-old students in lower secondary		15-year-old students in upper secondary	
			%	S.E.	%	S.E.	%	S.E.	%	S.E.
Countries and economies										
Australia	1	0	99.4	(0.16)	0.6	(0.16)	81.2	(0.68)	18.8	(0.68)
Austria	4	5	59.4	(1.34)	40.6	(1.34)	4.3	(0.94)	95.7	(0.94)
Belgium (Flemish Community)	4	3	78.5	(1.17)	21.5	(1.17)	2.9	(0.54)	97.1	(0.54)
Hong Kong-China	2	0	100.0	(0.00)	a	a	33.7	(0.84)	66.3	(0.84)
Croatia	5	0.5	77.0	(1.31)	23.0	(1.31)	0.2	(0.16)	99.8	(0.16)
Hungary	3	4	86.3	(1.07)	13.7	(1.07)	10.3	(1.57)	89.7	(1.57)
Ireland	4	0	74.3	(1.44)	25.7	(1.44)	61.3	(0.98)	38.7	(0.98)
Iceland	1	0	100.0	(0.00)	a	a	98.3	(0.11)	1.7	(0.11)
Italy	3	1	96.6	(0.28)	3.4	(0.28)	1.4	(0.30)	98.6	(0.30)
Korea	3	1	75.8	(1.82)	24.2	(1.82)	4.2	(0.89)	95.8	(0.89)
Latvia	1	0	99.2	(0.45)	0.8	(0.45)	97.0	(0.51)	3.0	(0.51)
Macao-China	1	0	98.7	(0.04)	1.3	(0.04)	60.0	(0.18)	40.0	(0.18)
Mexico	3	0	95.5	(0.54)	4.5	(0.54)	42.9	(0.97)	57.1	(0.97)
New Zealand	1	0	100.0	(0.00)	a	a	5.8	(0.36)	94.2	(0.36)
Poland	1	0	99.9	(0.09)	0.1	(0.09)	99.1	(0.30)	0.9	(0.30)
Portugal	3	0	84.4	(1.63)	15.6	(1.63)	43.2	(2.09)	56.8	(2.09)
Singapore	4	3	100.0	(0.00)	a	a	3.5	(0.22)	96.5	(0.22)
Serbia	m	m	23.6	(1.00)	76.4	(1.00)	2.1	(0.54)	97.9	(0.54)
Slovak Republic	5	4	91.4	(0.96)	8.6	(0.96)	38.0	(1.50)	62.0	(1.50)
Slovenia	3	1	47.6	(0.43)	52.4	(0.43)	3.1	(0.77)	96.9	(0.77)
Trinidad and Tobago	4	4	88.3	(0.19)	11.7	(0.19)	33.4	(0.44)	66.6	(0.44)
Regions										
Italy: Abruzzo	m	m	99.5	(0.09)	0.5	(0.09)	1.8	(0.11)	98.2	(0.11)
Italy: Basilicata	m	m	100.0	(0.00)	m	m	100.0	(0.00)	m	m
Italy: Bolzano	m	m	71.5	(0.59)	28.5	(0.59)	3.9	(1.46)	96.1	(1.46)
Italy: Calabria	m	m	100.0	(0.00)	m	m	1.1	(0.78)	98.9	(0.78)
Italy: Campania	m	m	100.0	(0.00)	m	m	0.9	(0.59)	99.1	(0.59)
Italy: Emilia Romagna	m	m	94.1	(1.63)	5.9	(1.63)	100.0	(0.00)	m	m
Italy: Friuli Venezia Giulia	m	m	98.4	(0.09)	1.6	(0.09)	2.8	(0.52)	97.2	(0.52)
Italy: Lazio	m	m	98.1	(0.51)	1.9	(0.51)	1.0	(1.00)	99.0	(1.00)
Italy: Liguria	m	m	96.8	(1.72)	3.2	(1.72)	1.0	(0.33)	99.0	(0.33)
Italy: Lombardia	m	m	93.1	(0.91)	6.9	(0.91)	1.5	(1.07)	98.5	(1.07)
Italy: Marche	m	m	100.0	(0.00)	m	m	0.5	(0.40)	99.5	(0.40)
Italy: Molise	m	m	99.9	(0.01)	0.1	(0.01)	1.0	(1.06)	99.0	(1.06)
Italy: Piemonte	m	m	94.8	(2.64)	5.2	(2.64)	2.9	(1.21)	97.1	(1.21)
Italy: Puglia	m	m	100.0	(0.00)	m	m	100.0	(0.00)	m	m
Italy: Sardegna	m	m	100.0	(0.00)	m	m	1.8	(0.78)	98.2	(0.78)
Italy: Sicilia	m	m	99.8	(0.22)	0.2	(0.22)	3.3	(2.09)	96.7	(2.09)
Italy: Toscana	m	m	100.0	(0.00)	m	m	1.6	(0.37)	98.4	(0.37)
Italy: Trento	m	m	78.2	(1.18)	21.8	(1.18)	0.5	(0.46)	99.5	(0.46)
Italy: Umbria	m	m	98.4	(0.26)	1.6	(0.26)	0.9	(1.24)	99.1	(1.24)
Italy: Valle d'Aosta	m	m	95.8	(0.27)	4.2	(0.27)	0.8	(0.22)	99.2	(0.22)
Italy: Veneto	m	m	89.0	(1.23)	11.0	(1.23)	1.3	(0.77)	98.7	(0.77)
Mexico: Aguascalientes	m	m	91.3	(2.65)	8.7	(2.65)	18.9	(2.16)	81.1	(2.16)
Mexico: Baja California	m	m	98.2	(1.79)	1.8	(1.79)	53.0	(3.49)	47.0	(3.49)
Mexico: Baja California Sur	m	m	95.6	(0.35)	4.4	(0.35)	40.7	(5.31)	59.3	(5.31)
Mexico: Campeche	m	m	98.2	(1.85)	1.8	(1.85)	49.9	(3.66)	50.1	(3.66)
Mexico: Chihuahua	m	m	95.2	(3.46)	4.8	(3.46)	26.2	(4.44)	73.8	(4.44)
Mexico: Colima	m	m	98.5	(0.19)	1.5	(0.19)	51.6	(5.22)	48.4	(5.22)
Mexico: Coahuila	m	m	92.9	(2.81)	7.1	(2.81)	41.2	(3.70)	58.8	(3.70)
Mexico: Chiapas	m	m	98.7	(1.31)	1.3	(1.31)	50.2	(3.61)	49.8	(3.61)
Mexico: Distrito Federal	m	m	89.5	(3.78)	10.5	(3.78)	39.6	(5.05)	60.4	(5.05)
Mexico: Durango	m	m	97.9	(2.08)	2.1	(2.08)	29.5	(4.32)	70.5	(4.32)
Mexico: Guerrero	m	m	98.2	(1.76)	1.8	(1.76)	61.4	(4.35)	38.6	(4.35)
Mexico: Guanajuato	m	m	95.5	(0.23)	4.5	(0.23)	49.6	(2.99)	50.4	(2.99)
Mexico: Hidalgo	m	m	97.8	(2.22)	2.2	(2.22)	23.2	(2.30)	76.8	(2.30)
Mexico: Jalisco	m	m	96.2	(0.25)	3.8	(0.25)	42.9	(2.64)	57.1	(2.64)
Mexico: Michoacán	m	m	91.1	(5.16)	8.9	(5.16)	33.7	(5.73)	66.3	(5.73)
Mexico: Morelos	m	m	94.3	(2.51)	5.7	(2.51)	49.2	(5.92)	50.8	(5.92)
Mexico: Mexico	m	m	94.1	(2.02)	5.9	(2.02)	30.3	(3.90)	69.7	(3.90)
Mexico: Nayarit	m	m	94.9	(1.42)	5.1	(1.42)	42.7	(4.34)	57.3	(4.34)
Mexico: Nuevo León	m	m	93.8	(3.26)	6.2	(3.26)	31.6	(9.32)	68.4	(9.32)
Mexico: Oaxaca	m	m	97.8	(2.17)	2.2	(2.17)	49.6	(5.17)	50.4	(5.17)
Mexico: Puebla	m	m	97.0	(0.34)	3.0	(0.34)	35.6	(4.60)	64.4	(4.60)
Mexico: Quintana Roo	m	m	94.8	(1.55)	5.2	(1.55)	61.0	(4.06)	39.0	(4.06)
Mexico: Querétaro	m	m	98.7	(1.38)	1.3	(1.38)	51.8	(4.59)	48.2	(4.59)
Mexico: Sinaloa	m	m	94.6	(3.30)	5.4	(3.30)	48.2	(4.51)	51.8	(4.51)
Mexico: San Luis Potosí	m	m	98.0	(0.42)	2.0	(0.42)	60.9	(3.77)	39.1	(3.77)
Mexico: Sonora	m	m	93.9	(0.34)	6.1	(0.34)	53.9	(5.02)	46.1	(5.02)
Mexico: Tamaulipas	m	m	96.0	(0.53)	4.0	(0.53)	50.3	(3.25)	49.7	(3.25)
Mexico: Tabasco	m	m	98.1	(1.88)	1.9	(1.88)	43.9	(4.95)	56.1	(4.95)
Mexico: Tlaxcala	m	m	97.3	(1.99)	2.7	(1.99)	46.4	(5.70)	53.6	(5.70)
Mexico: Veracruz	m	m	98.0	(1.97)	2.0	(1.97)	55.7	(4.58)	44.3	(4.58)
Mexico: Yucatán	m	m	98.0	(1.97)	2.0	(1.97)	47.6	(4.02)	52.4	(4.02)
Mexico: Zacatecas	m	m	98.4	(1.54)	1.6	(1.54)	28.2	(4.29)	71.8	(4.29)

1. Data from OECD (2010), *PISA 2009 Results: What Makes a School Successful? (Volume IV)*, PISA, OECD Publishing, Table IV.3.2a.
2. Data for Belgium (Flemish Community) is unavailable; data for Belgium as a whole presented instead.

StatLink http://dx.doi.org/10.1787/888932733754

[Part 1/2]

Table B1.2 Reading performance of students who do and do not expect to complete a university degree

	All students						Students in academic programme						Students in non-academic programme					
	Do not expect to complete a university degree		Expect to complete a university degree		Difference (Expect - Do not expect)		Do not expect to complete a university degree		Expect to complete a university degree		Difference (Expect - Do not expect)		Do not expect to complete a university degree		Expect to complete a university degree		Difference (Expect - Do not expect)	
	Mean	S.E.	Mean	S.E.	Diff.	S.E.	Mean	S.E.	Mean	S.E.	Diff.	S.E.	Mean	S.E.	Mean	S.E.	Diff.	S.E.
Countries and economies																		
Australia	461	(1.98)	558	(2.39)	**96.9**	(2.65)	461	(2.06)	558	(2.48)	**97.1**	(2.74)	454	(11.19)	c	c	c	c
Austria	451	(3.10)	542	(3.91)	**91.0**	(4.83)	497	(4.76)	552	(3.74)	**55.1**	(4.95)	411	(4.49)	420	(10.75)	9.4	(10.28)
Belgium (Flemish Community)	491	(2.31)	586	(3.27)	**94.9**	(3.76)	520	(2.67)	590	(3.17)	**69.8**	(3.78)	432	(2.89)	433	(16.47)	1.2	(16.05)
Hong Kong-China	507	(2.68)	565	(2.27)	**57.7**	(3.11)	507	(2.68)	565	(2.27)	**57.7**	(3.11)	a	a	a	a	a	a
Croatia	431	(2.96)	526	(2.55)	**95.0**	(3.33)	460	(4.00)	530	(2.58)	**69.2**	(4.08)	392	(3.01)	392	(11.77)	-0.4	(11.07)
Hungary	454	(3.82)	554	(2.82)	**99.9**	(4.64)	466	(4.71)	556	(2.79)	**89.7**	(5.33)	410	(7.37)	410	(20.29)	-0.6	(14.73)
Ireland	462	(3.66)	532	(2.78)	**69.8**	(3.51)	457	(3.60)	524	(3.04)	**67.0**	(3.71)	477	(6.72)	550	(4.57)	**73.2**	(7.59)
Iceland	472	(1.92)	541	(2.24)	**69.4**	(3.31)	472	(1.92)	541	(2.24)	**69.4**	(3.31)	a	a	a	a	a	a
Italy	455	(1.90)	536	(1.64)	**80.7**	(2.47)	458	(1.95)	536	(1.66)	**78.1**	(2.49)	401	(6.12)	361	(12.04)	**-40.3**	(10.87)
Korea	473	(5.75)	555	(2.94)	**81.9**	(5.71)	501	(5.28)	564	(3.10)	**63.2**	(5.79)	458	(7.27)	503	(6.99)	**44.2**	(7.50)
Latvia	470	(2.74)	531	(3.50)	**61.2**	(3.27)	470	(2.75)	532	(3.42)	**61.8**	(3.24)	c	c	c	c	c	c
Macao-China	471	(1.03)	520	(1.57)	**49.6**	(1.82)	471	(1.04)	520	(1.61)	**49.8**	(1.86)	c	c	c	c	c	c
Mexico	392	(2.20)	456	(1.68)	**63.8**	(2.16)	390	(2.26)	456	(1.72)	**66.2**	(2.24)	429	(6.26)	453	(4.11)	**23.8**	(5.67)
New Zealand	482	(2.79)	562	(2.66)	**79.2**	(3.32)	482	(2.79)	562	(2.66)	**79.2**	(3.32)	a	a	a	a	a	a
Poland	470	(2.46)	548	(2.87)	**78.1**	(2.94)	470	(2.46)	548	(2.87)	**78.2**	(2.94)	c	c	c	c	c	c
Portugal	444	(3.08)	534	(2.42)	**89.3**	(3.78)	451	(3.37)	536	(2.53)	**84.1**	(3.91)	424	(5.84)	503	(15.39)	**79.8**	(15.00)
Singapore	466	(2.24)	553	(1.40)	**86.5**	(2.87)	380	(11.42)	462	(7.57)	**82.8**	(11.67)	a	a	a	a	a	a
Serbia	401	(2.48)	478	(2.24)	**77.5**	(2.97)	461	(6.06)	508	(3.64)	**46.9**	(5.60)	397	(2.59)	460	(2.78)	**62.4**	(3.24)
Slovak Republic	437	(3.42)	531	(2.61)	**93.5**	(4.31)	446	(3.13)	531	(2.65)	**85.1**	(4.03)	387	(5.68)	c	c	c	c
Slovenia	459	(1.60)	533	(2.14)	**74.2**	(3.06)	517	(4.41)	559	(2.18)	**41.7**	(4.56)	432	(1.26)	451	(4.11)	**19.4**	(4.48)
Trinidad and Tobago	368	(3.09)	453	(1.88)	**85.3**	(4.19)	374	(3.49)	459	(1.98)	**84.8**	(4.67)	336	(6.45)	401	(4.57)	**65.1**	(8.38)
Regions																		
Italy: Abruzzo	445	(4.52)	529	(5.24)	**83.2**	(5.33)	446	(4.57)	529	(5.23)	**82.8**	(5.32)	c	c	c	c	c	c
Italy: Basilicata	438	(5.89)	517	(4.47)	**79.3**	(6.96)	438	(5.89)	517	(4.47)	**79.3**	(6.96)	c	c	c	c	c	c
Italy: Bolzano	475	(3.63)	547	(3.17)	**72.8**	(4.43)	496	(5.60)	557	(3.15)	**61.1**	(5.51)	436	(3.91)	c	c	c	c
Italy: Calabria	408	(6.33)	498	(4.02)	**89.9**	(6.89)	408	(6.33)	498	(4.02)	**89.9**	(6.89)	c	c	c	c	c	c
Italy: Campania	416	(7.06)	504	(5.84)	**88.2**	(7.85)	416	(7.06)	504	(5.84)	**88.2**	(7.85)	c	c	c	c	c	c
Italy: Emilia Romagna	469	(4.60)	559	(3.77)	**89.9**	(4.96)	479	(4.19)	561	(3.84)	**81.8**	(4.69)	c	c	c	c	c	c
Italy: Friuli Venezia Giulia	479	(5.67)	569	(3.75)	**89.9**	(6.37)	481	(5.92)	569	(3.74)	**88.0**	(6.58)	c	c	c	c	c	c
Italy: Lazio	446	(4.19)	522	(6.03)	**76.6**	(6.27)	449	(4.11)	523	(6.04)	**73.3**	(6.24)	c	c	c	c	c	c
Italy: Liguria	460	(10.90)	543	(5.58)	**83.0**	(9.84)	462	(11.45)	543	(5.55)	**81.1**	(10.37)	c	c	c	c	c	c
Italy: Lombardia	491	(6.50)	574	(5.73)	**82.7**	(8.21)	503	(6.54)	575	(5.89)	**71.5**	(7.90)	392	(12.76)	c	c	c	c
Italy: Marche	469	(8.38)	552	(5.23)	**83.0**	(7.55)	469	(8.38)	552	(5.23)	**83.0**	(7.55)	c	c	c	c	c	c
Italy: Molise	436	(3.55)	517	(3.87)	**80.6**	(5.28)	436	(3.57)	517	(3.87)	**80.5**	(5.31)	c	c	c	c	c	c
Italy: Piemonte	467	(5.19)	549	(6.44)	**82.4**	(6.39)	470	(5.50)	549	(6.44)	**79.9**	(6.45)	c	c	c	c	c	c
Italy: Puglia	457	(5.71)	537	(5.09)	**80.7**	(7.07)	457	(5.71)	537	(5.09)	**80.7**	(7.07)	c	c	c	c	c	c
Italy: Sardegna	435	(4.16)	520	(4.30)	**84.5**	(6.23)	435	(4.16)	520	(4.30)	**84.5**	(6.23)	c	c	c	c	c	c
Italy: Sicilia	418	(9.26)	509	(8.53)	**90.6**	(10.17)	418	(9.28)	509	(8.54)	**90.8**	(10.17)	c	c	c	c	c	c
Italy: Toscana	464	(5.19)	542	(4.98)	**77.9**	(5.75)	464	(5.19)	542	(4.98)	**77.9**	(5.75)	c	c	c	c	c	c
Italy: Trento	477	(3.51)	568	(3.97)	**91.0**	(5.39)	506	(3.51)	571	(3.86)	**64.8**	(5.28)	418	(8.09)	c	c	c	c
Italy: Umbria	456	(5.67)	545	(5.20)	**88.9**	(5.66)	458	(5.64)	546	(5.20)	**87.4**	(5.71)	c	c	c	c	c	c
Italy: Valle d'Aosta	489	(3.33)	562	(4.03)	**73.0**	(5.51)	493	(3.36)	563	(3.95)	**69.6**	(5.44)	c	c	c	c	c	c
Italy: Veneto	480	(5.92)	558	(5.27)	**77.4**	(7.01)	494	(6.20)	559	(5.32)	**65.0**	(7.17)	409	(13.73)	c	c	c	c
Mexico: Aguascalientes	420	(5.47)	472	(6.60)	**52.1**	(6.22)	415	(6.53)	472	(6.75)	**57.1**	(6.64)	c	c	c	c	c	c
Mexico: Baja California	397	(4.73)	460	(3.95)	**62.9**	(5.90)	396	(4.78)	460	(4.06)	**63.6**	(6.03)	c	c	c	c	c	c
Mexico: Baja California Sur	392	(7.78)	445	(5.58)	**52.6**	(6.00)	389	(7.96)	444	(5.78)	**54.5**	(6.11)	c	c	c	c	c	c
Mexico: Campeche	377	(5.47)	439	(5.08)	**62.6**	(6.63)	374	(5.54)	439	(5.12)	**64.4**	(6.78)	c	c	c	c	c	c
Mexico: Chihuahua	414	(7.86)	469	(5.49)	**55.2**	(7.74)	411	(7.48)	470	(5.64)	**58.9**	(7.35)	c	c	c	c	c	c
Mexico: Colima	401	(6.34)	458	(3.44)	**56.7**	(5.50)	401	(6.42)	458	(3.48)	**57.1**	(5.56)	c	c	c	c	c	c
Mexico: Coahuila	407	(6.93)	453	(5.47)	**46.7**	(6.68)	405	(7.56)	453	(5.86)	**47.3**	(6.90)	422	(17.15)	463	(15.68)	41.1	(21.81)
Mexico: Chiapas	330	(14.79)	405	(6.95)	**75.5**	(12.22)	329	(14.89)	405	(7.02)	**76.1**	(12.32)	c	c	c	c	c	c
Mexico: Distrito Federal	427	(12.00)	487	(6.15)	**60.1**	(10.38)	423	(13.56)	490	(6.47)	**67.0**	(11.31)	c	c	c	c	c	c
Mexico: Durango	397	(7.49)	453	(4.57)	**56.5**	(7.27)	396	(7.69)	454	(4.69)	**57.3**	(7.49)	c	c	c	c	c	c
Mexico: Guerrero	351	(7.27)	403	(7.79)	**51.6**	(7.43)	351	(7.42)	402	(7.94)	**51.5**	(7.55)	c	c	c	c	c	c
Mexico: Guanajuato	393	(5.09)	463	(4.82)	**69.9**	(5.65)	389	(5.20)	462	(4.94)	**72.9**	(5.78)	c	c	c	c	c	c
Mexico: Hidalgo	388	(6.31)	452	(6.33)	**63.2**	(7.29)	388	(6.62)	452	(6.39)	**64.0**	(7.46)	c	c	c	c	c	c
Mexico: Jalisco	410	(6.75)	462	(4.83)	**51.6**	(7.20)	409	(6.39)	462	(4.87)	**52.7**	(7.20)	c	c	c	c	c	c
Mexico: Michoacán	390	(5.03)	446	(3.93)	**56.2**	(5.70)	390	(5.75)	447	(4.19)	**57.4**	(5.99)	c	c	c	c	c	c
Mexico: Morelos	393	(13.63)	446	(11.35)	**52.3**	(6.28)	391	(14.55)	445	(11.72)	**53.7**	(6.61)	c	c	c	c	c	c
Mexico: Mexico	403	(8.45)	472	(6.57)	**69.0**	(8.66)	402	(9.09)	473	(6.82)	**71.5**	(9.22)	c	c	c	c	c	c
Mexico: Nayarit	396	(4.60)	442	(4.19)	**46.6**	(6.06)	393	(4.59)	441	(4.43)	**48.0**	(6.10)	c	c	c	c	c	c
Mexico: Nuevo León	409	(7.98)	483	(12.22)	**74.3**	(11.90)	408	(9.10)	484	(12.54)	**76.5**	(12.65)	418	(10.06)	c	c	c	c
Mexico: Oaxaca	359	(20.93)	427	(9.23)	**68.4**	(14.64)	358	(21.37)	427	(9.46)	**68.7**	(14.93)	c	c	c	c	c	c
Mexico: Puebla	405	(6.36)	456	(7.23)	**50.6**	(8.36)	403	(6.50)	455	(7.49)	**52.3**	(8.71)	c	c	c	c	c	c
Mexico: Quintana Roo	395	(6.29)	464	(9.86)	**69.1**	(8.34)	393	(6.34)	465	(10.45)	**72.6**	(8.88)	c	c	c	c	c	c
Mexico: Querétaro	402	(7.61)	475	(4.51)	**73.2**	(7.91)	401	(7.56)	475	(4.54)	**74.1**	(7.98)	c	c	c	c	c	c
Mexico: Sinaloa	393	(7.21)	439	(5.79)	**45.8**	(7.35)	390	(6.99)	437	(6.07)	**47.2**	(7.35)	c	c	c	c	c	c
Mexico: San Luis Potosí	375	(13.70)	439	(9.80)	**64.3**	(9.88)	373	(13.91)	439	(9.89)	**66.3**	(10.03)	c	c	c	c	c	c
Mexico: Sonora	386	(6.50)	441	(5.48)	**55.7**	(7.86)	384	(7.05)	442	(5.57)	**58.2**	(8.53)	c	c	c	c	c	c
Mexico: Tamaulipas	392	(9.25)	446	(6.26)	**53.5**	(6.11)	390	(9.60)	444	(6.45)	**54.1**	(6.32)	c	c	c	c	c	c
Mexico: Tabasco	368	(5.93)	419	(5.46)	**51.0**	(4.90)	366	(5.97)	419	(5.53)	**52.5**	(4.63)	c	c	c	c	c	c
Mexico: Tlaxcala	390	(4.72)	442	(2.83)	**51.6**	(5.04)	388	(4.74)	441	(2.89)	**53.2**	(5.18)	c	c	c	c	c	c
Mexico: Veracruz	395	(5.54)	452	(5.88)	**57.1**	(6.97)	393	(5.40)	451	(5.96)	**58.1**	(6.96)	c	c	c	c	c	c
Mexico: Yucatán	380	(6.10)	450	(7.24)	**69.9**	(6.50)	379	(6.19)	449	(7.45)	**70.2**	(6.69)	c	c	c	c	c	c
Mexico: Zacatecas	408	(9.77)	446	(5.22)	**37.6**	(10.78)	408	(9.97)	446	(5.25)	**37.7**	(10.96)	c	c	c	c	c	c

Note: Estimates statistically significantly different from 0 (zero) at a 95% confidence level are highlighted in bold.

StatLink http://dx.doi.org/10.1787/888932733773

[Part 2/2]

Table B1.2 Reading performance of students who do and do not expect to complete a university degree

	Students in lower secondary						Students in upper secondary					
	Do not expect to complete a university degree		Expect to complete a university degree		Difference (Expect - Do not expect)		Do not expect to complete a university degree		Expect to complete a university degree		Difference (Expect - Do not expect)	
	Mean	S.E.	Mean	S.E.	Diff.	S.E.	Mean	S.E.	Mean	S.E.	Diff.	S.E.
Countries and economies												
Australia	456	(2.34)	553	(2.50)	**96.5**	(2.70)	483	(3.79)	581	(4.31)	**98.3**	(5.41)
Austria	386	(9.49)	c	c	c	c	454	(3.18)	543	(3.90)	**89.0**	(4.95)
Belgium (Flemish Community)	407	(8.31)	c	c	**50.8**	(24.34)	494	(2.31)	588	(3.18)	**93.3**	(3.80)
Hong Kong-China	475	(4.24)	532	(3.49)	**57.3**	(4.49)	526	(2.74)	579	(2.45)	**53.5**	(3.34)
Croatia	c	c	c	c	c	c	432	(2.96)	526	(2.55)	**94.7**	(3.33)
Hungary	373	(7.83)	c	c	c	c	470	(3.13)	556	(2.77)	**86.0**	(4.16)
Ireland	451	(3.95)	521	(3.35)	**69.4**	(4.18)	480	(4.98)	548	(3.70)	**68.0**	(5.67)
Iceland	471	(1.87)	539	(2.26)	**67.9**	(3.23)	c	c	619	(11.22)	c	c
Italy	340	(23.35)	c	c	c	c	457	(1.82)	537	(1.67)	**79.3**	(2.30)
Korea	415	(26.12)	534	(11.74)	**119.7**	(33.08)	476	(5.96)	556	(2.99)	**80.6**	(5.85)
Latvia	468	(2.76)	529	(3.54)	**60.8**	(3.32)	522	(12.78)	564	(9.50)	**42.3**	(17.03)
Macao-China	452	(1.21)	495	(2.36)	**42.8**	(2.72)	509	(1.69)	542	(2.21)	**33.4**	(2.81)
Mexico	362	(3.11)	422	(4.35)	**60.3**	(4.04)	430	(1.72)	472	(1.66)	**41.4**	(1.96)
New Zealand	440	(8.66)	505	(8.92)	**64.3**	(13.15)	486	(2.77)	564	(2.69)	**78.5**	(3.28)
Poland	470	(2.46)	548	(2.88)	**77.5**	(2.88)	c	c	c	c	c	c
Portugal	416	(2.76)	486	(3.24)	**69.7**	(3.67)	499	(3.40)	547	(2.49)	**47.6**	(3.91)
Singapore	380	(11.42)	462	(7.57)	**82.8**	(11.67)	470	(2.34)	556	(1.45)	**86.0**	(2.89)
Serbia	354	(14.46)	c	c	c	c	403	(2.51)	479	(2.25)	**75.9**	(2.99)
Slovak Republic	419	(4.48)	496	(4.36)	**76.3**	(4.84)	451	(4.82)	546	(3.35)	**94.3**	(6.17)
Slovenia	414	(13.13)	c	c	c	c	461	(1.47)	535	(2.10)	**73.3**	(2.97)
Trinidad and Tobago	313	(4.05)	382	(3.77)	**68.7**	(6.16)	416	(3.65)	481	1.8776	**64.5**	(4.64)
Regions												
Italy: Abruzzo	c	c	c	c	c	c	450	(4.42)	529	(5.24)	**78.3**	(5.24)
Italy: Basilicata	c	c	c	c	c	c	438	(5.89)	517	(4.47)	**79.3**	(6.96)
Italy: Bolzano	c	c	c	c	c	c	480	(1.90)	549	(3.18)	**68.6**	(3.93)
Italy: Calabria	c	c	c	c	c	c	410	(6.15)	499	(4.02)	**89.5**	(6.88)
Italy: Campania	c	c	c	c	c	c	415	(7.14)	504	(5.84)	**88.8**	(7.81)
Italy: Emilia Romagna	c	c	c	c	c	c	469	(4.60)	559	(3.77)	**89.9**	(4.96)
Italy: Friuli Venezia Giulia	c	c	c	c	c	c	482	(5.32)	570	(3.60)	**87.0**	(5.56)
Italy: Lazio	c	c	c	c	c	c	447	(4.12)	524	(5.83)	**77.6**	(6.27)
Italy: Liguria	c	c	c	c	c	c	461	(11.00)	544	(5.52)	**82.8**	(9.82)
Italy: Lombardia	c	c	c	c	c	c	493	(6.40)	574	(5.73)	**80.4**	(8.63)
Italy: Marche	c	c	c	c	c	c	469	(8.48)	552	(5.23)	**82.7**	(7.65)
Italy: Molise	c	c	c	c	c	c	437	(3.65)	517	(3.87)	**80.1**	(5.42)
Italy: Piemonte	c	c	c	c	c	c	471	(5.37)	550	(6.29)	**79.3**	(6.64)
Italy: Puglia	c	c	c	c	c	c	457	(5.71)	537	(5.09)	**80.7**	(7.07)
Italy: Sardegna	c	c	c	c	c	c	437	(4.14)	520	(4.30)	**82.6**	(6.20)
Italy: Sicilia	c	c	c	c	c	c	427	(7.16)	511	(8.37)	**84.0**	(9.12)
Italy: Toscana	c	c	c	c	c	c	465	(5.18)	546	(4.49)	**80.8**	(5.61)
Italy: Trento	c	c	c	c	c	c	478	(3.57)	570	(3.77)	**91.8**	(5.31)
Italy: Umbria	c	c	c	c	c	c	457	(5.62)	545	(5.20)	**87.9**	(5.57)
Italy: Valle d'Aosta	c	c	c	c	c	c	491	(3.33)	562	(4.03)	**71.2**	(5.57)
Italy: Veneto	c	c	c	c	c	c	484	(5.65)	558	(5.27)	**73.8**	(6.77)
Mexico: Aguascalientes	360	(10.05)	405	(11.05)	**45.8**	(11.02)	443	(6.69)	482	(6.64)	**39.1**	(6.60)
Mexico: Baja California	377	(6.36)	431	(6.12)	**54.0**	(8.56)	446	(4.63)	476	(5.39)	**30.1**	(5.88)
Mexico: Baja California Sur	364	(10.78)	412	(15.45)	**48.0**	(10.26)	424	(4.54)	459	(4.24)	**35.2**	(5.21)
Mexico: Campeche	354	(6.26)	406	(10.23)	**51.3**	(10.01)	418	(5.97)	462	(5.82)	**43.5**	(6.44)
Mexico: Chihuahua	371	(9.22)	421	(17.16)	**50.3**	(15.15)	443	(7.31)	481	(5.32)	**37.5**	(8.56)
Mexico: Colima	378	(9.92)	432	(10.55)	**53.8**	(8.39)	443	(4.97)	479	(4.43)	**35.5**	(4.97)
Mexico: Coahuila	392	(10.44)	440	(13.16)	**48.8**	(11.78)	425	(5.74)	459	(6.14)	**34.3**	(5.59)
Mexico: Chiapas	306	(21.54)	378	(17.89)	**71.8**	(16.29)	370	(8.46)	422	(7.60)	**51.2**	(7.06)
Mexico: Distrito Federal	393	(20.17)	461	(17.31)	**68.3**	(13.44)	462	(7.70)	501	(6.16)	**39.1**	(7.65)
Mexico: Durango	361	(16.49)	425	(12.58)	**64.3**	(16.92)	425	(7.21)	459	(5.12)	**34.5**	(7.39)
Mexico: Guerrero	340	(8.61)	365	(13.49)	**25.3**	(11.76)	397	(7.74)	429	(6.58)	**32.3**	(7.31)
Mexico: Guanajuato	365	(6.54)	429	(5.03)	**64.4**	(6.70)	438	(4.60)	479	(6.08)	**41.0**	(6.23)
Mexico: Hidalgo	343	(12.85)	356	(12.90)	12.4	(8.53)	416	(6.59)	465	(6.29)	**48.5**	(6.77)
Mexico: Jalisco	386	(7.87)	433	(7.22)	**47.4**	(9.95)	438	(10.41)	478	(6.30)	**39.7**	(9.08)
Mexico: Michoacán	352	(8.00)	410	(16.03)	**58.1**	(14.82)	419	(6.87)	458	(4.63)	**39.1**	(5.37)
Mexico: Morelos	368	(19.35)	427	(24.60)	**58.9**	(10.32)	425	(7.31)	460	(5.96)	**34.5**	(8.15)
Mexico: Mexico	344	(9.38)	403	(11.69)	**59.1**	(14.16)	452	(6.55)	489	(6.16)	**36.9**	(6.53)
Mexico: Nayarit	375	(7.03)	430	(7.53)	**55.6**	(8.65)	417	(4.63)	449	(5.21)	**32.9**	(7.02)
Mexico: Nuevo León	374	(14.59)	447	(32.46)	73.0	(37.92)	437	(8.96)	493	(13.71)	**56.2**	(9.66)
Mexico: Oaxaca	325	(27.51)	384	(17.93)	**58.9**	(25.41)	418	(11.67)	453	(5.70)	**34.9**	(11.09)
Mexico: Puebla	382	(10.29)	444	(19.60)	**61.9**	(23.10)	424	(6.92)	461	(6.98)	**37.1**	(7.38)
Mexico: Quintana Roo	377	(7.03)	457	(19.06)	**80.0**	(17.06)	439	(6.62)	472	(5.76)	**33.1**	(5.34)
Mexico: Querétaro	381	(7.63)	455	(10.68)	**73.9**	(13.89)	451	(6.45)	486	(5.10)	**34.8**	(5.32)
Mexico: Sinaloa	373	(8.58)	407	(5.60)	**34.7**	(9.32)	422	(8.46)	460	(7.48)	**37.1**	(8.82)
Mexico: San Luis Potosí	356	(17.49)	418	(18.72)	**62.3**	(13.77)	420	(9.31)	459	(7.57)	**38.4**	(7.34)
Mexico: Sonora	366	(9.18)	411	(6.60)	**45.2**	(10.34)	425	(6.37)	465	(5.19)	**40.1**	(5.57)
Mexico: Tamaulipas	369	(13.78)	423	(13.94)	**53.8**	(8.09)	429	(5.85)	461	(6.12)	**32.4**	(7.56)
Mexico: Tabasco	344	(6.53)	385	(9.03)	**41.0**	(9.08)	394	(4.79)	437	(4.13)	**42.6**	(4.66)
Mexico: Tlaxcala	362	(7.02)	430	(4.68)	**68.1**	(7.30)	423	(4.48)	449	(3.23)	**25.7**	(4.90)
Mexico: Veracruz	378	(6.34)	426	(8.28)	**48.7**	(7.45)	428	(6.12)	473	(7.89)	**44.5**	(7.32)
Mexico: Yucatán	353	(7.16)	392	(11.87)	**39.1**	(8.92)	433	(9.35)	475	(7.40)	**41.8**	(6.02)
Mexico: Zacatecas	391	(21.22)	427	(15.21)	35.6	(20.52)	419	(9.52)	450	(5.01)	**30.9**	(10.69)

Note: Estimates statistically significantly different from 0 (zero) at a 95% confidence level are highlighted in bold.

StatLink http://dx.doi.org/10.1787/888932733773

[Part 1/2]

Table B1.3 Mathematics performance of students who do and do not expect to complete a university degree

	All students						Students in academic programme						Students in non-academic programme					
	Do not expect to complete a university degree		Expect to complete a university degree		Difference (Expect - Do not expect)		Do not expect to complete a university degree		Expect to complete a university degree		Difference (Expect - Do not expect)		Do not expect to complete a university degree		Expect to complete a university degree		Difference (Expect - Do not expect)	
	Mean	S.E.	Mean	S.E.	Diff.	S.E.	Mean	S.E.	Mean	S.E.	Diff.	S.E.	Mean	S.E.	Mean	S.E.	Diff.	S.E.
Countries and economies																		
Australia	466	(2.08)	552	(2.77)	**86.4**	(3.00)	466	(2.12)	553	(2.87)	**87.1**	(3.11)	471	(10.48)	c	c	30.5	(30.12)
Austria	474	(2.87)	567	(3.66)	**92.6**	(4.47)	516	(4.82)	576	(3.76)	**59.7**	(5.03)	438	(4.14)	463	(9.62)	**25.3**	(8.63)
Belgium (Flemish Community)	507	(3.06)	609	(3.74)	**102.1**	(4.23)	538	(3.18)	614	(3.65)	**75.2**	(4.04)	444	(3.34)	441	(14.01)	-2.6	(13.56)
Hong Kong-China	523	(3.08)	593	(2.88)	**70.3**	(3.43)	523	(3.08)	593	(2.88)	**70.3**	(3.43)	a	a	a	a	a	a
Croatia	420	(2.94)	505	(3.73)	**84.9**	(3.97)	446	(4.04)	508	(3.77)	**61.9**	(4.53)	386	(2.85)	399	(10.49)	13.5	(10.74)
Hungary	451	(3.89)	548	(3.87)	**96.3**	(5.13)	463	(4.96)	550	(3.86)	**86.8**	(5.92)	410	(5.33)	402	(13.25)	8.5	(11.79)
Ireland	457	(2.96)	518	(2.69)	**60.9**	(3.17)	455	(3.16)	513	(2.91)	**58.2**	(3.58)	466	(5.18)	532	(3.97)	**65.8**	(6.01)
Iceland	481	(1.93)	544	(2.07)	**62.5**	(3.09)	481	(1.93)	544	(2.07)	**62.5**	(3.09)	a	a	a	a	a	a
Italy	459	(1.97)	522	(2.28)	**63.2**	(2.50)	461	(2.07)	522	(2.28)	**61.6**	(2.53)	425	(6.30)	379	(13.42)	**-45.8**	(13.30)
Korea	476	(6.47)	563	(3.62)	**87.0**	(6.63)	510	(6.23)	574	(3.93)	**63.9**	(6.82)	457	(7.85)	498	(7.21)	**40.5**	(8.67)
Latvia	469	(3.04)	524	(3.94)	**54.8**	(4.20)	469	(3.06)	524	(3.84)	**55.1**	(4.11)	c	c	c	c	c	c
Macao-China	510	(1.22)	558	(1.72)	**48.4**	(2.23)	509	(1.23)	558	(1.76)	**48.5**	(2.26)	c	c	c	c	c	c
Mexico	389	(1.81)	445	(1.86)	**55.6**	(2.05)	388	(1.87)	445	(1.93)	**57.5**	(2.13)	418	(4.44)	438	(3.43)	**20.7**	(4.15)
New Zealand	489	(2.85)	551	(2.71)	**61.8**	(3.24)	489	(2.85)	551	(2.71)	**61.8**	(3.24)	a	a	a	a	a	a
Poland	465	(2.73)	540	(3.24)	**75.0**	(3.02)	465	(2.73)	540	(3.24)	**75.0**	(3.03)	c	c	c	c	c	c
Portugal	443	(2.63)	530	(3.00)	**87.0**	(3.88)	449	(2.70)	532	(3.09)	**83.4**	(3.79)	426	(6.01)	497	(16.73)	**70.3**	(16.89)
Singapore	503	(2.54)	589	(1.80)	**85.7**	(3.20)	439	(11.23)	524	(9.21)	**85.3**	(13.89)	a	a	a	a	a	a
Serbia	399	(3.03)	480	(3.01)	**80.7**	(3.73)	467	(9.15)	514	(5.98)	**46.8**	(8.22)	396	(3.13)	459	(3.28)	**63.3**	(3.69)
Slovak Republic	457	(3.29)	551	(4.04)	**94.3**	(4.74)	465	(3.21)	551	(4.10)	**86.6**	(4.65)	411	(6.35)	c	c	c	c
Slovenia	476	(1.81)	554	(2.31)	**77.9**	(3.17)	531	(4.71)	578	(2.48)	**47.4**	(4.82)	450	(1.50)	475	(4.58)	**25.3**	(5.24)
Trinidad and Tobago	377	(2.80)	442	(1.68)	**65.9**	(3.43)	383	(3.03)	449	(1.76)	**66.3**	(3.73)	345	(5.52)	382	(4.05)	**37.0**	(7.45)
Regions																		
Italy: Abruzzo	449	(5.31)	513	(8.81)	**64.6**	(7.91)	449	(5.36)	514	(8.81)	**64.3**	(7.91)	c	c	c	c	c	c
Italy: Basilicata	446	(5.31)	511	(5.15)	**64.5**	(6.34)	446	(5.31)	511	(5.15)	**64.5**	(6.34)	c	c	c	c	c	c
Italy: Bolzano	493	(3.64)	558	(3.77)	**65.3**	(4.82)	511	(5.87)	566	(3.85)	**55.0**	(6.19)	461	(3.15)	c	c	c	c
Italy: Calabria	416	(5.62)	475	(4.64)	**58.9**	(5.61)	416	(5.62)	475	(4.64)	**58.9**	(5.61)	c	c	c	c	c	c
Italy: Campania	418	(6.44)	488	(10.09)	**70.3**	(10.17)	418	(6.44)	488	(10.09)	**70.3**	(10.17)	c	c	c	c	c	c
Italy: Emilia Romagna	470	(5.58)	556	(4.86)	**85.6**	(6.60)	479	(5.48)	558	(4.94)	**78.8**	(6.25)	c	c	c	c	c	c
Italy: Friuli Venezia Giulia	484	(5.58)	553	(4.19)	**69.7**	(6.41)	485	(5.80)	553	(4.20)	**68.5**	(6.57)	c	c	c	c	c	c
Italy: Lazio	449	(4.62)	502	(8.05)	**52.7**	(7.16)	451	(4.72)	502	(8.06)	**50.4**	(7.15)	c	c	c	c	c	c
Italy: Liguria	463	(9.92)	538	(6.95)	**74.6**	(8.34)	467	(10.40)	538	(6.93)	**71.7**	(8.65)	c	c	c	c	c	c
Italy: Lombardia	490	(6.60)	560	(5.78)	**70.6**	(7.65)	499	(6.58)	561	(5.82)	**61.8**	(7.52)	412	(11.67)	c	c	c	c
Italy: Marche	478	(5.25)	537	(4.76)	**59.5**	(4.66)	478	(5.25)	537	(4.76)	**59.5**	(4.66)	c	c	c	c	c	c
Italy: Molise	435	(3.40)	510	(3.94)	**75.5**	(5.39)	435	(3.42)	510	(3.94)	**75.5**	(5.39)	c	c	c	c	c	c
Italy: Piemonte	467	(5.56)	539	(6.11)	**71.8**	(5.63)	470	(5.89)	540	(6.09)	**69.7**	(5.75)	c	c	c	c	c	c
Italy: Puglia	467	(8.34)	519	(7.22)	**52.1**	(8.07)	467	(8.34)	519	(7.22)	**52.1**	(8.07)	c	c	c	c	c	c
Italy: Sardegna	428	(5.20)	499	(5.51)	**70.5**	(6.85)	428	(5.20)	499	(5.51)	**70.5**	(6.85)	c	c	c	c	c	c
Italy: Sicilia	419	(9.34)	497	(9.48)	**77.4**	(9.55)	419	(9.37)	497	(9.49)	**77.4**	(9.56)	c	c	c	c	c	c
Italy: Toscana	474	(5.17)	530	(7.30)	**56.0**	(6.89)	474	(5.17)	530	(7.30)	**56.0**	(6.89)	c	c	c	c	c	c
Italy: Trento	491	(4.07)	558	(3.83)	**67.2**	(6.20)	514	(4.65)	560	(3.84)	**46.9**	(6.64)	445	(5.34)	c	c	c	c
Italy: Umbria	459	(4.07)	530	(5.29)	**70.6**	(5.58)	462	(4.09)	530	(5.29)	**68.8**	(5.66)	c	c	c	c	c	c
Italy: Valle d'Aosta	481	(3.41)	545	(4.00)	**63.9**	(5.54)	485	(3.53)	545	(3.99)	**59.7**	(5.66)	c	c	c	c	c	c
Italy: Veneto	488	(5.87)	548	(8.05)	**59.8**	(7.80)	496	(6.40)	550	(8.14)	**53.6**	(7.87)	450	(13.07)	c	c	c	c
Mexico: Aguascalientes	417	(6.46)	462	(7.77)	**45.2**	(6.12)	411	(8.05)	461	(8.06)	**50.1**	(6.57)	c	c	c	c	c	c
Mexico: Baja California	388	(6.47)	444	(5.38)	**55.9**	(6.56)	387	(6.62)	443	(5.51)	**56.4**	(6.75)	c	c	c	c	c	c
Mexico: Baja California Sur	393	(7.49)	437	(4.28)	**43.6**	(7.01)	392	(7.77)	437	(4.46)	**45.6**	(7.22)	c	c	c	c	c	c
Mexico: Campeche	375	(5.56)	433	(4.55)	**58.2**	(5.87)	373	(5.71)	433	(4.59)	**59.6**	(6.10)	c	c	c	c	c	c
Mexico: Chihuahua	416	(7.05)	461	(5.91)	**44.4**	(7.54)	415	(7.37)	462	(6.12)	**46.9**	(7.55)	c	c	c	c	c	c
Mexico: Colima	413	(5.96)	459	(3.32)	**46.4**	(6.56)	413	(6.04)	459	(3.38)	**46.3**	(6.66)	c	c	c	c	c	c
Mexico: Coahuila	399	(7.30)	438	(4.48)	**39.6**	(5.36)	398	(7.85)	438	(4.83)	**40.0**	(5.42)	406	(19.30)	442	(13.87)	36.5	(22.14)
Mexico: Chiapas	344	(10.18)	398	(6.92)	**53.7**	(7.95)	343	(10.23)	397	(7.02)	**54.2**	(8.00)	c	c	c	c	c	c
Mexico: Distrito Federal	416	(8.55)	472	(6.25)	**55.8**	(8.44)	415	(9.88)	475	(6.68)	**59.9**	(9.37)	c	c	c	c	c	c
Mexico: Durango	396	(6.60)	439	(3.89)	**42.6**	(6.60)	395	(6.50)	439	(3.93)	**44.0**	(6.68)	c	c	c	c	c	c
Mexico: Guerrero	361	(7.50)	401	(6.41)	**40.1**	(6.31)	360	(7.63)	400	(6.41)	**39.4**	(6.31)	c	c	c	c	c	c
Mexico: Guanajuato	399	(3.53)	457	(4.27)	**57.7**	(5.05)	396	(3.78)	457	(4.44)	**60.1**	(5.39)	c	c	c	c	c	c
Mexico: Hidalgo	393	(6.93)	447	(6.59)	**54.7**	(7.08)	393	(7.28)	448	(6.70)	**55.0**	(7.25)	c	c	c	c	c	c
Mexico: Jalisco	410	(6.67)	456	(5.96)	**45.8**	(6.85)	409	(6.46)	456	(6.03)	**46.8**	(6.94)	c	c	c	c	c	c
Mexico: Michoacán	389	(5.18)	436	(4.76)	**47.0**	(4.64)	390	(6.03)	437	(4.85)	**47.1**	(4.98)	c	c	c	c	c	c
Mexico: Morelos	388	(9.78)	437	(9.28)	**49.2**	(6.55)	388	(10.30)	436	(9.57)	**48.1**	(6.61)	c	c	c	c	c	c
Mexico: Mexico	392	(6.93)	451	(6.78)	**59.4**	(7.86)	390	(7.63)	453	(6.97)	**62.4**	(8.38)	c	c	c	c	c	c
Mexico: Nayarit	404	(4.43)	441	(3.99)	**36.8**	(5.67)	401	(4.59)	439	(4.25)	**37.8**	(5.82)	c	c	c	c	c	c
Mexico: Nuevo León	410	(7.32)	491	(13.91)	**80.6**	(12.80)	409	(8.31)	492	(14.09)	**82.4**	(13.24)	415	(10.54)	c	c	c	c
Mexico: Oaxaca	370	(15.50)	425	(7.13)	**54.6**	(13.27)	369	(15.81)	424	(7.20)	**55.1**	(13.46)	c	c	c	c	c	c
Mexico: Puebla	398	(6.14)	445	(7.34)	**46.6**	(7.69)	395	(6.20)	444	(7.59)	**48.9**	(7.97)	c	c	c	c	c	c
Mexico: Quintana Roo	382	(5.10)	448	(9.09)	**66.2**	(8.00)	381	(5.23)	450	(9.59)	**68.7**	(8.43)	c	c	c	c	c	c
Mexico: Querétaro	400	(5.71)	458	(5.46)	**57.5**	(8.97)	399	(5.77)	457	(5.53)	**58.3**	(9.07)	c	c	c	c	c	c
Mexico: Sinaloa	397	(7.01)	432	(5.72)	**35.0**	(7.63)	394	(6.92)	431	(6.04)	**36.4**	(7.85)	c	c	c	c	c	c
Mexico: San Luis Potosí	371	(8.89)	431	(9.96)	**60.1**	(8.36)	369	(8.99)	430	(10.05)	**61.9**	(8.38)	c	c	c	c	c	c
Mexico: Sonora	387	(8.50)	431	(5.55)	**44.3**	(8.60)	386	(9.37)	432	(5.15)	**46.4**	(9.50)	c	c	c	c	c	c
Mexico: Tamaulipas	387	(7.12)	426	(6.61)	**39.4**	(6.29)	385	(7.38)	425	(6.79)	**39.8**	(6.47)	c	c	c	c	c	c
Mexico: Tabasco	358	(6.76)	404	(6.54)	**45.9**	(4.22)	357	(6.89)	404	(6.62)	**46.6**	(4.10)	c	c	c	c	c	c
Mexico: Tlaxcala	385	(5.23)	428	(3.22)	**43.5**	(5.35)	383	(5.41)	428	(3.35)	**44.6**	(5.51)	c	c	c	c	c	c
Mexico: Veracruz	383	(5.98)	442	(8.00)	**58.7**	(7.11)	382	(6.01)	442	(8.12)	**59.5**	(7.27)	c	c	c	c	c	c
Mexico: Yucatán	374	(4.90)	435	(9.76)	**60.6**	(8.45)	374	(4.94)	434	(10.03)	**60.8**	(8.69)	c	c	c	c	c	c
Mexico: Zacatecas	408	(6.02)	442	(5.66)	**33.5**	(7.22)	407	(6.10)	442	(5.72)	**34.3**	(7.28)	c	c	c	c	c	c

Note: Estimates statistically significantly different from 0 (zero) at a 95% confidence level are highlighted in bold.

StatLink http://dx.doi.org/10.1787/888932733792

[Part 2/2]

Table B1.3 Mathematics performance of students who do and do not expect to complete a university degree

	Students in lower secondary						Students in upper secondary					
	Do not expect to complete a university degree		Expect to complete a university degree		Difference (Expect - Do not expect)		Do not expect to complete a university degree		Expect to complete a university degree		Difference (Expect - Do not expect)	
	Mean	S.E.	Mean	S.E.	Diff.	S.E.	Mean	S.E.	Mean	S.E.	Diff.	S.E.
Countries and economies												
Australia	461	(2.35)	545	(2.72)	**84.1**	(3.08)	485	(4.14)	583	(5.14)	**98.0**	(6.22)
Austria	401	(9.59)	c	c	**70.4**	(16.55)	478	(2.94)	569	(3.68)	**90.3**	(4.54)
Belgium (Flemish Community)	426	(9.69)	c	c	34.3	(23.24)	510	(3.05)	611	(3.63)	**100.8**	(4.26)
Hong Kong-China	485	(4.37)	554	(4.02)	**69.0**	(4.88)	544	(3.18)	610	(3.12)	**65.6**	(3.97)
Croatia	c	c	c	c	c	c	420	(2.93)	505	(3.73)	**84.6**	(3.96)
Hungary	371	(9.03)	c	c	c	c	467	(3.27)	549	(3.94)	**82.3**	(4.52)
Ireland	448	(3.42)	508	(3.36)	**60.8**	(4.27)	474	(4.09)	533	(3.17)	**59.0**	(4.79)
Iceland	480	(1.90)	540	(2.03)	**60.1**	(2.94)	c	c	651	(11.76)	c	c
Italy	339	(29.55)	c	c	c	c	461	(1.80)	523	(2.33)	**61.7**	(2.31)
Korea	421	(34.30)	533	(14.18)	**112.1**	(38.18)	478	(6.72)	564	(3.70)	**86.3**	(6.83)
Latvia	468	(3.07)	522	(3.93)	**53.9**	(4.19)	514	(16.80)	562	(10.79)	**47.1**	(21.29)
Macao-China	488	(1.48)	529	(3.05)	**40.9**	(3.53)	554	(2.22)	583	(2.29)	**29.1**	(3.51)
Mexico	365	(2.46)	416	(3.67)	**51.3**	(3.31)	421	(1.72)	459	(2.22)	**38.0**	(2.10)
New Zealand	444	(8.22)	496	(9.66)	**51.9**	(12.83)	493	(2.80)	554	(2.75)	**60.7**	(3.21)
Poland	465	(2.73)	539	(3.23)	**74.1**	(2.97)	c	c	c	c	c	c
Portugal	414	(2.44)	477	(3.26)	**62.5**	(3.67)	499	(3.15)	545	(3.15)	**46.0**	(3.88)
Singapore	439	(11.23)	524	(9.21)	**85.3**	(13.89)	505	(2.61)	591	(1.85)	**85.3**	(3.25)
Serbia	351	(15.68)	c	c	c	c	401	(3.07)	480	(3.02)	**79.0**	(3.75)
Slovak Republic	448	(4.70)	522	(4.85)	**74.2**	(4.27)	464	(4.31)	563	(5.47)	**99.7**	(6.82)
Slovenia	415	(15.13)	c	c	c	c	478	(1.71)	555	(2.25)	**76.4**	(3.17)
Trinidad and Tobago	337	(4.14)	377	(3.23)	**40.4**	(4.99)	411	(2.80)	467	1.716	**55.9**	(3.60)
Regions												
Italy: Abruzzo	c	c	c	c	c	c	454	(5.41)	513	(8.81)	**59.5**	(7.79)
Italy: Basilicata	c	c	c	c	c	c	446	(5.31)	511	(5.15)	**64.5**	(6.34)
Italy: Bolzano	c	c	c	c	c	c	499	(1.78)	560	(3.65)	**60.8**	(4.31)
Italy: Calabria	c	c	c	c	c	c	417	(5.77)	476	(4.68)	**59.1**	(5.81)
Italy: Campania	c	c	c	c	c	c	418	(6.53)	488	(10.09)	**70.2**	(10.20)
Italy: Emilia Romagna	c	c	c	c	c	c	470	(5.58)	556	(4.86)	**85.6**	(6.60)
Italy: Friuli Venezia Giulia	c	c	c	c	c	c	488	(4.97)	554	(4.14)	**65.3**	(5.38)
Italy: Lazio	c	c	c	c	c	c	450	(4.54)	504	(7.86)	**53.9**	(7.15)
Italy: Liguria	c	c	c	c	c	c	465	(9.97)	539	(6.85)	**74.1**	(8.10)
Italy: Lombardia	c	c	c	c	c	c	492	(6.70)	560	(5.78)	**68.5**	(7.89)
Italy: Marche	c	c	c	c	c	c	478	(5.24)	537	(4.76)	**59.2**	(4.65)
Italy: Molise	c	c	c	c	c	c	435	(3.46)	510	(3.94)	**75.2**	(5.44)
Italy: Piemonte	c	c	c	c	c	c	472	(5.93)	541	(5.82)	**69.0**	(5.70)
Italy: Puglia	c	c	c	c	c	c	467	(8.34)	519	(7.22)	**52.1**	(8.07)
Italy: Sardegna	c	c	c	c	c	c	430	(5.29)	499	(5.51)	**68.9**	(6.89)
Italy: Sicilia	c	c	c	c	c	c	430	(5.82)	500	(9.25)	**70.0**	(7.90)
Italy: Toscana	c	c	c	c	c	c	474	(5.16)	533	(7.22)	**58.3**	(6.86)
Italy: Trento	c	c	c	c	c	c	492	(4.08)	560	(3.80)	**67.8**	(6.17)
Italy: Umbria	c	c	c	c	c	c	461	(3.64)	530	(5.29)	**69.2**	(5.27)
Italy: Valle d'Aosta	c	c	c	c	c	c	482	(3.37)	545	(4.00)	**62.5**	(5.53)
Italy: Veneto	c	c	c	c	c	c	491	(5.76)	548	(8.05)	**57.4**	(7.68)
Mexico: Aguascalientes	372	(12.14)	402	(18.98)	29.8	(16.23)	434	(7.94)	471	(7.73)	**37.0**	(6.79)
Mexico: Baja California	369	(8.86)	407	(8.95)	**38.1**	(9.22)	433	(5.53)	464	(6.26)	**30.4**	(7.09)
Mexico: Baja California Sur	369	(10.23)	405	(11.36)	**35.8**	(10.18)	422	(5.06)	451	(3.10)	**29.9**	(6.46)
Mexico: Campeche	357	(8.01)	402	(8.57)	**45.2**	(7.83)	408	(4.67)	453	(5.12)	**45.6**	(5.63)
Mexico: Chihuahua	380	(11.27)	421	(20.74)	**40.7**	(20.12)	440	(9.37)	470	(5.87)	**29.7**	(8.74)
Mexico: Colima	396	(8.42)	435	(6.51)	**39.4**	(7.09)	442	(5.87)	477	(4.60)	**35.1**	(5.32)
Mexico: Coahuila	383	(11.12)	420	(10.32)	**36.9**	(5.52)	418	(5.32)	447	(4.44)	**28.9**	(4.72)
Mexico: Chiapas	330	(14.17)	376	(16.64)	**46.0**	(12.79)	368	(10.04)	411	(7.06)	**42.7**	(6.32)
Mexico: Distrito Federal	387	(13.63)	444	(11.61)	**56.5**	(10.07)	445	(8.04)	487	(7.80)	**41.6**	(6.61)
Mexico: Durango	365	(13.98)	403	(13.12)	**38.4**	(14.40)	421	(6.00)	446	(4.08)	**25.5**	(5.90)
Mexico: Guerrero	351	(9.79)	376	(11.77)	**24.1**	(9.53)	396	(5.52)	418	(7.22)	**22.4**	(7.02)
Mexico: Guanajuato	380	(4.55)	433	(5.29)	**52.9**	(6.80)	431	(4.47)	469	(5.52)	**37.8**	(6.44)
Mexico: Hidalgo	351	(11.50)	359	(11.39)	7.8	(10.74)	418	(8.18)	459	(6.75)	**41.1**	(7.31)
Mexico: Jalisco	387	(8.63)	426	(11.69)	**38.8**	(11.10)	437	(10.69)	473	(7.33)	**35.9**	(9.01)
Mexico: Michoacán	363	(10.73)	411	(18.11)	**48.0**	(12.89)	410	(7.75)	445	(5.12)	**35.1**	(5.43)
Mexico: Morelos	371	(13.75)	422	(18.29)	**50.5**	(9.78)	409	(8.50)	448	(7.11)	**39.7**	(9.43)
Mexico: Mexico	342	(7.86)	391	(8.32)	**48.9**	(11.12)	433	(6.90)	466	(7.29)	**32.8**	(5.76)
Mexico: Nayarit	393	(7.24)	428	(6.70)	**35.8**	(8.94)	415	(5.00)	448	(5.45)	**32.9**	(6.87)
Mexico: Nuevo León	379	(13.62)	460	(35.46)	**80.7**	(38.19)	435	(7.23)	499	(12.92)	**64.1**	(12.77)
Mexico: Oaxaca	346	(21.33)	398	(14.25)	**51.8**	(16.14)	412	(9.23)	440	(8.97)	**28.8**	(11.13)
Mexico: Puebla	375	(9.57)	437	(17.36)	**61.6**	(18.08)	416	(5.73)	448	(7.80)	**31.7**	(6.68)
Mexico: Quintana Roo	366	(5.69)	443	(17.27)	**77.8**	(16.05)	423	(7.57)	454	(5.23)	**31.0**	(6.90)
Mexico: Querétaro	385	(6.68)	451	(13.99)	**65.8**	(17.18)	435	(4.50)	461	(5.57)	**26.1**	(6.43)
Mexico: Sinaloa	383	(9.66)	411	(6.05)	**28.6**	(11.74)	418	(8.19)	446	(8.11)	**28.0**	(8.36)
Mexico: San Luis Potosí	353	(10.76)	412	(18.63)	**59.5**	(13.79)	413	(7.55)	448	(8.10)	**34.9**	(7.59)
Mexico: Sonora	371	(12.51)	409	(6.33)	**37.8**	(11.38)	418	(7.74)	449	(6.04)	**30.9**	(5.60)
Mexico: Tamaulipas	369	(10.78)	404	(11.92)	**35.2**	(8.27)	416	(5.31)	442	(8.65)	**25.5**	(8.18)
Mexico: Tabasco	338	(8.40)	378	(12.09)	**40.0**	(6.87)	380	(5.48)	417	(5.02)	**37.5**	(4.56)
Mexico: Tlaxcala	358	(9.53)	416	(5.89)	**57.7**	(7.17)	416	(4.38)	436	(4.38)	**19.9**	(4.36)
Mexico: Veracruz	369	(7.49)	422	(9.85)	**52.9**	(8.38)	411	(5.17)	458	(10.77)	**47.6**	(10.23)
Mexico: Yucatán	353	(5.53)	388	(10.68)	**34.5**	(9.25)	416	(7.53)	456	(11.58)	**39.2**	(8.26)
Mexico: Zacatecas	395	(15.11)	409	(19.90)	13.9	(17.40)	417	(5.32)	449	(5.61)	**32.0**	(6.89)

Note: Estimates statistically significantly different from 0 (zero) at a 95% confidence level are highlighted in bold.

StatLink http://dx.doi.org/10.1787/888932733792

[Part 1/1]

Table B1.4 Students with unrealistic expectations and potentially lost talent

	Students at or below PISA proficiency Level 2 in reading literacy		Students who expect to complete a university degree		Students at or below PISA proficiency Level 2 who expect to complete a university degree		Students at or above PISA proficiency Level 4 in reading literacy		Students who do *not* expect to complete a university degree		Students at or above PISA proficiency Level 4 who do *not* expect to complete a university degree		Students who do *not* expect to complete an upper secondary degree		Students at or above PISA proficiency Level 4 who expect to complete an upper secondary degree	
	%	S.E.	%	S.E.	%	S.E.	%	S.E.	%	S.E.	%	S.E.	%	S.E.	%	S.E.
Countries and economies																
Australia	34.7	(0.89)	61.2	(0.82)	30.0	(1.07)	36.8	(0.98)	38.8	(0.82)	12.9	(0.61)	24.8	(0.63)	6.9	(0.43)
Austria	51.7	(1.32)	28.1	(0.95)	9.9	(0.94)	22.3	(1.09)	71.9	(0.95)	41.2	(1.91)	55.7	(1.13)	34.0	(2.15)
Belgium (Flemish Community)	33.4	(1.03)	37.1	(1.03)	9.3	(1.08)	39.4	(1.20)	62.9	(1.03)	34.4	(1.36)	19.4	(0.79)	6.2	(0.48)
Hong Kong-China	24.3	(1.01)	47.2	(1.04)	24.2	(1.47)	44.3	(1.11)	52.8	(1.04)	35.7	(1.20)	27.1	(0.86)	12.8	(0.71)
Croatia	49.8	(1.55)	49.1	(1.21)	22.3	(1.09)	19.6	(1.11)	50.9	(1.21)	9.3	(1.23)	33.5	(1.05)	c	c
Hungary	41.3	(1.51)	41.1	(1.45)	11.5	(0.97)	27.7	(1.45)	58.9	(1.45)	20.9	(1.88)	28.9	(1.22)	6.2	(1.28)
Ireland	40.5	(1.35)	55.2	(1.07)	34.8	(1.66)	28.9	(1.16)	44.8	(1.07)	22.5	(1.36)	29.7	(0.96)	9.8	(0.94)
Iceland	39.0	(0.82)	44.7	(0.77)	24.5	(1.34)	30.4	(0.77)	55.3	(0.77)	31.2	(1.33)	29.5	(0.81)	11.8	(0.93)
Italy	45.1	(0.75)	40.9	(0.60)	19.8	(0.66)	26.1	(0.63)	59.1	(0.60)	30.0	(0.91)	41.7	(0.57)	16.9	(0.77)
Korea	21.2	(1.44)	80.9	(1.23)	52.3	(2.91)	45.8	(1.99)	19.1	(1.23)	5.2	(0.58)	5.3	(0.61)	c	c
Latvia	46.4	(1.71)	25.4	(1.18)	11.1	(0.74)	20.1	(1.28)	74.6	(1.18)	47.5	(2.15)	30.8	(1.31)	5.4	(0.76)
Macao-China	45.4	(0.66)	35.2	(0.59)	20.7	(0.72)	19.8	(0.50)	64.8	(0.59)	39.1	(1.37)	27.4	(0.62)	7.4	(0.81)
Mexico	73.1	(0.77)	55.8	(0.75)	47.1	(0.77)	5.7	(0.40)	44.2	(0.75)	11.4	(1.11)	28.7	(0.70)	3.1	(0.53)
New Zealand	33.7	(0.95)	52.5	(0.78)	29.2	(1.37)	40.6	(0.97)	47.5	(0.78)	26.9	(1.08)	23.6	(0.74)	9.4	(0.75)
Poland	39.5	(1.29)	41.5	(1.02)	17.9	(1.09)	29.5	(1.26)	58.5	(1.02)	28.7	(1.33)	28.7	(0.96)	2.6	(0.40)
Portugal	44.0	(1.62)	52.0	(1.57)	24.3	(1.36)	24.4	(1.17)	48.0	(1.57)	14.0	(1.16)	37.4	(1.45)	7.3	(0.92)
Singapore	31.0	(0.55)	70.1	(0.59)	45.1	(1.24)	41.4	(0.76)	29.9	(0.59)	11.0	(0.64)	2.7	(0.27)	c	c
Serbia	66.1	(1.15)	55.1	(1.32)	41.2	(1.57)	8.7	(0.62)	44.9	(1.32)	c	c	23.2	(1.03)	c	c
Slovak Republic	50.3	(1.32)	45.5	(0.97)	21.2	(1.17)	21.2	(0.92)	54.5	(0.97)	15.7	(1.71)	42.0	(1.01)	9.7	(1.13)
Slovenia	46.8	(0.63)	35.1	(0.73)	16.9	(0.91)	23.9	(0.67)	64.9	(0.73)	33.4	(1.64)	28.8	(0.59)	3.9	(0.68)
Trinidad and Tobago	69.9	(0.80)	69.4	(0.74)	60.5	(0.99)	11.2	(0.47)	30.6	(0.74)	7.1	(1.34)	18.9	(0.62)	c	c
Regions																
Italy: Abruzzo	47.8	(2.42)	44.3	(2.19)	21.4	(2.04)	22.7	(2.07)	55.7	(2.19)	22.2	(2.40)	38.0	(2.44)	9.3	(2.12)
Italy: Basilicata	51.8	(2.10)	45.7	(1.59)	25.2	(2.20)	18.8	(1.40)	54.3	(1.59)	18.3	(2.31)	35.6	(2.56)	c	c
Italy: Bolzano	43.3	(1.62)	23.4	(0.89)	9.6	(0.90)	25.9	(1.21)	76.6	(0.89)	51.8	(2.14)	62.7	(1.12)	37.3	(2.05)
Italy: Calabria	62.2	(2.29)	46.2	(2.37)	28.1	(1.86)	12.5	(1.56)	53.8	(2.37)	c	c	36.7	(2.09)	c	c
Italy: Campania	60.5	(2.99)	43.0	(2.75)	25.2	(1.74)	13.7	(2.15)	57.0	(2.75)	15.8	(2.47)	38.3	(1.92)	c	c
Italy: Emilia Romagna	38.7	(1.81)	40.2	(2.04)	15.0	(1.68)	34.5	(1.97)	59.8	(2.04)	30.8	(2.34)	42.2	(1.99)	17.4	(1.85)
Italy: Friuli Venezia Giulia	33.1	(2.28)	39.5	(2.02)	10.1	(1.84)	36.4	(2.29)	60.5	(2.02)	32.4	(1.91)	41.7	(2.63)	17.2	(1.68)
Italy: Lazio	48.0	(1.79)	48.6	(1.98)	28.3	(3.13)	23.9	(1.66)	51.4	(1.98)	21.8	(1.90)	34.6	(1.63)	11.5	(1.41)
Italy: Liguria	41.2	(3.53)	39.7	(2.69)	16.9	(2.23)	27.0	(2.38)	60.3	(2.69)	29.8	(2.98)	41.8	(3.08)	17.8	(1.92)
Italy: Lombardia	29.5	(2.46)	38.0	(2.08)	10.0	(1.96)	39.0	(2.75)	62.0	(2.08)	37.0	(3.52)	44.6	(1.89)	22.1	(2.92)
Italy: Marche	40.0	(3.21)	37.2	(1.77)	14.4	(1.92)	30.6	(2.09)	62.8	(1.77)	32.5	(1.75)	45.3	(1.74)	18.6	(1.92)
Italy: Molise	51.5	(1.78)	43.4	(1.41)	21.2	(1.80)	17.2	(1.44)	56.6	(1.41)	20.8	(3.70)	37.1	(1.63)	c	c
Italy: Piemonte	40.9	(2.90)	37.3	(2.21)	15.1	(2.00)	30.0	(2.19)	62.7	(2.21)	30.5	(2.33)	48.3	(2.47)	17.0	(1.34)
Italy: Puglia	43.6	(2.80)	41.3	(2.39)	16.9	(1.94)	24.6	(2.25)	58.7	(2.39)	26.3	(2.94)	43.6	(2.23)	20.2	(2.85)
Italy: Sardegna	53.9	(2.07)	43.2	(2.32)	22.8	(1.71)	19.6	(1.60)	56.8	(2.32)	23.9	(2.96)	39.8	(2.20)	10.8	(2.79)
Italy: Sicilia	57.8	(3.54)	42.2	(2.09)	22.8	(2.11)	16.1	(2.02)	57.8	(2.09)	19.2	(3.11)	39.8	(1.73)	c	c
Italy: Toscana	41.9	(2.18)	40.5	(1.45)	18.4	(1.75)	29.8	(1.67)	59.5	(1.45)	33.0	(2.54)	44.6	(1.47)	21.0	(2.78)
Italy: Trento	36.4	(1.53)	35.3	(1.20)	10.1	(1.38)	34.0	(1.41)	64.7	(1.20)	35.4	(2.24)	44.1	(1.49)	17.9	(1.97)
Italy: Umbria	42.5	(2.29)	42.1	(1.57)	17.6	(2.11)	28.8	(1.83)	57.9	(1.57)	26.5	(2.22)	40.0	(1.93)	14.5	(1.95)
Italy: Valle d'Aosta	33.5	(1.32)	35.1	(1.58)	13.8	(2.04)	35.2	(1.79)	64.9	(1.58)	42.6	(2.94)	48.1	(1.50)	29.2	(2.20)
Italy: Veneto	36.0	(2.52)	34.7	(2.00)	12.3	(1.55)	31.7	(2.19)	65.3	(2.00)	38.7	(2.61)	43.0	(2.27)	19.9	(1.97)
Mexico: Aguascalientes	64.9	(3.67)	56.4	(2.53)	47.1	(2.42)	9.2	(1.72)	43.6	(2.53)	c	c	22.3	(1.75)	c	c
Mexico: Baja California	73.1	(2.24)	51.6	(2.42)	42.0	(2.66)	5.4	(1.18)	48.4	(2.42)	c	c	29.2	(2.09)	c	c
Mexico: Baja California Sur	77.5	(2.24)	58.2	(3.18)	51.6	(3.39)	3.3	(0.88)	41.8	(3.18)	c	c	23.4	(2.57)	c	c
Mexico: Campeche	80.9	(1.97)	60.7	(2.57)	54.0	(2.69)	3.6	(1.03)	39.3	(2.57)	c	c	28.5	(2.32)	c	c
Mexico: Chihuahua	64.2	(3.47)	65.5	(2.73)	55.1	(2.82)	7.9	(1.44)	34.5	(2.73)	c	c	18.9	(2.57)	c	c
Mexico: Colima	69.3	(2.29)	62.3	(2.30)	53.4	(2.01)	6.3	(0.92)	37.7	(2.30)	c	c	25.3	(1.88)	c	c
Mexico: Coahuila	75.4	(3.60)	55.8	(2.89)	48.2	(3.27)	3.1	(0.68)	44.2	(2.89)	c	c	25.7	(2.36)	c	c
Mexico: Chiapas	89.5	(2.01)	52.4	(2.70)	49.0	(2.83)	c	c	47.6	(2.70)	c	c	38.0	(2.85)	c	c
Mexico: Distrito Federal	52.7	(3.65)	71.1	(2.05)	59.9	(2.64)	13.5	(1.97)	28.9	(2.05)	c	c	13.1	(1.42)	c	c
Mexico: Durango	75.9	(2.36)	52.8	(2.34)	45.5	(2.82)	4.0	(0.87)	47.2	(2.34)	c	c	31.1	(2.91)	c	c
Mexico: Guerrero	90.2	(1.42)	46.1	(3.23)	42.7	(3.17)	c	c	53.9	(3.23)	c	c	43.6	(3.06)	c	c
Mexico: Guanajuato	75.4	(2.20)	44.6	(2.46)	34.7	(2.39)	4.1	(0.98)	55.4	(2.46)	c	c	40.2	(2.51)	c	c
Mexico: Hidalgo	74.8	(2.72)	57.2	(3.03)	48.7	(3.04)	4.8	(1.14)	42.8	(3.03)	c	c	27.3	(2.96)	c	c
Mexico: Jalisco	69.3	(2.69)	58.5	(1.86)	50.3	(1.89)	6.4	(1.39)	41.5	(1.86)	c	c	25.4	(1.95)	c	c
Mexico: Michoacán	79.6	(2.12)	54.1	(2.09)	47.8	(2.14)	3.0	(0.90)	45.9	(2.09)	c	c	31.8	(1.93)	c	c
Mexico: Morelos	75.1	(4.03)	54.2	(3.22)	47.2	(2.83)	4.0	(1.12)	45.8	(3.22)	c	c	29.1	(3.79)	c	c
Mexico: Mexico	65.3	(3.57)	57.9	(2.56)	45.7	(2.92)	8.0	(1.77)	42.1	(2.56)	c	c	24.8	(2.59)	c	c
Mexico: Nayarit	80.8	(1.78)	57.8	(1.60)	53.0	(1.64)	3.5	(0.89)	42.2	(1.60)	c	c	25.8	(1.49)	c	c
Mexico: Nuevo León	62.4	(5.20)	56.3	(5.72)	41.2	(5.29)	11.7	(3.75)	43.7	(5.72)	c	c	28.5	(4.33)	c	c
Mexico: Oaxaca	79.9	(3.79)	53.3	(4.55)	48.5	(5.25)	2.9	(1.11)	46.7	(4.55)	c	c	35.9	(4.16)	c	c
Mexico: Puebla	73.1	(3.33)	60.0	(3.50)	52.1	(2.65)	4.9	(1.46)	40.0	(3.50)	c	c	23.9	(2.66)	c	c
Mexico: Quintana Roo	70.3	(4.39)	54.4	(3.44)	44.3	(2.83)	7.8	(2.63)	45.6	(3.44)	c	c	29.5	(3.11)	c	c
Mexico: Querétaro	69.4	(3.12)	52.6	(4.14)	39.5	(4.12)	7.1	(1.48)	47.4	(4.14)	c	c	32.8	(4.14)	c	c
Mexico: Sinaloa	79.0	(2.44)	58.1	(2.18)	53.2	(2.68)	3.8	(1.18)	41.9	(2.18)	c	c	27.2	(2.87)	c	c
Mexico: San Luis Potosí	81.2	(2.76)	42.2	(3.12)	37.0	(2.67)	2.8	(0.85)	57.8	(3.12)	c	c	43.1	(4.18)	c	c
Mexico: Sonora	79.3	(2.30)	56.6	(2.28)	50.4	(2.20)	3.2	(0.70)	43.4	(2.28)	c	c	28.3	(2.07)	c	c
Mexico: Tamaulipas	78.3	(2.75)	54.1	(3.03)	48.2	(3.28)	3.4	(0.89)	45.9	(3.03)	c	c	29.6	(2.72)	c	c
Mexico: Tabasco	87.6	(2.14)	47.9	(2.21)	44.1	(2.11)	c	c	52.1	(2.21)	c	c	34.6	(2.26)	c	c
Mexico: Tlaxcala	81.1	(1.87)	52.8	(2.99)	47.3	(3.24)	2.1	(0.50)	47.2	(2.99)	c	c	29.9	(3.26)	c	c
Mexico: Veracruz	77.8	(2.41)	50.9	(3.12)	43.2	(3.11)	4.4	(1.25)	49.1	(3.12)	c	c	32.8	(3.14)	c	c
Mexico: Yucatán	76.8	(3.45)	52.7	(2.66)	44.2	(2.45)	4.7	(1.48)	47.3	(2.66)	c	c	33.7	(2.45)	c	c
Mexico: Zacatecas	76.2	(3.04)	48.7	(2.19)	45.1	(1.43)	3.8	(1.25)	51.3	(2.19)	c	c	35.6	(2.29)	c	c

StatLink http://dx.doi.org/10.1787/888932733811

[Part 1/1]

Table B1.5 Student expectations in school systems with and without horizontal differentiation

	Intercept		Difference between school systems with at least two programmes for 15-year-old students and selection *after* age 13, and school systems with one programme		School systems with at least two programmes for 15-year-old students and selection *before* age 13, and school systems with one programme		Average annual growth in enrolment, from 1980 to 2009	
	Coeff.	S.E.	Coeff.	S.E.	Coeff.	S.E.	Coeff.	S.E.
Percentage of students who expect to complete a university degree	64.4	(7.89)	-3.4	(5.44)	-7.6	(5.96)	-8.2	(3.50)
Growth in university-degree expectations	15.9	(13.43)	-9.4	(7.11)	-6.4	(6.27)	-5.6	(5.90)
Percentage of ISCED-A students who expect to complete a university degree	73.2	(9.93)	-4.0	(6.84)	-7.1	(7.50)	-9.7	(4.40)
Percentage of students who expect to complete an upper secondary degree	14.8	(7.22)	6.4	(4.97)	10.4	(5.45)	4.2	(3.20)
Growth in upper secondary expectations	-17.0	(7.26)	8.9	(3.84)	9.0	(3.39)	5.9	(3.19)
Percentage of ISCED-A students who expect to complete an upper secondary degree	11.4	(8.22)	4.9	(5.66)	10.2	(6.21)	4.3	(3.64)

Notes: Each row represents a different OLS regression model with each observation representing a country or economy; all regression models include dummy variables for Korea and Latvia. Regional data for Italy and Mexico are not used.
Average yearly growth in enrolment rates for each country available in Table B1.16.

StatLink http://dx.doi.org/10.1787/888932733830

[Part 1/2]

Table B1.6 Relationship between low-performing students' experience in schools, school attributes, background characteristics and students' PISA reading scores

	Index of student-teacher relations		Index of attitudes towards school		Index of teacher stimulation of reading		School average disciplinary climate		Index of extracurricular activities		School implements ability grouping in some or all subjects		Learning time in language courses		School implements standardised tests and uses them to compare students or school		Percentage of certified teachers in the school	
	Coeff.	S.E.	Coeff.	S.E.	Coeff.	S.E.	Coeff.	S.E.	Coeff.	S.E.	Coeff.	S.E.	Coeff.	S.E.	Coeff.	S.E.	Coeff.	S.E.
Countries and economies																		
Australia	1.86	(1.94)	**6.42**	(1.76)	-2.56	(1.34)	3.48	(5.36)	1.37	(1.95)	0.06	(6.88)	-0.23	(1.82)	-2.28	(2.83)	-0.05	(0.07)
Austria	-0.11	(1.98)	-1.52	(2.46)	-1.90	(1.81)	5.74	(4.64)	-4.77	(3.34)	-4.72	(7.28)	-0.08	(5.04)	-4.08	(6.33)	**0.49**	(0.14)
Belgium (Flemish Community)	6.41	(5.32)	-5.39	(5.24)	-2.17	(5.71)	-2.09	(9.79)	-2.79	(4.48)	-8.12	(10.06)	-0.12	(5.24)	-0.19	(11.00)	0.09	(0.19)
Hong Kong-China	3.98	(3.83)	-0.98	(4.64)	0.92	(3.66)	11.18	(8.27)	-5.24	(3.91)	17.94	(15.18)	-4.58	(3.31)	0.15	(21.92)	0.37	(0.26)
Croatia	-3.81	(2.01)	**4.69**	(1.89)	2.34	(1.67)	**11.70**	(5.73)	6.35	(3.48)	-4.14	(3.86)	1.47	(2.31)	2.86	(4.84)	0.11	(0.11)
Hungary	-2.08	(2.48)	**4.98**	(2.20)	2.77	(2.47)	5.32	(6.12)	-0.70	(5.43)	4.33	(5.38)	3.57	(2.82)	0.89	(4.93)	**0.28**	(0.14)
Ireland	3.10	(3.61)	5.23	(3.83)	-1.35	(2.59)	8.14	(11.23)	4.50	(5.65)	8.91	(14.92)	3.02	(10.42)	-15.37	(10.18)	0.39	(0.49)
Iceland	3.51	(3.13)	2.16	(2.78)	2.91	(3.01)	6.95	(10.71)	-0.69	(4.55)	6.14	(6.03)	-1.58	(4.04)	-2.22	(9.02)	-0.12	(0.24)
Italy	**-3.63**	(1.69)	**4.12**	(1.49)	-1.75	(1.23)	**15.27**	(3.80)	1.57	(1.98)	1.90	(3.90)	-2.87	(1.75)	0.08	(3.54)	**0.16**	(0.08)
Korea	-0.30	(3.86)	3.73	(3.62)	1.39	(1.89)	28.05	(15.64)	-4.28	(3.63)	-3.08	(7.96)	-7.60	(9.41)	-0.21	(7.89)	0.20	(0.16)
Latvia	2.34	(2.16)	**7.54**	(2.24)	-3.57	(3.05)	**17.02**	(6.90)	-0.43	(3.85)	3.28	(4.77)	-1.73	(3.62)	1.04	(6.59)	-0.09	(0.10)
Macao-China	0.37	(2.40)	0.70	(3.22)	1.84	(2.83)	**32.96**	(11.40)	3.89	(4.62)	-3.09	(5.83)	-7.47	(7.94)	-6.76	(5.46)	0.12	(0.13)
Mexico	-0.20	(1.12)	**11.06**	(1.00)	1.64	(0.97)	**23.37**	(5.13)	2.30	(1.64)	3.66	(3.08)	**2.28**	(0.95)	-4.02	(3.06)	-0.05	(0.11)
New Zealand	-3.22	(2.62)	**4.98**	(2.17)	-0.77	(2.64)	9.09	(9.66)	0.11	(2.98)	-9.73	(13.98)	-1.53	(5.72)	4.72	(5.26)	0.00	(0.12)
Poland	-0.22	(2.25)	1.82	(2.31)	**4.04**	(1.94)	5.56	(4.91)	0.30	(3.04)	1.76	(4.22)	1.46	(8.86)	-5.43	(7.57)	0.05	(0.10)
Portugal	1.45	(3.06)	**7.74**	(2.45)	-3.26	(2.53)	12.47	(7.51)	4.59	(3.73)	11.00	(6.64)	2.43	(1.80)	-11.11	(6.19)	-0.11	(0.14)
Singapore	17.94	(16.46)	-11.36	(13.31)	-12.69	(10.48)	54.46	(34.93)	-17.73	(13.52)	0.00	(0.00)	-2.25	(6.82)	0.00	(0.00)	**1.33**	(0.59)
Serbia	-2.55	(1.44)	**7.92**	(1.99)	1.84	(1.78)	**24.96**	(7.32)	-0.14	(4.27)	5.20	(4.88)	-10.82	(7.53)	0.39	(4.42)	0.00	(0.08)
Slovak Republic	-1.43	(2.26)	4.27	(2.33)	0.55	(1.58)	4.41	(5.98)	0.37	(3.09)	-5.72	(4.86)	**-13.33**	(4.05)	-1.67	(7.26)	0.14	(0.21)
Slovenia	0.18	(1.89)	**3.56**	(1.68)	**3.37**	(1.24)	**9.50**	(3.29)	**7.33**	(2.54)	-3.70	(3.03)	**17.69**	(4.42)	-3.71	(3.79)	0.16	(0.16)
Trinidad and Tobago	1.62	(2.14)	**7.45**	(2.01)	-1.00	(1.88)	**22.95**	(7.43)	3.05	(2.35)	-1.12	(5.47)	1.92	(2.15)	7.27	(5.86)	-0.12	(0.11)
Regions																		
Italy: Abruzzo	3.56	(3.25)	-2.19	(3.83)	4.35	(5.20)	-2.22	(11.78)	-1.01	(5.73)	3.87	(11.27)	-0.08	(4.67)	10.07	(11.66)	-0.10	(0.21)
Italy: Basilicata	3.79	(4.21)	-0.07	(4.47)	0.03	(4.84)	**28.64**	(11.44)	-0.25	(5.76)	-14.22	(10.47)	-9.69	(5.13)	1.92	(8.55)	-0.27	(0.19)
Italy: Bolzano	-6.84	(3.89)	**8.10**	(3.96)	7.09	(4.96)	7.83	(6.39)	3.80	(4.83)	-7.00	(17.22)	-0.42	(7.01)	18.01	(9.40)	-0.09	(0.26)
Italy: Calabria	-3.20	(3.23)	0.01	(3.41)	-1.97	(3.57)	**30.47**	(12.86)	-10.66	(8.64)	9.61	(9.00)	-2.26	(5.48)	-3.34	(9.80)	0.05	(0.29)
Italy: Campania	-2.62	(4.93)	8.39	(5.02)	2.44	(4.29)	2.04	(13.97)	16.62	(8.69)	-24.13	(13.29)	-0.01	(5.76)	-15.83	(14.49)	-0.21	(0.20)
Italy: Emilia Romagna	1.30	(6.75)	2.37	(8.03)	-3.33	(6.59)	22.87	(13.46)	-7.10	(6.62)	-6.91	(18.04)	0.35	(5.50)	-0.56	(11.61)	0.35	(0.23)
Italy: Friuli Venezia Giulia	-3.98	(4.93)	3.67	(4.33)	-3.09	(4.58)	**33.52**	(12.87)	-0.76	(9.11)	-3.12	(12.08)	4.04	(7.65)	22.38	(13.51)	0.22	(0.24)
Italy: Lazio	-0.56	(4.47)	8.13	(5.02)	-5.66	(4.32)	**30.47**	(14.83)	-0.28	(7.51)	5.14	(9.75)	-2.47	(5.03)	3.52	(8.14)	0.42	(0.24)
Italy: Liguria	-5.20	(5.27)	**14.71**	(5.17)	-1.77	(5.25)	**35.85**	(12.92)	**-14.88**	(6.90)	2.25	(15.12)	-11.33	(8.43)	-5.60	(12.48)	0.26	(0.27)
Italy: Lombardia	-1.02	(4.81)	-0.56	(5.88)	1.67	(5.31)	12.11	(22.08)	22.78	(12.86)	-38.14	(22.19)	-1.16	(9.73)	10.77	(13.13)	**-0.40**	(0.19)
Italy: Marche	-0.54	(3.93)	8.71	(4.83)	0.14	(5.32)	13.81	(15.69)	-16.47	(11.67)	19.79	(13.90)	4.10	(7.13)	42.17	(21.86)	0.35	(0.25)
Italy: Molise	-0.90	(4.28)	5.20	(3.33)	-4.34	(6.04)	18.58	(10.36)	**12.61**	(5.65)	-4.75	(9.04)	-4.85	(4.36)	-3.54	(12.70)	0.14	(0.20)
Italy: Piemonte	-1.38	(4.05)	-1.54	(4.26)	-0.50	(4.06)	18.15	(13.98)	-9.55	(8.55)	-12.22	(9.34)	7.08	(5.23)	9.14	(15.26)	0.06	(0.21)
Italy: Puglia	-4.21	(6.40)	2.02	(4.75)	3.03	(3.91)	**30.35**	(9.45)	10.02	(6.90)	-0.32	(9.17)	1.47	(6.36)	5.92	(11.50)	-0.01	(0.19)
Italy: Sardegna	2.85	(5.78)	0.77	(5.69)	-8.05	(4.51)	9.78	(9.84)	-2.90	(7.10)	-0.46	(9.80)	-4.35	(4.41)	**28.34**	(12.76)	0.33	(0.26)
Italy: Sicilia	-6.16	(5.86)	8.49	(5.06)	-3.17	(4.77)	**28.76**	(13.68)	8.47	(10.44)	-13.60	(19.19)	1.48	(4.66)	-13.60	(14.88)	0.29	(0.28)
Italy: Toscana	-8.17	(8.36)	5.88	(6.25)	3.90	(6.35)	**31.46**	(12.50)	**20.41**	(9.36)	9.16	(16.05)	7.34	(5.38)	12.81	(14.30)	0.01	(0.27)
Italy: Trento	10.30	(6.33)	-8.76	(6.66)	-2.19	(4.95)	11.96	(17.44)	9.90	(6.55)	-12.60	(10.92)	-0.30	(7.36)	3.60	(16.91)	-0.02	(0.21)
Italy: Umbria	-1.45	(4.45)	6.38	(4.51)	7.84	(4.26)	1.05	(9.42)	-3.10	(6.11)	**-29.83**	(10.83)	0.52	(7.23)	**20.33**	(9.87)	-0.16	(0.19)
Italy: Valle d'Aosta	-1.22	(5.68)	2.33	(8.40)	-7.35	(7.59)	-14.07	(22.57)	-12.67	(28.87)	-5.91	(35.74)	9.65	(10.13)	11.58	(19.69)	-0.34	(0.83)
Italy: Veneto	1.46	(5.80)	8.00	(5.71)	-4.29	(4.52)	3.26	(16.53)	-10.92	(8.88)	3.08	(10.71)	-2.35	(8.15)	-9.27	(12.35)	**0.71**	(0.30)
Mexico: Aguascalientes	1.65	(3.59)	8.30	(4.25)	-0.11	(3.64)	**56.74**	(27.44)	-2.53	(5.10)	-3.31	(8.00)	4.01	(2.95)	-8.16	(12.09)	0.53	(0.47)
Mexico: Baja California	-1.65	(5.00)	**15.72**	(5.20)	4.60	(4.68)	12.73	(22.33)	10.07	(6.24)	-11.27	(13.30)	0.50	(4.34)	-5.93	(15.13)	-0.57	(0.37)
Mexico: Baja California Sur	2.09	(3.22)	5.47	(5.70)	-4.61	(4.91)	23.98	(36.83)	6.97	(12.59)	-12.05	(15.39)	8.86	(4.85)	-4.51	(12.22)	0.05	(0.53)
Mexico: Campeche	-5.35	(3.68)	**11.49**	(3.61)	-0.02	(5.27)	-6.73	(16.27)	-6.46	(8.57)	-9.97	(12.67)	**5.49**	(2.60)	0.00	(20.85)	-0.01	(0.42)
Mexico: Chihuahua	1.97	(4.73)	7.61	(4.27)	-1.64	(3.17)	**48.81**	(16.27)	-0.53	(8.23)	-3.76	(11.49)	7.52	(4.78)	-5.81	(8.26)	-0.48	(0.69)
Mexico: Colima	0.50	(5.19)	**8.95**	(4.19)	-1.70	(4.21)	43.27	(26.00)	-5.73	(7.15)	**-16.97**	(6.66)	3.54	(3.83)	14.49	(14.78)	-0.66	(0.36)
Mexico: Coahuila	4.27	(4.57)	**14.44**	(4.35)	-0.47	(4.51)	**-34.04**	(15.84)	-7.07	(6.70)	-7.55	(12.02)	4.40	(5.79)	-20.10	(11.35)	0.21	(0.78)
Mexico: Chiapas	-5.16	(5.73)	5.53	(4.87)	5.83	(4.26)	32.56	(25.43)	**16.67**	(7.09)	-20.27	(11.00)	8.54	(5.06)	3.70	(10.64)	2.15	(1.55)
Mexico: Distrito Federal	-4.91	(5.04)	**19.07**	(5.33)	-0.11	(5.06)	13.38	(24.57)	-25.18	(18.19)	1.40	(11.25)	1.61	(3.50)	18.23	(17.39)	**1.03**	(0.33)
Mexico: Durango	2.55	(4.48)	7.39	(4.25)	-1.32	(4.75)	6.57	(22.17)	7.97	(7.17)	**-19.42**	(9.59)	-7.09	(4.99)	1.87	(9.71)	-0.77	(1.73)
Mexico: Guerrero	-2.27	(3.87)	**8.53**	(3.48)	-3.15	(4.51)	24.47	(17.63)	2.75	(5.28)	9.89	(10.88)	-0.16	(3.55)	**-21.48**	(10.61)	**-2.71**	(0.80)
Mexico: Guanajuato	1.58	(4.79)	**13.58**	(4.30)	-4.78	(4.55)	**52.36**	(15.39)	6.10	(5.36)	-9.67	(11.29)	2.34	(4.29)	7.24	(13.05)	-0.12	(0.72)
Mexico: Hidalgo	0.66	(3.91)	**10.30**	(3.55)	-0.15	(6.98)	**36.90**	(18.74)	0.65	(5.40)	12.76	(21.94)	1.96	(3.15)	5.24	(11.95)	-1.32	(1.22)
Mexico: Jalisco	3.43	(4.63)	**10.82**	(4.98)	0.52	(3.28)	4.95	(11.24)	6.35	(3.63)	4.98	(8.25)	0.35	(5.05)	-2.58	(5.51)	-0.72	(0.41)
Mexico: Michoacán	-3.56	(3.86)	6.64	(4.19)	-1.00	(4.70)	19.58	(13.40)	4.02	(5.76)	-7.46	(9.54)	5.30	(3.72)	-9.46	(9.73)	0.13	(0.64)
Mexico: Morelos	2.70	(6.36)	6.99	(4.85)	1.90	(7.14)	**31.19**	(13.14)	-4.98	(5.42)	-10.47	(8.88)	1.14	(2.36)	-26.83	(13.87)	-0.41	(0.55)
Mexico: Mexico	3.91	(5.46)	7.49	(3.86)	5.69	(4.57)	**58.79**	(28.80)	-1.74	(6.28)	**55.73**	(14.45)	-1.64	(3.32)	**-31.93**	(11.99)	1.06	(1.15)
Mexico: Nayarit	3.56	(4.74)	6.56	(4.58)	2.97	(5.13)	21.27	(14.24)	**-20.53**	(6.64)	-4.23	(8.04)	1.64	(3.91)	1.73	(9.94)	0.08	(0.61)
Mexico: Nuevo León	8.62	(5.30)	5.84	(3.46)	4.62	(7.25)	-1.92	(23.36)	6.80	(7.56)	**41.46**	(14.97)	12.35	(9.50)	-15.81	(11.90)	-0.11	(0.16)
Mexico: Oaxaca	**6.62**	(3.01)	3.79	(6.17)	3.52	(5.27)	**66.22**	(15.80)	5.20	(5.69)	**41.02**	(14.07)	2.39	(3.72)	3.53	(8.53)	**-1.27**	(0.47)
Mexico: Puebla	0.88	(4.53)	**10.94**	(3.22)	**10.45**	(3.68)	22.51	(14.52)	15.40	(8.35)	-10.48	(14.38)	6.02	(6.11)	-9.41	(14.73)	-1.29	(1.38)
Mexico: Quintana Roo	-6.53	(5.51)	**9.62**	(3.36)	2.13	(3.62)	11.59	(11.63)	**-15.72**	(5.49)	-11.96	(9.33)	1.26	(7.24)	14.27	(13.33)	0.46	(0.39)
Mexico: Querétaro	-2.00	(4.04)	**8.56**	(3.66)	7.55	(4.10)	-0.96	(15.27)	8.60	(6.87)	-17.04	(10.54)	1.53	(3.23)	4.65	(14.52)	0.30	(0.36)
Mexico: Sinaloa	5.39	(6.36)	**10.72**	(3.15)	-1.03	(3.26)	-0.34	(13.18)	6.18	(6.37)	-0.69	(8.62)	5.58	(6.06)	-9.72	(11.53)	0.35	(0.39)
Mexico: San Luis Potosí—	-1.28	(3.20)	6.28	(4.63)	0.47	(6.74)	-15.40	(22.89)	-6.49	(8.88)	3.99	(10.88)	-2.92	(3.41)	21.49	(17.43)	-0.06	(0.42)
Mexico: Sonora	2.26	(4.82)	**16.47**	(4.03)	-0.05	(4.89)	**38.52**	(14.94)	3.65	(6.64)	-2.77	(8.26)	-2.92	(3.03)	0.00	(0.00)	0.29	(0.42)
Mexico: Tamaulipas	-2.09	(4.79)	6.00	(3.78)	0.77	(3.45)	22.20	(16.21)	**10.20**	(4.21)	-7.25	(7.71)	-0.17	(3.26)	1.29	(11.32)	**-0.64**	(0.23)
Mexico: Tabasco	-2.44	(3.88)	**10.29**	(4.90)	-0.97	(4.32)	3.93	(32.05)	-3.92	(3.82)	-10.08	(9.72)	0.05	(3.44)	-3.38	(9.18)	-0.43	(0.51)
Mexico: Tlaxcala	4.96	(4.77)	**12.53**	(3.11)	-3.50	(3.99)	19.51	(16.12)	2.15	(4.57)	16.55	(8.55)	3.94	(2.55)	-9.20	(12.10)	-0.82	(0.96)
Mexico: Veracruz	-1.01	(3.56)	**8.51**	(3.69)	2.35	(3.67)	15.20	(18.13)	2.62	(3.56)	3.24	(11.85)	0.83	(3.73)	-6.09	(8.56)	-0.51	(0.48)
Mexico: Yucatán	4.89	(4.90)	**8.90**	(3.95)	-4.36	(3.49)	**34.71**	(16.33)	3.48	(9.30)	6.21	(44.17)	1.13	(4.93)	11.56	(27.97)	-2.41	(1.55)
Mexico: Zacatecas	0.40	(7.24)	**16.77**	(5.82)	-6.94	(7.37)	**81.58**	(27.25)	-8.75	(8.86)	4.83	(11.61)	1.84	(4.65)	**-22.50**	(9.54)	0.17	(1.04)

Notes: Low-performing students are those who perform at or below PISA proficiency Level 2 in reading or mathematics.
Reading and mathematics scores and learning time rescaled so that each unit represents 100 score points and 100 minutes, respectively.
Estimates from ordinary least squares regression model.
Estimates in bold are statistically significantly different from zero at a 95% confidence level.

StatLink http://dx.doi.org/10.1787/888932733849

[Part 2/2]

Table B1.6 Relationship between low-performing students' experience in schools, school attributes, background characteristics and students' PISA reading scores

	Index of school material educational resources		Class size		Student in a non-academic ISCED programme		*PISA index of economic, social and cultural status*		Student is a girl		Student has an immigrant background		Student speaks another language at home		School average *PISA index of economic, social and cultural status*	
	Coeff.	S.E.	Coeff.	S.E.	Coeff.	S.E.	Coeff.	S.E.	Coeff.	S.E.	Coeff.	S.E.	Coeff.	S.E.	Coeff.	S.E.
Countries and economies																
Australia	-0.14	(1.45)	**0.94**	(0.35)	**-48.32**	(24.25)	4.76	(2.64)	**32.06**	(2.77)	3.26	(4.33)	**-15.30**	(4.48)	**16.70**	(5.96)
Austria	3.92	(2.47)	-0.57	(0.38)	**-17.02**	(6.36)	5.86	(3.65)	**34.55**	(4.43)	-10.25	(9.45)	-6.84	(8.50)	**20.03**	(6.67)
Belgium (Flemish Community)	4.59	(5.83)	1.15	(1.34)	-7.79	(11.89)	-4.76	(5.72)	**19.43**	(8.51)	-0.91	(18.50)	3.59	(14.00)	**43.70**	(12.34)
Hong Kong-China	5.00	(2.59)	0.49	(0.43)	c	c	-1.68	(4.12)	**24.78**	(6.60)	9.17	(5.68)	**-20.94**	(8.69)	16.26	(9.72)
Croatia	0.57	(2.00)	**0.58**	(0.24)	**-30.08**	(3.65)	2.18	(1.93)	**20.44**	(3.67)	0.63	(5.20)	-4.49	(15.41)	5.46	(5.42)
Hungary	-0.86	(2.50)	**1.11**	(0.37)	1.24	(7.17)	2.42	(3.29)	**22.53**	(3.94)	20.19	(10.44)	**-56.24**	(18.23)	**29.46**	(6.99)
Ireland	-3.22	(4.07)	0.87	(0.60)	-2.40	(11.42)	8.16	(4.64)	**29.49**	(6.30)	-6.73	(12.80)	-4.08	(13.68)	16.32	(12.37)
Iceland	2.23	(3.46)	**1.17**	(0.41)	c	c	3.93	(3.37)	**34.22**	(4.56)	-13.07	(19.85)	-12.44	(18.94)	-2.80	(10.17)
Italy	1.59	(2.20)	0.59	(0.31)	-6.41	(9.37)	0.66	(1.64)	**24.67**	(3.43)	**-19.73**	(6.20)	**-8.46**	(3.80)	**19.55**	(4.89)
Korea	4.54	(3.05)	1.36	(0.72)	-6.07	(11.11)	0.76	(3.39)	**25.74**	(5.22)	0.00	(0.00)	-36.46	(30.28)	-4.72	(10.49)
Latvia	-2.33	(2.91)	0.41	(0.36)	c	c	-1.66	(2.53)	**23.79**	(3.90)	-7.53	(7.01)	-0.94	(7.94)	**22.55**	(8.52)
Macao-China	2.03	(2.80)	**1.00**	(0.38)	11.36	(13.41)	2.76	(2.55)	**21.82**	(4.28)	-0.53	(4.99)	**-23.17**	(8.63)	7.43	(7.78)
Mexico	0.89	(1.70)	**0.47**	(0.12)	**10.43**	(5.15)	**2.34**	(0.74)	**13.16**	(2.02)	**-39.35**	(6.95)	**-31.44**	(8.20)	**16.62**	(2.56)
New Zealand	1.44	(2.73)	**0.74**	(0.37)	c	c	**7.67**	(2.90)	**31.62**	(4.75)	2.78	(6.20)	**-19.99**	(5.67)	13.09	(8.81)
Poland	-2.94	(2.37)	0.05	(0.45)	c	c	**12.34**	(2.37)	**34.37**	(3.28)	0.00	(0.00)	**-72.12**	(25.88)	0.08	(7.17)
Portugal	2.51	(4.51)	0.73	(0.77)	**-33.48**	(9.66)	**6.61**	(2.39)	**25.01**	(4.16)	5.16	(6.90)	-15.98	(14.57)	**15.72**	(6.22)
Singapore	-1.02	(8.06)	-0.71	(1.30)	c	c	-1.31	(13.62)	15.47	(17.68)	9.09	(22.62)	-42.29	(26.61)	32.28	(29.17)
Serbia	-1.23	(3.42)	**1.04**	(0.35)	-11.99	(7.04)	**5.94**	(2.01)	**26.36**	(2.58)	5.88	(5.41)	-10.06	(15.45)	**16.54**	(7.52)
Slovak Republic	-2.19	(2.43)	**0.72**	(0.30)	**-24.27**	(5.25)	4.10	(2.27)	**36.96**	(3.70)	19.61	(29.09)	**-20.52**	(6.46)	**32.70**	(9.13)
Slovenia	1.88	(2.10)	**0.91**	(0.31)	-2.70	(5.71)	3.22	(2.01)	**30.70**	(3.52)	1.59	(5.94)	-2.52	(7.92)	**23.18**	(5.88)
Trinidad and Tobago	1.29	(2.16)	0.38	(0.26)	**-13.95**	(6.05)	2.01	(2.55)	**31.03**	(4.96)	-7.47	(15.61)	**-54.34**	(14.06)	**58.71**	(6.42)
Regions																
Italy: Abruzzo	2.70	(9.67)	-0.90	(0.95)	**-49.75**	(18.91)	2.26	(6.00)	**20.06**	(8.09)	-0.65	(22.72)	-16.23	(12.25)	27.33	(14.41)
Italy: Basilicata	3.89	(2.77)	-1.06	(1.06)	c	c	6.31	(4.58)	**32.15**	(7.87)	0.00	(0.00)	7.18	(7.11)	20.63	(14.46)
Italy: Bolzano	-4.23	(5.35)	**2.61**	(0.82)	-14.18	(13.81)	5.59	(4.89)	**25.68**	(10.09)	**-44.84**	(16.07)	15.76	(10.15)	6.37	(18.41)
Italy: Calabria	0.26	(4.22)	0.53	(0.72)	c	c	5.19	(3.62)	**33.00**	(7.39)	-5.93	(14.54)	1.34	(7.19)	22.44	(16.09)
Italy: Campania	**-26.01**	(11.97)	0.57	(0.73)	c	c	-1.28	(4.82)	**25.86**	(10.93)	-73.81	(42.49)	0.53	(10.82)	19.73	(16.24)
Italy: Emilia Romagna	-6.23	(6.90)	-0.51	(1.52)	-11.74	(16.83)	-0.86	(6.86)	**22.07**	(10.97)	**-42.39**	(19.31)	-11.93	(18.10)	9.07	(19.50)
Italy: Friuli Venezia Giulia	8.47	(8.18)	-0.46	(1.26)	-46.61	(36.40)	3.42	(5.93)	**28.64**	(11.54)	**-41.13**	(20.85)	14.05	(8.64)	21.59	(21.41)
Italy: Lazio	-5.92	(6.44)	-0.76	(0.65)	-53.33	(28.18)	4.78	(4.74)	9.47	(8.59)	-6.41	(19.17)	-9.61	(16.91)	-6.78	(14.64)
Italy: Liguria	-8.62	(8.49)	-1.71	(1.80)	25.43	(35.67)	-0.81	(7.30)	**26.09**	(8.89)	-31.20	(24.12)	-12.39	(23.57)	14.77	(17.34)
Italy: Lombardia	8.72	(6.74)	1.07	(1.13)	**-106.99**	(37.98)	0.43	(5.60)	**36.31**	(9.76)	-29.76	(20.90)	-25.27	(19.80)	-48.07	(27.74)
Italy: Marche	-4.42	(4.90)	-1.21	(0.89)	c	c	3.10	(5.29)	9.21	(8.46)	-17.04	(12.10)	-12.39	(12.56)	28.62	(15.41)
Italy: Molise	-4.39	(7.91)	0.28	(0.78)	c	c	-0.95	(4.29)	**18.09**	(8.37)	12.04	(15.95)	-5.87	(8.59)	26.61	(15.72)
Italy: Piemonte	4.22	(6.20)	-0.13	(1.19)	**46.01**	(13.95)	5.71	(5.82)	**36.35**	(12.50)	-8.12	(18.60)	-2.30	(14.77)	**60.12**	(18.75)
Italy: Puglia	-0.06	(5.76)	1.32	(1.05)	c	c	1.08	(5.82)	11.86	(10.65)	10.30	(27.34)	-5.69	(11.82)	4.65	(15.92)
Italy: Sardegna	-3.60	(7.81)	1.01	(0.79)	c	c	-3.29	(4.91)	19.53	(12.28)	-37.93	(56.54)	-8.82	(11.31)	**30.90**	(11.86)
Italy: Sicilia	0.74	(10.94)	0.15	(1.65)	c	c	-2.35	(5.10)	17.64	(9.95)	-4.25	(35.17)	1.84	(14.88)	24.89	(16.24)
Italy: Toscana	**16.00**	(7.43)	-0.05	(1.05)	c	c	0.28	(6.97)	**35.32**	(7.91)	-6.96	(23.79)	-21.08	(22.43)	-3.87	(13.98)
Italy: Trento	-8.05	(7.17)	0.26	(0.83)	10.94	(24.17)	1.90	(7.60)	**32.01**	(11.56)	-15.43	(16.74)	4.67	(12.69)	44.21	(39.99)
Italy: Umbria	9.40	(4.89)	0.28	(0.70)	39.00	(27.69)	4.59	(4.49)	**18.47**	(7.79)	-9.69	(13.09)	-13.45	(10.22)	**36.88**	(10.19)
Italy: Valle d'Aosta	36.97	(36.83)	-1.60	(1.82)	-75.50	(74.33)	3.97	(8.69)	7.39	(13.71)	-9.76	(28.90)	-8.03	(25.16)	56.05	(38.48)
Italy: Veneto	-6.87	(6.23)	-1.19	(1.14)	11.81	(25.76)	2.60	(4.90)	**26.16**	(11.11)	-26.55	(15.26)	-12.68	(8.34)	33.98	(29.15)
Mexico: Aguascalientes	4.63	(8.83)	**0.84**	(0.37)	c	c	3.07	(3.03)	6.00	(6.84)	0.00	(0.00)	-18.85	(20.41)	**26.46**	(9.79)
Mexico: Baja California	-3.57	(6.75)	0.26	(0.33)	23.01	(13.37)	-1.35	(4.36)	10.69	(7.88)	**-35.76**	(17.01)	-19.76	(26.03)	8.81	(10.62)
Mexico: Baja California Sur	-0.35	(9.71)	0.65	(0.58)	45.72	(23.65)	2.57	(3.99)	14.68	(9.29)	**-53.52**	(20.44)	**63.09**	(25.75)	17.22	(15.93)
Mexico: Campeche	9.33	(6.73)	0.45	(0.47)	29.31	(23.73)	4.59	(3.84)	**15.47**	(7.86)	**-28.73**	(14.37)	32.08	(16.83)	15.21	(8.00)
Mexico: Chihuahua	**-13.62**	(5.58)	0.27	(0.54)	**46.90**	(18.71)	7.57	(5.93)	12.23	(6.92)	**-71.70**	(22.31)	-15.71	(35.03)	22.70	(13.62)
Mexico: Colima	2.29	(3.95)	0.41	(0.47)	c	c	2.89	(2.96)	11.00	(6.08)	37.11	(23.06)	-5.28	(56.18)	**19.76**	(8.94)
Mexico: Coahuila	-3.76	(6.33)	0.86	(0.58)	39.04	(32.77)	4.67	(4.70)	**17.88**	(9.02)	-20.25	(17.23)	0.00	(0.00)	**19.63**	(7.79)
Mexico: Chiapas	4.93	(7.28)	**1.33**	(0.56)	**41.74**	(17.65)	2.22	(3.62)	**17.35**	(7.13)	-18.74	(21.04)	**-49.77**	(20.68)	7.83	(7.59)
Mexico: Distrito Federal	**48.63**	(18.19)	0.08	(0.53)	**59.45**	(27.49)	3.96	(5.51)	-1.70	(7.59)	3.97	(23.53)	**-83.61**	(26.98)	-18.31	(23.54)
Mexico: Durango	-0.88	(5.68)	0.26	(0.31)	c	c	**5.90**	(2.17)	**18.15**	(7.01)	-42.46	(29.78)	0.00	(0.00)	0.55	(6.98)
Mexico: Guerrero	-2.52	(4.90)	-0.01	(0.44)	c	c	0.21	(4.90)	8.13	(7.58)	-33.54	(22.91)	-18.35	(19.15)	18.74	(10.74)
Mexico: Guanajuato	5.61	(7.89)	0.21	(0.71)	c	c	2.38	(3.31)	10.71	(5.77)	-31.66	(33.48)	-22.47	(43.09)	**28.14**	(7.30)
Mexico: Hidalgo	8.61	(8.29)	0.23	(0.63)	c	c	4.45	(2.80)	**14.30**	(7.05)	-33.00	(24.18)	**-62.49**	(26.20)	18.34	(9.86)
Mexico: Jalisco	4.25	(5.28)	0.38	(0.35)	6.02	(10.47)	**6.31**	(3.20)	9.05	(6.46)	**-74.70**	(12.95)	-31.39	(26.01)	12.01	(8.01)
Mexico: Michoacán	**10.33**	(5.22)	0.63	(0.32)	**-15.29**	(7.30)	3.61	(2.51)	**13.87**	(6.71)	-77.06	(39.54)	14.21	(27.50)	**21.81**	(5.99)
Mexico: Morelos	-1.78	(5.22)	**1.32**	(0.57)	c	c	-0.35	(4.99)	4.34	(11.32)	-43.58	(54.82)	63.76	(33.62)	**52.26**	(13.64)
Mexico: Mexico	**-25.96**	(12.45)	0.25	(0.46)	c	c	-0.70	(2.79)	8.58	(9.19)	-14.43	(28.76)	-27.04	(25.19)	**45.68**	(8.62)
Mexico: Nayarit	-5.67	(4.23)	0.01	(0.35)	-4.87	(16.37)	1.35	(3.43)	8.95	(7.19)	**-75.95**	(31.81)	**-58.24**	(29.38)	**28.16**	(10.22)
Mexico: Nuevo León	-1.25	(5.51)	-0.01	(0.55)	**46.08**	(20.89)	-3.55	(5.46)	18.60	(10.93)	**-52.23**	(21.56)	36.20	(56.67)	11.24	(13.24)
Mexico: Oaxaca	**-31.21**	(7.99)	-0.72	(0.49)	c	c	4.32	(4.28)	2.14	(8.06)	-8.91	(18.91)	-13.11	(15.17)	**21.62**	(5.35)
Mexico: Puebla	-2.39	(5.06)	-0.60	(0.46)	c	c	2.15	(3.67)	**14.42**	(5.18)	**-72.63**	(19.31)	27.29	(27.63)	**28.35**	(10.63)
Mexico: Quintana Roo	-4.71	(4.69)	-0.09	(0.59)	**55.24**	(21.90)	**7.07**	(3.57)	16.84	(8.61)	-32.56	(28.40)	-15.87	(17.63)	**32.62**	(11.12)
Mexico: Querétaro	-4.55	(5.50)	0.36	(0.35)	28.10	(16.18)	0.16	(3.09)	**15.81**	(6.88)	**-70.75**	(31.57)	17.97	(19.25)	**24.09**	(7.57)
Mexico: Sinaloa	-3.84	(5.29)	-0.12	(0.58)	c	c	**6.55**	(3.29)	16.82	(9.61)	30.13	(23.94)	15.33	(31.81)	22.44	(12.01)
Mexico: San Luis Potosí	-10.17	(12.26)	**1.15**	(0.47)	-4.79	(14.70)	6.66	(4.87)	**21.09**	(10.72)	**-115.36**	(31.89)	**-53.06**	(13.38)	11.01	(8.66)
Mexico: Sonora	3.87	(4.54)	**0.70**	(0.27)	15.57	(10.99)	6.46	(3.67)	**20.34**	(7.91)	-36.58	(23.34)	-31.20	(23.76)	2.64	(9.63)
Mexico: Tamaulipas	-0.57	(3.73)	0.50	(0.28)	22.54	(18.31)	2.71	(3.09)	13.63	(7.44)	**-59.72**	(23.12)	13.84	(38.30)	9.28	(5.83)
Mexico: Tabasco	6.83	(5.96)	1.20	(0.68)	c	c	3.95	(2.08)	**18.52**	(6.58)	**-32.94**	(16.39)	-32.17	(18.28)	-3.67	(15.69)
Mexico: Tlaxcala	1.24	(4.28)	0.34	(0.32)	**38.53**	(15.97)	3.08	(4.19)	8.88	(6.56)	-25.84	(25.43)	0.00	(0.00)	11.30	(9.34)
Mexico: Veracruz	2.42	(5.78)	0.22	(0.30)	1.88	(10.37)	4.55	(3.37)	**20.95**	(8.20)	**-90.50**	(34.11)	-41.19	(41.16)	10.23	(7.98)
Mexico: Yucatán	-6.43	(5.09)	0.18	(0.42)	c	c	-2.86	(3.10)	-2.39	(7.67)	-29.98	(32.50)	-7.07	(18.27)	**36.71**	(14.74)
Mexico: Zacatecas	5.41	(7.65)	0.30	(0.68)	c	c	4.96	(3.02)	**18.26**	(7.04)	-41.23	(25.54)	38.46	(24.86)	17.52	(9.50)

Notes: Low-performing students are those who perform at or below PISA proficiency Level 2 in reading or mathematics.
Reading and mathematics scores and learning time rescaled so that each unit represents 100 score points and 100 minutes, respectively.
Estimates from ordinary least squares regression model.
Estimates in bold are statistically significantly different from zero at a 95% confidence level.

StatLink http://dx.doi.org/10.1787/888932733849

[Part 1/3]

Table B1.7 Relationship between high-performing students' experience in schools, school attributes, background characteristics and students' expectation of completing a university degree

	Index of student-teacher relations		Index of attitudes towards school		Index of teacher stimulation of reading		School average disciplinary climate		Index of extracurricular activities		School implements ability grouping in some or all subjects		Learning time in language courses	
	Coeff.	S.E.	Coeff.	S.E.	Coeff.	S.E.	Coeff.	S.E.	Coeff.	S.E.	Coeff.	S.E.	Coeff.	S.E.
Countries and economies														
Australia	**0.15**	(0.06)	**0.48**	(0.06)	0.06	(0.06)	-0.04	(0.18)	**0.18**	(0.06)	-0.23	(0.19)	0.06	(0.09)
Austria	0.11	(0.08)	**0.17**	(0.06)	0.08	(0.08)	-0.20	(0.20)	0.00	(0.11)	-0.03	(0.20)	0.31	(0.22)
Belgium (Flemish Community)	0.12	(0.08)	**0.17**	(0.09)	0.14	(0.08)	-0.42	(0.22)	-0.03	(0.10)	-0.14	(0.17)	-0.15	(0.16)
Hong Kong-China	-0.06	(0.08)	0.11	(0.09)	0.00	(0.08)	-0.10	(0.25)	-0.07	(0.06)	-0.02	(0.13)	-0.05	(0.10)
Croatia	**0.41**	(0.13)	0.18	(0.12)	0.20	(0.14)	-0.39	(0.53)	0.03	(0.21)	**0.66**	(0.26)	**1.13**	(0.54)
Hungary	0.17	(0.11)	**0.24**	(0.12)	0.01	(0.08)	-0.11	(0.19)	0.14	(0.12)	0.07	(0.23)	-0.22	(0.13)
Ireland	**0.46**	(0.12)	**0.18**	(0.09)	-0.05	(0.11)	-0.19	(0.21)	-0.20	(0.12)	0.11	(0.50)	0.33	(0.40)
Iceland	0.13	(0.08)	-0.01	(0.10)	0.09	(0.09)	-0.22	(0.28)	0.09	(0.12)	-0.26	(0.17)	-0.01	(0.16)
Italy	**0.17**	(0.05)	**0.36**	(0.05)	0.06	(0.05)	**0.50**	(0.14)	**0.16**	(0.08)	-0.15	(0.11)	-0.06	(0.06)
Korea	0.17	(0.14)	0.02	(0.09)	-0.06	(0.11)	-0.19	(0.41)	-0.10	(0.14)	0.42	(0.39)	-0.02	(0.22)
Latvia	0.18	(0.10)	0.11	(0.10)	0.08	(0.07)	-0.31	(0.22)	**-0.21**	(0.11)	**0.29**	(0.15)	0.04	(0.13)
Macao-China	0.10	(0.06)	**0.14**	(0.06)	-0.03	(0.07)	-0.22	(0.30)	0.11	(0.06)	-0.10	(0.12)	-0.10	(0.18)
Mexico	0.13	(0.12)	**0.48**	(0.11)	0.15	(0.09)	0.18	(0.33)	-0.05	(0.12)	-0.42	(0.22)	0.14	(0.13)
New Zealand	**0.20**	(0.06)	**0.19**	(0.06)	0.09	(0.07)	0.03	(0.21)	-0.01	(0.07)	0.25	(0.25)	0.03	(0.14)
Poland	0.14	(0.08)	-0.08	(0.07)	**0.18**	(0.09)	-0.12	(0.16)	-0.07	(0.10)	0.04	(0.17)	-0.09	(0.30)
Portugal	**0.32**	(0.12)	0.19	(0.10)	0.23	(0.12)	-0.34	(0.34)	0.04	(0.14)	-0.07	(0.24)	-0.13	(0.14)
Singapore	-4.32	(10.69)	-2.00	(9.38)	**-19.65**	(6.78)	**-78.21**	(16.77)	-13.41	(10.90)	0.00	(0.00)	-4.38	(4.83)
Serbia	0.15	(0.26)	0.05	(0.22)	0.13	(0.18)	-0.11	(0.59)	**0.58**	(0.23)	-0.22	(0.35)	0.57	(0.96)
Slovak Republic	-0.15	(0.11)	0.19	(0.12)	-0.03	(0.09)	-0.01	(0.26)	0.03	(0.09)	0.12	(0.18)	-0.10	(0.18)
Slovenia	-0.03	(0.10)	0.05	(0.09)	0.09	(0.09)	-0.10	(0.12)	0.03	(0.11)	-0.13	(0.13)	-0.39	(0.61)
Trinidad and Tobago	0.35	(0.28)	**0.39**	(0.18)	-0.04	(0.23)	0.48	(0.54)	-0.26	(0.31)	-0.22	(0.43)	-0.27	(0.19)
Regions														
Italy: Abruzzo	**0.52**	(0.22)	0.08	(0.19)	0.11	(0.20)	0.43	(0.43)	0.31	(0.19)	-0.68	(0.38)	-0.02	(0.19)
Italy: Basilicata	**0.63**	(0.24)	0.08	(0.28)	**0.45**	(0.22)	1.74	(1.05)	0.41	(0.44)	-0.11	(0.44)	-0.14	(0.31)
Italy: Bolzano	-0.02	(0.12)	0.18	(0.12)	-0.21	(0.14)	-0.45	(0.26)	-0.04	(0.12)	0.35	(0.28)	-0.11	(0.28)
Italy: Calabria	0.19	(0.37)	**0.97**	(0.48)	-0.43	(0.34)	-1.54	(1.61)	**-1.54**	(0.52)	-0.70	(0.56)	**-0.62**	(0.30)
Italy: Campania	0.47	(0.36)	0.15	(0.29)	-0.14	(0.37)	-0.13	(1.56)	0.38	(0.31)	-0.52	(0.73)	0.43	(0.32)
Italy: Emilia Romagna	0.05	(0.12)	**0.44**	(0.13)	0.01	(0.12)	0.26	(0.33)	-0.04	(0.24)	0.21	(0.24)	-0.28	(0.22)
Italy: Friuli Venezia Giulia	-0.02	(0.17)	0.13	(0.17)	0.01	(0.15)	-0.45	(0.45)	-0.22	(0.20)	0.25	(0.26)	-0.05	(0.15)
Italy: Lazio	0.30	(0.23)	0.37	(0.19)	0.08	(0.11)	0.05	(0.44)	**0.58**	(0.28)	0.21	(0.37)	-0.16	(0.17)
Italy: Liguria	0.26	(0.18)	0.10	(0.17)	0.18	(0.18)	-0.69	(0.46)	0.50	(0.27)	0.54	(0.35)	-0.04	(0.22)
Italy: Lombardia	0.09	(0.12)	**0.55**	(0.13)	-0.14	(0.16)	-0.84	(0.55)	**0.53**	(0.17)	-0.39	(0.25)	0.04	(0.25)
Italy: Marche	0.02	(0.15)	**0.52**	(0.18)	-0.08	(0.14)	0.83	(0.49)	-0.13	(0.24)	-0.49	(0.31)	0.06	(0.19)
Italy: Molise	-0.12	(0.30)	0.08	(0.25)	0.70	(0.46)	0.77	(0.77)	0.21	(0.37)	-0.27	(0.70)	-0.18	(0.44)
Italy: Piemonte	**0.39**	(0.17)	0.14	(0.17)	0.19	(0.13)	-0.29	(0.45)	0.20	(0.22)	-0.01	(0.36)	0.18	(0.22)
Italy: Puglia	0.27	(0.16)	**0.51**	(0.23)	0.15	(0.20)	0.09	(0.38)	0.09	(0.27)	0.51	(0.44)	0.13	(0.26)
Italy: Sardegna	0.45	(0.29)	0.33	(0.33)	0.19	(0.36)	0.52	(0.63)	0.20	(0.25)	-0.33	(0.48)	-0.12	(0.30)
Italy: Sicilia	0.13	(0.26)	0.35	(0.28)	0.43	(0.27)	-1.32	(0.76)	0.03	(0.33)	0.54	(0.38)	-0.20	(0.16)
Italy: Toscana	0.04	(0.17)	**0.53**	(0.15)	-0.07	(0.13)	-0.33	(0.45)	0.23	(0.12)	-0.16	(0.27)	-0.03	(0.23)
Italy: Trento	**-0.54**	(0.18)	**0.79**	(0.22)	0.06	(0.14)	**1.67**	(0.58)	**-0.58**	(0.26)	-0.43	(0.34)	-0.13	(0.22)
Italy: Umbria	-0.09	(0.15)	0.26	(0.19)	0.26	(0.17)	-0.22	(0.44)	0.18	(0.17)	0.03	(0.33)	0.20	(0.23)
Italy: Valle d'Aosta	0.12	(0.17)	**0.35**	(0.17)	0.06	(0.18)	**-1.36**	(0.54)	0.66	(0.70)	-0.06	(0.41)	-0.09	(0.29)
Italy: Veneto	0.24	(0.14)	**0.32**	(0.15)	0.04	(0.16)	1.00	(0.80)	0.42	(0.26)	0.05	(0.28)	-0.14	(0.20)
Mexico: Aguascalientes	0.55	(0.82)	0.95	(0.53)	0.65	(0.67)	-3.78	(3.54)	0.41	(1.18)	-3.24	(2.00)	5.57	(3.22)
Mexico: Baja California	**-3.83**	(1.94)	2.40	(1.64)	2.79	(1.73)	1.01	(7.12)	**-3.44**	(1.69)	2.02	(1.59)	0.79	(3.29)
Mexico: Baja California Sur	**-20.48**	(5.43)	5.83	(10.64)	-16.00	(9.55)	1.95	(17.79)	0.75	(9.47)	-2.66	(24.28)	-9.98	(11.47)
Mexico: Campeche	5.40	(3.46)	-11.33	(7.35)	-3.09	(2.50)	-14.44	(35.14)	-4.64	(5.96)	9.80	(11.12)	**-13.99**	(2.73)
Mexico: Chihuahua	0.48	(0.44)	-0.37	(0.64)	0.48	(0.99)	-5.59	(5.22)	0.66	(2.03)	-5.58	(8.13)	**4.18**	(1.77)
Mexico: Colima	0.30	(0.67)	2.39	(1.90)	-0.67	(0.52)	-1.40	(7.93)	2.78	(2.57)	-8.06	(5.93)	-0.28	(1.17)
Mexico: Coahuila	-17.52	(15.46)	**81.83**	(12.39)	**-33.39**	(14.65)	-43.35	(67.14)	13.57	(21.20)	**-68.53**	(28.01)	30.65	(21.25)
Mexico: Chiapas	c	c	c	c	c	c	c	c	c	c	c	c	c	c
Mexico: Distrito Federal	0.42	(0.41)	**0.83**	(0.30)	0.09	(0.28)	0.29	(0.91)	-0.05	(0.58)	-0.40	(0.60)	0.36	(0.31)
Mexico: Durango	10.52	(7.32)	**-44.70**	(20.30)	**47.93**	(22.91)	-97.10	(63.18)	46.34	(58.37)	24.22	(67.18)	-24.24	(18.91)
Mexico: Guerrero	c	c	c	c	c	c	c	c	c	c	c	c	c	c
Mexico: Guanajuato	-1.29	(1.38)	-1.66	(1.08)	1.47	(1.70)	-6.28	(13.05)	-3.24	(3.13)	-30.05	(17.25)	-1.20	(0.83)
Mexico: Hidalgo	0.79	(1.12)	0.50	(1.58)	1.29	(0.76)	**-8.14**	(3.83)	**31.98**	(13.30)	**-7.94**	(3.92)	**6.67**	(2.89)
Mexico: Jalisco	1.57	(0.91)	1.11	(1.90)	0.15	(0.68)	2.03	(8.08)	**-4.68**	(2.19)	0.10	(2.14)	0.25	(0.53)
Mexico: Michoacán	c	c	c	c	c	c	c	c	c	c	c	c	c	c
Mexico: Morelos	**-11.72**	(2.94)	**7.62**	(2.70)	4.33	(2.70)	-2.73	(3.16)	-2.94	(3.95)	**11.77**	(3.15)	**-12.55**	(4.44)
Mexico: Mexico	**-98.49**	(8.95)	**128.98**	(12.00)	**158.23**	(15.58)	**1693.00**	(173.12)	**-106.96**	(12.74)	**366.37**	(47.90)	**-105.25**	(11.85)
Mexico: Nayarit	-5.49	(10.44)	**-40.38**	(20.22)	**-44.37**	(14.32)	**625.20**	(300.45)	-99.89	(53.58)	-1.29	(47.09)	36.32	(26.60)
Mexico: Nuevo León	0.69	(0.56)	0.24	(0.44)	0.78	(0.68)	2.35	(2.49)	**1.18**	(0.41)	0.80	(0.89)	0.04	(0.51)
Mexico: Oaxaca	33.31	(21.30)	**96.74**	(48.67)	-34.98	(42.90)	**-427.04**	(95.93)	**-43.30**	(22.00)	284.04	(218.29)	83.17	(140.29)
Mexico: Puebla	-0.73	(1.20)	0.58	(1.82)	1.46	(2.02)	-0.53	(5.79)	-1.39	(2.82)	**-22.71**	(9.10)	3.51	(3.04)
Mexico: Quintana Roo	**-112.16**	(22.62)	**66.80**	(7.35)	**156.31**	(17.72)	**-344.20**	(63.47)	-73.07	(56.23)	**-292.79**	(111.83)	**49.13**	(18.22)
Mexico: Querétaro	-1.11	(0.70)	**1.20**	(0.55)	0.64	(0.61)	1.43	(2.53)	0.17	(0.63)	0.63	(1.07)	-0.07	(0.49)
Mexico: Sinaloa	**-127.14**	(50.91)	**57.47**	(28.44)	**167.12**	(68.51)	**-324.41**	(142.69)	**-297.52**	(52.14)	284.58	(474.73)	**-333.01**	(120.21)
Mexico: San Luis Potosí	0.93	(14.20)	51.13	(36.19)	28.00	(20.49)	73.90	(80.60)	56.55	(36.14)	142.59	(135.14)	42.14	(36.12)
Mexico: Sonora	**-4.58**	(1.35)	6.94	(5.53)	**8.41**	(1.86)	**63.98**	(13.78)	**20.53**	(7.19)	**18.97**	(6.41)	**83.61**	(5.94)
Mexico: Tamaulipas	**14.68**	(6.79)	**18.13**	(7.88)	**-17.06**	(5.74)	31.28	(92.92)	38.70	(27.06)	-33.11	(30.95)	-5.72	(6.35)
Mexico: Tabasco	c	c	c	c	c	c	c	c	c	c	c	c	c	c
Mexico: Tlaxcala	c	c	c	c	c	c	c	c	c	c	c	c	c	c
Mexico: Veracruz	**397.44**	(177.63)	**-162.78**	(73.58)	-39.23	(23.40)	**-1885.23**	(783.32)	**141.25**	(64.72)	**-539.85**	(267.39)	**99.04**	(42.20)
Mexico: Yucatán	-8.30	(61.29)	22.61	(14.62)	**27.63**	(12.81)	475.04	(414.91)	-55.60	(33.10)	-306.86	(191.62)	18.04	(58.97)
Mexico: Zacatecas	1.30	(1.30)	-0.28	(0.86)	-0.21	(1.44)	17.39	(16.85)	-3.16	(2.74)	-5.03	(4.22)	1.87	(6.78)

Notes: High-performing students are those who perform at or above PISA proficiency Level 4 in reading or mathematics.
Reading and mathematics scores and learning time rescaled so that each unit represents 100 score points and 100 minutes, respectively.
Estimates from logistic regression model, presented in the logit scale.
Estimates in bold are statistically significantly different from zero at a 95% confidence level.

StatLink http://dx.doi.org/10.1787/888932733868

[Part 2/3]

Table B1.7 Relationship between high-performing students' experience in schools, school attributes, background characteristics and students' expectation of completing a university degree

	School implements standardised tests and uses them to compare students or school		Class size		Reading performance		Mathematics performance		Student in a non-academic ISCED programme		*PISA index of economic, social and cultural status*	
	Coeff.	S.E.	Coeff.	S.E.	Coeff.	S.E.	Coeff.	S.E.	Coeff.	S.E.	Coeff.	S.E.
Countries and economies												
Australia	-0.16	(0.11)	0.02	(0.01)	**0.70**	(0.15)	**0.80**	(0.17)	-0.30	(1.02)	**0.56**	(0.08)
Austria	-0.32	(0.19)	-0.01	(0.01)	0.08	(0.20)	**1.11**	(0.23)	-0.86	(0.52)	**0.53**	(0.08)
Belgium (Flemish Community)	0.06	(0.17)	0.01	(0.02)	0.12	(0.19)	**1.54**	(0.19)	-0.17	(1.42)	**0.60**	(0.06)
Hong Kong-China	0.57	(0.32)	**0.03**	(0.01)	**0.42**	(0.19)	**0.66**	(0.17)	a	a	**0.37**	(0.07)
Croatia	-0.03	(0.31)	-0.05	(0.03)	**1.66**	(0.33)	0.14	(0.32)	**-2.56**	(1.13)	**0.62**	(0.13)
Hungary	**-0.59**	(0.24)	0.01	(0.01)	**0.62**	(0.28)	0.36	(0.30)	**-14.02**	(0.93)	**0.62**	(0.10)
Ireland	0.10	(0.23)	-0.01	(0.02)	**1.20**	(0.30)	0.08	(0.25)	0.37	(0.32)	**0.68**	(0.14)
Iceland	0.07	(0.21)	0.02	(0.02)	**0.86**	(0.21)	0.25	(0.19)	a	a	**0.80**	(0.10)
Italy	0.01	(0.11)	0.02	(0.01)	**0.60**	(0.14)	**0.32**	(0.12)	**-2.62**	(0.78)	**0.33**	(0.04)
Korea	**0.78**	(0.30)	-0.02	(0.03)	**1.02**	(0.30)	0.08	(0.25)	**-1.25**	(0.36)	**0.51**	(0.13)
Latvia	**-0.59**	(0.24)	0.01	(0.02)	**1.58**	(0.27)	-0.27	(0.24)	a	a	**0.49**	(0.10)
Macao-China	-0.15	(0.12)	-0.01	(0.01)	**1.26**	(0.13)	0.02	(0.13)	0.56	(0.45)	**0.50**	(0.07)
Mexico	0.08	(0.24)	0.01	(0.01)	0.38	(0.37)	**0.78**	(0.35)	**-0.95**	(0.42)	**0.42**	(0.11)
New Zealand	-0.20	(0.13)	0.01	(0.01)	**1.21**	(0.20)	-0.19	(0.23)	a	a	**0.38**	(0.09)
Poland	-0.04	(0.20)	0.00	(0.02)	-0.21	(0.25)	**1.25**	(0.22)	a	a	**0.86**	(0.09)
Portugal	0.13	(0.27)	-0.01	(0.03)	**0.91**	(0.36)	0.54	(0.39)	-0.73	(0.56)	**0.59**	(0.10)
Singapore	-4.40	(31.19)	-0.70	(1.10)	11.82	(24.08)	6.86	(33.29)	a	a	7.54	(9.49)
Serbia	-0.08	(0.35)	-0.02	(0.04)	0.86	(0.53)	1.05	(0.57)	-0.81	(0.52)	**0.45**	(0.18)
Slovak Republic	0.59	(0.49)	0.03	(0.01)	0.09	(0.25)	**1.34**	(0.31)	-1.00	(1.00)	**0.52**	(0.12)
Slovenia	0.27	(0.15)	0.00	(0.02)	0.29	(0.26)	0.43	(0.24)	**-0.97**	(0.31)	**0.67**	(0.08)
Trinidad and Tobago	0.17	(0.43)	-0.01	(0.03)	0.57	(0.52)	0.41	(0.55)	**-2.08**	(1.04)	**0.64**	(0.23)
Regions												
Italy: Abruzzo	-0.38	(0.30)	-0.01	(0.03)	0.64	(0.63)	-0.20	(0.52)	c	c	0.27	(0.14)
Italy: Basilicata	0.14	(0.57)	0.02	(0.06)	0.59	(0.70)	0.78	(0.62)	c	c	0.30	(0.19)
Italy: Bolzano	0.03	(0.27)	0.02	(0.03)	0.54	(0.31)	**0.95**	(0.33)	**-15.66**	(0.72)	**0.42**	(0.13)
Italy: Calabria	**-1.36**	(0.54)	0.00	(0.07)	0.06	(0.87)	1.20	(0.95)	c	c	**0.96**	(0.37)
Italy: Campania	**-1.29**	(0.51)	-0.04	(0.07)	0.96	(0.72)	0.03	(0.56)	c	c	0.18	(0.26)
Italy: Emilia Romagna	-0.04	(0.18)	0.01	(0.04)	0.16	(0.46)	0.25	(0.32)	**-11.44**	(2.10)	0.27	(0.14)
Italy: Friuli Venezia Giulia	-0.57	(0.33)	**0.07**	(0.03)	0.21	(0.45)	0.67	(0.44)	**-9.58**	(1.32)	**0.43**	(0.18)
Italy: Lazio	-0.26	(0.24)	0.03	(0.04)	**0.89**	(0.42)	-0.22	(0.58)	c	c	0.07	(0.19)
Italy: Liguria	**0.99**	(0.31)	0.03	(0.04)	-0.25	(0.75)	**1.62**	(0.60)	c	c	**0.35**	(0.16)
Italy: Lombardia	0.35	(0.28)	-0.02	(0.03)	1.11	(0.58)	0.51	(0.38)	**-12.70**	(1.25)	**0.37**	(0.13)
Italy: Marche	-0.16	(0.37)	-0.03	(0.03)	0.40	(0.63)	0.12	(0.37)	c	c	**0.35**	(0.16)
Italy: Molise	0.25	(0.46)	-0.05	(0.06)	-0.40	(0.77)	0.27	(0.83)	c	c	0.27	(0.28)
Italy: Piemonte	0.36	(0.28)	0.06	(0.03)	0.31	(0.33)	**0.96**	(0.28)	-0.05	(0.60)	**0.62**	(0.11)
Italy: Puglia	-0.45	(0.43)	0.00	(0.04)	0.45	(0.46)	0.42	(0.44)	c	c	**0.47**	(0.15)
Italy: Sardegna	-0.55	(0.45)	0.04	(0.05)	-0.49	(0.71)	0.67	(0.62)	c	c	0.53	(0.27)
Italy: Sicilia	**1.29**	(0.38)	0.07	(0.05)	0.77	(0.69)	0.71	(0.59)	c	c	0.39	(0.25)
Italy: Toscana	0.24	(0.24)	-0.02	(0.03)	**0.67**	(0.29)	0.46	(0.37)	c	c	0.24	(0.15)
Italy: Trento	0.07	(0.31)	0.02	(0.03)	0.49	(0.46)	0.37	(0.42)	**-14.65**	(1.24)	**0.36**	(0.18)
Italy: Umbria	0.03	(0.31)	0.03	(0.03)	**1.22**	(0.59)	-0.52	(0.45)	c	c	**0.42**	(0.18)
Italy: Valle d'Aosta	-1.24	(0.74)	0.00	(0.06)	0.18	(0.51)	0.70	(0.60)	c	c	**0.61**	(0.19)
Italy: Veneto	-0.59	(0.39)	**-0.07**	(0.03)	**1.00**	(0.37)	-0.07	(0.27)	**-10.79**	(0.99)	**0.57**	(0.16)
Mexico: Aguascalientes	0.01	(1.49)	0.02	(0.06)	-1.07	(2.41)	4.51	(3.07)	3.24	(2.69)	**1.79**	(0.86)
Mexico: Baja California	10.69	(5.97)	0.18	(0.13)	1.22	(2.69)	8.34	(4.34)	**20.72**	(6.09)	0.02	(1.14)
Mexico: Baja California Sur	37.94	(20.46)	0.38	(0.30)	43.57	(24.90)	-43.57	(26.53)	c	c	7.90	(14.95)
Mexico: Campeche	7.20	(5.41)	0.05	(0.43)	**60.62**	(14.72)	**-40.06**	(16.90)	10.44	(24.74)	-4.53	(3.98)
Mexico: Chihuahua	2.52	(5.96)	-0.10	(0.17)	-0.04	(3.74)	0.65	(2.77)	-9.41	(14.73)	-0.17	(0.80)
Mexico: Colima	2.72	(7.51)	-0.04	(0.19)	12.06	(7.19)	-1.15	(2.97)	c	c	1.58	(1.06)
Mexico: Coahuila	-13.23	(20.90)	-2.11	(1.15)	**-99.56**	(32.05)	22.52	(105.12)	87.36	(61.52)	-13.25	(20.94)
Mexico: Chiapas	c	c	c	c	c	c	c	c	c	c	c	c
Mexico: Distrito Federal	0.36	(0.70)	0.03	(0.03)	0.91	(1.13)	-0.26	(0.88)	**12.79**	(2.97)	0.55	(0.61)
Mexico: Durango	-57.57	(56.06)	-2.30	(1.44)	16.75	(21.12)	32.36	(29.94)	c	c	**37.74**	(11.50)
Mexico: Guerrero	c	c	c	c	c	c	c	c	c	c	c	c
Mexico: Guanajuato	**-21.99**	(8.14)	0.14	(0.19)	-3.13	(4.98)	17.99	(13.45)	-25.48	(17.23)	1.62	(1.12)
Mexico: Hidalgo	**24.26**	(8.73)	0.05	(0.20)	0.00	(0.86)	0.98	(2.27)	c	c	**-1.60**	(0.69)
Mexico: Jalisco	5.39	(3.30)	0.08	(0.09)	-0.19	(1.71)	1.41	(1.58)	-6.30	(8.43)	0.57	(0.41)
Mexico: Michoacán	c	c	c	c	c	c	c	c	c	c	c	c
Mexico: Morelos	6.47	(4.38)	0.11	(0.19)	-2.77	(6.99)	-1.54	(11.85)	**-25.29**	(9.72)	**-4.77**	(1.70)
Mexico: Mexico	**869.55**	(89.59)	**5.79**	(2.62)	**92.65**	(15.71)	**-173.41**	(34.42)	c	c	**208.23**	(20.38)
Mexico: Nayarit	**-87.33**	(43.99)	**-9.16**	(3.39)	**-292.00**	(83.41)	**236.92**	(16.25)	**-189.19**	(56.98)	**46.43**	(14.59)
Mexico: Nuevo León	1.71	(2.19)	-0.03	(0.07)	-1.84	(2.18)	**3.87**	(1.54)	**-17.29**	(2.11)	-0.08	(0.42)
Mexico: Oaxaca	**171.61**	(83.97)	**-9.46**	(4.55)	**147.34**	(50.05)	**-223.92**	(103.40)	**309.53**	(141.08)	-2.69	(20.11)
Mexico: Puebla	-0.49	(6.13)	-0.02	(0.12)	4.76	(5.96)	-3.27	(2.77)	-4.21	(5.34)	0.29	(0.70)
Mexico: Quintana Roo	70.44	(78.01)	**3.19**	(0.51)	**-91.23**	(26.06)	**67.77**	(11.24)	6.02	(57.26)	**-49.12**	(6.12)
Mexico: Querétaro	2.79	(1.80)	0.07	(0.08)	-4.48	(3.17)	6.18	(3.25)	**17.16**	(1.62)	**1.06**	(0.38)
Mexico: Sinaloa	0.00	(0.00)	**-15.25**	(5.08)	-1.37	(98.70)	**-100.71**	(25.50)	-740.08	(932.66)	5.47	(16.29)
Mexico: San Luis Potosí	**147.60**	(65.49)	2.32	(2.00)	**188.70**	(44.87)	**204.51**	(70.39)	c	c	**41.40**	(8.02)
Mexico: Sonora	0.00	(0.00)	**-3.53**	(0.11)	**89.47**	(6.47)	**-101.24**	(16.55)	**-42.39**	(16.81)	**18.16**	(6.32)
Mexico: Tamaulipas	-17.58	(20.09)	-0.75	(2.39)	-19.07	(31.98)	42.53	(46.99)	-57.51	(78.02)	12.14	(7.02)
Mexico: Tabasco	c	c	c	c	c	c	c	c	c	c	c	c
Mexico: Tlaxcala	c	c	c	c	c	c	c	c	c	c	c	c
Mexico: Veracruz	**947.13**	(393.64)	**-33.30**	(15.34)	-6.70	(11.19)	**384.47**	(172.75)	c	c	**58.34**	(27.94)
Mexico: Yucatán	**255.16**	(124.23)	-4.65	(9.04)	**175.26**	(76.92)	**62.58**	(15.83)	119.88	(273.44)	-20.94	(11.02)
Mexico: Zacatecas	1.69	(3.68)	0.29	(0.26)	-5.52	(5.19)	-3.05	(3.82)	c	c	-0.23	(1.11)

Notes: High-performing students are those who perform at or above PISA proficiency Level 4 in reading or mathematics.
Reading and mathematics scores and learning time rescaled so that each unit represents 100 score points and 100 minutes, respectively.
Estimates from logistic regression model, presented in the logit scale.
Estimates in bold are statistically significantly different from zero at a 95% confidence level.

StatLink http://dx.doi.org/10.1787/888932733868

[Part 3/3]

Table B1.7 Relationship between high-performing students' experience in schools, school attributes, background characteristics and students' expectation of completing a university degree

	Student is a girl		Student has an immigrant background		Student speaks another language at home		School average *PISA index of economic, social and cultural status*		School average reading performance		School average mathematics performance	
	Coeff.	S.E.	Coeff.	S.E.	Coeff.	S.E.	Coeff.	S.E.	Coeff.	S.E.	Coeff.	S.E.
Countries and economies												
Australia	**0.69**	(0.12)	**0.79**	(0.17)	**1.48**	(0.43)	0.46	(0.27)	0.20	(0.36)	-0.16	(0.37)
Austria	**0.40**	(0.18)	**1.04**	(0.48)	-0.02	(0.43)	**1.95**	(0.24)	0.22	(0.40)	-0.45	(0.34)
Belgium (Flemish Community)	**0.48**	(0.15)	**1.23**	(0.31)	-0.04	(0.16)	**0.60**	(0.25)	**1.06**	(0.36)	-0.55	(0.37)
Hong Kong-China	-0.22	(0.16)	0.21	(0.12)	**0.72**	(0.27)	0.13	(0.12)	**1.19**	(0.34)	-0.56	(0.29)
Croatia	0.06	(0.27)	-0.09	(0.34)	-1.55	(0.96)	0.74	(0.64)	0.13	(0.75)	0.41	(0.57)
Hungary	0.34	(0.21)	-0.12	(0.60)	**12.84**	(0.95)	0.67	(0.38)	0.91	(0.52)	-0.26	(0.43)
Ireland	**0.56**	(0.20)	-0.14	(0.35)	**1.37**	(0.64)	0.38	(0.32)	**-1.52**	(0.50)	**1.40**	(0.56)
Iceland	0.25	(0.16)	**-12.42**	(1.81)	**13.70**	(1.25)	0.31	(0.30)	-0.47	(0.56)	0.08	(0.54)
Italy	0.13	(0.11)	-0.19	(0.32)	-0.14	(0.13)	**0.94**	(0.22)	0.20	(0.29)	-0.42	(0.25)
Korea	0.08	(0.21)	0.00	(0.00)	**11.05**	(1.23)	-0.08	(0.39)	0.50	(0.64)	-0.07	(0.56)
Latvia	-0.22	(0.21)	0.54	(0.32)	-0.05	(0.32)	0.26	(0.31)	-0.20	(0.59)	0.02	(0.54)
Macao-China	-0.14	(0.12)	0.02	(0.12)	0.24	(0.27)	0.30	(0.18)	-0.35	(0.33)	0.00	(0.30)
Mexico	0.38	(0.23)	-1.20	(0.63)	**12.82**	(0.60)	0.37	(0.23)	-0.39	(0.72)	-0.15	(0.71)
New Zealand	0.16	(0.15)	**0.52**	(0.20)	**1.07**	(0.29)	**0.55**	(0.22)	-0.24	(0.29)	0.02	(0.31)
Poland	**1.29**	(0.17)	0.00	(0.00)	0.15	(1.92)	-0.01	(0.26)	0.73	(0.42)	-0.75	(0.49)
Portugal	**0.91**	(0.32)	1.16	(0.87)	-0.40	(0.98)	-0.31	(0.27)	-0.66	(0.89)	1.37	(0.77)
Singapore	**-32.61**	(13.65)	**49.17**	(14.32)	5.95	(22.99)	**160.41**	(67.93)	-36.57	(56.49)	9.34	(40.18)
Serbia	**1.21**	(0.48)	0.23	(0.58)	-1.22	(1.46)	-0.16	(0.60)	0.78	(0.91)	-0.78	(0.68)
Slovak Republic	**0.90**	(0.21)	**10.55**	(1.31)	0.52	(0.37)	**1.38**	(0.41)	0.07	(0.49)	-0.45	(0.43)
Slovenia	0.34	(0.19)	0.14	(0.49)	0.41	(0.54)	0.42	(0.32)	0.76	(0.50)	-0.70	(0.40)
Trinidad and Tobago	0.01	(0.62)	**14.18**	(1.01)	**12.07**	(1.49)	**2.47**	(1.15)	0.01	(1.15)	-1.56	(1.39)
Regions												
Italy: Abruzzo	0.02	(0.28)	1.30	(0.95)	0.12	(0.98)	1.48	(0.92)	-0.87	(1.25)	0.20	(0.85)
Italy: Basilicata	0.74	(0.64)	**11.48**	(1.84)	-0.28	(0.54)	0.04	(0.87)	0.48	(1.58)	-0.45	(0.96)
Italy: Bolzano	0.30	(0.26)	0.85	(0.75)	-0.41	(0.29)	**1.90**	(0.55)	0.88	(0.62)	**-1.41**	(0.48)
Italy: Calabria	1.30	(0.68)	0.00	(0.00)	-1.11	(0.92)	0.17	(1.55)	3.29	(3.04)	-2.62	(2.15)
Italy: Campania	-0.59	(0.66)	0.00	(0.00)	-0.08	(0.91)	-0.30	(0.80)	0.37	(1.48)	1.10	(0.82)
Italy: Emilia Romagna	0.24	(0.31)	-0.85	(0.67)	0.34	(0.68)	0.05	(0.46)	0.90	(0.77)	0.90	(0.51)
Italy: Friuli Venezia Giulia	0.49	(0.32)	0.28	(0.69)	-0.48	(0.43)	**2.07**	(0.56)	**2.00**	(0.97)	**-1.45**	(0.64)
Italy: Lazio	0.34	(0.43)	0.13	(1.13)	0.48	(0.55)	0.62	(0.37)	0.79	(0.94)	-0.65	(0.67)
Italy: Liguria	0.25	(0.40)	-0.54	(1.00)	0.63	(0.52)	-0.17	(0.47)	**3.12**	(0.90)	-1.11	(0.89)
Italy: Lombardia	0.05	(0.25)	-0.52	(0.85)	-0.18	(0.72)	1.56	(1.04)	0.14	(0.93)	0.45	(0.83)
Italy: Marche	0.24	(0.39)	0.87	(0.78)	-0.31	(0.57)	0.43	(0.58)	1.29	(0.90)	-0.93	(0.77)
Italy: Molise	0.26	(0.89)	**12.63**	(2.28)	0.24	(0.91)	0.33	(0.82)	1.25	(1.67)	-0.34	(1.37)
Italy: Piemonte	0.53	(0.35)	**-1.63**	(0.49)	0.72	(0.71)	0.87	(0.65)	0.83	(0.83)	-0.85	(0.73)
Italy: Puglia	0.07	(0.32)	0.00	(0.00)	-0.22	(0.67)	**1.21**	(0.58)	**2.81**	(0.92)	**-2.12**	(0.64)
Italy: Sardegna	-0.45	(0.57)	**13.62**	(2.08)	-0.59	(0.96)	0.08	(0.57)	1.72	(0.96)	-1.58	(1.14)
Italy: Sicilia	0.27	(0.29)	0.00	(0.00)	-0.86	(0.85)	-0.92	(0.56)	**3.27**	(1.41)	-0.18	(0.84)
Italy: Toscana	0.19	(0.30)	-0.15	(0.59)	-0.72	(0.47)	**0.86**	(0.29)	1.21	(0.70)	-0.78	(0.71)
Italy: Trento	0.49	(0.35)	**1.69**	(0.60)	-0.25	(0.27)	1.33	(0.79)	1.61	(1.11)	-1.28	(0.79)
Italy: Umbria	-0.07	(0.31)	0.34	(0.67)	-0.19	(0.47)	**1.19**	(0.58)	-0.51	(0.75)	0.61	(0.72)
Italy: Valle d'Aosta	0.42	(0.41)	1.10	(1.19)	0.30	(0.46)	0.60	(0.63)	1.11	(1.20)	1.07	(1.11)
Italy: Veneto	0.26	(0.22)	2.10	(1.10)	0.28	(0.32)	0.63	(0.51)	0.54	(0.79)	0.70	(0.59)
Mexico: Aguascalientes	1.85	(1.44)	**13.27**	(1.90)	**12.02**	(2.77)	-0.50	(1.44)	4.63	(8.84)	-5.90	(5.42)
Mexico: Baja California	7.83	(4.93)	0.00	(0.00)	0.00	(0.00)	-0.21	(3.89)	6.99	(7.35)	-0.37	(9.73)
Mexico: Baja California Sur	6.16	(14.54)	0.00	(0.00)	0.00	(0.00)	-74.41	(48.81)	61.48	(71.22)	85.11	(55.60)
Mexico: Campeche	**-25.05**	(7.98)	0.00	(0.00)	**-28.59**	(5.05)	-1.64	(2.77)	-37.14	(31.44)	61.67	(35.89)
Mexico: Chihuahua	2.22	(2.51)	0.00	(0.00)	0.46	(10.22)	-1.53	(5.78)	19.41	(19.95)	-19.04	(19.65)
Mexico: Colima	-4.32	(3.48)	0.00	(0.00)	0.00	(0.00)	-5.16	(4.13)	13.23	(13.92)	0.90	(9.12)
Mexico: Coahuila	99.60	(57.00)	0.00	(0.00)	0.00	(0.00)	-73.55	(56.82)	137.95	(73.80)	142.93	(144.45)
Mexico: Chiapas	c	c	c	c	c	c	c	c	c	c	c	c
Mexico: Distrito Federal	-0.53	(0.75)	-0.44	(1.06)	**14.69**	(1.29)	-0.35	(0.79)	1.01	(2.83)	-1.83	(2.68)
Mexico: Durango	10.54	(18.07)	0.00	(0.00)	0.00	(0.00)	48.40	(55.54)	-213.57	(230.70)	101.12	(192.51)
Mexico: Guerrero	c	c	c	c	c	c	c	c	c	c	c	c
Mexico: Guanajuato	7.53	(5.78)	0.00	(0.00)	0.00	(0.00)	-4.03	(6.07)	24.30	(21.58)	0.59	(7.41)
Mexico: Hidalgo	1.22	(1.43)	0.00	(0.00)	0.00	(0.00)	**8.68**	(4.16)	**-70.75**	(26.76)	**34.74**	(13.77)
Mexico: Jalisco	-0.70	(1.73)	0.00	(0.00)	**12.85**	(2.93)	-0.40	(2.97)	5.65	(12.31)	-4.49	(7.49)
Mexico: Michoacán	c	c	c	c	c	c	c	c	c	c	c	c
Mexico: Morelos	3.22	(3.94)	0.00	(0.00)	0.00	(0.00)	**14.12**	(3.10)	**42.91**	(14.95)	-27.60	(16.82)
Mexico: Mexico	**-209.27**	(19.04)	0.00	(0.00)	0.00	(0.00)	**265.60**	(50.34)	562.58	(300.86)	**-2064.84**	(258.93)
Mexico: Nayarit	**37.09**	(8.29)	**-95.74**	(23.20)	0.00	(0.00)	**137.09**	(52.61)	-445.43	(276.59)	178.22	(184.19)
Mexico: Nuevo León	2.26	(1.16)	**17.30**	(2.79)	0.00	(0.00)	**4.30**	(1.25)	**-6.39**	(2.63)	-0.54	(2.04)
Mexico: Oaxaca	50.91	(78.41)	0.00	(0.00)	-89.97	(181.69)	73.39	(84.30)	55.20	(329.37)	**745.55**	(226.43)
Mexico: Puebla	0.02	(2.44)	0.00	(0.00)	0.00	(0.00)	2.35	(4.23)	-17.04	(21.02)	13.69	(18.55)
Mexico: Quintana Roo	33.47	(29.59)	**-350.07**	(73.71)	**-622.16**	(180.55)	**431.68**	(66.45)	-888.38	(698.15)	177.68	(777.18)
Mexico: Querétaro	3.83	(2.54)	0.00	(0.00)	**15.48**	(1.10)	-0.22	(1.34)	8.29	(5.30)	-6.88	(4.67)
Mexico: Sinaloa	37.32	(31.04)	0.00	(0.00)	0.00	(0.00)	-1480.93	(1531.37)	**1840.28**	(615.68)	715.98	(1443.98)
Mexico: San Luis Potosí	-61.54	(38.12)	0.00	(0.00)	0.00	(0.00)	**63.34**	(28.11)	44.68	(130.56)	-273.97	(294.08)
Mexico: Sonora	-4.43	(10.46)	0.00	(0.00)	0.00	(0.00)	-27.86	(19.49)	**116.84**	(36.90)	-10.64	(10.31)
Mexico: Tamaulipas	**64.14**	(23.11)	0.00	(0.00)	0.00	(0.00)	22.97	(38.08)	**-230.58**	(82.20)	111.55	(86.66)
Mexico: Tabasco	c	c	c	c	c	c	c	c	c	c	c	c
Mexico: Tlaxcala	c	c	c	c	c	c	c	c	c	c	c	c
Mexico: Veracruz	**436.65**	(186.58)	0.00	(0.00)	0.00	(0.00)	391.52	(220.04)	-701.50	(426.85)	**-406.47**	(131.50)
Mexico: Yucatán	-65.33	(51.47)	0.00	(0.00)	0.00	(0.00)	116.29	(98.75)	-169.65	(174.50)	-110.49	(276.55)
Mexico: Zacatecas	-0.06	(2.87)	0.00	(0.00)	0.00	(0.00)	4.90	(4.67)	-6.28	(10.93)	10.72	(9.23)

Notes: High-performing students are those who perform at or above PISA proficiency Level 4 in reading or mathematics.
Reading and mathematics scores and learning time rescaled so that each unit represents 100 score points and 100 minutes, respectively.
Estimates from logistic regression model, presented in the logit scale.
Estimates in bold are statistically significantly different from zero at a 95% confidence level.
StatLink http://dx.doi.org/10.1787/888932733868

[Part 1/2]

Table B1.8 Percentage of students who expect to complete an upper secondary degree, but not more, by ISCED type and ISCED level programme

	Percentage of students who expect to complete an upper secondary degree, but not more													
	All, 2009		All, 2003		Change between 2003 and 2009		Academic programme		Non-academic programme		Lower secondary		Upper secondary	
	%	S.E.	%	S.E.	Diff.	S.E.	%	S.E.	%	S.E.	%	S.E.	%	S.E.
Countries and economies														
Australia	21.1	(0.55)	16.4	(0.45)	4.7	(0.67)	20.9	(0.57)	44.5	(6.57)	20.9	(0.60)	21.7	(1.17)
Austria	53.0	(1.16)	51.9	(1.17)	1.1	(1.50)	46.1	(1.30)	63.1	(2.30)	61.6	(2.97)	52.6	(1.20)
Belgium (Flemish Community)	18.0	(0.76)	19.8	(0.83)	-1.7	(1.11)	15.5	(0.83)	27.2	(1.50)	40.4	(4.52)	17.4	(0.76)
Hong Kong-China	24.1	(0.82)	29.4	(1.05)	-5.3	(1.23)	24.1	(0.82)	a	a	22.2	(1.17)	25.1	(1.04)
Croatia	33.5	(1.05)	m	m	m	m	21.8	(0.99)	72.5	(1.33)	c	c	33.4	(1.04)
Hungary	27.6	(1.18)	22.3	(0.85)	5.3	(1.46)	22.4	(1.44)	60.3	(2.62)	58.8	(3.98)	24.0	(1.35)
Ireland	24.0	(0.81)	17.2	(0.76)	6.8	(1.10)	23.8	(0.89)	24.5	(1.88)	22.5	(0.92)	26.3	(1.47)
Iceland	27.2	(0.82)	29.8	(0.71)	-2.6	(1.10)	27.2	(0.82)	a	a	27.6	(0.83)	4.7	(2.74)
Italy	38.6	(0.58)	35.1	(1.14)	3.5	(1.28)	37.4	(0.57)	74.3	(1.44)	49.2	(7.52)	38.5	(0.57)
Korea	5.2	(0.61)	5.0	(0.51)	0.2	(0.73)	2.0	(0.28)	15.1	(2.00)	6.3	(2.18)	5.1	(0.63)
Latvia	26.7	(1.25)	25.9	(1.37)	0.8	(2.01)	26.5	(1.24)	c	c	27.0	(1.27)	15.3	(5.07)
Macao-China	18.0	(0.53)	31.2	(1.43)	-13.2	(1.40)	17.9	(0.52)	c	c	24.6	(0.75)	8.1	(0.58)
Mexico	20.2	(0.44)	25.9	(0.99)	-5.8	(1.04)	19.7	(0.45)	30.1	(2.27)	25.3	(0.82)	16.3	(0.47)
New Zealand	22.5	(0.72)	29.8	(0.89)	-7.3	(1.09)	22.5	(0.72)	a	a	28.5	(2.51)	22.1	(0.73)
Poland	27.8	(0.91)	30.0	(0.93)	-2.2	(1.40)	27.8	(0.92)	c	c	28.1	(0.93)	c	c
Portugal	29.5	(0.95)	26.5	(0.92)	2.9	(1.18)	25.9	(1.10)	48.9	(3.74)	44.0	(0.97)	18.4	(1.03)
Singapore	2.1	(0.23)	m	m	m	m	2.6	(1.15)	a	a	2.6	(1.15)	2.1	(0.22)
Serbia	22.4	(0.97)	m	m	m	m	2.5	(0.50)	28.5	(1.16)	63.3	(5.03)	21.6	(0.96)
Slovak Republic	39.6	(0.92)	36.3	(1.25)	3.3	(1.53)	37.1	(0.96)	66.1	(2.38)	45.3	(1.44)	36.0	(1.15)
Slovenia	26.9	(0.57)	m	m	m	m	9.8	(0.78)	42.3	(0.99)	45.8	(6.70)	26.3	(0.57)
Trinidad and Tobago	15.0	(0.55)	m	m	m	m	14.4	(0.58)	19.6	(1.62)	22.9	(1.17)	11.1	(0.63)
Regions														
Italy: Abruzzo	34.9	(2.32)	m	m	m	m	34.6	(2.33)	c	c	c	c	34.0	(2.34)
Italy: Basilicata	33.7	(2.42)	m	m	m	m	33.7	(2.42)	m	m	33.7	(2.42)	m	m
Italy: Bolzano	59.8	(1.16)	m	m	m	m	51.5	(1.43)	80.6	(1.90)	c	c	59.0	(1.12)
Italy: Calabria	33.3	(2.03)	m	m	m	m	33.3	(2.03)	m	m	c	c	33.3	(2.05)
Italy: Campania	35.2	(1.81)	m	m	m	m	35.2	(1.81)	m	m	c	c	35.0	(1.78)
Italy: Emilia Romagna	39.2	(2.08)	m	m	m	m	38.3	(2.24)	c	c	39.2	(2.08)	m	m
Italy: Friuli Venezia Giulia	38.6	(2.44)	m	m	m	m	38.0	(2.48)	c	c	c	c	38.0	(2.52)
Italy: Lazio	32.4	(1.49)	m	m	m	m	31.7	(1.49)	c	c	c	c	32.2	(1.49)
Italy: Liguria	39.3	(2.62)	m	m	m	m	37.8	(2.55)	c	c	c	c	39.3	(2.64)
Italy: Lombardia	41.9	(2.03)	m	m	m	m	39.2	(2.17)	78.2	(2.46)	c	c	41.3	(2.00)
Italy: Marche	42.2	(1.53)	m	m	m	m	42.2	(1.53)	m	m	c	c	42.0	(1.53)
Italy: Molise	32.7	(1.34)	m	m	m	m	32.6	(1.34)	c	c	c	c	32.6	(1.36)
Italy: Piemonte	44.9	(2.37)	m	m	m	m	42.9	(2.18)	c	c	c	c	44.6	(2.44)
Italy: Puglia	41.0	(2.22)	m	m	m	m	41.0	(2.22)	m	m	41.1	(2.22)	m	m
Italy: Sardegna	36.1	(2.03)	m	m	m	m	36.1	(2.03)	m	m	c	c	35.9	(2.05)
Italy: Sicilia	34.1	(1.45)	m	m	m	m	34.1	(1.45)	c	c	c	c	34.7	(1.34)
Italy: Toscana	42.0	(1.45)	m	m	m	m	42.0	(1.45)	m	m	c	c	42.4	(1.46)
Italy: Trento	41.7	(1.60)	m	m	m	m	34.3	(1.80)	68.2	(3.48)	c	c	41.9	(1.57)
Italy: Umbria	37.2	(1.85)	m	m	m	m	36.3	(1.88)	c	c	c	c	36.6	(1.66)
Italy: Valle d'Aosta	44.8	(1.48)	m	m	m	m	43.2	(1.47)	c	c	c	c	44.7	(1.49)
Italy: Veneto	41.7	(2.19)	m	m	m	m	37.4	(2.39)	75.9	(2.07)	c	c	41.3	(2.19)
Mexico: Aguascalientes	17.7	(1.57)	m	m	m	m	16.9	(1.66)	c	c	25.5	(2.94)	15.9	(1.89)
Mexico: Baja California	19.1	(1.89)	m	m	m	m	19.0	(1.94)	c	c	24.7	(3.38)	12.8	(1.62)
Mexico: Baja California Sur	17.2	(1.55)	m	m	m	m	17.1	(1.59)	c	c	20.8	(3.07)	14.8	(1.42)
Mexico: Campeche	20.2	(1.85)	m	m	m	m	19.8	(1.91)	c	c	25.5	(2.93)	15.0	(2.29)
Mexico: Chihuahua	16.0	(2.10)	m	m	m	m	15.6	(2.26)	c	c	25.9	(4.84)	12.5	(2.25)
Mexico: Colima	19.1	(1.50)	m	m	m	m	19.0	(1.52)	c	c	26.1	(2.93)	11.8	(1.45)
Mexico: Coahuila	20.5	(2.32)	m	m	m	m	19.5	(2.43)	33.6	(9.66)	26.8	(4.82)	16.1	(2.21)
Mexico: Chiapas	24.0	(1.63)	m	m	m	m	24.0	(1.65)	c	c	28.5	(2.47)	19.4	(1.86)
Mexico: Distrito Federal	9.5	(0.81)	m	m	m	m	8.8	(0.87)	c	c	14.0	(2.22)	6.6	(0.93)
Mexico: Durango	23.5	(2.52)	m	m	m	m	23.7	(2.55)	c	c	29.6	(7.98)	21.0	(1.63)
Mexico: Guerrero	23.4	(1.91)	m	m	m	m	23.2	(1.93)	c	c	27.8	(2.12)	16.4	(2.17)
Mexico: Guanajuato	23.8	(1.83)	m	m	m	m	23.3	(1.87)	c	c	25.6	(2.56)	22.0	(2.64)
Mexico: Hidalgo	20.9	(2.30)	m	m	m	m	20.4	(2.29)	c	c	34.1	(4.40)	16.9	(2.53)
Mexico: Jalisco	19.9	(1.72)	m	m	m	m	19.2	(1.73)	c	c	24.3	(3.19)	16.6	(1.71)
Mexico: Michoacán	23.4	(1.74)	m	m	m	m	21.3	(1.47)	c	c	27.9	(3.31)	21.2	(2.26)
Mexico: Morelos	22.3	(2.01)	m	m	m	m	20.8	(1.67)	c	c	25.1	(2.87)	19.6	(2.85)
Mexico: Mexico	18.2	(1.62)	m	m	m	m	16.8	(1.68)	c	c	22.7	(2.35)	16.2	(1.93)
Mexico: Nayarit	18.2	(1.25)	m	m	m	m	18.3	(1.28)	c	c	18.6	(2.03)	17.9	(1.46)
Mexico: Nuevo León	21.8	(3.02)	m	m	m	m	19.5	(2.97)	55.7	(1.61)	27.3	(3.82)	19.2	(3.54)
Mexico: Oaxaca	23.6	(2.84)	m	m	m	m	23.5	(2.92)	c	c	30.0	(5.89)	17.3	(2.06)
Mexico: Puebla	18.4	(2.36)	m	m	m	m	18.4	(2.43)	c	c	22.6	(5.91)	16.1	(2.10)
Mexico: Quintana Roo	20.8	(2.13)	m	m	m	m	20.9	(2.24)	c	c	25.0	(3.31)	14.3	(1.56)
Mexico: Querétaro	21.9	(2.80)	m	m	m	m	21.9	(2.83)	c	c	32.3	(4.12)	10.7	(0.96)
Mexico: Sinaloa	20.0	(2.45)	m	m	m	m	20.4	(2.60)	c	c	26.4	(5.20)	14.1	(1.12)
Mexico: San Luis Potosí	26.0	(2.53)	m	m	m	m	25.6	(2.58)	c	c	26.9	(3.97)	24.5	(1.88)
Mexico: Sonora	20.4	(1.45)	m	m	m	m	19.6	(1.54)	c	c	25.9	(1.96)	14.0	(1.64)
Mexico: Tamaulipas	20.0	(1.94)	m	m	m	m	19.9	(2.02)	c	c	24.4	(3.38)	15.6	(2.18)
Mexico: Tabasco	26.7	(1.87)	m	m	m	m	26.3	(1.78)	c	c	30.9	(3.42)	23.5	(1.86)
Mexico: Tlaxcala	22.9	(1.98)	m	m	m	m	23.0	(2.02)	c	c	27.7	(3.77)	18.7	(1.42)
Mexico: Veracruz	23.5	(2.49)	m	m	m	m	23.4	(2.54)	c	c	27.1	(4.07)	18.9	(2.18)
Mexico: Yucatán	22.4	(1.35)	m	m	m	m	22.3	(1.37)	c	c	31.7	(1.70)	13.9	(1.66)
Mexico: Zacatecas	24.2	(2.46)	m	m	m	m	23.9	(2.48)	c	c	25.6	(6.48)	23.7	(2.85)

1. Data from OECD (2010), *PISA 2009 Results: What Makes a School Successful? (Volume IV)*, PISA, OECD Publishing, Table IV.3.2a.
2. Data for Belgium (Flemish Community) is unavailable; data for Belgium as a whole is presented instead.

StatLink http://dx.doi.org/10.1787/888932733887

[Part 2/2]
Table B1.8 Percentage of students who expect to complete an upper secondary degree, but not more, by ISCED type and ISCED level programme

	Number of programmes for 15-year-olds[1, 2]	Additional years of selection into these programmes before 15[1, 2]	15-year-old students in an academic programme		15-year-old students in a non-academic programme		15-year-old students in lower secondary		15-year-old students in upper secondary	
			%	S.E.	%	S.E.	%	S.E.	%	S.E.
Countries and economies										
Australia	1	0	99.4	(0.16)	0.6	(0.16)	81.2	(0.68)	18.8	(0.68)
Austria	4	5	59.4	(1.34)	40.6	(1.34)	4.3	(0.94)	95.7	(0.94)
Belgium (Flemish Community)	4	3	78.5	(1.17)	21.5	(1.17)	2.9	(0.54)	97.1	(0.54)
Hong Kong-China	2	0	100.0	(0.00)	a	a	33.7	(0.84)	66.3	(0.84)
Croatia	5	0.5	77.0	(1.31)	23.0	(1.31)	0.2	(0.16)	99.8	(0.16)
Hungary	3	4	86.3	(1.07)	13.7	(1.07)	10.3	(1.57)	89.7	(1.57)
Ireland	4	0	74.3	(1.44)	25.7	(1.44)	61.3	(0.98)	38.7	(0.98)
Iceland	1	0	100.0	(0.00)	a	a	98.3	(0.11)	1.7	(0.11)
Italy	3	1	96.6	(0.28)	3.4	(0.28)	1.4	(0.30)	98.6	(0.30)
Korea	3	1	75.8	(1.82)	24.2	(1.82)	4.2	(0.89)	95.8	(0.89)
Latvia	1	0	99.2	(0.45)	0.8	(0.45)	97.0	(0.51)	3.0	(0.51)
Macao-China	1	0	98.7	(0.04)	1.3	(0.04)	60.0	(0.18)	40.0	(0.18)
Mexico	3	0	95.5	(0.54)	4.5	(0.54)	42.9	(0.97)	57.1	(0.97)
New Zealand	1	0	100.0	(0.00)	a	a	5.8	(0.36)	94.2	(0.36)
Poland	1	0	99.9	(0.09)	0.1	(0.09)	99.1	(0.30)	0.9	(0.30)
Portugal	3	0	84.4	(1.63)	15.6	(1.63)	43.2	(2.09)	56.8	(2.09)
Singapore	4	3	100.0	(0.00)	a	a	3.5	(0.22)	96.5	(0.22)
Serbia	m	m	23.6	(1.00)	76.4	(1.00)	2.1	(0.54)	97.9	(0.54)
Slovak Republic	5	4	91.4	(0.96)	8.6	(0.96)	38.0	(1.50)	62.0	(1.50)
Slovenia	3	1	47.6	(0.43)	52.4	(0.43)	3.1	(0.77)	96.9	(0.77)
Trinidad and Tobago	4	4	88.3	(0.19)	11.7	(0.19)	33.4	(0.44)	66.6	(0.44)
Regions										
Italy: Abruzzo	m	m	99.5	(0.09)	0.5	(0.09)	1.8	(0.11)	98.2	(0.11)
Italy: Basilicata	m	m	100.0	(0.00)	m	m	100.0	(0.00)	m	m
Italy: Bolzano	m	m	71.5	(0.59)	28.5	(0.59)	3.9	(1.46)	96.1	(1.46)
Italy: Calabria	m	m	100.0	(0.00)	m	m	1.1	(0.78)	98.9	(0.78)
Italy: Campania	m	m	100.0	(0.00)	m	m	0.9	(0.59)	99.1	(0.59)
Italy: Emilia Romagna	m	m	94.1	(1.63)	5.9	(1.63)	100.0	(0.00)	m	m
Italy: Friuli Venezia Giulia	m	m	98.4	(0.09)	1.6	(0.09)	2.8	(0.52)	97.2	(0.52)
Italy: Lazio	m	m	98.1	(0.51)	1.9	(0.51)	1.0	(1.00)	99.0	(1.00)
Italy: Liguria	m	m	96.8	(1.72)	3.2	(1.72)	1.0	(0.33)	99.0	(0.33)
Italy: Lombardia	m	m	93.1	(0.91)	6.9	(0.91)	1.5	(1.07)	98.5	(1.07)
Italy: Marche	m	m	100.0	(0.00)	m	m	0.5	(0.40)	99.5	(0.40)
Italy: Molise	m	m	99.9	(0.01)	0.1	(0.01)	1.0	(1.06)	99.0	(1.06)
Italy: Piemonte	m	m	94.8	(2.64)	5.2	(2.64)	2.9	(1.21)	97.1	(1.21)
Italy: Puglia	m	m	100.0	(0.00)	m	m	100.0	(0.00)	m	m
Italy: Sardegna	m	m	100.0	(0.00)	m	m	1.8	(0.78)	98.2	(0.78)
Italy: Sicilia	m	m	99.8	(0.22)	0.2	(0.22)	3.3	(2.09)	96.7	(2.09)
Italy: Toscana	m	m	100.0	(0.00)	m	m	1.6	(0.37)	98.4	(0.37)
Italy: Trento	m	m	78.2	(1.18)	21.8	(1.18)	0.5	(0.46)	99.5	(0.46)
Italy: Umbria	m	m	98.4	(0.26)	1.6	(0.26)	0.9	(1.24)	99.1	(1.24)
Italy: Valle d'Aosta	m	m	95.8	(0.27)	4.2	(0.27)	0.8	(0.22)	99.2	(0.22)
Italy: Veneto	m	m	89.0	(1.23)	11.0	(1.23)	1.3	(0.77)	98.7	(0.77)
Mexico: Aguascalientes	m	m	91.3	(2.65)	8.7	(2.65)	18.9	(2.16)	81.1	(2.16)
Mexico: Baja California	m	m	98.2	(1.79)	1.8	(1.79)	53.0	(3.49)	47.0	(3.49)
Mexico: Baja California Sur	m	m	95.6	(0.35)	4.4	(0.35)	40.7	(5.31)	59.3	(5.31)
Mexico: Campeche	m	m	98.2	(1.85)	1.8	(1.85)	49.9	(3.66)	50.1	(3.66)
Mexico: Chihuahua	m	m	95.2	(3.46)	4.8	(3.46)	26.2	(4.44)	73.8	(4.44)
Mexico: Colima	m	m	98.5	(0.19)	1.5	(0.19)	51.6	(5.22)	48.4	(5.22)
Mexico: Coahuila	m	m	92.9	(2.81)	7.1	(2.81)	41.2	(3.70)	58.8	(3.70)
Mexico: Chiapas	m	m	98.7	(1.31)	1.3	(1.31)	50.2	(3.61)	49.8	(3.61)
Mexico: Distrito Federal	m	m	89.5	(3.78)	10.5	(3.78)	39.6	(5.05)	60.4	(5.05)
Mexico: Durango	m	m	97.9	(2.08)	2.1	(2.08)	29.5	(4.32)	70.5	(4.32)
Mexico: Guerrero	m	m	98.2	(1.76)	1.8	(1.76)	61.4	(4.35)	38.6	(4.35)
Mexico: Guanajuato	m	m	95.5	(0.23)	4.5	(0.23)	49.6	(2.99)	50.4	(2.99)
Mexico: Hidalgo	m	m	97.8	(2.22)	2.2	(2.22)	23.2	(2.30)	76.8	(2.30)
Mexico: Jalisco	m	m	96.2	(0.25)	3.8	(0.25)	42.9	(2.64)	57.1	(2.64)
Mexico: Michoacán	m	m	91.1	(5.16)	8.9	(5.16)	33.7	(5.73)	66.3	(5.73)
Mexico: Morelos	m	m	94.3	(2.51)	5.7	(2.51)	49.2	(5.92)	50.8	(5.92)
Mexico: Mexico	m	m	94.1	(2.02)	5.9	(2.02)	30.3	(3.90)	69.7	(3.90)
Mexico: Nayarit	m	m	94.9	(1.42)	5.1	(1.42)	42.7	(4.34)	57.3	(4.34)
Mexico: Nuevo León	m	m	93.8	(3.26)	6.2	(3.26)	31.6	(9.32)	68.4	(9.32)
Mexico: Oaxaca	m	m	97.8	(2.17)	2.2	(2.17)	49.6	(5.17)	50.4	(5.17)
Mexico: Puebla	m	m	97.0	(0.34)	3.0	(0.34)	35.6	(4.60)	64.4	(4.60)
Mexico: Quintana Roo	m	m	94.8	(1.55)	5.2	(1.55)	61.0	(4.06)	39.0	(4.06)
Mexico: Querétaro	m	m	98.7	(1.38)	1.3	(1.38)	51.8	(4.59)	48.2	(4.59)
Mexico: Sinaloa	m	m	94.6	(3.30)	5.4	(3.30)	48.2	(4.51)	51.8	(4.51)
Mexico: San Luis Potosí	m	m	98.0	(0.42)	2.0	(0.42)	60.9	(3.77)	39.1	(3.77)
Mexico: Sonora	m	m	93.9	(0.34)	6.1	(0.34)	53.9	(5.02)	46.1	(5.02)
Mexico: Tamaulipas	m	m	96.0	(0.53)	4.0	(0.53)	50.3	(3.25)	49.7	(3.25)
Mexico: Tabasco	m	m	98.1	(1.88)	1.9	(1.88)	43.9	(4.95)	56.1	(4.95)
Mexico: Tlaxcala	m	m	97.3	(1.99)	2.7	(1.99)	46.4	(5.70)	53.6	(5.70)
Mexico: Veracruz	m	m	98.0	(1.97)	2.0	(1.97)	55.7	(4.58)	44.3	(4.58)
Mexico: Yucatán	m	m	98.0	(1.97)	2.0	(1.97)	47.6	(4.02)	52.4	(4.02)
Mexico: Zacatecas	m	m	98.4	(1.54)	1.6	(1.54)	28.2	(4.29)	71.8	(4.29)

1. Data from OECD (2010), *PISA 2009 Results: What Makes a School Successful? (Volume IV)*, PISA, OECD Publishing, Table IV.3.2a.
2. Data for Belgium (Flemish Community) is unavailable; data for Belgium as a whole is presented instead.
StatLink http://dx.doi.org/10.1787/888932733887

[Part 1/1]

Table B1.9 Students who expect to drop out before completing upper secondary education and students who expect to obtain a vocational post-secondary degree

	Students who do not expect to complete upper secondary education or higher (drop out)		Students who expect to complete vocational post-secondary education (ISCED 4 or 5B)		Students who do not expect to complete a university degree	
	%	S.E.	%	S.E.	%	S.E.
Countries and economies						
Australia	3.7	(0.22)	14.0	(0.36)	38.8	(0.82)
Austria	2.7	(0.25)	16.2	(0.86)	71.9	(0.95)
Belgium (Flemish Community)	1.4	(0.18)	43.5	(0.91)	62.9	(1.03)
Hong Kong-China	2.9	(0.22)	25.8	(0.76)	52.8	(1.04)
Croatia	c	c	17.4	(0.62)	50.9	(1.21)
Hungary	1.3	(0.32)	30.1	(1.07)	58.9	(1.45)
Ireland	5.7	(0.39)	15.1	(0.66)	44.8	(1.07)
Iceland	2.3	(0.29)	25.8	(0.71)	55.3	(0.77)
Italy	3.0	(0.21)	17.5	(0.42)	59.1	(0.60)
Korea	c	c	13.8	(0.76)	19.1	(1.23)
Latvia	4.1	(0.41)	43.8	(0.90)	74.6	(1.18)
Macao-China	9.4	(0.42)	37.4	(0.62)	64.8	(0.59)
Mexico	8.6	(0.40)	15.4	(0.32)	44.2	(0.75)
New Zealand	1.1	(0.15)	23.9	(0.65)	47.5	(0.78)
Poland	0.9	(0.15)	29.9	(0.76)	58.5	(1.02)
Portugal	8.0	(0.75)	10.5	(0.41)	48.0	(1.57)
Singapore	0.6	(0.11)	27.1	(0.56)	29.9	(0.59)
Serbia	0.7	(0.16)	21.7	(0.67)	44.9	(1.32)
Slovak Republic	2.5	(0.34)	12.5	(0.63)	54.5	(0.97)
Slovenia	2.0	(0.26)	36.0	(0.81)	64.9	(0.73)
Trinidad and Tobago	3.9	(0.36)	11.6	(0.55)	30.6	(0.74)
Regions						
Italy: Abruzzo	3.1	(0.65)	17.7	(1.03)	55.7	(2.19)
Italy: Basilicata	c	c	18.7	(1.84)	54.3	(1.59)
Italy: Bolzano	2.9	(0.44)	14.0	(0.79)	76.6	(0.89)
Italy: Calabria	3.5	(0.56)	17.1	(1.26)	53.8	(2.37)
Italy: Campania	3.0	(0.61)	18.7	(1.43)	57.0	(2.75)
Italy: Emilia Romagna	3.0	(0.56)	17.6	(1.50)	59.8	(2.04)
Italy: Friuli Venezia Giulia	3.1	(0.72)	18.8	(1.64)	60.5	(2.02)
Italy: Lazio	2.2	(0.47)	16.8	(1.18)	51.4	(1.98)
Italy: Liguria	2.6	(0.78)	18.4	(1.21)	60.3	(2.69)
Italy: Lombardia	2.7	(0.66)	17.4	(1.42)	62.0	(2.08)
Italy: Marche	3.0	(0.60)	17.6	(1.22)	62.8	(1.77)
Italy: Molise	4.4	(0.99)	19.5	(1.43)	56.6	(1.41)
Italy: Piemonte	3.4	(0.50)	14.4	(0.85)	62.7	(2.21)
Italy: Puglia	2.6	(0.52)	15.0	(1.33)	58.7	(2.39)
Italy: Sardegna	3.8	(0.71)	17.0	(1.49)	56.8	(2.32)
Italy: Sicilia	5.7	(1.54)	18.0	(1.58)	57.8	(2.09)
Italy: Toscana	2.6	(0.54)	15.0	(0.82)	59.5	(1.45)
Italy: Trento	2.4	(0.45)	20.5	(1.28)	64.7	(1.20)
Italy: Umbria	2.8	(0.35)	18.0	(1.51)	57.9	(1.57)
Italy: Valle d'Aosta	c	c	16.8	(1.11)	64.9	(1.58)
Italy: Veneto	c	c	22.3	(1.80)	65.3	(2.00)
Mexico: Aguascalientes	4.6	(0.62)	21.3	(1.55)	43.6	(2.53)
Mexico: Baja California	10.0	(0.82)	19.2	(1.58)	48.4	(2.42)
Mexico: Baja California Sur	6.2	(1.50)	18.3	(1.58)	41.8	(3.18)
Mexico: Campeche	8.3	(1.60)	10.8	(0.90)	39.3	(2.57)
Mexico: Chihuahua	c	c	15.7	(1.13)	34.5	(2.73)
Mexico: Colima	6.2	(0.99)	12.4	(1.05)	37.7	(2.30)
Mexico: Coahuila	c	c	18.5	(1.26)	44.2	(2.89)
Mexico: Chiapas	14.0	(2.29)	9.6	(1.00)	47.6	(2.70)
Mexico: Distrito Federal	3.6	(1.02)	15.8	(1.41)	28.9	(2.05)
Mexico: Durango	7.6	(2.18)	16.0	(1.47)	47.2	(2.34)
Mexico: Guerrero	20.2	(1.94)	10.3	(1.32)	53.9	(3.23)
Mexico: Guanajuato	16.5	(2.18)	15.2	(1.10)	55.4	(2.46)
Mexico: Hidalgo	6.5	(1.76)	15.5	(1.62)	42.8	(3.03)
Mexico: Jalisco	5.4	(0.64)	16.1	(1.50)	41.5	(1.86)
Mexico: Michoacán	8.3	(1.51)	14.2	(1.20)	45.9	(2.09)
Mexico: Morelos	6.8	(2.59)	16.7	(1.63)	45.8	(3.22)
Mexico: Mexico	6.6	(1.68)	17.3	(1.21)	42.1	(2.56)
Mexico: Nayarit	7.7	(1.03)	16.3	(1.61)	42.2	(1.60)
Mexico: Nuevo León	6.8	(1.87)	15.1	(1.81)	43.7	(5.72)
Mexico: Oaxaca	12.4	(3.23)	10.8	(1.45)	46.7	(4.55)
Mexico: Puebla	5.5	(0.62)	16.1	(1.52)	40.0	(3.50)
Mexico: Quintana Roo	8.7	(1.40)	16.0	(1.41)	45.6	(3.44)
Mexico: Querétaro	10.9	(2.28)	14.6	(1.38)	47.4	(4.14)
Mexico: Sinaloa	7.2	(1.53)	14.7	(1.30)	41.9	(2.18)
Mexico: San Luis Potosí	17.2	(3.83)	14.7	(1.75)	57.8	(3.12)
Mexico: Sonora	8.0	(1.16)	15.1	(1.26)	43.4	(2.28)
Mexico: Tamaulipas	9.6	(1.41)	16.3	(1.44)	45.9	(3.03)
Mexico: Tabasco	7.9	(1.74)	17.5	(1.28)	52.1	(2.21)
Mexico: Tlaxcala	7.1	(1.60)	17.2	(1.10)	47.2	(2.99)
Mexico: Veracruz	9.3	(1.33)	16.3	(1.35)	49.1	(3.12)
Mexico: Yucatán	11.3	(1.58)	13.6	(1.18)	47.3	(2.66)
Mexico: Zacatecas	11.4	(2.33)	15.7	(1.28)	51.3	(2.19)

StatLink http://dx.doi.org/10.1787/888932733906

[Part 1/1]

Table B1.10 Socio-economic differences in expectations of completing a university degree

	Students who expect to complete a university degree								Students who expect to complete a university degree (after accounting for reading and mathematics performance)							
	High ESCS		Low ESCS		Difference (High - Low ESCS)		Odds ratio (High/Low ESCS)		High ESCS		Low ESCS		Adjusted difference (High - Low ESCS)		Odds ratio (High/Low ESCS)	
	%	S.E.	%	S.E.	Diff.	S.E.	O.R.	S.E.	%	S.E.	%	S.E.	Diff.	S.E.	O.R.	S.E.
Countries and economies																
Australia	80.6	(0.81)	42.6	(1.09)	**38.0**	(1.21)	**5.61**	(0.34)	71.9	(0.80)	58.8	(0.92)	**13.1**	(0.86)	**2.84**	(0.19)
Austria	46.3	(1.41)	13.6	(1.15)	**32.7**	(1.72)	**5.48**	(0.59)	30.2	(1.33)	18.4	(1.07)	**11.8**	(1.16)	**2.78**	(0.34)
Belgium (Flemish Community)	60.4	(1.53)	17.3	(1.21)	**43.1**	(1.76)	**7.30**	(0.70)	35.9	(1.71)	23.7	(1.53)	**12.2**	(1.32)	**3.24**	(0.33)
Hong Kong-China	64.8	(1.53)	32.3	(1.23)	**32.5**	(1.88)	**3.86**	(0.32)	67.2	(1.64)	55.6	(1.13)	**11.6**	(0.73)	**2.79**	(0.24)
Croatia	71.4	(1.49)	28.4	(1.57)	**43.1**	(2.14)	**6.32**	(0.66)	69.3	(1.70)	50.4	(1.29)	**18.9**	(1.25)	**4.29**	(0.47)
Hungary	69.0	(1.89)	16.4	(1.18)	**52.6**	(2.13)	11.33	(1.33)	57.1	(1.93)	37.5	(1.54)	**19.6**	(1.28)	**4.29**	(0.39)
Ireland	73.2	(1.36)	37.4	(1.62)	**35.7**	(2.04)	**4.56**	(0.43)	67.3	(1.56)	54.3	(1.20)	**13.0**	(1.24)	**2.67**	(0.27)
Iceland	68.2	(1.39)	25.1	(1.25)	**43.1**	(1.89)	**6.41**	(0.60)	47.6	(0.94)	28.8	(1.16)	**18.8**	(1.15)	**4.71**	(0.46)
Italy	60.7	(0.84)	22.0	(0.68)	**38.6**	(1.00)	**5.46**	(0.27)	53.2	(0.91)	38.7	(0.62)	**14.5**	(0.57)	**3.38**	(0.16)
Korea	93.4	(0.71)	63.6	(2.48)	**29.8**	(2.52)	8.15	(1.22)	95.2	(0.54)	89.2	(0.67)	**6.0**	(0.36)	**4.54**	(0.62)
Latvia	42.4	(1.87)	11.7	(1.37)	**30.8**	(2.15)	**5.58**	(0.79)	34.7	(1.58)	21.4	(1.07)	**13.3**	(1.26)	**3.41**	(0.49)
Macao-China	48.7	(1.09)	24.3	(0.98)	**24.4**	(1.45)	**2.96**	(0.20)	53.7	(1.53)	40.7	(0.89)	**13.0**	(0.85)	**2.65**	(0.19)
Mexico	74.9	(0.68)	38.6	(1.13)	**36.3**	(1.23)	**4.75**	(0.26)	74.1	(0.83)	66.7	(0.60)	**7.4**	(0.35)	**2.71**	(0.15)
New Zealand	70.2	(1.30)	38.1	(1.27)	**32.1**	(1.81)	**3.84**	(0.32)	62.4	(1.56)	51.0	(0.94)	**11.3**	(1.33)	**2.26**	(0.21)
Poland	67.1	(1.34)	23.1	(1.08)	**44.0**	(1.48)	**6.80**	(0.50)	63.4	(1.67)	43.3	(1.20)	**20.1**	(1.05)	**3.71**	(0.33)
Portugal	77.0	(1.34)	29.2	(1.77)	**47.8**	(2.04)	**8.10**	(0.85)	71.4	(1.31)	57.5	(1.18)	**13.9**	(0.78)	**3.94**	(0.39)
Singapore	86.0	(0.86)	54.6	(1.21)	**31.4**	(1.55)	**5.12**	(0.47)	85.7	(1.06)	78.2	(0.75)	**7.5**	(0.53)	**2.70**	(0.27)
Serbia	77.1	(1.18)	34.9	(1.43)	**42.2**	(1.86)	**6.27**	(0.57)	72.1	(1.54)	55.7	(1.15)	**16.4**	(1.03)	**4.11**	(0.43)
Slovak Republic	65.7	(1.35)	25.1	(1.63)	**40.5**	(2.26)	**5.69**	(0.64)	58.9	(2.03)	43.4	(1.31)	**15.4**	(1.53)	**2.84**	(0.34)
Slovenia	57.8	(1.45)	17.2	(0.91)	**40.7**	(1.67)	**6.61**	(0.56)	45.9	(1.32)	29.1	(0.82)	**16.8**	(1.04)	**3.55**	(0.32)
Trinidad and Tobago	81.7	(1.09)	59.8	(1.46)	**21.8**	(1.88)	**2.99**	(0.29)	79.1	(1.41)	73.9	(0.89)	**5.1**	(0.75)	**1.81**	(0.21)
Regions																
Italy: Abruzzo	61.5	(2.79)	25.5	(2.38)	**35.9**	(3.36)	**4.65**	(0.74)	54.3	(3.21)	41.2	(2.41)	**13.2**	(1.66)	**2.78**	(0.52)
Italy: Basilicata	63.6	(2.47)	29.1	(2.73)	**34.5**	(3.71)	**4.25**	(0.73)	59.3	(2.71)	46.9	(2.05)	**12.3**	(1.90)	**2.65**	(0.42)
Italy: Bolzano	38.3	(2.13)	10.7	(1.34)	**27.6**	(2.50)	5.20	(0.85)	33.3	(2.65)	19.9	(1.11)	**13.4**	(1.96)	**3.46**	(0.57)
Italy: Calabria	68.6	(2.93)	25.8	(2.18)	**42.8**	(3.97)	6.28	(1.21)	62.8	(3.75)	47.7	(2.50)	**15.1**	(2.09)	3.96	(0.72)
Italy: Campania	65.0	(3.69)	23.6	(2.69)	**41.3**	(4.26)	6.00	(1.23)	60.1	(3.25)	44.0	(2.27)	**16.1**	(1.79)	3.58	(0.73)
Italy: Emilia Romagna	64.5	(2.39)	18.8	(1.59)	**45.7**	(2.90)	7.85	(1.17)	47.9	(2.63)	33.8	(2.11)	**14.1**	(1.53)	**3.75**	(0.59)
Italy: Friuli Venezia Giulia	59.0	(2.92)	19.3	(1.99)	**39.7**	(3.95)	6.01	(1.19)	51.0	(3.11)	33.5	(2.02)	**17.5**	(2.42)	3.77	(0.80)
Italy: Lazio	64.1	(2.75)	34.4	(3.85)	**29.7**	(4.65)	3.41	(0.70)	57.2	(3.19)	45.6	(2.99)	**11.6**	(2.27)	2.23	(0.49)
Italy: Liguria	59.3	(2.86)	23.6	(3.40)	**35.7**	(4.86)	4.72	(1.14)	48.3	(3.19)	34.2	(2.27)	**14.0**	(2.26)	3.30	(0.61)
Italy: Lombardia	57.7	(2.96)	16.4	(2.30)	**41.4**	(2.92)	6.98	(1.14)	48.2	(3.50)	31.9	(2.28)	**16.3**	(1.91)	**3.93**	(0.58)
Italy: Marche	55.2	(2.77)	19.7	(2.16)	**35.5**	(3.08)	**5.01**	(0.78)	49.4	(3.36)	33.5	(1.73)	**15.9**	(2.26)	**3.51**	(0.58)
Italy: Molise	62.2	(2.83)	27.2	(2.60)	**35.0**	(4.00)	4.41	(0.82)	52.2	(3.09)	41.4	(1.64)	**10.8**	(2.36)	2.66	(0.59)
Italy: Piemonte	61.1	(2.62)	16.6	(1.58)	**44.4**	(2.75)	7.87	(1.11)	53.9	(2.94)	34.7	(1.99)	**19.2**	(1.98)	**4.55**	(0.68)
Italy: Puglia	58.7	(2.97)	24.6	(2.65)	**34.2**	(3.37)	**4.37**	(0.69)	55.8	(2.92)	42.3	(2.16)	**13.5**	(1.86)	**3.08**	(0.52)
Italy: Sardegna	62.2	(2.73)	27.9	(3.54)	**34.2**	(3.41)	**4.24**	(0.69)	54.1	(2.89)	42.4	(2.09)	**11.7**	(1.77)	**2.91**	(0.48)
Italy: Sicilia	63.9	(2.94)	22.5	(1.83)	**41.4**	(3.41)	6.09	(0.99)	54.8	(3.64)	41.1	(2.68)	**13.7**	(1.37)	**3.46**	(0.48)
Italy: Toscana	55.8	(2.66)	24.5	(2.39)	**31.4**	(4.05)	3.90	(0.75)	49.7	(2.72)	35.4	(2.17)	**14.3**	(2.15)	2.83	(0.56)
Italy: Trento	56.3	(2.77)	17.6	(2.18)	**38.7**	(3.77)	6.03	(1.20)	45.4	(3.20)	29.8	(1.83)	**15.6**	(2.50)	3.59	(0.78)
Italy: Umbria	63.1	(2.10)	22.2	(1.80)	**40.9**	(3.03)	**5.99**	(0.91)	51.4	(3.07)	35.6	(2.09)	**15.8**	(2.02)	**3.66**	(0.61)
Italy: Valle d'Aosta	55.3	(2.98)	17.2	(2.22)	**38.1**	(3.75)	5.95	(1.18)	46.8	(3.33)	31.9	(2.03)	**14.9**	(2.44)	3.94	(0.82)
Italy: Veneto	54.3	(3.86)	16.7	(1.84)	**37.6**	(4.58)	5.94	(1.30)	47.0	(3.62)	29.5	(2.12)	**17.5**	(2.35)	4.37	(0.78)
Mexico: Aguascalientes	78.0	(2.92)	38.1	(2.31)	**39.9**	(3.60)	5.76	(1.09)	76.8	(3.20)	67.6	(2.53)	**9.2**	(0.97)	3.95	(0.83)
Mexico: Baja California	68.3	(2.43)	37.5	(3.62)	**30.8**	(3.88)	**3.59**	(0.61)	67.1	(3.92)	59.8	(2.62)	**7.3**	(1.75)	2.27	(0.49)
Mexico: Baja California Sur	72.9	(2.47)	46.2	(3.82)	**26.7**	(3.19)	**3.13**	(0.42)	72.8	(2.66)	65.9	(2.38)	**7.0**	(1.06)	**2.10**	(0.28)
Mexico: Campeche	79.9	(2.38)	44.1	(3.69)	**35.8**	(4.21)	5.05	(1.02)	81.5	(2.29)	74.7	(2.16)	**6.7**	(0.65)	3.18	(0.69)
Mexico: Chihuahua	85.2	(2.51)	48.7	(4.78)	**36.5**	(5.02)	6.07	(1.55)	83.9	(2.50)	76.1	(1.92)	**7.8**	(1.10)	3.65	(1.04)
Mexico: Colima	76.5	(3.12)	50.4	(3.57)	**26.2**	(3.65)	**3.21**	(0.56)	74.7	(2.91)	69.7	(2.28)	**5.0**	(0.88)	1.86	(0.38)
Mexico: Coahuila	74.4	(3.33)	39.5	(5.11)	**34.9**	(7.07)	4.45	(1.44)	74.6	(4.62)	65.0	(3.25)	**9.6**	(2.03)	3.23	(1.25)
Mexico: Chiapas	69.3	(2.82)	39.8	(3.69)	**29.6**	(4.40)	3.43	(0.66)	68.9	(3.92)	63.1	(3.28)	**5.7**	(0.85)	**2.09**	(0.33)
Mexico: Distrito Federal	82.6	(3.39)	57.5	(4.68)	**25.1**	(7.40)	3.51	(1.38)	82.5	(2.69)	77.4	(1.63)	**5.1**	(1.36)	1.95	(0.66)
Mexico: Durango	70.3	(3.01)	37.3	(3.55)	**33.1**	(5.73)	3.99	(1.03)	70.4	(2.86)	62.7	(2.03)	**7.7**	(1.52)	2.78	(0.66)
Mexico: Guerrero	63.4	(5.18)	33.0	(3.83)	**30.4**	(6.10)	3.52	(0.94)	70.9	(4.83)	62.1	(3.71)	**8.8**	(1.71)	2.64	(0.73)
Mexico: Guanajuato	70.7	(3.17)	20.2	(2.24)	**50.5**	(3.50)	9.55	(1.77)	76.4	(3.36)	63.4	(3.10)	**13.0**	(0.74)	5.01	(1.08)
Mexico: Hidalgo	76.1	(3.87)	40.9	(5.02)	**35.2**	(6.02)	4.59	(1.29)	75.7	(4.18)	69.5	(3.40)	**6.2**	(1.32)	2.13	(0.64)
Mexico: Jalisco	76.2	(3.12)	39.3	(2.21)	**36.9**	(3.87)	4.96	(0.98)	78.2	(2.91)	69.3	(2.43)	**8.9**	(0.76)	**3.30**	(0.56)
Mexico: Michoacán	68.9	(2.44)	39.0	(3.08)	**29.9**	(3.93)	**3.46**	(0.60)	68.1	(3.68)	62.1	(2.83)	**6.1**	(1.29)	1.85	(0.32)
Mexico: Morelos	71.7	(3.26)	41.1	(4.34)	**30.6**	(4.77)	3.63	(0.77)	74.3	(3.57)	66.1	(2.68)	**8.3**	(1.60)	2.42	(0.61)
Mexico: Mexico	74.8	(3.41)	42.8	(3.70)	**31.9**	(4.43)	3.96	(0.83)	76.1	(3.05)	68.9	(2.35)	**7.2**	(1.04)	**2.70**	(0.43)
Mexico: Nayarit	71.3	(2.83)	42.3	(3.65)	**29.0**	(4.13)	**3.39**	(0.62)	74.5	(2.70)	67.7	(1.86)	**6.8**	(1.22)	2.39	(0.52)
Mexico: Nuevo León	79.2	(4.32)	33.4	(2.91)	**45.8**	(5.03)	7.61	(2.12)	74.6	(4.36)	63.9	(3.14)	**10.7**	(1.58)	3.96	(1.06)
Mexico: Oaxaca	65.4	(4.36)	39.0	(4.61)	**26.5**	(4.87)	2.96	(0.62)	79.7	(4.34)	72.4	(3.21)	**7.3**	(1.90)	2.72	(0.79)
Mexico: Puebla	78.9	(2.53)	45.0	(3.76)	**33.9**	(5.02)	4.58	(1.10)	78.3	(3.29)	71.5	(2.41)	**6.9**	(1.11)	2.56	(0.64)
Mexico: Quintana Roo	76.5	(2.76)	34.1	(3.41)	**42.4**	(4.19)	6.31	(1.30)	75.7	(3.03)	66.4	(2.43)	**9.4**	(1.03)	**3.40**	(0.60)
Mexico: Querétaro	80.0	(3.91)	31.0	(3.56)	**49.0**	(4.94)	8.89	(2.37)	77.8	(4.96)	68.0	(4.38)	**9.8**	(0.95)	3.96	(1.07)
Mexico: Sinaloa	76.4	(2.14)	44.2	(3.20)	**32.2**	(3.78)	**4.10**	(0.71)	74.2	(2.91)	67.4	(2.12)	**6.8**	(1.31)	**2.84**	(0.45)
Mexico: San Luis Potosí	62.8	(2.83)	25.4	(3.63)	**37.4**	(5.35)	4.97	(1.30)	64.3	(3.19)	54.9	(2.20)	**9.3**	(1.81)	2.51	(0.69)
Mexico: Sonora	70.4	(4.16)	43.0	(3.60)	**27.4**	(4.46)	3.15	(0.64)	71.1	(3.14)	64.9	(2.28)	**6.3**	(1.29)	1.99	(0.42)
Mexico: Tamaulipas	68.5	(2.70)	37.9	(3.12)	**30.5**	(2.44)	**3.55**	(0.38)	72.6	(2.19)	64.3	(2.59)	**8.3**	(0.98)	**2.60**	(0.39)
Mexico: Tabasco	59.2	(4.86)	36.2	(2.59)	**23.0**	(6.21)	2.56	(0.67)	58.2	(5.68)	54.0	(3.59)	4.3	(2.26)	1.62	(0.36)
Mexico: Tlaxcala	70.3	(3.19)	38.2	(3.85)	**32.1**	(3.84)	**3.83**	(0.65)	74.9	(2.80)	66.3	(2.59)	**8.6**	(0.79)	**2.97**	(0.50)
Mexico: Veracruz	72.4	(3.56)	33.0	(5.45)	**39.4**	(6.33)	5.32	(1.55)	76.8	(4.11)	68.2	(3.42)	**8.6**	(1.19)	3.16	(0.89)
Mexico: Yucatán	72.2	(2.72)	35.0	(3.64)	**37.3**	(4.61)	4.84	(1.03)	69.1	(3.87)	63.0	(2.95)	**6.1**	(1.25)	2.28	(0.51)
Mexico: Zacatecas	65.7	(3.60)	29.5	(3.83)	**36.3**	(6.36)	4.59	(1.35)	73.1	(4.55)	64.0	(3.56)	**9.1**	(1.26)	3.90	(0.86)

Notes: ESCS is the *PISA index of economic, social and cultural status.*

High and Low ESCS correspond to the top and bottom thirds of ESCS within each country or economy.

Accounting for reading performance is done by assuming students have a score equal to that of the country average; see OECD (2010), *PISA 2009 Results: What Students Know and Can Do (Volume I)*, PISA, OECD Publishing, Tables I.2.3 and I.3.3.

Differences statistically significantly different from 0 (zero) and odds ratio (O.R.) statistically significantly different from 1 (one) at a 95% confidence level are highlighted in bold.

StatLink http://dx.doi.org/10.1787/888932733925

[Part 1/1]

Table B1.11 Socio-economic differences in expectations of completing, at most, upper secondary school

	Students who expect to complete, at most, an upper secondary school degree								Students who expect to complete, at most, an upper secondary school degree (after accounting for reading and mathematics performance)							
	High ESCS		Low ESCS		Difference (High - Low ESCS)		Odds ratio (High/Low ESCS)		High ESCS		Low ESCS		Adjusted difference (High - Low ESCS)		Odds ratio (High/Low ESCS)	
	%	S.E.	%	S.E.	Diff.	S.E.	O.R.	S.E.	%	S.E.	%	S.E.	Diff.	S.E.	O.R.	S.E.
Countries and economies																
Australia	10.0	(0.56)	32.2	(0.91)	**-22.2**	(1.03)	**0.23**	(0.02)	14.0	(0.48)	20.3	(0.56)	**-6.2**	(0.46)	**0.40**	(0.03)
Austria	38.5	(1.35)	64.5	(1.86)	**-25.9**	(1.91)	**0.35**	(0.03)	45.0	(1.32)	54.8	(1.26)	**-9.8**	(1.18)	**0.52**	(0.04)
Belgium (Flemish Community)	9.7	(0.80)	26.3	(1.36)	**-16.6**	(1.53)	**0.30**	(0.03)	13.4	(0.76)	16.5	(0.79)	**-3.0**	(0.56)	**0.54**	(0.06)
Hong Kong-China	11.6	(0.99)	35.8	(1.35)	**-24.2**	(1.53)	**0.23**	(0.02)	9.5	(0.76)	14.7	(0.70)	**-5.2**	(0.25)	**0.32**	(0.04)
Croatia	17.1	(1.10)	51.0	(1.52)	**-33.9**	(1.77)	**0.20**	(0.02)	14.9	(1.04)	24.6	(1.01)	**-9.7**	(0.61)	**0.32**	(0.03)
Hungary	13.0	(1.39)	43.2	(1.49)	**-30.3**	(1.95)	**0.20**	(0.03)	16.7	(1.54)	21.9	(1.51)	**-5.2**	(0.76)	**0.50**	(0.07)
Ireland	13.5	(0.96)	35.9	(1.57)	**-22.4**	(1.71)	**0.28**	(0.03)	15.9	(1.04)	21.8	(0.81)	**-5.9**	(0.73)	**0.47**	(0.05)
Iceland	13.0	(1.15)	41.1	(1.53)	**-28.1**	(1.94)	**0.21**	(0.03)	22.0	(0.84)	32.8	(1.24)	**-10.7**	(1.18)	**0.28**	(0.04)
Italy	21.7	(0.65)	55.6	(0.89)	**-33.8**	(1.00)	**0.22**	(0.01)	24.7	(0.63)	35.7	(0.56)	**-11.0**	(0.42)	**0.31**	(0.01)
Korea	1.2	(0.29)	10.7	(1.38)	**-9.5**	(1.42)	**0.10**	(0.03)	1.1	(0.23)	2.3	(0.26)	**-1.2**	(0.13)	**0.20**	(0.06)
Latvia	9.5	(1.20)	43.7	(2.00)	**-34.2**	(2.30)	**0.14**	(0.02)	11.3	(1.03)	20.1	(1.02)	**-8.8**	(0.75)	**0.24**	(0.04)
Macao-China	11.1	(0.61)	25.5	(1.03)	**-14.4**	(1.24)	**0.37**	(0.03)	7.2	(0.56)	11.1	(0.51)	**-3.9**	(0.22)	**0.41**	(0.04)
Mexico	9.6	(0.41)	29.9	(0.84)	**-20.3**	(0.99)	**0.25**	(0.02)	9.9	(0.52)	13.1	(0.42)	**-3.1**	(0.17)	**0.36**	(0.03)
New Zealand	10.4	(0.88)	34.7	(1.34)	**-24.3**	(1.61)	**0.22**	(0.02)	12.9	(0.92)	19.5	(0.71)	**-6.5**	(0.71)	**0.42**	(0.06)
Poland	8.3	(0.78)	46.2	(1.29)	**-37.9**	(1.40)	**0.11**	(0.01)	7.0	(0.77)	15.3	(0.87)	**-8.2**	(0.37)	**0.21**	(0.03)
Portugal	13.5	(1.06)	44.2	(1.39)	**-30.7**	(1.75)	**0.20**	(0.02)	16.3	(0.95)	23.7	(0.74)	**-7.4**	(0.48)	**0.30**	(0.03)
Singapore	0.8	(0.25)	4.0	(0.45)	**-3.2**	(0.49)	**0.20**	(0.06)	0.6	(0.19)	0.7	(0.17)	**-0.2**	(0.06)	**0.53**	(0.18)
Serbia	7.9	(0.79)	38.0	(1.25)	**-30.1**	(1.46)	**0.14**	(0.02)	8.0	(0.75)	15.5	(0.79)	**-7.5**	(0.36)	**0.22**	(0.03)
Slovak Republic	23.7	(1.13)	56.6	(1.67)	**-32.9**	(2.05)	**0.24**	(0.02)	27.1	(1.48)	36.3	(1.10)	**-9.2**	(1.19)	**0.46**	(0.05)
Slovenia	8.8	(0.69)	43.7	(1.44)	**-34.9**	(1.64)	**0.12**	(0.01)	11.9	(0.73)	21.3	(0.72)	**-9.4**	(0.52)	**0.24**	(0.03)
Trinidad and Tobago	8.2	(0.76)	21.2	(1.19)	**-13.0**	(1.61)	**0.33**	(0.05)	9.0	(0.95)	11.2	(0.63)	**-2.2**	(0.48)	**0.57**	(0.10)
Regions																
Italy: Abruzzo	21.3	(2.13)	53.3	(3.09)	**-31.9**	(3.20)	**0.24**	(0.04)	21.6	(2.01)	32.1	(2.01)	**-10.4**	(1.37)	**0.36**	(0.05)
Italy: Basilicata	17.8	(2.08)	49.2	(2.92)	**-31.4**	(3.10)	**0.22**	(0.04)	17.5	(2.48)	27.3	(2.14)	**-9.8**	(1.17)	**0.33**	(0.06)
Italy: Bolzano	42.1	(2.40)	75.6	(2.12)	**-33.4**	(3.29)	**0.24**	(0.04)	42.3	(2.58)	58.0	(1.43)	**-15.7**	(1.83)	**0.30**	(0.05)
Italy: Calabria	16.0	(2.20)	50.7	(2.12)	**-34.7**	(2.99)	**0.19**	(0.03)	16.5	(2.42)	26.3	(2.28)	**-9.8**	(0.89)	**0.28**	(0.05)
Italy: Campania	19.5	(2.39)	51.6	(2.21)	**-32.1**	(3.51)	**0.23**	(0.04)	20.3	(2.32)	29.3	(1.84)	**-9.0**	(0.82)	**0.37**	(0.07)
Italy: Emilia Romagna	18.0	(1.53)	57.0	(3.06)	**-39.1**	(3.32)	**0.16**	(0.03)	26.3	(2.04)	38.7	(2.11)	**-12.4**	(1.39)	**0.24**	(0.04)
Italy: Friuli Venezia Giulia	21.1	(2.47)	56.3	(3.01)	**-35.2**	(3.71)	**0.21**	(0.04)	22.4	(2.35)	36.0	(2.02)	**-13.5**	(1.49)	**0.30**	(0.06)
Italy: Lazio	19.8	(1.83)	46.2	(3.88)	**-26.4**	(4.26)	**0.29**	(0.05)	23.3	(1.72)	31.2	(1.90)	**-7.9**	(1.71)	**0.42**	(0.08)
Italy: Liguria	21.7	(2.31)	54.1	(3.67)	**-32.4**	(4.16)	**0.24**	(0.05)	26.3	(1.86)	38.2	(2.02)	**-11.9**	(1.19)	**0.31**	(0.05)
Italy: Lombardia	24.7	(2.46)	60.5	(2.84)	**-35.8**	(3.41)	**0.21**	(0.03)	28.4	(1.97)	40.4	(2.08)	**-12.0**	(1.40)	**0.35**	(0.06)
Italy: Marche	24.8	(2.05)	60.6	(2.57)	**-35.8**	(2.95)	**0.21**	(0.03)	25.9	(2.41)	39.4	(2.05)	**-13.4**	(1.52)	**0.28**	(0.04)
Italy: Molise	18.4	(1.95)	46.5	(3.18)	**-28.1**	(3.55)	**0.26**	(0.05)	21.1	(2.05)	28.3	(1.51)	**-7.2**	(1.48)	**0.40**	(0.08)
Italy: Piemonte	24.6	(2.07)	64.0	(2.83)	**-39.4**	(3.12)	**0.18**	(0.03)	26.5	(1.89)	41.8	(1.87)	**-15.3**	(1.61)	**0.27**	(0.04)
Italy: Puglia	23.7	(2.05)	59.6	(2.99)	**-36.0**	(3.48)	**0.21**	(0.03)	20.4	(2.44)	32.9	(2.00)	**-12.5**	(1.25)	**0.27**	(0.04)
Italy: Sardegna	20.2	(2.10)	49.8	(3.87)	**-29.6**	(4.20)	**0.26**	(0.05)	22.9	(2.26)	31.4	(1.75)	**-8.5**	(1.51)	**0.35**	(0.07)
Italy: Sicilia	16.0	(1.57)	49.5	(3.30)	**-33.5**	(3.60)	**0.19**	(0.03)	19.9	(2.07)	29.6	(1.58)	**-9.7**	(1.29)	**0.25**	(0.04)
Italy: Toscana	27.2	(2.07)	55.9	(2.53)	**-28.7**	(3.43)	**0.29**	(0.05)	28.8	(1.81)	42.1	(1.97)	**-13.3**	(1.56)	**0.39**	(0.06)
Italy: Trento	26.5	(2.33)	56.0	(2.60)	**-29.6**	(3.17)	**0.28**	(0.04)	29.2	(2.30)	39.3	(1.66)	**-10.1**	(1.69)	**0.43**	(0.07)
Italy: Umbria	20.3	(2.14)	54.7	(3.13)	**-34.4**	(3.81)	**0.21**	(0.04)	25.7	(2.10)	36.6	(1.93)	**-10.9**	(1.55)	**0.31**	(0.06)
Italy: Valle d'Aosta	27.2	(2.60)	60.9	(2.65)	**-33.7**	(3.83)	**0.24**	(0.04)	29.3	(2.51)	42.3	(1.73)	**-13.0**	(1.70)	**0.30**	(0.05)
Italy: Veneto	25.4	(3.50)	60.0	(2.78)	**-34.6**	(4.75)	**0.23**	(0.05)	26.3	(3.27)	39.4	(2.46)	**-13.0**	(1.77)	**0.30**	(0.06)
Mexico: Aguascalientes	7.0	(1.39)	27.8	(2.59)	**-20.8**	(2.95)	**0.20**	(0.05)	7.5	(1.39)	10.9	(1.27)	**-3.3**	(0.37)	**0.27**	(0.08)
Mexico: Baja California	12.0	(1.98)	23.5	(3.59)	**-11.5**	(3.42)	**0.45**	(0.10)	12.7	(2.31)	14.6	(1.77)	**-2.0**	(0.90)	**0.63**	(0.13)
Mexico: Baja California Sur	9.1	(1.87)	22.1	(2.13)	**-13.0**	(2.15)	**0.35**	(0.07)	9.9	(2.04)	12.8	(1.70)	**-2.8**	(0.56)	**0.43**	(0.12)
Mexico: Campeche	9.8	(1.77)	27.3	(2.61)	**-17.5**	(3.34)	**0.29**	(0.07)	9.9	(2.17)	12.9	(2.01)	**-3.0**	(0.44)	**0.40**	(0.12)
Mexico: Chihuahua	5.1	(1.44)	28.0	(3.50)	**-22.9**	(3.30)	**0.14**	(0.04)	6.7	(1.54)	9.4	(1.42)	**-2.8**	(0.47)	**0.28**	(0.10)
Mexico: Colima	11.0	(2.06)	27.3	(3.09)	**-16.3**	(4.06)	**0.33**	(0.10)	10.9	(1.74)	13.3	(1.32)	**-2.4**	(0.63)	**0.54**	(0.17)
Mexico: Coahuila	6.7	(1.38)	34.5	(3.15)	**-27.8**	(2.34)	**0.14**	(0.02)	7.5	(1.17)	12.1	(1.60)	**-4.6**	(0.56)	**0.19**	(0.03)
Mexico: Chiapas	18.0	(2.40)	27.8	(2.81)	**-9.8**	(2.79)	**0.57**	(0.09)	17.5	(3.01)	19.4	(2.48)	**-1.9**	(0.68)	**0.75**	(0.12)
Mexico: Distrito Federal	4.8	(2.35)	14.5	(3.40)	-9.7	(4.95)	**0.30**	(0.21)	4.9	(2.07)	6.2	(1.41)	-1.3	(0.77)	0.69	(0.45)
Mexico: Durango	13.0	(1.62)	34.4	(3.43)	**-21.3**	(3.75)	**0.29**	(0.06)	12.4	(1.73)	16.2	(1.78)	**-3.8**	(0.75)	**0.37**	(0.07)
Mexico: Guerrero	16.0	(2.69)	26.2	(2.59)	**-10.2**	(3.34)	**0.54**	(0.12)	14.4	(2.37)	17.2	(2.05)	**-2.8**	(0.63)	**0.65**	(0.17)
Mexico: Guanajuato	11.4	(1.48)	31.0	(3.48)	**-19.7**	(3.63)	**0.28**	(0.06)	11.1	(2.02)	14.9	(1.72)	**-3.8**	(0.58)	**0.38**	(0.10)
Mexico: Hidalgo	9.0	(1.95)	32.2	(4.18)	**-23.2**	(4.34)	**0.21**	(0.06)	7.4	(2.07)	10.7	(2.09)	**-3.2**	(0.43)	**0.31**	(0.11)
Mexico: Jalisco	10.2	(1.47)	28.9	(2.74)	**-18.6**	(2.97)	**0.28**	(0.06)	10.7	(1.77)	14.0	(1.50)	**-3.3**	(0.57)	**0.42**	(0.08)
Mexico: Michoacán	12.8	(1.58)	29.8	(2.71)	**-17.1**	(3.27)	**0.34**	(0.07)	16.5	(2.14)	18.6	(1.77)	**-2.1**	(0.78)	**0.59**	(0.13)
Mexico: Morelos	10.6	(1.90)	30.0	(3.18)	**-19.5**	(3.86)	**0.28**	(0.07)	10.9	(2.28)	14.4	(1.69)	**-3.4**	(0.89)	**0.37**	(0.10)
Mexico: Mexico	8.8	(2.00)	29.3	(2.65)	**-20.5**	(3.61)	**0.23**	(0.07)	7.9	(1.82)	10.9	(1.72)	**-2.9**	(0.38)	**0.32**	(0.09)
Mexico: Nayarit	13.4	(1.72)	24.4	(2.67)	**-11.0**	(2.76)	**0.48**	(0.09)	12.4	(1.52)	14.3	(1.16)	**-1.8**	(0.64)	**0.66**	(0.14)
Mexico: Nuevo León	8.9	(2.33)	34.3	(3.23)	**-25.3**	(4.24)	**0.19**	(0.06)	11.4	(2.74)	15.8	(2.09)	**-4.4**	(0.97)	**0.30**	(0.08)
Mexico: Oaxaca	11.5	(2.44)	34.7	(5.16)	**-23.2**	(5.63)	**0.24**	(0.08)	3.2	(1.40)	6.2	(1.83)	**-2.9**	(0.54)	**0.23**	(0.09)
Mexico: Puebla	8.1	(1.58)	28.1	(3.08)	**-20.0**	(3.80)	**0.22**	(0.07)	8.9	(1.78)	11.6	(1.45)	**-2.7**	(0.56)	**0.36**	(0.15)
Mexico: Quintana Roo	10.1	(2.43)	34.1	(2.36)	**-23.9**	(3.32)	**0.22**	(0.06)	9.2	(1.88)	13.0	(1.71)	**-3.7**	(0.44)	**0.31**	(0.10)
Mexico: Querétaro	7.0	(1.65)	33.9	(4.15)	**-26.9**	(4.07)	**0.15**	(0.04)	9.2	(2.20)	12.7	(2.21)	**-3.5**	(0.41)	**0.28**	(0.07)
Mexico: Sinaloa	12.8	(1.73)	26.0	(3.66)	**-13.2**	(3.49)	**0.42**	(0.08)	12.5	(1.34)	15.4	(1.35)	**-2.9**	(0.94)	**0.55**	(0.13)
Mexico: San Luis Potosí	14.9	(2.88)	34.9	(5.53)	**-20.0**	(6.37)	**0.33**	(0.11)	12.9	(3.34)	16.8	(2.77)	**-3.8**	(0.94)	**0.44**	(0.16)
Mexico: Sonora	10.6	(1.64)	28.1	(1.85)	**-17.4**	(2.15)	**0.30**	(0.05)	10.1	(1.72)	13.3	(1.33)	**-3.2**	(0.65)	**0.42**	(0.10)
Mexico: Tamaulipas	11.7	(1.28)	28.5	(2.81)	**-16.8**	(3.19)	**0.33**	(0.06)	9.4	(1.78)	12.9	(1.60)	**-3.5**	(0.59)	**0.46**	(0.10)
Mexico: Tabasco	19.8	(3.24)	35.6	(2.50)	**-15.8**	(4.13)	**0.45**	(0.10)	18.4	(3.15)	20.8	(2.35)	**-2.4**	(1.13)	**0.59**	(0.14)
Mexico: Tlaxcala	13.4	(2.33)	30.3	(3.41)	**-16.9**	(3.33)	**0.36**	(0.07)	12.1	(2.87)	15.2	(2.46)	**-3.1**	(0.57)	**0.47**	(0.10)
Mexico: Veracruz	7.2	(2.01)	34.2	(5.54)	**-26.9**	(6.36)	**0.15**	(0.06)	7.1	(2.90)	10.8	(2.80)	**-3.7**	(0.48)	**0.20**	(0.09)
Mexico: Yucatán	11.1	(1.84)	30.4	(1.97)	**-19.3**	(2.53)	**0.29**	(0.06)	12.7	(1.92)	15.4	(1.62)	**-2.7**	(0.44)	**0.44**	(0.11)
Mexico: Zacatecas	12.6	(1.90)	31.1	(3.69)	**-18.5**	(3.80)	**0.32**	(0.07)	10.5	(2.20)	14.4	(2.08)	**-3.9**	(0.62)	**0.37**	(0.09)

Notes: ESCS is the *PISA index of economic, social and cultural status.*
High and Low ESCS correspond to the top and bottom thirds of ESCS within each country or economy.
Accounting for reading performance is done by assuming students have a score equal to that of the country average; see OECD (2010), *PISA 2009 Results: What Students Know and Can Do (Volume I)*, PISA, OECD Publishing, Tables I.2.3 and I.3.3.
Differences statistically significantly different from 0 (zero) and odds ratio (O.R.) statistically significantly different from 1 (one) at a 95% confidence level are highlighted in bold.

StatLink http://dx.doi.org/10.1787/888932733944

[Part 1/1]

Table B1.12 Gender differences in expectations of completing a university degree

	Students who expect to complete a university degree								Students who expect to complete a university degree (after accounting for reading and mathematics performance)							
	Girls		Boys		Difference (Girls - Boys)		Odds ratio (Girls/Boys)		Girls		Boys		Adjusted difference (Girls - Boys)		Odds ratio (Girls/Boys)	
	%	S.E.	%	S.E.	Diff.	S.E.	O.R.	S.E.	%	S.E.	%	S.E.	Diff.	S.E.	O.R.	S.E.
Countries and economies																
Australia	67.9	(0.92)	54.0	(1.19)	**13.9**	(1.33)	**1.80**	(0.10)	70.4	(0.88)	54.6	(1.22)	**15.8**	(1.46)	**1.98**	(0.12)
Austria	29.8	(1.65)	26.3	(1.13)	3.5	(2.10)	1.19	(0.12)	23.1	(1.61)	17.3	(1.26)	**5.8**	(1.99)	**1.43**	(0.18)
Belgium (Flemish Community)	39.0	(1.43)	35.3	(1.61)	3.7	(2.25)	1.17	(0.11)	30.1	(1.80)	23.0	(1.76)	**7.1**	(2.06)	**1.44**	(0.16)
Hong Kong-China	47.0	(1.50)	47.3	(1.65)	-0.3	(2.39)	0.99	(0.09)	46.2	(1.75)	45.4	(1.33)	0.8	(2.32)	1.03	(0.10)
Croatia	58.1	(1.86)	41.0	(1.47)	**17.0**	(2.31)	**1.99**	(0.19)	51.7	(2.00)	42.3	(1.85)	**9.5**	(2.86)	**1.46**	(0.17)
Hungary	46.9	(1.87)	35.3	(1.86)	**11.6**	(2.30)	**1.62**	(0.16)	39.1	(1.92)	30.4	(1.81)	**8.8**	(2.25)	**1.47**	(0.15)
Ireland	60.2	(1.10)	50.3	(1.64)	**9.9**	(1.82)	**1.49**	(0.11)	59.1	(1.47)	49.9	(1.80)	**9.2**	(2.26)	**1.45**	(0.13)
Iceland	49.7	(1.01)	39.5	(1.00)	**10.2**	(1.30)	**1.51**	(0.08)	46.6	(1.18)	38.8	(1.19)	**7.8**	(1.73)	**1.38**	(0.10)
Italy	48.3	(0.92)	33.7	(0.86)	**14.6**	(1.30)	**1.84**	(0.10)	41.1	(0.92)	34.2	(0.92)	**6.9**	(1.41)	**1.34**	(0.08)
Korea	83.8	(1.64)	78.2	(1.90)	**5.6**	(2.64)	1.44	(0.25)	86.6	(1.30)	85.9	(1.28)	0.7	(2.10)	1.06	(0.19)
Latvia	29.8	(1.48)	20.9	(1.29)	**9.0**	(1.56)	**1.61**	(0.13)	22.8	(1.33)	20.0	(1.48)	2.8	(1.95)	1.18	(0.14)
Macao-China	37.4	(0.81)	33.1	(0.83)	**4.2**	(1.13)	**1.20**	(0.06)	32.2	(0.91)	33.3	(0.99)	-1.1	(1.36)	0.95	(0.06)
Mexico	63.1	(0.73)	48.4	(0.96)	**14.6**	(0.77)	**1.82**	(0.06)	64.4	(0.70)	47.4	(0.79)	**17.0**	(0.87)	**2.01**	(0.07)
New Zealand	60.2	(0.98)	44.9	(1.05)	**15.3**	(1.36)	**1.85**	(0.10)	56.0	(1.24)	47.8	(1.45)	**8.2**	(1.99)	**1.39**	(0.11)
Poland	50.6	(1.26)	32.2	(1.24)	**18.4**	(1.48)	**2.15**	(0.14)	49.3	(1.66)	27.4	(1.38)	**22.0**	(2.07)	**2.58**	(0.24)
Portugal	60.1	(1.67)	43.5	(1.63)	**16.6**	(1.22)	**1.96**	(0.10)	60.3	(1.71)	42.4	(1.49)	**18.0**	(2.02)	**2.07**	(0.17)
Singapore	74.1	(0.89)	66.3	(0.87)	**7.8**	(1.32)	**1.46**	(0.09)	75.6	(1.00)	71.7	(1.03)	**3.9**	(1.56)	**1.22**	(0.10)
Serbia	62.7	(1.52)	47.5	(1.64)	**15.2**	(1.72)	**1.86**	(0.13)	65.5	(1.56)	46.6	(1.85)	**18.9**	(2.48)	**2.18**	(0.23)
Slovak Republic	53.4	(1.41)	37.4	(1.23)	**16.0**	(1.76)	**1.92**	(0.14)	48.8	(1.72)	35.4	(2.26)	**13.4**	(3.06)	**1.74**	(0.23)
Slovenia	38.8	(1.01)	31.6	(0.99)	**7.2**	(1.38)	**1.37**	(0.08)	32.4	(1.40)	29.9	(1.33)	2.4	(2.16)	1.12	(0.11)
Trinidad and Tobago	78.3	(0.83)	59.9	(1.05)	**18.5**	(1.20)	**2.42**	(0.14)	77.6	(1.01)	62.9	(1.14)	**14.7**	(1.46)	**2.04**	(0.15)
Regions																
Italy: Abruzzo	53.1	(3.33)	36.4	(2.55)	**16.7**	(3.75)	**1.98**	(0.31)	43.8	(3.57)	38.4	(2.55)	5.3	(3.76)	1.25	(0.19)
Italy: Basilicata	56.2	(2.15)	36.1	(2.29)	**20.2**	(3.16)	**2.28**	(0.30)	54.4	(2.82)	33.9	(2.61)	**20.5**	(3.74)	**2.32**	(0.37)
Italy: Bolzano	25.8	(1.31)	20.9	(1.07)	**4.9**	(1.61)	**1.32**	(0.12)	19.3	(1.47)	18.0	(1.65)	1.3	(2.30)	1.09	(0.17)
Italy: Calabria	55.9	(3.07)	36.8	(3.00)	**19.1**	(3.46)	**2.18**	(0.32)	46.6	(3.04)	40.9	(3.01)	5.7	(3.36)	1.26	(0.17)
Italy: Campania	55.0	(3.70)	33.7	(3.62)	**21.3**	(4.38)	2.40	(0.45)	48.8	(3.70)	32.0	(3.19)	**16.8**	(5.03)	2.02	(0.44)
Italy: Emilia Romagna	42.2	(2.90)	38.0	(1.97)	4.2	(2.83)	1.19	(0.14)	38.7	(3.51)	31.6	(2.77)	7.0	(4.22)	1.36	(0.25)
Italy: Friuli Venezia Giulia	49.7	(2.50)	29.9	(2.39)	**19.8**	(3.28)	**2.32**	(0.33)	38.3	(2.74)	29.2	(2.75)	**9.0**	(3.43)	1.50	(0.23)
Italy: Lazio	59.6	(1.74)	39.0	(2.72)	**20.6**	(2.53)	**2.30**	(0.25)	54.3	(2.64)	41.4	(3.49)	**12.9**	(3.52)	**1.68**	(0.24)
Italy: Liguria	45.8	(3.18)	34.4	(3.81)	**11.4**	(4.59)	1.61	(0.32)	40.2	(3.30)	30.9	(3.09)	**9.3**	(4.63)	1.50	(0.31)
Italy: Lombardia	43.2	(3.83)	33.3	(2.75)	9.9	(5.07)	1.52	(0.33)	34.0	(4.19)	31.6	(2.55)	2.3	(5.15)	1.11	(0.26)
Italy: Marche	45.4	(2.29)	30.3	(2.53)	**15.2**	(3.76)	**1.92**	(0.32)	35.2	(3.59)	30.6	(2.34)	4.6	(4.93)	1.23	(0.27)
Italy: Molise	52.4	(2.22)	35.0	(1.93)	**17.5**	(3.11)	**2.05**	(0.27)	49.6	(2.95)	31.4	(2.52)	**18.2**	(4.54)	2.15	(0.42)
Italy: Piemonte	42.6	(2.98)	31.8	(3.03)	**10.8**	(4.17)	1.59	(0.29)	37.7	(3.30)	28.5	(2.73)	**9.2**	(4.34)	1.52	(0.30)
Italy: Puglia	50.7	(3.31)	31.5	(2.61)	**19.2**	(3.54)	**2.23**	(0.33)	39.4	(3.93)	34.6	(2.53)	4.8	(4.68)	1.23	(0.24)
Italy: Sardegna	49.8	(2.87)	36.0	(2.97)	**13.8**	(3.33)	**1.77**	(0.24)	43.9	(2.34)	34.8	(3.33)	**9.1**	(3.97)	1.47	(0.25)
Italy: Sicilia	48.0	(3.19)	36.0	(2.58)	**12.0**	(3.69)	**1.64**	(0.25)	41.4	(3.50)	34.4	(3.39)	7.0	(4.68)	1.35	(0.27)
Italy: Toscana	50.8	(2.14)	31.1	(2.60)	**19.7**	(3.52)	**2.29**	(0.36)	43.8	(2.10)	30.8	(3.33)	**13.0**	(3.87)	1.75	(0.31)
Italy: Trento	43.5	(2.70)	27.7	(1.79)	**15.8**	(3.78)	**2.01**	(0.33)	32.2	(2.94)	25.5	(2.11)	6.8	(3.82)	1.39	(0.26)
Italy: Umbria	48.1	(2.07)	35.6	(2.17)	**12.5**	(2.86)	**1.68**	(0.20)	40.4	(2.93)	34.5	(3.11)	5.9	(4.05)	1.29	(0.23)
Italy: Valle d'Aosta	37.8	(2.36)	32.4	(1.73)	**5.5**	(2.68)	1.27	(0.15)	33.8	(3.21)	28.3	(2.39)	5.5	(4.16)	1.29	(0.25)
Italy: Veneto	41.0	(3.18)	28.1	(2.87)	**12.9**	(4.63)	1.78	(0.37)	31.2	(2.92)	28.2	(2.74)	3.0	(3.50)	1.16	(0.19)
Mexico: Aguascalientes	62.0	(2.95)	50.5	(2.92)	**11.5**	(2.79)	**1.60**	(0.18)	62.0	(2.29)	51.7	(3.04)	**10.3**	(3.65)	1.52	(0.23)
Mexico: Baja California	60.6	(2.88)	42.6	(2.78)	**18.0**	(2.91)	**2.07**	(0.25)	61.8	(4.27)	41.3	(3.09)	**20.6**	(5.66)	2.30	(0.55)
Mexico: Baja California Sur	66.8	(3.59)	49.5	(3.09)	**17.3**	(2.40)	**2.05**	(0.22)	67.6	(3.03)	49.1	(2.97)	**18.5**	(3.06)	**2.16**	(0.29)
Mexico: Campeche	65.9	(2.29)	55.6	(3.69)	**10.3**	(3.45)	**1.55**	(0.22)	69.2	(3.29)	55.1	(2.87)	**14.1**	(4.07)	1.83	(0.33)
Mexico: Chihuahua	73.3	(3.07)	56.5	(3.37)	**16.8**	(3.60)	**2.12**	(0.35)	75.7	(2.81)	57.4	(3.28)	**18.3**	(4.71)	2.31	(0.52)
Mexico: Colima	71.3	(3.37)	53.3	(2.67)	**18.0**	(4.14)	2.18	(0.41)	73.9	(2.85)	53.4	(3.07)	**20.6**	(4.53)	2.48	(0.51)
Mexico: Coahuila	66.4	(3.57)	44.7	(3.57)	**21.7**	(4.40)	2.45	(0.46)	67.2	(4.98)	41.8	(3.18)	**25.4**	(6.18)	2.86	(0.78)
Mexico: Chiapas	58.7	(3.40)	46.9	(2.71)	**11.8**	(2.93)	**1.61**	(0.19)	53.1	(2.77)	49.3	(2.98)	3.8	(3.59)	1.16	(0.17)
Mexico: Distrito Federal	74.3	(2.66)	67.6	(2.89)	6.7	(3.63)	1.38	(0.25)	78.2	(2.37)	68.9	(2.46)	**9.3**	(4.22)	1.62	(0.36)
Mexico: Durango	61.2	(2.54)	43.4	(2.85)	**17.9**	(2.76)	**2.06**	(0.24)	61.9	(2.63)	41.3	(3.58)	**20.6**	(3.62)	**2.31**	(0.35)
Mexico: Guerrero	51.4	(4.16)	40.8	(3.30)	**10.6**	(3.99)	1.53	(0.25)	49.2	(6.06)	41.6	(3.45)	7.6	(6.42)	1.36	(0.35)
Mexico: Guanajuato	49.1	(2.64)	39.8	(2.77)	**9.2**	(2.32)	**1.45**	(0.14)	46.9	(2.97)	36.1	(3.18)	**10.7**	(3.86)	1.56	(0.25)
Mexico: Hidalgo	65.8	(3.37)	48.4	(3.62)	**17.4**	(3.50)	**2.05**	(0.30)	66.7	(3.62)	48.0	(4.49)	**18.7**	(4.93)	2.17	(0.45)
Mexico: Jalisco	66.2	(2.32)	51.1	(2.20)	**15.2**	(2.73)	**1.88**	(0.22)	66.2	(2.35)	52.4	(2.60)	**13.8**	(3.89)	**1.78**	(0.29)
Mexico: Michoacán	59.6	(3.02)	47.8	(2.18)	**11.8**	(3.00)	**1.61**	(0.20)	62.0	(3.02)	45.3	(2.66)	**16.8**	(3.63)	**1.98**	(0.30)
Mexico: Morelos	60.3	(3.76)	45.2	(3.81)	**15.1**	(4.42)	1.84	(0.33)	62.8	(3.79)	42.0	(2.85)	**20.8**	(5.46)	2.33	(0.54)
Mexico: Mexico	68.4	(2.53)	46.9	(3.42)	**21.5**	(3.55)	**2.45**	(0.37)	70.3	(1.78)	45.6	(2.46)	**24.8**	(2.79)	**2.83**	(0.34)
Mexico: Nayarit	66.7	(3.16)	49.1	(2.93)	**17.6**	(5.04)	2.08	(0.45)	66.6	(4.16)	49.7	(3.62)	**16.9**	(6.86)	2.02	(0.59)
Mexico: Nuevo León	61.5	(4.68)	52.2	(9.26)	9.4	(8.88)	1.47	(0.53)	69.6	(4.46)	48.4	(4.50)	**21.3**	(4.79)	2.45	(0.51)
Mexico: Oaxaca	61.8	(4.66)	46.0	(5.21)	**15.7**	(3.87)	**1.89**	(0.30)	60.5	(5.54)	46.9	(6.60)	**13.5**	(5.30)	1.73	(0.37)
Mexico: Puebla	66.6	(3.62)	53.0	(4.37)	**13.7**	(3.50)	**1.77**	(0.26)	70.4	(2.79)	50.3	(4.67)	**20.1**	(4.75)	2.35	(0.47)
Mexico: Quintana Roo	59.9	(3.91)	49.3	(3.67)	**10.6**	(3.19)	**1.53**	(0.20)	62.3	(3.48)	47.4	(3.19)	**14.9**	(4.63)	1.83	(0.35)
Mexico: Querétaro	58.5	(3.55)	46.2	(5.19)	**12.3**	(3.47)	**1.64**	(0.23)	55.4	(3.13)	43.5	(4.32)	**11.9**	(3.95)	1.61	(0.26)
Mexico: Sinaloa	64.9	(2.50)	50.5	(2.69)	**14.3**	(2.91)	**1.81**	(0.22)	65.7	(3.70)	51.7	(2.34)	**14.0**	(3.55)	**1.79**	(0.28)
Mexico: San Luis Potosí	45.9	(4.29)	38.0	(3.26)	8.0	(4.35)	1.39	(0.25)	44.1	(3.81)	34.8	(4.49)	9.2	(5.52)	1.47	(0.35)
Mexico: Sonora	66.3	(2.56)	47.0	(2.79)	**19.2**	(2.68)	**2.21**	(0.25)	64.9	(2.42)	48.7	(2.39)	**16.3**	(2.73)	**1.95**	(0.23)
Mexico: Tamaulipas	67.0	(3.05)	41.1	(3.57)	**26.0**	(3.07)	**2.92**	(0.38)	68.8	(3.70)	37.8	(3.36)	**31.0**	(3.70)	**3.63**	(0.61)
Mexico: Tabasco	54.9	(2.45)	41.2	(2.63)	**13.7**	(2.77)	**1.74**	(0.20)	56.8	(2.87)	38.7	(2.17)	**18.1**	(3.61)	**2.08**	(0.31)
Mexico: Tlaxcala	61.1	(3.48)	44.0	(3.45)	**17.1**	(3.20)	**2.00**	(0.27)	62.6	(3.33)	40.7	(3.35)	**21.8**	(3.80)	**2.43**	(0.39)
Mexico: Veracruz	58.7	(3.53)	43.3	(3.14)	**15.4**	(2.38)	**1.86**	(0.18)	62.4	(3.34)	38.9	(2.33)	**23.5**	(2.78)	**2.61**	(0.31)
Mexico: Yucatán	58.9	(2.84)	46.4	(3.46)	**12.5**	(3.60)	**1.66**	(0.24)	60.7	(3.04)	44.4	(3.11)	**16.3**	(4.59)	1.94	(0.37)
Mexico: Zacatecas	56.0	(3.09)	39.4	(3.49)	**16.7**	(4.98)	1.96	(0.40)	58.3	(3.53)	35.7	(3.91)	**22.6**	(5.76)	2.52	(0.62)

Notes: Accounting for reading performance is done by assuming students have a score equal to that of the country average; see OECD (2010), *PISA 2009 Results: What Students Know and Can Do (Volume I)*, PISA, OECD Publishing, Tables I.2.3 and I.3.3.
Differences statistically significantly different from 0 (zero) and odds ratio (O.R.) statistically significantly different from 1 (one) at a 95% confidence level are highlighted in bold.

StatLink http://dx.doi.org/10.1787/888932733963

[Part 1/1]

Table B1.13 Gender differences in expectations of completing, at most, upper secondary school

	Students who expect to complete, at most, an upper secondary school degree								Students who expect to complete, at most, an upper secondary school degree (after accounting for reading and mathematics performance)							
	Girls		Boys		Difference (Girls - Boys)		Odds ratio (Girls/Boys)		Girls		Boys		Adjusted difference (Girls - Boys)		Odds ratio (Girls/Boys)	
	%	S.E.	%	S.E.	Diff.	S.E.	O.R.	S.E.	%	S.E.	%	S.E.	Diff.	S.E.	O.R.	S.E.
Countries and economies																
Australia	16.9	(0.65)	25.7	(0.89)	**-8.8**	(1.06)	**0.59**	(0.04)	15.5	(0.53)	21.8	(0.85)	**-6.3**	(1.00)	**0.66**	(0.04)
Austria	53.7	(1.97)	52.3	(1.06)	1.3	(2.20)	1.06	(0.09)	53.6	(2.05)	54.7	(1.27)	-1.2	(2.47)	0.95	(0.09)
Belgium (Flemish Community)	13.3	(0.80)	22.6	(1.20)	**-9.3**	(1.45)	**0.53**	(0.05)	11.4	(0.87)	20.9	(1.39)	**-9.5**	(1.77)	**0.49**	(0.06)
Hong Kong-China	21.9	(0.99)	26.1	(1.32)	**-4.2**	(1.68)	**0.79**	(0.07)	19.5	(1.06)	23.5	(1.18)	**-4.0**	(1.62)	**0.79**	(0.08)
Croatia	24.1	(1.55)	41.9	(1.32)	**-17.8**	(2.02)	**0.44**	(0.04)	20.2	(1.42)	35.1	(1.68)	**-14.9**	(2.31)	**0.47**	(0.06)
Hungary	22.3	(1.44)	32.9	(1.50)	**-10.6**	(1.73)	**0.59**	(0.05)	19.4	(1.78)	27.5	(1.84)	**-8.1**	(1.79)	**0.63**	(0.07)
Ireland	22.1	(0.90)	25.9	(1.32)	**-3.7**	(1.58)	**0.81**	(0.07)	20.6	(1.21)	23.6	(1.39)	-3.0	(2.02)	0.84	(0.10)
Iceland	24.7	(1.07)	29.8	(1.07)	**-5.1**	(1.38)	**0.77**	(0.05)	25.0	(1.17)	26.3	(1.21)	-1.3	(1.74)	0.93	(0.09)
Italy	32.1	(0.66)	44.8	(0.84)	**-12.7**	(1.04)	**0.58**	(0.03)	34.1	(0.74)	41.6	(0.93)	**-7.6**	(1.29)	**0.72**	(0.04)
Korea	4.0	(0.55)	6.2	(1.01)	-2.2	(1.13)	**0.63**	(0.14)	2.5	(0.34)	3.4	(0.46)	-0.9	(0.59)	**0.74**	(0.15)
Latvia	21.1	(1.47)	32.5	(1.61)	**-11.4**	(1.78)	**0.55**	(0.05)	17.7	(1.56)	28.8	(1.80)	**-11.1**	(2.40)	**0.53**	(0.07)
Macao-China	13.2	(0.69)	22.6	(0.71)	**-9.4**	(0.92)	**0.52**	(0.04)	11.8	(0.68)	19.5	(0.84)	**-7.8**	(1.07)	**0.55**	(0.05)
Mexico	17.2	(0.49)	23.2	(0.59)	**-6.1**	(0.62)	**0.68**	(0.03)	15.0	(0.47)	22.7	(0.62)	**-7.7**	(0.72)	**0.60**	(0.03)
New Zealand	19.9	(0.78)	25.0	(1.15)	**-5.1**	(1.34)	**0.74**	(0.06)	19.6	(0.89)	19.3	(1.18)	0.3	(1.55)	1.02	(0.10)
Poland	19.7	(1.05)	36.1	(1.27)	**-16.4**	(1.47)	**0.43**	(0.03)	14.5	(1.00)	28.3	(1.49)	**-13.9**	(1.84)	**0.43**	(0.05)
Portugal	25.8	(1.23)	33.3	(1.00)	**-7.6**	(1.24)	**0.69**	(0.04)	24.9	(1.21)	30.6	(0.99)	**-5.7**	(1.61)	**0.75**	(0.06)
Singapore	2.0	(0.30)	2.3	(0.30)	-0.4	(0.39)	0.84	(0.16)	1.0	(0.19)	0.7	(0.18)	0.2	(0.21)	1.34	(0.34)
Serbia	15.8	(1.27)	29.1	(1.21)	**-13.3**	(1.50)	**0.46**	(0.04)	12.0	(1.04)	21.8	(1.01)	**-9.7**	(1.43)	**0.49**	(0.06)
Slovak Republic	32.7	(1.43)	46.6	(1.29)	**-13.9**	(2.03)	**0.56**	(0.05)	31.7	(1.56)	43.6	(1.98)	**-11.9**	(2.79)	**0.60**	(0.07)
Slovenia	23.5	(0.78)	30.2	(0.92)	**-6.7**	(1.26)	**0.71**	(0.05)	22.3	(1.07)	21.9	(1.17)	0.3	(1.81)	1.02	(0.11)
Trinidad and Tobago	9.8	(0.59)	20.7	(0.90)	**-10.9**	(1.05)	**0.41**	(0.03)	8.4	(0.60)	17.9	(1.03)	**-9.5**	(1.18)	**0.42**	(0.04)
Regions																
Italy: Abruzzo	28.7	(3.26)	40.5	(2.89)	**-11.8**	(4.01)	**0.59**	(0.11)	28.2	(2.83)	38.0	(2.56)	**-9.8**	(3.41)	**0.64**	(0.10)
Italy: Basilicata	25.9	(2.76)	40.8	(2.88)	**-14.9**	(3.15)	**0.51**	(0.08)	23.4	(2.49)	39.5	(2.90)	**-16.1**	(3.63)	**0.47**	(0.08)
Italy: Bolzano	57.6	(1.64)	61.9	(1.39)	**-4.3**	(1.97)	**0.84**	(0.07)	58.3	(1.97)	63.5	(1.80)	-5.2	(2.85)	**0.80**	(0.10)
Italy: Calabria	26.6	(2.78)	39.7	(2.33)	**-13.1**	(2.63)	**0.55**	(0.07)	26.6	(2.51)	35.1	(2.97)	**-8.5**	(2.89)	**0.67**	(0.09)
Italy: Campania	26.8	(2.30)	41.8	(2.82)	**-15.1**	(3.58)	**0.51**	(0.08)	27.9	(2.64)	38.2	(2.30)	**-10.4**	(3.78)	**0.62**	(0.11)
Italy: Emilia Romagna	35.1	(2.74)	43.6	(1.97)	**-8.5**	(2.37)	**0.70**	(0.07)	32.0	(2.64)	45.6	(2.44)	**-13.6**	(2.88)	**0.56**	(0.07)
Italy: Friuli Venezia Giulia	29.7	(2.71)	46.9	(2.53)	**-17.3**	(2.66)	**0.48**	(0.06)	32.9	(2.79)	42.2	(2.50)	**-9.2**	(3.12)	**0.67**	(0.09)
Italy: Lazio	23.8	(2.00)	39.9	(2.03)	**-16.1**	(2.74)	**0.47**	(0.06)	23.9	(2.09)	36.6	(2.47)	**-12.7**	(3.32)	**0.54**	(0.09)
Italy: Liguria	36.1	(3.24)	42.0	(3.27)	-5.9	(3.91)	0.78	(0.13)	35.5	(3.17)	41.3	(3.02)	-5.8	(4.66)	0.78	(0.15)
Italy: Lombardia	35.3	(2.69)	47.8	(3.12)	**-12.4**	(4.39)	**0.60**	(0.11)	37.8	(2.98)	44.2	(3.25)	-6.4	(4.53)	0.77	(0.14)
Italy: Marche	36.3	(1.93)	47.2	(1.91)	**-10.9**	(2.63)	**0.64**	(0.07)	38.2	(2.61)	44.8	(2.46)	**-6.6**	(3.31)	**0.76**	(0.10)
Italy: Molise	25.8	(1.83)	39.1	(1.90)	**-13.4**	(2.58)	**0.54**	(0.07)	24.0	(2.21)	35.7	(2.46)	**-11.7**	(3.59)	**0.57**	(0.10)
Italy: Piemonte	40.3	(2.87)	49.8	(2.86)	**-9.5**	(3.42)	**0.68**	(0.09)	39.9	(3.03)	49.9	(2.33)	**-10.1**	(3.35)	**0.67**	(0.09)
Italy: Puglia	34.1	(2.55)	48.4	(2.87)	**-14.3**	(3.18)	**0.55**	(0.07)	39.6	(3.10)	40.7	(2.90)	-1.1	(4.26)	0.95	(0.17)
Italy: Sardegna	31.6	(2.31)	41.0	(2.73)	**-9.4**	(2.95)	**0.66**	(0.08)	33.4	(2.13)	36.0	(2.98)	-2.7	(3.39)	0.89	(0.13)
Italy: Sicilia	29.8	(2.36)	38.8	(2.04)	**-9.0**	(3.25)	**0.67**	(0.10)	31.9	(2.74)	35.1	(3.38)	-3.1	(4.92)	0.87	(0.19)
Italy: Toscana	33.0	(2.57)	50.1	(2.47)	**-17.1**	(3.76)	**0.49**	(0.08)	36.8	(2.84)	46.2	(3.20)	**-9.4**	(4.51)	**0.68**	(0.13)
Italy: Trento	35.8	(2.91)	47.1	(2.52)	**-11.3**	(4.34)	**0.63**	(0.11)	39.3	(2.87)	42.7	(2.72)	-3.4	(4.44)	0.87	(0.16)
Italy: Umbria	31.4	(2.28)	43.4	(2.50)	**-11.9**	(3.15)	**0.60**	(0.08)	32.4	(2.33)	40.6	(2.77)	**-8.2**	(3.41)	**0.70**	(0.10)
Italy: Valle d'Aosta	41.5	(2.04)	48.1	(2.11)	**-6.6**	(2.90)	**0.77**	(0.09)	39.3	(2.46)	50.0	(2.67)	**-10.7**	(4.01)	**0.65**	(0.11)
Italy: Veneto	33.0	(2.19)	50.7	(3.21)	**-17.7**	(3.81)	**0.48**	(0.08)	33.0	(2.37)	49.6	(3.21)	**-16.6**	(3.44)	**0.50**	(0.07)
Mexico: Aguascalientes	16.1	(1.95)	19.4	(1.93)	-3.3	(2.19)	0.80	(0.12)	14.6	(1.99)	17.6	(2.03)	-3.0	(3.00)	0.80	(0.18)
Mexico: Baja California	15.6	(1.48)	22.7	(2.96)	**-7.1**	(2.82)	**0.63**	(0.11)	13.9	(2.03)	20.5	(2.59)	**-6.6**	(3.07)	**0.63**	(0.14)
Mexico: Baja California Sur	12.8	(1.83)	21.8	(2.32)	**-9.1**	(2.83)	**0.52**	(0.11)	11.3	(1.76)	21.8	(2.65)	**-10.5**	(3.39)	**0.46**	(0.12)
Mexico: Campeche	17.9	(1.84)	22.4	(2.54)	-4.5	(2.48)	**0.75**	(0.11)	16.0	(1.88)	21.8	(2.47)	**-5.8**	(2.56)	**0.68**	(0.11)
Mexico: Chihuahua	13.2	(2.12)	19.1	(3.32)	-5.8	(3.61)	**0.65**	(0.17)	9.8	(1.46)	16.9	(2.97)	**-7.1**	(3.53)	**0.54**	(0.16)
Mexico: Colima	13.8	(1.93)	24.6	(2.34)	**-10.8**	(3.01)	**0.49**	(0.10)	9.5	(1.49)	24.6	(2.46)	**-15.1**	(3.22)	**0.32**	(0.08)
Mexico: Coahuila	17.9	(2.66)	23.1	(2.39)	**-5.2**	(1.96)	**0.73**	(0.09)	15.8	(2.60)	23.6	(2.95)	**-7.7**	(2.51)	**0.61**	(0.10)
Mexico: Chiapas	23.2	(2.34)	24.7	(2.43)	-1.5	(3.50)	0.92	(0.18)	23.2	(2.84)	24.1	(2.89)	-0.9	(4.74)	0.95	(0.25)
Mexico: Distrito Federal	7.4	(0.93)	12.0	(1.39)	**-4.6**	(1.66)	**0.59**	(0.11)	4.2	(0.67)	10.7	(1.53)	**-6.5**	(1.54)	**0.37**	(0.08)
Mexico: Durango	20.5	(1.99)	27.0	(3.90)	-6.5	(3.46)	**0.70**	(0.12)	17.8	(2.09)	28.4	(4.19)	**-10.6**	(3.62)	**0.55**	(0.10)
Mexico: Guerrero	19.7	(2.44)	27.1	(2.77)	**-7.5**	(3.62)	**0.66**	(0.14)	18.5	(2.78)	27.8	(3.19)	**-9.3**	(4.20)	**0.59**	(0.14)
Mexico: Guanajuato	20.5	(2.12)	27.3	(2.21)	**-6.8**	(2.38)	**0.69**	(0.09)	16.6	(1.94)	29.6	(2.28)	**-13.0**	(2.53)	**0.47**	(0.07)
Mexico: Hidalgo	18.9	(2.41)	22.8	(2.52)	**-3.9**	(1.75)	**0.79**	(0.08)	16.9	(1.96)	22.3	(3.02)	**-5.4**	(2.26)	**0.71**	(0.09)
Mexico: Jalisco	16.8	(1.86)	22.9	(2.70)	**-6.1**	(3.13)	**0.68**	(0.13)	14.8	(1.48)	21.4	(2.12)	**-6.6**	(2.46)	**0.64**	(0.10)
Mexico: Michoacán	22.0	(2.44)	25.1	(3.21)	-3.1	(4.43)	0.84	(0.21)	18.5	(2.32)	24.9	(3.23)	-6.4	(4.36)	**0.69**	(0.18)
Mexico: Morelos	19.9	(3.20)	25.9	(3.37)	-6.0	(5.28)	0.71	(0.22)	17.0	(2.69)	25.6	(3.60)	-8.6	(5.54)	**0.60**	(0.20)
Mexico: Mexico	13.7	(1.75)	22.9	(2.31)	**-9.3**	(2.54)	**0.53**	(0.09)	10.3	(1.31)	23.5	(2.29)	**-13.3**	(2.19)	**0.37**	(0.06)
Mexico: Nayarit	13.2	(1.59)	23.1	(1.80)	**-9.8**	(2.34)	**0.51**	(0.09)	12.6	(2.18)	21.4	(2.25)	**-8.8**	(3.72)	**0.53**	(0.15)
Mexico: Nuevo León	18.6	(2.35)	24.3	(5.24)	-5.7	(5.33)	0.71	(0.21)	14.0	(2.22)	23.2	(3.32)	**-9.2**	(3.50)	**0.54**	(0.12)
Mexico: Oaxaca	20.9	(4.73)	25.9	(2.21)	-5.0	(4.34)	0.76	(0.20)	20.6	(5.47)	25.4	(2.85)	-4.8	(4.21)	0.76	(0.20)
Mexico: Puebla	15.8	(2.34)	21.2	(3.05)	**-5.4**	(2.54)	**0.70**	(0.11)	13.0	(1.91)	20.8	(3.22)	**-7.8**	(2.92)	**0.57**	(0.11)
Mexico: Quintana Roo	20.6	(2.76)	21.0	(1.95)	-0.3	(2.10)	0.98	(0.13)	18.2	(2.62)	19.9	(1.63)	-1.7	(2.70)	0.89	(0.16)
Mexico: Querétaro	19.3	(2.20)	24.7	(3.80)	**-5.5**	(2.64)	**0.73**	(0.10)	19.4	(1.75)	22.5	(3.33)	-3.1	(2.54)	0.83	(0.12)
Mexico: Sinaloa	15.5	(2.04)	25.0	(3.33)	**-9.5**	(2.44)	**0.55**	(0.07)	14.6	(2.64)	24.6	(3.24)	**-10.0**	(2.55)	**0.52**	(0.09)
Mexico: San Luis Potosí	25.1	(3.52)	26.9	(2.57)	-1.8	(3.61)	0.91	(0.17)	24.4	(3.39)	26.4	(2.92)	-2.0	(4.01)	0.90	(0.19)
Mexico: Sonora	17.9	(1.68)	22.8	(2.02)	**-4.8**	(2.28)	**0.74**	(0.10)	16.9	(1.72)	20.1	(1.81)	-3.2	(2.28)	0.81	(0.12)
Mexico: Tamaulipas	14.2	(1.65)	25.9	(2.95)	**-11.6**	(2.79)	**0.47**	(0.08)	10.8	(1.37)	27.8	(3.45)	**-16.9**	(3.59)	**0.32**	(0.07)
Mexico: Tabasco	25.0	(1.87)	28.4	(2.56)	-3.3	(2.54)	0.84	(0.11)	21.6	(2.69)	28.3	(2.60)	**-6.7**	(3.37)	**0.70**	(0.13)
Mexico: Tlaxcala	18.7	(2.39)	27.3	(2.24)	**-8.6**	(2.26)	**0.61**	(0.08)	17.3	(1.91)	25.4	(2.44)	**-8.0**	(2.76)	**0.62**	(0.10)
Mexico: Veracruz	19.7	(2.36)	27.2	(2.85)	**-7.5**	(1.71)	**0.66**	(0.06)	18.5	(2.33)	25.8	(2.87)	**-7.3**	(2.98)	**0.65**	(0.11)
Mexico: Yucatán	21.3	(1.89)	23.5	(2.08)	-2.2	(2.94)	0.88	(0.15)	19.4	(1.82)	22.3	(2.07)	-2.9	(3.11)	0.84	(0.16)
Mexico: Zacatecas	23.8	(3.07)	24.7	(3.58)	-1.0	(4.43)	0.95	(0.23)	20.6	(2.59)	26.9	(3.66)	-6.3	(3.99)	**0.71**	(0.15)

Notes: Accounting for reading performance is done by assuming students have a score equal to that of the country average; see OECD (2010), *PISA 2009 Results: What Students Know and Can Do (Volume I)*, PISA, OECD Publishing, Tables I.2.3 and I.3.3.

Differences statistically significantly different from 0 (zero) and odds ratio (O.R.) statistically significantly different from 1 (one) at a 95% confidence level are highlighted in bold.

StatLink http://dx.doi.org/10.1787/888932733982

[Part 1/1]

Table B1.14 Percentage of students who expect to complete a university degree, enrolment and graduation rates

	Percentage of students who expect to complete a university degree						Percentage of students graduating from ISCED 5B programmes[1, 4]	Percentage of students graduating from ISCED 5A programmes[1, 4]	Average annual growth in gross enrolment ratios from 1980 to 2009[2, 4]	Average annual growth in gross enrolment ratios from 2003 to 2009[3, 4]	Change in gross enrolment ratio from 2003 to 2009
	All, 2009		All, 2003		Change between 2003 and 2009						
	%	S.E.	%	S.E.	Diff.	S.E.					
Countries and economies											
Australia	61.2	(0.82)	62.8	(0.80)	-1.6	(1.20)	19.8	59.1	2.25	1.32	7.94
Austria	28.1	(0.95)	24.3	(1.29)	3.8	(1.52)	10.1	29.3	1.32	1.82	10.90
Belgium (Flemish Community)	37.1	(1.03)	37.6	(1.19)	-0.5	(1.47)	29.3	19.1	1.57	0.63	3.81
Hong Kong-China	47.2	(1.04)	52.3	(1.43)	-5.1	(1.82)	m	m	1.29	4.87	29.20
Croatia	49.1	(1.21)	m	m	m	m	m	m	1.26	1.72	10.34
Hungary	41.1	(1.46)	53.2	(1.36)	-12.2	(1.96)	5.1	37.4	2.05	1.71	10.25
Ireland	55.2	(1.07)	53.5	(1.07)	1.7	(1.51)	25.6	47.1	1.71	0.65	3.92
Iceland	44.7	(0.77)	36.1	(0.79)	8.6	(1.15)	2.2	52.0	2.11	1.70	10.22
Italy	40.9	(0.60)	52.1	(1.20)	-11.2	(1.38)	0.5	31.8	1.73	1.71	10.26
Korea	80.9	(1.23)	78.3	(0.96)	2.5	(1.56)	29.7	44.5	3.16	1.90	11.39
Latvia	25.4	(1.18)	24.9	(1.53)	0.6	(2.04)	m	m	2.26	-0.96	-5.77
Macao-China	35.2	(0.59)	48.9	(1.54)	-13.6	(1.59)	m	m	2.16	-2.37	-14.22
Mexico	55.8	(0.75)	49.1	(1.50)	6.7	(1.69)	1.4	19.4	0.46	0.83	5.01
New Zealand	52.5	(0.78)	38.8	(0.92)	13.7	(1.31)	31.2	52.9	2.16	0.88	5.29
Poland	41.5	(1.03)	30.1	(0.98)	11.3	(1.35)	1.0	50.2	2.17	1.85	11.08
Portugal	52.0	(1.57)	52.2	(1.38)	-0.2	(2.03)	0.6	40.0	2.02	0.95	5.73
Singapore	70.1	(0.59)	m	m	m	m	m	m	m	m	m
Serbia	55.1	(1.32)	m	m	m	m	m	m	0.93	0.93	5.57
Slovak Republic	45.5	(0.97)	43.0	(1.34)	2.5	(1.64)	0.7	61.4	2.48	3.96	23.79
Slovenia	35.1	(0.73)	m	m	m	m	27.7	27.1	2.81	3.22	19.30
Trinidad and Tobago	69.4	(0.74)	m	m	m	m	m	m	0.22	1.53	9.18
Regions											
Italy: Abruzzo	44.3	(2.19)	m	m	m	m	m	m	m	m	m
Italy: Basilicata	45.7	(1.59)	m	m	m	m	m	m	m	m	m
Italy: Bolzano	23.4	(0.89)	m	m	m	m	m	m	m	m	m
Italy: Calabria	46.2	(2.37)	m	m	m	m	m	m	m	m	m
Italy: Campania	43.0	(2.75)	m	m	m	m	m	m	m	m	m
Italy: Emilia Romagna	40.2	(2.04)	m	m	m	m	m	m	m	m	m
Italy: Friuli Venezia Giulia	39.5	(2.02)	m	m	m	m	m	m	m	m	m
Italy: Lazio	48.6	(1.98)	m	m	m	m	m	m	m	m	m
Italy: Liguria	39.7	(2.69)	m	m	m	m	m	m	m	m	m
Italy: Lombardia	38.0	(2.08)	m	m	m	m	m	m	m	m	m
Italy: Marche	37.2	(1.77)	m	m	m	m	m	m	m	m	m
Italy: Molise	43.4	(1.41)	m	m	m	m	m	m	m	m	m
Italy: Piemonte	37.3	(2.21)	m	m	m	m	m	m	m	m	m
Italy: Puglia	41.3	(2.39)	m	m	m	m	m	m	m	m	m
Italy: Sardegna	43.2	(2.32)	m	m	m	m	m	m	m	m	m
Italy: Sicilia	42.2	(2.09)	m	m	m	m	m	m	m	m	m
Italy: Toscana	40.5	(1.45)	m	m	m	m	m	m	m	m	m
Italy: Trento	35.3	(1.20)	m	m	m	m	m	m	m	m	m
Italy: Umbria	42.1	(1.57)	m	m	m	m	m	m	m	m	m
Italy: Valle d'Aosta	35.1	(1.58)	m	m	m	m	m	m	m	m	m
Italy: Veneto	34.7	(2.00)	m	m	m	m	m	m	m	m	m
Mexico: Aguascalientes	56.4	(2.53)	m	m	m	m	m	m	m	m	m
Mexico: Baja California	51.6	(2.42)	m	m	m	m	m	m	m	m	m
Mexico: Baja California Sur	58.2	(3.18)	m	m	m	m	m	m	m	m	m
Mexico: Campeche	60.7	(2.57)	m	m	m	m	m	m	m	m	m
Mexico: Chihuahua	65.5	(2.73)	m	m	m	m	m	m	m	m	m
Mexico: Colima	62.3	(2.30)	m	m	m	m	m	m	m	m	m
Mexico: Coahuila	55.8	(2.89)	m	m	m	m	m	m	m	m	m
Mexico: Chiapas	52.4	(2.70)	m	m	m	m	m	m	m	m	m
Mexico: Distrito Federal	71.1	(2.05)	m	m	m	m	m	m	m	m	m
Mexico: Durango	52.8	(2.34)	m	m	m	m	m	m	m	m	m
Mexico: Guerrero	46.1	(3.23)	m	m	m	m	m	m	m	m	m
Mexico: Guanajuato	44.6	(2.46)	m	m	m	m	m	m	m	m	m
Mexico: Hidalgo	57.2	(3.03)	m	m	m	m	m	m	m	m	m
Mexico: Jalisco	58.5	(1.86)	m	m	m	m	m	m	m	m	m
Mexico: Michoacán	54.1	(2.09)	m	m	m	m	m	m	m	m	m
Mexico: Morelos	54.2	(3.22)	m	m	m	m	m	m	m	m	m
Mexico: Mexico	57.9	(2.56)	m	m	m	m	m	m	m	m	m
Mexico: Nayarit	57.8	(1.60)	m	m	m	m	m	m	m	m	m
Mexico: Nuevo León	56.3	(5.72)	m	m	m	m	m	m	m	m	m
Mexico: Oaxaca	53.3	(4.55)	m	m	m	m	m	m	m	m	m
Mexico: Puebla	60.0	(3.50)	m	m	m	m	m	m	m	m	m
Mexico: Quintana Roo	54.4	(3.44)	m	m	m	m	m	m	m	m	m
Mexico: Querétaro	52.6	(4.14)	m	m	m	m	m	m	m	m	m
Mexico: Sinaloa	58.1	(2.18)	m	m	m	m	m	m	m	m	m
Mexico: San Luis Potosí	42.2	(3.12)	m	m	m	m	m	m	m	m	m
Mexico: Sonora	56.6	(2.28)	m	m	m	m	m	m	m	m	m
Mexico: Tamaulipas	54.1	(3.03)	m	m	m	m	m	m	m	m	m
Mexico: Tabasco	47.9	(2.21)	m	m	m	m	m	m	m	m	m
Mexico: Tlaxcala	52.8	(2.99)	m	m	m	m	m	m	m	m	m
Mexico: Veracruz	50.9	(3.12)	m	m	m	m	m	m	m	m	m
Mexico: Yucatán	52.7	(2.66)	m	m	m	m	m	m	m	m	m
Mexico: Zacatecas	48.7	(2.19)	m	m	m	m	m	m	m	m	m

1. Data from OECD (2011), *Education at a Glance 2011: OECD Indicators*, OECD Publishing, Table A3.3 (first-degree graduation rates).
2. Linear regression from 1980 to 2009 data from World Bank EdStats, see Table B1.16 for the complete series from 1980 to 2009.
3. Linear regression from 2003 to 2009 data from World Bank EdStats, see Table B1.16 for complete series from 1980 to 2009.
4. Data for Belgium (Flemish Community) is unavailable; data for Belgium as a whole presented instead.

StatLink http://dx.doi.org/10.1787/888932734001

[Part 1/2]

Table B1.15 Patterns of expectations of upward and downward mobility

	Students who expect to complete a university degree and whose parents do not have such a degree (upward mobility), 2009		Students who do not expect to complete a university degree and at least one of whose parents have such a degree (downward mobility), 2009		Students who expect to complete a university degree, 2009		Mothers with a university degree, 2009		Fathers with a university degree, 2009		Students who expect to complete a university degree and whose parents do not have such a degree (upward mobility), 2003		Students who do not expect to complete a university degree and at least one of whose parents does have such a degree (downward mobility), 2003		Students who expect to complete a university degree, 2003	
	%	S.E.	%	S.E.	%	S.E.	%	S.E.	%	S.E.	%	S.E.	%	S.E.	%	S.E.
Countries and economies																
Australia	29.0	(0.51)	8.3	(0.33)	61.2	(0.82)	28.8	(0.70)	27.8	(0.68)	23.1	(0.61)	13.2	(0.51)	62.8	(0.80)
Austria	17.6	(0.85)	7.8	(0.42)	28.1	(0.95)	9.1	(0.57)	13.6	(0.62)	9.4	(0.58)	27.9	(0.78)	24.3	(1.29)
Belgium (Flemish Community)	15.9	(0.70)	14.7	(0.63)	37.1	(1.03)	24.2	(0.81)	25.7	(0.97)	9.9	(0.60)	25.3	(0.78)	37.6	(1.19)
Hong Kong-China	38.0	(0.81)	2.9	(0.32)	47.2	(1.04)	6.3	(0.65)	10.3	(0.93)	44.2	(1.21)	3.4	(0.32)	52.3	(1.43)
Croatia	30.2	(0.98)	6.9	(0.42)	49.1	(1.21)	17.2	(0.82)	17.5	(0.76)	m	m	m	m	m	m
Hungary	21.2	(0.90)	9.1	(0.54)	41.1	(1.45)	23.1	(1.03)	18.7	(0.98)	27.5	(0.93)	6.9	(0.43)	53.2	(1.36)
Ireland	31.7	(0.94)	9.5	(0.48)	55.2	(1.07)	23.6	(0.89)	20.2	(0.92)	27.5	(0.86)	13.5	(0.56)	53.5	(1.07)
Iceland	16.0	(0.60)	15.7	(0.63)	44.7	(0.77)	33.7	(0.73)	28.4	(0.60)	14.9	(0.52)	18.7	(0.66)	36.1	(0.79)
Italy	25.5	(0.51)	10.9	(0.29)	40.9	(0.60)	18.7	(0.39)	18.5	(0.39)	29.1	(0.85)	11.4	(0.55)	52.1	(1.20)
Korea	39.7	(1.38)	4.5	(0.40)	80.9	(1.23)	27.8	(1.19)	40.2	(1.50)	44.9	(1.30)	3.5	(0.27)	78.3	(0.96)
Latvia	11.3	(0.72)	19.4	(0.94)	25.4	(1.18)	27.8	(1.16)	15.1	(0.81)	7.6	(0.86)	41.9	(2.05)	24.9	(1.53)
Macao-China	31.0	(0.60)	2.2	(0.19)	35.2	(0.59)	3.8	(0.27)	4.8	(0.23)	44.4	(1.56)	2.5	(0.44)	48.9	(1.54)
Mexico	37.4	(0.58)	6.2	(0.23)	55.8	(0.75)	15.7	(0.59)	17.8	(0.71)	28.5	(0.82)	10.3	(0.43)	49.1	(1.50)
New Zealand	29.8	(0.76)	10.1	(0.44)	52.5	(0.78)	23.9	(0.80)	20.0	(0.73)	17.6	(0.66)	18.6	(0.57)	38.8	(0.92)
Poland	24.7	(0.70)	5.3	(0.36)	41.5	(1.02)	17.8	(0.90)	12.5	(0.78)	17.4	(0.67)	9.5	(0.52)	30.1	(0.98)
Portugal	33.9	(1.24)	4.7	(0.31)	52.0	(1.57)	17.7	(1.00)	15.1	(1.04)	35.2	(1.12)	8.9	(0.55)	52.2	(1.38)
Singapore	47.8	(0.69)	2.8	(0.25)	70.1	(0.59)	15.6	(0.47)	21.2	(0.60)	m	m	m	m	m	m
Serbia	36.4	(0.91)	5.7	(0.35)	55.1	(1.32)	16.2	(0.62)	16.4	(0.60)	m	m	m	m	m	m
Slovak Republic	30.9	(0.87)	7.6	(0.39)	45.5	(0.97)	14.7	(0.72)	14.8	(0.69)	24.8	(0.85)	8.3	(0.36)	43.0	(1.34)
Slovenia	20.0	(0.57)	8.3	(0.48)	35.1	(0.73)	17.9	(0.62)	14.6	(0.54)	m	m	m	m	m	m
Trinidad and Tobago	54.1	(0.81)	4.7	(0.39)	69.4	(0.74)	12.7	(0.51)	13.0	(0.62)	m	m	m	m	m	m
Regions																
Italy: Abruzzo	27.9	(1.66)	12.4	(1.13)	44.3	(2.19)	21.3	(1.03)	19.5	(1.12)	m	m	m	m	m	m
Italy: Basilicata	33.4	(1.57)	6.9	(0.71)	45.7	(1.59)	13.4	(1.04)	13.7	(1.15)	m	m	m	m	m	m
Italy: Bolzano	14.8	(0.71)	12.6	(0.82)	23.4	(0.89)	14.2	(0.83)	14.2	(0.88)	m	m	m	m	m	m
Italy: Calabria	30.3	(1.70)	6.0	(0.70)	46.2	(2.37)	14.4	(1.50)	15.8	(1.39)	m	m	m	m	m	m
Italy: Campania	30.3	(1.87)	7.6	(1.03)	43.0	(2.75)	14.7	(1.65)	13.7	(1.41)	m	m	m	m	m	m
Italy: Emilia Romagna	20.9	(1.37)	14.5	(1.12)	40.2	(2.04)	24.8	(1.70)	23.7	(1.79)	m	m	m	m	m	m
Italy: Friuli Venezia Giulia	24.5	(1.39)	10.9	(0.72)	39.5	(2.02)	17.9	(1.24)	18.4	(1.15)	m	m	m	m	m	m
Italy: Lazio	27.7	(1.90)	15.6	(1.30)	48.6	(1.98)	27.4	(2.13)	26.4	(2.28)	m	m	m	m	m	m
Italy: Liguria	22.7	(2.09)	14.3	(0.97)	39.7	(2.69)	22.8	(1.48)	22.9	(1.55)	m	m	m	m	m	m
Italy: Lombardia	21.9	(1.28)	12.4	(0.85)	38.0	(2.08)	21.2	(1.13)	20.1	(1.17)	m	m	m	m	m	m
Italy: Marche	23.5	(1.29)	12.1	(1.10)	37.2	(1.77)	17.6	(1.16)	17.2	(1.48)	m	m	m	m	m	m
Italy: Molise	28.0	(1.34)	11.0	(0.95)	43.4	(1.41)	18.8	(1.32)	18.2	(1.35)	m	m	m	m	m	m
Italy: Piemonte	21.3	(1.70)	11.4	(1.18)	37.3	(2.21)	19.4	(1.31)	19.3	(1.34)	m	m	m	m	m	m
Italy: Puglia	31.8	(2.00)	6.5	(0.65)	41.3	(2.39)	9.5	(0.83)	12.0	(0.93)	m	m	m	m	m	m
Italy: Sardegna	29.0	(1.41)	7.5	(0.96)	43.2	(2.32)	15.6	(1.16)	14.0	(1.42)	m	m	m	m	m	m
Italy: Sicilia	26.2	(1.55)	7.6	(0.76)	42.2	(2.09)	15.5	(1.43)	18.1	(2.04)	m	m	m	m	m	m
Italy: Toscana	23.4	(1.23)	14.8	(0.96)	40.5	(1.45)	24.7	(1.30)	20.8	(1.43)	m	m	m	m	m	m
Italy: Trento	20.9	(1.28)	12.6	(1.21)	35.3	(1.20)	19.5	(1.20)	17.9	(1.10)	m	m	m	m	m	m
Italy: Umbria	23.3	(0.96)	13.8	(0.94)	42.1	(1.57)	24.0	(1.04)	22.4	(1.29)	m	m	m	m	m	m
Italy: Valle d'Aosta	21.1	(1.43)	13.1	(1.10)	35.1	(1.58)	19.9	(1.32)	14.9	(1.01)	m	m	m	m	m	m
Italy: Veneto	22.0	(1.54)	11.9	(1.05)	34.7	(2.00)	16.1	(1.26)	17.4	(1.55)	m	m	m	m	m	m
Mexico: Aguascalientes	33.8	(1.82)	7.7	(1.28)	56.4	(2.53)	19.2	(2.37)	22.1	(3.04)	m	m	m	m	m	m
Mexico: Baja California	36.0	(1.75)	7.5	(0.47)	51.6	(2.42)	14.8	(1.44)	17.1	(1.87)	m	m	m	m	m	m
Mexico: Baja California Sur	40.8	(2.11)	8.4	(0.92)	58.2	(3.18)	15.2	(1.70)	17.3	(1.93)	m	m	m	m	m	m
Mexico: Campeche	39.4	(2.33)	6.2	(0.94)	60.7	(2.57)	16.3	(2.49)	20.9	(3.08)	m	m	m	m	m	m
Mexico: Chihuahua	40.7	(1.36)	5.4	(0.82)	65.5	(2.73)	18.7	(1.91)	21.9	(1.94)	m	m	m	m	m	m
Mexico: Colima	42.5	(1.70)	7.0	(0.98)	62.3	(2.30)	16.8	(1.32)	19.5	(1.59)	m	m	m	m	m	m
Mexico: Coahuila	32.5	(1.67)	8.7	(1.12)	55.8	(2.89)	19.7	(2.76)	21.5	(2.24)	m	m	m	m	m	m
Mexico: Chiapas	40.1	(2.12)	4.9	(0.95)	52.4	(2.70)	9.0	(1.48)	14.0	(2.11)	m	m	m	m	m	m
Mexico: Distrito Federal	42.7	(2.58)	6.0	(1.24)	71.1	(2.05)	23.6	(2.68)	25.2	(2.78)	m	m	m	m	m	m
Mexico: Durango	36.8	(2.01)	7.7	(0.94)	52.8	(2.34)	14.3	(1.12)	16.2	(1.23)	m	m	m	m	m	m
Mexico: Guerrero	31.6	(2.18)	7.8	(1.35)	46.1	(3.23)	14.5	(1.18)	16.4	(1.90)	m	m	m	m	m	m
Mexico: Guanajuato	28.4	(1.29)	4.6	(0.60)	44.6	(2.46)	14.0	(1.72)	14.8	(1.69)	m	m	m	m	m	m
Mexico: Hidalgo	42.3	(2.45)	3.2	(0.67)	57.2	(3.03)	11.4	(2.06)	13.1	(2.01)	m	m	m	m	m	m
Mexico: Jalisco	37.7	(1.34)	8.0	(1.29)	58.5	(1.86)	17.8	(2.00)	20.1	(2.51)	m	m	m	m	m	m
Mexico: Michoacán	38.3	(1.43)	6.0	(0.68)	54.1	(2.09)	14.0	(1.46)	15.2	(1.43)	m	m	m	m	m	m
Mexico: Morelos	38.5	(2.22)	6.1	(1.34)	54.2	(3.22)	14.4	(2.09)	15.9	(2.36)	m	m	m	m	m	m
Mexico: Mexico	40.3	(1.84)	4.6	(0.92)	57.9	(2.56)	14.1	(1.36)	15.5	(2.08)	m	m	m	m	m	m
Mexico: Nayarit	37.5	(1.69)	8.9	(0.95)	57.8	(1.60)	18.1	(1.31)	20.7	(1.95)	m	m	m	m	m	m
Mexico: Nuevo León	26.2	(2.81)	9.3	(0.96)	56.3	(5.72)	27.2	(6.47)	31.7	(8.15)	m	m	m	m	m	m
Mexico: Oaxaca	41.4	(3.87)	6.8	(1.30)	53.3	(4.55)	10.5	(1.11)	14.4	(1.53)	m	m	m	m	m	m
Mexico: Puebla	38.4	(3.17)	4.9	(1.36)	60.0	(3.50)	18.0	(5.12)	20.2	(6.18)	m	m	m	m	m	m
Mexico: Quintana Roo	32.8	(1.90)	7.8	(0.79)	54.4	(3.44)	17.9	(2.99)	23.1	(3.74)	m	m	m	m	m	m
Mexico: Querétaro	35.0	(2.13)	4.9	(0.97)	52.6	(4.14)	14.4	(2.06)	16.4	(2.37)	m	m	m	m	m	m
Mexico: Sinaloa	36.2	(2.08)	8.8	(1.08)	58.1	(2.18)	17.5	(2.08)	23.6	(3.36)	m	m	m	m	m	m
Mexico: San Luis Potosí	30.3	(1.93)	7.1	(0.68)	42.2	(3.12)	13.7	(1.80)	12.3	(1.44)	m	m	m	m	m	m
Mexico: Sonora	40.6	(1.72)	6.9	(0.87)	56.6	(2.28)	14.8	(1.68)	15.5	(1.61)	m	m	m	m	m	m
Mexico: Tamaulipas	37.3	(2.31)	8.6	(0.90)	54.1	(3.03)	16.4	(1.97)	17.2	(2.18)	m	m	m	m	m	m
Mexico: Tabasco	36.1	(1.30)	8.8	(2.17)	47.9	(2.21)	13.8	(1.70)	13.8	(1.14)	m	m	m	m	m	m
Mexico: Tlaxcala	38.6	(2.15)	5.3	(0.67)	52.8	(2.99)	12.6	(1.24)	12.6	(0.98)	m	m	m	m	m	m
Mexico: Veracruz	37.7	(2.54)	3.4	(0.64)	50.9	(3.12)	10.1	(1.42)	12.2	(1.57)	m	m	m	m	m	m
Mexico: Yucatán	38.9	(1.80)	5.6	(0.80)	52.7	(2.66)	11.6	(1.31)	14.0	(1.68)	m	m	m	m	m	m
Mexico: Zacatecas	35.0	(1.35)	6.2	(0.85)	48.7	(2.19)	11.4	(1.47)	14.0	(1.37)	m	m	m	m	m	m

Notes: Differences and regression estimates statistically significantly different from 0 (zero) at a 95% confidence level are highlighted in bold.

The strength of the socio-economic gradient is the percentage of the variance of reading performance explained in an OLS regression where the *PISA index of economic, social and cultural status* is the only covariate in the model. The slope of the socio-economic gradient is the estimated coefficient of this regression model.

1. Linear regression from 1980 to 2009 data from World Bank EdStats, see Table B1.16 for complete series from 1980 to 2009.
2. Linear regression from 2003 to 2009 data from World Bank EdStats, see Table B1.16 for complete series from 1980 to 2009.
3. Data for Belgium (Flemish Community) is unavailable; data for Belgium as a whole is presented instead.

StatLink http://dx.doi.org/10.1787/888932734020

[Part 2/2]

Table B1.15 Patterns of expectations of upward and downward mobility

	Mothers with a university degree, 2003		Fathers with a university degree, 2003		Difference in the expectation of upward mobility (2009 - 2003)		Difference in the expectation of downward mobility (2009 - 2003)		Average annual growth in gross tertiary enrolment ratios from 1980 to 2009[1,2]	Average yearly growth in tertiary education gross enrolment ratios from 2003 to 2009[2,3]	Strength of the socio-economic gradient		Slope of the socio-economic gradient	
	%	S.E.	%	S.E.	Diff.	S.E.	Diff.	S.E.			%	S.E.	Slope	S.E.
Countries and economies														
Australia	38.3	(0.80)	38.8	(0.77)	**6.0**	(0.77)	**-5.0**	(0.63)	2.25	1.32	**12.7**	(0.85)	**46.0**	(1.80)
Austria	21.2	(0.88)	36.1	(0.94)	**8.2**	(1.02)	**-20.1**	(0.92)	1.32	1.82	**16.6**	(1.39)	**48.0**	(2.30)
Belgium (Flemish Community)	39.2	(0.81)	39.8	(0.86)	**5.9**	(0.93)	**-10.6**	(0.94)	1.57	0.63	**16.5**	(1.31)	**41.5**	(2.00)
Hong Kong-China	6.5	(0.50)	9.8	(0.74)	**-6.1**	(1.41)	-0.4	(0.46)	1.29	4.87	**4.5**	(1.08)	**17.0**	(2.20)
Croatia	m	m	m	m	m	m	m	m	1.26	1.72	**11.0**	(1.34)	**32.0**	(2.00)
Hungary	25.0	(0.83)	21.8	(0.96)	**-6.3**	(1.33)	**2.2**	(0.70)	2.05	1.71	**26.0**	(2.17)	**48.0**	(2.20)
Ireland	27.1	(1.05)	26.4	(1.04)	**4.1**	(1.35)	**-4.0**	(0.82)	1.71	0.65	**12.6**	(1.17)	**39.0**	(2.00)
Iceland	26.6	(0.72)	28.6	(0.86)	1.2	(0.75)	**-3.0**	(0.91)	2.11	1.70	**6.2**	(0.81)	**27.0**	(1.80)
Italy	25.6	(0.79)	24.8	(0.81)	**-3.6**	(1.00)	-0.5	(0.60)	1.73	1.71	**11.8**	(0.74)	**32.0**	(1.30)
Korea	21.2	(1.30)	34.7	(1.32)	**-5.2**	(1.77)	**1.0**	(0.48)	3.16	1.90	**11.0**	(1.51)	**32.0**	(2.50)
Latvia	50.8	(1.87)	40.6	(1.85)	**3.7**	(1.33)	**-22.5**	(2.25)	2.26	-0.96	**10.3**	(1.69)	**29.0**	(2.60)
Macao-China	5.0	(0.62)	5.4	(0.68)	**-13.4**	(1.55)	-0.3	(0.45)	2.16	-2.37	**1.8**	(0.35)	**12.0**	(1.20)
Mexico	20.7	(1.07)	24.1	(1.19)	**8.9**	(1.07)	**-4.2**	(0.52)	0.46	0.83	**14.5**	(0.99)	**25.0**	(1.00)
New Zealand	31.0	(0.67)	23.8	(0.65)	**12.2**	(1.01)	**-8.5**	(0.71)	2.16	0.88	**16.6**	(1.08)	**52.0**	(1.90)
Poland	16.7	(0.71)	14.5	(0.71)	**7.3**	(0.98)	**-4.3**	(0.61)	2.17	1.85	**14.8**	(1.38)	**39.0**	(1.90)
Portugal	21.0	(1.01)	19.0	(0.98)	-1.3	(1.60)	**-4.2**	(0.63)	2.02	0.95	**16.5**	(1.60)	**30.0**	(1.60)
Singapore	m	m	m	m	m	m	m	m	m	m	**15.3**	(1.11)	**47.0**	(1.70)
Serbia	m	m	m	m	m	m	m	m	0.93	0.93	**9.8**	(1.02)	**27.0**	(1.60)
Slovak Republic	17.4	(0.67)	19.7	(0.96)	**6.0**	(1.17)	-0.7	(0.53)	2.48	3.96	**14.6**	(1.48)	**41.0**	(2.30)
Slovenia	m	m	m	m	m	m	m	m	2.81	3.22	**14.3**	(1.06)	**39.0**	(1.50)
Trinidad and Tobago	m	m	m	m	m	m	m	m	0.22	1.53	**9.7**	(0.86)	**38.0**	(1.70)
Regions														
Italy: Abruzzo	m	m	m	m	m	m	m	m	m	m	**12.8**	(2.93)	**33.8**	(4.69)
Italy: Basilicata	m	m	m	m	m	m	m	m	m	m	**9.3**	(1.77)	**27.6**	(3.03)
Italy: Bolzano	m	m	m	m	m	m	m	m	m	m	**6.6**	(1.82)	**27.4**	(3.65)
Italy: Calabria	m	m	m	m	m	m	m	m	m	m	**12.0**	(1.68)	**28.4**	(2.27)
Italy: Campania	m	m	m	m	m	m	m	m	m	m	**9.3**	(2.33)	**27.3**	(4.26)
Italy: Emilia Romagna	m	m	m	m	m	m	m	m	m	m	**21.9**	(3.02)	**44.3**	(3.34)
Italy: Friuli Venezia Giulia	m	m	m	m	m	m	m	m	m	m	**11.0**	(2.23)	**33.6**	(4.21)
Italy: Lazio	m	m	m	m	m	m	m	m	m	m	**10.0**	(2.47)	**29.6**	(3.68)
Italy: Liguria	m	m	m	m	m	m	m	m	m	m	**8.2**	(3.00)	**28.6**	(6.72)
Italy: Lombardia	m	m	m	m	m	m	m	m	m	m	**14.1**	(2.48)	**33.9**	(3.28)
Italy: Marche	m	m	m	m	m	m	m	m	m	m	**8.1**	(1.46)	**28.3**	(3.79)
Italy: Molise	m	m	m	m	m	m	m	m	m	m	**13.0**	(1.93)	**30.1**	(2.41)
Italy: Piemonte	m	m	m	m	m	m	m	m	m	m	**13.5**	(3.09)	**35.1**	(3.19)
Italy: Puglia	m	m	m	m	m	m	m	m	m	m	**7.6**	(1.72)	**24.2**	(2.78)
Italy: Sardegna	m	m	m	m	m	m	m	m	m	m	**8.1**	(2.11)	**24.5**	(3.29)
Italy: Sicilia	m	m	m	m	m	m	m	m	m	m	**14.6**	(3.66)	**34.7**	(5.55)
Italy: Toscana	m	m	m	m	m	m	m	m	m	m	**7.4**	(1.91)	**27.6**	(3.60)
Italy: Trento	m	m	m	m	m	m	m	m	m	m	**10.8**	(2.36)	**34.2**	(3.88)
Italy: Umbria	m	m	m	m	m	m	m	m	m	m	**12.5**	(2.12)	**35.4**	(2.96)
Italy: Valle d'Aosta	m	m	m	m	m	m	m	m	m	m	**8.4**	(1.89)	**27.1**	(3.26)
Italy: Veneto	m	m	m	m	m	m	m	m	m	m	**8.2**	(2.48)	**27.2**	(4.81)
Mexico: Aguascalientes	m	m	m	m	m	m	m	m	m	m	**11.6**	(2.59)	**21.2**	(2.42)
Mexico: Baja California	m	m	m	m	m	m	m	m	m	m	**9.2**	(2.75)	**20.4**	(2.88)
Mexico: Baja California Sur	m	m	m	m	m	m	m	m	m	m	**8.5**	(1.88)	**20.8**	(2.41)
Mexico: Campeche	m	m	m	m	m	m	m	m	m	m	**12.1**	(3.53)	**19.3**	(2.93)
Mexico: Chihuahua	m	m	m	m	m	m	m	m	m	m	**17.9**	(3.77)	**27.2**	(3.33)
Mexico: Colima	m	m	m	m	m	m	m	m	m	m	**10.8**	(1.81)	**21.2**	(1.78)
Mexico: Coahuila	m	m	m	m	m	m	m	m	m	m	**9.0**	(2.75)	**18.7**	(2.98)
Mexico: Chiapas	m	m	m	m	m	m	m	m	m	m	**11.4**	(3.58)	**23.7**	(4.73)
Mexico: Distrito Federal	m	m	m	m	m	m	m	m	m	m	**11.7**	(3.72)	**24.1**	(4.74)
Mexico: Durango	m	m	m	m	m	m	m	m	m	m	**11.6**	(3.30)	**21.8**	(3.73)
Mexico: Guerrero	m	m	m	m	m	m	m	m	m	m	**7.0**	(2.74)	**16.6**	(3.30)
Mexico: Guanajuato	m	m	m	m	m	m	m	m	m	m	**18.9**	(3.10)	**27.1**	(2.66)
Mexico: Hidalgo	m	m	m	m	m	m	m	m	m	m	**23.8**	(4.22)	**30.1**	(2.46)
Mexico: Jalisco	m	m	m	m	m	m	m	m	m	m	**10.1**	(3.39)	**20.4**	(3.56)
Mexico: Michoacán	m	m	m	m	m	m	m	m	m	m	**14.6**	(2.54)	**22.5**	(2.36)
Mexico: Morelos	m	m	m	m	m	m	m	m	m	m	**10.3**	(4.84)	**22.2**	(6.60)
Mexico: Mexico	m	m	m	m	m	m	m	m	m	m	**8.1**	(3.66)	**20.3**	(4.59)
Mexico: Nayarit	m	m	m	m	m	m	m	m	m	m	**7.3**	(2.71)	**15.3**	(2.79)
Mexico: Nuevo León	m	m	m	m	m	m	m	m	m	m	10.8	(7.04)	**23.3**	(8.42)
Mexico: Oaxaca	m	m	m	m	m	m	m	m	m	m	3.8	(4.12)	15.2	(8.09)
Mexico: Puebla	m	m	m	m	m	m	m	m	m	m	**12.7**	(3.42)	**18.9**	(2.91)
Mexico: Quintana Roo	m	m	m	m	m	m	m	m	m	m	**21.0**	(4.21)	**31.1**	(3.83)
Mexico: Querétaro	m	m	m	m	m	m	m	m	m	m	**27.0**	(3.41)	**31.8**	(2.41)
Mexico: Sinaloa	m	m	m	m	m	m	m	m	m	m	**11.1**	(3.70)	**20.8**	(3.73)
Mexico: San Luis Potosí	m	m	m	m	m	m	m	m	m	m	**13.8**	(2.94)	**25.1**	(4.84)
Mexico: Sonora	m	m	m	m	m	m	m	m	m	m	**11.1**	(3.16)	**23.5**	(3.39)
Mexico: Tamaulipas	m	m	m	m	m	m	m	m	m	m	**8.0**	(2.88)	**18.8**	(4.27)
Mexico: Tabasco	m	m	m	m	m	m	m	m	m	m	**8.4**	(2.92)	**17.6**	(3.25)
Mexico: Tlaxcala	m	m	m	m	m	m	m	m	m	m	**5.6**	(1.91)	**15.3**	(2.80)
Mexico: Veracruz	m	m	m	m	m	m	m	m	m	m	**13.9**	(3.97)	**22.2**	(3.28)
Mexico: Yucatán	m	m	m	m	m	m	m	m	m	m	**19.1**	(3.83)	**27.9**	(3.24)
Mexico: Zacatecas	m	m	m	m	m	m	m	m	m	m	5.9	(3.71)	**14.2**	(4.99)

Notes: Differences and regression estimates statistically significantly different from 0 (zero) at a 95% confidence level are highlighted in bold.

The strength of the socio-economic gradient is the percentage of the variance of reading performance explained in an OLS regression where the *PISA index of economic, social and cultural status* is the only covariate in the model. The slope of the socio-economic gradient is the estimated coefficient of this regression model.

1. Linear regression from 1980 to 2009 data from World Bank EdStats, see Table B1.16 for complete series from 1980 to 2009.

2. Linear regression from 2003 to 2009 data from World Bank EdStats, see Table B1.16 for complete series from 1980 to 2009.

3. Data for Belgium (Flemish Community) is unavailable; data for Belgium as a whole is presented instead.

StatLink http://dx.doi.org/10.1787/888932734020

[Part 1/2]

Table B1.16 Gross tertiary enrolment ratios and average growth in enrolment ratios from 1980 to 2009

	Average annual growth in gross enrolment ratios from 1980 to 2009[1]	Average annual growth in gross enrolment ratios from 2003 to 2009[2]	Gross enrolment ratio									
			1980	1981	1982	1983	1984	1985	1986	1987	1988	1989
Countries and economies												
Australia	2.25	1.32	25.1	25.6	25.7	26.5	27.0	27.8	29.1	29.1	30.8	32.1
Austria	1.32	1.82	21.1	22.0	22.1	22.6	23.5	25.0	26.3	27.5	29.3	30.6
Belgium	1.57	0.63	25.0	24.5	26.6	27.4	28.5	31.1	31.7	32.9	33.8	35.5
Hong Kong-China	1.29	4.87	10.0	10.3	10.8	12.0	12.6	m	m	m	m	m
Croatia	1.26	1.72	m	19.0	m	m	m	m	17.7	m	m	m
Hungary	2.05	1.71	13.1	13.4	14.3	14.6	15.1	15.5	15.6	15.4	15.2	14.8
Ireland	1.71	0.65	16.6	18.1	19.6	20.8	20.7	21.5	22.4	23.4	24.7	26.2
Iceland	2.11	1.70	19.7	20.4	21.2	22.9	23.4	20.7	21.1	21.3	21.5	23.2
Italy	1.73	1.71	27.4	27.2	m	25.2	25.2	26.0	25.7	24.8	26.3	27.9
Korea	3.16	1.90	12.8	15.3	19.5	24.2	28.3	31.6	34.0	35.0	35.4	35.7
Latvia	2.26	-0.96	m	23.7	23.7	23.5	23.3	23.2	22.8	22.7	23.1	23.6
Maca-China	2.16	-2.37	m	m	m	m	m	m	m	m	25.4	26.4
Mexico	0.46	0.83	13.0	13.8	14.5	14.9	15.5	m	16.1	15.8	16.4	15.7
New Zealand	2.16	0.88	26.6	27.5	27.6	27.8	31.0	30.9	33.4	35.0	38.7	41.8
Poland	2.17	1.85	18.2	18.1	17.3	16.4	16.5	16.5	17.1	17.5	18.2	19.8
Portugal	2.02	0.95	11.2	11.5	11.7	12.0	12.1	13.4	12.2	15.3	m	m
Singapore	m	m	m	m	m	m	m	m	m	m	m	m
Serbia	0.93	0.93	m	m	m	m	m	m	m	m	m	m
Slovak Republic	2.48	3.96	m	m	m	m	m	m	m	m	m	m
Slovenia	2.81	3.22	m	19.1	18.2	18.2	19.1	19.4	20.8	21.8	21.9	22.1
Trinidad and Tobago	0.22	1.53	4.5	4.4	4.4	4.0	3.9	4.5	5.3	5.4	5.3	6.2
Regions												
Italy: Abruzzo	m	m	m	m	m	m	m	m	m	m	m	m
Italy: Basilicata	m	m	m	m	m	m	m	m	m	m	m	m
Italy: Bolzano	m	m	m	m	m	m	m	m	m	m	m	m
Italy: Calabria	m	m	m	m	m	m	m	m	m	m	m	m
Italy: Campania	m	m	m	m	m	m	m	m	m	m	m	m
Italy: Emilia Romagna	m	m	m	m	m	m	m	m	m	m	m	m
Italy: Friuli Venezia Giulia	m	m	m	m	m	m	m	m	m	m	m	m
Italy: Lazio	m	m	m	m	m	m	m	m	m	m	m	m
Italy: Liguria	m	m	m	m	m	m	m	m	m	m	m	m
Italy: Lombardia	m	m	m	m	m	m	m	m	m	m	m	m
Italy: Marche	m	m	m	m	m	m	m	m	m	m	m	m
Italy: Molise	m	m	m	m	m	m	m	m	m	m	m	m
Italy: Piemonte	m	m	m	m	m	m	m	m	m	m	m	m
Italy: Puglia	m	m	m	m	m	m	m	m	m	m	m	m
Italy: Sardegna	m	m	m	m	m	m	m	m	m	m	m	m
Italy: Sicilia	m	m	m	m	m	m	m	m	m	m	m	m
Italy: Toscana	m	m	m	m	m	m	m	m	m	m	m	m
Italy: Trento	m	m	m	m	m	m	m	m	m	m	m	m
Italy: Umbria	m	m	m	m	m	m	m	m	m	m	m	m
Italy: Valle d'Aosta	m	m	m	m	m	m	m	m	m	m	m	m
Italy: Veneto	m	m	m	m	m	m	m	m	m	m	m	m
Mexico: Aguascalientes	m	m	m	m	m	m	m	m	m	m	m	m
Mexico: Baja California	m	m	m	m	m	m	m	m	m	m	m	m
Mexico: Baja California Sur	m	m	m	m	m	m	m	m	m	m	m	m
Mexico: Campeche	m	m	m	m	m	m	m	m	m	m	m	m
Mexico: Chihuahua	m	m	m	m	m	m	m	m	m	m	m	m
Mexico: Colima	m	m	m	m	m	m	m	m	m	m	m	m
Mexico: Coahuila	m	m	m	m	m	m	m	m	m	m	m	m
Mexico: Chiapas	m	m	m	m	m	m	m	m	m	m	m	m
Mexico: Distrito Federal	m	m	m	m	m	m	m	m	m	m	m	m
Mexico: Durango	m	m	m	m	m	m	m	m	m	m	m	m
Mexico: Guerrero	m	m	m	m	m	m	m	m	m	m	m	m
Mexico: Guanajuato	m	m	m	m	m	m	m	m	m	m	m	m
Mexico: Hidalgo	m	m	m	m	m	m	m	m	m	m	m	m
Mexico: Jalisco	m	m	m	m	m	m	m	m	m	m	m	m
Mexico: Michoacán	m	m	m	m	m	m	m	m	m	m	m	m
Mexico: Morelos	m	m	m	m	m	m	m	m	m	m	m	m
Mexico: Mexico	m	m	m	m	m	m	m	m	m	m	m	m
Mexico: Nayarit	m	m	m	m	m	m	m	m	m	m	m	m
Mexico: Nuevo León	m	m	m	m	m	m	m	m	m	m	m	m
Mexico: Oaxaca	m	m	m	m	m	m	m	m	m	m	m	m
Mexico: Puebla	m	m	m	m	m	m	m	m	m	m	m	m
Mexico: Quintana Roo	m	m	m	m	m	m	m	m	m	m	m	m
Mexico: Querétaro	m	m	m	m	m	m	m	m	m	m	m	m
Mexico: Sinaloa	m	m	m	m	m	m	m	m	m	m	m	m
Mexico: San Luis Potosí	m	m	m	m	m	m	m	m	m	m	m	m
Mexico: Sonora	m	m	m	m	m	m	m	m	m	m	m	m
Mexico: Tamaulipas	m	m	m	m	m	m	m	m	m	m	m	m
Mexico: Tabasco	m	m	m	m	m	m	m	m	m	m	m	m
Mexico: Tlaxcala	m	m	m	m	m	m	m	m	m	m	m	m
Mexico: Veracruz	m	m	m	m	m	m	m	m	m	m	m	m
Mexico: Yucatán	m	m	m	m	m	m	m	m	m	m	m	m
Mexico: Zacatecas	m	m	m	m	m	m	m	m	m	m	m	m

1. Linear regression from 1980 to 2009 data where the dependent variable is the gross enrolment ratio and the independent variable is the year; coefficient for year is presented.
2. Linear regression from 2003 to 2009 data where the dependent variable is the gross enrolment ratio and the independent variable is the year; coefficient for year is presented.
Source: World Bank EdStats.

StatLink http://dx.doi.org/10.1787/888932734039

[Part 2/2]

Table B1.16 Gross tertiary enrolment ratios and average growth in enrolment ratios from 1980 to 2009

	Gross enrolment ratio																			
	1990	1991	1992	1993	1994	1995	1996	1997	1998	1999	2000	2001	2002	2003	2004	2005	2006	2007	2008	2009
Countries and economies																				
Australia	35.1	38.6	40.3	66.5	67.5	70.4	74.0	78.3	66.4	65.4	65.5	66.7	76.3	74.1	72.2	72.4	72.6	75.0	77.0	82.3
Austria	32.6	34.7	37.7	40.0	42.6	45.4	47.8	49.4	51.8	53.6	55.7	56.2	47.0	47.4	48.1	48.3	49.3	50.3	54.7	59.3
Belgium	37.8	39.4	m	45.5	48.6	54.0	55.6	m	m	56.7	57.8	58.6	59.8	60.8	62.3	62.3	62.6	62.1	63.0	66.3
Hong Kong-China	m	m	19.4	20.1	21.6	m	m	m	m	m	m	m	m	30.7	31.2	32.4	33.3	42.2	55.6	56.6
Croatia	22.7	23.9	23.0	25.4	26.8	26.5	27.7	27.4	28.7	30.5	30.8	33.2	36.0	39.1	m	43.9	45.1	47.0	49.3	48.9
Hungary	14.6	14.4	14.7	15.7	18.8	21.7	24.4	26.6	31.1	33.8	37.3	40.7	45.0	51.7	58.9	63.9	66.8	67.2	65.0	62.5
Ireland	27.5	29.2	32.5	34.6	37.2	38.0	39.7	41.3	43.6	45.9	48.6	50.5	53.6	55.6	58.2	58.3	58.9	61.2	58.3	60.6
Iceland	25.5	24.9	29.6	27.4	34.0	35.5	35.9	37.8	38.5	40.0	45.5	47.7	54.3	62.6	69.0	71.0	72.9	72.3	74.6	74.3
Italy	29.4	31.6	33.6	35.8	39.7	40.8	41.5	45.7	46.9	47.2	48.6	51.9	55.0	58.5	62.2	64.4	66.0	67.1	67.2	m
Korea	36.8	38.3	40.2	44.0	45.5	48.9	53.6	62.4	66.0	72.5	78.3	83.2	86.9	88.8	90.5	91.8	93.7	96.1	98.1	100.0
Latvia	24.6	25.1	25.6	24.4	22.8	23.2	27.3	33.4	42.5	50.3	56.3	63.4	67.4	71.3	74.8	74.9	73.6	71.3	69.2	67.3
Maca-China	29.7	25.4	26.0	26.2	24.3	m	m	29.0	m	27.8	26.7	47.3	64.3	76.6	67.0	59.1	55.7	54.7	56.5	62.9
Mexico	15.2	14.7	m	13.8	14.0	14.4	15.3	16.0	17.1	18.2	19.6	20.5	21.7	22.8	23.9	24.7	25.4	26.3	27.2	27.9
New Zealand	39.3	45.5	52.0	57.8	60.1	58.5	58.8	62.7	60.9	64.1	66.0	67.3	68.5	70.2	84.8	81.4	78.9	79.1	78.5	83.5
Poland	20.4	21.7	21.5	23.8	27.4	31.0	35.0	39.5	38.9	44.8	49.7	55.1	58.4	60.2	61.7	64.1	65.6	66.9	69.4	71.4
Portugal	19.3	23.0	23.7	30.5	33.9	36.7	39.0	m	43.7	45.1	48.1	51.0	53.4	55.4	56.1	55.7	55.3	56.9	60.2	61.2
Singapore	m	m	m	m	m	m	m	m	m	m	m	m	m	m	m	m	m	m	m	m
Serbia	m	m	m	m	m	m	m	m	m	m	m	m	m	m	m	m	m	48.0	48.7	49.8
Slovak Republic	m	m	m	16.1	17.1	18.7	20.2	22.1	24.5	26.3	28.8	30.4	32.3	33.9	35.9	40.3	44.8	50.1	53.6	55.8
Slovenia	24.3	23.8	27.1	27.5	29.2	29.7	32.6	36.0	45.5	52.6	55.6	60.8	66.6	69.1	72.4	79.5	83.0	85.5	86.7	87.6
Trinidad and Tobago	m	6.5	6.8	7.4	m	m	m	m	m	5.8	5.8	6.2	8.5	8.5	11.5	11.6	m	m	m	m
Regions																				
Italy: Abruzzo	m	m	m	m	m	m	m	m	m	m	m	m	m	m	m	m	m	m	m	m
Italy: Basilicata	m	m	m	m	m	m	m	m	m	m	m	m	m	m	m	m	m	m	m	m
Italy: Bolzano	m	m	m	m	m	m	m	m	m	m	m	m	m	m	m	m	m	m	m	m
Italy: Calabria	m	m	m	m	m	m	m	m	m	m	m	m	m	m	m	m	m	m	m	m
Italy: Campania	m	m	m	m	m	m	m	m	m	m	m	m	m	m	m	m	m	m	m	m
Italy: Emilia Romagna	m	m	m	m	m	m	m	m	m	m	m	m	m	m	m	m	m	m	m	m
Italy: Friuli Venezia Giulia	m	m	m	m	m	m	m	m	m	m	m	m	m	m	m	m	m	m	m	m
Italy: Lazio	m	m	m	m	m	m	m	m	m	m	m	m	m	m	m	m	m	m	m	m
Italy: Liguria	m	m	m	m	m	m	m	m	m	m	m	m	m	m	m	m	m	m	m	m
Italy: Lombardia	m	m	m	m	m	m	m	m	m	m	m	m	m	m	m	m	m	m	m	m
Italy: Marche	m	m	m	m	m	m	m	m	m	m	m	m	m	m	m	m	m	m	m	m
Italy: Molise	m	m	m	m	m	m	m	m	m	m	m	m	m	m	m	m	m	m	m	m
Italy: Piemonte	m	m	m	m	m	m	m	m	m	m	m	m	m	m	m	m	m	m	m	m
Italy: Puglia	m	m	m	m	m	m	m	m	m	m	m	m	m	m	m	m	m	m	m	m
Italy: Sardegna	m	m	m	m	m	m	m	m	m	m	m	m	m	m	m	m	m	m	m	m
Italy: Sicilia	m	m	m	m	m	m	m	m	m	m	m	m	m	m	m	m	m	m	m	m
Italy: Toscana	m	m	m	m	m	m	m	m	m	m	m	m	m	m	m	m	m	m	m	m
Italy: Trento	m	m	m	m	m	m	m	m	m	m	m	m	m	m	m	m	m	m	m	m
Italy: Umbria	m	m	m	m	m	m	m	m	m	m	m	m	m	m	m	m	m	m	m	m
Italy: Valle d'Aosta	m	m	m	m	m	m	m	m	m	m	m	m	m	m	m	m	m	m	m	m
Italy: Veneto	m	m	m	m	m	m	m	m	m	m	m	m	m	m	m	m	m	m	m	m
Mexico: Aguascalientes	m	m	m	m	m	m	m	m	m	m	m	m	m	m	m	m	m	m	m	m
Mexico: Baja California	m	m	m	m	m	m	m	m	m	m	m	m	m	m	m	m	m	m	m	m
Mexico: Baja California Sur	m	m	m	m	m	m	m	m	m	m	m	m	m	m	m	m	m	m	m	m
Mexico: Campeche	m	m	m	m	m	m	m	m	m	m	m	m	m	m	m	m	m	m	m	m
Mexico: Chihuahua	m	m	m	m	m	m	m	m	m	m	m	m	m	m	m	m	m	m	m	m
Mexico: Colima	m	m	m	m	m	m	m	m	m	m	m	m	m	m	m	m	m	m	m	m
Mexico: Coahuila	m	m	m	m	m	m	m	m	m	m	m	m	m	m	m	m	m	m	m	m
Mexico: Chiapas	m	m	m	m	m	m	m	m	m	m	m	m	m	m	m	m	m	m	m	m
Mexico: Distrito Federal	m	m	m	m	m	m	m	m	m	m	m	m	m	m	m	m	m	m	m	m
Mexico: Durango	m	m	m	m	m	m	m	m	m	m	m	m	m	m	m	m	m	m	m	m
Mexico: Guerrero	m	m	m	m	m	m	m	m	m	m	m	m	m	m	m	m	m	m	m	m
Mexico: Guanajuato	m	m	m	m	m	m	m	m	m	m	m	m	m	m	m	m	m	m	m	m
Mexico: Hidalgo	m	m	m	m	m	m	m	m	m	m	m	m	m	m	m	m	m	m	m	m
Mexico: Jalisco	m	m	m	m	m	m	m	m	m	m	m	m	m	m	m	m	m	m	m	m
Mexico: Michoacán	m	m	m	m	m	m	m	m	m	m	m	m	m	m	m	m	m	m	m	m
Mexico: Morelos	m	m	m	m	m	m	m	m	m	m	m	m	m	m	m	m	m	m	m	m
Mexico: Mexico	m	m	m	m	m	m	m	m	m	m	m	m	m	m	m	m	m	m	m	m
Mexico: Nayarit	m	m	m	m	m	m	m	m	m	m	m	m	m	m	m	m	m	m	m	m
Mexico: Nuevo León	m	m	m	m	m	m	m	m	m	m	m	m	m	m	m	m	m	m	m	m
Mexico: Oaxaca	m	m	m	m	m	m	m	m	m	m	m	m	m	m	m	m	m	m	m	m
Mexico: Puebla	m	m	m	m	m	m	m	m	m	m	m	m	m	m	m	m	m	m	m	m
Mexico: Quintana Roo	m	m	m	m	m	m	m	m	m	m	m	m	m	m	m	m	m	m	m	m
Mexico: Querétaro	m	m	m	m	m	m	m	m	m	m	m	m	m	m	m	m	m	m	m	m
Mexico: Sinaloa	m	m	m	m	m	m	m	m	m	m	m	m	m	m	m	m	m	m	m	m
Mexico: San Luis Potosí	m	m	m	m	m	m	m	m	m	m	m	m	m	m	m	m	m	m	m	m
Mexico: Sonora	m	m	m	m	m	m	m	m	m	m	m	m	m	m	m	m	m	m	m	m
Mexico: Tamaulipas	m	m	m	m	m	m	m	m	m	m	m	m	m	m	m	m	m	m	m	m
Mexico: Tabasco	m	m	m	m	m	m	m	m	m	m	m	m	m	m	m	m	m	m	m	m
Mexico: Tlaxcala	m	m	m	m	m	m	m	m	m	m	m	m	m	m	m	m	m	m	m	m
Mexico: Veracruz	m	m	m	m	m	m	m	m	m	m	m	m	m	m	m	m	m	m	m	m
Mexico: Yucatán	m	m	m	m	m	m	m	m	m	m	m	m	m	m	m	m	m	m	m	m
Mexico: Zacatecas	m	m	m	m	m	m	m	m	m	m	m	m	m	m	m	m	m	m	m	m

1. Linear regression from 1980 to 2009 data where the dependent variable is the gross enrolment ratio and the independent variable is the year; coefficient for year is presented.
2. Linear regression from 2003 to 2009 data where the dependent variable is the gross enrolment ratio and the independent variable is the year; coefficient for year is presented.
Source: World Bank EdStats.
StatLink http://dx.doi.org/10.1787/888932734039

[Part 1/2]

Table B2.1 How countries and economies use and distribute marks to students, in the local scale

	Possible values for student marks	Minimum passing mark	Percentage of students with failing marks	
			%	S.E.
Countries and economies				
Austria	Five: {1,2,3,4,5}	4 [2]	2.42	(0.29)
Belgium (Flemish Community)	One hundred: {0-100}	50	3.54	(0.42)
Croatia	Six: {1,2,3,4,5,6}	2	1.81	(0.20)
Hungary	Five: {1,2,3,4,5}	2	2.23	(0.40)
Iceland	Ten: {1-10}	6	8.37	(0.45)
Ireland	One hundred: {0-100}	40	2.77	(0.34)
Italy	Ten: {1-10}	6	14.81	(0.42)
Latvia	Ten: {1-10}	6	34.85	(1.35)
Macao-China[1]	Variable	a	11.65	(0.41)
Mexico[1]	Variable	a	8.25	(0.31)
New Zealand[1]	Variable	a	13.97	(0.52)
Poland	Six: {1,2,3,4,5,6}	1	2.36	(0.26)
Portugal: ISCED2	Five: {1,2,3,4,5}	3	30.92	(1.50)
Portugal: ISCED3	Twenty: {1-20}	10	7.09	(0.59)
Serbia	Five: {1,2,3,4,5}	2	3.57	(0.41)
Singapore	One hundred: {0-100}	50	15.38	(0.60)
Slovak Republic	Six: {1,2,3,4,5,6}	5 [2]	0.89	(0.21)
Trinidad and Tobago	One hundred: {0-100}	50	9.49	(0.54)
Regions				
Italy: Abruzzo	Ten: {1-10}	6	16.45	(1.16)
Italy: Basilicata	Ten: {1-10}	6	16.78	(1.23)
Italy: Bolzano	Ten: {1-10}	6	7.70	(0.81)
Italy: Calabria	Ten: {1-10}	6	17.13	(1.10)
Italy: Campania	Ten: {1-10}	6	24.27	(1.52)
Italy: Emilia Romagna	Ten: {1-10}	6	10.39	(1.37)
Italy: Friuli Venezia Giulia	Ten: {1-10}	6	15.01	(1.00)
Italy: Lazio	Ten: {1-10}	6	17.30	(1.36)
Italy: Liguria	Ten: {1-10}	6	13.52	(1.11)
Italy: Lombardia	Ten: {1-10}	6	10.67	(1.19)
Italy: Marche	Ten: {1-10}	6	13.47	(1.49)
Italy: Molise	Ten: {1-10}	6	16.19	(1.58)
Italy: Piemonte	Ten: {1-10}	6	9.75	(1.40)
Italy: Puglia	Ten: {1-10}	6	14.02	(1.28)
Italy: Sardegna	Ten: {1-10}	6	18.11	(1.16)
Italy: Sicilia	Ten: {1-10}	6	17.33	(1.70)
Italy: Toscana	Ten: {1-10}	6	14.73	(1.10)
Italy: Trento	Ten: {1-10}	6	8.22	(0.85)
Italy: Umbria	Ten: {1-10}	6	12.65	(0.87)
Italy: Valle d'Aosta	Ten: {1-10}	6	11.84	(1.12)
Italy: Veneto	Ten: {1-10}	6	11.44	(0.99)
Mexico: Aguascalientes[1]	Variable	a	7.65	(0.77)
Mexico: Baja California[1]	Variable	a	7.96	(0.89)
Mexico: Baja California Sur[1]	Variable	a	8.04	(1.01)
Mexico: Campeche[1]	Variable	a	8.07	(1.38)
Mexico: Chihuahua[1]	Variable	a	8.65	(1.33)
Mexico: Colima[1]	Variable	a	4.31	(0.72)
Mexico: Coahuila[1]	Variable	a	7.55	(1.68)
Mexico: Chiapas[1]	Variable	a	7.01	(0.93)
Mexico: Distrito Federal[1]	Variable	a	11.76	(1.20)
Mexico: Durango[1]	Variable	a	6.54	(0.89)
Mexico: Guerrero[1]	Variable	a	7.58	(0.77)
Mexico: Guanajuato[1]	Variable	a	10.08	(1.27)
Mexico: Hidalgo[1]	Variable	a	6.82	(1.00)
Mexico: Jalisco[1]	Variable	a	8.72	(0.80)
Mexico: Michoacán[1]	Variable	a	7.50	(1.60)
Mexico: Morelos[1]	Variable	a	9.13	(1.25)
Mexico: Mexico[1]	Variable	a	8.50	(1.34)
Mexico: Nayarit[1]	Variable	a	7.70	(1.18)
Mexico: Nuevo León[1]	Variable	a	10.03	(2.04)
Mexico: Oaxaca[1]	Variable	a	7.54	(1.22)
Mexico: Puebla[1]	Variable	a	8.28	(1.30)
Mexico: Quintana Roo[1]	Variable	a	6.41	(0.98)
Mexico: Querétaro[1]	Variable	a	7.02	(1.23)
Mexico: Sinaloa[1]	Variable	a	8.55	(1.65)
Mexico: San Luis Potosí[1]	Variable	a	7.94	(1.49)
Mexico: Sonora[1]	Variable	a	5.84	(0.99)
Mexico: Tamaulipas[1]	Variable	a	7.48	(0.79)
Mexico: Tabasco[1]	Variable	a	5.02	(0.78)
Mexico: Tlaxcala[1]	Variable	a	9.25	(1.44)
Mexico: Veracruz[1]	Variable	a	7.00	(1.64)
Mexico: Yucatán[1]	Variable	a	7.43	(0.69)
Mexico: Zacatecas[1]	Variable	a	5.99	(1.21)

1. Macao-China, Mexico and New Zealand distributed, in the Educational Career questionnaire, the alternative question on whether students received a passing or failing mark. Results for these countries and economies are thus based on a dichotomous variable, and this restricted information does not allow for the calculation of mean, standard deviation and percentiles.
2. In Austria and the Slovak Republic, marks closer to the value 1 (one) signal better appraisal.

StatLink http://dx.doi.org/10.1787/888932734058

[Part 2/2]

Table B2.1 How countries and economies use and distribute marks to students, in the local scale

	Distribution of passing marks in local scale											
	Mean	S.E.	Std. Dev.	S.E.	5th percentile	S.E.	95th percentile	S.E.	Minimum	S.E.	Maximum	S.E.
Countries and economies												
Austria	2.59	(0.02)	0.92	(0.01)	1.00	(0.00)	4.00	(0.00)	1.00	(0.00)	4.00	(0.00)
Belgium (Flemish Community)	70.92	(0.28)	9.41	(0.16)	55.00	(0.00)	86.00	(1.00)	50.00	(0.00)	100.00	(0.00)
Croatia	3.56	(0.03)	0.99	(0.01)	2.00	(0.00)	5.00	(0.00)	2.00	(0.00)	6.00	(0.00)
Hungary	3.67	(0.03)	0.97	(0.01)	2.00	(0.00)	5.00	(0.00)	2.00	(0.00)	5.00	(0.00)
Iceland	7.78	(0.02)	1.10	(0.01)	6.00	(0.00)	9.00	(0.00)	6.00	(0.00)	10.00	(0.00)
Ireland	70.60	(0.31)	12.78	(0.15)	48.00	(0.00)	93.00	(0.00)	40.00	(0.00)	100.00	(0.00)
Italy	6.76	(0.01)	0.81	(0.01)	6.00	(0.00)	8.00	(0.00)	6.00	(0.00)	10.00	(0.00)
Latvia	6.88	(0.03)	0.90	(0.02)	6.00	(0.00)	8.00	(1.40)	6.00	(0.00)	10.00	(0.00)
Macao-China[1]	a	a	a	a	a	a	a	a	a	a	a	a
Mexico[1]	a	a	a	a	a	a	a	a	a	a	a	a
New Zealand[1]	a	a	a	a	a	a	a	a	a	a	a	a
Poland	3.41	(0.02)	1.00	(0.01)	2.00	(0.00)	5.00	(0.00)	2.00	(0.00)	6.00	(0.00)
Portugal: ISCED2	3.24	(0.01)	0.49	(0.02)	3.00	(0.00)	4.00	(0.00)	3.00	(0.00)	5.00	(0.00)
Portugal: ISCED3	13.24	(0.07)	2.22	(0.03)	10.00	(0.00)	17.00	(0.00)	10.00	(0.00)	20.00	(0.00)
Serbia	3.49	(0.03)	1.02	(0.01)	2.00	(0.00)	5.00	(0.00)	2.00	(0.00)	5.00	(0.00)
Singapore	61.52	(0.12)	7.90	(0.11)	50.00	(0.00)	76.00	(1.32)	50.00	(0.00)	100.00	(0.00)
Slovak Republic	2.47	(0.02)	0.95	(0.01)	1.00	(0.00)	4.00	(0.00)	1.00	(0.00)	6.00	(0.00)
Trinidad and Tobago	71.79	(0.20)	11.43	(0.11)	53.00	(0.22)	91.00	(1.47)	50.00	(0.00)	100.00	(0.00)
Regions												
Italy: Abruzzo	6.83	(0.03)	0.83	(0.03)	6.00	(0.00)	8.00	(0.00)	6.00	(0.00)	10.00	(0.00)
Italy: Basilicata	6.72	(0.03)	0.81	(0.02)	6.00	(0.00)	8.00	(0.00)	6.00	(0.00)	10.00	(0.00)
Italy: Bolzano	7.13	(0.03)	0.89	(0.01)	6.00	(0.00)	9.00	(0.00)	6.00	(0.00)	10.00	(0.00)
Italy: Calabria	6.74	(0.03)	0.80	(0.03)	6.00	(0.00)	8.00	(0.00)	6.00	(0.00)	10.00	(0.00)
Italy: Campania	6.50	(0.03)	0.70	(0.03)	6.00	(0.00)	8.00	(0.00)	6.00	(0.00)	10.00	(0.00)
Italy: Emilia Romagna	6.86	(0.04)	0.82	(0.02)	6.00	(0.00)	8.00	(0.00)	6.00	(0.00)	10.00	(0.00)
Italy: Friuli Venezia Giulia	6.78	(0.03)	0.82	(0.02)	6.00	(0.00)	8.00	(0.00)	6.00	(0.00)	10.00	(0.00)
Italy: Lazio	6.75	(0.04)	0.82	(0.03)	6.00	(0.00)	8.00	(0.00)	6.00	(0.00)	10.00	(0.00)
Italy: Liguria	6.76	(0.03)	0.80	(0.02)	6.00	(0.00)	8.00	(0.00)	6.00	(0.00)	10.00	(0.00)
Italy: Lombardia	6.77	(0.03)	0.80	(0.03)	6.00	(0.00)	8.00	(0.00)	6.00	(0.00)	10.00	(0.00)
Italy: Marche	6.76	(0.03)	0.78	(0.02)	6.00	(0.00)	8.00	(0.00)	6.00	(0.00)	10.00	(0.00)
Italy: Molise	6.73	(0.03)	0.80	(0.03)	6.00	(0.00)	8.00	(0.00)	6.00	(0.00)	10.00	(0.00)
Italy: Piemonte	6.93	(0.03)	0.83	(0.01)	6.00	(0.00)	8.00	(0.00)	6.00	(0.00)	10.00	(0.00)
Italy: Puglia	6.79	(0.04)	0.82	(0.03)	6.00	(0.00)	8.00	(0.00)	6.00	(0.00)	10.00	(0.00)
Italy: Sardegna	6.84	(0.04)	0.86	(0.03)	6.00	(0.00)	8.00	(0.00)	6.00	(0.00)	10.00	(0.00)
Italy: Sicilia	6.75	(0.04)	0.85	(0.02)	6.00	(0.00)	8.00	(0.00)	6.00	(0.00)	10.00	(0.00)
Italy: Toscana	6.73	(0.04)	0.77	(0.03)	6.00	(0.00)	8.00	(0.00)	6.00	(0.00)	10.00	(0.00)
Italy: Trento	6.87	(0.03)	0.85	(0.02)	6.00	(0.00)	8.00	(0.00)	6.00	(0.00)	10.00	(0.00)
Italy: Umbria	6.84	(0.03)	0.85	(0.02)	6.00	(0.00)	8.00	(0.00)	6.00	(0.00)	10.00	(0.00)
Italy: Valle d'Aosta	6.79	(0.03)	0.81	(0.02)	6.00	(0.00)	8.00	(0.00)	6.00	(0.00)	10.00	(0.00)
Italy: Veneto	6.73	(0.03)	0.76	(0.02)	6.00	(0.00)	8.00	(0.00)	6.00	(0.00)	10.00	(0.00)
Mexico: Aguascalientes[1]	a	a	a	a	a	a	a	a	a	a	a	a
Mexico: Baja California[1]	a	a	a	a	a	a	a	a	a	a	a	a
Mexico: Baja California Sur[1]	a	a	a	a	a	a	a	a	a	a	a	a
Mexico: Campeche[1]	a	a	a	a	a	a	a	a	a	a	a	a
Mexico: Chihuahua[1]	a	a	a	a	a	a	a	a	a	a	a	a
Mexico: Colima[1]	a	a	a	a	a	a	a	a	a	a	a	a
Mexico: Coahuila[1]	a	a	a	a	a	a	a	a	a	a	a	a
Mexico: Chiapas[1]	a	a	a	a	a	a	a	a	a	a	a	a
Mexico: Distrito Federal[1]	a	a	a	a	a	a	a	a	a	a	a	a
Mexico: Durango[1]	a	a	a	a	a	a	a	a	a	a	a	a
Mexico: Guerrero[1]	a	a	a	a	a	a	a	a	a	a	a	a
Mexico: Guanajuato[1]	a	a	a	a	a	a	a	a	a	a	a	a
Mexico: Hidalgo[1]	a	a	a	a	a	a	a	a	a	a	a	a
Mexico: Jalisco[1]	a	a	a	a	a	a	a	a	a	a	a	a
Mexico: Michoacán[1]	a	a	a	a	a	a	a	a	a	a	a	a
Mexico: Morelos[1]	a	a	a	a	a	a	a	a	a	a	a	a
Mexico: Mexico[1]	a	a	a	a	a	a	a	a	a	a	a	a
Mexico: Nayarit[1]	a	a	a	a	a	a	a	a	a	a	a	a
Mexico: Nuevo León[1]	a	a	a	a	a	a	a	a	a	a	a	a
Mexico: Oaxaca[1]	a	a	a	a	a	a	a	a	a	a	a	a
Mexico: Puebla[1]	a	a	a	a	a	a	a	a	a	a	a	a
Mexico: Quintana Roo[1]	a	a	a	a	a	a	a	a	a	a	a	a
Mexico: Querétaro[1]	a	a	a	a	a	a	a	a	a	a	a	a
Mexico: Sinaloa[1]	a	a	a	a	a	a	a	a	a	a	a	a
Mexico: San Luis Potosí[1]	a	a	a	a	a	a	a	a	a	a	a	a
Mexico: Sonora[1]	a	a	a	a	a	a	a	a	a	a	a	a
Mexico: Tamaulipas[1]	a	a	a	a	a	a	a	a	a	a	a	a
Mexico: Tabasco[1]	a	a	a	a	a	a	a	a	a	a	a	a
Mexico: Tlaxcala[1]	a	a	a	a	a	a	a	a	a	a	a	a
Mexico: Veracruz[1]	a	a	a	a	a	a	a	a	a	a	a	a
Mexico: Yucatán[1]	a	a	a	a	a	a	a	a	a	a	a	a
Mexico: Zacatecas[1]	a	a	a	a	a	a	a	a	a	a	a	a

1. Macao-China, Mexico and New Zealand distributed, in the Educational Career questionnaire, the alternative question on whether students received a passing or failing mark. Results for these countries and economies are thus based on a dichotomous variable, and this restricted information does not allow for the calculation of mean, standard deviation and percentiles.
2. In Austria and the Slovak Republic, marks closer to the value 1 (one) signal better appraisal.

StatLink http://dx.doi.org/10.1787/888932734058

[Part 1/2]

Table B2.2 How countries and economies use and distribute marks to students, in a comparable scale

	Possible values	Minimum passing mark	Percentage of students with failing marks	
			%	S.E.
Countries and economies				
Austria	Five: {1,2,3,4,5}	4 [2]	2.42	(0.29)
Belgium (Flemish Community)	One hundred: {0-100}	50	3.54	(0.42)
Croatia	Six: {1,2,3,4,5,6}	2	1.81	(0.20)
Hungary	Five: {1,2,3,4,5}	2	2.23	(0.40)
Iceland	Ten: {1-10}	6	8.37	(0.45)
Ireland	One hundred: {0-100}	40	2.77	(0.34)
Italy	Ten: {1-10}	6	14.81	(0.42)
Latvia	Ten: {1-10}	6	34.85	(1.35)
Macao-China[1]	Variable	a	11.65	(0.41)
Mexico[1]	Variable	a	8.25	(0.31)
New Zealand[1]	Variable	a	13.97	(0.52)
Poland	Six: {1,2,3,4,5,6}	1	2.36	(0.26)
Portugal: ISCED2	Five: {1,2,3,4,5}	3	30.92	(1.50)
Portugal: ISCED3	Twenty: {1-20}	10	7.09	(0.59)
Serbia	Five: {1,2,3,4,5}	2	3.57	(0.41)
Singapore	One hundred: {0-100}	50	15.38	(0.60)
Slovak Republic	Six: {1,2,3,4,5,6}	5 [2]	0.89	(0.21)
Trinidad and Tobago	One hundred: {0-100}	50	9.49	(0.54)
Regions				
Italy: Abruzzo	Ten: {1-10}	6	16.45	(1.16)
Italy: Basilicata	Ten: {1-10}	6	16.78	(1.23)
Italy: Bolzano	Ten: {1-10}	6	7.70	(0.81)
Italy: Calabria	Ten: {1-10}	6	17.13	(1.10)
Italy: Campania	Ten: {1-10}	6	24.27	(1.52)
Italy: Emilia Romagna	Ten: {1-10}	6	10.39	(1.37)
Italy: Friuli Venezia Giulia	Ten: {1-10}	6	15.01	(1.00)
Italy: Lazio	Ten: {1-10}	6	17.30	(1.36)
Italy: Liguria	Ten: {1-10}	6	13.52	(1.11)
Italy: Lombardia	Ten: {1-10}	6	10.67	(1.19)
Italy: Marche	Ten: {1-10}	6	13.47	(1.49)
Italy: Molise	Ten: {1-10}	6	16.19	(1.58)
Italy: Piemonte	Ten: {1-10}	6	9.75	(1.40)
Italy: Puglia	Ten: {1-10}	6	14.02	(1.28)
Italy: Sardegna	Ten: {1-10}	6	18.11	(1.16)
Italy: Sicilia	Ten: {1-10}	6	17.33	(1.70)
Italy: Toscana	Ten: {1-10}	6	14.73	(1.10)
Italy: Trento	Ten: {1-10}	6	8.22	(0.85)
Italy: Umbria	Ten: {1-10}	6	12.65	(0.87)
Italy: Valle d'Aosta	Ten: {1-10}	6	11.84	(1.12)
Italy: Veneto	Ten: {1-10}	6	11.44	(0.99)
Mexico: Aguascalientes[1]	Variable	a	7.65	(0.77)
Mexico: Baja California[1]	Variable	a	7.96	(0.89)
Mexico: Baja California Sur[1]	Variable	a	8.04	(1.01)
Mexico: Campeche[1]	Variable	a	8.07	(1.38)
Mexico: Chihuahua[1]	Variable	a	8.65	(1.33)
Mexico: Colima[1]	Variable	a	4.31	(0.72)
Mexico: Coahuila[1]	Variable	a	7.55	(1.68)
Mexico: Chiapas[1]	Variable	a	7.01	(0.93)
Mexico: Distrito Federal[1]	Variable	a	11.76	(1.20)
Mexico: Durango[1]	Variable	a	6.54	(0.89)
Mexico: Guerrero[1]	Variable	a	7.58	(0.77)
Mexico: Guanajuato[1]	Variable	a	10.08	(1.27)
Mexico: Hidalgo[1]	Variable	a	6.82	(1.00)
Mexico: Jalisco[1]	Variable	a	8.72	(0.80)
Mexico: Michoacán[1]	Variable	a	7.50	(1.60)
Mexico: Morelos[1]	Variable	a	9.13	(1.25)
Mexico: Mexico[1]	Variable	a	8.50	(1.34)
Mexico: Nayarit[1]	Variable	a	7.70	(1.18)
Mexico: Nuevo León[1]	Variable	a	10.03	(2.04)
Mexico: Oaxaca[1]	Variable	a	7.54	(1.22)
Mexico: Puebla[1]	Variable	a	8.28	(1.30)
Mexico: Quintana Roo[1]	Variable	a	6.41	(0.98)
Mexico: Querétaro[1]	Variable	a	7.02	(1.23)
Mexico: Sinaloa[1]	Variable	a	8.55	(1.65)
Mexico: San Luis Potosí[1]	Variable	a	7.94	(1.49)
Mexico: Sonora[1]	Variable	a	5.84	(0.99)
Mexico: Tamaulipas[1]	Variable	a	7.48	(0.79)
Mexico: Tabasco[1]	Variable	a	5.02	(0.78)
Mexico: Tlaxcala[1]	Variable	a	9.25	(1.44)
Mexico: Veracruz[1]	Variable	a	7.00	(1.64)
Mexico: Yucatán[1]	Variable	a	7.43	(0.69)
Mexico: Zacatecas[1]	Variable	a	5.99	(1.21)

1. Macao-China, Mexico and New Zealand distributed, in the Educational Career questionnaire, the alternative question on whether students received a passing or failing mark. Results for these countries and economies are thus based on a dichotomous variable, and this restricted information does not allow for the calculation of mean, standard deviation and percentiles.
2. In Austria and the Slovak Republic, marks closer to the value 1 (one) signal better appraisal.

StatLink http://dx.doi.org/10.1787/888932734077

[Part 2/2]

Table B2.2 How countries and economies use and distribute marks to students, in a comparable scale

	Distribution of passing marks in scale from 50 (minimum passing mark) to 100 (maximum mark)											
	Mean	S.E.	Std. Dev.	S.E.	5th percentile	S.E.	95th percentile	S.E.	Minimum	S.E.	Maximum	S.E.
Countries and economies												
Austria	73.45	(0.39)	15.28	(0.13)	50.00	(0.00)	100.00	(0.00)	50.00	(0.00)	100.00	(0.00)
Belgium (Flemish Community)	70.92	(0.28)	9.41	(0.16)	55.00	(0.00)	86.00	(1.00)	50.00	(0.00)	100.00	(0.00)
Croatia	69.47	(0.33)	12.39	(0.11)	50.00	(0.00)	87.50	(0.00)	50.00	(0.00)	100.00	(0.00)
Hungary	77.86	(0.52)	16.19	(0.19)	50.00	(0.00)	100.00	(0.00)	50.00	(0.00)	100.00	(0.00)
Iceland	72.25	(0.25)	13.73	(0.12)	50.00	(0.00)	87.50	(0.00)	50.00	(0.00)	100.00	(0.00)
Ireland	75.50	(0.26)	10.65	(0.12)	56.67	(0.00)	94.17	(0.00)	50.00	(0.00)	100.00	(0.00)
Italy	59.50	(0.11)	10.11	(0.09)	50.00	(0.00)	75.00	(0.00)	50.00	(0.00)	100.00	(0.00)
Latvia	60.96	(0.40)	11.27	(0.30)	50.00	(0.00)	75.00	(17.46)	50.00	(0.00)	100.00	(0.00)
Macao-China[1]	a	a	a	a	a	a	a	a	a	a	a	a
Mexico[1]	a	a	a	a	a	a	a	a	a	a	a	a
New Zealand[1]	a	a	a	a	a	a	a	a	a	a	a	a
Poland	67.58	(0.30)	12.55	(0.14)	50.00	(0.00)	87.50	(0.00)	50.00	(0.00)	100.00	(0.00)
Portugal: ISCED2	55.89	(0.32)	12.20	(0.38)	50.00	(0.00)	75.00	(0.00)	50.00	(0.00)	100.00	(0.00)
Portugal: ISCED3	66.18	(0.37)	11.08	(0.16)	50.00	(0.00)	85.00	(0.00)	50.00	(0.00)	100.00	(0.00)
Serbia	74.84	(0.50)	17.06	(0.17)	50.00	(0.00)	100.00	(0.00)	50.00	(0.00)	100.00	(0.00)
Singapore	61.52	(0.12)	7.90	(0.11)	50.00	(0.00)	76.00	(1.32)	50.00	(0.00)	100.00	(0.00)
Slovak Republic	85.31	(0.22)	9.53	(0.11)	70.00	(0.00)	100.00	(0.00)	50.00	(0.00)	100.00	(0.00)
Trinidad and Tobago	71.79	(0.20)	11.43	(0.11)	53.00	(0.22)	91.00	(1.47)	50.00	(0.00)	100.00	(0.00)
Regions												
Italy: Abruzzo	60.42	(0.43)	10.34	(0.32)	50.00	(0.00)	75.00	(0.00)	50.00	(0.00)	100.00	(0.00)
Italy: Basilicata	58.96	(0.37)	10.10	(0.25)	50.00	(0.00)	75.00	(0.00)	50.00	(0.00)	100.00	(0.00)
Italy: Bolzano	64.14	(0.38)	11.11	(0.16)	50.00	(0.00)	87.50	(0.00)	50.00	(0.00)	100.00	(0.00)
Italy: Calabria	59.19	(0.40)	10.05	(0.32)	50.00	(0.00)	75.00	(0.00)	50.00	(0.00)	100.00	(0.00)
Italy: Campania	56.30	(0.41)	8.79	(0.32)	50.00	(0.00)	75.00	(0.00)	50.00	(0.00)	100.00	(0.00)
Italy: Emilia Romagna	60.79	(0.46)	10.21	(0.29)	50.00	(0.00)	75.00	(0.00)	50.00	(0.00)	100.00	(0.00)
Italy: Friuli Venezia Giulia	59.77	(0.38)	10.22	(0.27)	50.00	(0.00)	75.00	(0.00)	50.00	(0.00)	100.00	(0.00)
Italy: Lazio	59.32	(0.46)	10.23	(0.39)	50.00	(0.00)	75.00	(0.00)	50.00	(0.00)	100.00	(0.00)
Italy: Liguria	59.50	(0.37)	10.04	(0.26)	50.00	(0.00)	75.00	(0.00)	50.00	(0.00)	100.00	(0.00)
Italy: Lombardia	59.60	(0.32)	10.01	(0.32)	50.00	(0.00)	75.00	(0.00)	50.00	(0.00)	100.00	(0.00)
Italy: Marche	59.45	(0.39)	9.70	(0.28)	50.00	(0.00)	75.00	(0.00)	50.00	(0.00)	100.00	(0.00)
Italy: Molise	59.06	(0.39)	9.94	(0.31)	50.00	(0.00)	75.00	(0.00)	50.00	(0.00)	100.00	(0.00)
Italy: Piemonte	61.68	(0.41)	10.33	(0.18)	50.00	(0.00)	75.00	(0.00)	50.00	(0.00)	100.00	(0.00)
Italy: Puglia	59.85	(0.51)	10.30	(0.38)	50.00	(0.00)	75.00	(0.00)	50.00	(0.00)	100.00	(0.00)
Italy: Sardegna	60.47	(0.54)	10.81	(0.40)	50.00	(0.00)	75.00	(0.00)	50.00	(0.00)	100.00	(0.00)
Italy: Sicilia	59.35	(0.45)	10.57	(0.30)	50.00	(0.00)	75.00	(0.00)	50.00	(0.00)	100.00	(0.00)
Italy: Toscana	59.15	(0.45)	9.63	(0.34)	50.00	(0.00)	75.00	(0.00)	50.00	(0.00)	100.00	(0.00)
Italy: Trento	60.82	(0.38)	10.67	(0.26)	50.00	(0.00)	75.00	(0.00)	50.00	(0.00)	100.00	(0.00)
Italy: Umbria	60.44	(0.43)	10.57	(0.25)	50.00	(0.00)	75.00	(0.00)	50.00	(0.00)	100.00	(0.00)
Italy: Valle d'Aosta	59.85	(0.39)	10.10	(0.31)	50.00	(0.00)	75.00	(0.00)	50.00	(0.00)	100.00	(0.00)
Italy: Veneto	59.18	(0.36)	9.44	(0.26)	50.00	(0.00)	75.00	(0.00)	50.00	(0.00)	100.00	(0.00)
Mexico: Aguascalientes[1]	a	a	a	a	a	a	a	a	a	a	a	a
Mexico: Baja California[1]	a	a	a	a	a	a	a	a	a	a	a	a
Mexico: Baja California Sur[1]	a	a	a	a	a	a	a	a	a	a	a	a
Mexico: Campeche[1]	a	a	a	a	a	a	a	a	a	a	a	a
Mexico: Chihuahua[1]	a	a	a	a	a	a	a	a	a	a	a	a
Mexico: Colima[1]	a	a	a	a	a	a	a	a	a	a	a	a
Mexico: Coahuila[1]	a	a	a	a	a	a	a	a	a	a	a	a
Mexico: Chiapas[1]	a	a	a	a	a	a	a	a	a	a	a	a
Mexico: Distrito Federal[1]	a	a	a	a	a	a	a	a	a	a	a	a
Mexico: Durango[1]	a	a	a	a	a	a	a	a	a	a	a	a
Mexico: Guerrero[1]	a	a	a	a	a	a	a	a	a	a	a	a
Mexico: Guanajuato[1]	a	a	a	a	a	a	a	a	a	a	a	a
Mexico: Hidalgo[1]	a	a	a	a	a	a	a	a	a	a	a	a
Mexico: Jalisco[1]	a	a	a	a	a	a	a	a	a	a	a	a
Mexico: Michoacán[1]	a	a	a	a	a	a	a	a	a	a	a	a
Mexico: Morelos[1]	a	a	a	a	a	a	a	a	a	a	a	a
Mexico: Mexico[1]	a	a	a	a	a	a	a	a	a	a	a	a
Mexico: Nayarit[1]	a	a	a	a	a	a	a	a	a	a	a	a
Mexico: Nuevo León[1]	a	a	a	a	a	a	a	a	a	a	a	a
Mexico: Oaxaca[1]	a	a	a	a	a	a	a	a	a	a	a	a
Mexico: Puebla[1]	a	a	a	a	a	a	a	a	a	a	a	a
Mexico: Quintana Roo[1]	a	a	a	a	a	a	a	a	a	a	a	a
Mexico: Querétaro[1]	a	a	a	a	a	a	a	a	a	a	a	a
Mexico: Sinaloa[1]	a	a	a	a	a	a	a	a	a	a	a	a
Mexico: San Luis Potosí[1]	a	a	a	a	a	a	a	a	a	a	a	a
Mexico: Sonora[1]	a	a	a	a	a	a	a	a	a	a	a	a
Mexico: Tamaulipas[1]	a	a	a	a	a	a	a	a	a	a	a	a
Mexico: Tabasco[1]	a	a	a	a	a	a	a	a	a	a	a	a
Mexico: Tlaxcala[1]	a	a	a	a	a	a	a	a	a	a	a	a
Mexico: Veracruz[1]	a	a	a	a	a	a	a	a	a	a	a	a
Mexico: Yucatán[1]	a	a	a	a	a	a	a	a	a	a	a	a
Mexico: Zacatecas[1]	a	a	a	a	a	a	a	a	a	a	a	a

1. Macao-China, Mexico and New Zealand distributed, in the Educational Career questionnaire, the alternative question on whether students received a passing or failing mark. Results for these countries and economies are thus based on a dichotomous variable, and this restricted information does not allow for the calculation of mean, standard deviation and percentiles.
2. In Austria and the Slovak Republic, marks closer to the value 1 (one) signal better appraisal.

StatLink http://dx.doi.org/10.1787/888932734077

[Part 1/2]

Table B2.3 Correlation between the marks received by students in their language-of-assessment course and student characteristics

	Reading performance		Metacognition strategies: Understanding and remembering		Metacognition strategies: Effective summarising strategies		Approaches to learning: Memorisation strategies		Approaches to learning: Elaboration strategies		Approaches to learning: Control strategies		Engagement: Enjoyment of reading		Engagement: Attitudes toward school	
	Corr.	S.E.	Corr.	S.E.	Corr.	S.E.	Corr.	S.E.	Corr.	S.E.	Corr.	S.E.	Corr.	S.E.	Corr.	S.E.
Countries and economies																
Austria	**0.222**	(0.020)	**0.129**	(0.014)	**0.154**	(0.016)	**0.067**	(0.015)	**0.079**	(0.016)	**0.173**	(0.020)	**0.210**	(0.018)	**0.084**	(0.015)
Belgium (Flemish Community)	**0.190**	(0.024)	**0.133**	(0.020)	**0.125**	(0.020)	0.039	(0.020)	**0.076**	(0.015)	**0.164**	(0.021)	**0.220**	(0.021)	**0.100**	(0.019)
Croatia	**0.469**	(0.021)	**0.224**	(0.019)	**0.280**	(0.018)	**0.061**	(0.018)	**0.070**	(0.017)	**0.186**	(0.015)	**0.333**	(0.015)	**0.052**	(0.016)
Hungary	**0.502**	(0.019)	**0.245**	(0.019)	**0.289**	(0.020)	**0.092**	(0.018)	**0.065**	(0.017)	**0.181**	(0.016)	**0.367**	(0.018)	**0.130**	(0.021)
Iceland	**0.408**	(0.013)	**0.185**	(0.017)	**0.219**	(0.017)	**0.124**	(0.021)	**0.147**	(0.017)	**0.256**	(0.019)	**0.234**	(0.019)	**0.215**	(0.018)
Ireland	**0.289**	(0.020)	**0.088**	(0.018)	**0.143**	(0.018)	**0.087**	(0.019)	**0.122**	(0.019)	**0.208**	(0.019)	**0.287**	(0.019)	**0.109**	(0.017)
Italy	**0.391**	(0.011)	**0.175**	(0.009)	**0.200**	(0.010)	0.001	(0.012)	**0.128**	(0.008)	**0.233**	(0.011)	**0.296**	(0.007)	**0.109**	(0.010)
Latvia	**0.508**	(0.022)	**0.254**	(0.019)	**0.253**	(0.019)	**0.064**	(0.022)	**0.099**	(0.021)	**0.199**	(0.021)	**0.372**	(0.017)	**0.132**	(0.024)
Macao-China[1]	**0.259**	(0.012)	**0.095**	(0.014)	**0.095**	(0.014)	**0.071**	(0.015)	**0.092**	(0.014)	**0.126**	(0.014)	**0.176**	(0.014)	**0.069**	(0.013)
Mexico[1]	**0.083**	(0.011)	**0.020**	(0.008)	**0.048**	(0.009)	**0.063**	(0.008)	**0.085**	(0.008)	**0.121**	(0.008)	**0.110**	(0.007)	**0.062**	(0.008)
New Zealand[1]	**0.267**	(0.015)	**0.144**	(0.014)	**0.172**	(0.014)	**0.111**	(0.017)	**0.078**	(0.016)	**0.218**	(0.016)	**0.193**	(0.015)	**0.143**	(0.016)
Poland	**0.575**	(0.014)	**0.232**	(0.016)	**0.325**	(0.014)	**0.131**	(0.015)	**0.112**	(0.015)	**0.302**	(0.015)	**0.404**	(0.013)	**0.056**	(0.015)
Portugal: ISCED2	**0.411**	(0.024)	**0.193**	(0.023)	**0.265**	(0.020)	0.030	(0.024)	**0.191**	(0.023)	**0.273**	(0.023)	**0.255**	(0.022)	**0.174**	(0.016)
Portugal: ISCED3	**0.467**	(0.022)	**0.177**	(0.013)	**0.161**	(0.018)	-0.026	(0.020)	**0.220**	(0.017)	**0.351**	(0.018)	**0.311**	(0.018)	**0.126**	(0.018)
Serbia	**0.456**	(0.020)	**0.242**	(0.020)	**0.256**	(0.017)	**-0.043**	(0.017)	**0.107**	(0.016)	**0.189**	(0.011)	**0.341**	(0.014)	**0.092**	(0.018)
Singapore	**0.219**	(0.018)	**0.057**	(0.019)	**0.091**	(0.017)	0.001	(0.014)	**0.069**	(0.019)	**0.113**	(0.015)	**0.182**	(0.016)	**0.041**	(0.018)
Slovak Republic	**0.562**	(0.018)	**0.210**	(0.019)	**0.308**	(0.019)	**-0.116**	(0.025)	**0.088**	(0.023)	**0.243**	(0.022)	**0.337**	(0.016)	**0.106**	(0.020)
Trinidad and Tobago	**0.227**	(0.020)	**0.076**	(0.017)	**0.058**	(0.018)	**0.121**	(0.020)	**0.126**	(0.017)	**0.206**	(0.016)	**0.171**	(0.018)	**0.092**	(0.021)
Regions																
Italy: Abruzzo	**0.429**	(0.032)	**0.227**	(0.030)	**0.240**	(0.041)	0.037	(0.030)	**0.193**	(0.025)	**0.294**	(0.030)	**0.353**	(0.025)	**0.170**	(0.033)
Italy: Basilicata	**0.473**	(0.030)	**0.239**	(0.042)	**0.324**	(0.031)	0.045	(0.032)	**0.189**	(0.030)	**0.323**	(0.038)	**0.350**	(0.029)	**0.157**	(0.020)
Italy: Bolzano	**0.375**	(0.037)	**0.172**	(0.042)	**0.213**	(0.043)	**0.073**	(0.025)	**0.061**	(0.023)	**0.176**	(0.030)	**0.238**	(0.030)	**0.154**	(0.028)
Italy: Calabria	**0.433**	(0.034)	**0.171**	(0.030)	**0.236**	(0.025)	0.019	(0.034)	**0.102**	(0.029)	**0.237**	(0.031)	**0.364**	(0.023)	**0.107**	(0.035)
Italy: Campania	**0.349**	(0.031)	**0.110**	(0.038)	**0.117**	(0.040)	0.011	(0.034)	**0.157**	(0.030)	**0.238**	(0.036)	**0.306**	(0.028)	**0.128**	(0.033)
Italy: Emilia Romagna	**0.382**	(0.044)	**0.142**	(0.035)	**0.207**	(0.026)	0.009	(0.025)	**0.145**	(0.031)	**0.235**	(0.030)	**0.349**	(0.026)	**0.172**	(0.039)
Italy: Friuli Venezia Giulia	**0.375**	(0.039)	**0.190**	(0.040)	**0.173**	(0.044)	**0.060**	(0.031)	**0.159**	(0.029)	**0.271**	(0.032)	**0.301**	(0.032)	**0.194**	(0.026)
Italy: Lazio	**0.366**	(0.035)	**0.224**	(0.027)	**0.255**	(0.040)	0.010	(0.035)	**0.176**	(0.027)	**0.281**	(0.032)	**0.354**	(0.023)	**0.110**	(0.042)
Italy: Liguria	**0.313**	(0.027)	**0.157**	(0.034)	**0.172**	(0.029)	0.013	(0.049)	**0.143**	(0.036)	**0.268**	(0.033)	**0.230**	(0.042)	**0.124**	(0.022)
Italy: Lombardia	**0.351**	(0.028)	**0.158**	(0.030)	**0.178**	(0.028)	-0.026	(0.033)	**0.112**	(0.024)	**0.185**	(0.028)	**0.268**	(0.026)	**0.090**	(0.023)
Italy: Marche	**0.371**	(0.026)	**0.195**	(0.027)	**0.181**	(0.033)	**0.080**	(0.037)	**0.175**	(0.024)	**0.251**	(0.032)	**0.326**	(0.034)	**0.132**	(0.029)
Italy: Molise	**0.425**	(0.033)	**0.228**	(0.032)	**0.233**	(0.041)	0.007	(0.045)	**0.122**	(0.051)	**0.286**	(0.051)	**0.329**	(0.033)	0.051	(0.036)
Italy: Piemonte	**0.341**	(0.038)	**0.098**	(0.027)	**0.150**	(0.035)	0.033	(0.034)	**0.144**	(0.023)	**0.242**	(0.031)	**0.267**	(0.030)	**0.145**	(0.046)
Italy: Puglia	**0.415**	(0.024)	**0.163**	(0.024)	**0.165**	(0.029)	-0.042	(0.042)	**0.138**	(0.032)	**0.227**	(0.041)	**0.294**	(0.022)	**0.099**	(0.035)
Italy: Sardegna	**0.388**	(0.030)	**0.185**	(0.032)	**0.188**	(0.050)	**0.110**	(0.037)	**0.191**	(0.045)	**0.345**	(0.032)	**0.327**	(0.027)	**0.244**	(0.037)
Italy: Sicilia	**0.430**	(0.043)	**0.217**	(0.037)	**0.209**	(0.038)	0.011	(0.063)	**0.128**	(0.033)	**0.273**	(0.049)	**0.352**	(0.020)	**0.082**	(0.029)
Italy: Toscana	**0.364**	(0.027)	**0.233**	(0.024)	**0.210**	(0.022)	0.021	(0.029)	**0.147**	(0.030)	**0.264**	(0.024)	**0.323**	(0.031)	**0.195**	(0.026)
Italy: Trento	**0.316**	(0.025)	**0.158**	(0.030)	**0.194**	(0.026)	0.037	(0.026)	**0.136**	(0.027)	**0.208**	(0.027)	**0.280**	(0.028)	**0.146**	(0.029)
Italy: Umbria	**0.383**	(0.037)	**0.143**	(0.024)	**0.192**	(0.034)	**-0.088**	(0.028)	**0.101**	(0.030)	**0.213**	(0.036)	**0.295**	(0.032)	**0.084**	(0.032)
Italy: Valle d'Aosta	**0.274**	(0.032)	**0.131**	(0.032)	**0.102**	(0.038)	**0.082**	(0.035)	**0.102**	(0.037)	**0.223**	(0.036)	**0.209**	(0.038)	**0.088**	(0.042)
Italy: Veneto	**0.363**	(0.033)	**0.119**	(0.037)	**0.174**	(0.030)	-0.012	(0.038)	**0.184**	(0.027)	**0.248**	(0.034)	**0.250**	(0.023)	**0.134**	(0.034)
Mexico: Aguascalientes[1]	**0.109**	(0.027)	0.055	(0.035)	0.034	(0.031)	0.007	(0.039)	0.055	(0.037)	0.050	(0.046)	**0.141**	(0.036)	**0.084**	(0.036)
Mexico: Baja California[1]	**0.138**	(0.034)	0.071	(0.037)	0.071	(0.041)	0.045	(0.040)	**0.129**	(0.030)	**0.152**	(0.044)	**0.111**	(0.030)	**0.096**	(0.032)
Mexico: Baja California Sur[1]	**0.121**	(0.044)	0.027	(0.029)	0.052	(0.041)	**0.091**	(0.032)	**0.095**	(0.033)	**0.131**	(0.039)	0.045	(0.029)	0.037	(0.041)
Mexico: Campeche[1]	**0.167**	(0.030)	0.000	(0.034)	0.066	(0.034)	**0.067**	(0.023)	**0.080**	(0.037)	**0.132**	(0.040)	**0.102**	(0.039)	0.059	(0.032)
Mexico: Chihuahua[1]	**0.169**	(0.062)	0.031	(0.030)	0.020	(0.030)	0.052	(0.035)	0.025	(0.039)	0.077	(0.043)	**0.063**	(0.028)	0.117	(0.068)
Mexico: Colima[1]	**0.103**	(0.034)	0.064	(0.034)	0.041	(0.029)	0.036	(0.028)	0.036	(0.033)	0.051	(0.040)	**0.079**	(0.031)	**0.093**	(0.028)
Mexico: Coahuila[1]	**0.101**	(0.050)	**0.054**	(0.026)	0.059	(0.035)	**0.081**	(0.037)	**0.073**	(0.030)	**0.142**	(0.040)	0.029	(0.028)	0.032	(0.050)
Mexico: Chiapas[1]	0.056	(0.049)	-0.026	(0.026)	0.028	(0.040)	**0.100**	(0.037)	**0.124**	(0.053)	0.092	(0.059)	**0.090**	(0.027)	**0.096**	(0.040)
Mexico: Distrito Federal[1]	**0.094**	(0.026)	0.049	(0.029)	0.035	(0.032)	-0.002	(0.029)	**0.093**	(0.045)	**0.123**	(0.038)	**0.121**	(0.028)	**0.090**	(0.024)
Mexico: Durango[1]	**0.131**	(0.047)	0.067	(0.040)	**0.133**	(0.033)	**0.136**	(0.032)	**0.120**	(0.034)	**0.161**	(0.027)	**0.143**	(0.039)	**0.133**	(0.052)
Mexico: Guerrero[1]	**0.103**	(0.040)	0.031	(0.031)	0.010	(0.036)	0.034	(0.040)	0.007	(0.040)	**0.074**	(0.038)	0.054	(0.037)	**0.135**	(0.024)
Mexico: Guanajuato[1]	-0.022	(0.041)	0.018	(0.044)	0.024	(0.042)	**0.078**	(0.034)	**0.088**	(0.033)	**0.086**	(0.036)	**0.080**	(0.028)	-0.031	(0.026)
Mexico: Hidalgo[1]	**0.067**	(0.032)	-0.046	(0.032)	0.031	(0.034)	0.048	(0.029)	**0.063**	(0.031)	**0.085**	(0.029)	**0.088**	(0.043)	**0.107**	(0.030)
Mexico: Jalisco[1]	**0.174**	(0.039)	0.007	(0.055)	**0.110**	(0.043)	**0.097**	(0.028)	**0.112**	(0.035)	**0.171**	(0.036)	**0.119**	(0.027)	**0.091**	(0.039)
Mexico: Michoacán[1]	0.043	(0.047)	0.054	(0.058)	**0.096**	(0.030)	**0.126**	(0.026)	**0.138**	(0.044)	**0.181**	(0.030)	**0.119**	(0.024)	0.027	(0.031)
Mexico: Morelos[1]	**0.171**	(0.037)	0.002	(0.036)	**0.079**	(0.029)	**0.061**	(0.029)	**0.102**	(0.039)	**0.131**	(0.034)	**0.166**	(0.037)	**0.127**	(0.035)
Mexico: Mexico[1]	**0.137**	(0.046)	**0.057**	(0.028)	**0.116**	(0.038)	**0.062**	(0.028)	**0.118**	(0.022)	**0.175**	(0.029)	**0.154**	(0.022)	0.042	(0.032)
Mexico: Nayarit[1]	**0.074**	(0.032)	-0.006	(0.031)	-0.031	(0.043)	0.029	(0.035)	-0.014	(0.048)	0.045	(0.038)	0.058	(0.049)	0.038	(0.049)
Mexico: Nuevo León[1]	0.039	(0.053)	0.021	(0.029)	0.032	(0.043)	0.053	(0.042)	**0.079**	(0.031)	**0.120**	(0.035)	0.085	(0.049)	0.058	(0.040)
Mexico: Oaxaca[1]	**0.203**	(0.064)	-0.075	(0.048)	0.054	(0.049)	0.048	(0.081)	-0.035	(0.040)	**0.085**	(0.034)	**0.083**	(0.026)	0.067	(0.065)
Mexico: Puebla[1]	0.076	(0.039)	0.005	(0.033)	0.043	(0.023)	0.003	(0.033)	0.024	(0.028)	0.047	(0.026)	**0.138**	(0.032)	0.026	(0.034)
Mexico: Quintana Roo[1]	**0.105**	(0.021)	**0.071**	(0.036)	**0.066**	(0.033)	**0.102**	(0.033)	0.031	(0.032)	**0.107**	(0.038)	**0.073**	(0.034)	0.053	(0.033)
Mexico: Querétaro[1]	0.023	(0.032)	**0.068**	(0.030)	0.061	(0.034)	0.057	(0.033)	0.046	(0.033)	**0.074**	(0.026)	**0.119**	(0.030)	0.062	(0.033)
Mexico: Sinaloa[1]	**0.134**	(0.051)	0.044	(0.028)	**0.083**	(0.029)	**0.136**	(0.034)	**0.085**	(0.037)	**0.130**	(0.051)	**0.146**	(0.026)	**0.062**	(0.030)
Mexico: San Luis Potosí[1]	0.074	(0.059)	0.046	(0.038)	**0.069**	(0.031)	0.044	(0.067)	0.052	(0.035)	**0.119**	(0.039)	**0.132**	(0.031)	0.021	(0.028)
Mexico: Sonora[1]	0.053	(0.041)	0.018	(0.024)	-0.011	(0.030)	**0.133**	(0.048)	**0.099**	(0.027)	**0.167**	(0.034)	0.066	(0.047)	**0.090**	(0.027)
Mexico: Tamaulipas[1]	**0.150**	(0.026)	0.047	(0.031)	0.045	(0.034)	**0.129**	(0.033)	**0.217**	(0.035)	**0.200**	(0.032)	**0.088**	(0.018)	0.060	(0.031)
Mexico: Tabasco[1]	0.060	(0.051)	0.056	(0.029)	0.016	(0.030)	**0.094**	(0.033)	**0.117**	(0.036)	**0.133**	(0.028)	**0.091**	(0.029)	**0.084**	(0.021)
Mexico: Tlaxcala[1]	**0.130**	(0.037)	0.020	(0.040)	0.055	(0.037)	**0.086**	(0.028)	**0.095**	(0.043)	**0.146**	(0.028)	0.084	(0.048)	**0.102**	(0.051)
Mexico: Veracruz[1]	0.091	(0.059)	-0.031	(0.035)	0.035	(0.044)	0.060	(0.040)	**0.103**	(0.028)	**0.129**	(0.029)	**0.140**	(0.030)	**0.082**	(0.034)
Mexico: Yucatán[1]	**0.096**	(0.035)	0.046	(0.025)	**0.071**	(0.030)	**0.094**	(0.033)	**0.098**	(0.034)	**0.135**	(0.037)	**0.099**	(0.026)	**0.077**	(0.027)
Mexico: Zacatecas[1]	0.095	(0.074)	**0.069**	(0.034)	0.044	(0.034)	0.047	(0.042)	-0.002	(0.034)	0.052	(0.042)	0.038	(0.029)	0.037	(0.035)

Notes: To facilitate comparability, marks in all countries and economies have been standardised so that higher values indicate better appraisals and that all countries and economies have a mean mark of 0 (zero) with a standard deviation of 1 (one).

Logistic models that account for the dichotomous nature of observed marks in Macao-China, Mexico and New Zealand, and Tobit models that account for the censored nature of failing marks in Austria, Croatia, Hungary, Poland, Serbia and the Slovak Republic do not yield substantively different results.

Correlations statistically significantly different from 0 (zero) at a 95% confidence level are highlighted in bold.

1. Macao-China, Mexico and New Zealand distributed, in the Educational Career questionnaire, the alternative question on whether students received a passing or failing mark. Results for these countries and economies are thus based on a dichotomous variable that does not capture the full variability of marks received by students. Estimates for these countries and economies are probably underestimated.

StatLink http://dx.doi.org/10.1787/888932734096

[Part 2/2]

Table B2.3 Correlation between the marks received by students in their language-of-assessment course and student characteristics

	Student-teacher relations		Student background									
			Student is a girl		*PISA index of economic, social and cultural status*		Student with an immigrant background		Student speaks other language at home		Student attended ISCED 0 for more than one year	
	Corr.	S.E.	Corr.	S.E.	Corr.	S.E.	Corr.	S.E.	Corr.	S.E.	Corr.	S.E.
Countries and economies												
Austria	**0.161**	(0.015)	**0.139**	(0.018)	**0.135**	(0.019)	**-0.110**	(0.016)	**-0.129**	(0.016)	-0.002	(0.020)
Belgium (Flemish Community)	**0.127**	(0.020)	**0.125**	(0.016)	**0.077**	(0.021)	**-0.061**	(0.024)	**-0.068**	(0.016)	**0.037**	(0.019)
Croatia	**0.099**	(0.016)	**0.246**	(0.018)	**0.175**	(0.020)	**-0.036**	(0.016)	-0.011	(0.025)	**0.050**	(0.019)
Hungary	**0.186**	(0.018)	**0.206**	(0.026)	**0.312**	(0.021)	-0.010	(0.016)	-0.033	(0.027)	0.023	(0.019)
Iceland	**0.211**	(0.019)	**0.121**	(0.016)	**0.247**	(0.019)	**-0.049**	(0.019)	-0.031	(0.017)	**0.052**	(0.018)
Ireland	**0.126**	(0.017)	**0.104**	(0.019)	**0.213**	(0.021)	-0.009	(0.017)	0.003	(0.020)	0.032	(0.021)
Italy	**0.150**	(0.010)	**0.197**	(0.009)	**0.195**	(0.009)	**-0.045**	(0.009)	**-0.093**	(0.011)	**0.091**	(0.011)
Latvia	**0.181**	(0.020)	**0.296**	(0.019)	**0.227**	(0.028)	0.026	(0.021)	0.013	(0.020)	0.023	(0.022)
Macao-China[1]	**0.054**	(0.013)	**0.126**	(0.014)	**0.073**	(0.012)	**0.040**	(0.014)	-0.024	(0.014)	**0.076**	(0.016)
Mexico[1]	**0.075**	(0.007)	**0.037**	(0.008)	0.001	(0.011)	-0.006	(0.009)	-0.004	(0.008)	0.015	(0.008)
New Zealand[1]	**0.168**	(0.014)	**0.110**	(0.014)	**0.155**	(0.018)	0.007	(0.015)	**-0.062**	(0.017)	0.018	(0.014)
Poland	**0.177**	(0.018)	**0.320**	(0.015)	**0.335**	(0.015)	-0.006	(0.003)	-0.019	(0.019)	**0.102**	(0.015)
Portugal: ISCED2	**0.178**	(0.020)	**0.155**	(0.021)	**0.218**	(0.024)	0.031	(0.022)	0.018	(0.024)	**0.107**	(0.023)
Portugal: ISCED3	**0.221**	(0.021)	**0.167**	(0.018)	**0.243**	(0.027)	**-0.040**	(0.018)	0.007	(0.016)	**0.095**	(0.022)
Serbia	**0.044**	(0.014)	**0.192**	(0.017)	**0.214**	(0.017)	0.020	(0.014)	**-0.030**	(0.013)	**0.053**	(0.016)
Singapore	**0.052**	(0.015)	0.001	(0.016)	**0.187**	(0.018)	-0.033	(0.017)	**-0.218**	(0.017)	0.017	(0.018)
Slovak Republic	**0.168**	(0.020)	**0.283**	(0.019)	**0.284**	(0.020)	0.014	(0.010)	**-0.075**	(0.028)	**0.087**	(0.017)
Trinidad and Tobago	**0.076**	(0.018)	**0.089**	(0.019)	**0.175**	(0.018)	0.018	(0.024)	-0.013	(0.026)	-0.009	(0.021)
Regions												
Italy: Abruzzo	**0.206**	(0.023)	**0.261**	(0.035)	**0.201**	(0.023)	**-0.110**	(0.037)	**-0.109**	(0.035)	**0.126**	(0.028)
Italy: Basilicata	**0.192**	(0.027)	**0.174**	(0.032)	**0.193**	(0.027)	-0.053	(0.028)	**-0.121**	(0.050)	**0.073**	(0.027)
Italy: Bolzano	**0.159**	(0.027)	**0.174**	(0.024)	**0.072**	(0.028)	-0.154	(0.084)	**0.132**	(0.031)	0.061	(0.031)
Italy: Calabria	**0.144**	(0.038)	**0.261**	(0.033)	**0.198**	(0.024)	-0.036	(0.036)	**-0.102**	(0.031)	0.047	(0.028)
Italy: Campania	**0.175**	(0.042)	**0.237**	(0.027)	**0.219**	(0.036)	-0.035	(0.023)	**-0.200**	(0.038)	**0.082**	(0.033)
Italy: Emilia Romagna	**0.201**	(0.028)	**0.204**	(0.030)	**0.188**	(0.033)	**-0.138**	(0.029)	**-0.128**	(0.037)	**0.074**	(0.024)
Italy: Friuli Venezia Giulia	**0.215**	(0.026)	**0.142**	(0.028)	**0.191**	(0.028)	-0.060	(0.036)	**-0.111**	(0.030)	**0.109**	(0.044)
Italy: Lazio	**0.169**	(0.052)	**0.229**	(0.027)	**0.180**	(0.031)	-0.017	(0.036)	-0.048	(0.029)	0.051	(0.028)
Italy: Liguria	**0.135**	(0.042)	**0.146**	(0.032)	**0.082**	(0.031)	**-0.122**	(0.036)	-0.022	(0.033)	**0.089**	(0.032)
Italy: Lombardia	**0.147**	(0.035)	**0.160**	(0.033)	**0.198**	(0.029)	**-0.108**	(0.033)	**-0.097**	(0.035)	0.047	(0.032)
Italy: Marche	**0.133**	(0.029)	**0.229**	(0.023)	**0.175**	(0.029)	**-0.070**	(0.028)	-0.056	(0.040)	**0.076**	(0.032)
Italy: Molise	0.064	(0.038)	**0.167**	(0.034)	**0.222**	(0.029)	**-0.100**	(0.023)	**-0.149**	(0.039)	**0.114**	(0.028)
Italy: Piemonte	**0.174**	(0.036)	**0.151**	(0.034)	**0.176**	(0.030)	-0.048	(0.043)	**-0.070**	(0.036)	**0.087**	(0.035)
Italy: Puglia	**0.162**	(0.039)	**0.171**	(0.035)	**0.207**	(0.031)	-0.010	(0.027)	**-0.100**	(0.032)	**0.117**	(0.026)
Italy: Sardegna	**0.248**	(0.030)	**0.179**	(0.032)	**0.169**	(0.051)	-0.054	(0.092)	**-0.140**	(0.043)	0.065	(0.033)
Italy: Sicilia	**0.099**	(0.034)	**0.176**	(0.030)	**0.274**	(0.042)	0.022	(0.012)	**-0.078**	(0.038)	**0.143**	(0.037)
Italy: Toscana	**0.239**	(0.027)	**0.227**	(0.036)	**0.122**	(0.030)	**-0.066**	(0.021)	**-0.063**	(0.027)	**0.118**	(0.038)
Italy: Trento	**0.144**	(0.031)	**0.118**	(0.042)	**0.159**	(0.029)	**-0.087**	(0.027)	-0.022	(0.035)	**0.099**	(0.034)
Italy: Umbria	**0.103**	(0.040)	**0.164**	(0.028)	**0.237**	(0.032)	**-0.100**	(0.042)	**-0.096**	(0.024)	**0.084**	(0.025)
Italy: Valle d'Aosta	**0.105**	(0.033)	**0.151**	(0.035)	0.064	(0.040)	-0.003	(0.039)	0.026	(0.035)	**0.073**	(0.037)
Italy: Veneto	**0.175**	(0.030)	**0.204**	(0.028)	**0.094**	(0.042)	**-0.112**	(0.043)	**-0.106**	(0.035)	**0.137**	(0.033)
Mexico: Aguascalientes[1]	**0.067**	(0.024)	-0.018	(0.031)	-0.030	(0.028)	**0.021**	(0.005)	**0.019**	(0.004)	-0.011	(0.027)
Mexico: Baja California[1]	**0.111**	(0.020)	-0.015	(0.035)	**0.079**	(0.024)	-0.046	(0.062)	0.005	(0.041)	-0.057	(0.033)
Mexico: Baja California Sur[1]	**0.071**	(0.028)	-0.020	(0.028)	**0.061**	(0.030)	**0.034**	(0.013)	-0.035	(0.051)	0.020	(0.040)
Mexico: Campeche[1]	**0.115**	(0.028)	**0.072**	(0.035)	0.008	(0.047)	-0.024	(0.035)	-0.072	(0.048)	0.060	(0.044)
Mexico: Chihuahua[1]	0.026	(0.063)	0.024	(0.029)	0.026	(0.059)	-0.013	(0.042)	**0.021**	(0.006)	0.046	(0.033)
Mexico: Colima[1]	**0.151**	(0.046)	**0.061**	(0.030)	0.042	(0.040)	**0.020**	(0.004)	**0.014**	(0.005)	0.039	(0.031)
Mexico: Coahuila[1]	**0.053**	(0.027)	**0.078**	(0.030)	0.027	(0.046)	**0.014**	(0.005)	-0.028	(0.037)	-0.062	(0.032)
Mexico: Chiapas[1]	0.072	(0.046)	-0.019	(0.030)	-0.061	(0.044)	-0.002	(0.034)	-0.009	(0.045)	0.017	(0.039)
Mexico: Distrito Federal[1]	**0.069**	(0.024)	-0.007	(0.036)	-0.003	(0.033)	-0.013	(0.034)	**0.027**	(0.006)	**0.088**	(0.036)
Mexico: Durango[1]	**0.162**	(0.039)	-0.013	(0.042)	0.038	(0.031)	-0.029	(0.049)	**0.024**	(0.012)	0.030	(0.040)
Mexico: Guerrero[1]	0.027	(0.033)	0.037	(0.028)	-0.019	(0.038)	-0.023	(0.045)	-0.024	(0.048)	-0.021	(0.043)
Mexico: Guanajuato[1]	-0.007	(0.033)	**0.058**	(0.028)	-0.040	(0.044)	**0.021**	(0.006)	**0.020**	(0.006)	0.025	(0.035)
Mexico: Hidalgo[1]	**0.127**	(0.040)	0.017	(0.030)	-0.003	(0.034)	-0.001	(0.032)	**-0.073**	(0.031)	**-0.054**	(0.023)
Mexico: Jalisco[1]	**0.146**	(0.030)	**0.098**	(0.041)	**0.120**	(0.035)	-0.043	(0.070)	-0.040	(0.052)	0.042	(0.032)
Mexico: Michoacán[1]	0.077	(0.049)	0.027	(0.050)	-0.020	(0.033)	**0.022**	(0.007)	**0.017**	(0.005)	0.027	(0.038)
Mexico: Morelos[1]	**0.069**	(0.035)	0.061	(0.042)	-0.015	(0.032)	-0.072	(0.057)	**0.025**	(0.007)	0.019	(0.024)
Mexico: Mexico[1]	0.036	(0.031)	**0.090**	(0.034)	0.034	(0.039)	**0.041**	(0.009)	-0.063	(0.054)	0.037	(0.038)
Mexico: Nayarit[1]	0.051	(0.035)	-0.005	(0.032)	-0.044	(0.047)	**0.030**	(0.007)	**0.023**	(0.006)	0.050	(0.032)
Mexico: Nuevo León[1]	0.067	(0.042)	-0.034	(0.059)	0.058	(0.067)	**0.037**	(0.010)	**0.026**	(0.008)	0.011	(0.036)
Mexico: Oaxaca[1]	**0.094**	(0.031)	0.080	(0.056)	**-0.115**	(0.049)	**0.051**	(0.012)	-0.079	(0.083)	0.101	(0.080)
Mexico: Puebla[1]	**0.068**	(0.029)	0.014	(0.018)	0.045	(0.061)	-0.078	(0.089)	0.035	(0.021)	-0.033	(0.026)
Mexico: Quintana Roo[1]	**0.100**	(0.033)	0.054	(0.031)	0.023	(0.036)	-0.022	(0.038)	-0.038	(0.042)	**0.057**	(0.024)
Mexico: Querétaro[1]	0.053	(0.032)	-0.009	(0.042)	-0.006	(0.038)	-0.016	(0.043)	**0.019**	(0.007)	0.016	(0.029)
Mexico: Sinaloa[1]	**0.102**	(0.037)	0.069	(0.043)	0.019	(0.038)	**0.031**	(0.005)	0.007	(0.004)	0.047	(0.026)
Mexico: San Luis Potosí[1]	**0.135**	(0.038)	**0.088**	(0.027)	-0.010	(0.049)	-0.056	(0.083)	0.011	(0.029)	0.006	(0.033)
Mexico: Sonora[1]	**0.088**	(0.034)	0.038	(0.028)	-0.011	(0.033)	-0.046	(0.060)	-0.002	(0.025)	0.003	(0.035)
Mexico: Tamaulipas[1]	**0.114**	(0.054)	0.016	(0.039)	**0.086**	(0.038)	0.001	(0.051)	0.007	(0.004)	0.029	(0.027)
Mexico: Tabasco[1]	**0.125**	(0.026)	0.043	(0.030)	-0.003	(0.025)	-0.111	(0.064)	**0.027**	(0.008)	-0.010	(0.023)
Mexico: Tlaxcala[1]	**0.104**	(0.024)	0.007	(0.024)	**0.073**	(0.026)	**0.034**	(0.009)	**0.018**	(0.007)	0.011	(0.033)
Mexico: Veracruz[1]	**0.083**	(0.031)	0.053	(0.045)	0.019	(0.049)	0.017	(0.017)	0.028	(0.015)	-0.047	(0.030)
Mexico: Yucatán[1]	**0.067**	(0.028)	0.046	(0.035)	0.021	(0.028)	-0.092	(0.050)	0.003	(0.041)	0.001	(0.028)
Mexico: Zacatecas[1]	**0.095**	(0.040)	0.067	(0.051)	-0.029	(0.036)	-0.192	(0.148)	-0.032	(0.047)	**-0.089**	(0.034)

Notes: To facilitate comparability, marks in all countries and economies have been standardised so that higher values indicate better appraisals and that all countries and economies have a mean mark of 0 (zero) with a standard deviation of 1 (one).

Logistic models that account for the dichotomous nature of observed marks in Macao-China, Mexico and New Zealand, and Tobit models that account for the censored nature of failing marks in Austria, Croatia, Hungary, Poland, Serbia and the Slovak Republic do not yield substantively different results.

Correlations statistically significantly different from 0 (zero) at a 95% confidence level are highlighted in bold.

1. Macao-China, Mexico and New Zealand distributed, in the Educational Career questionnaire, the alternative question on whether students received a passing or failing mark. Results for these countries and economies are thus based on a dichotomous variable that does not capture the full variability of marks received by students. Estimates for these countries and economies are probably underestimated.

StatLink http://dx.doi.org/10.1787/888932734096

[Part 1/2]

Table B2.4 Correlation between the marks received by students in their language-of-assessment course and student characteristics, after accounting for students' PISA reading scores

	Metacognition strategies				Approaches to learning						Engagement			
	Understanding and remembering		Effective summarising strategies		Memorisation strategies		Elaboration strategies		Control strategies		Enjoyment of reading		Attitudes towards school	
	Corr.	S.E.	Corr.	S.E.	Corr.	S.E.	Corr.	S.E.	Corr.	S.E.	Corr.	S.E.	Corr.	S.E.
Countries and economies														
Austria	**0.032**	(0.015)	**0.051**	(0.016)	**0.090**	(0.015)	**0.076**	(0.016)	**0.140**	(0.020)	**0.122**	(0.016)	**0.098**	(0.016)
Belgium (Flemish Community)	**0.040**	(0.017)	0.017	(0.020)	**0.068**	(0.021)	**0.067**	(0.014)	**0.107**	(0.020)	**0.148**	(0.022)	**0.091**	(0.020)
Croatia	**0.042**	(0.019)	**0.064**	(0.018)	**0.083**	(0.017)	**0.093**	(0.016)	**0.128**	(0.015)	**0.185**	(0.015)	**0.076**	(0.014)
Hungary	**0.056**	(0.017)	**0.035**	(0.015)	**0.104**	(0.015)	**0.078**	(0.016)	**0.117**	(0.014)	**0.169**	(0.021)	**0.108**	(0.018)
Iceland	**0.046**	(0.017)	**0.043**	(0.018)	**0.150**	(0.022)	**0.118**	(0.018)	**0.171**	(0.020)	0.038	(0.021)	**0.136**	(0.018)
Ireland	-0.017	(0.017)	0.019	(0.020)	**0.080**	(0.019)	**0.111**	(0.020)	**0.136**	(0.019)	**0.168**	(0.018)	**0.080**	(0.018)
Italy	**0.026**	(0.009)	**0.029**	(0.012)	**0.047**	(0.012)	**0.115**	(0.008)	**0.140**	(0.011)	**0.162**	(0.009)	**0.103**	(0.010)
Latvia	**0.085**	(0.021)	**0.045**	(0.020)	**0.100**	(0.020)	**0.084**	(0.019)	**0.122**	(0.018)	**0.194**	(0.020)	**0.062**	(0.021)
Macao-China[1]	**0.033**	(0.014)	0.021	(0.015)	**0.048**	(0.015)	**0.046**	(0.014)	**0.074**	(0.014)	**0.095**	(0.013)	**0.057**	(0.013)
Mexico[1]	-0.007	(0.008)	**0.016**	(0.008)	**0.063**	(0.008)	**0.080**	(0.008)	**0.104**	(0.007)	**0.095**	(0.007)	**0.040**	(0.007)
New Zealand[1]	**0.043**	(0.015)	**0.045**	(0.015)	**0.107**	(0.017)	**0.076**	(0.016)	**0.140**	(0.017)	**0.073**	(0.018)	**0.112**	(0.015)
Poland	**0.052**	(0.017)	**0.071**	(0.018)	**0.110**	(0.017)	**0.080**	(0.015)	**0.167**	(0.017)	**0.197**	(0.018)	**0.080**	(0.018)
Portugal: ISCED2	**0.047**	(0.023)	**0.080**	(0.019)	0.015	(0.024)	**0.125**	(0.022)	**0.150**	(0.021)	**0.156**	(0.020)	**0.124**	(0.014)
Portugal: ISCED3	**0.041**	(0.017)	0.010	(0.018)	0.027	(0.019)	**0.165**	(0.018)	**0.240**	(0.021)	**0.177**	(0.019)	**0.122**	(0.017)
Serbia	**0.075**	(0.020)	**0.055**	(0.016)	**0.042**	(0.015)	**0.102**	(0.015)	**0.138**	(0.013)	**0.231**	(0.015)	**0.073**	(0.017)
Singapore	-0.015	(0.019)	-0.018	(0.016)	**0.030**	(0.014)	**0.066**	(0.019)	**0.059**	(0.016)	**0.101**	(0.016)	0.023	(0.018)
Slovak Republic	0.022	(0.021)	**0.059**	(0.021)	0.015	(0.024)	0.038	(0.021)	**0.119**	(0.022)	**0.149**	(0.018)	**0.089**	(0.019)
Trinidad and Tobago	-0.008	(0.017)	-0.034	(0.019)	**0.112**	(0.020)	**0.128**	(0.016)	**0.153**	(0.016)	**0.117**	(0.019)	**0.051**	(0.021)
Regions														
Italy: Abruzzo	**0.074**	(0.037)	0.054	(0.044)	**0.090**	(0.028)	**0.168**	(0.028)	**0.196**	(0.030)	**0.208**	(0.030)	**0.149**	(0.029)
Italy: Basilicata	0.070	(0.041)	**0.124**	(0.032)	**0.113**	(0.033)	**0.161**	(0.036)	**0.209**	(0.041)	**0.200**	(0.031)	**0.144**	(0.022)
Italy: Bolzano	0.026	(0.038)	0.043	(0.035)	**0.104**	(0.029)	**0.052**	(0.026)	**0.095**	(0.029)	**0.087**	(0.037)	**0.135**	(0.025)
Italy: Calabria	0.001	(0.035)	0.049	(0.030)	**0.077**	(0.023)	**0.064**	(0.028)	**0.136**	(0.026)	**0.224**	(0.022)	**0.118**	(0.037)
Italy: Campania	-0.011	(0.034)	-0.029	(0.040)	**0.080**	(0.024)	**0.140**	(0.029)	**0.165**	(0.036)	**0.197**	(0.032)	**0.105**	(0.033)
Italy: Emilia Romagna	0.003	(0.031)	0.031	(0.033)	**0.061**	(0.025)	**0.099**	(0.031)	**0.134**	(0.032)	**0.209**	(0.023)	**0.158**	(0.041)
Italy: Friuli Venezia Giulia	0.042	(0.027)	-0.005	(0.031)	**0.070**	(0.031)	**0.132**	(0.032)	**0.146**	(0.033)	**0.150**	(0.035)	**0.161**	(0.026)
Italy: Lazio	**0.100**	(0.033)	**0.108**	(0.048)	0.022	(0.034)	**0.133**	(0.028)	**0.188**	(0.037)	**0.220**	(0.028)	**0.092**	(0.044)
Italy: Liguria	0.047	(0.031)	0.030	(0.031)	0.044	(0.041)	**0.123**	(0.030)	**0.185**	(0.021)	**0.107**	(0.039)	**0.102**	(0.021)
Italy: Lombardia	0.035	(0.032)	0.033	(0.033)	0.004	(0.035)	**0.093**	(0.035)	**0.082**	(0.032)	**0.131**	(0.033)	**0.086**	(0.026)
Italy: Marche	0.039	(0.024)	0.028	(0.030)	**0.102**	(0.031)	**0.130**	(0.024)	**0.135**	(0.030)	**0.180**	(0.036)	**0.110**	(0.028)
Italy: Molise	**0.072**	(0.031)	0.047	(0.040)	0.030	(0.044)	**0.103**	(0.047)	**0.171**	(0.050)	**0.165**	(0.034)	0.048	(0.035)
Italy: Piemonte	-0.040	(0.026)	0.005	(0.030)	0.052	(0.032)	**0.119**	(0.031)	**0.161**	(0.034)	**0.146**	(0.030)	**0.139**	(0.043)
Italy: Puglia	0.025	(0.029)	0.014	(0.037)	0.006	(0.047)	**0.119**	(0.034)	**0.122**	(0.050)	**0.161**	(0.029)	**0.070**	(0.035)
Italy: Sardegna	0.038	(0.029)	0.050	(0.042)	**0.120**	(0.038)	**0.143**	(0.049)	**0.250**	(0.036)	**0.179**	(0.023)	**0.219**	(0.036)
Italy: Sicilia	0.039	(0.025)	0.021	(0.039)	0.061	(0.062)	**0.118**	(0.029)	**0.162**	(0.039)	**0.208**	(0.023)	**0.075**	(0.028)
Italy: Toscana	**0.080**	(0.025)	**0.056**	(0.024)	0.053	(0.032)	**0.122**	(0.030)	**0.144**	(0.026)	**0.187**	(0.031)	**0.152**	(0.024)
Italy: Trento	0.046	(0.033)	**0.062**	(0.027)	**0.071**	(0.029)	**0.121**	(0.027)	**0.123**	(0.029)	**0.163**	(0.030)	**0.143**	(0.030)
Italy: Umbria	0.004	(0.026)	0.020	(0.028)	-0.050	(0.028)	**0.073**	(0.029)	**0.112**	(0.037)	**0.145**	(0.030)	**0.067**	(0.031)
Italy: Valle d'Aosta	0.019	(0.034)	-0.013	(0.037)	**0.098**	(0.037)	**0.080**	(0.036)	**0.146**	(0.037)	**0.102**	(0.039)	0.067	(0.042)
Italy: Veneto	-0.042	(0.034)	-0.007	(0.028)	0.007	(0.040)	**0.138**	(0.025)	**0.135**	(0.034)	**0.092**	(0.024)	**0.113**	(0.034)
Mexico: Aguascalientes[1]	0.016	(0.034)	-0.016	(0.030)	-0.003	(0.038)	0.038	(0.036)	0.015	(0.045)	**0.115**	(0.035)	0.041	(0.031)
Mexico: Baja California[1]	0.018	(0.039)	0.017	(0.040)	0.034	(0.039)	**0.115**	(0.027)	**0.114**	(0.041)	0.070	(0.037)	0.046	(0.032)
Mexico: Baja California Sur[1]	-0.012	(0.027)	0.010	(0.033)	**0.087**	(0.034)	**0.090**	(0.032)	**0.107**	(0.040)	0.012	(0.035)	0.013	(0.036)
Mexico: Campeche[1]	**-0.059**	(0.030)	0.002	(0.032)	**0.076**	(0.025)	**0.077**	(0.032)	**0.108**	(0.038)	0.074	(0.041)	0.023	(0.033)
Mexico: Chihuahua[1]	-0.027	(0.024)	-0.051	(0.026)	0.045	(0.037)	0.013	(0.039)	0.034	(0.037)	0.017	(0.035)	0.071	(0.051)
Mexico: Colima[1]	0.034	(0.039)	0.001	(0.034)	0.032	(0.027)	0.029	(0.032)	0.027	(0.038)	0.053	(0.028)	**0.067**	(0.027)
Mexico: Coahuila[1]	0.025	(0.036)	0.024	(0.040)	**0.074**	(0.037)	**0.070**	(0.030)	**0.124**	(0.038)	0.010	(0.029)	0.003	(0.047)
Mexico: Chiapas[1]	-0.032	(0.029)	0.017	(0.045)	**0.102**	(0.038)	**0.124**	(0.051)	0.082	(0.053)	**0.083**	(0.029)	**0.089**	(0.041)
Mexico: Distrito Federal[1]	0.015	(0.029)	-0.017	(0.035)	0.003	(0.030)	0.087	(0.046)	**0.100**	(0.038)	**0.094**	(0.026)	**0.072**	(0.023)
Mexico: Durango[1]	0.043	(0.039)	**0.098**	(0.044)	**0.135**	(0.033)	**0.117**	(0.034)	**0.130**	(0.035)	**0.118**	(0.042)	**0.100**	(0.049)
Mexico: Guerrero[1]	0.003	(0.033)	-0.022	(0.050)	0.044	(0.038)	0.008	(0.038)	0.058	(0.041)	0.039	(0.038)	**0.091**	(0.022)
Mexico: Guanajuato[1]	0.029	(0.037)	0.045	(0.037)	**0.080**	(0.034)	**0.089**	(0.033)	**0.097**	(0.033)	**0.085**	(0.026)	-0.028	(0.023)
Mexico: Hidalgo[1]	**-0.074**	(0.033)	0.005	(0.037)	0.052	(0.030)	**0.062**	(0.031)	**0.074**	(0.027)	0.083	(0.044)	**0.094**	(0.032)
Mexico: Jalisco[1]	-0.056	(0.055)	0.045	(0.048)	**0.089**	(0.031)	**0.093**	(0.034)	**0.130**	(0.031)	**0.075**	(0.023)	0.042	(0.039)
Mexico: Michoacán[1]	0.046	(0.070)	**0.084**	(0.032)	**0.125**	(0.026)	**0.138**	(0.044)	**0.176**	(0.029)	**0.113**	(0.023)	0.014	(0.035)
Mexico: Morelos[1]	-0.028	(0.036)	0.032	(0.029)	0.054	(0.028)	0.080	(0.042)	**0.092**	(0.036)	**0.128**	(0.036)	**0.077**	(0.028)
Mexico: Mexico[1]	0.001	(0.027)	**0.049**	(0.025)	**0.060**	(0.029)	**0.100**	(0.023)	**0.140**	(0.023)	**0.125**	(0.018)	0.004	(0.022)
Mexico: Nayarit[1]	-0.037	(0.030)	-0.061	(0.041)	0.028	(0.037)	-0.021	(0.048)	0.025	(0.039)	0.043	(0.049)	0.017	(0.050)
Mexico: Nuevo León[1]	0.002	(0.031)	0.020	(0.035)	0.050	(0.040)	**0.076**	(0.030)	**0.113**	(0.029)	0.076	(0.042)	0.049	(0.037)
Mexico: Oaxaca[1]	-0.103	(0.057)	0.011	(0.054)	0.060	(0.082)	-0.037	(0.038)	0.061	(0.037)	0.054	(0.029)	0.001	(0.076)
Mexico: Puebla[1]	-0.024	(0.028)	0.010	(0.029)	0.007	(0.035)	0.014	(0.028)	0.030	(0.024)	**0.127**	(0.038)	0.006	(0.032)
Mexico: Quintana Roo[1]	0.032	(0.036)	0.023	(0.037)	**0.105**	(0.032)	0.031	(0.032)	**0.086**	(0.038)	0.055	(0.033)	0.020	(0.030)
Mexico: Querétaro[1]	**0.059**	(0.024)	0.052	(0.033)	0.056	(0.033)	0.043	(0.034)	**0.070**	(0.028)	**0.117**	(0.031)	0.057	(0.035)
Mexico: Sinaloa[1]	0.004	(0.030)	0.044	(0.030)	**0.136**	(0.036)	0.075	(0.040)	0.098	(0.059)	**0.120**	(0.022)	0.021	(0.034)
Mexico: San Luis Potosí[1]	0.024	(0.031)	0.040	(0.032)	0.044	(0.066)	0.046	(0.034)	**0.104**	(0.036)	**0.121**	(0.030)	0.005	(0.024)
Mexico: Sonora[1]	-0.003	(0.027)	-0.039	(0.038)	**0.132**	(0.047)	**0.097**	(0.028)	**0.161**	(0.031)	0.056	(0.053)	**0.086**	(0.024)
Mexico: Tamaulipas[1]	-0.007	(0.025)	-0.011	(0.033)	**0.121**	(0.031)	**0.209**	(0.034)	**0.171**	(0.028)	**0.059**	(0.019)	0.017	(0.034)
Mexico: Tabasco[1]	0.030	(0.022)	0.006	(0.024)	**0.097**	(0.032)	**0.118**	(0.035)	**0.126**	(0.026)	**0.085**	(0.030)	**0.071**	(0.021)
Mexico: Tlaxcala[1]	-0.022	(0.039)	0.002	(0.034)	**0.087**	(0.028)	**0.081**	(0.039)	**0.114**	(0.024)	0.060	(0.046)	0.067	(0.047)
Mexico: Veracruz[1]	-0.061	(0.036)	-0.002	(0.037)	0.061	(0.040)	**0.095**	(0.029)	**0.109**	(0.030)	**0.124**	(0.024)	**0.056**	(0.027)
Mexico: Yucatán[1]	0.017	(0.028)	0.039	(0.031)	**0.093**	(0.033)	**0.097**	(0.033)	**0.117**	(0.036)	**0.088**	(0.026)	0.046	(0.025)
Mexico: Zacatecas[1]	0.046	(0.031)	0.010	(0.025)	0.047	(0.040)	-0.005	(0.030)	0.026	(0.045)	0.018	(0.032)	0.023	(0.041)

Notes: To facilitate comparability, marks in all countries and economies have been standardised so that higher values indicate better appraisals and that all countries and economies have a mean mark of 0 (zero) with a standard deviation of 1 (one).

Logistic models that account for the dichotomous nature of observed marks in Macao-China, Mexico and New Zealand, and Tobit models that account for the censored nature of failing marks in Austria, Croatia, Hungary, Poland, Serbia and the Slovak Republic do not yield substantively different results.

Correlations statistically significantly different from 0 (zero) at a 95% confidence level are highlighted in bold.

1. Macao-China, Mexico and New Zealand distributed, in the Educational Career questionnaire, the alternative question on whether students received a passing or failing mark. Results for these countries and economies are thus based on a dichotomous variable that does not capture the full variability of marks received by students. Estimates for these countries and economies are probably underestimated.

StatLink http://dx.doi.org/10.1787/888932734115

[Part 2/2]

Table B2.4 Correlation between the marks received by students in their language-of-assessment course and student characteristics, after accounting for students' PISA reading scores

	Student-teacher relations		Student background									
			Student is a girl		*PISA index of economic, social and cultural status*		Student with an immigrant background		Student speaks other language at home		Student attended ISCED 0 for more than one year	
	Corr.	S.E.	Corr.	S.E.	Corr.	S.E.	Corr.	S.E.	Corr.	S.E.	Corr.	S.E.
Countries and economies												
Austria	**0.155**	(0.015)	**0.097**	(0.019)	**0.050**	(0.019)	**-0.065**	(0.015)	**-0.091**	(0.016)	-0.033	(0.019)
Belgium (Flemish Community)	**0.113**	(0.020)	**0.093**	(0.015)	0.005	(0.018)	-0.023	(0.023)	**-0.051**	(0.017)	-0.001	(0.018)
Croatia	**0.115**	(0.017)	**0.129**	(0.015)	0.020	(0.018)	-0.007	(0.014)	0.000	(0.028)	**-0.029**	(0.015)
Hungary	**0.176**	(0.018)	**0.123**	(0.022)	**0.077**	(0.019)	-0.017	(0.016)	0.002	(0.011)	-0.019	(0.017)
Iceland	**0.114**	(0.020)	0.025	(0.015)	**0.164**	(0.019)	0.003	(0.022)	0.023	(0.020)	0.019	(0.018)
Ireland	**0.072**	(0.017)	**0.049**	(0.018)	**0.122**	(0.021)	0.008	(0.016)	0.016	(0.019)	0.034	(0.020)
Italy	**0.148**	(0.011)	**0.114**	(0.009)	**0.068**	(0.009)	0.021	(0.011)	0.000	(0.010)	0.019	(0.011)
Latvia	**0.131**	(0.021)	**0.182**	(0.020)	**0.072**	(0.026)	0.028	(0.018)	**0.060**	(0.024)	-0.022	(0.021)
Macao-China[1]	**0.039**	(0.013)	**0.070**	(0.014)	**0.039**	(0.012)	**0.029**	(0.014)	0.027	(0.015)	**0.033**	(0.015)
Mexico[1]	**0.068**	(0.007)	**0.024**	(0.008)	**-0.034**	(0.011)	0.005	(0.009)	0.011	(0.008)	0.003	(0.009)
New Zealand[1]	**0.117**	(0.015)	**0.055**	(0.014)	**0.051**	(0.016)	0.023	(0.016)	-0.012	(0.017)	-0.015	(0.014)
Poland	**0.148**	(0.020)	**0.198**	(0.015)	**0.146**	(0.018)	-0.018	(0.009)	0.015	(0.022)	0.020	(0.016)
Portugal: ISCED2	**0.171**	(0.019)	**0.078**	(0.024)	**0.071**	(0.022)	0.036	(0.023)	0.027	(0.025)	0.038	(0.023)
Portugal: ISCED3	**0.212**	(0.020)	**0.111**	(0.019)	**0.114**	(0.026)	-0.015	(0.017)	0.010	(0.021)	**0.057**	(0.023)
Serbia	**0.093**	(0.014)	**0.100**	(0.017)	**0.082**	(0.015)	-0.004	(0.013)	-0.015	(0.014)	0.022	(0.017)
Singapore	0.029	(0.015)	**-0.034**	(0.016)	**0.115**	(0.017)	**-0.037**	(0.016)	**-0.164**	(0.016)	-0.021	(0.017)
Slovak Republic	**0.143**	(0.021)	**0.159**	(0.021)	**0.093**	(0.019)	0.009	(0.010)	0.013	(0.020)	**0.054**	(0.017)
Trinidad and Tobago	**0.056**	(0.018)	**0.040**	(0.019)	**0.115**	(0.019)	0.019	(0.025)	0.011	(0.026)	-0.029	(0.020)
Regions												
Italy: Abruzzo	**0.161**	(0.023)	**0.163**	(0.031)	**0.069**	(0.024)	-0.049	(0.030)	-0.013	(0.032)	**0.060**	(0.024)
Italy: Basilicata	**0.192**	(0.026)	**0.068**	(0.029)	0.049	(0.033)	**-0.071**	(0.027)	-0.037	(0.045)	0.041	(0.034)
Italy: Bolzano	**0.175**	(0.027)	**0.098**	(0.025)	-0.032	(0.027)	-0.059	(0.056)	**0.164**	(0.036)	-0.020	(0.027)
Italy: Calabria	**0.160**	(0.035)	**0.157**	(0.037)	0.047	(0.032)	-0.005	(0.036)	0.000	(0.030)	0.006	(0.027)
Italy: Campania	**0.167**	(0.042)	**0.153**	(0.035)	**0.117**	(0.032)	0.009	(0.018)	**-0.123**	(0.035)	0.047	(0.031)
Italy: Emilia Romagna	**0.174**	(0.027)	**0.159**	(0.028)	0.021	(0.031)	-0.010	(0.027)	0.006	(0.035)	-0.045	(0.026)
Italy: Friuli Venezia Giulia	**0.200**	(0.022)	0.028	(0.027)	**0.078**	(0.028)	0.034	(0.046)	-0.029	(0.036)	0.007	(0.036)
Italy: Lazio	**0.153**	(0.052)	**0.154**	(0.030)	**0.071**	(0.032)	0.050	(0.048)	0.057	(0.030)	-0.014	(0.031)
Italy: Liguria	**0.112**	(0.043)	0.069	(0.039)	-0.005	(0.031)	-0.057	(0.035)	0.041	(0.035)	0.026	(0.024)
Italy: Lombardia	**0.149**	(0.038)	**0.079**	(0.031)	**0.071**	(0.032)	0.003	(0.039)	0.002	(0.036)	-0.029	(0.029)
Italy: Marche	**0.124**	(0.027)	**0.149**	(0.030)	**0.075**	(0.026)	0.005	(0.029)	0.018	(0.047)	-0.010	(0.032)
Italy: Molise	0.061	(0.035)	0.060	(0.033)	**0.072**	(0.031)	**-0.069**	(0.021)	-0.052	(0.041)	0.057	(0.029)
Italy: Piemonte	**0.152**	(0.037)	**0.100**	(0.035)	0.054	(0.038)	0.057	(0.041)	0.033	(0.038)	0.016	(0.036)
Italy: Puglia	**0.128**	(0.046)	0.061	(0.037)	**0.101**	(0.032)	0.047	(0.034)	-0.051	(0.038)	**0.071**	(0.025)
Italy: Sardegna	**0.210**	(0.035)	**0.080**	(0.036)	0.060	(0.051)	-0.032	(0.100)	-0.086	(0.051)	0.038	(0.033)
Italy: Sicilia	**0.113**	(0.038)	**0.088**	(0.035)	**0.127**	(0.034)	**0.030**	(0.012)	0.011	(0.042)	**0.080**	(0.039)
Italy: Toscana	**0.212**	(0.025)	**0.143**	(0.036)	0.029	(0.032)	-0.005	(0.030)	-0.018	(0.024)	0.041	(0.039)
Italy: Trento	**0.131**	(0.033)	0.056	(0.040)	0.058	(0.030)	-0.005	(0.027)	**0.071**	(0.032)	0.033	(0.030)
Italy: Umbria	**0.097**	(0.035)	**0.091**	(0.030)	**0.105**	(0.034)	-0.008	(0.037)	-0.008	(0.026)	-0.001	(0.028)
Italy: Valle d'Aosta	**0.084**	(0.034)	**0.122**	(0.035)	-0.018	(0.043)	0.048	(0.039)	**0.074**	(0.034)	0.032	(0.038)
Italy: Veneto	**0.163**	(0.032)	**0.103**	(0.040)	-0.009	(0.041)	-0.030	(0.037)	0.002	(0.033)	**0.065**	(0.033)
Mexico: Aguascalientes[1]	**0.057**	(0.025)	-0.036	(0.030)	**-0.073**	(0.025)	**0.027**	(0.008)	**0.017**	(0.005)	-0.023	(0.028)
Mexico: Baja California[1]	**0.103**	(0.019)	-0.036	(0.035)	0.038	(0.022)	-0.008	(0.069)	0.018	(0.039)	**-0.080**	(0.033)
Mexico: Baja California Sur[1]	**0.063**	(0.027)	-0.045	(0.030)	0.026	(0.022)	**0.052**	(0.014)	-0.038	(0.054)	0.012	(0.039)
Mexico: Campeche[1]	**0.109**	(0.027)	0.050	(0.036)	-0.054	(0.047)	0.017	(0.030)	-0.049	(0.044)	0.018	(0.039)
Mexico: Chihuahua[1]	0.021	(0.059)	0.002	(0.035)	-0.054	(0.040)	0.012	(0.043)	**0.026**	(0.013)	0.025	(0.030)
Mexico: Colima[1]	**0.144**	(0.047)	0.044	(0.029)	0.007	(0.036)	**0.028**	(0.006)	**0.012**	(0.005)	0.022	(0.029)
Mexico: Coahuila[1]	0.047	(0.026)	**0.059**	(0.029)	-0.002	(0.038)	**0.018**	(0.007)	-0.030	(0.036)	**-0.070**	(0.032)
Mexico: Chiapas[1]	0.068	(0.042)	-0.028	(0.033)	-0.077	(0.044)	0.006	(0.031)	0.012	(0.035)	0.011	(0.043)
Mexico: Distrito Federal[1]	**0.072**	(0.024)	-0.018	(0.034)	-0.040	(0.030)	-0.009	(0.035)	**0.031**	(0.010)	**0.077**	(0.036)
Mexico: Durango[1]	**0.156**	(0.039)	-0.032	(0.046)	-0.007	(0.021)	-0.009	(0.051)	0.053	(0.029)	0.016	(0.041)
Mexico: Guerrero[1]	0.015	(0.033)	0.019	(0.025)	-0.050	(0.040)	-0.010	(0.045)	0.000	(0.042)	-0.036	(0.039)
Mexico: Guanajuato[1]	-0.006	(0.034)	**0.063**	(0.028)	-0.033	(0.041)	**0.020**	(0.006)	**0.020**	(0.006)	0.028	(0.034)
Mexico: Hidalgo[1]	**0.123**	(0.040)	0.008	(0.027)	-0.046	(0.031)	0.005	(0.035)	-0.055	(0.034)	**-0.065**	(0.023)
Mexico: Jalisco[1]	**0.131**	(0.029)	0.063	(0.045)	**0.065**	(0.033)	-0.019	(0.070)	-0.016	(0.051)	0.015	(0.029)
Mexico: Michoacán[1]	0.074	(0.050)	0.024	(0.049)	-0.040	(0.029)	**0.028**	(0.011)	**0.015**	(0.005)	0.020	(0.034)
Mexico: Morelos[1]	0.053	(0.038)	0.043	(0.041)	**-0.075**	(0.038)	-0.047	(0.055)	**0.024**	(0.006)	-0.015	(0.032)
Mexico: Mexico[1]	0.025	(0.031)	**0.067**	(0.033)	-0.005	(0.034)	**0.064**	(0.017)	-0.049	(0.054)	0.019	(0.043)
Mexico: Nayarit[1]	0.040	(0.036)	-0.021	(0.032)	-0.071	(0.044)	**0.039**	(0.011)	**0.025**	(0.007)	0.045	(0.032)
Mexico: Nuevo León[1]	0.062	(0.040)	-0.040	(0.058)	0.048	(0.073)	**0.039**	(0.010)	**0.027**	(0.011)	0.006	(0.038)
Mexico: Oaxaca[1]	0.045	(0.038)	0.038	(0.047)	**-0.180**	(0.060)	**0.072**	(0.031)	-0.021	(0.071)	0.044	(0.060)
Mexico: Puebla[1]	**0.059**	(0.029)	0.007	(0.021)	0.019	(0.056)	-0.067	(0.084)	0.037	(0.021)	-0.044	(0.026)
Mexico: Quintana Roo[1]	**0.090**	(0.033)	0.043	(0.033)	-0.028	(0.038)	0.003	(0.036)	-0.014	(0.048)	0.034	(0.025)
Mexico: Querétaro[1]	0.051	(0.033)	-0.012	(0.041)	-0.021	(0.039)	-0.015	(0.043)	**0.018**	(0.006)	0.010	(0.028)
Mexico: Sinaloa[1]	**0.080**	(0.040)	0.048	(0.045)	-0.031	(0.047)	**0.047**	(0.008)	0.007	(0.004)	0.028	(0.024)
Mexico: San Luis Potosí[1]	**0.125**	(0.034)	**0.075**	(0.031)	-0.042	(0.033)	-0.047	(0.082)	0.022	(0.030)	-0.004	(0.034)
Mexico: Sonora[1]	**0.082**	(0.033)	0.026	(0.026)	-0.030	(0.028)	-0.040	(0.057)	0.000	(0.026)	-0.004	(0.037)
Mexico: Tamaulipas[1]	0.096	(0.050)	-0.010	(0.038)	0.047	(0.038)	0.016	(0.052)	0.006	(0.003)	0.024	(0.022)
Mexico: Tabasco[1]	**0.119**	(0.029)	0.032	(0.028)	-0.022	(0.028)	-0.105	(0.061)	**0.032**	(0.010)	-0.023	(0.021)
Mexico: Tlaxcala[1]	**0.097**	(0.024)	-0.012	(0.025)	0.044	(0.027)	**0.054**	(0.016)	**0.026**	(0.010)	-0.004	(0.033)
Mexico: Veracruz[1]	**0.074**	(0.034)	0.037	(0.051)	-0.021	(0.041)	0.029	(0.018)	**0.035**	(0.018)	-0.056	(0.031)
Mexico: Yucatán[1]	**0.064**	(0.026)	0.031	(0.036)	-0.024	(0.030)	-0.080	(0.048)	0.031	(0.044)	-0.023	(0.026)
Mexico: Zacatecas[1]	**0.082**	(0.039)	0.054	(0.047)	-0.055	(0.040)	-0.186	(0.146)	-0.031	(0.047)	**-0.091**	(0.037)

Notes: To facilitate comparability, marks in all countries and economies have been standardised so that higher values indicate better appraisals and that all countries and economies have a mean mark of 0 (zero) with a standard deviation of 1 (one).

Logistic models that account for the dichotomous nature of observed marks in Macao-China, Mexico and New Zealand, and Tobit models that account for the censored nature of failing marks in Austria, Croatia, Hungary, Poland, Serbia and the Slovak Republic do not yield substantively different results.

Correlations statistically significantly different from 0 (zero) at a 95% confidence level are highlighted in bold.

1. Macao-China, Mexico and New Zealand distributed, in the Educational Career questionnaire, the alternative question on whether students received a passing or failing mark. Results for these countries and economies are thus based on a dichotomous variable that does not capture the full variability of marks received by students. Estimates for these countries and economies are probably underestimated.

StatLink http://dx.doi.org/10.1787/888932734115

[Part 1/7]

Table B2.5 Within-school correlation between the marks received by students in their language-of-assessment course and student characteristics

	Reading performance				Metacognition strategies: Understanding and remembering			
	Average corr.	S.E.	Percentage of schools with positive correlation	Percentage of schools with negative correlation	Average corr.	S.E.	Percentage of schools with positive correlation	Percentage of schools with negative correlation
Countries and economies								
Austria	**0.252**	(0.113)	63.66	4.91	**0.086**	(0.028)	66.33	30.29
Belgium (Flemish Community)	**0.239**	(0.091)	56.98	6.17	**0.146**	(0.010)	70.50	27.62
Croatia	**0.300**	(0.078)	76.38	1.24	**0.144**	(0.029)	67.47	23.26
Hungary	**0.331**	(0.132)	65.95	5.08	**0.146**	(0.010)	67.57	28.78
Iceland	0.406	(0.211)	57.28	0.00	0.178	(0.212)	27.32	1.82
Ireland	**0.243**	(0.077)	65.83	7.36	**0.088**	(0.017)	61.38	29.94
Italy	**0.322**	(0.108)	73.68	2.05	**0.118**	(0.037)	66.18	26.50
Latvia	**0.470**	(0.111)	79.99	2.41	**0.184**	(0.013)	76.07	15.94
Macao-China[1]	**0.215**	(0.106)	54.76	9.52	0.088	(0.093)	16.67	11.90
Mexico[1]	0.135	(0.121)	23.64	43.07	0.005	(0.012)	28.25	67.47
New Zealand[1]	**0.276**	(0.082)	61.17	10.72	**0.094**	(0.046)	51.41	35.18
Poland	**0.574**	(0.073)	95.32	0.00	**0.233**	(0.013)	84.47	10.90
Portugal: ISCED2	**0.348**	(0.095)	70.72	5.37	**0.141**	(0.010)	69.32	27.36
Portugal: ISCED3	**0.458**	(0.089)	89.87	0.88	**0.200**	(0.020)	84.94	13.54
Serbia	**0.327**	(0.107)	80.78	0.00	**0.167**	(0.049)	73.78	19.33
Singapore	0.132	(0.214)	21.26	1.69	0.029	(0.189)	9.74	5.94
Slovak Republic	**0.544**	(0.084)	90.16	0.00	**0.205**	(0.008)	74.12	22.84
Trinidad and Tobago	0.143	(0.227)	11.73	1.37	0.016	(0.212)	6.89	6.96
Regions								
Italy: Abruzzo	**0.354**	(0.088)	84.57	2.79	**0.115**	(0.040)	60.80	27.71
Italy: Basilicata	**0.359**	(0.130)	70.45	0.00	**0.177**	(0.068)	66.64	22.25
Italy: Bolzano	0.337	(0.194)	38.52	1.17	0.190	(0.186)	29.96	3.50
Italy: Calabria	**0.341**	(0.115)	70.35	1.29	**0.167**	(0.015)	68.95	24.75
Italy: Campania	**0.269**	(0.089)	74.11	8.74	**0.054**	(0.011)	58.82	38.26
Italy: Emilia Romagna	**0.281**	(0.077)	68.32	7.33	**0.039**	(0.009)	55.41	41.37
Italy: Friuli Venezia Giulia	**0.424**	(0.132)	75.46	0.00	**0.146**	(0.064)	64.63	20.50
Italy: Lazio	**0.317**	(0.127)	71.22	0.00	**0.240**	(0.009)	83.49	12.83
Italy: Liguria	**0.291**	(0.093)	76.80	0.00	**0.094**	(0.037)	67.83	22.26
Italy: Lombardia	**0.308**	(0.107)	77.30	0.00	**0.130**	(0.008)	71.54	28.46
Italy: Marche	**0.295**	(0.111)	63.72	0.00	**0.183**	(0.028)	79.29	17.49
Italy: Molise	0.322	(0.202)	50.27	2.32	0.158	(0.180)	39.00	0.00
Italy: Piemonte	**0.253**	(0.107)	64.60	7.57	**0.060**	(0.011)	60.27	29.14
Italy: Puglia	**0.319**	(0.099)	76.89	0.00	**0.061**	(0.008)	56.32	38.12
Italy: Sardegna	**0.335**	(0.101)	72.89	1.42	**0.164**	(0.009)	74.49	21.20
Italy: Sicilia	**0.372**	(0.105)	79.76	0.00	**0.054**	(0.014)	68.00	27.48
Italy: Toscana	**0.368**	(0.093)	86.59	0.00	**0.229**	(0.012)	76.05	18.78
Italy: Trento	0.293	(0.156)	48.14	2.58	0.121	(0.134)	48.22	17.74
Italy: Umbria	**0.365**	(0.111)	72.49	0.00	0.082	(0.067)	55.12	28.87
Italy: Valle d'Aosta	0.339	(0.204)	71.43	0.00	0.131	(0.192)	9.52	4.76
Italy: Veneto	**0.366**	(0.095)	76.88	0.00	**0.118**	(0.008)	64.37	23.03
Mexico: Aguascalientes[1]	0.155	(0.080)	22.63	41.22	-0.014	(0.036)	28.28	65.59
Mexico: Baja California[1]	0.142	(0.106)	44.50	19.62	-0.007	(0.009)	53.71	46.29
Mexico: Baja California Sur[1]	0.152	(0.127)	19.61	45.29	0.079	(0.056)	38.94	53.87
Mexico: Campeche[1]	0.153	(0.139)	30.83	32.09	**-0.083**	(0.023)	33.04	65.75
Mexico: Chihuahua[1]	0.058	(0.122)	20.09	57.65	**-0.043**	(0.004)	27.27	72.73
Mexico: Colima[1]	0.234	(0.122)	32.07	42.82	**0.139**	(0.046)	32.70	63.38
Mexico: Coahuila[1]	0.076	(0.117)	13.35	41.72	**0.106**	(0.014)	44.42	55.17
Mexico: Chiapas[1]	-0.005	(0.123)	16.15	37.45	**-0.020**	(0.004)	24.66	75.34
Mexico: Distrito Federal[1]	0.117	(0.083)	28.45	32.52	**0.128**	(0.008)	46.11	47.19
Mexico: Durango[1]	0.078	(0.127)	28.47	34.95	**0.070**	(0.016)	39.85	59.48
Mexico: Guerrero[1]	0.066	(0.155)	36.53	16.11	0.007	(0.005)	37.60	58.91
Mexico: Guanajuato[1]	0.105	(0.151)	13.61	42.56	**0.110**	(0.003)	28.77	71.05
Mexico: Hidalgo[1]	0.131	(0.113)	18.62	54.50	**-0.225**	(0.002)	11.84	84.63
Mexico: Jalisco[1]	**0.250**	(0.122)	36.07	34.78	**-0.117**	(0.001)	24.19	75.81
Mexico: Michoacán[1]	0.094	(0.110)	34.16	15.94	**-0.020**	(0.003)	44.60	55.40
Mexico: Morelos[1]	0.159	(0.122)	32.94	35.48	-0.048	(0.026)	20.35	68.29
Mexico: Mexico[1]	0.160	(0.106)	27.21	27.92	**0.028**	(0.005)	43.40	43.45
Mexico: Nayarit[1]	**0.275**	(0.126)	28.57	42.76	-0.037	(0.040)	19.67	76.96
Mexico: Nuevo León[1]	0.176	(0.106)	25.40	50.54	**-0.041**	(0.017)	24.34	64.24
Mexico: Oaxaca[1]	0.181	(0.104)	27.24	61.81	**-0.103**	(0.005)	10.03	89.97
Mexico: Puebla[1]	0.076	(0.106)	9.98	55.84	**0.006**	(0.001)	16.08	79.07
Mexico: Quintana Roo[1]	0.177	(0.092)	27.23	39.68	**0.100**	(0.027)	34.18	63.88
Mexico: Querétaro[1]	0.003	(0.213)	16.79	52.27	**0.128**	(0.029)	35.85	55.95
Mexico: Sinaloa[1]	0.105	(0.149)	18.52	52.35	**0.046**	(0.005)	27.42	72.58
Mexico: San Luis Potosí[1]	0.251	(0.136)	16.63	58.71	**0.221**	(0.007)	28.61	71.39
Mexico: Sonora[1]	**0.179**	(0.084)	34.12	38.92	**-0.053**	(0.003)	35.52	64.48
Mexico: Tamaulipas[1]	0.112	(0.088)	13.29	39.71	**0.022**	(0.002)	36.64	63.13
Mexico: Tabasco[1]	**0.217**	(0.101)	19.99	45.31	**0.089**	(0.001)	30.87	69.13
Mexico: Tlaxcala[1]	0.079	(0.107)	32.40	27.69	-0.043	(0.024)	42.83	54.28
Mexico: Veracruz[1]	0.187	(0.128)	23.55	58.47	**-0.109**	(0.006)	10.26	82.39
Mexico: Yucatán[1]	0.151	(0.110)	30.23	10.28	**0.069**	(0.007)	48.17	50.98
Mexico: Zacatecas[1]	**0.300**	(0.108)	26.72	59.74	**0.075**	(0.014)	34.23	62.69

Notes: To facilitate comparability, marks in all countries and economies have been standardised so that higher values indicate better appraisals and that all countries and economies have a mean mark of 0 (zero) with a standard deviation of 1 (one).

Logistic models that account for the dichotomous nature of observed marks in Macao-China, Mexico and New Zealand, and Tobit models that account for the censored nature of failing marks in Austria, Croatia, Hungary, Poland, Serbia and the Slovak Republic do not yield substantively different results.

Correlations statistically significantly different from 0 (zero) at a 95% confidence level are highlighted in bold.

1. Macao-China, Mexico and New Zealand distributed, in the Educational Career questionnaire, the alternative question on whether students received a passing or failing mark. Results for these countries and economies are thus based on a dichotomous variable that does not capture the full variability of marks received by students. Estimates for these countries and economies are probably underestimated.

StatLink http://dx.doi.org/10.1787/888932734134

[Part 2/7]

Table B2.5 Within-school correlation between the marks received by students in their language-of-assessment course and student characteristics

	Metacognition strategies				Approaches to learning			
	Effective summarising strategies				Memorisation strategies			
	Average corr.	S.E.	Percentage of schools with positive correlation	Percentage of schools with negative correlation	Average corr.	S.E.	Percentage of schools with positive correlation	Percentage of schools with negative correlation
Countries and economies								
Austria	**0.149**	(0.028)	77.98	17.28	**0.088**	(0.027)	60.99	33.68
Belgium (Flemish Community)	**0.138**	(0.013)	67.89	27.32	**0.027**	(0.008)	47.20	48.57
Croatia	**0.198**	(0.025)	80.65	15.67	0.047	(0.026)	60.17	37.60
Hungary	**0.177**	(0.008)	77.45	19.97	**0.147**	(0.011)	74.49	24.69
Iceland	0.232	(0.201)	32.55	1.87	0.112	(0.237)	19.55	4.47
Ireland	**0.147**	(0.017)	71.13	24.35	**0.082**	(0.016)	58.86	34.06
Italy	**0.116**	(0.037)	67.44	25.06	0.033	(0.039)	49.46	42.97
Latvia	**0.243**	(0.013)	79.98	13.05	**0.061**	(0.014)	57.28	35.42
Macao-China[1]	0.083	(0.097)	16.67	11.90	0.064	(0.101)	11.90	9.52
Mexico[1]	**0.048**	(0.012)	32.23	66.62	**0.110**	(0.012)	40.09	58.69
New Zealand[1]	**0.151**	(0.045)	63.18	27.66	**0.093**	(0.045)	57.76	34.41
Poland	**0.315**	(0.011)	91.34	8.01	**0.162**	(0.014)	80.03	17.73
Portugal: ISCED2	**0.190**	(0.014)	74.85	23.79	**0.039**	(0.012)	53.56	44.10
Portugal: ISCED3	**0.192**	(0.019)	77.41	17.53	-0.026	(0.020)	44.23	51.77
Serbia	**0.199**	(0.049)	79.51	16.00	0.014	(0.042)	47.71	45.63
Singapore	0.056	(0.194)	12.83	3.39	0.021	(0.182)	11.60	9.18
Slovak Republic	**0.283**	(0.009)	84.35	15.06	**-0.071**	(0.010)	31.52	64.00
Trinidad and Tobago	0.017	(0.224)	5.53	2.74	0.121	(0.216)	13.10	1.42
Regions								
Italy: Abruzzo	**0.124**	(0.032)	55.97	20.46	-0.029	(0.041)	30.48	47.59
Italy: Basilicata	**0.224**	(0.065)	71.91	11.94	0.072	(0.069)	52.17	34.70
Italy: Bolzano	0.167	(0.187)	19.84	1.17	0.094	(0.181)	20.62	9.34
Italy: Calabria	**0.149**	(0.014)	72.06	25.45	**-0.050**	(0.017)	40.73	50.44
Italy: Campania	**0.050**	(0.012)	62.31	34.28	**0.032**	(0.009)	56.74	40.95
Italy: Emilia Romagna	**0.113**	(0.009)	68.88	27.47	**0.055**	(0.012)	50.62	37.43
Italy: Friuli Venezia Giulia	**0.183**	(0.060)	65.47	23.21	-0.022	(0.079)	37.75	42.51
Italy: Lazio	**0.248**	(0.008)	81.71	18.29	**0.042**	(0.010)	45.79	48.78
Italy: Liguria	**0.114**	(0.033)	66.59	30.45	0.046	(0.034)	51.86	31.10
Italy: Lombardia	**0.100**	(0.013)	76.42	22.79	-0.007	(0.015)	49.22	50.78
Italy: Marche	**0.085**	(0.028)	73.75	23.69	**0.101**	(0.028)	59.22	35.32
Italy: Molise	0.137	(0.192)	25.05	2.36	0.069	(0.209)	14.51	5.79
Italy: Piemonte	**0.135**	(0.011)	65.52	27.91	0.018	(0.009)	57.70	41.37
Italy: Puglia	**0.067**	(0.008)	60.20	33.34	**0.020**	(0.007)	57.72	40.35
Italy: Sardegna	**0.186**	(0.011)	70.09	28.26	**0.122**	(0.010)	61.59	34.13
Italy: Sicilia	0.014	(0.019)	54.60	26.34	**0.062**	(0.012)	48.23	43.41
Italy: Toscana	**0.203**	(0.011)	80.68	19.32	**0.061**	(0.011)	52.34	44.30
Italy: Trento	0.099	(0.118)	40.58	22.66	0.086	(0.127)	39.24	13.84
Italy: Umbria	**0.150**	(0.070)	69.88	11.26	-0.023	(0.069)	24.42	53.46
Italy: Valle d'Aosta	0.100	(0.182)	19.05	9.52	0.057	(0.195)	9.52	4.76
Italy: Veneto	**0.077**	(0.007)	69.87	28.61	**0.043**	(0.007)	48.03	50.03
Mexico: Aguascalientes[1]	0.007	(0.040)	28.35	60.82	-0.012	(0.045)	29.42	65.00
Mexico: Baja California[1]	**0.105**	(0.010)	65.25	34.75	**0.036**	(0.005)	53.86	45.95
Mexico: Baja California Sur[1]	0.003	(0.062)	23.05	69.35	0.036	(0.054)	22.53	71.93
Mexico: Campeche[1]	**-0.064**	(0.017)	25.14	73.64	**0.148**	(0.018)	49.66	49.13
Mexico: Chihuahua[1]	0.005	(0.004)	20.39	79.61	**0.074**	(0.003)	40.77	59.23
Mexico: Colima[1]	-0.043	(0.035)	22.35	70.90	**0.093**	(0.034)	33.23	60.63
Mexico: Coahuila[1]	**0.145**	(0.011)	56.14	43.46	**0.087**	(0.008)	41.90	57.70
Mexico: Chiapas[1]	**-0.075**	(0.003)	23.19	73.89	**0.170**	(0.003)	48.73	51.27
Mexico: Distrito Federal[1]	**0.051**	(0.007)	44.03	55.97	-0.004	(0.008)	27.08	60.38
Mexico: Durango[1]	**0.192**	(0.014)	51.38	47.49	**0.097**	(0.023)	56.53	42.35
Mexico: Guerrero[1]	-0.006	(0.005)	37.71	61.70	**-0.019**	(0.005)	43.88	56.12
Mexico: Guanajuato[1]	**0.082**	(0.007)	30.14	69.65	**0.155**	(0.006)	49.42	50.58
Mexico: Hidalgo[1]	**-0.161**	(0.001)	18.26	81.74	**0.056**	(0.001)	32.81	67.19
Mexico: Jalisco[1]	**0.105**	(0.001)	38.31	61.69	**0.245**	(0.003)	52.26	45.79
Mexico: Michoacán[1]	**0.059**	(0.002)	60.03	39.17	**0.090**	(0.002)	55.89	42.31
Mexico: Morelos[1]	**0.067**	(0.023)	39.51	54.04	**0.216**	(0.025)	49.74	49.49
Mexico: Mexico[1]	**0.030**	(0.007)	36.76	63.24	**0.083**	(0.009)	46.86	52.46
Mexico: Nayarit[1]	-0.045	(0.037)	23.92	72.32	**0.102**	(0.049)	36.92	58.53
Mexico: Nuevo León[1]	**0.085**	(0.022)	21.88	77.50	**0.048**	(0.019)	30.56	68.82
Mexico: Oaxaca[1]	**0.194**	(0.010)	33.34	66.66	**-0.055**	(0.013)	17.23	82.77
Mexico: Puebla[1]	**0.079**	(0.001)	25.19	74.81	**0.055**	(0.002)	27.13	72.87
Mexico: Quintana Roo[1]	**0.190**	(0.036)	43.77	53.97	**0.202**	(0.022)	40.56	57.21
Mexico: Querétaro[1]	**0.064**	(0.021)	38.05	60.90	**0.147**	(0.023)	30.47	68.49
Mexico: Sinaloa[1]	**0.089**	(0.005)	29.06	70.94	**0.224**	(0.002)	40.37	59.63
Mexico: San Luis Potosí[1]	**0.121**	(0.018)	23.98	61.32	-0.011	(0.022)	19.86	79.83
Mexico: Sonora[1]	-0.003	(0.003)	31.19	68.81	**0.251**	(0.002)	52.95	46.33
Mexico: Tamaulipas[1]	**0.066**	(0.002)	37.90	62.10	**0.301**	(0.001)	56.38	43.62
Mexico: Tabasco[1]	**0.116**	(0.002)	33.87	66.13	**0.375**	(0.003)	53.43	44.43
Mexico: Tlaxcala[1]	-0.007	(0.030)	47.21	49.42	**0.110**	(0.029)	69.22	27.89
Mexico: Veracruz[1]	**-0.018**	(0.005)	17.98	82.02	**0.168**	(0.003)	36.60	63.40
Mexico: Yucatán[1]	**0.051**	(0.009)	52.52	41.27	**0.170**	(0.004)	76.28	23.53
Mexico: Zacatecas[1]	**0.100**	(0.025)	29.95	69.13	**0.165**	(0.015)	33.53	65.55

Notes: To facilitate comparability, marks in all countries and economies have been standardised so that higher values indicate better appraisals and that all countries and economies have a mean mark of 0 (zero) with a standard deviation of 1 (one).

Logistic models that account for the dichotomous nature of observed marks in Macao-China, Mexico and New Zealand, and Tobit models that account for the censored nature of failing marks in Austria, Croatia, Hungary, Poland, Serbia and the Slovak Republic do not yield substantively different results.

Correlations statistically significantly different from 0 (zero) at a 95% confidence level are highlighted in bold.

1. Macao-China, Mexico and New Zealand distributed, in the Educational Career questionnaire, the alternative question on whether students received a passing or failing mark. Results for these countries and economies are thus based on a dichotomous variable that does not capture the full variability of marks received by students. Estimates for these countries and economies are probably underestimated.

StatLink http://dx.doi.org/10.1787/888932734134

[Part 3/7]

Table B2.5 Within-school correlation between the marks received by students in their language-of-assessment course and student characteristics

	Approaches to learning							
	Elaboration strategies				Control strategies			
	Average corr.	S.E.	Percentage of schools with positive correlation	Percentage of schools with negative correlation	Average corr.	S.E.	Percentage of schools with positive correlation	Percentage of schools with negative correlation
Countries and economies								
Austria	0.041	(0.029)	51.70	41.52	**0.170**	(0.026)	70.29	25.51
Belgium (Flemish Community)	**0.051**	(0.009)	55.65	37.36	**0.127**	(0.011)	68.09	29.44
Croatia	**0.072**	(0.025)	63.28	31.80	**0.126**	(0.024)	74.61	23.07
Hungary	**0.074**	(0.008)	55.91	38.19	**0.120**	(0.008)	69.23	29.96
Iceland	0.131	(0.232)	18.39	1.78	0.227	(0.236)	31.72	0.00
Ireland	**0.104**	(0.016)	58.17	32.67	**0.195**	(0.015)	80.46	13.57
Italy	**0.132**	(0.037)	64.97	27.65	**0.227**	(0.036)	78.39	16.31
Latvia	**0.118**	(0.015)	62.79	30.92	**0.155**	(0.013)	70.69	26.06
Macao-China[1]	0.076	(0.092)	14.29	9.52	0.121	(0.091)	30.95	9.52
Mexico[1]	**0.142**	(0.012)	39.76	59.34	**0.165**	(0.012)	45.41	54.14
New Zealand[1]	0.071	(0.042)	53.86	38.68	**0.230**	(0.044)	70.96	23.08
Poland	**0.137**	(0.013)	68.69	24.50	**0.319**	(0.014)	88.22	7.24
Portugal: ISCED2	**0.151**	(0.011)	67.21	26.24	**0.224**	(0.011)	81.70	16.73
Portugal: ISCED3	**0.240**	(0.017)	82.24	14.90	**0.388**	(0.016)	95.88	2.23
Serbia	**0.122**	(0.045)	68.52	23.56	**0.180**	(0.044)	81.95	13.10
Singapore	0.070	(0.185)	18.49	2.82	0.095	(0.184)	19.29	1.69
Slovak Republic	**0.056**	(0.008)	58.05	39.33	**0.216**	(0.008)	77.07	21.36
Trinidad and Tobago	0.138	(0.204)	15.18	0.68	0.180	(0.202)	19.40	1.42
Regions								
Italy: Abruzzo	**0.125**	(0.039)	75.74	13.29	**0.224**	(0.040)	81.90	15.13
Italy: Basilicata	**0.196**	(0.065)	72.53	14.20	**0.291**	(0.067)	80.60	9.22
Italy: Bolzano	0.036	(0.190)	8.17	4.67	0.197	(0.183)	29.96	2.33
Italy: Calabria	**0.082**	(0.015)	62.37	23.89	**0.198**	(0.017)	71.19	24.41
Italy: Campania	**0.162**	(0.009)	71.08	27.76	**0.203**	(0.009)	75.89	19.10
Italy: Emilia Romagna	**0.176**	(0.010)	67.02	32.12	**0.214**	(0.011)	76.54	19.08
Italy: Friuli Venezia Giulia	0.069	(0.070)	50.93	33.90	**0.143**	(0.065)	60.63	29.27
Italy: Lazio	**0.193**	(0.011)	68.69	27.00	**0.290**	(0.011)	76.31	22.80
Italy: Liguria	**0.148**	(0.032)	73.90	23.88	**0.237**	(0.024)	80.05	10.77
Italy: Lombardia	**0.054**	(0.011)	57.21	42.79	**0.178**	(0.008)	82.84	17.16
Italy: Marche	**0.179**	(0.022)	78.86	14.77	**0.234**	(0.023)	89.02	9.12
Italy: Molise	0.140	(0.169)	16.84	5.79	0.276	(0.165)	47.89	2.89
Italy: Piemonte	**0.085**	(0.011)	69.69	24.63	**0.209**	(0.011)	78.30	12.13
Italy: Puglia	**0.117**	(0.007)	73.13	26.87	**0.202**	(0.006)	83.39	15.35
Italy: Sardegna	**0.157**	(0.007)	70.27	28.86	**0.299**	(0.009)	83.95	12.39
Italy: Sicilia	**0.210**	(0.014)	60.23	20.76	**0.278**	(0.011)	76.08	19.68
Italy: Toscana	**0.051**	(0.009)	55.05	44.95	**0.212**	(0.013)	77.66	19.52
Italy: Trento	0.125	(0.116)	41.05	19.29	0.135	(0.119)	49.50	20.72
Italy: Umbria	0.133	(0.074)	56.23	24.06	**0.207**	(0.069)	69.82	14.42
Italy: Valle d'Aosta	0.055	(0.186)	9.52	4.76	0.205	(0.185)	23.81	0.00
Italy: Veneto	**0.180**	(0.005)	81.79	18.21	**0.265**	(0.006)	96.29	3.71
Mexico: Aguascalientes[1]	**0.114**	(0.036)	32.68	65.13	0.044	(0.042)	37.78	58.39
Mexico: Baja California[1]	**0.067**	(0.003)	57.70	37.63	**0.156**	(0.004)	70.58	29.23
Mexico: Baja California Sur[1]	0.055	(0.045)	29.73	66.12	**0.089**	(0.044)	28.66	63.90
Mexico: Campeche[1]	**0.099**	(0.020)	35.61	63.17	**0.129**	(0.018)	54.60	40.56
Mexico: Chihuahua[1]	**0.061**	(0.002)	32.50	67.27	**0.143**	(0.004)	45.28	54.72
Mexico: Colima[1]	0.023	(0.036)	29.43	66.65	0.013	(0.030)	29.79	58.83
Mexico: Coahuila[1]	**0.136**	(0.014)	41.35	58.25	**0.115**	(0.011)	49.60	49.79
Mexico: Chiapas[1]	**0.247**	(0.005)	52.95	46.36	**0.295**	(0.005)	56.85	43.15
Mexico: Distrito Federal[1]	0.008	(0.005)	29.56	69.90	**0.077**	(0.006)	41.98	58.02
Mexico: Durango[1]	**0.205**	(0.015)	61.86	35.62	**0.155**	(0.017)	54.26	43.64
Mexico: Guerrero[1]	**0.017**	(0.007)	31.97	65.15	**0.067**	(0.008)	48.67	49.32
Mexico: Guanajuato[1]	**0.199**	(0.005)	50.76	49.24	**0.153**	(0.007)	46.93	53.07
Mexico: Hidalgo[1]	**0.089**	(0.001)	33.29	66.71	**0.091**	(0.001)	33.55	66.45
Mexico: Jalisco[1]	**0.293**	(0.004)	57.75	42.25	**0.295**	(0.002)	64.15	35.85
Mexico: Michoacán[1]	**0.190**	(0.003)	62.54	37.46	**0.136**	(0.002)	67.20	32.80
Mexico: Morelos[1]	**0.220**	(0.018)	53.51	45.98	**0.195**	(0.026)	58.07	40.91
Mexico: Mexico[1]	**0.150**	(0.011)	53.23	46.09	**0.179**	(0.012)	50.75	49.25
Mexico: Nayarit[1]	**0.097**	(0.041)	45.29	50.96	**0.128**	(0.040)	38.75	57.87
Mexico: Nuevo León[1]	-0.014	(0.021)	38.34	60.16	-0.013	(0.017)	40.73	58.78
Mexico: Oaxaca[1]	**0.041**	(0.012)	21.82	78.18	**0.099**	(0.006)	34.22	65.78
Mexico: Puebla[1]	**0.053**	(0.002)	27.42	72.58	**0.049**	(0.003)	31.94	68.06
Mexico: Quintana Roo[1]	**0.094**	(0.029)	28.97	68.79	**0.235**	(0.033)	53.67	44.71
Mexico: Querétaro[1]	**0.047**	(0.019)	19.13	79.65	**0.150**	(0.024)	36.85	61.93
Mexico: Sinaloa[1]	**0.154**	(0.004)	33.04	66.96	**0.259**	(0.003)	43.74	56.26
Mexico: San Luis Potosí[1]	**0.195**	(0.034)	34.34	65.66	**0.272**	(0.014)	38.72	61.28
Mexico: Sonora[1]	**0.133**	(0.006)	40.99	49.30	**0.267**	(0.005)	54.15	45.85
Mexico: Tamaulipas[1]	**0.344**	(0.003)	56.55	43.45	**0.314**	(0.001)	54.24	45.76
Mexico: Tabasco[1]	**0.344**	(0.003)	54.27	45.73	**0.334**	(0.003)	57.06	42.94
Mexico: Tlaxcala[1]	**0.068**	(0.026)	53.30	43.80	**0.146**	(0.033)	83.62	13.49
Mexico: Veracruz[1]	**0.254**	(0.002)	31.09	68.91	**0.226**	(0.004)	37.31	62.69
Mexico: Yucatán[1]	**0.131**	(0.010)	54.55	39.23	**0.190**	(0.005)	59.08	40.74
Mexico: Zacatecas[1]	0.021	(0.020)	17.16	82.11	**0.149**	(0.024)	20.62	78.65

Notes: To facilitate comparability, marks in all countries and economies have been standardised so that higher values indicate better appraisals and that all countries and economies have a mean mark of 0 (zero) with a standard deviation of 1 (one).

Logistic models that account for the dichotomous nature of observed marks in Macao-China, Mexico and New Zealand, and Tobit models that account for the censored nature of failing marks in Austria, Croatia, Hungary, Poland, Serbia and the Slovak Republic do not yield substantively different results.

Correlations statistically significantly different from 0 (zero) at a 95% confidence level are highlighted in bold.

1. Macao-China, Mexico and New Zealand distributed, in the Educational Career questionnaire, the alternative question on whether students received a passing or failing mark. Results for these countries and economies are thus based on a dichotomous variable that does not capture the full variability of marks received by students. Estimates for these countries and economies are probably underestimated.

StatLink http://dx.doi.org/10.1787/888932734134

[Part 4/7]

Table B2.5 Within-school correlation between the marks received by students in their language-of-assessment course and student characteristics

	Engagement							
	Enjoyment of reading				Attitudes towards school			
	Average corr.	S.E.	Percentage of schools with positive correlation	Percentage of schools with negative correlation	Average corr.	S.E.	Percentage of schools with positive correlation	Percentage of schools with negative correlation
Countries and economies								
Austria	**0.223**	(0.027)	83.35	10.11	**0.095**	(0.032)	64.07	29.04
Belgium (Flemish Community)	**0.185**	(0.011)	73.38	24.69	**0.115**	(0.012)	65.50	30.32
Croatia	**0.253**	(0.026)	86.04	5.61	**0.058**	(0.027)	63.16	30.47
Hungary	**0.229**	(0.011)	78.48	20.32	**0.116**	(0.010)	72.37	27.16
Iceland	0.192	(0.224)	33.98	0.87	0.205	(0.219)	28.00	0.95
Ireland	**0.267**	(0.015)	87.58	8.49	**0.092**	(0.018)	58.27	26.53
Italy	**0.229**	(0.036)	80.72	14.01	**0.128**	(0.039)	63.88	28.56
Latvia	**0.341**	(0.013)	89.41	9.43	**0.177**	(0.015)	67.34	26.58
Macao-China[1]	0.160	(0.090)	50.00	9.52	0.071	(0.098)	16.67	9.52
Mexico[1]	**0.165**	(0.011)	45.74	53.72	**0.094**	(0.012)	39.07	59.04
New Zealand[1]	**0.192**	(0.044)	71.88	20.66	**0.185**	(0.043)	64.72	24.75
Poland	**0.412**	(0.012)	96.56	1.32	**0.076**	(0.014)	54.18	39.12
Portugal: ISCED2	**0.239**	(0.010)	83.40	16.60	**0.151**	(0.014)	70.44	27.11
Portugal: ISCED3	**0.335**	(0.017)	88.60	8.64	**0.135**	(0.021)	71.85	22.10
Serbia	**0.298**	(0.048)	86.61	7.99	0.048	(0.052)	59.03	34.83
Singapore	0.154	(0.186)	26.32	2.26	0.042	(0.198)	14.25	7.06
Slovak Republic	**0.312**	(0.008)	89.37	9.90	**0.110**	(0.011)	66.43	31.66
Trinidad and Tobago	0.161	(0.210)	18.60	1.37	0.048	(0.210)	12.44	4.79
Regions								
Italy: Abruzzo	**0.256**	(0.031)	77.10	12.86	**0.199**	(0.034)	72.43	23.49
Italy: Basilicata	**0.266**	(0.062)	78.83	9.45	**0.144**	(0.061)	71.61	15.17
Italy: Bolzano	0.203	(0.190)	23.35	13.62	0.170	(0.203)	24.12	4.67
Italy: Calabria	**0.170**	(0.011)	88.35	10.36	0.026	(0.015)	50.21	48.12
Italy: Campania	**0.251**	(0.007)	85.28	14.06	**0.123**	(0.008)	75.82	18.89
Italy: Emilia Romagna	**0.326**	(0.012)	89.99	9.46	**0.223**	(0.009)	75.41	22.87
Italy: Friuli Venezia Giulia	**0.172**	(0.066)	62.05	25.78	0.110	(0.072)	57.10	29.53
Italy: Lazio	**0.296**	(0.009)	93.22	6.10	**0.179**	(0.009)	73.90	24.69
Italy: Liguria	**0.179**	(0.028)	78.85	17.69	**0.168**	(0.035)	74.56	16.71
Italy: Lombardia	**0.168**	(0.011)	70.78	21.89	**0.055**	(0.013)	47.80	44.46
Italy: Marche	**0.260**	(0.030)	80.61	17.35	**0.145**	(0.025)	74.57	24.28
Italy: Molise	0.236	(0.160)	42.61	5.79	0.131	(0.193)	24.57	5.21
Italy: Piemonte	**0.216**	(0.010)	76.39	23.61	**0.184**	(0.011)	68.48	22.01
Italy: Puglia	**0.204**	(0.009)	88.47	5.10	**0.085**	(0.008)	64.38	31.26
Italy: Sardegna	**0.225**	(0.011)	80.76	16.44	**0.180**	(0.011)	78.86	9.91
Italy: Sicilia	**0.289**	(0.019)	85.68	7.17	**0.109**	(0.017)	58.47	37.11
Italy: Toscana	**0.290**	(0.013)	87.51	10.70	**0.115**	(0.010)	68.97	26.13
Italy: Trento	0.219	(0.112)	56.80	14.84	0.140	(0.125)	47.90	15.22
Italy: Umbria	**0.244**	(0.072)	77.25	13.50	0.091	(0.081)	61.46	22.06
Italy: Valle d'Aosta	0.208	(0.167)	38.10	4.76	0.098	(0.193)	9.52	0.00
Italy: Veneto	**0.125**	(0.005)	82.18	17.82	**0.153**	(0.008)	67.24	28.97
Mexico: Aguascalientes[1]	**0.143**	(0.028)	47.74	48.43	0.038	(0.039)	29.47	67.80
Mexico: Baja California[1]	**0.177**	(0.003)	73.05	26.50	**0.073**	(0.008)	48.66	48.73
Mexico: Baja California Sur[1]	-0.027	(0.047)	13.76	80.01	0.065	(0.065)	29.59	66.25
Mexico: Campeche[1]	**0.090**	(0.019)	54.84	44.35	**0.053**	(0.021)	39.60	58.65
Mexico: Chihuahua[1]	**0.066**	(0.005)	46.70	53.06	**0.011**	(0.002)	35.20	64.80
Mexico: Colima[1]	**0.194**	(0.026)	46.11	49.98	**0.128**	(0.035)	40.04	55.48
Mexico: Coahuila[1]	-0.018	(0.016)	28.02	71.38	0.005	(0.017)	32.23	67.17
Mexico: Chiapas[1]	**0.159**	(0.004)	58.64	41.36	**0.128**	(0.003)	52.62	47.38
Mexico: Distrito Federal[1]	**0.155**	(0.007)	55.68	43.30	**0.116**	(0.004)	51.43	45.56
Mexico: Durango[1]	**0.232**	(0.009)	56.58	42.52	**0.315**	(0.028)	41.65	57.23
Mexico: Guerrero[1]	**-0.095**	(0.006)	41.20	58.34	**0.172**	(0.006)	53.19	33.50
Mexico: Guanajuato[1]	**0.242**	(0.004)	52.15	47.85	**0.069**	(0.006)	37.10	62.90
Mexico: Hidalgo[1]	**0.126**	(0.002)	28.71	69.39	**0.249**	(0.001)	38.38	61.62
Mexico: Jalisco[1]	**0.217**	(0.002)	53.10	46.90	**0.167**	(0.002)	41.60	58.40
Mexico: Michoacán[1]	**0.090**	(0.002)	63.00	37.00	**-0.053**	(0.002)	33.55	66.45
Mexico: Morelos[1]	**0.220**	(0.023)	56.26	36.93	**0.073**	(0.019)	45.93	53.05
Mexico: Mexico[1]	**0.229**	(0.008)	63.57	36.43	**-0.031**	(0.005)	35.62	59.58
Mexico: Nayarit[1]	**0.126**	(0.045)	47.25	48.98	0.047	(0.057)	24.11	72.89
Mexico: Nuevo León[1]	**0.068**	(0.019)	36.55	62.95	**0.165**	(0.022)	43.01	56.37
Mexico: Oaxaca[1]	**0.105**	(0.009)	25.64	74.36	**0.089**	(0.010)	26.25	73.23
Mexico: Puebla[1]	**0.266**	(0.003)	36.77	63.23	**0.017**	(0.003)	23.02	74.55
Mexico: Quintana Roo[1]	**0.190**	(0.031)	44.22	53.51	-0.043	(0.027)	25.31	72.74
Mexico: Querétaro[1]	**0.283**	(0.019)	47.35	51.61	0.034	(0.022)	27.78	71.18
Mexico: Sinaloa[1]	**0.266**	(0.001)	49.22	50.78	**0.252**	(0.005)	40.27	59.73
Mexico: San Luis Potosí[1]	**0.243**	(0.006)	36.01	62.99	**0.187**	(0.004)	32.99	67.01
Mexico: Sonora[1]	**0.151**	(0.004)	47.36	52.64	**0.180**	(0.003)	54.71	45.29
Mexico: Tamaulipas[1]	**0.077**	(0.002)	37.85	61.48	**0.101**	(0.002)	39.41	60.59
Mexico: Tabasco[1]	**0.197**	(0.002)	35.93	63.44	**0.202**	(0.003)	46.49	53.51
Mexico: Tlaxcala[1]	0.056	(0.032)	48.81	47.81	**0.063**	(0.023)	57.42	40.17
Mexico: Veracruz[1]	**0.181**	(0.002)	34.72	65.28	**0.143**	(0.005)	43.04	55.92
Mexico: Yucatán[1]	**0.186**	(0.008)	70.59	28.40	**0.145**	(0.004)	67.82	31.16
Mexico: Zacatecas[1]	**0.172**	(0.015)	29.88	69.39	**0.063**	(0.025)	22.94	76.33

Notes: To facilitate comparability, marks in all countries and economies have been standardised so that higher values indicate better appraisals and that all countries and economies have a mean mark of 0 (zero) with a standard deviation of 1 (one).

Logistic models that account for the dichotomous nature of observed marks in Macao-China, Mexico and New Zealand, and Tobit models that account for the censored nature of failing marks in Austria, Croatia, Hungary, Poland, Serbia and the Slovak Republic do not yield substantively different results.

Correlations statistically significantly different from 0 (zero) at a 95% confidence level are highlighted in bold.

1. Macao-China, Mexico and New Zealand distributed, in the Educational Career questionnaire, the alternative question on whether students received a passing or failing mark. Results for these countries and economies are thus based on a dichotomous variable that does not capture the full variability of marks received by students. Estimates for these countries and economies are probably underestimated.

StatLink http://dx.doi.org/10.1787/888932734134

[Part 5/7]

Table B2.5 Within-school correlation between the marks received by students in their language-of-assessment course and student characteristics

	Student-teacher relations				Student background: Student is a girl			
	Average corr.	S.E.	Percentage of schools with positive correlation	Percentage of schools with negative correlation	Average corr.	S.E.	Percentage of schools with positive correlation	Percentage of schools with negative correlation
Countries and economies								
Austria	**0.159**	(0.030)	68.14	26.84	**0.122**	(0.027)	60.01	36.01
Belgium (Flemish Community)	**0.033**	(0.010)	58.68	38.90	**0.162**	(0.009)	67.70	29.28
Croatia	**0.123**	(0.025)	67.43	28.44	**0.162**	(0.026)	72.83	24.65
Hungary	**0.186**	(0.011)	78.97	16.65	**0.185**	(0.006)	69.07	25.71
Iceland	0.177	(0.219)	22.88	2.60	0.120	(0.220)	20.11	6.42
Ireland	**0.126**	(0.019)	65.97	24.09	**0.104**	(0.019)	37.27	54.17
Italy	**0.159**	(0.038)	71.38	22.01	**0.144**	(0.036)	61.56	32.49
Latvia	**0.178**	(0.016)	65.69	19.26	**0.249**	(0.012)	79.84	14.76
Macao-China[1]	0.047	(0.107)	4.76	9.52	0.129	(0.088)	35.71	26.19
Mexico[1]	**0.093**	(0.012)	38.87	60.16	**0.049**	(0.011)	35.13	64.19
New Zealand[1]	**0.166**	(0.044)	60.57	28.55	**0.131**	(0.045)	45.06	48.44
Poland	**0.193**	(0.014)	73.86	22.87	**0.335**	(0.008)	91.10	7.61
Portugal: ISCED2	**0.159**	(0.012)	62.24	31.69	**0.148**	(0.008)	73.43	22.49
Portugal: ISCED3	**0.204**	(0.021)	77.84	17.99	**0.180**	(0.019)	80.15	19.20
Serbia	**0.109**	(0.046)	67.93	25.92	**0.176**	(0.041)	75.14	20.51
Singapore	0.065	(0.191)	15.11	2.82	-0.013	(0.193)	9.71	20.88
Slovak Republic	**0.219**	(0.008)	79.48	15.73	**0.265**	(0.007)	83.92	15.53
Trinidad and Tobago	0.063	(0.217)	11.77	2.05	0.107	(0.225)	7.53	29.45
Regions								
Italy: Abruzzo	**0.153**	(0.034)	75.20	17.66	**0.207**	(0.031)	72.23	16.83
Italy: Basilicata	**0.135**	(0.069)	56.86	34.81	0.089	(0.063)	44.87	42.70
Italy: Bolzano	0.166	(0.193)	25.29	1.17	0.207	(0.188)	31.13	5.84
Italy: Calabria	**0.041**	(0.015)	68.74	27.62	**0.163**	(0.014)	63.18	36.29
Italy: Campania	**0.226**	(0.009)	80.02	13.03	**0.141**	(0.011)	62.02	35.08
Italy: Emilia Romagna	**0.179**	(0.009)	74.08	24.36	**0.133**	(0.008)	68.41	29.19
Italy: Friuli Venezia Giulia	0.091	(0.066)	55.49	34.28	**0.135**	(0.062)	63.84	24.98
Italy: Lazio	**0.234**	(0.010)	72.44	21.91	**0.160**	(0.007)	61.41	37.51
Italy: Liguria	**0.129**	(0.035)	71.93	20.62	0.044	(0.043)	49.55	46.75
Italy: Lombardia	**0.074**	(0.011)	64.90	32.56	**0.054**	(0.008)	49.73	43.89
Italy: Marche	**0.142**	(0.021)	72.90	18.56	**0.189**	(0.030)	69.54	21.86
Italy: Molise	0.120	(0.185)	21.61	5.21	0.120	(0.160)	12.30	19.83
Italy: Piemonte	**0.148**	(0.013)	81.25	13.81	**0.066**	(0.010)	66.78	30.16
Italy: Puglia	**0.130**	(0.009)	74.12	25.88	**0.170**	(0.008)	63.06	30.79
Italy: Sardegna	**0.251**	(0.010)	79.13	20.35	**0.075**	(0.009)	61.97	36.90
Italy: Sicilia	**0.195**	(0.018)	68.81	22.41	**0.279**	(0.014)	77.12	17.94
Italy: Toscana	**0.254**	(0.013)	83.99	16.01	**0.224**	(0.008)	74.27	22.97
Italy: Trento	0.136	(0.136)	45.97	10.90	0.127	(0.119)	40.00	27.38
Italy: Umbria	**0.191**	(0.068)	69.90	13.50	0.055	(0.071)	47.23	31.86
Italy: Valle d'Aosta	0.148	(0.185)	14.29	0.00	0.163	(0.182)	19.05	19.05
Italy: Veneto	**0.135**	(0.010)	75.29	22.75	**0.178**	(0.006)	58.36	41.64
Mexico: Aguascalientes[1]	**0.082**	(0.040)	43.33	49.03	**-0.082**	(0.034)	21.52	75.75
Mexico: Baja California[1]	**0.121**	(0.004)	66.70	33.10	**0.067**	(0.004)	50.85	44.79
Mexico: Baja California Sur[1]	0.054	(0.055)	27.20	66.30	**-0.116**	(0.049)	11.19	85.35
Mexico: Campeche[1]	**0.144**	(0.018)	61.17	37.61	**0.103**	(0.022)	46.27	52.52
Mexico: Chihuahua[1]	**0.112**	(0.004)	40.27	55.82	**0.016**	(0.002)	34.70	65.30
Mexico: Colima[1]	**0.292**	(0.036)	45.40	51.80	**0.083**	(0.038)	33.71	59.75
Mexico: Coahuila[1]	**0.134**	(0.023)	42.00	57.40	**0.095**	(0.012)	45.21	51.29
Mexico: Chiapas[1]	**0.074**	(0.004)	39.98	60.02	**-0.145**	(0.005)	21.80	78.20
Mexico: Distrito Federal[1]	0.003	(0.005)	37.12	62.88	0.002	(0.004)	41.72	58.28
Mexico: Durango[1]	**0.397**	(0.017)	70.50	28.37	**-0.062**	(0.013)	41.63	57.93
Mexico: Guerrero[1]	**-0.041**	(0.007)	27.69	62.15	**0.067**	(0.007)	44.59	55.41
Mexico: Guanajuato[1]	**-0.151**	(0.004)	29.35	70.65	**0.122**	(0.005)	40.72	58.97
Mexico: Hidalgo[1]	**0.242**	(0.001)	43.04	56.96	**0.060**	(0.001)	26.95	70.89
Mexico: Jalisco[1]	**0.223**	(0.002)	63.87	36.13	**0.246**	(0.002)	52.08	47.92
Mexico: Michoacán[1]	**0.073**	(0.003)	46.53	50.36	0.001	(0.002)	46.44	53.56
Mexico: Morelos[1]	**0.063**	(0.023)	41.28	57.70	-0.004	(0.024)	35.51	60.68
Mexico: Mexico[1]	**0.119**	(0.011)	49.79	49.54	**0.050**	(0.008)	45.58	54.42
Mexico: Nayarit[1]	**0.228**	(0.042)	38.55	57.70	-0.021	(0.037)	28.01	68.98
Mexico: Nuevo León[1]	-0.013	(0.025)	34.99	64.07	-0.036	(0.019)	27.13	70.89
Mexico: Oaxaca[1]	**0.023**	(0.003)	22.16	77.84	**0.034**	(0.005)	15.12	84.36
Mexico: Puebla[1]	**-0.007**	(0.003)	22.62	77.38	-0.001	(0.001)	22.02	77.98
Mexico: Quintana Roo[1]	0.012	(0.021)	38.53	58.96	**0.150**	(0.028)	46.93	51.12
Mexico: Querétaro[1]	**0.085**	(0.018)	38.48	60.30	**0.181**	(0.023)	35.49	61.20
Mexico: Sinaloa[1]	**0.267**	(0.003)	44.12	55.88	**0.045**	(0.003)	35.41	64.59
Mexico: San Luis Potosí[1]	**0.323**	(0.002)	33.61	66.39	**0.144**	(0.004)	35.13	64.87
Mexico: Sonora[1]	**0.147**	(0.006)	54.52	45.48	**0.081**	(0.002)	44.63	55.37
Mexico: Tamaulipas[1]	**0.147**	(0.002)	48.69	49.16	**0.025**	(0.001)	28.30	70.61
Mexico: Tabasco[1]	**0.120**	(0.003)	40.61	59.40	**0.040**	(0.002)	37.27	62.73
Mexico: Tlaxcala[1]	**0.107**	(0.036)	68.71	28.39	0.066	(0.035)	52.04	39.04
Mexico: Veracruz[1]	**0.166**	(0.006)	31.30	68.70	**0.109**	(0.003)	31.93	68.07
Mexico: Yucatán[1]	**0.042**	(0.003)	53.08	46.74	**-0.059**	(0.007)	46.01	52.46
Mexico: Zacatecas[1]	**0.372**	(0.017)	34.90	64.55	**0.183**	(0.022)	24.28	74.99

Notes: To facilitate comparability, marks in all countries and economies have been standardised so that higher values indicate better appraisals and that all countries and economies have a mean mark of 0 (zero) with a standard deviation of 1 (one).

Logistic models that account for the dichotomous nature of observed marks in Macao-China, Mexico and New Zealand, and Tobit models that account for the censored nature of failing marks in Austria, Croatia, Hungary, Poland, Serbia and the Slovak Republic do not yield substantively different results.

Correlations statistically significantly different from 0 (zero) at a 95% confidence level are highlighted in bold.

1. Macao-China, Mexico and New Zealand distributed, in the Educational Career questionnaire, the alternative question on whether students received a passing or failing mark. Results for these countries and economies are thus based on a dichotomous variable that does not capture the full variability of marks received by students. Estimates for these countries and economies are probably underestimated.

StatLink http://dx.doi.org/10.1787/888932734134

[Part 6/7]

Table B2.5 Within-school correlation between the marks received by students in their language-of-assessment course and student characteristics

	Student background							
	PISA index of economic, social and cultural status				Student with an immigrant background			
	Average corr.	S.E.	Percentage of schools with positive correlation	Percentage of schools with negative correlation	Average corr.	S.E.	Percentage of schools with positive correlation	Percentage of schools with negative correlation
Countries and economies								
Austria	**0.091**	(0.027)	61.33	35.61	-0.077	(0.023)	21.65	71.54
Belgium (Flemish Community)	**0.052**	(0.010)	53.44	42.41	-0.126	(0.008)	24.26	74.71
Croatia	**0.079**	(0.026)	58.27	39.29	-0.035	(0.030)	30.68	66.28
Hungary	**0.106**	(0.010)	58.76	36.97	-0.062	(0.004)	11.12	88.88
Iceland	0.223	(0.222)	32.79	0.95	-0.066	(0.142)	1.82	70.08
Ireland	**0.133**	(0.015)	74.24	20.23	0.006	(0.012)	39.44	55.20
Italy	**0.110**	(0.038)	64.84	28.44	-0.056	(0.032)	20.48	76.62
Latvia	**0.202**	(0.014)	74.38	21.48	-0.065	(0.010)	11.78	87.82
Macao-China[1]	0.078	(0.097)	21.43	11.90	0.034	(0.100)	9.52	14.29
Mexico[1]	**0.040**	(0.011)	34.97	63.16	-0.011	(0.005)	14.36	85.61
New Zealand[1]	**0.130**	(0.045)	52.55	37.37	0.000	(0.043)	38.04	51.74
Poland	**0.289**	(0.013)	87.50	9.65	-0.034	(0.003)	0.00	100.00
Portugal: ISCED2	**0.129**	(0.011)	68.09	30.31	0.105	(0.015)	36.04	62.51
Portugal: ISCED3	**0.219**	(0.021)	89.87	7.40	-0.051	(0.023)	15.84	81.51
Serbia	0.075	(0.047)	61.90	33.95	-0.020	(0.031)	36.15	60.01
Singapore	0.134	(0.192)	16.04	5.24	-0.055	(0.178)	3.14	17.61
Slovak Republic	**0.224**	(0.011)	76.89	19.97	0.059	(0.003)	4.73	94.86
Trinidad and Tobago	0.139	(0.204)	16.50	1.37	0.000	(0.162)	2.86	68.71
Regions								
Italy: Abruzzo	0.034	(0.039)	58.83	31.52	-0.101	(0.015)	25.78	72.23
Italy: Basilicata	0.128	(0.067)	63.71	22.11	-0.245	(0.023)	0.00	98.15
Italy: Bolzano	0.079	(0.197)	20.62	2.33	-0.095	(0.160)	0.00	50.20
Italy: Calabria	**0.050**	(0.015)	55.35	36.08	0.010	(0.013)	13.12	86.88
Italy: Campania	**0.084**	(0.009)	69.79	28.94	0.047	(0.006)	7.97	92.03
Italy: Emilia Romagna	**0.088**	(0.009)	61.69	29.07	0.012	(0.010)	36.12	56.73
Italy: Friuli Venezia Giulia	**0.148**	(0.068)	63.31	22.91	-0.096	(0.060)	27.31	61.76
Italy: Lazio	**0.051**	(0.008)	62.08	36.24	-0.013	(0.009)	37.20	60.79
Italy: Liguria	0.056	(0.042)	56.22	39.31	-0.265	(0.022)	9.56	89.70
Italy: Lombardia	**0.166**	(0.009)	77.09	16.28	-0.115	(0.017)	20.97	79.04
Italy: Marche	**0.151**	(0.031)	85.62	12.64	-0.084	(0.025)	23.03	75.23
Italy: Molise	0.118	(0.187)	22.20	2.89	-0.092	(0.069)	2.89	66.42
Italy: Piemonte	**0.190**	(0.010)	72.09	20.98	-0.005	(0.009)	42.57	55.34
Italy: Puglia	**0.083**	(0.007)	69.16	25.43	-0.001	(0.005)	11.15	88.85
Italy: Sardegna	**0.107**	(0.010)	68.24	30.64	-0.193	(0.006)	6.94	93.06
Italy: Sicilia	**0.181**	(0.015)	69.89	30.11	0.005	(0.007)	3.28	96.72
Italy: Toscana	**-0.028**	(0.011)	42.26	55.51	-0.047	(0.013)	18.51	80.06
Italy: Trento	0.089	(0.124)	42.74	19.79	-0.075	(0.110)	11.89	58.33
Italy: Umbria	**0.169**	(0.073)	64.28	17.93	-0.050	(0.052)	26.38	66.29
Italy: Valle d'Aosta	0.076	(0.198)	4.76	0.00	-0.002	(0.147)	4.76	38.10
Italy: Veneto	**0.091**	(0.006)	56.21	42.18	-0.045	(0.006)	34.85	62.09
Mexico: Aguascalientes[1]	**-0.066**	(0.033)	20.16	77.10	0.072	(0.000)	6.23	93.77
Mexico: Baja California[1]	**0.223**	(0.003)	62.66	37.15	-0.154	(0.001)	35.03	64.97
Mexico: Baja California Sur[1]	0.074	(0.049)	37.24	57.22	0.064	(0.012)	33.78	64.84
Mexico: Campeche[1]	**0.038**	(0.018)	42.94	56.25	0.089	(0.006)	21.50	78.50
Mexico: Chihuahua[1]	**0.064**	(0.003)	49.15	50.85	0.058	(0.001)	21.06	78.94
Mexico: Colima[1]	0.024	(0.034)	30.73	64.23	0.081	(0.001)	11.28	88.72
Mexico: Coahuila[1]	**0.048**	(0.011)	41.28	58.11	0.045	(0.000)	0.22	99.78
Mexico: Chiapas[1]	**0.082**	(0.003)	41.87	58.13	0.029	(0.006)	34.70	65.30
Mexico: Distrito Federal[1]	**0.043**	(0.005)	48.95	50.62	-0.181	(0.001)	13.26	86.74
Mexico: Durango[1]	**-0.033**	(0.016)	35.08	62.84	0.065	(0.009)	15.90	83.89
Mexico: Guerrero[1]	**-0.097**	(0.009)	29.65	70.35	-0.059	(0.011)	12.01	87.99
Mexico: Guanajuato[1]	**0.069**	(0.004)	39.02	53.78	0.067	(0.002)	3.97	96.03
Mexico: Hidalgo[1]	**0.084**	(0.001)	27.53	69.82	-0.093	(0.000)	13.19	86.81
Mexico: Jalisco[1]	**-0.036**	(0.002)	32.14	65.91	-0.140	(0.000)	6.49	93.51
Mexico: Michoacán[1]	-0.003	(0.004)	38.52	61.48	0.077	(0.001)	13.11	86.89
Mexico: Morelos[1]	**-0.062**	(0.024)	19.65	76.78	-0.322	(0.010)	14.74	85.00
Mexico: Mexico[1]	**0.062**	(0.010)	42.76	48.05	0.129	(0.004)	31.24	68.76
Mexico: Nayarit[1]	**-0.160**	(0.039)	16.26	80.36	0.058	(0.012)	15.53	83.71
Mexico: Nuevo León[1]	0.032	(0.017)	32.96	66.30	0.095	(0.002)	15.18	84.82
Mexico: Oaxaca[1]	**-0.027**	(0.004)	22.77	77.23	0.147	(0.003)	21.00	79.00
Mexico: Puebla[1]	**-0.087**	(0.001)	13.97	86.03	0.095	(0.000)	7.62	92.38
Mexico: Quintana Roo[1]	**-0.054**	(0.024)	16.30	81.76	-0.043	(0.007)	23.33	76.02
Mexico: Querétaro[1]	**0.079**	(0.016)	34.21	64.92	-0.140	(0.000)	4.40	95.60
Mexico: Sinaloa[1]	**0.078**	(0.003)	29.95	70.05	0.062	(0.001)	12.76	87.24
Mexico: San Luis Potosí[1]	**0.195**	(0.013)	31.29	68.71	-0.054	(0.000)	6.43	93.57
Mexico: Sonora[1]	**0.023**	(0.003)	33.13	66.87	-0.006	(0.011)	14.19	85.81
Mexico: Tamaulipas[1]	**0.134**	(0.002)	41.99	58.01	-0.099	(0.000)	12.05	87.95
Mexico: Tabasco[1]	**0.073**	(0.002)	40.25	59.59	-0.194	(0.003)	19.11	80.89
Mexico: Tlaxcala[1]	0.019	(0.027)	51.00	46.11	0.116	(0.006)	40.01	59.03
Mexico: Veracruz[1]	**0.154**	(0.005)	39.17	60.83	0.007	(0.001)	4.28	95.72
Mexico: Yucatán[1]	**0.078**	(0.005)	48.42	51.40	-0.300	(0.002)	8.36	91.64
Mexico: Zacatecas[1]	-0.025	(0.015)	25.21	74.24	-0.937	(0.000)	0.72	99.28

Notes: To facilitate comparability, marks in all countries and economies have been standardised so that higher values indicate better appraisals and that all countries and economies have a mean mark of 0 (zero) with a standard deviation of 1 (one).

Logistic models that account for the dichotomous nature of observed marks in Macao-China, Mexico and New Zealand, and Tobit models that account for the censored nature of failing marks in Austria, Croatia, Hungary, Poland, Serbia and the Slovak Republic do not yield substantively different results.

Correlations statistically significantly different from 0 (zero) at a 95% confidence level are highlighted in bold.

1. Macao-China, Mexico and New Zealand distributed, in the Educational Career questionnaire, the alternative question on whether students received a passing or failing mark. Results for these countries and economies are thus based on a dichotomous variable that does not capture the full variability of marks received by students. Estimates for these countries and economies are probably underestimated.

StatLink http://dx.doi.org/10.1787/888932734134

[Part 7/7]

Table B2.5 Within-school correlation between the marks received by students in their language-of-assessment course and student characteristics

	Student background							
	Student speaks another language at home				Student attended ISCED 0 for more than one year			
	Average corr.	S.E.	Percentage of schools with positive correlation	Percentage of schools with negative correlation	Average corr.	S.E.	Percentage of schools with positive correlation	Percentage of schools with negative correlation
Countries and economies								
Austria	**-0.101**	(0.023)	19.27	78.78	-0.020	(0.024)	43.99	52.90
Belgium (Flemish Community)	**-0.081**	(0.014)	39.75	53.09	**0.080**	(0.013)	33.04	66.25
Croatia	**-0.094**	(0.018)	9.05	89.53	0.028	(0.027)	52.05	42.83
Hungary	**-0.047**	(0.008)	2.06	97.94	**0.016**	(0.006)	33.23	64.98
Iceland	-0.062	(0.143)	2.69	56.73	0.066	(0.168)	11.35	28.74
Ireland	**-0.036**	(0.016)	19.17	76.77	0.012	(0.020)	50.26	43.92
Italy	**-0.079**	(0.036)	27.07	66.63	0.032	(0.031)	47.84	46.07
Latvia	**0.079**	(0.012)	28.39	68.98	**-0.038**	(0.013)	36.98	50.29
Macao-China[1]	-0.009	(0.072)	21.43	50.00	0.077	(0.114)	9.52	23.81
Mexico[1]	**-0.043**	(0.004)	8.87	91.12	0.022	(0.012)	26.87	71.50
New Zealand[1]	**-0.105**	(0.047)	39.42	54.73	0.050	(0.044)	46.47	42.32
Poland	**0.019**	(0.008)	5.48	94.52	**0.075**	(0.013)	58.54	33.65
Portugal: ISCED2	**0.062**	(0.011)	20.60	76.36	**0.053**	(0.012)	55.36	33.53
Portugal: ISCED3	-0.014	(0.023)	7.06	92.28	**0.073**	(0.021)	58.13	35.56
Serbia	-0.059	(0.045)	7.39	90.98	-0.013	(0.050)	45.97	48.08
Singapore	-0.188	(0.189)	3.75	28.25	0.002	(0.176)	7.62	23.98
Slovak Republic	**-0.101**	(0.008)	13.42	84.37	**0.104**	(0.010)	57.72	38.60
Trinidad and Tobago	-0.001	(0.164)	4.86	62.71	-0.034	(0.212)	4.18	8.33
Regions								
Italy: Abruzzo	-0.011	(0.050)	33.92	63.11	**0.096**	(0.036)	54.32	35.53
Italy: Basilicata	-0.100	(0.074)	24.47	61.95	**0.125**	(0.042)	49.43	39.91
Italy: Bolzano	0.072	(0.175)	19.46	43.19	-0.116	(0.168)	5.84	29.96
Italy: Calabria	**-0.115**	(0.020)	20.92	72.29	**0.043**	(0.017)	44.37	54.44
Italy: Campania	**-0.113**	(0.013)	24.34	70.80	**0.032**	(0.008)	51.68	46.92
Italy: Emilia Romagna	**-0.039**	(0.013)	37.66	59.05	0.020	(0.011)	52.34	37.58
Italy: Friuli Venezia Giulia	**-0.191**	(0.066)	25.30	63.90	**0.212**	(0.060)	58.56	30.28
Italy: Lazio	**0.052**	(0.013)	50.35	48.98	-0.013	(0.009)	37.98	59.32
Italy: Liguria	-0.047	(0.028)	35.04	62.71	**0.114**	(0.027)	72.43	23.10
Italy: Lombardia	**-0.162**	(0.010)	19.09	80.91	**-0.035**	(0.010)	27.81	63.22
Italy: Marche	-0.012	(0.025)	43.92	53.10	**0.077**	(0.021)	57.15	35.18
Italy: Molise	-0.124	(0.158)	10.56	30.94	0.086	(0.133)	22.22	19.36
Italy: Piemonte	**-0.122**	(0.007)	32.57	59.43	**0.090**	(0.007)	61.47	35.29
Italy: Puglia	**-0.061**	(0.007)	23.37	76.63	**0.102**	(0.011)	54.47	45.53
Italy: Sardegna	**-0.094**	(0.008)	25.08	74.92	**0.099**	(0.006)	48.66	48.54
Italy: Sicilia	**-0.073**	(0.018)	18.68	68.04	**-0.146**	(0.014)	36.87	61.03
Italy: Toscana	**-0.053**	(0.011)	21.87	74.16	**0.148**	(0.010)	69.59	27.35
Italy: Trento	0.064	(0.122)	31.67	31.45	0.075	(0.099)	39.09	32.54
Italy: Umbria	-0.051	(0.065)	28.37	51.80	0.069	(0.070)	50.22	33.19
Italy: Valle d'Aosta	-0.004	(0.177)	4.76	9.52	0.088	(0.152)	9.52	9.52
Italy: Veneto	**-0.095**	(0.009)	22.76	70.38	**0.123**	(0.008)	69.83	30.17
Mexico: Aguascalientes[1]	**0.069**	(0.001)	15.01	84.99	0.036	(0.036)	30.67	66.52
Mexico: Baja California[1]	-0.003	(0.002)	21.17	78.83	**-0.070**	(0.005)	24.04	75.77
Mexico: Baja California Sur[1]	**-0.184**	(0.001)	3.44	96.56	0.013	(0.059)	18.00	77.85
Mexico: Campeche[1]	**-0.112**	(0.009)	12.35	87.65	**0.076**	(0.028)	30.99	67.66
Mexico: Chihuahua[1]	**0.050**	(0.001)	9.72	90.28	**0.081**	(0.004)	34.37	65.40
Mexico: Colima[1]	**0.102**	(0.009)	9.09	90.35	**0.166**	(0.052)	27.01	69.64
Mexico: Coahuila[1]	-0.585	(0.000)	1.31	98.69	**-0.040**	(0.008)	21.94	77.66
Mexico: Chiapas[1]	**-0.092**	(0.006)	6.03	93.97	**0.031**	(0.005)	31.12	67.54
Mexico: Distrito Federal[1]	**0.048**	(0.001)	7.42	92.58	**0.112**	(0.009)	48.55	50.95
Mexico: Durango[1]	**0.516**	(0.005)	5.27	94.73	-0.042	(0.023)	26.86	72.01
Mexico: Guerrero[1]	**-0.375**	(0.002)	4.69	95.31	0.006	(0.006)	37.70	61.84
Mexico: Guanajuato[1]	**0.059**	(0.000)	4.42	95.58	**0.170**	(0.005)	33.49	66.51
Mexico: Hidalgo[1]	0.000	(0.001)	16.59	83.41	**-0.104**	(0.001)	7.92	92.08
Mexico: Jalisco[1]	**-0.109**	(0.001)	11.03	88.97	**0.101**	(0.003)	35.77	64.23
Mexico: Michoacán[1]	0.050	(0.000)	3.03	96.97	**0.067**	(0.006)	43.82	55.83
Mexico: Morelos[1]	**0.060**	(0.004)	12.27	87.48	**0.074**	(0.024)	27.55	68.88
Mexico: Mexico[1]	**-0.225**	(0.009)	6.83	93.17	**0.092**	(0.008)	44.03	46.77
Mexico: Nayarit[1]	**0.054**	(0.001)	3.43	96.57	**0.257**	(0.040)	41.14	55.86
Mexico: Nuevo León[1]	**0.122**	(0.000)	2.34	97.66	**-0.117**	(0.019)	12.77	86.58
Mexico: Oaxaca[1]	**0.066**	(0.004)	28.01	71.99	**0.053**	(0.006)	15.46	84.54
Mexico: Puebla[1]	**0.028**	(0.000)	9.44	90.56	**-0.097**	(0.001)	14.66	85.34
Mexico: Quintana Roo[1]	**-0.060**	(0.003)	15.00	85.00	**0.060**	(0.030)	21.60	76.78
Mexico: Querétaro[1]	**0.061**	(0.000)	3.60	96.40	**0.134**	(0.026)	37.78	53.85
Mexico: Sinaloa[1]	0.080	(0.000)	1.01	98.99	**-0.037**	(0.004)	20.22	79.28
Mexico: San Luis Potosí[1]	**-0.025**	(0.000)	7.15	92.85	**0.024**	(0.001)	12.25	87.37
Mexico: Sonora[1]	**0.049**	(0.000)	15.62	84.38	-0.007	(0.007)	26.01	73.99
Mexico: Tamaulipas[1]	**0.034**	(0.000)	0.23	99.77	**0.018**	(0.003)	34.40	65.60
Mexico: Tabasco[1]	**0.043**	(0.000)	3.11	96.89	0.002	(0.004)	19.29	80.71
Mexico: Tlaxcala[1]	**0.041**	(0.000)	6.30	93.70	-0.039	(0.022)	13.96	71.64
Mexico: Veracruz[1]	**0.060**	(0.001)	5.53	94.47	**-0.051**	(0.001)	15.39	84.61
Mexico: Yucatán[1]	**0.091**	(0.003)	47.28	52.72	**-0.088**	(0.003)	38.23	60.67
Mexico: Zacatecas[1]	**-0.318**	(0.006)	2.13	97.68	**-0.283**	(0.015)	3.27	95.82

Notes: To facilitate comparability, marks in all countries and economies have been standardised so that higher values indicate better appraisals and that all countries and economies have a mean mark of 0 (zero) with a standard deviation of 1 (one).
Logistic models that account for the dichotomous nature of observed marks in Macao-China, Mexico and New Zealand, and Tobit models that account for the censored nature of failing marks in Austria, Croatia, Hungary, Poland, Serbia and the Slovak Republic do not yield substantively different results.
Correlations statistically significantly different from 0 (zero) at a 95% confidence level are highlighted in bold.
1. Macao-China, Mexico and New Zealand distributed, in the Educational Career questionnaire, the alternative question on whether students received a passing or failing mark. Results for these countries and economies are thus based on a dichotomous variable that does not capture the full variability of marks received by students. Estimates for these countries and economies are probably underestimated.

StatLink http://dx.doi.org/10.1787/888932734134

[Part 1/6]

Table B2.6 Within-school correlation between the marks received by students in their language-of-assessment course and student characteristics, after accounting for students' PISA reading scores

	Metacognition strategies							
	Understanding and remembering				Effective summarising strategies			
	Average corr.	S.E.	Percentage of schools with positive correlation	Percentage of schools with negative correlation	Average corr.	S.E.	Percentage of schools with positive correlation	Percentage of schools with negative correlation
Countries and economies								
Austria	0.007	(0.027)	52.89	42.49	**0.066**	(0.029)	64.11	30.83
Belgium (Flemish Community)	**0.069**	(0.011)	57.30	34.42	**0.048**	(0.013)	55.03	40.22
Croatia	0.043	(0.031)	56.11	39.95	**0.079**	(0.026)	57.17	35.87
Hungary	**0.059**	(0.011)	57.83	38.10	**0.036**	(0.009)	54.53	39.96
Iceland	0.063	(0.217)	10.67	6.23	0.050	(0.225)	13.35	4.47
Ireland	0.014	(0.020)	47.79	46.65	**0.052**	(0.017)	50.23	43.77
Italy	0.036	(0.038)	51.84	38.64	0.023	(0.038)	50.60	40.47
Latvia	0.014	(0.013)	46.21	46.99	**0.069**	(0.013)	65.23	29.56
Macao-China[1]	0.043	(0.097)	4.76	11.90	0.024	(0.098)	2.38	11.90
Mexico[1]	**-0.025**	(0.012)	26.00	72.15	0.005	(0.012)	30.59	68.74
New Zealand[1]	-0.007	(0.046)	37.31	49.79	0.033	(0.047)	45.13	44.72
Poland	**0.045**	(0.012)	51.74	42.61	**0.036**	(0.014)	52.47	41.60
Portugal: ISCED2	0.009	(0.011)	52.80	45.06	**0.030**	(0.013)	55.49	38.94
Portugal: ISCED3	**0.069**	(0.023)	58.83	31.90	0.046	(0.024)	51.17	42.62
Serbia	0.050	(0.044)	54.81	40.95	0.066	(0.049)	55.92	36.14
Singapore	-0.002	(0.193)	9.74	8.75	-0.016	(0.194)	9.12	8.81
Slovak Republic	**0.034**	(0.009)	51.86	44.37	**0.036**	(0.009)	58.26	38.49
Trinidad and Tobago	-0.002	(0.218)	5.48	5.53	-0.025	(0.221)	2.74	7.63
Regions								
Italy: Abruzzo	0.047	(0.039)	54.24	31.05	-0.057	(0.034)	37.48	57.84
Italy: Basilicata	0.086	(0.068)	53.12	33.08	0.067	(0.063)	50.28	29.15
Italy: Bolzano	0.141	(0.193)	22.96	4.67	0.021	(0.188)	4.67	14.79
Italy: Calabria	**0.064**	(0.011)	56.66	39.32	**0.032**	(0.014)	57.51	42.49
Italy: Campania	-0.011	(0.010)	52.79	42.22	**-0.043**	(0.010)	34.31	56.03
Italy: Emilia Romagna	**-0.031**	(0.009)	49.57	49.17	**0.054**	(0.009)	59.40	36.31
Italy: Friuli Venezia Giulia	0.068	(0.065)	56.38	26.92	0.008	(0.063)	37.77	35.01
Italy: Lazio	**0.208**	(0.009)	76.28	22.82	**0.142**	(0.009)	65.71	29.74
Italy: Liguria	0.031	(0.037)	52.92	37.18	0.028	(0.032)	50.17	46.87
Italy: Lombardia	**0.057**	(0.007)	61.03	38.97	0.019	(0.010)	53.95	42.80
Italy: Marche	**0.106**	(0.024)	67.98	30.87	-0.013	(0.026)	61.52	34.01
Italy: Molise	0.089	(0.175)	18.05	4.70	0.030	(0.193)	17.44	9.37
Italy: Piemonte	0.024	(0.015)	54.79	34.81	**0.055**	(0.012)	48.92	47.06
Italy: Puglia	**-0.039**	(0.007)	25.16	54.06	**-0.023**	(0.008)	51.82	41.60
Italy: Sardegna	**0.080**	(0.009)	51.81	36.08	**0.075**	(0.009)	57.23	37.77
Italy: Sicilia	**-0.100**	(0.024)	29.25	49.47	-0.013	(0.022)	43.13	38.15
Italy: Toscana	**0.123**	(0.013)	74.86	22.00	**0.092**	(0.010)	64.31	28.86
Italy: Trento	0.073	(0.137)	37.24	25.88	0.022	(0.123)	32.92	27.03
Italy: Umbria	-0.007	(0.069)	42.30	42.71	0.045	(0.071)	45.57	40.03
Italy: Valle d'Aosta	0.061	(0.186)	9.52	4.76	-0.008	(0.194)	9.52	9.52
Italy: Veneto	**0.018**	(0.008)	43.88	53.43	**-0.051**	(0.007)	53.51	46.49
Mexico: Aguascalientes[1]	-0.060	(0.040)	23.40	72.77	-0.058	(0.046)	21.71	70.11
Mexico: Baja California[1]	**-0.030**	(0.006)	44.73	55.08	**0.079**	(0.009)	53.73	45.99
Mexico: Baja California Sur[1]	0.045	(0.053)	34.43	53.87	-0.039	(0.065)	23.32	70.44
Mexico: Campeche[1]	**-0.165**	(0.023)	23.32	75.47	**-0.099**	(0.018)	25.21	73.58
Mexico: Chihuahua[1]	**-0.083**	(0.004)	25.17	74.83	**-0.015**	(0.003)	24.12	75.88
Mexico: Colima[1]	0.028	(0.043)	24.03	72.61	**-0.091**	(0.038)	18.91	72.61
Mexico: Coahuila[1]	**0.077**	(0.017)	37.48	58.82	**0.112**	(0.011)	51.35	48.05
Mexico: Chiapas[1]	**-0.037**	(0.005)	23.41	76.59	**-0.042**	(0.004)	34.29	65.71
Mexico: Distrito Federal[1]	**0.123**	(0.009)	49.88	50.12	**0.023**	(0.004)	30.59	64.96
Mexico: Durango[1]	**0.046**	(0.018)	37.87	61.23	**0.158**	(0.013)	51.05	48.05
Mexico: Guerrero[1]	**0.025**	(0.004)	35.39	61.47	**-0.077**	(0.005)	37.24	62.41
Mexico: Guanajuato[1]	**0.075**	(0.006)	27.14	72.86	**0.072**	(0.008)	27.62	72.38
Mexico: Hidalgo[1]	**-0.266**	(0.002)	11.37	88.17	**-0.215**	(0.001)	14.91	83.91
Mexico: Jalisco[1]	**-0.125**	(0.002)	23.79	76.21	**-0.051**	(0.001)	31.90	68.10
Mexico: Michoacán[1]	**-0.029**	(0.003)	44.95	55.05	**0.024**	(0.003)	56.21	43.79
Mexico: Morelos[1]	**-0.078**	(0.025)	18.95	79.78	0.037	(0.022)	35.46	60.87
Mexico: Mexico[1]	**-0.027**	(0.005)	33.32	57.48	**-0.046**	(0.007)	36.16	63.84
Mexico: Nayarit[1]	**-0.120**	(0.040)	7.73	88.90	**-0.181**	(0.039)	21.20	74.67
Mexico: Nuevo León[1]	-0.005	(0.018)	36.11	62.95	**0.122**	(0.022)	26.48	72.19
Mexico: Oaxaca[1]	**-0.106**	(0.003)	9.79	90.21	**0.187**	(0.003)	36.63	63.37
Mexico: Puebla[1]	**-0.016**	(0.001)	18.20	79.38	**0.048**	(0.001)	27.93	72.07
Mexico: Quintana Roo[1]	0.025	(0.030)	29.11	68.95	**0.107**	(0.034)	41.21	55.85
Mexico: Querétaro[1]	**0.132**	(0.028)	36.68	55.29	**0.074**	(0.020)	38.43	60.87
Mexico: Sinaloa[1]	**-0.030**	(0.005)	21.34	78.66	**0.072**	(0.005)	28.84	71.16
Mexico: San Luis Potosí[1]	**0.162**	(0.007)	26.31	73.69	0.030	(0.022)	22.59	77.18
Mexico: Sonora[1]	**-0.140**	(0.004)	24.89	75.11	**-0.063**	(0.003)	19.35	80.65
Mexico: Tamaulipas[1]	**-0.044**	(0.003)	27.87	71.90	**0.051**	(0.002)	32.59	67.41
Mexico: Tabasco[1]	**0.028**	(0.003)	24.24	75.76	**0.072**	(0.002)	32.70	67.05
Mexico: Tlaxcala[1]	-0.061	(0.033)	45.62	48.57	**-0.090**	(0.032)	39.14	57.97
Mexico: Veracruz[1]	**-0.147**	(0.005)	11.33	88.67	**-0.058**	(0.003)	16.84	83.16
Mexico: Yucatán[1]	**0.070**	(0.006)	51.24	48.58	**0.092**	(0.008)	52.09	47.72
Mexico: Zacatecas[1]	**-0.042**	(0.017)	10.78	87.63	**-0.149**	(0.025)	7.71	91.74

Notes: To facilitate comparability, marks in all countries and economies have been standardised so that higher values indicate better appraisals and that all countries and economies have a mean mark of 0 (zero) with a standard deviation of 1 (one).

Logistic models that account for the dichotomous nature of observed marks in Macao-China, Mexico and New Zealand, and Tobit models that account for the censored nature of failing marks in Austria, Croatia, Hungary, Poland, Serbia and the Slovak Republic do not yield substantively different results.

Correlations statistically significantly different from 0 (zero) at a 95% confidence level are highlighted in bold.

1. Macao-China, Mexico and New Zealand distributed, in the Educational Career questionnaire, the alternative question on whether students received a passing or failing mark. Results for these countries and economies are thus based on a dichotomous variable that does not capture the full variability of marks received by students. Estimates for these countries and economies are probably underestimated.

StatLink http://dx.doi.org/10.1787/888932734153

[Part 2/6]

Table B2.6 Within-school correlation between the marks received by students in their language-of-assessment course and student characteristics, after accounting for students' PISA reading scores

	Approaches to learning											
	Memorisation strategies				Elaboration strategies				Control strategies			
	Average corr.	S.E.	Percentage of schools with positive correlation	Percentage of schools with negative correlation	Average corr.	S.E.	Percentage of schools with positive correlation	Percentage of schools with negative correlation	Average corr.	S.E.	Percentage of schools with positive correlation	Percentage of schools with negative correlation
Countries and economies												
Austria	**0.119**	(0.026)	62.86	31.20	0.035	(0.026)	52.32	40.17	**0.151**	(0.027)	67.48	26.46
Belgium (Flemish Community)	**0.026**	(0.009)	55.27	41.77	**0.041**	(0.008)	54.46	39.82	**0.092**	(0.010)	63.71	32.23
Croatia	**0.065**	(0.026)	60.97	34.21	**0.091**	(0.025)	61.20	29.96	**0.108**	(0.024)	69.52	25.42
Hungary	**0.155**	(0.009)	67.81	28.32	**0.115**	(0.007)	59.93	39.87	**0.127**	(0.007)	65.57	33.37
Iceland	0.150	(0.217)	23.15	1.78	0.092	(0.222)	18.47	3.51	0.159	(0.232)	21.03	0.00
Ireland	**0.103**	(0.016)	61.70	34.99	**0.094**	(0.018)	56.72	33.25	**0.145**	(0.016)	73.26	20.16
Italy	0.069	(0.037)	55.76	35.30	**0.120**	(0.037)	60.48	30.23	**0.177**	(0.036)	72.54	23.04
Latvia	**0.094**	(0.016)	61.99	31.46	**0.098**	(0.015)	60.77	32.52	**0.106**	(0.016)	68.10	26.02
Macao-China[1]	0.053	(0.101)	9.52	9.52	0.035	(0.094)	4.76	11.90	0.072	(0.098)	11.90	9.52
Mexico[1]	**0.125**	(0.013)	40.39	58.59	**0.139**	(0.013)	41.46	57.55	**0.144**	(0.014)	43.25	55.76
New Zealand[1]	**0.094**	(0.045)	56.24	34.73	0.055	(0.043)	51.59	38.47	**0.136**	(0.045)	63.04	28.23
Poland	**0.143**	(0.014)	72.48	23.19	**0.089**	(0.014)	65.09	29.98	**0.194**	(0.015)	74.36	16.01
Portugal: ISCED2	**0.034**	(0.012)	47.59	50.83	**0.094**	(0.010)	62.64	35.85	**0.140**	(0.013)	61.82	33.80
Portugal: ISCED3	0.035	(0.018)	51.18	41.12	**0.203**	(0.017)	78.65	19.91	**0.291**	(0.018)	86.49	11.18
Serbia	0.041	(0.041)	57.73	37.02	**0.091**	(0.045)	67.94	27.37	**0.145**	(0.045)	75.63	18.23
Singapore	0.036	(0.184)	11.84	8.61	0.066	(0.188)	16.42	3.39	0.066	(0.187)	15.01	6.88
Slovak Republic	0.008	(0.011)	42.49	52.85	-0.019	(0.010)	48.57	50.77	**0.106**	(0.011)	57.51	38.44
Trinidad and Tobago	0.094	(0.213)	10.32	2.10	0.117	(0.206)	9.65	1.37	0.145	(0.205)	19.35	1.42
Regions												
Italy: Abruzzo	**0.082**	(0.041)	57.88	34.84	**0.119**	(0.040)	75.03	13.61	**0.164**	(0.041)	80.18	16.11
Italy: Basilicata	**0.131**	(0.067)	62.90	21.56	**0.206**	(0.061)	74.65	14.16	**0.231**	(0.067)	80.14	9.68
Italy: Bolzano	0.160	(0.179)	26.46	7.00	0.047	(0.193)	20.62	5.84	0.166	(0.185)	24.12	3.50
Italy: Calabria	**-0.080**	(0.012)	45.47	54.53	**0.043**	(0.018)	53.21	36.29	**0.140**	(0.019)	63.29	33.41
Italy: Campania	**0.099**	(0.009)	67.43	27.77	**0.153**	(0.009)	70.72	26.82	**0.193**	(0.009)	79.45	20.55
Italy: Emilia Romagna	**0.104**	(0.011)	52.26	25.39	**0.166**	(0.009)	64.41	31.84	**0.191**	(0.010)	73.81	23.29
Italy: Friuli Venezia Giulia	0.000	(0.077)	47.20	37.33	0.064	(0.069)	56.83	31.03	0.091	(0.066)	48.67	40.15
Italy: Lazio	**0.117**	(0.010)	51.30	45.83	**0.189**	(0.011)	67.81	28.66	**0.256**	(0.011)	77.20	22.80
Italy: Liguria	0.069	(0.036)	53.62	34.55	**0.109**	(0.032)	64.20	30.27	**0.182**	(0.028)	73.31	15.33
Italy: Lombardia	0.012	(0.010)	59.65	34.08	**0.055**	(0.008)	50.11	34.88	**0.132**	(0.008)	71.69	27.25
Italy: Marche	**0.133**	(0.027)	69.62	23.85	**0.159**	(0.027)	77.68	16.69	**0.179**	(0.026)	76.66	17.62
Italy: Molise	0.098	(0.203)	14.58	5.79	0.135	(0.169)	14.53	5.79	0.242	(0.165)	38.55	2.89
Italy: Piemonte	**0.042**	(0.010)	54.82	37.48	**0.063**	(0.013)	51.07	35.44	**0.183**	(0.013)	79.44	17.42
Italy: Puglia	**0.057**	(0.006)	63.08	36.92	**0.103**	(0.006)	60.05	39.11	**0.131**	(0.005)	77.40	22.60
Italy: Sardegna	**0.126**	(0.009)	60.61	34.52	**0.079**	(0.008)	54.11	40.75	**0.195**	(0.008)	63.90	31.99
Italy: Sicilia	**0.079**	(0.012)	56.67	35.36	**0.202**	(0.013)	61.23	34.50	**0.208**	(0.013)	68.91	31.09
Italy: Toscana	**0.137**	(0.013)	56.48	37.79	**0.059**	(0.012)	50.69	37.01	**0.112**	(0.019)	71.81	25.07
Italy: Trento	0.128	(0.124)	43.74	15.26	0.127	(0.115)	49.50	15.16	0.111	(0.117)	40.40	24.97
Italy: Umbria	-0.016	(0.065)	27.40	54.09	0.116	(0.077)	57.80	24.98	**0.143**	(0.070)	60.73	19.74
Italy: Valle d'Aosta	0.072	(0.195)	14.29	0.00	0.059	(0.180)	9.52	4.76	0.156	(0.195)	23.81	0.00
Italy: Veneto	**0.075**	(0.007)	52.78	41.01	**0.164**	(0.008)	83.68	16.32	**0.224**	(0.009)	86.27	10.95
Mexico: Aguascalientes[1]	-0.003	(0.044)	29.85	65.11	**0.108**	(0.040)	32.13	64.59	0.022	(0.043)	30.24	59.21
Mexico: Baja California[1]	**0.077**	(0.005)	49.35	50.45	**0.070**	(0.005)	55.85	39.79	**0.146**	(0.005)	61.93	37.87
Mexico: Baja California Sur[1]	-0.003	(0.055)	26.34	68.12	0.031	(0.046)	28.36	67.49	0.041	(0.053)	27.65	66.81
Mexico: Campeche[1]	**0.135**	(0.018)	41.58	53.17	**0.083**	(0.019)	51.62	47.17	**0.112**	(0.018)	55.73	39.43
Mexico: Chihuahua[1]	**0.141**	(0.002)	39.00	61.00	**0.122**	(0.002)	40.70	59.07	**0.167**	(0.004)	45.28	54.72
Mexico: Colima[1]	**0.136**	(0.037)	33.39	54.11	0.004	(0.036)	26.69	69.39	-0.019	(0.031)	25.95	59.23
Mexico: Coahuila[1]	**0.073**	(0.010)	41.69	57.70	**0.120**	(0.015)	41.14	58.25	**0.080**	(0.008)	46.50	52.90
Mexico: Chiapas[1]	**0.155**	(0.003)	52.17	47.83	**0.223**	(0.006)	51.43	47.05	**0.270**	(0.004)	55.04	44.96
Mexico: Distrito Federal[1]	-0.002	(0.009)	30.01	69.99	**0.012**	(0.005)	31.62	68.38	**0.047**	(0.006)	34.07	65.93
Mexico: Durango[1]	**0.157**	(0.022)	53.10	45.78	**0.113**	(0.017)	61.04	36.63	**0.201**	(0.021)	58.02	40.90
Mexico: Guerrero[1]	0.009	(0.008)	44.31	55.69	**0.109**	(0.005)	42.41	54.08	**0.129**	(0.007)	56.63	40.23
Mexico: Guanajuato[1]	**0.186**	(0.006)	48.79	51.21	**0.186**	(0.007)	50.52	49.48	**0.154**	(0.007)	43.69	53.31
Mexico: Hidalgo[1]	**0.061**	(0.001)	33.01	66.99	**0.059**	(0.001)	32.70	67.30	**0.044**	(0.001)	33.48	66.52
Mexico: Jalisco[1]	**0.274**	(0.003)	58.43	39.62	**0.319**	(0.004)	58.36	41.64	**0.238**	(0.003)	62.08	37.92
Mexico: Michoacán[1]	**0.079**	(0.003)	49.97	48.22	**0.189**	(0.003)	62.54	37.46	**0.115**	(0.002)	62.02	37.98
Mexico: Morelos[1]	**0.192**	(0.026)	44.91	53.91	**0.140**	(0.020)	43.95	55.28	**0.179**	(0.027)	47.23	51.50
Mexico: Mexico[1]	**0.138**	(0.009)	51.66	44.23	**0.126**	(0.011)	53.91	46.09	**0.099**	(0.011)	49.67	47.56
Mexico: Nayarit[1]	0.048	(0.049)	34.92	60.95	0.034	(0.040)	23.40	72.85	0.025	(0.042)	26.49	70.89
Mexico: Nuevo León[1]	**0.040**	(0.019)	30.52	68.99	-0.003	(0.021)	38.34	60.16	-0.009	(0.017)	29.59	69.92
Mexico: Oaxaca[1]	**-0.038**	(0.006)	16.48	81.88	**0.053**	(0.010)	27.81	72.19	**0.081**	(0.002)	28.22	71.78
Mexico: Puebla[1]	**0.063**	(0.003)	30.40	69.60	**0.049**	(0.002)	27.54	72.46	**0.031**	(0.003)	31.04	68.96
Mexico: Quintana Roo[1]	**0.220**	(0.023)	43.13	55.25	**0.081**	(0.030)	26.01	72.38	**0.191**	(0.033)	49.88	48.83
Mexico: Querétaro[1]	**0.224**	(0.023)	30.87	67.92	**0.041**	(0.020)	16.80	82.15	**0.178**	(0.025)	36.72	62.24
Mexico: Sinaloa[1]	**0.270**	(0.001)	40.57	59.43	**0.167**	(0.004)	29.95	60.38	**0.257**	(0.003)	48.23	51.77
Mexico: San Luis Potosí[1]	-0.003	(0.024)	20.41	79.59	**0.131**	(0.045)	33.12	66.88	**0.176**	(0.043)	41.97	58.03
Mexico: Sonora[1]	**0.247**	(0.003)	52.51	47.49	**0.111**	(0.005)	31.29	68.71	**0.228**	(0.004)	52.76	47.24
Mexico: Tamaulipas[1]	**0.300**	(0.002)	50.11	49.89	**0.348**	(0.003)	56.83	43.17	**0.303**	(0.002)	53.35	46.65
Mexico: Tabasco[1]	**0.170**	(0.003)	45.29	54.71	**0.139**	(0.003)	45.87	53.87	**0.193**	(0.003)	48.29	51.07
Mexico: Tlaxcala[1]	**0.095**	(0.030)	63.20	33.43	**0.110**	(0.027)	66.26	30.37	**0.157**	(0.031)	76.39	21.20
Mexico: Veracruz[1]	**0.185**	(0.003)	34.16	65.84	**0.284**	(0.002)	40.05	59.64	**0.243**	(0.004)	34.44	65.56
Mexico: Yucatán[1]	**0.182**	(0.005)	76.84	22.98	**0.124**	(0.011)	54.10	39.68	**0.188**	(0.006)	60.21	39.61
Mexico: Zacatecas[1]	**0.256**	(0.016)	35.44	63.34	**0.113**	(0.020)	30.72	68.54	**0.176**	(0.024)	31.65	67.43

Notes: To facilitate comparability, marks in all countries and economies have been standardised so that higher values indicate better appraisals and that all countries and economies have a mean mark of 0 (zero) with a standard deviation of 1 (one).

Logistic models that account for the dichotomous nature of observed marks in Macao-China, Mexico and New Zealand, and Tobit models that account for the censored nature of failing marks in Austria, Croatia, Hungary, Poland, Serbia and the Slovak Republic do not yield substantively different results.

Correlations statistically significantly different from 0 (zero) at a 95% confidence level are highlighted in bold.

1. Macao-China, Mexico and New Zealand distributed, in the Educational Career questionnaire, the alternative question on whether students received a passing or failing mark. Results for these countries and economies are thus based on a dichotomous variable that does not capture the full variability of marks received by students. Estimates for these countries and economies are probably underestimated.

StatLink http://dx.doi.org/10.1787/888932734153

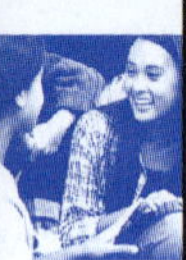

[Part 3/6]

Table B2.6 Within-school correlation between the marks received by students in their language-of-assessment course and student characteristics, after accounting for students' PISA reading scores

	Engagement							
	Enjoyment of reading				Attitudes towards school			
	Average corr.	S.E.	Percentage of schools with positive correlation	Percentage of schools with negative correlation	Average corr.	S.E.	Percentage of schools with positive correlation	Percentage of schools with negative correlation
Countries and economies								
Austria	**0.134**	(0.027)	69.98	26.08	**0.119**	(0.030)	70.11	26.43
Belgium (Flemish Community)	**0.097**	(0.011)	69.08	27.80	**0.132**	(0.011)	65.14	28.58
Croatia	**0.182**	(0.027)	78.82	19.11	**0.070**	(0.028)	61.16	33.92
Hungary	**0.163**	(0.010)	68.48	29.47	**0.101**	(0.009)	62.67	35.92
Iceland	-0.009	(0.227)	11.36	8.20	0.151	(0.213)	22.02	3.64
Ireland	**0.162**	(0.018)	71.67	22.17	**0.078**	(0.018)	61.16	31.30
Italy	**0.149**	(0.037)	69.10	24.63	**0.123**	(0.039)	64.51	29.29
Latvia	**0.160**	(0.015)	69.60	27.68	**0.129**	(0.012)	57.87	37.54
Macao-China[1]	0.096	(0.096)	26.19	11.90	0.062	(0.098)	11.90	9.52
Mexico[1]	**0.140**	(0.011)	43.61	55.41	**0.044**	(0.013)	32.48	65.39
New Zealand[1]	0.037	(0.045)	51.57	40.57	**0.134**	(0.044)	55.63	35.09
Poland	**0.201**	(0.014)	81.23	14.28	**0.079**	(0.013)	59.15	32.33
Portugal: ISCED2	**0.143**	(0.010)	65.99	26.19	**0.101**	(0.016)	67.13	30.21
Portugal: ISCED3	**0.214**	(0.022)	78.87	16.75	**0.132**	(0.020)	73.59	22.20
Serbia	**0.244**	(0.051)	80.85	14.68	0.034	(0.048)	58.55	35.77
Singapore	0.121	(0.192)	21.82	2.26	0.033	(0.200)	13.14	7.06
Slovak Republic	**0.154**	(0.007)	69.86	27.79	**0.058**	(0.011)	56.84	38.09
Trinidad and Tobago	0.116	(0.211)	12.44	3.49	0.009	(0.207)	9.11	6.23
Regions								
Italy: Abruzzo	**0.161**	(0.032)	56.72	37.00	**0.211**	(0.037)	70.88	18.16
Italy: Basilicata	**0.198**	(0.064)	74.95	14.78	0.100	(0.062)	56.37	30.41
Italy: Bolzano	0.103	(0.198)	27.63	2.33	0.148	(0.207)	24.12	4.67
Italy: Calabria	**0.104**	(0.015)	75.90	20.61	0.003	(0.014)	42.95	52.74
Italy: Campania	**0.214**	(0.007)	82.30	17.04	**0.119**	(0.008)	77.65	21.49
Italy: Emilia Romagna	**0.261**	(0.011)	89.54	7.37	**0.229**	(0.008)	75.77	24.23
Italy: Friuli Venezia Giulia	**0.167**	(0.070)	66.33	23.48	**0.152**	(0.071)	61.51	24.57
Italy: Lazio	**0.222**	(0.009)	78.80	19.42	**0.165**	(0.009)	70.62	26.64
Italy: Liguria	**0.082**	(0.031)	58.91	37.62	**0.144**	(0.034)	65.34	24.72
Italy: Lombardia	**0.049**	(0.008)	57.41	41.41	**0.056**	(0.006)	57.93	39.97
Italy: Marche	**0.165**	(0.027)	73.04	20.07	**0.140**	(0.026)	68.48	28.03
Italy: Molise	0.165	(0.164)	33.47	5.79	0.124	(0.193)	22.90	0.00
Italy: Piemonte	**0.157**	(0.011)	59.60	31.93	**0.207**	(0.010)	68.59	25.28
Italy: Puglia	**0.124**	(0.008)	74.71	14.99	**0.055**	(0.009)	60.79	33.71
Italy: Sardegna	**0.113**	(0.011)	68.45	25.62	**0.200**	(0.010)	86.36	10.38
Italy: Sicilia	**0.253**	(0.013)	78.81	17.32	**0.094**	(0.017)	61.33	34.80
Italy: Toscana	**0.130**	(0.015)	62.80	26.20	**0.115**	(0.010)	71.97	21.32
Italy: Trento	0.131	(0.120)	46.99	17.67	0.142	(0.127)	45.06	19.48
Italy: Umbria	**0.160**	(0.075)	64.81	15.35	0.082	(0.080)	63.70	21.73
Italy: Valle d'Aosta	0.108	(0.185)	23.81	4.76	0.117	(0.197)	19.05	0.00
Italy: Veneto	**0.020**	(0.005)	63.06	36.94	**0.134**	(0.008)	61.07	35.13
Mexico: Aguascalientes[1]	**0.096**	(0.031)	36.68	54.01	-0.027	(0.042)	19.36	72.68
Mexico: Baja California[1]	**0.135**	(0.004)	68.82	30.98	**0.019**	(0.007)	47.59	52.21
Mexico: Baja California Sur[1]	-0.037	(0.049)	13.76	80.01	0.046	(0.065)	28.48	68.06
Mexico: Campeche[1]	**0.063**	(0.020)	47.43	51.36	**0.044**	(0.021)	32.52	59.26
Mexico: Chihuahua[1]	**0.047**	(0.004)	44.96	55.04	**0.031**	(0.002)	39.06	57.68
Mexico: Colima[1]	**0.166**	(0.026)	36.49	59.59	0.028	(0.035)	31.08	56.98
Mexico: Coahuila[1]	**-0.061**	(0.014)	25.92	73.68	-0.005	(0.017)	39.46	59.94
Mexico: Chiapas[1]	**0.205**	(0.004)	58.64	41.36	**0.161**	(0.003)	51.68	48.32
Mexico: Distrito Federal[1]	**0.129**	(0.007)	55.68	44.32	**0.055**	(0.004)	38.16	60.92
Mexico: Durango[1]	**0.203**	(0.011)	55.89	42.98	**0.248**	(0.031)	29.02	69.63
Mexico: Guerrero[1]	**-0.036**	(0.004)	46.10	49.53	**0.070**	(0.006)	42.64	57.36
Mexico: Guanajuato[1]	**0.216**	(0.004)	44.41	55.59	**0.035**	(0.008)	36.85	62.90
Mexico: Hidalgo[1]	**0.083**	(0.002)	28.36	68.99	**0.236**	(0.001)	31.46	68.54
Mexico: Jalisco[1]	**0.207**	(0.002)	59.26	40.74	**0.072**	(0.002)	38.94	61.06
Mexico: Michoacán[1]	**0.065**	(0.002)	39.35	60.65	**-0.097**	(0.003)	25.09	74.91
Mexico: Morelos[1]	**0.143**	(0.024)	48.90	47.52	**0.054**	(0.021)	43.46	55.53
Mexico: Mexico[1]	**0.172**	(0.008)	63.57	36.43	**-0.054**	(0.006)	35.94	64.06
Mexico: Nayarit[1]	0.071	(0.046)	44.73	50.48	-0.082	(0.058)	21.60	72.53
Mexico: Nuevo León[1]	0.033	(0.018)	25.05	73.98	**0.051**	(0.021)	34.73	62.51
Mexico: Oaxaca[1]	**0.049**	(0.007)	21.29	75.42	**-0.038**	(0.006)	22.85	77.15
Mexico: Puebla[1]	**0.259**	(0.003)	34.34	64.23	**0.010**	(0.003)	22.88	77.12
Mexico: Quintana Roo[1]	**0.129**	(0.030)	44.53	53.21	**-0.107**	(0.028)	25.99	72.07
Mexico: Querétaro[1]	**0.267**	(0.020)	47.09	51.69	0.035	(0.022)	25.77	73.19
Mexico: Sinaloa[1]	**0.265**	(0.001)	47.98	52.02	**0.224**	(0.005)	37.62	61.15
Mexico: San Luis Potosí[1]	**0.102**	(0.008)	36.47	63.53	-0.025	(0.020)	12.70	73.85
Mexico: Sonora[1]	**0.085**	(0.004)	37.72	62.28	**0.133**	(0.003)	41.71	58.29
Mexico: Tamaulipas[1]	**0.038**	(0.003)	30.20	69.80	**0.081**	(0.002)	36.86	60.59
Mexico: Tabasco[1]	**0.160**	(0.002)	36.19	63.81	**0.163**	(0.003)	36.68	63.32
Mexico: Tlaxcala[1]	**0.096**	(0.034)	57.29	39.82	**0.094**	(0.024)	57.42	40.17
Mexico: Veracruz[1]	**0.162**	(0.003)	34.72	64.97	**0.037**	(0.005)	19.89	72.76
Mexico: Yucatán[1]	**0.172**	(0.008)	68.82	30.17	**0.078**	(0.005)	63.06	29.88
Mexico: Zacatecas[1]	**0.153**	(0.014)	29.58	69.69	**0.286**	(0.027)	22.63	76.82

Notes: To facilitate comparability, marks in all countries and economies have been standardised so that higher values indicate better appraisals and that all countries and economies have a mean mark of 0 (zero) with a standard deviation of 1 (one).

Logistic models that account for the dichotomous nature of observed marks in Macao-China, Mexico and New Zealand, and Tobit models that account for the censored nature of failing marks in Austria, Croatia, Hungary, Poland, Serbia and the Slovak Republic do not yield substantively different results.

Correlations statistically significantly different from 0 (zero) at a 95% confidence level are highlighted in bold.

1. Macao-China, Mexico and New Zealand distributed, in the Educational Career questionnaire, the alternative question on whether students received a passing or failing mark. Results for these countries and economies are thus based on a dichotomous variable that does not capture the full variability of marks received by students. Estimates for these countries and economies are probably underestimated.

StatLink http://dx.doi.org/10.1787/888932734153

[Part 4/6]

Table B2.6 Within-school correlation between the marks received by students in their language-of-assessment course and student characteristics, after accounting for students' PISA reading scores

	Student-teacher relations				Student background – Student is a girl			
	Average corr.	S.E.	Percentage of schools with positive correlation	Percentage of schools with negative correlation	Average corr.	S.E.	Percentage of schools with positive correlation	Percentage of schools with negative correlation
Countries and economies								
Austria	**0.152**	(0.030)	68.52	23.17	**0.096**	(0.028)	57.84	38.02
Belgium (Flemish Community)	**0.027**	(0.009)	55.57	39.31	**0.103**	(0.009)	59.42	36.29
Croatia	**0.126**	(0.027)	66.57	26.30	**0.104**	(0.025)	63.37	31.94
Hungary	**0.206**	(0.009)	78.23	20.07	**0.115**	(0.007)	66.46	31.01
Iceland	0.101	(0.224)	15.83	3.47	0.026	(0.213)	14.95	13.49
Ireland	**0.088**	(0.018)	59.62	29.68	**0.086**	(0.021)	37.19	55.85
Italy	**0.145**	(0.038)	66.50	25.34	**0.088**	(0.036)	55.99	38.42
Latvia	**0.138**	(0.014)	63.94	29.37	**0.116**	(0.012)	61.07	29.25
Macao-China[1]	0.033	(0.108)	2.38	9.52	0.095	(0.087)	16.67	26.19
Mexico[1]	**0.069**	(0.012)	38.33	61.02	0.019	(0.011)	31.83	67.46
New Zealand[1]	**0.109**	(0.044)	61.61	30.16	0.062	(0.046)	40.14	50.40
Poland	**0.176**	(0.012)	71.24	25.24	**0.201**	(0.008)	79.11	20.89
Portugal: ISCED2	**0.151**	(0.011)	66.29	27.42	**0.086**	(0.008)	64.03	33.64
Portugal: ISCED3	**0.193**	(0.021)	74.51	23.08	**0.131**	(0.021)	73.20	24.04
Serbia	**0.130**	(0.046)	70.00	23.89	**0.116**	(0.049)	60.69	34.82
Singapore	0.051	(0.195)	14.58	3.39	-0.031	(0.195)	9.15	23.70
Slovak Republic	**0.184**	(0.009)	66.32	29.02	**0.124**	(0.007)	62.49	36.90
Trinidad and Tobago	0.038	(0.212)	10.41	2.74	0.055	(0.230)	7.53	29.45
Regions								
Italy: Abruzzo	**0.161**	(0.035)	82.72	11.51	**0.148**	(0.035)	66.73	27.00
Italy: Basilicata	0.116	(0.068)	54.80	33.56	0.036	(0.068)	41.54	46.35
Italy: Bolzano	0.160	(0.189)	25.29	2.33	0.142	(0.188)	21.79	9.34
Italy: Calabria	**0.045**	(0.016)	58.44	36.07	**0.094**	(0.014)	51.61	46.68
Italy: Campania	**0.217**	(0.008)	79.47	15.81	**0.124**	(0.010)	62.01	35.37
Italy: Emilia Romagna	**0.157**	(0.010)	69.83	25.53	**0.081**	(0.008)	70.46	28.90
Italy: Friuli Venezia Giulia	**0.224**	(0.066)	70.07	19.65	0.049	(0.062)	49.35	33.62
Italy: Lazio	**0.218**	(0.010)	72.54	22.61	**0.154**	(0.006)	60.00	38.92
Italy: Liguria	**0.110**	(0.036)	61.42	24.21	0.002	(0.040)	41.85	52.44
Italy: Lombardia	**0.055**	(0.012)	60.15	38.08	**-0.032**	(0.006)	43.40	50.56
Italy: Marche	**0.123**	(0.021)	71.98	25.10	**0.119**	(0.028)	65.16	31.46
Italy: Molise	0.122	(0.181)	21.61	5.21	0.085	(0.167)	15.20	16.98
Italy: Piemonte	**0.126**	(0.012)	60.74	17.73	**0.022**	(0.010)	56.25	34.88
Italy: Puglia	**0.118**	(0.008)	68.58	30.50	**0.124**	(0.007)	61.32	38.68
Italy: Sardegna	**0.288**	(0.009)	77.72	18.93	**0.022**	(0.007)	51.12	48.88
Italy: Sicilia	**0.162**	(0.017)	67.00	26.29	**0.207**	(0.012)	65.55	30.83
Italy: Toscana	**0.227**	(0.015)	81.33	15.57	**0.128**	(0.015)	73.02	26.98
Italy: Trento	0.106	(0.139)	48.58	15.96	0.066	(0.119)	28.33	30.63
Italy: Umbria	**0.150**	(0.066)	61.95	14.93	0.013	(0.069)	38.48	46.11
Italy: Valle d'Aosta	0.082	(0.185)	9.52	4.76	0.109	(0.171)	19.05	19.05
Italy: Veneto	**0.106**	(0.009)	60.63	34.66	**0.128**	(0.006)	54.82	45.18
Mexico: Aguascalientes[1]	0.069	(0.040)	41.67	50.69	**-0.113**	(0.034)	20.90	76.92
Mexico: Baja California[1]	**0.135**	(0.004)	65.77	34.03	**0.013**	(0.005)	41.50	58.30
Mexico: Baja California Sur[1]	0.030	(0.053)	31.01	60.33	**-0.175**	(0.045)	10.44	85.35
Mexico: Campeche[1]	**0.137**	(0.020)	54.79	44.00	**0.057**	(0.024)	42.23	52.52
Mexico: Chihuahua[1]	**0.137**	(0.003)	43.53	56.47	**0.018**	(0.002)	26.37	73.63
Mexico: Colima[1]	**0.273**	(0.036)	44.28	51.80	0.034	(0.039)	26.09	68.45
Mexico: Coahuila[1]	**0.122**	(0.021)	38.10	61.30	**0.078**	(0.013)	40.71	58.89
Mexico: Chiapas[1]	**0.039**	(0.004)	47.67	48.89	**-0.151**	(0.004)	18.36	81.64
Mexico: Distrito Federal[1]	-0.001	(0.005)	35.52	64.20	-0.002	(0.004)	41.72	58.28
Mexico: Durango[1]	**0.378**	(0.016)	70.50	28.37	**-0.057**	(0.014)	40.68	58.65
Mexico: Guerrero[1]	**0.038**	(0.009)	44.87	55.13	**0.019**	(0.006)	44.20	55.80
Mexico: Guanajuato[1]	**-0.180**	(0.004)	28.24	71.76	**0.104**	(0.004)	40.60	59.40
Mexico: Hidalgo[1]	**0.237**	(0.001)	42.62	57.38	**0.022**	(0.001)	26.68	73.32
Mexico: Jalisco[1]	**0.123**	(0.002)	42.01	57.99	**0.063**	(0.002)	29.65	70.35
Mexico: Michoacán[1]	**0.067**	(0.003)	47.21	49.68	**-0.014**	(0.002)	46.79	53.21
Mexico: Morelos[1]	**0.070**	(0.024)	30.32	68.41	**-0.054**	(0.024)	38.15	61.09
Mexico: Mexico[1]	**0.096**	(0.011)	49.79	49.54	0.015	(0.008)	41.46	54.42
Mexico: Nayarit[1]	**0.155**	(0.043)	36.00	60.25	**-0.105**	(0.039)	28.01	68.98
Mexico: Nuevo León[1]	**-0.067**	(0.026)	24.51	74.75	**0.049**	(0.019)	27.14	72.11
Mexico: Oaxaca[1]	**-0.035**	(0.004)	19.98	80.02	**-0.012**	(0.003)	16.68	83.32
Mexico: Puebla[1]	**-0.023**	(0.003)	25.04	74.96	**-0.007**	(0.001)	19.59	80.41
Mexico: Quintana Roo[1]	-0.026	(0.022)	37.83	59.66	**0.120**	(0.027)	47.61	50.45
Mexico: Querétaro[1]	**0.105**	(0.019)	44.79	54.00	**0.195**	(0.025)	35.49	63.47
Mexico: Sinaloa[1]	**0.271**	(0.004)	47.42	52.58	0.000	(0.003)	32.07	67.93
Mexico: San Luis Potosí[1]	**0.312**	(0.002)	33.81	66.19	**0.119**	(0.004)	33.78	66.22
Mexico: Sonora[1]	**0.123**	(0.005)	54.97	45.03	**0.034**	(0.002)	41.34	58.66
Mexico: Tamaulipas[1]	**0.134**	(0.002)	48.29	51.71	**-0.012**	(0.001)	26.58	73.42
Mexico: Tabasco[1]	**-0.030**	(0.002)	37.82	62.18	**0.082**	(0.002)	29.14	70.86
Mexico: Tlaxcala[1]	**0.118**	(0.036)	63.18	33.93	**0.095**	(0.036)	56.94	39.69
Mexico: Veracruz[1]	**0.116**	(0.006)	29.06	70.94	**0.045**	(0.003)	25.42	74.58
Mexico: Yucatán[1]	**-0.027**	(0.004)	53.23	46.59	**-0.043**	(0.006)	44.10	55.72
Mexico: Zacatecas[1]	**0.356**	(0.018)	34.59	64.68	**0.202**	(0.022)	24.28	74.99

Notes: To facilitate comparability, marks in all countries and economies have been standardised so that higher values indicate better appraisals and that all countries and economies have a mean mark of 0 (zero) with a standard deviation of 1 (one).

Logistic models that account for the dichotomous nature of observed marks in Macao-China, Mexico and New Zealand, and Tobit models that account for the censored nature of failing marks in Austria, Croatia, Hungary, Poland, Serbia and the Slovak Republic do not yield substantively different results.

Correlations statistically significantly different from 0 (zero) at a 95% confidence level are highlighted in bold.

1. Macao-China, Mexico and New Zealand distributed, in the Educational Career questionnaire, the alternative question on whether students received a passing or failing mark. Results for these countries and economies are thus based on a dichotomous variable that does not capture the full variability of marks received by students. Estimates for these countries and economies are probably underestimated.

StatLink http://dx.doi.org/10.1787/888932734153

[Part 5/6]

Table B2.6 Within-school correlation between the marks received by students in their language-of-assessment course and student characteristics, after accounting for students' PISA reading scores

	Student background							
	PISA index of economic, social and cultural status				Student with an immigrant background			
	Average corr.	S.E.	Percentage of schools with positive correlation	Percentage of schools with negative correlation	Average corr.	S.E.	Percentage of schools with positive correlation	Percentage of schools with negative correlation
Countries and economies								
Austria	**0.073**	(0.026)	60.96	29.63	-0.053	(0.024)	27.77	69.97
Belgium (Flemish Community)	**0.050**	(0.008)	49.83	46.31	-0.087	(0.008)	26.13	70.14
Croatia	0.034	(0.026)	46.15	48.66	-0.012	(0.031)	34.32	59.44
Hungary	**0.064**	(0.009)	58.56	38.71	-0.006	(0.004)	14.79	85.21
Iceland	0.145	(0.223)	21.80	1.82	0.023	(0.144)	3.55	68.27
Ireland	**0.071**	(0.014)	59.74	33.23	0.031	(0.012)	40.90	56.43
Italy	**0.088**	(0.038)	60.62	31.82	0.009	(0.031)	25.43	71.95
Latvia	**0.123**	(0.013)	63.85	32.02	-0.077	(0.010)	11.29	87.34
Macao-China[1]	0.058	(0.099)	16.67	11.90	0.021	(0.101)	9.52	14.29
Mexico[1]	**0.039**	(0.012)	33.95	64.64	0.020	(0.006)	13.51	86.45
New Zealand[1]	0.039	(0.044)	48.68	43.18	0.015	(0.044)	37.44	53.56
Poland	**0.147**	(0.013)	73.77	22.50	-0.084	(0.005)	0.00	100.00
Portugal: ISCED2	**0.058**	(0.010)	55.09	40.78	0.099	(0.015)	27.40	68.27
Portugal: ISCED3	**0.153**	(0.020)	76.28	20.09	0.004	(0.022)	16.81	79.75
Serbia	0.044	(0.044)	58.69	37.04	-0.039	(0.034)	35.73	60.08
Singapore	0.110	(0.194)	13.82	6.37	-0.055	(0.185)	4.83	17.05
Slovak Republic	**0.141**	(0.009)	67.54	31.22	0.047	(0.003)	4.73	94.66
Trinidad and Tobago	0.144	(0.210)	16.57	2.05	-0.010	(0.183)	2.81	68.71
Regions								
Italy: Abruzzo	-0.005	(0.043)	56.64	34.82	-0.059	(0.016)	27.26	72.00
Italy: Basilicata	0.102	(0.068)	59.77	30.67	-0.206	(0.021)	1.33	96.82
Italy: Bolzano	0.052	(0.194)	21.79	3.50	0.019	(0.154)	13.62	51.36
Italy: Calabria	0.017	(0.019)	47.58	39.74	0.033	(0.008)	13.12	86.88
Italy: Campania	**0.080**	(0.008)	64.83	34.31	0.138	(0.010)	8.25	90.81
Italy: Emilia Romagna	**0.060**	(0.008)	59.10	40.90	0.110	(0.009)	46.68	47.25
Italy: Friuli Venezia Giulia	0.038	(0.069)	38.86	42.17	0.112	(0.065)	52.89	37.86
Italy: Lazio	0.015	(0.008)	44.38	49.99	0.014	(0.009)	40.92	59.08
Italy: Liguria	0.066	(0.042)	59.25	36.18	-0.171	(0.021)	19.53	79.73
Italy: Lombardia	**0.152**	(0.011)	70.15	22.64	-0.031	(0.017)	27.91	70.39
Italy: Marche	**0.149**	(0.027)	76.24	20.65	-0.069	(0.021)	33.47	64.78
Italy: Molise	0.114	(0.190)	22.73	7.06	-0.073	(0.082)	2.89	64.10
Italy: Piemonte	**0.180**	(0.009)	71.10	18.39	0.061	(0.009)	45.97	51.12
Italy: Puglia	**0.070**	(0.006)	69.99	30.01	0.015	(0.007)	15.21	84.79
Italy: Sardegna	**0.058**	(0.010)	61.04	36.31	-0.148	(0.006)	6.94	93.06
Italy: Sicilia	**0.121**	(0.019)	69.89	26.91	0.006	(0.005)	3.28	96.72
Italy: Toscana	-0.009	(0.012)	47.28	46.67	-0.015	(0.011)	25.34	74.66
Italy: Trento	0.059	(0.125)	38.62	24.50	-0.026	(0.104)	11.89	54.72
Italy: Umbria	0.115	(0.067)	67.95	19.66	-0.009	(0.042)	29.81	59.41
Italy: Valle d'Aosta	0.105	(0.197)	14.29	0.00	0.084	(0.155)	14.29	28.57
Italy: Veneto	**0.089**	(0.006)	56.89	36.44	0.019	(0.007)	44.83	55.17
Mexico: Aguascalientes[1]	**-0.083**	(0.034)	26.31	70.41	0.127	(0.003)	6.23	93.77
Mexico: Baja California[1]	**0.225**	(0.004)	59.65	37.52	-0.107	(0.001)	35.03	64.97
Mexico: Baja California Sur[1]	0.078	(0.054)	37.24	57.22	0.067	(0.017)	33.09	64.84
Mexico: Campeche[1]	0.018	(0.017)	42.94	56.66	0.082	(0.006)	21.50	78.50
Mexico: Chihuahua[1]	**0.064**	(0.003)	49.15	50.85	0.011	(0.001)	16.09	83.91
Mexico: Colima[1]	-0.010	(0.033)	28.97	65.99	0.099	(0.001)	11.28	88.72
Mexico: Coahuila[1]	**0.028**	(0.012)	36.84	62.55	0.055	(0.000)	0.22	99.78
Mexico: Chiapas[1]	**0.102**	(0.005)	40.83	59.17	0.053	(0.006)	36.28	63.72
Mexico: Distrito Federal[1]	**0.012**	(0.006)	44.55	52.00	-0.186	(0.002)	13.26	86.74
Mexico: Durango[1]	**-0.061**	(0.020)	29.71	69.16	-0.020	(0.004)	15.90	83.89
Mexico: Guerrero[1]	0.007	(0.010)	39.16	59.63	-0.005	(0.014)	10.21	89.79
Mexico: Guanajuato[1]	**0.014**	(0.004)	32.81	59.13	0.066	(0.001)	3.97	96.03
Mexico: Hidalgo[1]	**0.105**	(0.001)	24.64	75.36	-0.091	(0.001)	10.54	89.46
Mexico: Jalisco[1]	**-0.074**	(0.002)	32.14	67.86	-0.135	(0.000)	6.49	93.51
Mexico: Michoacán[1]	**-0.020**	(0.004)	38.52	61.48	0.097	(0.002)	13.11	86.89
Mexico: Morelos[1]	**-0.057**	(0.025)	16.58	82.15	-0.316	(0.011)	14.16	85.59
Mexico: Mexico[1]	**0.058**	(0.011)	42.45	57.55	0.135	(0.007)	27.13	72.87
Mexico: Nayarit[1]	**-0.181**	(0.039)	26.81	68.47	0.273	(0.017)	15.53	83.71
Mexico: Nuevo León[1]	-0.032	(0.018)	30.67	68.71	0.047	(0.003)	15.18	84.82
Mexico: Oaxaca[1]	-0.003	(0.012)	11.42	88.58	0.278	(0.003)	21.00	79.00
Mexico: Puebla[1]	**-0.097**	(0.001)	15.98	83.28	0.147	(0.000)	7.62	92.38
Mexico: Quintana Roo[1]	-0.046	(0.025)	11.42	72.90	0.014	(0.013)	23.33	76.02
Mexico: Querétaro[1]	**0.087**	(0.018)	32.66	66.14	-0.117	(0.000)	4.40	95.60
Mexico: Sinaloa[1]	**0.070**	(0.003)	32.29	67.71	0.042	(0.002)	8.27	91.73
Mexico: San Luis Potosí[1]	**0.134**	(0.018)	32.45	67.55	-0.018	(0.000)	6.43	93.57
Mexico: Sonora[1]	-0.001	(0.003)	33.27	66.73	0.090	(0.011)	14.19	85.81
Mexico: Tamaulipas[1]	**0.130**	(0.002)	38.59	58.58	-0.069	(0.001)	11.49	88.52
Mexico: Tabasco[1]	**0.038**	(0.002)	35.10	64.90	-0.049	(0.003)	17.64	82.36
Mexico: Tlaxcala[1]	0.037	(0.026)	54.86	42.25	0.092	(0.008)	26.57	72.46
Mexico: Veracruz[1]	**0.181**	(0.006)	39.17	60.83	0.083	(0.001)	4.28	95.72
Mexico: Yucatán[1]	**0.144**	(0.005)	55.35	38.43	-0.284	(0.002)	8.36	91.64
Mexico: Zacatecas[1]	-0.005	(0.014)	25.21	74.24	-0.938	(0.000)	0.72	99.28

Notes: To facilitate comparability, marks in all countries and economies have been standardised so that higher values indicate better appraisals and that all countries and economies have a mean mark of 0 (zero) with a standard deviation of 1 (one).

Logistic models that account for the dichotomous nature of observed marks in Macao-China, Mexico and New Zealand, and Tobit models that account for the censored nature of failing marks in Austria, Croatia, Hungary, Poland, Serbia and the Slovak Republic do not yield substantively different results.

Correlations statistically significantly different from 0 (zero) at a 95% confidence level are highlighted in bold.

1. Macao-China, Mexico and New Zealand distributed, in the Educational Career questionnaire, the alternative question on whether students received a passing or failing mark. Results for these countries and economies are thus based on a dichotomous variable that does not capture the full variability of marks received by students. Estimates for these countries and economies are probably underestimated.

StatLink http://dx.doi.org/10.1787/888932734153

[Part 6/6]

Table B2.6 Within-school correlation between the marks received by students in their language-of-assessment course and student characteristics, after accounting for students' PISA reading scores

	Student background							
	Student speaks another language at home				Student attended ISCED 0 for more than one year			
	Average corr.	S.E.	Percentage of schools with positive correlation	Percentage of schools with negative correlation	Average corr.	S.E.	Percentage of schools with positive correlation	Percentage of schools with negative correlation
Countries and economies								
Austria	**-0.069**	(0.024)	20.57	75.73	-0.027	(0.023)	39.89	56.29
Belgium (Flemish Community)	**-0.053**	(0.014)	41.62	52.27	**0.038**	(0.009)	29.18	70.00
Croatia	**-0.109**	(0.019)	9.43	89.15	0.011	(0.028)	45.81	48.90
Hungary	-0.025	(0.013)	4.09	95.91	**0.027**	(0.006)	32.41	66.75
Iceland	0.009	(0.140)	5.29	56.74	0.037	(0.178)	12.22	29.60
Ireland	0.003	(0.017)	21.90	71.45	0.028	(0.019)	55.51	39.75
Italy	-0.050	(0.036)	31.26	63.25	-0.016	(0.032)	40.45	52.79
Latvia	**0.053**	(0.014)	23.96	72.93	**-0.066**	(0.014)	37.32	54.95
Macao-China[1]	0.023	(0.068)	19.05	45.24	0.044	(0.114)	4.76	21.43
Mexico[1]	**-0.031**	(0.004)	8.30	91.69	0.016	(0.012)	27.57	71.80
New Zealand[1]	-0.044	(0.047)	41.33	52.53	0.009	(0.045)	36.00	53.79
Poland	**0.140**	(0.008)	6.15	93.85	**0.060**	(0.013)	59.30	35.86
Portugal: ISCED2	**0.071**	(0.010)	19.36	77.70	-0.014	(0.012)	51.85	45.95
Portugal: ISCED3	0.012	(0.030)	8.31	90.42	**0.071**	(0.020)	62.41	34.53
Serbia	-0.031	(0.045)	10.54	88.29	-0.018	(0.050)	43.41	49.40
Singapore	-0.164	(0.190)	4.88	24.29	-0.017	(0.178)	7.04	27.15
Slovak Republic	**-0.033**	(0.009)	16.38	82.04	**0.084**	(0.009)	56.50	38.20
Trinidad and Tobago	0.025	(0.174)	4.11	62.71	-0.041	(0.210)	4.18	8.97
Regions								
Italy: Abruzzo	0.002	(0.050)	35.95	60.07	0.078	(0.042)	49.72	42.12
Italy: Basilicata	-0.089	(0.071)	25.45	57.38	0.063	(0.045)	39.82	51.77
Italy: Bolzano	0.153	(0.153)	18.29	44.36	-0.152	(0.172)	3.50	29.96
Italy: Calabria	**-0.127**	(0.018)	17.99	78.01	**-0.032**	(0.012)	36.30	59.19
Italy: Campania	**-0.114**	(0.012)	27.75	69.29	-0.015	(0.008)	41.97	52.21
Italy: Emilia Romagna	**0.040**	(0.013)	45.00	50.92	**-0.019**	(0.009)	41.27	49.64
Italy: Friuli Venezia Giulia	0.096	(0.071)	52.69	33.60	**0.153**	(0.059)	53.73	36.25
Italy: Lazio	**0.101**	(0.012)	54.55	43.35	**-0.074**	(0.011)	33.68	64.19
Italy: Liguria	**0.051**	(0.025)	41.76	56.76	**0.078**	(0.028)	65.31	28.33
Italy: Lombardia	**-0.135**	(0.006)	25.55	74.45	**-0.074**	(0.008)	29.20	66.92
Italy: Marche	-0.011	(0.022)	43.45	45.55	**0.061**	(0.019)	59.67	34.72
Italy: Molise	-0.102	(0.178)	7.67	28.62	0.032	(0.129)	9.92	19.36
Italy: Piemonte	**-0.069**	(0.008)	44.82	52.98	**0.027**	(0.007)	44.38	53.72
Italy: Puglia	**-0.054**	(0.007)	24.22	74.90	**0.053**	(0.010)	44.70	42.55
Italy: Sardegna	**-0.130**	(0.007)	23.31	76.69	**0.068**	(0.007)	47.30	48.54
Italy: Sicilia	**-0.095**	(0.016)	19.59	75.69	**-0.179**	(0.011)	35.62	63.63
Italy: Toscana	**-0.025**	(0.012)	25.44	67.57	**0.091**	(0.012)	58.14	31.90
Italy: Trento	0.087	(0.122)	33.11	26.85	0.046	(0.099)	41.93	32.54
Italy: Umbria	0.007	(0.062)	41.50	41.91	0.004	(0.067)	41.81	39.54
Italy: Valle d'Aosta	0.029	(0.184)	9.52	0.00	0.082	(0.162)	14.29	14.29
Italy: Veneto	**-0.074**	(0.006)	23.89	67.46	**0.047**	(0.006)	43.32	55.24
Mexico: Aguascalientes[1]	**0.051**	(0.001)	12.11	87.89	0.024	(0.033)	31.10	65.62
Mexico: Baja California[1]	**0.143**	(0.004)	21.17	78.83	**-0.107**	(0.005)	17.53	82.27
Mexico: Baja California Sur[1]	**-0.156**	(0.001)	3.44	96.56	0.034	(0.060)	18.00	75.77
Mexico: Campeche[1]	**-0.120**	(0.011)	10.30	89.29	**0.086**	(0.030)	32.72	59.06
Mexico: Chihuahua[1]	**0.004**	(0.001)	3.95	96.05	**0.069**	(0.004)	27.80	71.98
Mexico: Colima[1]	**-0.052**	(0.011)	1.62	97.82	**0.185**	(0.053)	34.47	62.17
Mexico: Coahuila[1]	-0.584	(0.000)	1.31	98.69	**-0.043**	(0.009)	21.94	77.12
Mexico: Chiapas[1]	**-0.147**	(0.005)	6.03	93.97	**0.066**	(0.004)	32.14	67.86
Mexico: Distrito Federal[1]	**0.027**	(0.004)	7.42	92.58	**0.114**	(0.009)	48.93	51.07
Mexico: Durango[1]	**0.538**	(0.004)	5.27	94.73	**-0.065**	(0.022)	22.32	76.55
Mexico: Guerrero[1]	**-0.294**	(0.003)	4.69	95.31	**-0.095**	(0.007)	35.11	64.89
Mexico: Guanajuato[1]	**0.056**	(0.000)	4.42	95.58	**0.173**	(0.005)	31.64	66.51
Mexico: Hidalgo[1]	**0.014**	(0.002)	16.59	83.41	**-0.136**	(0.001)	7.92	92.08
Mexico: Jalisco[1]	**-0.079**	(0.001)	11.03	88.97	**0.076**	(0.003)	33.82	66.18
Mexico: Michoacán[1]	0.038	(0.000)	3.03	96.97	**0.044**	(0.006)	43.82	55.83
Mexico: Morelos[1]	**-0.123**	(0.005)	2.38	97.36	**0.085**	(0.024)	27.14	69.30
Mexico: Mexico[1]	**-0.224**	(0.008)	6.83	93.17	**0.041**	(0.008)	44.03	55.97
Mexico: Nayarit[1]	**0.087**	(0.002)	2.98	97.02	**0.279**	(0.041)	37.98	59.02
Mexico: Nuevo León[1]	**0.122**	(0.000)	2.34	97.66	**-0.101**	(0.018)	12.58	86.77
Mexico: Oaxaca[1]	**0.134**	(0.004)	28.01	71.99	**0.138**	(0.005)	18.76	81.24
Mexico: Puebla[1]	**0.050**	(0.000)	9.44	90.56	**-0.102**	(0.001)	14.13	85.87
Mexico: Quintana Roo[1]	**-0.052**	(0.003)	14.38	85.62	-0.002	(0.029)	21.49	76.89
Mexico: Querétaro[1]	**0.077**	(0.000)	3.01	96.99	**0.149**	(0.027)	38.16	53.64
Mexico: Sinaloa[1]	0.086	(0.000)	1.01	98.99	**-0.053**	(0.004)	18.99	81.01
Mexico: San Luis Potosí[1]	**0.009**	(0.000)	10.79	89.21	**0.024**	(0.001)	12.72	87.28
Mexico: Sonora[1]	**0.027**	(0.000)	15.62	84.38	0.002	(0.007)	26.01	73.99
Mexico: Tamaulipas[1]	**0.035**	(0.000)	0.23	99.77	**0.010**	(0.003)	27.75	72.25
Mexico: Tabasco[1]	**0.008**	(0.000)	0.70	99.30	**0.033**	(0.005)	19.96	79.40
Mexico: Tlaxcala[1]	**0.034**	(0.001)	6.30	93.70	**-0.086**	(0.024)	14.56	83.99
Mexico: Veracruz[1]	**0.091**	(0.001)	4.36	95.64	**-0.016**	(0.002)	23.30	76.70
Mexico: Yucatán[1]	**0.019**	(0.002)	41.25	58.75	**-0.026**	(0.004)	46.57	53.25
Mexico: Zacatecas[1]	**-0.330**	(0.006)	1.40	98.42	**-0.278**	(0.014)	3.27	95.82

Notes: To facilitate comparability, marks in all countries and economies have been standardised so that higher values indicate better appraisals and that all countries and economies have a mean mark of 0 (zero) with a standard deviation of 1 (one).

Logistic models that account for the dichotomous nature of observed marks in Macao-China, Mexico and New Zealand, and Tobit models that account for the censored nature of failing marks in Austria, Croatia, Hungary, Poland, Serbia and the Slovak Republic do not yield substantively different results.

Correlations statistically significantly different from 0 (zero) at a 95% confidence level are highlighted in bold.

1. Macao-China, Mexico and New Zealand distributed, in the Educational Career questionnaire, the alternative question on whether students received a passing or failing mark. Results for these countries and economies are thus based on a dichotomous variable that does not capture the full variability of marks received by students. Estimates for these countries and economies are probably underestimated.

StatLink http://dx.doi.org/10.1787/888932734153

[Part 1/3]

Table B2.7 How students' learning strategies, approaches to learning, engagement and background characteristics relate to the marks they receive in their language-of-assessment course

	Intercept		Reading performance		Metacognition strategies: Understanding and remembering		Metacognition strategies: Effective summarising strategies		Approaches to learning: Memorisation strategies		Approaches to learning: Elaboration strategies		Approaches to learning: Control strategies	
	Coeff.	S.E.	Coeff.	S.E.	Coeff.	S.E.	Coeff.	S.E.	Coeff.	S.E.	Coeff.	S.E.	Coeff.	S.E.
Countries and economies														
Austria	0.31	(0.24)	**0.36**	(0.03)	0.01	(0.02)	0.02	(0.02)	0.02	(0.02)	-0.01	(0.02)	**0.09**	(0.03)
Belgium (Flemish Community)	-0.53	(0.47)	**0.23**	(0.04)	0.01	(0.02)	-0.02	(0.03)	0.03	(0.02)	0.01	(0.02)	**0.07**	(0.02)
Croatia	**-2.76**	(0.36)	**0.41**	(0.03)	0.00	(0.02)	**0.05**	(0.02)	0.03	(0.02)	0.04	(0.02)	0.03	(0.02)
Hungary	**-2.24**	(0.38)	**0.41**	(0.04)	0.03	(0.02)	0.00	(0.02)	0.03	(0.02)	0.01	(0.02)	0.03	(0.02)
Iceland	**-1.48**	(0.25)	**0.41**	(0.02)	0.01	(0.02)	0.02	(0.02)	**0.08**	(0.03)	-0.02	(0.02)	**0.07**	(0.02)
Ireland	**-0.65**	(0.30)	**0.26**	(0.03)	**-0.05**	(0.02)	0.03	(0.02)	0.00	(0.02)	0.04	(0.02)	**0.05**	(0.02)
Italy	**-1.10**	(0.15)	**0.43**	(0.02)	0.01	(0.01)	0.02	(0.01)	**-0.04**	(0.01)	**0.04**	(0.01)	**0.07**	(0.01)
Latvia	**-1.11**	(0.52)	**0.60**	(0.04)	**0.06**	(0.02)	0.00	(0.02)	0.02	(0.03)	0.02	(0.03)	0.04	(0.03)
Macao-China[1]	**-3.02**	(0.71)	**0.98**	(0.08)	0.04	(0.06)	0.00	(0.05)	-0.07	(0.08)	0.00	(0.07)	**0.20**	(0.08)
Mexico[1]	**2.17**	(0.69)	**0.62**	(0.07)	**-0.10**	(0.04)	0.04	(0.04)	0.02	(0.04)	**0.09**	(0.04)	**0.22**	(0.04)
New Zealand[1]	-0.01	(0.73)	**0.53**	(0.07)	-0.01	(0.06)	0.06	(0.06)	0.00	(0.08)	-0.03	(0.08)	**0.28**	(0.08)
Poland	-0.44	(0.44)	**0.57**	(0.02)	0.00	(0.02)	0.03	(0.02)	0.00	(0.02)	-0.03	(0.02)	**0.10**	(0.02)
Portugal: ISCED2	**-1.35**	(0.40)	**0.47**	(0.05)	0.01	(0.02)	**0.04**	(0.02)	**-0.09**	(0.03)	0.03	(0.04)	**0.11**	(0.04)
Portugal: ISCED3	-1.19	(0.99)	**0.65**	(0.04)	0.01	(0.02)	-0.02	(0.02)	**-0.04**	(0.02)	0.03	(0.03)	**0.15**	(0.03)
Serbia	**-1.28**	(0.32)	**0.45**	(0.03)	**0.06**	(0.02)	0.02	(0.02)	-0.02	(0.02)	0.01	(0.02)	**0.06**	(0.02)
Singapore	**-0.74**	(0.27)	**0.10**	(0.03)	-0.03	(0.02)	0.00	(0.02)	0.01	(0.02)	0.03	(0.02)	0.01	(0.02)
Slovak Republic	**-1.58**	(0.36)	**0.59**	(0.02)	-0.02	(0.02)	**0.04**	(0.02)	**-0.04**	(0.02)	**-0.05**	(0.02)	**0.08**	(0.02)
Trinidad and Tobago	**-0.82**	(0.23)	**0.13**	(0.04)	0.00	(0.02)	**-0.04**	(0.02)	**0.05**	(0.02)	**0.05**	(0.02)	**0.06**	(0.02)
Regions														
Italy: Abruzzo	-0.48	(0.54)	**0.47**	(0.05)	0.02	(0.03)	0.01	(0.05)	0.01	(0.03)	0.06	(0.03)	**0.12**	(0.04)
Italy: Basilicata	**-1.62**	(0.57)	**0.44**	(0.05)	-0.02	(0.04)	**0.13**	(0.03)	0.04	(0.04)	**0.07**	(0.03)	**0.09**	(0.04)
Italy: Bolzano	**-1.37**	(0.50)	**0.41**	(0.05)	-0.02	(0.03)	0.04	(0.04)	0.06	(0.03)	0.00	(0.03)	0.04	(0.04)
Italy: Calabria	-1.24	(0.65)	**0.50**	(0.06)	-0.05	(0.03)	0.06	(0.04)	-0.02	(0.03)	-0.04	(0.04)	0.04	(0.03)
Italy: Campania	-0.51	(0.46)	**0.28**	(0.06)	-0.02	(0.04)	-0.03	(0.05)	-0.03	(0.04)	0.06	(0.04)	**0.09**	(0.05)
Italy: Emilia Romagna	-1.04	(0.63)	**0.42**	(0.06)	-0.04	(0.03)	0.03	(0.05)	-0.02	(0.03)	**0.05**	(0.02)	0.06	(0.04)
Italy: Friuli Venezia Giulia	0.09	(0.62)	**0.56**	(0.06)	0.04	(0.04)	-0.07	(0.04)	-0.04	(0.04)	0.02	(0.03)	**0.11**	(0.05)
Italy: Lazio	-0.71	(0.56)	**0.34**	(0.06)	**0.08**	(0.04)	0.04	(0.07)	**-0.11**	(0.04)	0.04	(0.03)	**0.13**	(0.05)
Italy: Liguria	-0.48	(0.33)	**0.39**	(0.06)	0.02	(0.04)	0.02	(0.03)	-0.06	(0.05)	0.02	(0.03)	**0.18**	(0.04)
Italy: Lombardia	-0.50	(0.57)	**0.39**	(0.06)	0.03	(0.04)	0.03	(0.04)	-0.02	(0.03)	0.05	(0.03)	0.03	(0.04)
Italy: Marche	-0.54	(0.38)	**0.52**	(0.04)	**0.07**	(0.03)	-0.01	(0.04)	0.03	(0.04)	**0.05**	(0.02)	0.00	(0.04)
Italy: Molise	-0.72	(0.46)	**0.43**	(0.06)	**0.07**	(0.03)	0.06	(0.04)	-0.01	(0.04)	0.00	(0.04)	**0.17**	(0.05)
Italy: Piemonte	**-1.02**	(0.43)	**0.49**	(0.06)	-0.07	(0.03)	0.00	(0.04)	-0.04	(0.03)	0.03	(0.03)	**0.10**	(0.03)
Italy: Puglia	-0.83	(0.56)	**0.50**	(0.07)	0.00	(0.03)	-0.02	(0.03)	-0.06	(0.04)	**0.10**	(0.04)	0.07	(0.04)
Italy: Sardegna	**-1.35**	(0.54)	**0.59**	(0.08)	0.00	(0.04)	-0.02	(0.06)	0.02	(0.05)	0.04	(0.03)	**0.19**	(0.05)
Italy: Sicilia	**-1.10**	(0.38)	**0.37**	(0.05)	0.03	(0.03)	0.07	(0.05)	-0.09	(0.05)	0.01	(0.03)	**0.09**	(0.04)
Italy: Toscana	-0.38	(0.36)	**0.41**	(0.05)	**0.06**	(0.03)	0.03	(0.03)	-0.05	(0.03)	**0.07**	(0.03)	0.04	(0.03)
Italy: Trento	-0.67	(0.37)	**0.33**	(0.05)	-0.03	(0.04)	0.05	(0.03)	0.01	(0.03)	0.03	(0.03)	0.06	(0.03)
Italy: Umbria	0.25	(0.37)	**0.44**	(0.05)	-0.03	(0.03)	0.03	(0.03)	**-0.09**	(0.03)	0.03	(0.03)	**0.16**	(0.05)
Italy: Valle d'Aosta	**-1.15**	(0.55)	**0.51**	(0.07)	0.02	(0.04)	-0.03	(0.05)	0.03	(0.04)	-0.01	(0.03)	**0.10**	(0.04)
Italy: Veneto	-0.31	(0.45)	**0.51**	(0.04)	-0.06	(0.04)	0.02	(0.03)	-0.07	(0.04)	**0.10**	(0.02)	**0.12**	(0.03)
Mexico: Aguascalientes[1]	2.76	(1.86)	**1.66**	(0.27)	0.05	(0.14)	-0.17	(0.14)	0.04	(0.15)	0.27	(0.15)	-0.14	(0.18)
Mexico: Baja California[1]	1.93	(1.91)	**1.22**	(0.33)	-0.02	(0.16)	0.04	(0.17)	-0.04	(0.13)	0.20	(0.12)	0.21	(0.18)
Mexico: Baja California Sur[1]	0.09	(2.22)	**0.78**	(0.32)	-0.15	(0.16)	0.02	(0.18)	0.12	(0.21)	0.08	(0.16)	0.25	(0.26)
Mexico: Campeche[1]	**-4.05**	(1.88)	**1.02**	(0.28)	-0.31	(0.17)	-0.02	(0.18)	-0.05	(0.16)	0.08	(0.15)	0.32	(0.25)
Mexico: Chihuahua[1]	-5.14	(2.64)	**0.93**	(0.43)	-0.05	(0.14)	-0.23	(0.16)	0.07	(0.17)	-0.02	(0.14)	0.14	(0.16)
Mexico: Colima[1]	**9.72**	(3.43)	0.70	(0.37)	0.32	(0.20)	-0.13	(0.21)	0.05	(0.18)	0.11	(0.17)	-0.19	(0.28)
Mexico: Coahuila[1]	-1.12	(2.98)	0.25	(0.31)	**0.32**	(0.15)	0.06	(0.19)	-0.07	(0.26)	0.04	(0.25)	**0.56**	(0.23)
Mexico: Chiapas[1]	0.64	(2.02)	0.36	(0.30)	-0.07	(0.16)	-0.07	(0.25)	0.35	(0.26)	0.32	(0.20)	-0.19	(0.29)
Mexico: Distrito Federal[1]	0.76	(1.44)	**0.70**	(0.22)	-0.05	(0.11)	-0.17	(0.12)	-0.02	(0.13)	0.10	(0.16)	0.22	(0.12)
Mexico: Durango[1]	-0.06	(3.59)	0.67	(0.43)	0.08	(0.28)	0.11	(0.19)	0.27	(0.18)	0.43	(0.30)	-0.05	(0.28)
Mexico: Guerrero[1]	**7.53**	(2.54)	**1.03**	(0.36)	-0.02	(0.20)	-0.04	(0.17)	0.12	(0.22)	0.11	(0.26)	0.13	(0.20)
Mexico: Guanajuato[1]	**5.76**	(2.61)	**0.78**	(0.22)	-0.05	(0.12)	0.04	(0.13)	0.24	(0.14)	0.14	(0.18)	0.19	(0.16)
Mexico: Hidalgo[1]	6.35	(4.27)	**0.72**	(0.24)	**-0.53**	(0.14)	0.22	(0.20)	0.05	(0.20)	-0.10	(0.22)	0.17	(0.25)
Mexico: Jalisco[1]	2.21	(2.60)	0.39	(0.32)	-0.25	(0.20)	0.07	(0.21)	-0.02	(0.19)	0.06	(0.16)	0.13	(0.19)
Mexico: Michoacán[1]	-0.58	(2.43)	0.23	(0.48)	0.02	(0.31)	**0.33**	(0.15)	0.30	(0.20)	0.09	(0.31)	**0.52**	(0.19)
Mexico: Morelos[1]	0.40	(2.17)	0.30	(0.35)	-0.15	(0.13)	0.15	(0.13)	-0.08	(0.20)	0.23	(0.23)	0.19	(0.19)
Mexico: Mexico[1]	0.30	(2.14)	**0.75**	(0.36)	-0.18	(0.15)	0.21	(0.12)	-0.27	(0.18)	0.08	(0.15)	**0.62**	(0.19)
Mexico: Nayarit[1]	-4.80	(3.09)	0.48	(0.32)	-0.01	(0.16)	-0.28	(0.22)	0.05	(0.19)	-0.09	(0.20)	0.13	(0.23)
Mexico: Nuevo León[1]	**10.68**	(3.54)	**0.76**	(0.20)	-0.02	(0.10)	0.04	(0.13)	-0.09	(0.15)	0.03	(0.13)	**0.40**	(0.19)
Mexico: Oaxaca[1]	0.73	(2.07)	0.61	(0.49)	-0.52	(0.42)	0.43	(0.26)	-0.12	(0.38)	-0.16	(0.27)	**0.46**	(0.21)
Mexico: Puebla[1]	4.05	(3.19)	0.41	(0.30)	-0.10	(0.17)	0.07	(0.16)	0.08	(0.18)	-0.09	(0.15)	-0.18	(0.14)
Mexico: Quintana Roo[1]	1.15	(3.40)	**1.11**	(0.41)	0.20	(0.14)	-0.18	(0.18)	0.30	(0.24)	-0.31	(0.20)	0.16	(0.28)
Mexico: Querétaro[1]	-1.84	(3.26)	0.29	(0.30)	0.10	(0.15)	0.11	(0.14)	0.15	(0.19)	0.04	(0.18)	0.06	(0.20)
Mexico: Sinaloa[1]	-4.88	(5.39)	**0.70**	(0.29)	-0.12	(0.11)	**0.24**	(0.09)	**0.48**	(0.23)	-0.13	(0.22)	0.02	(0.37)
Mexico: San Luis Potosí[1]	**5.80**	(2.54)	**0.69**	(0.31)	-0.18	(0.13)	**0.42**	(0.13)	0.07	(0.21)	**-0.32**	(0.15)	**0.46**	(0.17)
Mexico: Sonora[1]	**10.36**	(4.20)	0.61	(0.40)	0.02	(0.16)	-0.14	(0.20)	-0.21	(0.16)	-0.29	(0.23)	**0.82**	(0.32)
Mexico: Tamaulipas[1]	-1.58	(1.98)	**0.85**	(0.33)	0.01	(0.10)	-0.04	(0.16)	-0.42	(0.23)	**0.83**	(0.28)	0.39	(0.24)
Mexico: Tabasco[1]	**7.74**	(3.16)	0.13	(0.46)	0.05	(0.14)	0.00	(0.18)	-0.13	(0.23)	0.20	(0.16)	0.18	(0.23)
Mexico: Tlaxcala[1]	0.94	(2.33)	0.42	(0.30)	-0.22	(0.17)	0.02	(0.15)	-0.15	(0.12)	0.00	(0.21)	**0.44**	(0.16)
Mexico: Veracruz[1]	-5.87	(4.62)	0.63	(0.37)	-0.30	(0.19)	-0.01	(0.24)	0.15	(0.19)	**0.27**	(0.12)	0.15	(0.16)
Mexico: Yucatán[1]	3.09	(2.02)	**0.86**	(0.28)	0.02	(0.14)	0.18	(0.14)	0.13	(0.15)	0.30	(0.16)	0.07	(0.18)
Mexico: Zacatecas[1]	1.12	(3.74)	0.05	(0.30)	0.19	(0.23)	-0.04	(0.17)	-0.25	(0.26)	-0.05	(0.22)	0.30	(0.28)

Notes: To facilitate comparability, marks in all countries and economies have been standardised so that higher values indicate better appraisals and that all countries and economies have a mean mark of 0 (zero) with a standard deviation of 1 (one). Reading scores have been scaled so that one unit equals 100 PISA reading score points. Tobit models that account for the censored nature of failing marks in Austria, Croatia, Hungary, Poland, Serbia and the Slovak Republic do not yield substantively different results.

Estimates statistically significantly different from 0 (zero) at a 95% confidence level are highlighted in bold.

1. Macao-China, Mexico and New Zealand distributed, in the Educational Career questionnaire, the alternative question on whether students received a passing or failing mark. Results for these countries and economies are thus based on a dichotomous variable that does not capture the full variability of marks received by students. Estimates for these countries and economies are based on a logistic regression predicting whether a student received a passing or failing mark.

StatLink http://dx.doi.org/10.1787/888932734172

[Part 2/3]

Table B2.7 How students' learning strategies, approaches to learning, engagement and background characteristics relate to the marks they receive in their language-of-assessment course

	Engagement						Student background					
	Enjoyment of reading		Attitudes towards school		Student-teacher relations		Student is a girl		*PISA index of economic, social and cultural status*		Student with an immigrant background	
	Coeff.	S.E.	Coeff.	S.E.	Coeff.	S.E.	Coeff.	S.E.	Coeff.	S.E.	Coeff.	S.E.
Countries and economies												
Austria	**0.06**	(0.02)	0.02	(0.02)	**0.10**	(0.02)	**0.15**	(0.04)	**0.08**	(0.02)	-0.01	(0.08)
Belgium (Flemish Community)	**0.12**	(0.02)	**0.05**	(0.02)	**0.07**	(0.03)	**0.10**	(0.04)	0.02	(0.02)	-0.11	(0.09)
Croatia	**0.12**	(0.02)	0.00	(0.02)	**0.07**	(0.02)	**0.16**	(0.03)	0.02	(0.02)	-0.04	(0.04)
Hungary	**0.09**	(0.03)	-0.01	(0.02)	**0.14**	(0.02)	**0.20**	(0.04)	**0.07**	(0.02)	-0.13	(0.10)
Iceland	-0.01	(0.02)	**0.06**	(0.02)	0.04	(0.02)	0.05	(0.03)	**0.17**	(0.02)	0.05	(0.18)
Ireland	**0.13**	(0.02)	0.03	(0.02)	0.01	(0.02)	**0.10**	(0.04)	**0.11**	(0.03)	-0.05	(0.07)
Italy	**0.08**	(0.01)	0.02	(0.01)	**0.09**	(0.01)	**0.16**	(0.02)	**0.08**	(0.01)	0.06	(0.05)
Latvia	**0.11**	(0.03)	0.01	(0.02)	**0.12**	(0.02)	**0.25**	(0.04)	**0.08**	(0.02)	0.10	(0.08)
Macao-China[1]	**0.36**	(0.10)	0.12	(0.08)	0.07	(0.07)	**0.43**	(0.11)	**0.18**	(0.06)	0.18	(0.10)
Mexico[1]	**0.30**	(0.05)	0.02	(0.03)	**0.14**	(0.03)	0.02	(0.07)	0.02	(0.04)	0.13	(0.30)
New Zealand[1]	0.09	(0.07)	**0.15**	(0.05)	**0.26**	(0.06)	**0.25**	(0.10)	**0.21**	(0.08)	0.06	(0.15)
Poland	**0.08**	(0.01)	0.00	(0.01)	**0.09**	(0.02)	**0.30**	(0.03)	**0.18**	(0.02)	0.00	(0.00)
Portugal: ISCED2	**0.08**	(0.03)	0.02	(0.02)	**0.13**	(0.02)	0.06	(0.05)	**0.06**	(0.02)	-0.05	(0.08)
Portugal: ISCED3	**0.06**	(0.02)	0.02	(0.02)	**0.13**	(0.02)	**0.14**	(0.04)	**0.13**	(0.02)	-0.10	(0.09)
Serbia	**0.21**	(0.02)	0.02	(0.02)	**0.03**	(0.01)	**0.09**	(0.03)	**0.08**	(0.01)	0.00	(0.04)
Singapore	**0.11**	(0.02)	0.01	(0.02)	0.00	(0.02)	-0.06	(0.04)	**0.06**	(0.02)	**-0.10**	(0.05)
Slovak Republic	**0.08**	(0.02)	0.01	(0.02)	**0.12**	(0.02)	**0.28**	(0.04)	**0.13**	(0.02)	0.03	(0.14)
Trinidad and Tobago	**0.12**	(0.02)	0.01	(0.02)	0.01	(0.02)	0.03	(0.04)	**0.12**	(0.02)	0.16	(0.15)
Regions												
Italy: Abruzzo	**0.08**	(0.03)	-0.01	(0.03)	**0.10**	(0.03)	**0.25**	(0.06)	0.02	(0.03)	-0.26	(0.21)
Italy: Basilicata	**0.12**	(0.04)	0.04	(0.03)	**0.13**	(0.03)	0.01	(0.06)	0.01	(0.03)	**-0.63**	(0.32)
Italy: Bolzano	0.05	(0.03)	0.04	(0.03)	**0.11**	(0.03)	**0.16**	(0.06)	0.04	(0.03)	-0.30	(0.32)
Italy: Calabria	**0.18**	(0.04)	0.06	(0.04)	**0.10**	(0.04)	**0.19**	(0.08)	**0.08**	(0.03)	0.21	(0.23)
Italy: Campania	**0.14**	(0.04)	0.02	(0.03)	**0.11**	(0.05)	**0.24**	(0.07)	**0.09**	(0.03)	0.16	(0.27)
Italy: Emilia Romagna	**0.13**	(0.04)	0.07	(0.05)	**0.09**	(0.03)	**0.19**	(0.07)	**0.08**	(0.03)	-0.14	(0.11)
Italy: Friuli Venezia Giulia	**0.09**	(0.04)	0.07	(0.04)	**0.12**	(0.03)	0.01	(0.07)	**0.12**	(0.03)	0.04	(0.13)
Italy: Lazio	**0.17**	(0.04)	-0.06	(0.04)	**0.09**	(0.05)	**0.23**	(0.07)	0.05	(0.03)	-0.13	(0.14)
Italy: Liguria	0.00	(0.04)	0.05	(0.03)	0.05	(0.05)	0.09	(0.08)	-0.02	(0.04)	**-0.33**	(0.15)
Italy: Lombardia	0.04	(0.03)	-0.01	(0.03)	**0.11**	(0.04)	0.11	(0.06)	**0.09**	(0.03)	-0.07	(0.19)
Italy: Marche	**0.11**	(0.04)	0.05	(0.03)	**0.07**	(0.02)	**0.20**	(0.06)	**0.11**	(0.03)	-0.02	(0.08)
Italy: Molise	**0.12**	(0.05)	0.02	(0.03)	0.00	(0.04)	0.02	(0.07)	0.02	(0.04)	-0.29	(0.20)
Italy: Piemonte	0.05	(0.04)	0.06	(0.04)	**0.11**	(0.04)	0.11	(0.07)	**0.11**	(0.04)	0.05	(0.19)
Italy: Puglia	0.06	(0.03)	-0.01	(0.03)	**0.11**	(0.03)	**0.14**	(0.06)	0.04	(0.03)	0.29	(0.38)
Italy: Sardegna	**0.08**	(0.03)	0.07	(0.04)	**0.11**	(0.04)	0.06	(0.08)	0.05	(0.05)	0.57	(0.49)
Italy: Sicilia	**0.21**	(0.04)	**0.08**	(0.03)	0.03	(0.04)	0.07	(0.06)	**0.15**	(0.04)	0.40	(0.21)
Italy: Toscana	**0.10**	(0.04)	0.05	(0.03)	**0.10**	(0.03)	**0.20**	(0.07)	0.04	(0.03)	-0.12	(0.14)
Italy: Trento	**0.08**	(0.03)	**0.09**	(0.03)	0.05	(0.03)	0.06	(0.07)	**0.11**	(0.03)	0.01	(0.11)
Italy: Umbria	0.06	(0.04)	0.01	(0.04)	0.05	(0.03)	**0.18**	(0.05)	**0.10**	(0.04)	-0.04	(0.15)
Italy: Valle d'Aosta	0.01	(0.05)	0.00	(0.04)	0.05	(0.04)	**0.19**	(0.07)	0.04	(0.04)	0.19	(0.16)
Italy: Veneto	0.01	(0.03)	0.03	(0.04)	**0.11**	(0.03)	**0.19**	(0.07)	0.05	(0.03)	-0.14	(0.15)
Mexico: Aguascalientes[1]	**0.54**	(0.20)	0.07	(0.13)	0.06	(0.13)	-0.36	(0.30)	-0.11	(0.13)	**14.16**	(1.05)
Mexico: Baja California[1]	0.08	(0.29)	0.00	(0.19)	**0.38**	(0.18)	-0.34	(0.35)	**0.43**	(0.14)	0.00	(0.99)
Mexico: Baja California Sur[1]	0.11	(0.24)	-0.16	(0.18)	**0.28**	(0.11)	-0.25	(0.27)	0.09	(0.16)	1.71	(1.21)
Mexico: Campeche[1]	0.02	(0.29)	-0.16	(0.08)	**0.42**	(0.14)	0.12	(0.29)	-0.11	(0.19)	-0.20	(0.61)
Mexico: Chihuahua[1]	0.08	(0.20)	0.16	(0.20)	-0.01	(0.18)	0.15	(0.23)	**-0.30**	(0.13)	0.60	(1.14)
Mexico: Colima[1]	0.12	(0.29)	0.20	(0.18)	**0.80**	(0.25)	0.41	(0.27)	-0.14	(0.14)	**13.27**	(0.66)
Mexico: Coahuila[1]	**-0.43**	(0.20)	-0.19	(0.23)	0.26	(0.17)	0.51	(0.28)	0.14	(0.14)	**12.04**	(1.24)
Mexico: Chiapas[1]	0.30	(0.26)	0.29	(0.22)	0.14	(0.19)	-0.14	(0.35)	0.01	(0.15)	-0.05	(1.01)
Mexico: Distrito Federal[1]	**0.27**	(0.11)	0.18	(0.10)	0.13	(0.13)	-0.29	(0.22)	-0.11	(0.15)	-0.59	(0.82)
Mexico: Durango[1]	0.22	(0.37)	0.11	(0.25)	**0.45**	(0.21)	-0.19	(0.33)	0.05	(0.12)	**12.24**	(1.08)
Mexico: Guerrero[1]	-0.08	(0.26)	**0.49**	(0.16)	0.09	(0.22)	0.30	(0.29)	-0.08	(0.20)	-1.34	(1.23)
Mexico: Guanajuato[1]	0.10	(0.14)	-0.15	(0.11)	-0.14	(0.15)	**0.51**	(0.21)	0.10	(0.09)	**13.22**	(0.93)
Mexico: Hidalgo[1]	0.64	(0.33)	0.22	(0.13)	0.23	(0.22)	-0.27	(0.22)	0.03	(0.16)	**13.14**	(1.11)
Mexico: Jalisco[1]	0.20	(0.22)	0.19	(0.24)	0.20	(0.16)	0.36	(0.36)	0.08	(0.13)	**14.66**	(1.39)
Mexico: Michoacán[1]	0.07	(0.22)	-0.32	(0.30)	0.23	(0.27)	-0.14	(0.32)	-0.04	(0.15)	**13.25**	(0.66)
Mexico: Morelos[1]	0.50	(0.31)	0.10	(0.16)	0.13	(0.18)	-0.04	(0.31)	-0.02	(0.11)	-0.71	(0.94)
Mexico: Mexico[1]	**0.54**	(0.20)	-0.23	(0.13)	-0.09	(0.14)	0.43	(0.29)	0.07	(0.14)	**14.76**	(0.53)
Mexico: Nayarit[1]	0.15	(0.28)	0.02	(0.22)	0.18	(0.15)	-0.26	(0.29)	-0.06	(0.16)	**12.98**	(1.56)
Mexico: Nuevo León[1]	0.25	(0.20)	0.09	(0.11)	0.14	(0.14)	-0.33	(0.27)	0.05	(0.18)	2.19	(1.22)
Mexico: Oaxaca[1]	0.29	(0.30)	0.27	(0.35)	0.10	(0.23)	-0.19	(0.35)	-0.16	(0.18)	**13.91**	(1.03)
Mexico: Puebla[1]	**0.86**	(0.21)	-0.08	(0.15)	0.25	(0.14)	-0.19	(0.20)	-0.09	(0.13)	-1.51	(1.05)
Mexico: Quintana Roo[1]	0.34	(0.30)	-0.07	(0.19)	**0.37**	(0.18)	0.00	(0.30)	-0.23	(0.16)	-0.10	(0.81)
Mexico: Querétaro[1]	**0.39**	(0.17)	0.06	(0.17)	0.08	(0.14)	-0.22	(0.34)	0.19	(0.14)	0.18	(1.30)
Mexico: Sinaloa[1]	0.44	(0.33)	-0.19	(0.12)	**0.33**	(0.16)	0.01	(0.47)	-0.04	(0.15)	**14.21**	(0.96)
Mexico: San Luis Potosí[1]	0.28	(0.22)	**-0.31**	(0.13)	**0.33**	(0.13)	0.54	(0.34)	0.07	(0.16)	**12.48**	(1.06)
Mexico: Sonora[1]	0.27	(0.25)	0.13	(0.15)	0.31	(0.18)	-0.18	(0.34)	-0.10	(0.14)	**13.14**	(1.18)
Mexico: Tamaulipas[1]	-0.03	(0.14)	-0.07	(0.15)	0.25	(0.33)	-0.05	(0.44)	0.23	(0.29)	0.42	(1.24)
Mexico: Tabasco[1]	0.26	(0.31)	0.15	(0.12)	**0.55**	(0.22)	0.06	(0.34)	-0.07	(0.14)	**-2.11**	(0.72)
Mexico: Tlaxcala[1]	0.07	(0.33)	0.18	(0.22)	0.24	(0.13)	-0.50	(0.27)	0.13	(0.18)	**14.09**	(0.93)
Mexico: Veracruz[1]	0.45	(0.27)	0.19	(0.25)	0.17	(0.17)	0.20	(0.56)	0.36	(0.22)	**14.28**	(0.75)
Mexico: Yucatán[1]	0.26	(0.27)	0.09	(0.15)	0.00	(0.15)	0.51	(0.34)	0.06	(0.11)	-1.24	(0.72)
Mexico: Zacatecas[1]	-0.15	(0.33)	0.03	(0.21)	0.24	(0.19)	0.79	(0.52)	**0.35**	(0.15)	**11.88**	(0.65)

Notes: To facilitate comparability, marks in all countries and economies have been standardised so that higher values indicate better appraisals and that all countries and economies have a mean mark of 0 (zero) with a standard deviation of 1 (one). Reading scores have been scaled so that one unit equals 100 PISA reading score points. Tobit models that account for the censored nature of failing marks in Austria, Croatia, Hungary, Poland, Serbia and the Slovak Republic do not yield substantively different results.

Estimates statistically significantly different from 0 (zero) at a 95% confidence level are highlighted in bold.

1. Macao-China, Mexico and New Zealand distributed, in the Educational Career questionnaire, the alternative question on whether students received a passing or failing mark. Results for these countries and economies are thus based on a dichotomous variable that does not capture the full variability of marks received by students. Estimates for these countries and economies are based on a logistic regression predicting whether a student received a passing or failing mark.

StatLink http://dx.doi.org/10.1787/888932734172

[Part 3/3]

Table B2.7 How students' learning strategies, approaches to learning, engagement and background characteristics relate to the marks they receive in their language-of-assessment course

	Student background				Contextual effects					
	Student speaks another language at home		Student attended ISCED 0 for more than one year		School average reading performance		School average ESCS		R-squared	
	Coeff.	S.E.	Coeff.	S.E.	Coeff.	S.E.	Coeff.	S.E.	R^2	S.E.
Countries and economies										
Austria	**-0.26**	(0.10)	-0.10	(0.05)	**-0.42**	(0.06)	0.11	(0.10)	**0.14**	(0.01)
Belgium (Flemish Community)	**-0.09**	(0.04)	-0.05	(0.10)	-0.11	(0.09)	-0.12	(0.12)	**0.10**	(0.01)
Croatia	0.09	(0.21)	-0.06	(0.03)	**0.16**	(0.07)	-0.02	(0.08)	**0.27**	(0.02)
Hungary	-0.03	(0.14)	-0.04	(0.07)	0.02	(0.09)	0.10	(0.09)	**0.31**	(0.02)
Iceland	0.04	(0.13)	0.06	(0.07)	**-0.14**	(0.05)	-0.05	(0.04)	**0.24**	(0.01)
Ireland	0.04	(0.10)	0.04	(0.04)	**-0.15**	(0.07)	0.05	(0.08)	**0.15**	(0.02)
Italy	0.04	(0.03)	**0.09**	(0.03)	**-0.25**	(0.03)	0.04	(0.04)	**0.21**	(0.01)
Latvia	**0.15**	(0.06)	-0.04	(0.04)	**-0.39**	(0.11)	**0.22**	(0.07)	**0.35**	(0.02)
Macao-China[1]	0.23	(0.22)	**0.28**	(0.13)	0.00	(0.13)	**-0.40**	(0.17)	a	a
Mexico[1]	0.22	(0.24)	-0.03	(0.08)	**-0.59**	(0.15)	-0.15	(0.09)	a	a
New Zealand[1]	**-0.39**	(0.17)	-0.18	(0.12)	-0.15	(0.14)	0.03	(0.21)	a	a
Poland	0.01	(0.23)	0.00	(0.03)	**-0.49**	(0.09)	0.06	(0.07)	**0.44**	(0.01)
Portugal: ISCED2	0.03	(0.17)	0.05	(0.05)	-0.17	(0.10)	0.08	(0.06)	**0.25**	(0.02)
Portugal: ISCED3	0.12	(0.21)	0.06	(0.04)	**-0.48**	(0.18)	-0.06	(0.08)	**0.32**	(0.02)
Serbia	-0.05	(0.09)	0.06	(0.03)	**-0.18**	(0.08)	0.14	(0.08)	**0.26**	(0.02)
Singapore	**-0.24**	(0.03)	**-0.13**	(0.06)	**0.11**	(0.05)	0.09	(0.07)	**0.10**	(0.01)
Slovak Republic	0.11	(0.07)	**0.08**	(0.04)	**-0.31**	(0.07)	**0.20**	(0.10)	**0.37**	(0.02)
Trinidad and Tobago	0.13	(0.15)	-0.05	(0.04)	0.04	(0.05)	-0.02	(0.07)	**0.10**	(0.01)
Regions										
Italy: Abruzzo	0.10	(0.11)	0.12	(0.09)	**-0.41**	(0.13)	**0.45**	(0.11)	**0.30**	(0.03)
Italy: Basilicata	0.11	(0.10)	0.05	(0.11)	-0.13	(0.12)	0.06	(0.14)	**0.29**	(0.03)
Italy: Bolzano	**0.36**	(0.10)	-0.08	(0.08)	-0.10	(0.11)	-0.02	(0.15)	**0.22**	(0.04)
Italy: Calabria	0.07	(0.06)	-0.03	(0.09)	**-0.27**	(0.12)	0.06	(0.17)	**0.28**	(0.03)
Italy: Campania	-0.11	(0.09)	**0.20**	(0.09)	**-0.30**	(0.09)	0.15	(0.11)	**0.22**	(0.03)
Italy: Emilia Romagna	-0.05	(0.11)	-0.13	(0.08)	-0.17	(0.13)	-0.15	(0.14)	**0.25**	(0.03)
Italy: Friuli Venezia Giulia	-0.03	(0.07)	-0.06	(0.09)	**-0.56**	(0.13)	0.17	(0.16)	**0.24**	(0.02)
Italy: Lazio	0.20	(0.11)	0.12	(0.11)	**-0.28**	(0.13)	0.17	(0.10)	**0.24**	(0.03)
Italy: Liguria	**0.28**	(0.13)	0.10	(0.08)	**-0.31**	(0.09)	0.01	(0.11)	**0.16**	(0.03)
Italy: Lombardia	0.01	(0.13)	-0.10	(0.07)	**-0.27**	(0.11)	0.03	(0.12)	**0.17**	(0.02)
Italy: Marche	0.08	(0.11)	-0.01	(0.10)	**-0.42**	(0.08)	0.04	(0.14)	**0.25**	(0.03)
Italy: Molise	-0.03	(0.12)	0.13	(0.09)	**-0.32**	(0.11)	**0.25**	(0.11)	**0.28**	(0.04)
Italy: Piemonte	0.10	(0.13)	0.10	(0.09)	**-0.26**	(0.09)	-0.07	(0.11)	**0.21**	(0.03)
Italy: Puglia	-0.07	(0.12)	0.17	(0.10)	**-0.35**	(0.13)	**0.32**	(0.15)	**0.25**	(0.03)
Italy: Sardegna	**-0.34**	(0.17)	**0.25**	(0.10)	**-0.37**	(0.11)	0.15	(0.13)	**0.30**	(0.04)
Italy: Sicilia	0.12	(0.13)	**0.21**	(0.11)	**-0.21**	(0.08)	-0.05	(0.08)	**0.25**	(0.03)
Italy: Toscana	0.06	(0.11)	0.11	(0.11)	**-0.39**	(0.10)	0.10	(0.16)	**0.25**	(0.03)
Italy: Trento	**0.22**	(0.07)	0.16	(0.09)	**-0.20**	(0.09)	0.06	(0.14)	**0.17**	(0.03)
Italy: Umbria	0.06	(0.08)	0.05	(0.08)	**-0.52**	(0.08)	**0.38**	(0.10)	**0.24**	(0.03)
Italy: Valle d'Aosta	0.14	(0.09)	0.05	(0.12)	**-0.31**	(0.13)	-0.29	(0.15)	**0.16**	(0.03)
Italy: Veneto	0.03	(0.05)	0.08	(0.11)	**-0.46**	(0.11)	-0.07	(0.10)	**0.22**	(0.02)
Mexico: Aguascalientes[1]	**12.64**	(1.20)	0.03	(0.25)	**-1.69**	(0.51)	-0.14	(0.23)	a	a
Mexico: Baja California[1]	0.23	(1.64)	**-1.02**	(0.35)	-0.85	(0.48)	-0.47	(0.32)	a	a
Mexico: Baja California Sur[1]	-0.76	(1.49)	0.44	(0.38)	-0.23	(0.60)	-0.11	(0.40)	a	a
Mexico: Campeche[1]	-1.03	(0.61)	0.31	(0.29)	0.41	(0.45)	-0.37	(0.22)	a	a
Mexico: Chihuahua[1]	**13.35**	(0.98)	0.33	(0.25)	0.57	(0.83)	-0.34	(0.35)	a	a
Mexico: Colima[1]	**13.07**	(0.78)	0.34	(0.43)	**-2.01**	(0.66)	**1.20**	(0.57)	a	a
Mexico: Coahuila[1]	-1.92	(1.08)	-0.81	(0.48)	0.70	(0.68)	-0.42	(0.33)	a	a
Mexico: Chiapas[1]	0.85	(0.93)	-0.01	(0.42)	0.00	(0.50)	-0.32	(0.37)	a	a
Mexico: Distrito Federal[1]	**13.88**	(0.62)	**0.58**	(0.23)	-0.54	(0.38)	-0.11	(0.29)	a	a
Mexico: Durango[1]	**13.82**	(1.04)	0.43	(0.32)	-0.05	(0.96)	-0.20	(0.43)	a	a
Mexico: Guerrero[1]	**15.16**	(0.58)	-0.30	(0.45)	**-2.08**	(0.50)	0.45	(0.40)	a	a
Mexico: Guanajuato[1]	**12.81**	(0.74)	-0.05	(0.25)	**-1.64**	(0.49)	-0.24	(0.29)	a	a
Mexico: Hidalgo[1]	-0.71	(0.77)	-0.42	(0.34)	-1.38	(0.90)	0.25	(0.38)	a	a
Mexico: Jalisco[1]	**13.88**	(1.43)	-0.02	(0.35)	-0.23	(0.46)	0.47	(0.31)	a	a
Mexico: Michoacán[1]	**13.14**	(0.68)	0.10	(0.48)	0.41	(0.42)	**-0.66**	(0.29)	a	a
Mexico: Morelos[1]	**10.89**	(1.40)	-0.08	(0.37)	0.04	(0.60)	-0.61	(0.35)	a	a
Mexico: Mexico[1]	**-2.89**	(0.86)	-0.01	(0.33)	-0.35	(0.65)	-0.40	(0.35)	a	a
Mexico: Nayarit[1]	**12.11**	(1.33)	0.21	(0.37)	0.98	(0.77)	**-1.13**	(0.43)	a	a
Mexico: Nuevo León[1]	**12.78**	(1.10)	0.08	(0.26)	**-2.47**	(0.68)	0.91	(0.51)	a	a
Mexico: Oaxaca[1]	0.58	(1.01)	-0.04	(0.53)	-0.32	(0.69)	-0.36	(0.26)	a	a
Mexico: Puebla[1]	**14.27**	(0.75)	-0.40	(0.31)	-0.58	(0.69)	0.56	(0.38)	a	a
Mexico: Quintana Roo[1]	-0.99	(0.65)	0.18	(0.24)	-0.76	(0.84)	-0.11	(0.56)	a	a
Mexico: Querétaro[1]	**13.35**	(1.61)	0.01	(0.27)	0.57	(0.74)	**-0.81**	(0.39)	a	a
Mexico: Sinaloa[1]	**12.84**	(0.93)	0.09	(0.25)	0.95	(1.07)	-0.48	(0.61)	a	a
Mexico: San Luis Potosí[1]	-0.53	(0.80)	0.11	(0.29)	**-1.48**	(0.51)	-0.27	(0.36)	a	a
Mexico: Sonora[1]	-0.74	(0.89)	0.32	(0.32)	**-2.23**	(0.77)	0.28	(0.43)	a	a
Mexico: Tamaulipas[1]	**9.68**	(1.69)	-0.02	(0.23)	0.19	(0.62)	-0.57	(0.53)	a	a
Mexico: Tabasco[1]	**13.65**	(0.91)	-0.05	(0.32)	**-1.16**	(0.50)	0.40	(0.48)	a	a
Mexico: Tlaxcala[1]	0.00	(0.00)	-0.42	(0.34)	0.18	(0.57)	0.20	(0.32)	a	a
Mexico: Veracruz[1]	0.59	(1.11)	-0.61	(0.35)	1.11	(0.81)	**-1.22**	(0.46)	a	a
Mexico: Yucatán[1]	-0.01	(0.62)	-0.45	(0.31)	**-0.93**	(0.44)	-0.03	(0.25)	a	a
Mexico: Zacatecas[1]	**12.92**	(0.70)	**-1.38**	(0.64)	0.45	(0.68)	-0.74	(0.39)	a	a

Notes: To facilitate comparability, marks in all countries and economies have been standardised so that higher values indicate better appraisals and that all countries and economies have a mean mark of 0 (zero) with a standard deviation of 1 (one). Reading scores have been scaled so that one unit equals 100 PISA reading score points. Tobit models that account for the censored nature of failing marks in Austria, Croatia, Hungary, Poland, Serbia and the Slovak Republic do not yield substantively different results.

Estimates statistically significantly different from 0 (zero) at a 95% confidence level are highlighted in bold.

1. Macao-China, Mexico and New Zealand distributed, in the Educational Career questionnaire, the alternative question on whether students received a passing or failing mark. Results for these countries and economies are thus based on a dichotomous variable that does not capture the full variability of marks received by students. Estimates for these countries and economies are based on a logistic regression predicting whether a student received a passing or failing mark.

StatLink http://dx.doi.org/10.1787/888932734172

[Part 1/2]

Table B2.8 The types of schools that overestimate the marks they give to students in their language-of-assessment course with respect to students' PISA reading scores, learning strategies, approaches to learning and attitudes towards school

	Students in schools that inflate marks (schools with average studentised residuals above 0.5)		Students in schools that inflate marks (schools with more than 75% of students with positive residuals)		Private vs. public school		Selective vs. non-selective school	
	%	S.E.	%	S.E.	Difference in residual (private - public)	S.E.	Difference in residual (selective - non-selective)	S.E.
Countries and economies								
Austria	**12.97**	(2.15)	**44.66**	(3.81)	-0.11	(0.08)	**-0.30**	(0.06)
Belgium (Flemish Community)	**8.85**	(1.88)	**20.81**	(3.47)	-0.01	(0.07)	-0.04	(0.06)
Croatia	**7.73**	(1.62)	**13.58**	(2.67)	0.03	(0.26)	**-0.20**	(0.09)
Hungary	**10.17**	(2.41)	**24.47**	(3.75)	-0.14	(0.07)	-0.24	(0.13)
Iceland	**7.87**	(0.14)	**13.23**	(0.18)	**-0.41**	(0.02)	**0.13**	(0.02)
Ireland	**4.46**	(1.87)	**11.10**	(2.94)	0.01	(0.05)	-0.05	(0.04)
Italy	**13.75**	(1.30)	**51.58**	(1.67)	**0.37**	(0.07)	-0.02	(0.03)
Latvia	**11.65**	(2.43)	**20.65**	(2.87)	0.14	(0.14)	**-0.12**	(0.06)
Macao-China[1]	**0.55**	(0.00)	**82.77**	(0.04)	**-0.12**	(0.00)	**0.07**	(0.00)
Mexico[1]	**8.17**	(1.14)	**71.65**	(0.80)	-0.04	(0.04)	0.00	(0.03)
New Zealand[1]	**2.82**	(1.29)	**63.02**	(2.37)	0.00	(0.08)	0.06	(0.03)
Poland	**13.28**	(2.44)	**12.04**	(2.25)	0.07	(0.09)	0.02	(0.07)
Portugal: ISCED2	**10.07**	(2.83)	**43.08**	(4.46)	**0.17**	(0.08)	0.09	(0.06)
Portugal: ISCED3	**10.72**	(2.71)	**23.11**	(4.35)	0.08	(0.14)	0.01	(0.07)
Serbia	**12.03**	(2.72)	**27.49**	(3.58)	-0.40	(0.39)	0.24	(0.18)
Singapore	**6.32**	(0.10)	**20.63**	(0.26)	0.00	(0.18)	**0.05**	(0.00)
Slovak Republic	**14.77**	(3.14)	**15.60**	(3.20)	0.06	(0.10)	-0.09	(0.06)
Trinidad and Tobago	**12.00**	(0.20)	**29.44**	(0.31)	**0.03**	(0.00)	**0.05**	(0.00)
Regions								
Italy: Abruzzo	7.11	(4.06)	c	c	**0.50**	(0.05)	-0.10	(0.14)
Italy: Basilicata	**7.08**	(2.84)	c	c	0.00	(0.00)	0.06	(0.07)
Italy: Bolzano	**15.20**	(0.45)	c	c	**-0.09**	(0.03)	-0.05	(0.05)
Italy: Calabria	**13.66**	(4.88)	4.18	(2.93)	**-0.22**	(0.04)	**0.19**	(0.09)
Italy: Campania	5.14	(3.05)	**92.36**	(3.12)	**0.14**	(0.05)	-0.02	(0.15)
Italy: Emilia Romagna	**11.04**	(4.90)	**21.14**	(5.79)	0.14	(0.14)	0.05	(0.09)
Italy: Friuli Venezia Giulia	**8.96**	(3.56)	2.25	(1.74)	**0.45**	(0.03)	**0.16**	(0.05)
Italy: Lazio	**2.92**	(0.08)	**68.91**	(7.05)	**0.62**	(0.11)	0.05	(0.08)
Italy: Liguria	**8.45**	(4.23)	c	c	-0.14	(0.18)	**-0.24**	(0.10)
Italy: Lombardia	**5.52**	(2.04)	**89.23**	(3.99)	**0.41**	(0.10)	-0.07	(0.06)
Italy: Marche	7.33	(3.86)	1.50	(1.47)	**0.26**	(0.06)	-0.03	(0.10)
Italy: Molise	**5.67**	(1.00)	c	c	0.00	(0.00)	**-0.13**	(0.04)
Italy: Piemonte	**10.95**	(4.92)	**42.93**	(7.23)	0.26	(0.13)	0.20	(0.11)
Italy: Puglia	**11.61**	(4.09)	**56.87**	(7.16)	0.00	(0.00)	-0.09	(0.09)
Italy: Sardegna	**10.05**	(3.24)	8.00	(5.34)	**0.48**	(0.04)	-0.03	(0.09)
Italy: Sicilia	**9.11**	(3.74)	**82.11**	(5.65)	**0.13**	(0.05)	-0.02	(0.12)
Italy: Toscana	6.63	(3.74)	**25.87**	(7.29)	**-0.74**	(0.04)	0.08	(0.10)
Italy: Trento	**6.90**	(2.99)	c	c	0.20	(0.11)	0.07	(0.06)
Italy: Umbria	**10.58**	(3.24)	c	c	**0.49**	(0.19)	0.08	(0.08)
Italy: Valle d'Aosta	**8.50**	(0.28)	c	c	**0.22**	(0.01)	**-0.31**	(0.01)
Italy: Veneto	**7.76**	(2.59)	**47.83**	(7.15)	**0.65**	(0.25)	**0.18**	(0.08)
Mexico: Aguascalientes[1]	3.53	(2.47)	1.30	(1.24)	**-0.17**	(0.06)	-0.05	(0.08)
Mexico: Baja California[1]	c	c	**57.66**	(3.95)	-0.07	(0.06)	-0.07	(0.09)
Mexico: Baja California Sur[1]	4.72	(3.46)	c	c	**0.16**	(0.07)	-0.08	(0.05)
Mexico: Campeche[1]	4.44	(2.79)	c	c	0.06	(0.11)	-0.07	(0.09)
Mexico: Chihuahua[1]	c	c	**48.82**	(8.54)	0.10	(0.15)	0.06	(0.09)
Mexico: Colima[1]	c	c	c	c	-0.16	(0.12)	-0.01	(0.06)
Mexico: Coahuila[1]	10.89	(7.57)	**45.70**	(5.46)	-0.14	(0.11)	-0.06	(0.08)
Mexico: Chiapas[1]	2.76	(2.71)	**82.76**	(4.40)	0.03	(0.10)	**-0.20**	(0.08)
Mexico: Distrito Federal[1]	1.26	(1.21)	**100.00**	(0.00)	-0.05	(0.15)	0.20	(0.10)
Mexico: Durango[1]	**5.01**	(1.93)	**13.75**	(3.41)	**0.16**	(0.06)	0.05	(0.09)
Mexico: Guerrero[1]	8.05	(6.78)	**67.58**	(5.22)	0.00	(0.00)	0.01	(0.10)
Mexico: Guanajuato[1]	1.22	(1.18)	**86.57**	(3.83)	-0.26	(0.19)	**-0.23**	(0.11)
Mexico: Hidalgo[1]	1.74	(1.76)	**24.55**	(5.86)	**0.18**	(0.05)	0.03	(0.09)
Mexico: Jalisco[1]	2.18	(1.96)	**91.79**	(2.09)	-0.09	(0.17)	0.22	(0.12)
Mexico: Michoacán[1]	c	c	**79.19**	(5.40)	0.04	(0.08)	-0.17	(0.16)
Mexico: Morelos[1]	10.95	(8.61)	**40.56**	(10.50)	0.08	(0.15)	-0.09	(0.10)
Mexico: Mexico[1]	2.92	(1.95)	**100.00**	(0.00)	0.06	(0.18)	0.14	(0.10)
Mexico: Nayarit[1]	14.08	(9.30)	**21.66**	(4.11)	-0.07	(0.07)	-0.09	(0.10)
Mexico: Nuevo León[1]	15.94	(12.29)	**65.83**	(6.43)	0.11	(0.15)	0.02	(0.13)
Mexico: Oaxaca[1]	18.90	(11.54)	**61.80**	(6.91)	**0.11**	(0.05)	-0.10	(0.11)
Mexico: Puebla[1]	**18.34**	(4.48)	**96.91**	(1.88)	0.18	(0.13)	-0.10	(0.10)
Mexico: Quintana Roo[1]	**3.45**	(0.98)	**7.59**	(1.10)	-0.06	(0.11)	-0.06	(0.07)
Mexico: Querétaro[1]	**5.19**	(0.89)	**28.83**	(7.61)	-0.28	(0.15)	**-0.19**	(0.08)
Mexico: Sinaloa[1]	13.79	(9.03)	**56.40**	(4.97)	**0.23**	(0.09)	-0.02	(0.17)
Mexico: San Luis Potosí[1]	**16.09**	(6.59)	**57.73**	(5.61)	0.13	(0.15)	-0.16	(0.12)
Mexico: Sonora[1]	2.79	(2.80)	**51.27**	(6.06)	0.03	(0.10)	**-0.16**	(0.07)
Mexico: Tamaulipas[1]	2.17	(1.94)	**52.17**	(5.45)	**0.14**	(0.05)	0.01	(0.08)
Mexico: Tabasco[1]	c	c	**44.97**	(5.38)	**0.21**	(0.05)	0.09	(0.06)
Mexico: Tlaxcala[1]	8.44	(7.76)	16.80	(10.37)	**-0.90**	(0.25)	**0.20**	(0.08)
Mexico: Veracruz[1]	8.55	(5.16)	**99.18**	(0.84)	-0.48	(0.29)	0.12	(0.14)
Mexico: Yucatán[1]	c	c	**25.09**	(7.67)	-0.10	(0.06)	0.00	(0.05)
Mexico: Zacatecas[1]	6.85	(4.71)	**21.91**	(6.44)	**-0.68**	(0.32)	0.05	(0.09)

Notes: Each column represents a different model where the dependent variable is the residual of an OLS regression model of student marks after accounting for socio-economic status, metacognition strategies, approaches to learning and reading performance. Students with positive residuals have inflated grades because their grades overestimate their cognitive and non-cognitive skills.

Logistic models that account for the dichotomous nature of observed marks in Macao-China, Mexico and New Zealand, and Tobit models that account for the censored nature of failing marks in Austria, Croatia, Hungary, Poland, Serbia and the Slovak Republic do not yield substantively different results.

Estimates statistically significantly different from 0 (zero) at a 95% confidence level are highlighted in bold.

1. Macao-China, Mexico and New Zealand distributed, in the Educational Career questionnaire, the alternative question on whether students received a passing or failing mark. Results for these countries and economies are thus based on a dichotomous variable that does not capture the full variability of marks received by students. Estimates for these countries and economies are based on a logistic regression predicting whether a student received a passing or failing mark.

StatLink http://dx.doi.org/10.1787/888932734191

[Part 2/2]

Table B2.8 The types of schools that overestimate the marks they give to students in their language-of-assessment course with respect to students' PISA reading scores, learning strategies, approaches to learning and attitudes towards school

	There is constant pressure from parents vs. no constant pressure		School implements standardised tests at least once a year vs. school does not implement standardised tests		School implements standardised tests at least once a year vs. school does not implement standardised tests		Socio-economic status of the school	
	Difference in residual (constant - no constant pressure)	S.E.	Difference in residual (implements - does not implement)	S.E.	Difference in absolute residual (implements - does not implement)	S.E.	Coeff.	S.E.
Countries and economies								
Austria	0.13	(0.14)	0.05	(0.07)	-0.03	(0.04)	**-0.19**	(0.06)
Belgium (Flemish Community)	-0.05	(0.08)	0.00	(0.07)	-0.05	(0.04)	**-0.15**	(0.06)
Croatia	0.08	(0.11)	0.00	(0.05)	0.01	(0.03)	0.04	(0.05)
Hungary	**0.15**	(0.07)	**-0.14**	(0.07)	-0.01	(0.04)	0.01	(0.05)
Iceland	**-0.19**	(0.01)	**-0.04**	(0.00)	**-0.03**	(0.00)	**-0.08**	(0.00)
Ireland	-0.02	(0.05)	0.04	(0.04)	0.01	(0.03)	-0.03	(0.05)
Italy	0.01	(0.04)	0.00	(0.03)	-0.01	(0.02)	**-0.07**	(0.02)
Latvia	0.11	(0.11)	0.11	(0.17)	-0.12	(0.10)	-0.02	(0.07)
Macao-China[1]	**0.05**	(0.00)	**0.11**	(0.00)	**0.00**	(0.00)	**-0.07**	(0.00)
Mexico[1]	-0.02	(0.03)	0.02	(0.03)	0.02	(0.02)	**-0.04**	(0.02)
New Zealand[1]	-0.05	(0.03)	0.01	(0.04)	**-0.05**	(0.03)	-0.05	(0.04)
Poland	-0.12	(0.07)	0.00	(0.09)	-0.03	(0.06)	**-0.14**	(0.06)
Portugal: ISCED2	0.11	(0.12)	0.03	(0.07)	0.00	(0.04)	-0.02	(0.05)
Portugal: ISCED3	-0.04	(0.12)	-0.11	(0.09)	-0.08	(0.05)	**-0.13**	(0.06)
Serbia	-0.02	(0.16)	-0.02	(0.06)	0.02	(0.03)	0.00	(0.06)
Singapore	**0.01**	(0.01)	**0.05**	(0.01)	-0.01	(0.01)	**0.14**	(0.00)
Slovak Republic	0.12	(0.09)	0.01	(0.11)	0.02	(0.08)	-0.09	(0.07)
Trinidad and Tobago	**-0.03**	(0.00)	**0.08**	(0.01)	**-0.01**	(0.00)	0.00	(0.00)
Regions								
Italy: Abruzzo	0.09	(0.07)	-0.18	(0.09)	-0.04	(0.06)	**0.13**	(0.04)
Italy: Basilicata	-0.03	(0.08)	-0.05	(0.05)	0.05	(0.03)	0.02	(0.07)
Italy: Bolzano	**-0.83**	(0.11)	0.01	(0.01)	**0.03**	(0.00)	**-0.27**	(0.04)
Italy: Calabria	0.33	(0.17)	0.04	(0.12)	-0.09	(0.07)	0.02	(0.08)
Italy: Campania	0.18	(0.21)	0.13	(0.08)	0.01	(0.07)	-0.03	(0.08)
Italy: Emilia Romagna	-0.08	(0.12)	0.10	(0.09)	0.08	(0.05)	**-0.21**	(0.07)
Italy: Friuli Venezia Giulia	-0.04	(0.07)	**-0.14**	(0.06)	-0.05	(0.03)	**-0.26**	(0.09)
Italy: Lazio	**-0.24**	(0.08)	-0.12	(0.10)	0.11	(0.07)	0.08	(0.13)
Italy: Liguria	-0.10	(0.07)	**-0.20**	(0.07)	-0.02	(0.04)	**-0.27**	(0.09)
Italy: Lombardia	-0.05	(0.13)	-0.06	(0.08)	**-0.09**	(0.04)	**-0.16**	(0.07)
Italy: Marche	**-0.28**	(0.11)	0.06	(0.10)	0.04	(0.05)	**-0.21**	(0.09)
Italy: Molise	**-0.04**	(0.01)	-0.01	(0.03)	**-0.06**	(0.03)	0.01	(0.02)
Italy: Piemonte	0.04	(0.09)	-0.06	(0.10)	0.03	(0.06)	**-0.24**	(0.06)
Italy: Puglia	0.00	(0.10)	0.08	(0.09)	0.02	(0.05)	0.13	(0.09)
Italy: Sardegna	0.06	(0.15)	-0.13	(0.11)	0.08	(0.08)	0.03	(0.11)
Italy: Sicilia	0.06	(0.30)	**0.23**	(0.10)	-0.04	(0.06)	0.01	(0.06)
Italy: Toscana	**-0.38**	(0.04)	-0.08	(0.10)	-0.03	(0.05)	-0.18	(0.09)
Italy: Trento	0.08	(0.11)	0.04	(0.06)	0.00	(0.04)	**-0.21**	(0.07)
Italy: Umbria	**0.28**	(0.07)	0.03	(0.07)	0.02	(0.05)	-0.10	(0.06)
Italy: Valle d'Aosta	0.00	(0.00)	**0.14**	(0.01)	**0.04**	(0.00)	**-0.56**	(0.01)
Italy: Veneto	0.04	(0.06)	0.05	(0.09)	0.01	(0.04)	**-0.38**	(0.09)
Mexico: Aguascalientes[1]	0.00	(0.10)	-0.07	(0.09)	0.00	(0.05)	**-0.11**	(0.04)
Mexico: Baja California[1]	0.04	(0.09)	0.11	(0.09)	0.06	(0.04)	-0.05	(0.05)
Mexico: Baja California Sur[1]	**0.15**	(0.05)	-0.09	(0.06)	**0.07**	(0.03)	0.00	(0.05)
Mexico: Campeche[1]	**-0.23**	(0.10)	**-0.20**	(0.07)	**0.12**	(0.03)	0.02	(0.04)
Mexico: Chihuahua[1]	-0.03	(0.07)	0.09	(0.10)	-0.04	(0.06)	-0.03	(0.06)
Mexico: Colima[1]	0.00	(0.06)	0.01	(0.06)	0.05	(0.04)	0.05	(0.05)
Mexico: Coahuila[1]	0.10	(0.11)	-0.02	(0.11)	0.04	(0.04)	0.00	(0.08)
Mexico: Chiapas[1]	0.10	(0.07)	-0.12	(0.08)	0.04	(0.04)	-0.05	(0.06)
Mexico: Distrito Federal[1]	0.05	(0.12)	0.08	(0.10)	-0.05	(0.07)	-0.07	(0.07)
Mexico: Durango[1]	-0.01	(0.05)	0.22	(0.17)	-0.14	(0.14)	0.07	(0.06)
Mexico: Guerrero[1]	0.14	(0.10)	0.11	(0.08)	-0.01	(0.05)	0.02	(0.04)
Mexico: Guanajuato[1]	-0.21	(0.18)	0.11	(0.10)	-0.02	(0.07)	**-0.14**	(0.07)
Mexico: Hidalgo[1]	0.07	(0.08)	-0.07	(0.09)	0.00	(0.07)	-0.05	(0.04)
Mexico: Jalisco[1]	-0.15	(0.11)	-0.04	(0.07)	**0.12**	(0.03)	**0.15**	(0.07)
Mexico: Michoacán[1]	0.06	(0.12)	0.00	(0.10)	**0.15**	(0.07)	-0.02	(0.07)
Mexico: Morelos[1]	0.09	(0.09)	-0.05	(0.16)	-0.10	(0.07)	-0.13	(0.08)
Mexico: Mexico[1]	**-0.24**	(0.09)	-0.04	(0.15)	-0.05	(0.07)	-0.05	(0.07)
Mexico: Nayarit[1]	0.12	(0.08)	**0.30**	(0.08)	**-0.12**	(0.04)	**-0.14**	(0.05)
Mexico: Nuevo León[1]	**0.27**	(0.13)	-0.07	(0.15)	**0.16**	(0.06)	0.04	(0.12)
Mexico: Oaxaca[1]	0.02	(0.08)	0.11	(0.10)	-0.05	(0.07)	-0.07	(0.05)
Mexico: Puebla[1]	-0.17	(0.09)	-0.11	(0.07)	**0.08**	(0.04)	0.04	(0.06)
Mexico: Quintana Roo[1]	**0.17**	(0.06)	-0.09	(0.06)	0.02	(0.05)	-0.04	(0.04)
Mexico: Querétaro[1]	**0.24**	(0.09)	0.25	(0.17)	-0.10	(0.14)	-0.08	(0.05)
Mexico: Sinaloa[1]	**0.20**	(0.09)	**-0.28**	(0.06)	**-0.12**	(0.05)	0.00	(0.07)
Mexico: San Luis Potosí[1]	-0.18	(0.10)	0.10	(0.12)	0.04	(0.05)	-0.06	(0.09)
Mexico: Sonora[1]	0.01	(0.21)	-0.16	(0.09)	-0.02	(0.04)	**-0.09**	(0.05)
Mexico: Tamaulipas[1]	**-0.30**	(0.11)	0.09	(0.06)	0.07	(0.04)	0.03	(0.08)
Mexico: Tabasco[1]	0.10	(0.05)	-0.06	(0.09)	-0.05	(0.04)	-0.01	(0.04)
Mexico: Tlaxcala[1]	0.09	(0.10)	0.10	(0.15)	0.03	(0.09)	**0.14**	(0.06)
Mexico: Veracruz[1]	-0.06	(0.13)	0.09	(0.16)	-0.03	(0.12)	-0.05	(0.06)
Mexico: Yucatán[1]	-0.03	(0.08)	0.08	(0.07)	-0.02	(0.04)	-0.03	(0.03)
Mexico: Zacatecas[1]	0.07	(0.05)	-0.11	(0.07)	**0.13**	(0.03)	**-0.09**	(0.04)

Notes: Each column represents a different model where the dependent variable is the residual of an OLS regression model of student marks after accounting for socio-economic status, metacognition strategies, approaches to learning and reading performance. Students with positive residuals have inflated grades because their grades overestimate their cognitive and non-cognitive skills.

Logistic models that account for the dichotomous nature of observed marks in Macao-China, Mexico and New Zealand, and Tobit models that account for the censored nature of failing marks in Austria, Croatia, Hungary, Poland, Serbia and the Slovak Republic do not yield substantively different results.

Estimates statistically significantly different from 0 (zero) at a 95% confidence level are highlighted in bold.

1. Macao-China, Mexico and New Zealand distributed, in the Educational Career questionnaire, the alternative question on whether students received a passing or failing mark. Results for these countries and economies are thus based on a dichotomous variable that does not capture the full variability of marks received by students. Estimates for these countries and economies are based on a logistic regression predicting whether a student received a passing or failing mark.

StatLink http://dx.doi.org/10.1787/888932734191

[Part 1/1]

Table B3.1 Relationship between students' information about their own performance and prospects and their expectation of completing a university degree

	Information about students' own performance and prospects							
	Marks		Reading performance		Mathematics performance		Non-academic programme	
	Coeff.	S.E.	Coeff.	S.E.	Coeff.	S.E.	Coeff.	S.E.
Countries and economies								
Austria	**0.26**	(0.04)	0.23	(0.13)	**0.84**	(0.10)	**-1.75**	(0.19)
Belgium (Flemish Community)	**0.26**	(0.07)	**0.64**	(0.15)	**1.15**	(0.13)	**-1.18**	(0.32)
Croatia	**0.44**	(0.06)	**1.17**	(0.10)	**0.38**	(0.09)	**-2.13**	(0.19)
Hungary	**0.57**	(0.06)	**1.21**	(0.15)	**0.46**	(0.11)	**-1.59**	(0.18)
Iceland	**0.49**	(0.05)	**0.52**	(0.09)	**0.32**	(0.08)	c	c
Ireland	**0.37**	(0.05)	**0.51**	(0.10)	**0.54**	(0.10)	-0.12	(0.10)
Italy	**0.33**	(0.02)	**1.06**	(0.07)	-0.02	(0.06)	**-2.40**	(0.24)
Latvia	**0.34**	(0.05)	**0.80**	(0.14)	**0.28**	(0.13)	-0.81	(1.42)
Macao-China[1]	**0.12**	(0.03)	**0.80**	(0.06)	**0.30**	(0.06)	**-0.68**	(0.25)
Mexico[1]	**0.09**	(0.02)	**0.89**	(0.05)	**0.39**	(0.05)	**-0.72**	(0.10)
New Zealand[1]	**0.17**	(0.03)	**1.12**	(0.08)	**-0.21**	(0.09)	c	c
Poland	**0.84**	(0.05)	**0.36**	(0.10)	**0.65**	(0.09)	c	c
Portugal: ISCED2	**0.57**	(0.07)	**1.18**	(0.13)	0.22	(0.12)	**-1.51**	(0.27)
Portugal: ISCED3	**0.52**	(0.07)	**0.42**	(0.15)	**0.34**	(0.09)	**-1.96**	(0.32)
Serbia	**0.61**	(0.05)	**0.55**	(0.10)	**0.66**	(0.09)	**-1.61**	(0.13)
Singapore	**0.60**	(0.29)	1.01	(0.69)	**1.23**	(0.41)	c	c
Slovak Republic	**0.58**	(0.07)	**0.67**	(0.14)	**0.77**	(0.12)	**-2.30**	(0.42)
Trinidad and Tobago	**0.20**	(0.05)	**0.64**	(0.10)	0.17	(0.10)	-0.17	(0.14)
Regions								
Italy: Abruzzo	**0.37**	(0.08)	**1.26**	(0.19)	0.06	(0.17)	0.17	(2.12)
Italy: Basilicata	**0.36**	(0.10)	**1.20**	(0.16)	0.16	(0.15)	0.00	(0.00)
Italy: Bolzano	**0.21**	(0.07)	**0.62**	(0.13)	0.25	(0.13)	**-1.73**	(0.20)
Italy: Calabria	**0.26**	(0.06)	**1.39**	(0.15)	0.09	(0.14)	0.00	(0.00)
Italy: Campania	**0.39**	(0.09)	**1.26**	(0.12)	0.16	(0.16)	0.00	(0.00)
Italy: Emilia Romagna	**0.17**	(0.07)	**0.85**	(0.12)	**0.55**	(0.11)	-0.25	(0.29)
Italy: Friuli Venezia Giulia	**0.29**	(0.07)	**1.57**	(0.16)	-0.03	(0.15)	**-2.45**	(1.15)
Italy: Lazio	**0.31**	(0.08)	**1.20**	(0.14)	-0.18	(0.16)	-1.13	(0.67)
Italy: Liguria	**0.17**	(0.09)	**0.88**	(0.16)	**0.56**	(0.14)	-1.57	(1.64)
Italy: Lombardia	**0.34**	(0.10)	**1.10**	(0.25)	0.36	(0.22)	-1.93	(1.14)
Italy: Marche	**0.29**	(0.10)	**1.30**	(0.16)	-0.05	(0.14)	0.00	(0.00)
Italy: Molise	**0.29**	(0.09)	**1.15**	(0.18)	**0.51**	(0.16)	**-10.57**	(0.38)
Italy: Piemonte	**0.36**	(0.08)	**0.99**	(0.22)	0.18	(0.21)	**-2.58**	(0.78)
Italy: Puglia	**0.60**	(0.08)	**1.71**	(0.18)	**-0.47**	(0.18)	0.00	(0.00)
Italy: Sardegna	**0.42**	(0.08)	**0.93**	(0.19)	**0.49**	(0.23)	0.00	(0.00)
Italy: Sicilia	**0.33**	(0.08)	**0.99**	(0.18)	0.30	(0.21)	**-12.76**	(1.46)
Italy: Toscana	**0.33**	(0.10)	**1.20**	(0.18)	-0.16	(0.17)	0.00	(0.00)
Italy: Trento	**0.17**	(0.08)	**1.43**	(0.25)	-0.23	(0.21)	**-2.13**	(0.33)
Italy: Umbria	**0.46**	(0.08)	**1.16**	(0.16)	0.07	(0.15)	**-1.66**	(0.84)
Italy: Valle d'Aosta	0.03	(0.11)	**1.22**	(0.21)	0.08	(0.18)	**-14.57**	(0.19)
Italy: Veneto	**0.35**	(0.09)	**1.02**	(0.23)	0.16	(0.25)	**-2.19**	(0.22)
Mexico: Aguascalientes[1]	-0.03	(0.08)	**0.96**	(0.23)	0.15	(0.25)	**-1.08**	(0.22)
Mexico: Baja California[1]	0.04	(0.05)	**1.26**	(0.20)	0.15	(0.20)	**0.37**	(0.10)
Mexico: Baja California Sur[1]	0.06	(0.08)	**0.96**	(0.16)	0.21	(0.22)	-0.53	(0.34)
Mexico: Campeche[1]	0.06	(0.09)	**0.90**	(0.27)	**0.73**	(0.21)	**-2.13**	(0.16)
Mexico: Chihuahua[1]	-0.06	(0.08)	**1.26**	(0.20)	-0.01	(0.21)	**-0.93**	(0.39)
Mexico: Colima[1]	**0.20**	(0.07)	**0.86**	(0.19)	0.31	(0.27)	-0.23	(0.30)
Mexico: Coahuila[1]	-0.07	(0.07)	**1.00**	(0.22)	0.30	(0.20)	-0.38	(0.45)
Mexico: Chiapas[1]	0.00	(0.11)	**1.45**	(0.14)	**-0.33**	(0.14)	**-0.35**	(0.10)
Mexico: Distrito Federal[1]	0.10	(0.07)	**0.76**	(0.26)	**0.55**	(0.22)	**-0.55**	(0.19)
Mexico: Durango[1]	**0.18**	(0.08)	**1.17**	(0.17)	-0.04	(0.19)	**-0.80**	(0.15)
Mexico: Guerrero[1]	**0.17**	(0.07)	**1.01**	(0.25)	0.04	(0.24)	-0.03	(0.14)
Mexico: Guanajuato[1]	0.00	(0.05)	**1.15**	(0.16)	**0.57**	(0.16)	**-0.88**	(0.15)
Mexico: Hidalgo[1]	**0.18**	(0.05)	**1.05**	(0.15)	0.16	(0.13)	**-1.42**	(0.14)
Mexico: Jalisco[1]	**0.27**	(0.07)	**0.83**	(0.19)	0.31	(0.17)	**-1.14**	(0.42)
Mexico: Michoacán[1]	0.01	(0.09)	**1.19**	(0.23)	0.19	(0.20)	**-0.81**	(0.26)
Mexico: Morelos[1]	0.12	(0.06)	0.27	(0.22)	**0.81**	(0.20)	**-1.07**	(0.40)
Mexico: Mexico[1]	**0.20**	(0.07)	**0.91**	(0.18)	0.35	(0.22)	**-1.01**	(0.22)
Mexico: Nayarit[1]	-0.03	(0.09)	**1.18**	(0.17)	0.08	(0.18)	-0.14	(0.39)
Mexico: Nuevo León[1]	**0.12**	(0.06)	0.34	(0.51)	**1.13**	(0.54)	**-1.51**	(0.20)
Mexico: Oaxaca[1]	0.14	(0.12)	**0.81**	(0.15)	0.23	(0.34)	0.23	(0.27)
Mexico: Puebla[1]	0.05	(0.06)	**0.89**	(0.29)	**0.44**	(0.17)	**-0.91**	(0.42)
Mexico: Quintana Roo[1]	0.01	(0.06)	**0.67**	(0.20)	**0.63**	(0.20)	0.13	(0.31)
Mexico: Querétaro[1]	-0.05	(0.08)	**1.49**	(0.19)	0.07	(0.27)	**-1.11**	(0.13)
Mexico: Sinaloa[1]	0.09	(0.05)	**0.94**	(0.23)	0.12	(0.30)	-0.25	(0.22)
Mexico: San Luis Potosí[1]	0.01	(0.08)	**0.46**	(0.21)	**0.87**	(0.22)	**-1.85**	(0.30)
Mexico: Sonora[1]	**0.16**	(0.06)	**0.99**	(0.17)	0.26	(0.24)	-0.73	(0.41)
Mexico: Tamaulipas[1]	0.14	(0.11)	**1.20**	(0.18)	0.04	(0.21)	**-0.73**	(0.19)
Mexico: Tabasco[1]	0.03	(0.08)	**0.60**	(0.15)	**0.76**	(0.14)	**-1.36**	(0.08)
Mexico: Tlaxcala[1]	0.05	(0.08)	**1.15**	(0.15)	**0.26**	(0.12)	**-0.67**	(0.10)
Mexico: Veracruz[1]	0.04	(0.07)	**0.65**	(0.21)	**0.87**	(0.22)	**-1.14**	(0.10)
Mexico: Yucatán[1]	**0.14**	(0.05)	**0.97**	(0.18)	**0.50**	(0.21)	0.04	(0.08)
Mexico: Zacatecas[1]	-0.02	(0.12)	0.56	(0.34)	**0.46**	(0.18)	**-0.79**	(0.11)

Notes: Estimates from a logistic regression model including marks for the language of assessment course, PISA reading and mathematics scores and ISCED programme. Marks are standardised at the country level. Reading and mathematics scores scaled so that one unit represents 100 score points.

Estimates statistically significantly different from 0 (zero) at a 95% confidence level are highlighted in bold.

1. Macao-China, Mexico and New Zealand distributed, in the Educational Career questionnaire, the alternative question on whether students received a passing or failing mark. Results for these countries and economies are thus based on a dichotomous variable that does not capture the full variability of marks received by students. Estimates for these countries and economies are probably underestimated.

StatLink http://dx.doi.org/10.1787/888932734210

[Part 1/1]

Table B3.2 Relationship between students' information about their own performance and prospects, contextual effects, and their expectation of completing a university degree

	Information about students' own performance and prospects								Contextual effects					
	Marks		Reading performance		Mathematics performance		Non-academic programme		School average marks		School average reading performance		School average mathematics performance	
	Coeff.	S.E.	Coeff.	S.E.	Coeff.	S.E.	Coeff.	S.E.	Coeff.	S.E.	Coeff.	S.E.	Coeff.	S.E.
Countries and economies														
Austria	**0.28**	(0.04)	-0.15	(0.13)	**0.98**	(0.12)	**-1.12**	(0.30)	0.09	(0.24)	**1.18**	(0.28)	-0.40	(0.24)
Belgium (Flemish Community)	**0.35**	(0.07)	-0.01	(0.15)	**1.26**	(0.12)	**-1.09**	(0.33)	-0.19	(0.19)	**1.61**	(0.26)	**-0.58**	(0.23)
Croatia	**0.39**	(0.05)	**0.83**	(0.10)	**0.38**	(0.09)	**-1.87**	(0.20)	0.36	(0.20)	**0.77**	(0.27)	-0.09	(0.25)
Hungary	**0.47**	(0.05)	**0.81**	(0.18)	0.18	(0.15)	**-0.93**	(0.22)	0.32	(0.16)	**1.11**	(0.34)	0.03	(0.26)
Iceland	**0.55**	(0.05)	**0.56**	(0.09)	**0.22**	(0.09)	0.00	(0.00)	**-0.35**	(0.13)	-0.11	(0.23)	0.47	(0.24)
Ireland	**0.34**	(0.05)	**0.57**	(0.12)	**0.49**	(0.12)	-0.11	(0.10)	0.36	(0.19)	-0.24	(0.21)	0.17	(0.25)
Italy	**0.32**	(0.02)	**0.38**	(0.05)	**0.20**	(0.05)	**-2.02**	(0.27)	**0.43**	(0.13)	**1.36**	(0.15)	**-0.67**	(0.14)
Latvia	**0.40**	(0.05)	**0.75**	(0.15)	0.17	(0.12)	-0.63	(1.48)	-0.32	(0.18)	0.11	(0.33)	0.50	(0.30)
Macao-China[1]	**0.12**	(0.03)	**0.96**	(0.07)	**0.16**	(0.07)	**-0.73**	(0.26)	0.21	(0.18)	**-0.87**	(0.18)	**0.81**	(0.18)
Mexico[1]	**0.12**	(0.02)	**0.71**	(0.06)	**0.30**	(0.06)	**-0.73**	(0.09)	-0.16	(0.09)	**0.37**	(0.13)	0.12	(0.15)
New Zealand[1]	**0.16**	(0.04)	**1.12**	(0.09)	**-0.21**	(0.10)	0.00	(0.00)	0.13	(0.19)	-0.06	(0.25)	0.00	(0.22)
Poland	**0.88**	(0.05)	**0.20**	(0.10)	**0.69**	(0.09)	**11.97**	(1.89)	0.08	(0.19)	**0.78**	(0.27)	-0.30	(0.31)
Portugal: ISCED2	**0.53**	(0.07)	**1.07**	(0.14)	0.25	(0.13)	**-1.54**	(0.27)	0.34	(0.22)	0.37	(0.30)	-0.27	(0.33)
Portugal: ISCED3	**0.60**	(0.07)	**0.38**	(0.14)	0.17	(0.10)	**-1.89**	(0.32)	-0.40	(0.24)	0.24	(0.54)	**0.81**	(0.41)
Serbia	**0.61**	(0.04)	**0.26**	(0.10)	**0.82**	(0.10)	**-1.41**	(0.16)	0.12	(0.15)	**1.01**	(0.27)	**-0.68**	(0.21)
Singapore	0.55	(0.33)	0.73	(0.69)	**1.33**	(0.42)	0.00	(0.00)	0.55	(1.04)	1.47	(1.53)	-0.68	(1.19)
Slovak Republic	**0.53**	(0.07)	**0.32**	(0.13)	**0.87**	(0.12)	**-2.09**	(0.37)	**0.60**	(0.19)	**0.77**	(0.24)	**-0.52**	(0.22)
Trinidad and Tobago	**0.18**	(0.05)	**0.67**	(0.10)	-0.05	(0.13)	-0.13	(0.15)	0.12	(0.12)	-0.29	(0.22)	**0.56**	(0.23)
Regions														
Italy: Abruzzo	**0.31**	(0.11)	**0.56**	(0.28)	0.11	(0.20)	1.45	(2.28)	**1.13**	(0.30)	**1.11**	(0.45)	-0.13	(0.37)
Italy: Basilicata	**0.34**	(0.09)	**0.51**	(0.17)	0.18	(0.15)	0.00	(0.00)	0.62	(0.36)	**1.48**	(0.44)	-0.47	(0.42)
Italy: Bolzano	**0.25**	(0.08)	0.16	(0.19)	**0.51**	(0.17)	**-1.29**	(0.30)	-0.22	(0.17)	**1.37**	(0.33)	**-0.74**	(0.28)
Italy: Calabria	**0.28**	(0.08)	**0.52**	(0.20)	0.26	(0.19)	0.00	(0.00)	0.47	(0.47)	1.11	(0.60)	0.23	(0.68)
Italy: Campania	**0.37**	(0.08)	**0.45**	(0.19)	0.00	(0.20)	0.00	(0.00)	0.75	(0.41)	**1.47**	(0.34)	0.16	(0.30)
Italy: Emilia Romagna	**0.21**	(0.07)	0.27	(0.15)	**0.40**	(0.15)	0.95	(0.72)	0.08	(0.44)	**1.47**	(0.48)	-0.07	(0.39)
Italy: Friuli Venezia Giulia	**0.40**	(0.07)	0.41	(0.22)	0.32	(0.23)	-0.75	(1.19)	0.17	(0.34)	**2.65**	(0.49)	**-1.00**	(0.45)
Italy: Lazio	**0.23**	(0.08)	**0.95**	(0.19)	**-0.39**	(0.20)	0.09	(1.78)	**1.56**	(0.36)	-0.02	(0.38)	0.63	(0.34)
Italy: Liguria	0.22	(0.11)	0.31	(0.23)	**0.61**	(0.13)	-0.66	(1.71)	0.27	(0.40)	**1.08**	(0.38)	0.10	(0.29)
Italy: Lombardia	**0.34**	(0.09)	0.46	(0.26)	**0.39**	(0.15)	-0.98	(1.26)	**0.96**	(0.49)	**1.12**	(0.36)	-0.05	(0.50)
Italy: Marche	**0.37**	(0.08)	0.39	(0.20)	0.18	(0.19)	0.00	(0.00)	0.47	(0.48)	**1.40**	(0.54)	-0.34	(0.50)
Italy: Molise	**0.30**	(0.09)	**0.47**	(0.24)	0.38	(0.23)	**-9.92**	(0.29)	0.43	(0.26)	**1.22**	(0.39)	0.27	(0.39)
Italy: Piemonte	**0.44**	(0.10)	0.30	(0.19)	0.04	(0.18)	**-1.92**	(0.90)	0.58	(0.48)	0.95	(0.66)	0.41	(0.62)
Italy: Puglia	**0.58**	(0.10)	**0.43**	(0.19)	0.30	(0.18)	0.00	(0.00)	0.76	(0.47)	**2.27**	(0.44)	**-1.41**	(0.34)
Italy: Sardegna	**0.44**	(0.08)	-0.11	(0.23)	**0.91**	(0.26)	0.00	(0.00)	0.37	(0.26)	**1.97**	(0.50)	-0.64	(0.67)
Italy: Sicilia	**0.27**	(0.09)	0.17	(0.17)	**0.61**	(0.16)	**-13.50**	(1.58)	0.86	(0.46)	**1.29**	(0.37)	-0.68	(0.46)
Italy: Toscana	**0.37**	(0.10)	0.32	(0.23)	0.28	(0.17)	0.00	(0.00)	0.53	(0.47)	**1.45**	(0.44)	-0.78	(0.48)
Italy: Trento	**0.20**	(0.10)	**0.43**	(0.21)	0.22	(0.20)	-0.88	(0.53)	0.07	(0.34)	**2.78**	(0.55)	**-1.28**	(0.51)
Italy: Umbria	**0.39**	(0.08)	**0.58**	(0.16)	0.07	(0.15)	-1.43	(0.76)	**1.17**	(0.25)	**0.65**	(0.30)	0.09	(0.29)
Italy: Valle d'Aosta	**0.25**	(0.12)	0.26	(0.25)	0.27	(0.23)	**-13.36**	(0.35)	**-1.18**	(0.53)	**2.51**	(0.43)	-0.79	(0.42)
Italy: Veneto	**0.40**	(0.09)	0.39	(0.20)	-0.04	(0.15)	**-1.48**	(0.46)	**1.28**	(0.60)	1.05	(0.62)	0.45	(0.61)
Mexico: Aguascalientes[1]	0.02	(0.08)	**0.60**	(0.20)	0.17	(0.21)	**-1.11**	(0.23)	-0.04	(0.30)	1.40	(0.75)	-0.75	(0.74)
Mexico: Baja California[1]	0.10	(0.05)	**1.17**	(0.22)	-0.12	(0.24)	**0.31**	(0.13)	-0.58	(0.48)	0.59	(0.43)	0.37	(0.45)
Mexico: Baja California Sur[1]	0.10	(0.08)	**0.81**	(0.18)	-0.02	(0.24)	-0.65	(0.35)	-0.45	(0.44)	0.26	(0.56)	0.80	(0.56)
Mexico: Campeche[1]	0.10	(0.09)	**0.88**	(0.29)	0.34	(0.25)	**-2.14**	(0.22)	-0.31	(0.29)	-0.35	(0.46)	**1.32**	(0.53)
Mexico: Chihuahua[1]	0.01	(0.09)	**1.23**	(0.24)	**-0.64**	(0.25)	**-0.76**	(0.38)	**-0.54**	(0.23)	0.13	(0.52)	**1.26**	(0.54)
Mexico: Colima[1]	**0.16**	(0.07)	**0.81**	(0.23)	0.04	(0.30)	-0.35	(0.30)	0.72	(0.38)	0.00	(0.34)	0.71	(0.48)
Mexico: Coahuila[1]	-0.04	(0.06)	**1.08**	(0.28)	-0.14	(0.22)	-0.34	(0.52)	-0.30	(0.61)	-0.21	(0.70)	1.20	(0.65)
Mexico: Chiapas[1]	0.01	(0.11)	**1.54**	(0.23)	-0.43	(0.27)	**-0.34**	(0.16)	-0.07	(0.52)	-0.24	(0.45)	0.27	(0.60)
Mexico: Distrito Federal[1]	0.15	(0.08)	**0.65**	(0.31)	0.33	(0.24)	**-0.42**	(0.18)	-0.34	(0.26)	-0.09	(0.44)	0.69	(0.53)
Mexico: Durango[1]	**0.16**	(0.07)	**0.99**	(0.22)	-0.17	(0.24)	**-1.01**	(0.23)	0.92	(0.95)	0.44	(0.49)	0.35	(0.56)
Mexico: Guerrero[1]	**0.14**	(0.06)	**0.50**	(0.20)	**0.40**	(0.19)	-0.10	(0.18)	1.07	(0.79)	**1.75**	(0.60)	**-1.55**	(0.79)
Mexico: Guanajuato[1]	**0.10**	(0.05)	**0.62**	(0.22)	**0.55**	(0.18)	**-1.06**	(0.23)	-0.27	(0.43)	1.09	(0.64)	0.09	(0.85)
Mexico: Hidalgo[1]	**0.15**	(0.06)	**0.67**	(0.14)	**0.33**	(0.15)	**-1.77**	(0.19)	0.90	(0.49)	**1.68**	(0.53)	**-1.30**	(0.48)
Mexico: Jalisco[1]	**0.28**	(0.06)	0.42	(0.26)	**0.54**	(0.21)	**-1.12**	(0.55)	-0.25	(0.34)	**1.82**	(0.50)	**-1.31**	(0.45)
Mexico: Michoacán[1]	-0.01	(0.09)	**1.19**	(0.34)	0.22	(0.24)	**-0.85**	(0.26)	0.19	(0.25)	-0.01	(0.70)	-0.05	(0.60)
Mexico: Morelos[1]	0.14	(0.07)	0.31	(0.21)	**0.73**	(0.23)	**-0.95**	(0.41)	-0.32	(0.37)	-0.38	(0.90)	0.63	(1.05)
Mexico: Mexico[1]	**0.23**	(0.08)	**0.72**	(0.21)	0.20	(0.24)	**-0.93**	(0.24)	-0.16	(0.23)	0.31	(0.43)	0.22	(0.49)
Mexico: Nayarit[1]	0.08	(0.10)	**1.21**	(0.21)	-0.15	(0.22)	-0.27	(0.42)	**-0.77**	(0.31)	-0.04	(0.69)	0.65	(0.58)
Mexico: Nuevo León[1]	**0.18**	(0.06)	0.47	(0.41)	0.39	(0.39)	**-1.23**	(0.14)	-0.02	(0.28)	-0.32	(0.73)	**1.51**	(0.71)
Mexico: Oaxaca[1]	0.13	(0.10)	0.63	(0.40)	0.35	(0.36)	0.23	(0.31)	0.01	(0.78)	0.54	(1.32)	-0.52	(1.56)
Mexico: Puebla[1]	0.04	(0.06)	**0.73**	(0.36)	0.24	(0.18)	**-1.21**	(0.42)	0.05	(0.31)	0.10	(0.50)	0.77	(0.44)
Mexico: Quintana Roo[1]	0.05	(0.07)	0.24	(0.31)	**0.81**	(0.27)	0.01	(0.34)	-0.38	(0.58)	1.34	(0.88)	-0.85	(0.87)
Mexico: Querétaro[1]	0.07	(0.08)	**0.68**	(0.23)	0.31	(0.25)	**-1.27**	(0.22)	-0.76	(0.41)	**1.26**	(0.59)	0.04	(0.75)
Mexico: Sinaloa[1]	**0.15**	(0.05)	**0.72**	(0.21)	0.19	(0.30)	-0.25	(0.28)	-0.44	(0.34)	1.02	(0.59)	-0.64	(0.59)
Mexico: San Luis Potosí[1]	0.04	(0.08)	**0.76**	(0.19)	**0.47**	(0.20)	**-1.98**	(0.19)	-0.31	(0.45)	**-1.24**	(0.52)	**1.60**	(0.59)
Mexico: Sonora[1]	**0.19**	(0.07)	**0.86**	(0.21)	0.24	(0.25)	-0.74	(0.39)	-0.15	(0.40)	0.50	(0.43)	-0.09	(0.45)
Mexico: Tamaulipas[1]	0.18	(0.11)	**1.16**	(0.23)	-0.01	(0.23)	**-0.80**	(0.17)	**-1.02**	(0.49)	-0.15	(0.57)	0.64	(0.47)
Mexico: Tabasco[1]	0.02	(0.07)	**0.49**	(0.17)	**0.83**	(0.19)	**-1.41**	(0.18)	0.16	(0.56)	0.47	(0.42)	-0.34	(0.56)
Mexico: Tlaxcala[1]	0.08	(0.09)	**0.90**	(0.14)	**0.39**	(0.14)	**-0.81**	(0.12)	-0.36	(0.44)	**1.75**	(0.86)	-1.19	(0.85)
Mexico: Veracruz[1]	0.07	(0.09)	**0.45**	(0.17)	**0.78**	(0.24)	**-1.23**	(0.10)	-0.06	(0.54)	0.50	(0.53)	0.24	(0.51)
Mexico: Yucatán[1]	**0.18**	(0.05)	**0.39**	(0.20)	**0.68**	(0.25)	0.05	(0.13)	0.21	(0.46)	**1.97**	(0.46)	**-1.41**	(0.59)
Mexico: Zacatecas[1]	0.05	(0.13)	**0.64**	(0.29)	0.15	(0.17)	**-1.00**	(0.18)	**-0.83**	(0.38)	-0.43	(0.50)	**1.17**	(0.54)

Notes: Estimates from a logistic regression model including marks for the language of assessment course, PISA reading and math scores, ISCED programme, and schools' average marks, PISA reading and mathematics scores. Marks are standardised at the country level. Reading and mathematics scores are scaled so that one unit represents 100 score points.

Estimates statistically significantly different from 0 (zero) at a 95% confidence level are highlighted in bold.

1. Macao-China, Mexico and New Zealand distributed, in the Educational Career questionnaire, the alternative question on whether students received a passing or failing mark. Results for these countries and economies are thus based on a dichotomous variable that does not capture the full variability of marks received by students. Estimates for these countries and economies are probably underestimated.

StatLink http://dx.doi.org/10.1787/888932734229

[Part 1/2]

Table B3.3 Relationship between students' marks, performance and programme, background characteristics, contextual effects, and expectation of completing a university degree

	Information about students' own performance and prospects								Contextual effects					
	Marks		Reading performance		Mathematics performance		Non-academic programme		School average marks		School average reading performance		School average mathematics performance	
	Coeff.	S.E.	Coeff.	S.E.	Coeff.	S.E.	Coeff.	S.E.	Coeff.	S.E.	Coeff.	S.E.	Coeff.	S.E.
Countries and economies														
Austria	**0.27**	(0.05)	-0.28	(0.18)	**1.25**	(0.17)	**-0.95**	(0.32)	-0.02	(0.24)	**0.63**	(0.25)	**-0.60**	(0.24)
Belgium (Flemish Community)	**0.37**	(0.06)	-0.21	(0.17)	**1.59**	(0.15)	**-1.13**	(0.35)	-0.11	(0.19)	**1.36**	(0.27)	**-0.73**	(0.27)
Croatia	**0.41**	(0.06)	**0.78**	(0.14)	**0.51**	(0.13)	**-1.76**	(0.21)	**0.53**	(0.20)	0.10	(0.29)	-0.36	(0.25)
Hungary	**0.46**	(0.06)	**0.65**	(0.22)	0.26	(0.19)	**-0.83**	(0.22)	0.18	(0.19)	**0.78**	(0.33)	-0.07	(0.28)
Iceland	**0.47**	(0.06)	**0.54**	(0.11)	**0.24**	(0.10)	0.00	(0.00)	**-0.48**	(0.15)	0.26	(0.26)	-0.28	(0.27)
Ireland	**0.30**	(0.06)	**0.41**	(0.13)	**0.58**	(0.14)	-0.11	(0.10)	0.19	(0.20)	**-0.56**	(0.22)	0.11	(0.27)
Italy	**0.30**	(0.03)	**0.20**	(0.05)	**0.38**	(0.06)	**-1.47**	(0.29)	0.11	(0.12)	**0.74**	(0.18)	**-0.62**	(0.16)
Latvia	**0.34**	(0.05)	**0.78**	(0.20)	0.09	(0.17)	**-12.08**	(1.07)	**-0.37**	(0.17)	0.02	(0.36)	0.02	(0.32)
Macao-China[1]	**0.11**	(0.04)	**1.02**	(0.08)	0.12	(0.09)	-0.51	(0.28)	0.34	(0.19)	**-0.50**	(0.22)	0.17	(0.21)
Mexico[1]	**0.11**	(0.02)	**0.17**	(0.07)	**0.92**	(0.08)	**-0.65**	(0.09)	-0.01	(0.08)	**0.56**	(0.13)	**-0.58**	(0.15)
New Zealand[1]	**0.14**	(0.04)	**1.13**	(0.11)	-0.22	(0.12)	0.00	(0.00)	-0.01	(0.16)	**-0.55**	(0.23)	-0.08	(0.20)
Poland	**0.70**	(0.05)	**-0.41**	(0.12)	**1.23**	(0.12)	**13.48**	(1.72)	0.03	(0.18)	**0.72**	(0.30)	**-1.03**	(0.33)
Portugal: ISCED2	**0.53**	(0.07)	**0.67**	(0.21)	**0.62**	(0.19)	**-1.34**	(0.26)	0.25	(0.22)	0.12	(0.34)	**-0.86**	(0.37)
Portugal: ISCED3	**0.50**	(0.08)	0.22	(0.16)	**0.31**	(0.15)	**-1.69**	(0.32)	-0.34	(0.24)	-0.04	(0.55)	0.54	(0.45)
Serbia	**0.57**	(0.05)	-0.07	(0.13)	**1.16**	(0.12)	**-0.96**	(0.15)	-0.05	(0.14)	**0.70**	(0.27)	**-0.88**	(0.21)
Singapore	**0.79**	(0.39)	1.00	(0.94)	1.50	(0.84)	0.00	(0.00)	1.00	(1.34)	0.98	(2.24)	-1.50	(2.03)
Slovak Republic	**0.48**	(0.07)	0.16	(0.15)	**1.02**	(0.16)	**-2.12**	(0.39)	**0.48**	(0.19)	0.46	(0.24)	**-0.69**	(0.23)
Trinidad and Tobago	**0.10**	(0.05)	**0.44**	(0.12)	0.19	(0.14)	-0.08	(0.15)	0.13	(0.12)	-0.40	(0.23)	0.33	(0.27)
Regions														
Italy: Abruzzo	**0.30**	(0.13)	0.43	(0.29)	0.23	(0.23)	1.57	(1.71)	**0.78**	(0.38)	0.51	(0.63)	0.01	(0.46)
Italy: Basilicata	**0.38**	(0.10)	0.07	(0.20)	**0.61**	(0.20)	0.00	(0.00)	0.60	(0.36)	0.63	(0.43)	-0.40	(0.38)
Italy: Bolzano	**0.28**	(0.09)	0.03	(0.25)	**0.62**	(0.26)	**-0.77**	(0.29)	0.06	(0.26)	0.57	(0.34)	**-0.65**	(0.33)
Italy: Calabria	**0.21**	(0.08)	0.41	(0.26)	0.38	(0.28)	0.00	(0.00)	0.45	(0.46)	0.21	(0.62)	-0.04	(0.61)
Italy: Campania	**0.30**	(0.11)	0.16	(0.22)	0.26	(0.23)	0.00	(0.00)	0.22	(0.41)	**1.02**	(0.32)	0.12	(0.29)
Italy: Emilia Romagna	**0.24**	(0.08)	0.11	(0.23)	**0.55**	(0.21)	0.76	(0.52)	0.07	(0.33)	0.39	(0.55)	0.19	(0.38)
Italy: Friuli Venezia Giulia	**0.33**	(0.09)	0.25	(0.26)	0.47	(0.28)	**-11.97**	(0.35)	0.24	(0.34)	**1.58**	(0.45)	-0.73	(0.41)
Italy: Lazio	**0.20**	(0.08)	**0.77**	(0.16)	-0.14	(0.22)	0.64	(1.93)	**1.45**	(0.49)	-0.05	(0.44)	0.44	(0.44)
Italy: Liguria	**0.28**	(0.14)	0.12	(0.33)	**0.98**	(0.21)	0.10	(1.76)	0.23	(0.45)	**0.87**	(0.43)	-0.25	(0.31)
Italy: Lombardia	**0.31**	(0.09)	0.52	(0.28)	0.34	(0.20)	-0.48	(1.15)	0.62	(0.38)	-0.42	(0.45)	0.48	(0.47)
Italy: Marche	**0.35**	(0.09)	0.29	(0.33)	0.26	(0.32)	0.00	(0.00)	0.18	(0.41)	0.61	(0.41)	-0.25	(0.38)
Italy: Molise	**0.36**	(0.11)	0.02	(0.30)	**0.71**	(0.31)	**-9.00**	(1.48)	-0.23	(0.30)	0.40	(0.48)	0.04	(0.47)
Italy: Piemonte	**0.32**	(0.10)	0.27	(0.25)	0.35	(0.25)	-1.24	(1.11)	0.53	(0.49)	-0.04	(0.63)	0.18	(0.55)
Italy: Puglia	**0.59**	(0.10)	0.12	(0.25)	**0.53**	(0.23)	0.00	(0.00)	0.15	(0.60)	**1.65**	(0.42)	**-1.26**	(0.33)
Italy: Sardegna	**0.40**	(0.11)	-0.25	(0.28)	**1.03**	(0.31)	0.00	(0.00)	0.33	(0.25)	**1.55**	(0.55)	-0.54	(0.67)
Italy: Sicilia	**0.25**	(0.12)	-0.08	(0.23)	**0.88**	(0.24)	**-14.33**	(1.35)	0.67	(0.43)	**1.35**	(0.60)	-0.68	(0.45)
Italy: Toscana	**0.36**	(0.12)	0.17	(0.25)	**0.51**	(0.23)	0.00	(0.00)	0.14	(0.36)	**1.11**	(0.37)	-0.79	(0.43)
Italy: Trento	0.22	(0.11)	0.19	(0.28)	0.50	(0.26)	-0.74	(0.60)	-0.53	(0.43)	**2.43**	(0.65)	**-1.42**	(0.52)
Italy: Umbria	**0.37**	(0.09)	**0.63**	(0.21)	0.16	(0.19)	-0.57	(0.47)	0.29	(0.29)	0.05	(0.31)	0.00	(0.30)
Italy: Valle d'Aosta	0.20	(0.13)	0.26	(0.32)	0.38	(0.33)	**-13.47**	(0.38)	**-1.14**	(0.56)	**1.86**	(0.59)	-0.74	(0.50)
Italy: Veneto	**0.42**	(0.11)	**0.48**	(0.23)	-0.02	(0.14)	**-1.24**	(0.49)	**1.12**	(0.48)	-0.19	(0.39)	0.66	(0.40)
Mexico: Aguascalientes[1]	0.03	(0.08)	0.02	(0.20)	**0.75**	(0.21)	**-0.66**	(0.24)	-0.10	(0.38)	0.93	(0.79)	-0.93	(0.74)
Mexico: Baja California[1]	0.08	(0.06)	**0.63**	(0.25)	0.59	(0.32)	**0.52**	(0.15)	-0.29	(0.53)	**1.25**	(0.51)	-1.18	(0.61)
Mexico: Baja California Sur[1]	0.08	(0.09)	0.36	(0.23)	0.48	(0.32)	-0.51	(0.36)	-0.32	(0.46)	0.21	(0.64)	0.36	(0.58)
Mexico: Campeche[1]	0.06	(0.08)	0.37	(0.30)	**1.03**	(0.30)	**-1.78**	(0.23)	-0.11	(0.35)	-0.08	(0.50)	0.38	(0.76)
Mexico: Chihuahua[1]	0.01	(0.08)	0.54	(0.30)	0.01	(0.34)	-0.52	(0.43)	0.01	(0.29)	0.06	(0.74)	0.79	(0.60)
Mexico: Colima[1]	0.15	(0.08)	0.00	(0.28)	**0.92**	(0.33)	-0.15	(0.33)	0.35	(0.41)	0.66	(0.37)	-0.43	(0.44)
Mexico: Coahuila[1]	**-0.12**	(0.06)	0.23	(0.26)	**0.72**	(0.27)	-0.11	(0.20)	-0.17	(0.48)	0.20	(0.80)	-0.60	(0.81)
Mexico: Chiapas[1]	0.04	(0.13)	**1.23**	(0.40)	0.01	(0.41)	**-0.90**	(0.20)	0.22	(0.40)	-0.42	(0.60)	-0.10	(0.68)
Mexico: Distrito Federal[1]	**0.19**	(0.09)	0.19	(0.34)	**0.82**	(0.36)	**-0.64**	(0.25)	-0.36	(0.23)	0.51	(0.42)	0.11	(0.55)
Mexico: Durango[1]	0.13	(0.09)	0.29	(0.31)	**0.64**	(0.31)	**-1.07**	(0.24)	1.10	(0.97)	0.31	(0.61)	0.15	(0.58)
Mexico: Guerrero[1]	**0.16**	(0.08)	0.22	(0.32)	**0.71**	(0.27)	**-0.32**	(0.15)	0.70	(0.79)	1.13	(0.62)	**-1.54**	(0.66)
Mexico: Guanajuato[1]	0.07	(0.06)	0.22	(0.26)	**0.96**	(0.21)	-0.09	(0.26)	-0.32	(0.37)	0.79	(0.68)	-0.86	(0.82)
Mexico: Hidalgo[1]	0.12	(0.07)	-0.20	(0.26)	**1.34**	(0.31)	**-1.65**	(0.22)	**0.91**	(0.46)	**1.50**	(0.66)	**-2.13**	(0.44)
Mexico: Jalisco[1]	**0.26**	(0.06)	0.04	(0.35)	**0.85**	(0.33)	-0.78	(0.63)	-0.53	(0.33)	**1.77**	(0.52)	**-1.68**	(0.45)
Mexico: Michoacán[1]	-0.04	(0.11)	0.61	(0.38)	**0.98**	(0.29)	**-1.09**	(0.30)	0.44	(0.29)	0.34	(0.75)	-1.08	(0.61)
Mexico: Morelos[1]	0.16	(0.09)	-0.32	(0.34)	**1.38**	(0.32)	**-1.04**	(0.36)	-0.03	(0.36)	0.04	(0.82)	-0.45	(0.92)
Mexico: Mexico[1]	**0.17**	(0.08)	0.12	(0.23)	**1.10**	(0.23)	**-0.64**	(0.24)	-0.07	(0.20)	**0.91**	(0.36)	**-1.06**	(0.41)
Mexico: Nayarit[1]	0.11	(0.11)	**0.87**	(0.34)	0.27	(0.35)	-0.23	(0.44)	-0.59	(0.31)	-0.31	(0.70)	0.13	(0.72)
Mexico: Nuevo León[1]	**0.14**	(0.06)	-0.13	(0.38)	**1.16**	(0.39)	**-0.77**	(0.23)	-0.05	(0.26)	0.10	(0.67)	0.55	(0.68)
Mexico: Oaxaca[1]	**0.18**	(0.07)	0.03	(0.37)	**1.07**	(0.48)	-0.30	(0.21)	0.56	(0.87)	0.26	(1.04)	-0.42	(1.23)
Mexico: Puebla[1]	0.04	(0.06)	-0.02	(0.37)	**1.12**	(0.23)	**-0.89**	(0.19)	0.00	(0.23)	0.53	(0.54)	-0.24	(0.52)
Mexico: Quintana Roo[1]	0.03	(0.08)	-0.31	(0.31)	**1.33**	(0.31)	0.15	(0.36)	-0.41	(0.67)	1.54	(1.07)	-1.38	(1.12)
Mexico: Querétaro[1]	0.06	(0.08)	0.03	(0.30)	**0.92**	(0.35)	**-1.17**	(0.21)	-0.38	(0.39)	1.10	(0.59)	-0.62	(0.69)
Mexico: Sinaloa[1]	**0.13**	(0.07)	0.13	(0.26)	**0.81**	(0.33)	0.12	(0.31)	-0.19	(0.23)	0.95	(0.60)	-1.30	(0.68)
Mexico: San Luis Potosí[1]	0.01	(0.09)	0.43	(0.23)	**0.89**	(0.26)	**-1.73**	(0.16)	-0.22	(0.35)	**-1.39**	(0.64)	0.56	(0.59)
Mexico: Sonora[1]	**0.25**	(0.08)	0.33	(0.27)	**0.78**	(0.33)	-0.66	(0.40)	-0.36	(0.43)	0.77	(0.42)	-0.72	(0.43)
Mexico: Tamaulipas[1]	0.21	(0.12)	0.01	(0.27)	**1.34**	(0.28)	0.06	(0.24)	-0.71	(0.40)	0.77	(0.70)	**-1.16**	(0.53)
Mexico: Tabasco[1]	0.00	(0.08)	0.01	(0.21)	**1.41**	(0.27)	**-0.92**	(0.17)	-0.04	(0.54)	0.52	(0.48)	-0.88	(0.61)
Mexico: Tlaxcala[1]	0.11	(0.08)	0.17	(0.20)	**1.14**	(0.21)	0.05	(0.33)	-0.48	(0.37)	**1.78**	(0.81)	**-1.79**	(0.79)
Mexico: Veracruz[1]	0.00	(0.09)	-0.12	(0.24)	**1.34**	(0.28)	**-1.29**	(0.10)	0.51	(0.58)	-0.17	(0.61)	0.24	(0.60)
Mexico: Yucatán[1]	**0.16**	(0.04)	-0.09	(0.22)	**1.22**	(0.28)	0.21	(0.19)	0.27	(0.52)	**2.13**	(0.58)	**-1.86**	(0.63)
Mexico: Zacatecas[1]	0.08	(0.09)	-0.02	(0.29)	**0.92**	(0.25)	-0.29	(0.16)	-0.13	(0.25)	0.26	(0.36)	-0.69	(0.52)

Notes: Estimates from a logistic regression model including marks for the language of assessment course, PISA reading and math scores, ISCED programme, schools' average marks, and student background characteristics. Marks are standardised at the country level. Reading and mathematics scores are scaled so that one unit represents 100 score points.

Estimates statistically significantly different from 0 (zero) at a 95% confidence level are highlighted in bold.

1. Macao-China, Mexico and New Zealand distributed, in the Educational Career questionnaire, the alternative question on whether students received a passing or failing mark. Results for these countries and economies are thus based on a dichotomous variable that does not capture the full variability of marks received by students. Estimates for these countries and economies are probably underestimated.

StatLink http://dx.doi.org/10.1787/888932734248

[Part 2/2]

Table B3.3 Relationship between students' marks, performance and programme, background characteristics, contextual effects, and expectation of completing a university degree

	Student background characteristics									
	PISA index of economic, social and cultural status		School average *PISA index of economic, social and cultural status*		Student is a girl		Student has immigrant status		Student speaks another language at home	
	Coeff.	S.E.	Coeff.	S.E.	Coeff.	S.E.	Coeff.	S.E.	Coeff.	S.E.
Countries and economies										
Austria	**0.49**	(0.07)	**1.28**	(0.22)	**0.33**	(0.15)	**1.13**	(0.22)	0.10	(0.27)
Belgium (Flemish Community)	**0.53**	(0.07)	0.38	(0.26)	**0.32**	(0.12)	**1.45**	(0.26)	0.02	(0.12)
Croatia	**0.62**	(0.07)	**0.92**	(0.24)	0.21	(0.13)	0.18	(0.16)	0.49	(0.35)
Hungary	**0.66**	(0.05)	0.26	(0.19)	**0.30**	(0.12)	-0.49	(0.28)	0.74	(0.79)
Iceland	**0.75**	(0.06)	**0.70**	(0.15)	**0.28**	(0.08)	**1.43**	(0.41)	0.22	(0.35)
Ireland	**0.54**	(0.06)	0.22	(0.19)	**0.45**	(0.10)	0.13	(0.16)	0.20	(0.22)
Italy	**0.35**	(0.02)	**1.03**	(0.14)	**0.37**	(0.06)	-0.13	(0.13)	0.03	(0.09)
Latvia	**0.60**	(0.06)	0.28	(0.19)	0.09	(0.14)	0.09	(0.21)	-0.09	(0.19)
Macao-China[1]	**0.46**	(0.04)	**0.28**	(0.10)	-0.11	(0.08)	-0.01	(0.07)	0.13	(0.16)
Mexico[1]	**0.34**	(0.02)	**0.13**	(0.06)	**0.85**	(0.04)	-0.14	(0.16)	**0.69**	(0.15)
New Zealand[1]	**0.46**	(0.06)	**0.56**	(0.15)	**0.34**	(0.08)	**0.66**	(0.10)	**0.67**	(0.11)
Poland	**0.74**	(0.06)	**0.39**	(0.16)	**0.94**	(0.12)	**-13.59**	(1.73)	-0.05	(0.62)
Portugal: ISCED2	**0.59**	(0.07)	**0.53**	(0.15)	**0.74**	(0.17)	0.00	(0.22)	0.37	(0.49)
Portugal: ISCED3	**0.45**	(0.06)	0.03	(0.14)	**0.52**	(0.13)	0.14	(0.24)	-0.03	(0.76)
Serbia	**0.62**	(0.05)	**0.78**	(0.22)	**0.79**	(0.11)	0.08	(0.12)	0.10	(0.28)
Singapore	0.61	(0.58)	3.25	(1.73)	-0.26	(0.64)	0.94	(0.89)	1.50	(1.11)
Slovak Republic	**0.48**	(0.07)	**0.79**	(0.23)	**0.42**	(0.12)	0.76	(0.60)	0.10	(0.23)
Trinidad and Tobago	**0.29**	(0.06)	**0.47**	(0.20)	**0.75**	(0.09)	-0.59	(0.32)	0.17	(0.28)
Regions										
Italy: Abruzzo	**0.21**	(0.09)	0.74	(0.44)	0.25	(0.16)	0.56	(0.46)	-0.32	(0.33)
Italy: Basilicata	**0.30**	(0.08)	**1.05**	(0.40)	**0.76**	(0.21)	0.20	(1.03)	-0.03	(0.26)
Italy: Bolzano	**0.44**	(0.09)	**1.52**	(0.38)	0.17	(0.16)	-0.08	(0.34)	**-0.81**	(0.22)
Italy: Calabria	**0.42**	(0.11)	**0.98**	(0.46)	**0.44**	(0.18)	-0.21	(0.70)	-0.23	(0.25)
Italy: Campania	**0.31**	(0.08)	**0.87**	(0.24)	0.36	(0.23)	-0.33	(0.32)	-0.26	(0.19)
Italy: Emilia Romagna	**0.39**	(0.08)	**0.77**	(0.34)	0.31	(0.21)	0.08	(0.33)	0.30	(0.22)
Italy: Friuli Venezia Giulia	**0.44**	(0.09)	**1.42**	(0.38)	**0.40**	(0.20)	0.26	(0.32)	-0.16	(0.22)
Italy: Lazio	**0.43**	(0.10)	0.03	(0.31)	**0.53**	(0.23)	0.22	(0.45)	0.39	(0.31)
Italy: Liguria	**0.45**	(0.11)	0.71	(0.39)	**0.50**	(0.19)	**0.83**	(0.39)	-0.14	(0.40)
Italy: Lombardia	**0.39**	(0.08)	**1.74**	(0.81)	0.13	(0.21)	-0.23	(0.48)	0.10	(0.46)
Italy: Marche	**0.49**	(0.09)	**1.43**	(0.31)	0.28	(0.22)	0.30	(0.49)	-0.01	(0.35)
Italy: Molise	0.13	(0.12)	**1.71**	(0.37)	**0.52**	(0.26)	0.09	(0.70)	**-0.69**	(0.25)
Italy: Piemonte	**0.50**	(0.09)	**1.55**	(0.44)	0.30	(0.26)	-0.16	(0.51)	0.42	(0.50)
Italy: Puglia	**0.25**	(0.09)	**1.09**	(0.44)	**0.53**	(0.20)	0.06	(0.87)	-0.28	(0.31)
Italy: Sardegna	**0.33**	(0.11)	0.19	(0.35)	**0.38**	(0.19)	-1.40	(1.30)	-0.18	(0.24)
Italy: Sicilia	**0.38**	(0.08)	0.38	(0.55)	0.39	(0.24)	**-14.77**	(1.58)	0.20	(0.35)
Italy: Toscana	**0.47**	(0.11)	**0.74**	(0.23)	**0.51**	(0.20)	0.41	(0.39)	0.32	(0.45)
Italy: Trento	**0.37**	(0.12)	**0.84**	(0.41)	0.44	(0.23)	0.67	(0.44)	-0.26	(0.19)
Italy: Umbria	**0.42**	(0.11)	**1.60**	(0.37)	0.26	(0.24)	**0.91**	(0.33)	**-0.41**	(0.20)
Italy: Valle d'Aosta	**0.52**	(0.13)	0.61	(0.39)	0.22	(0.24)	0.83	(0.44)	-0.08	(0.26)
Italy: Veneto	**0.44**	(0.10)	**1.68**	(0.41)	0.13	(0.21)	**1.09**	(0.41)	0.04	(0.19)
Mexico: Aguascalientes[1]	**0.39**	(0.07)	0.25	(0.22)	**0.77**	(0.15)	1.05	(0.93)	0.19	(1.07)
Mexico: Baja California[1]	0.18	(0.09)	**0.58**	(0.24)	**0.85**	(0.24)	0.23	(0.37)	1.26	(0.95)
Mexico: Baja California Sur[1]	**0.27**	(0.08)	0.31	(0.19)	**0.90**	(0.14)	-0.80	(0.55)	**-1.74**	(0.84)
Mexico: Campeche[1]	**0.35**	(0.08)	0.00	(0.17)	**0.61**	(0.21)	0.14	(0.59)	-0.22	(0.29)
Mexico: Chihuahua[1]	**0.44**	(0.10)	0.14	(0.28)	**0.83**	(0.24)	-0.60	(0.93)	0.78	(1.08)
Mexico: Colima[1]	**0.23**	(0.07)	0.16	(0.18)	**1.01**	(0.21)	0.19	(0.65)	0.82	(1.82)
Mexico: Coahuila[1]	**0.37**	(0.13)	**0.63**	(0.32)	**1.28**	(0.28)	-0.47	(1.36)	0.02	(0.93)
Mexico: Chiapas[1]	**0.22**	(0.07)	**0.44**	(0.16)	0.34	(0.20)	-0.75	(0.47)	-0.09	(0.30)
Mexico: Distrito Federal[1]	**0.36**	(0.14)	-0.34	(0.17)	**0.62**	(0.22)	0.30	(0.85)	-0.12	(0.82)
Mexico: Durango[1]	**0.32**	(0.08)	0.09	(0.19)	**0.88**	(0.20)	**-14.85**	(1.11)	**2.75**	(0.73)
Mexico: Guerrero[1]	**0.28**	(0.09)	**0.75**	(0.13)	**0.62**	(0.25)	0.36	(0.69)	**1.09**	(0.43)
Mexico: Guanajuato[1]	**0.48**	(0.07)	0.40	(0.21)	**0.71**	(0.17)	-0.83	(1.16)	0.48	(3.01)
Mexico: Hidalgo[1]	**0.24**	(0.07)	0.41	(0.35)	**1.09**	(0.26)	-0.78	(0.90)	-0.33	(0.37)
Mexico: Jalisco[1]	**0.45**	(0.10)	0.08	(0.18)	**0.75**	(0.21)	-0.02	(1.30)	0.55	(0.50)
Mexico: Michoacán[1]	**0.35**	(0.06)	0.03	(0.26)	**0.89**	(0.20)	**-13.36**	(0.93)	1.30	(1.24)
Mexico: Morelos[1]	**0.48**	(0.12)	0.39	(0.30)	**1.13**	(0.26)	0.25	(0.67)	**14.39**	(0.95)
Mexico: Mexico[1]	**0.34**	(0.07)	0.16	(0.18)	**1.12**	(0.15)	0.17	(0.54)	1.07	(0.60)
Mexico: Nayarit[1]	**0.27**	(0.07)	0.21	(0.20)	0.58	(0.35)	**-1.69**	(0.82)	-0.12	(1.27)
Mexico: Nuevo León[1]	**0.33**	(0.09)	0.20	(0.28)	**0.91**	(0.20)	**1.37**	(0.50)	**13.29**	(1.82)
Mexico: Oaxaca[1]	**0.38**	(0.12)	0.21	(0.31)	**0.70**	(0.22)	-0.22	(0.84)	0.70	(0.37)
Mexico: Puebla[1]	**0.29**	(0.07)	0.13	(0.17)	**1.08**	(0.20)	-0.51	(1.37)	-1.12	(0.97)
Mexico: Quintana Roo[1]	**0.50**	(0.07)	0.07	(0.21)	**0.88**	(0.21)	0.28	(0.37)	0.36	(0.43)
Mexico: Querétaro[1]	**0.27**	(0.08)	0.36	(0.28)	**0.79**	(0.19)	**1.16**	(0.42)	**1.80**	(0.21)
Mexico: Sinaloa[1]	**0.32**	(0.06)	0.25	(0.32)	**0.79**	(0.17)	-1.48	(1.40)	**-13.21**	(1.43)
Mexico: San Luis Potosí[1]	**0.33**	(0.10)	**0.58**	(0.28)	**0.60**	(0.29)	-0.03	(0.92)	0.50	(0.52)
Mexico: Sonora[1]	**0.42**	(0.10)	-0.12	(0.18)	**0.82**	(0.13)	0.18	(0.99)	0.86	(0.59)
Mexico: Tamaulipas[1]	**0.42**	(0.07)	0.21	(0.24)	**1.65**	(0.19)	-1.15	(0.80)	**-13.84**	(1.50)
Mexico: Tabasco[1]	0.15	(0.14)	0.21	(0.21)	**0.80**	(0.18)	-0.82	(0.68)	0.89	(0.67)
Mexico: Tlaxcala[1]	**0.50**	(0.08)	0.12	(0.18)	**1.11**	(0.17)	-1.77	(1.11)	**13.46**	(1.36)
Mexico: Veracruz[1]	**0.55**	(0.12)	0.01	(0.21)	**1.04**	(0.13)	-0.32	(0.67)	**0.71**	(0.35)
Mexico: Yucatán[1]	**0.25**	(0.06)	-0.03	(0.15)	**0.83**	(0.20)	0.76	(0.55)	0.17	(0.28)
Mexico: Zacatecas[1]	**0.21**	(0.10)	**0.88**	(0.14)	**1.17**	(0.26)	1.78	(1.65)	-0.08	(1.02)

Notes: Estimates from a logistic regression model including marks for the language of assessment course, PISA reading and math scores, ISCED programme, schools' average marks, and student background characteristics. Marks are standardised at the country level. Reading and mathematics scores are scaled so that one unit represents 100 score points.

Estimates statistically significantly different from 0 (zero) at a 95% confidence level are highlighted in bold.

1. Macao-China, Mexico and New Zealand distributed, in the Educational Career questionnaire, the alternative question on whether students received a passing or failing mark. Results for these countries and economies are thus based on a dichotomous variable that does not capture the full variability of marks received by students. Estimates for these countries and economies are probably underestimated.

StatLink http://dx.doi.org/10.1787/888932734248

[Part 1/2]

Table B3.4 Relationship between students' marks, other tests, performance and programme, background characteristics, contextual effects, and expectation of completing a university degree

	Information about students' own performance and prospects														Contextual effects					
	Marks		Reading performance		Mathematics performance		Non-academic programme		Testing		Marks x academic programme		Marks x Testing		School average marks		School average reading performance		School average mathematics performance	
	Coeff.	S.E.	Coeff.	S.E.	Coeff.	S.E.	Coeff.	S.E.	Coeff.	S.E.	Coeff.	S.E.	Coeff.	S.E.	Coeff.	S.E.	Coeff.	S.E.	Coeff.	S.E.
Countries and economies																				
Austria	0.10	(0.19)	-0.27	(0.19)	**1.23**	(0.18)	**-1.00**	(0.34)	-0.25	(0.16)	0.19	(0.20)	0.00	(0.09)	-0.02	(0.24)	**0.63**	(0.25)	**-0.60**	(0.24)
Belgium (Flemish Community)	0.55	(0.51)	-0.16	(0.18)	**1.51**	(0.16)	**-1.40**	(0.46)	-0.07	(0.13)	-0.26	(0.50)	0.28	(0.16)	-0.11	(0.19)	**1.36**	(0.27)	**-0.73**	(0.27)
Croatia	0.06	(0.17)	**0.79**	(0.14)	**0.49**	(0.14)	**-1.85**	(0.21)	0.06	(0.14)	0.22	(0.17)	**0.26**	(0.11)	**0.53**	(0.20)	0.10	(0.29)	-0.36	(0.25)
Hungary	0.08	(0.24)	**0.63**	(0.23)	0.27	(0.20)	**-1.00**	(0.22)	-0.29	(0.17)	0.34	(0.24)	0.06	(0.13)	0.18	(0.19)	**0.78**	(0.33)	-0.07	(0.28)
Iceland	**0.56**	(0.15)	**0.50**	(0.12)	**0.28**	(0.11)	0.00	(0.00)	-0.04	(0.12)	0.00	(0.00)	-0.10	(0.15)	**-0.48**	(0.15)	0.26	(0.26)	-0.28	(0.27)
Ireland	**0.43**	(0.12)	**0.40**	(0.15)	**0.59**	(0.16)	-0.20	(0.11)	0.03	(0.11)	**-0.28**	(0.11)	0.14	(0.10)	0.19	(0.20)	**-0.56**	(0.22)	0.11	(0.27)
Italy	-0.14	(0.26)	**0.22**	(0.06)	**0.37**	(0.06)	**-1.26**	(0.27)	0.09	(0.10)	0.39	(0.26)	0.08	(0.06)	0.11	(0.12)	**0.74**	(0.18)	**-0.62**	(0.16)
Latvia	**159.36**	(25.34)	**0.81**	(0.18)	0.08	(0.15)	0.00	(0.00)	0.11	(0.28)	**-158.72**	(25.35)	-0.31	(0.20)	**-0.37**	(0.17)	0.02	(0.36)	0.02	(0.32)
Macao-China[1]	-0.26	(0.51)	**1.02**	(0.08)	0.12	(0.09)	-0.33	(0.32)	-0.10	(0.07)	0.38	(0.50)	0.00	(0.08)	0.34	(0.19)	**-0.50**	(0.22)	0.17	(0.21)
Mexico[1]	-0.11	(0.13)	**0.18**	(0.07)	**0.91**	(0.08)	**-0.63**	(0.11)	0.00	(0.05)	0.20	(0.12)	0.03	(0.05)	-0.01	(0.08)	**0.56**	(0.13)	**-0.58**	(0.15)
New Zealand[1]	**0.23**	(0.08)	**1.13**	(0.12)	-0.22	(0.13)	0.00	(0.00)	-0.14	(0.10)	0.00	(0.00)	-0.11	(0.09)	-0.01	(0.16)	**-0.55**	(0.23)	-0.08	(0.20)
Poland	**22.63**	(2.71)	**-0.42**	(0.13)	**1.24**	(0.12)	0.00	(0.00)	-0.07	(0.19)	**-21.94**	(2.72)	0.01	(0.16)	0.03	(0.18)	**0.72**	(0.30)	**-1.03**	(0.33)
Portugal: ISCED2	**0.94**	(0.32)	**0.69**	(0.22)	**0.62**	(0.20)	**-1.42**	(0.34)	0.05	(0.24)	-0.34	(0.29)	-0.11	(0.25)	0.25	(0.22)	0.12	(0.34)	**-0.86**	(0.37)
Portugal: ISCED3	**0.48**	(0.19)	0.17	(0.16)	**0.32**	(0.16)	**-1.72**	(0.30)	-0.34	(0.21)	0.29	(0.16)	-0.25	(0.17)	-0.34	(0.24)	-0.04	(0.55)	0.54	(0.45)
Serbia	**0.57**	(0.08)	-0.06	(0.14)	**1.18**	(0.12)	**-1.02**	(0.14)	-0.15	(0.10)	0.08	(0.15)	-0.05	(0.11)	-0.05	(0.14)	**0.70**	(0.27)	**-0.88**	(0.21)
Singapore	**45.34**	(13.85)	1.00	(0.94)	1.50	(0.84)	0.00	(0.00)	0.00	(0.00)	0.00	(0.00)	**-44.55**	(14.00)	1.00	(1.34)	0.98	(2.24)	-1.50	(2.03)
Slovak Republic	0.70	(0.47)	0.20	(0.15)	**1.00**	(0.16)	**-2.10**	(0.39)	0.28	(0.27)	-0.04	(0.43)	-0.20	(0.20)	**0.48**	(0.19)	0.46	(0.24)	**-0.69**	(0.23)
Trinidad and Tobago	-0.05	(0.18)	**0.43**	(0.13)	0.14	(0.16)	-0.01	(0.16)	**0.24**	(0.12)	0.16	(0.16)	0.03	(0.12)	0.13	(0.12)	-0.40	(0.23)	0.33	(0.27)
Regions																				
Italy: Abruzzo	**-15.00**	(1.54)	0.51	(0.31)	0.11	(0.23)	**-17.27**	(0.84)	0.16	(0.25)	**15.36**	(1.51)	-0.05	(0.16)	**0.90**	(0.43)	0.48	(0.71)	0.17	(0.50)
Italy: Basilicata	**0.49**	(0.20)	0.08	(0.22)	**0.65**	(0.21)	0.00	(0.00)	**-0.45**	(0.18)	0.00	(0.00)	-0.21	(0.24)	0.60	(0.32)	0.65	(0.46)	-0.60	(0.37)
Italy: Bolzano	**-0.70**	(0.32)	0.30	(0.27)	0.46	(0.29)	**-0.73**	(0.33)	0.30	(0.19)	**1.02**	(0.32)	-0.18	(0.16)	0.27	(0.28)	-0.03	(0.38)	**-0.74**	(0.36)
Italy: Calabria	**0.29**	(0.13)	0.22	(0.23)	**0.61**	(0.27)	0.00	(0.00)	-0.03	(0.20)	0.00	(0.00)	-0.11	(0.15)	0.32	(0.51)	0.80	(0.60)	-0.35	(0.62)
Italy: Campania	**0.41**	(0.13)	0.33	(0.24)	0.16	(0.26)	0.00	(0.00)	-0.29	(0.24)	0.00	(0.00)	-0.16	(0.19)	**0.68**	(0.30)	**0.74**	(0.33)	0.25	(0.28)
Italy: Emilia Romagna	0.11	(0.21)	0.08	(0.22)	**0.57**	(0.21)	0.92	(0.54)	0.02	(0.19)	0.25	(0.17)	-0.19	(0.18)	0.08	(0.33)	0.41	(0.56)	0.19	(0.37)
Italy: Friuli Venezia Giulia	-0.03	(0.16)	0.25	(0.26)	0.47	(0.29)	**-11.86**	(0.37)	-0.20	(0.21)	**0.51**	(0.14)	**-0.28**	(0.14)	0.11	(0.40)	**1.62**	(0.45)	-0.79	(0.42)
Italy: Lazio	-0.61	(0.60)	**0.87**	(0.18)	-0.23	(0.23)	0.22	(0.48)	**0.63**	(0.24)	1.01	(0.57)	-0.28	(0.17)	**1.67**	(0.46)	-0.29	(0.45)	0.70	(0.50)
Italy: Liguria	-0.18	(0.93)	0.06	(0.39)	**1.03**	(0.22)	0.38	(1.96)	-0.13	(0.29)	0.47	(0.92)	-0.06	(0.25)	0.29	(0.45)	0.62	(0.57)	-0.08	(0.43)
Italy: Lombardia	1.14	(1.76)	0.52	(0.29)	0.32	(0.20)	-1.32	(2.64)	0.09	(0.34)	-1.15	(1.72)	**0.47**	(0.19)	0.62	(0.39)	-0.46	(0.46)	0.58	(0.48)
Italy: Marche	0.39	(0.21)	0.41	(0.35)	0.15	(0.33)	0.00	(0.00)	**-0.46**	(0.20)	0.00	(0.00)	0.02	(0.20)	0.27	(0.40)	0.75	(0.49)	-0.27	(0.47)
Italy: Molise	**-17.21**	(2.95)	-0.03	(0.30)	**0.72**	(0.30)	0.00	(0.00)	0.15	(0.17)	**17.37**	(2.97)	0.26	(0.23)	-0.38	(0.31)	0.38	(0.49)	0.06	(0.47)
Italy: Piemonte	**1.12**	(0.57)	0.29	(0.27)	0.32	(0.25)	**-2.70**	(0.78)	0.34	(0.22)	-0.91	(0.52)	0.26	(0.19)	0.45	(0.46)	-0.05	(0.63)	0.20	(0.55)
Italy: Puglia	**0.48**	(0.14)	0.12	(0.26)	**0.52**	(0.24)	0.00	(0.00)	-0.02	(0.23)	0.00	(0.00)	0.18	(0.25)	0.14	(0.60)	**1.67**	(0.46)	**-1.26**	(0.34)
Italy: Sardegna	**0.44**	(0.13)	-0.18	(0.27)	**0.92**	(0.29)	0.00	(0.00)	0.02	(0.23)	0.00	(0.00)	-0.08	(0.19)	0.31	(0.31)	**1.46**	(0.66)	-0.41	(0.80)
Italy: Sicilia	0.11	(0.60)	-0.06	(0.22)	**0.87**	(0.23)	**-13.92**	(1.42)	0.32	(0.31)	0.19	(0.66)	-0.11	(0.19)	0.50	(0.43)	**1.43**	(0.56)	-0.69	(0.47)
Italy: Toscana	0.30	(0.17)	0.14	(0.27)	**0.50**	(0.24)	0.00	(0.00)	0.14	(0.28)	0.00	(0.00)	0.13	(0.16)	-0.15	(0.38)	**1.19**	(0.42)	-0.74	(0.44)
Italy: Trento	0.25	(0.54)	0.19	(0.32)	0.48	(0.31)	-0.83	(0.53)	-0.21	(0.24)	0.08	(0.57)	-0.19	(0.21)	-0.59	(0.50)	**2.57**	(0.65)	**-1.23**	(0.54)
Italy: Umbria	**-0.72**	(0.17)	**0.62**	(0.22)	0.11	(0.19)	-0.45	(0.30)	-0.24	(0.22)	**0.97**	(0.19)	0.22	(0.17)	0.29	(0.29)	0.16	(0.35)	-0.05	(0.33)
Italy: Valle d'Aosta	-0.35	(0.29)	0.20	(0.32)	0.44	(0.34)	**-13.03**	(0.40)	**-0.61**	(0.23)	0.50	(0.28)	0.19	(0.26)	-0.79	(0.63)	**1.54**	(0.60)	-0.60	(0.50)
Italy: Veneto	**-0.57**	(0.20)	**0.51**	(0.24)	-0.01	(0.14)	-0.89	(0.52)	-0.25	(0.27)	**0.93**	(0.22)	0.20	(0.24)	**1.20**	(0.51)	-0.16	(0.44)	0.56	(0.43)
Mexico: Aguascalientes[1]	**-3.33**	(0.38)	0.02	(0.21)	**0.72**	(0.22)	0.41	(0.23)	**0.51**	(0.19)	**3.70**	(0.30)	-0.36	(0.30)	-0.07	(0.35)	0.36	(0.81)	-0.40	(0.73)
Mexico: Baja California[1]	**-3.65**	(0.39)	**0.65**	(0.24)	0.58	(0.32)	**1.80**	(0.26)	0.35	(0.21)	**3.65**	(0.38)	0.12	(0.10)	-0.46	(0.54)	**1.51**	(0.59)	**-1.41**	(0.71)
Mexico: Baja California Sur[1]	-0.05	(0.35)	0.48	(0.25)	0.43	(0.33)	**-1.02**	(0.49)	-0.31	(0.19)	0.25	(0.35)	-0.19	(0.17)	-0.48	(0.49)	0.30	(0.70)	0.09	(0.68)
Mexico: Campeche[1]	**-0.52**	(0.04)	0.35	(0.31)	**1.09**	(0.31)	-0.56	(0.41)	**1.23**	(0.31)	**4.49**	(0.27)	**-3.92**	(0.26)	-0.08	(0.37)	-0.12	(0.53)	0.41	(0.81)
Mexico: Chihuahua[1]	**3.37**	(0.45)	0.56	(0.31)	-0.03	(0.34)	**-1.56**	(0.44)	0.12	(0.18)	**-3.41**	(0.47)	0.14	(0.11)	-0.12	(0.33)	0.25	(0.81)	0.72	(0.64)
Mexico: Colima[1]	-0.08	(0.12)	0.08	(0.31)	**1.04**	(0.37)	0.00	(0.00)	-0.33	(0.20)	0.00	(0.00)	0.30	(0.17)	0.25	(0.46)	0.50	(0.46)	-0.55	(0.42)
Mexico: Coahuila[1]	-0.60	(0.95)	0.25	(0.29)	**0.74**	(0.30)	0.00	(0.00)	-0.38	(0.29)	0.60	(0.98)	-0.14	(0.15)	-0.46	(0.37)	-0.11	(0.83)	-0.16	(0.88)
Mexico: Chiapas[1]	**-3.90**	(0.93)	**1.38**	(0.31)	0.03	(0.33)	0.00	(0.00)	0.05	(0.21)	**3.57**	(0.84)	**0.59**	(0.28)	0.22	(0.47)	-0.27	(0.51)	-0.34	(0.57)
Mexico: Distrito Federal[1]	-0.32	(0.27)	0.27	(0.36)	**0.78**	(0.39)	-0.38	(0.29)	**0.41**	(0.19)	0.36	(0.27)	0.22	(0.13)	-0.39	(0.22)	0.39	(0.47)	0.27	(0.63)
Mexico: Durango[1]	**-3.02**	(0.82)	0.33	(0.31)	0.61	(0.32)	0.00	(0.00)	0.02	(0.24)	**3.46**	(0.84)	-0.41	(0.25)	1.06	(0.99)	0.06	(0.68)	0.28	(0.68)
Mexico: Guerrero[1]	**0.38**	(0.03)	-0.02	(0.34)	**0.78**	(0.30)	-0.24	(0.18)	-0.06	(0.23)	-0.17	(0.11)	-0.13	(0.17)	0.83	(0.82)	1.14	(0.68)	-1.38	(0.82)
Mexico: Guanajuato[1]	-0.25	(0.91)	0.27	(0.26)	**0.96**	(0.23)	0.00	(0.00)	0.14	(0.23)	0.35	(0.90)	-0.05	(0.11)	-0.33	(0.40)	0.79	(0.71)	-0.95	(0.87)
Mexico: Hidalgo[1]	**-4.86**	(0.74)	-0.15	(0.27)	**1.28**	(0.30)	0.00	(0.00)	-0.43	(0.32)	**4.94**	(0.73)	0.04	(0.15)	0.68	(0.43)	**1.57**	(0.68)	**-1.96**	(0.47)
Mexico: Jalisco[1]	**2.94**	(0.56)	-0.06	(0.34)	**0.92**	(0.35)	**-1.58**	(0.60)	0.01	(0.12)	**-2.66**	(0.55)	-0.04	(0.11)	-0.39	(0.28)	**1.83**	(0.54)	**-1.60**	(0.42)
Mexico: Michoacán[1]	-0.76	(0.49)	0.58	(0.40)	**1.05**	(0.30)	**-0.98**	(0.32)	0.02	(0.17)	0.63	(0.46)	0.14	(0.20)	0.43	(0.29)	0.31	(0.79)	-1.01	(0.66)
Mexico: Morelos[1]	0.32	(0.23)	-0.38	(0.37)	**1.49**	(0.31)	-1.00	(0.57)	-0.14	(0.35)	-0.09	(0.20)	-0.06	(0.15)	-0.41	(0.32)	0.74	(0.85)	-1.28	(0.97)
Mexico: Mexico[1]	**3.12**	(0.35)	0.08	(0.23)	**1.15**	(0.23)	**-1.63**	(0.27)	**0.54**	(0.15)	**-2.95**	(0.29)	0.00	(0.22)	-0.06	(0.19)	**1.08**	(0.35)	**-1.19**	(0.40)
Mexico: Nayarit[1]	**4.06**	(0.42)	**0.87**	(0.38)	0.27	(0.37)	**-1.22**	(0.44)	0.28	(0.21)	**-3.97**	(0.45)	-0.01	(0.19)	**-0.75**	(0.36)	-0.46	(0.73)	0.43	(0.74)
Mexico: Nuevo León[1]	**7.42**	(0.41)	-0.15	(0.39)	**1.17**	(0.41)	**-2.09**	(0.21)	**0.88**	(0.14)	**-3.53**	(0.24)	**-3.76**	(0.20)	-0.05	(0.26)	0.11	(0.66)	0.53	(0.68)
Mexico: Oaxaca[1]	**-3.31**	(0.46)	0.17	(0.35)	0.87	(0.45)	0.56	(0.31)	0.08	(0.36)	**3.48**	(0.40)	0.06	(0.25)	0.54	(0.88)	0.23	(1.38)	-0.34	(1.57)
Mexico: Puebla[1]	**-3.40**	(0.43)	-0.01	(0.37)	**1.11**	(0.24)	0.11	(0.23)	-0.28	(0.25)	**3.25**	(0.38)	0.20	(0.20)	-0.05	(0.24)	0.52	(0.55)	-0.26	(0.52)
Mexico: Quintana Roo[1]	0.03	(0.33)	-0.37	(0.32)	**1.40**	(0.30)	0.10	(0.36)	-0.10	(0.21)	-0.02	(0.36)	0.06	(0.20)	-0.48	(0.76)	1.59	(1.12)	-1.43	(1.18)
Mexico: Querétaro[1]	**-3.84**	(0.78)	0.02	(0.32)	**0.87**	(0.38)	0.00	(0.00)	0.42	(0.22)	**3.89**	(0.72)	0.01	(0.25)	-0.53	(0.38)	**1.23**	(0.57)	-0.73	(0.68)
Mexico: Sinaloa[1]	**3.77**	(1.21)	0.13	(0.26)	**0.87**	(0.34)	0.00	(0.00)	0.00	(0.00)	0.21	(0.78)	**-3.85**	(0.51)	-0.24	(0.22)	0.78	(0.60)	-1.14	(0.67)
Mexico: San Luis Potosí[1]	**3.33**	(0.11)	0.39	(0.25)	**0.97**	(0.29)	**-2.56**	(0.18)	-0.04	(0.17)	**-3.10**	(0.09)	**-0.31**	(0.12)	-0.09	(0.38)	**-1.39**	(0.66)	0.50	(0.62)
Mexico: Sonora[1]	-0.14	(0.58)	0.33	(0.28)	**0.76**	(0.34)	**-0.84**	(0.41)	-0.01	(0.20)	0.43	(0.58)	-0.05	(0.39)	-0.29	(0.41)	0.68	(0.44)	-0.56	(0.49)
Mexico: Tamaulipas[1]	0.85	(0.64)	0.21	(0.23)	**1.14**	(0.25)	0.11	(0.31)	0.00	(0.25)	-0.28	(0.60)	**-0.55**	(0.26)	-0.43	(0.39)	0.56	(0.73)	-1.06	(0.55)
Mexico: Tabasco[1]	**-0.59**	(0.19)	-0.09	(0.19)	**1.47**	(0.26)	**-0.81**	(0.28)	-0.26	(0.19)	**0.33**	(0.11)	0.36	(0.19)	0.05	(0.58)	0.37	(0.67)	-0.70	(0.83)
Mexico: Tlaxcala[1]	-0.27	(0.29)	0.22	(0.22)	**1.06**	(0.22)	0.08	(0.37)	-0.08	(0.19)	0.38	(0.26)	0.08	(0.15)	-0.26	(0.43)	1.46	(0.84)	-1.63	(0.87)
Mexico: Veracruz[1]	**2.63**	(0.52)	-0.11	(0.26)	**1.35**	(0.30)	**-2.10**	(0.21)	-0.04	(0.26)	**-2.62**	(0.49)	-0.04	(0.19)	0.62	(0.63)	-0.34	(0.74)	0.31	(0.66)
Mexico: Yucatán[1]	**-3.15**	(0.42)	-0.08	(0.22)	**1.17**	(0.29)	**1.17**	(0.24)	-0.08	(0.27)	**3.24**	(0.41)	0.10	(0.10)	0.09	(0.55)	**2.13**	(0.60)	**-1.88**	(0.69)
Mexico: Zacatecas[1]	**3.33**	(0.38)	-0.08	(0.29)	**0.97**	(0.27)	**-1.30**	(0.24)	-0.14	(0.20)	**-3.20**	(0.42)	-0.08	(0.19)	-0.20	(0.34)	0.32	(0.34)	-0.69	(0.52)

Notes: Estimates from a logistic regression model including marks for the language of assessment course, PISA reading and mathematics scores, ISCED programme, schools' average marks, and student background characteristics. Marks are standardised at the country level and interaction terms. Reading and mathematics scores are scaled so that one unit represents 100 score points.

Estimates statistically significantly different from 0 (zero) at a 95% confidence level are highlighted in bold.

1. Macao-China, Mexico and New Zealand distributed, in the Educational Career questionnaire, the alternative question on whether students received a passing or failing mark. Results for these countries and economies are thus based on a dichotomous variable that does not capture the full variability of marks received by students. Estimates for these countries and economies are probably underestimated.

StatLink http://dx.doi.org/10.1787/888932734267

[Part 2/2]

Table B3.4 Relationship between students' marks, other tests, performance and programme, background characteristics, contextual effects, and expectation of completing a university degree

	Student background characteristics									
	PISA index of economic, social and cultural status		School average *PISA index of economic, social and cultural status*		Student is a girl		Student has immigrant status		Student speaks another language at home	
	Coeff.	S.E.	Coeff.	S.E.	Coeff.	S.E.	Coeff.	S.E.	Coeff.	S.E.
Countries and economies										
Austria	**0.49**	(0.07)	**1.28**	(0.22)	**0.33**	(0.15)	**1.13**	(0.22)	0.10	(0.27)
Belgium (Flemish Community)	**0.53**	(0.07)	0.38	(0.26)	**0.32**	(0.12)	**1.45**	(0.26)	0.02	(0.12)
Croatia	**0.62**	(0.07)	**0.92**	(0.24)	0.21	(0.13)	0.18	(0.16)	0.49	(0.35)
Hungary	**0.66**	(0.05)	0.26	(0.19)	**0.30**	(0.12)	-0.49	(0.28)	0.74	(0.79)
Iceland	**0.75**	(0.06)	**0.70**	(0.15)	**0.28**	(0.08)	**1.43**	(0.41)	0.22	(0.35)
Ireland	**0.54**	(0.06)	0.22	(0.19)	**0.45**	(0.10)	0.13	(0.16)	0.20	(0.22)
Italy	**0.35**	(0.02)	**1.03**	(0.14)	**0.37**	(0.06)	-0.13	(0.13)	-0.03	(0.09)
Latvia	**0.60**	(0.06)	0.28	(0.19)	0.09	(0.14)	0.09	(0.21)	-0.09	(0.19)
Macao-China[1]	**0.46**	(0.04)	**0.28**	(0.10)	-0.11	(0.08)	-0.01	(0.07)	0.13	(0.16)
Mexico[1]	**0.34**	(0.02)	**0.13**	(0.06)	**0.85**	(0.04)	-0.14	(0.16)	**0.69**	(0.15)
New Zealand[1]	**0.46**	(0.06)	**0.56**	(0.15)	**0.34**	(0.08)	**0.66**	(0.10)	**0.67**	(0.11)
Poland	**0.74**	(0.06)	**0.39**	(0.16)	**0.94**	(0.12)	**-13.59**	(1.73)	-0.05	(0.62)
Portugal: ISCED2	**0.59**	(0.07)	**0.53**	(0.15)	**0.74**	(0.17)	0.00	(0.22)	0.37	(0.49)
Portugal: ISCED3	**0.45**	(0.06)	0.03	(0.14)	**0.52**	(0.13)	0.14	(0.24)	-0.03	(0.76)
Serbia	**0.62**	(0.05)	**0.78**	(0.22)	**0.79**	(0.11)	0.08	(0.12)	0.10	(0.28)
Singapore	0.61	(0.58)	3.25	(1.73)	-0.26	(0.64)	0.94	(0.89)	1.50	(1.11)
Slovak Republic	**0.48**	(0.07)	**0.79**	(0.23)	**0.42**	(0.12)	0.76	(0.60)	0.10	(0.23)
Trinidad and Tobago	**0.29**	(0.06)	**0.47**	(0.20)	**0.75**	(0.09)	-0.59	(0.32)	0.17	(0.28)
Regions										
Italy: Abruzzo	**0.26**	(0.10)	0.58	(0.44)	0.31	(0.16)	0.61	(0.48)	-0.21	(0.33)
Italy: Basilicata	**0.35**	(0.09)	**0.95**	(0.47)	**0.86**	(0.21)	-0.34	(1.11)	-0.18	(0.26)
Italy: Bolzano	**0.46**	(0.09)	**1.99**	(0.40)	0.05	(0.19)	0.57	(0.40)	**-0.52**	(0.25)
Italy: Calabria	**0.50**	(0.11)	0.79	(0.43)	**0.56**	(0.18)	-0.29	(0.81)	-0.32	(0.24)
Italy: Campania	**0.31**	(0.08)	**0.61**	(0.24)	0.32	(0.25)	-0.22	(0.34)	-0.26	(0.22)
Italy: Emilia Romagna	**0.39**	(0.08)	**0.77**	(0.35)	0.32	(0.21)	0.08	(0.33)	0.30	(0.22)
Italy: Friuli Venezia Giulia	**0.43**	(0.10)	**1.51**	(0.40)	**0.39**	(0.20)	0.25	(0.34)	-0.16	(0.22)
Italy: Lazio	**0.42**	(0.10)	0.02	(0.31)	0.41	(0.21)	-0.06	(0.44)	0.44	(0.33)
Italy: Liguria	**0.42**	(0.13)	**1.03**	(0.41)	**0.53**	(0.18)	**0.89**	(0.45)	-0.29	(0.43)
Italy: Lombardia	**0.40**	(0.08)	**1.68**	(0.80)	0.16	(0.19)	-0.28	(0.50)	0.10	(0.45)
Italy: Marche	**0.49**	(0.10)	**1.14**	(0.27)	0.29	(0.24)	0.52	(0.47)	0.05	(0.37)
Italy: Molise	0.11	(0.12)	**1.78**	(0.37)	0.49	(0.28)	0.34	(0.67)	**-0.58**	(0.25)
Italy: Piemonte	**0.51**	(0.09)	**1.40**	(0.42)	0.30	(0.27)	-0.07	(0.54)	0.45	(0.52)
Italy: Puglia	**0.25**	(0.09)	**1.07**	(0.43)	**0.51**	(0.21)	0.01	(0.83)	-0.29	(0.35)
Italy: Sardegna	**0.29**	(0.12)	0.20	(0.38)	0.36	(0.18)	-0.05	(0.99)	-0.30	(0.29)
Italy: Sicilia	**0.38**	(0.08)	0.37	(0.51)	0.36	(0.23)	**-14.66**	(1.53)	0.26	(0.36)
Italy: Toscana	**0.45**	(0.11)	**0.75**	(0.22)	**0.46**	(0.22)	0.17	(0.42)	0.06	(0.47)
Italy: Trento	**0.35**	(0.13)	0.81	(0.45)	**0.56**	(0.26)	0.27	(0.41)	-0.17	(0.21)
Italy: Umbria	**0.34**	(0.11)	**1.55**	(0.39)	0.14	(0.23)	**0.82**	(0.36)	-0.37	(0.24)
Italy: Valle d'Aosta	**0.53**	(0.13)	0.62	(0.40)	0.27	(0.25)	0.81	(0.45)	-0.09	(0.25)
Italy: Veneto	**0.44**	(0.10)	**1.63**	(0.42)	0.12	(0.21)	**1.11**	(0.41)	0.05	(0.20)
Mexico: Aguascalientes[1]	**0.38**	(0.07)	0.31	(0.21)	**0.79**	(0.17)	1.05	(0.89)	0.01	(0.99)
Mexico: Baja California[1]	0.18	(0.09)	**0.57**	(0.25)	**0.86**	(0.24)	0.24	(0.37)	1.21	(0.92)
Mexico: Baja California Sur[1]	**0.25**	(0.07)	0.32	(0.20)	**0.89**	(0.14)	-1.04	(0.59)	**-1.74**	(0.86)
Mexico: Campeche[1]	**0.36**	(0.08)	0.00	(0.19)	**0.64**	(0.21)	0.18	(0.61)	-0.23	(0.31)
Mexico: Chihuahua[1]	**0.45**	(0.11)	0.09	(0.29)	**0.83**	(0.24)	-0.64	(0.92)	0.73	(1.08)
Mexico: Colima[1]	**0.23**	(0.08)	0.17	(0.21)	**0.99**	(0.21)	0.32	(0.64)	**13.34**	(0.79)
Mexico: Coahuila[1]	**0.31**	(0.10)	0.60	(0.39)	**1.36**	(0.24)	-0.48	(1.32)	0.08	(0.97)
Mexico: Chiapas[1]	**0.25**	(0.07)	**0.46**	(0.21)	**0.35**	(0.17)	-0.80	(0.53)	-0.02	(0.33)
Mexico: Distrito Federal[1]	**0.40**	(0.15)	**-0.48**	(0.21)	**0.72**	(0.21)	0.37	(0.82)	-0.13	(0.82)
Mexico: Durango[1]	**0.32**	(0.08)	0.13	(0.18)	**0.85**	(0.20)	**-14.18**	(1.24)	**2.55**	(0.66)
Mexico: Guerrero[1]	**0.23**	(0.09)	**0.65**	(0.19)	**0.67**	(0.28)	0.42	(0.69)	0.39	(0.39)
Mexico: Guanajuato[1]	**0.45**	(0.06)	**0.43**	(0.20)	**0.72**	(0.18)	-0.87	(1.16)	0.45	(3.04)
Mexico: Hidalgo[1]	**0.24**	(0.07)	0.26	(0.35)	**1.09**	(0.27)	-0.95	(0.90)	-0.29	(0.43)
Mexico: Jalisco[1]	**0.39**	(0.08)	0.20	(0.15)	**0.79**	(0.17)	0.83	(1.57)	0.42	(0.47)
Mexico: Michoacán[1]	**0.32**	(0.07)	0.02	(0.26)	**1.01**	(0.21)	**-13.51**	(0.86)	1.29	(1.21)
Mexico: Morelos[1]	**0.47**	(0.13)	0.26	(0.27)	**1.23**	(0.28)	-0.08	(0.87)	**14.23**	(0.82)
Mexico: Mexico[1]	**0.34**	(0.07)	0.10	(0.16)	**1.12**	(0.15)	0.27	(0.57)	1.05	(0.56)
Mexico: Nayarit[1]	**0.28**	(0.07)	0.23	(0.19)	0.61	(0.38)	-1.61	(0.95)	0.40	(1.28)
Mexico: Nuevo León[1]	**0.34**	(0.09)	0.21	(0.29)	**0.88**	(0.20)	**1.39**	(0.50)	**14.29**	(0.81)
Mexico: Oaxaca[1]	**0.38**	(0.13)	0.29	(0.32)	**0.65**	(0.21)	-0.21	(0.84)	0.74	(0.38)
Mexico: Puebla[1]	**0.29**	(0.07)	0.13	(0.16)	**1.07**	(0.20)	-0.48	(1.37)	-1.08	(0.97)
Mexico: Quintana Roo[1]	**0.50**	(0.07)	0.06	(0.21)	**0.88**	(0.22)	0.30	(0.37)	0.28	(0.44)
Mexico: Querétaro[1]	**0.29**	(0.08)	0.37	(0.31)	**0.81**	(0.20)	**1.02**	(0.41)	**1.80**	(0.19)
Mexico: Sinaloa[1]	**0.32**	(0.06)	0.26	(0.32)	**0.86**	(0.17)	-1.44	(1.41)	**-13.26**	(1.43)
Mexico: San Luis Potosí[1]	**0.34**	(0.10)	**0.58**	(0.29)	0.60	(0.31)	-0.10	(0.88)	0.46	(0.53)
Mexico: Sonora[1]	**0.42**	(0.11)	-0.14	(0.18)	**0.83**	(0.14)	0.18	(0.97)	0.89	(0.59)
Mexico: Tamaulipas[1]	**0.42**	(0.08)	0.28	(0.26)	**1.59**	(0.19)	-1.49	(0.90)	**-13.85**	(1.83)
Mexico: Tabasco[1]	0.18	(0.16)	0.10	(0.18)	**0.87**	(0.17)	-0.90	(0.75)	0.12	(0.72)
Mexico: Tlaxcala[1]	**0.46**	(0.08)	0.13	(0.18)	**1.07**	(0.18)	-1.56	(1.10)	**13.38**	(1.33)
Mexico: Veracruz[1]	**0.58**	(0.13)	0.06	(0.23)	**1.05**	(0.15)	-0.33	(0.81)	0.76	(0.44)
Mexico: Yucatán[1]	**0.25**	(0.06)	-0.05	(0.16)	**0.82**	(0.20)	0.71	(0.54)	0.27	(0.30)
Mexico: Zacatecas[1]	**0.19**	(0.09)	**0.87**	(0.16)	**1.20**	(0.27)	1.70	(1.60)	0.20	(1.17)

Notes: Estimates from a logistic regression model including marks for the language of assessment course, PISA reading and mathematics scores, ISCED programme, schools' average marks, and student background characteristics. Marks are standardised at the country level and interaction terms. Reading and mathematics scores are scaled so that one unit represents 100 score points.

Estimates statistically significantly different from 0 (zero) at a 95% confidence level are highlighted in bold.

1. Macao-China, Mexico and New Zealand distributed, in the Educational Career questionnaire, the alternative question on whether students received a passing or failing mark. Results for these countries and economies are thus based on a dichotomous variable that does not capture the full variability of marks received by students. Estimates for these countries and economies are probably underestimated.

StatLink http://dx.doi.org/10.1787/888932734267

[Part 1/1]

Table B3.5 Relationship between students' background characteristics and their expectation of completing a university degree

	Student background characteristics							
	Student is a girl		*PISA index of economic, social and cultural status*		Student has an immigrant background		Student speaks another language at home	
	Coeff.	S.E.	Coeff.	S.E.	Coeff.	S.E.	Coeff.	S.E.
Countries and economies								
Austria	**0.29**	(0.10)	**1.16**	(0.06)	**0.69**	(0.18)	0.04	(0.24)
Belgium (Flemish Community)	**0.26**	(0.10)	**1.03**	(0.06)	0.37	(0.30)	-0.05	(0.14)
Croatia	**0.81**	(0.10)	**1.07**	(0.06)	0.05	(0.12)	0.32	(0.35)
Hungary	**0.73**	(0.10)	**1.33**	(0.05)	-0.18	(0.27)	0.03	(0.52)
Iceland	**0.55**	(0.07)	**1.02**	(0.06)	**1.02**	(0.36)	0.01	(0.30)
Ireland	**0.43**	(0.08)	**0.86**	(0.06)	-0.02	(0.15)	0.08	(0.21)
Italy	**0.67**	(0.06)	**0.79**	(0.02)	**-0.32**	(0.11)	**-0.41**	(0.08)
Latvia	**0.55**	(0.09)	**0.90**	(0.06)	0.10	(0.19)	-0.19	(0.20)
Macao-China[1]	**0.17**	(0.06)	**0.63**	(0.04)	0.05	(0.06)	-0.16	(0.10)
Mexico[1]	**0.74**	(0.03)	**0.58**	(0.02)	**-0.87**	(0.15)	0.19	(0.13)
New Zealand[1]	**0.71**	(0.06)	**0.82**	(0.05)	**0.67**	(0.10)	0.17	(0.10)
Poland	**1.00**	(0.07)	**1.18**	(0.04)	**-9.99**	(1.42)	-0.28	(0.50)
Portugal: ISCED2	**0.83**	(0.10)	**0.95**	(0.06)	0.06	(0.18)	0.31	(0.36)
Portugal: ISCED3	**0.73**	(0.09)	**0.74**	(0.05)	0.00	(0.18)	-0.10	(0.57)
Serbia	**0.83**	(0.08)	**1.00**	(0.05)	**0.30**	(0.11)	-0.19	(0.27)
Singapore	**0.34**	(0.09)	**0.79**	(0.06)	**0.57**	(0.14)	**-0.36**	(0.09)
Slovak Republic	**0.76**	(0.08)	**1.08**	(0.06)	0.47	(0.53)	-0.33	(0.29)
Trinidad and Tobago	**0.87**	(0.08)	**0.55**	(0.05)	-0.51	(0.32)	-0.20	(0.30)
Regions								
Italy: Abruzzo	**0.75**	(0.15)	**0.75**	(0.07)	-0.18	(0.46)	**-0.71**	(0.34)
Italy: Basilicata	**0.93**	(0.16)	**0.77**	(0.09)	0.19	(0.94)	-0.26	(0.33)
Italy: Bolzano	**0.41**	(0.11)	**0.89**	(0.08)	**-0.64**	(0.32)	**-0.90**	(0.15)
Italy: Calabria	**0.92**	(0.16)	**0.87**	(0.10)	-0.59	(0.86)	-0.41	(0.21)
Italy: Campania	**0.72**	(0.19)	**0.77**	(0.09)	0.08	(0.68)	**-0.85**	(0.24)
Italy: Emilia Romagna	**0.29**	(0.14)	**0.86**	(0.07)	**-0.54**	(0.26)	-0.22	(0.20)
Italy: Friuli Venezia Giulia	**0.91**	(0.17)	**0.95**	(0.11)	-0.12	(0.28)	-0.34	(0.21)
Italy: Lazio	**1.02**	(0.15)	**0.75**	(0.09)	0.03	(0.39)	-0.15	(0.32)
Italy: Liguria	**0.52**	(0.17)	**0.71**	(0.13)	0.12	(0.36)	-0.41	(0.41)
Italy: Lombardia	**0.46**	(0.21)	**0.87**	(0.08)	-0.46	(0.30)	-0.53	(0.36)
Italy: Marche	**0.77**	(0.15)	**0.86**	(0.09)	-0.10	(0.40)	-0.42	(0.33)
Italy: Molise	**0.74**	(0.17)	**0.70**	(0.10)	-0.45	(0.65)	**-1.22**	(0.25)
Italy: Piemonte	**0.62**	(0.22)	**1.07**	(0.09)	-0.46	(0.36)	-0.06	(0.40)
Italy: Puglia	**0.95**	(0.15)	**0.78**	(0.07)	-0.87	(0.76)	-0.37	(0.28)
Italy: Sardegna	**0.69**	(0.12)	**0.70**	(0.10)	-1.63	(1.05)	-0.56	(0.29)
Italy: Sicilia	**0.56**	(0.18)	**0.83**	(0.05)	**-13.10**	(1.04)	-0.06	(0.26)
Italy: Toscana	**0.88**	(0.17)	**0.78**	(0.10)	0.04	(0.32)	0.12	(0.34)
Italy: Trento	**0.76**	(0.17)	**0.82**	(0.10)	0.04	(0.27)	**-0.45**	(0.18)
Italy: Umbria	**0.69**	(0.14)	**0.94**	(0.09)	0.12	(0.33)	**-0.55**	(0.19)
Italy: Valle d'Aosta	**0.42**	(0.15)	**0.86**	(0.11)	0.35	(0.38)	-0.16	(0.24)
Italy: Veneto	**0.64**	(0.19)	**0.91**	(0.12)	0.42	(0.31)	**-0.45**	(0.20)
Mexico: Aguascalientes[1]	**0.70**	(0.14)	**0.63**	(0.07)	0.51	(0.98)	0.22	(1.07)
Mexico: Baja California[1]	**0.87**	(0.14)	**0.52**	(0.07)	**-0.94**	(0.35)	0.49	(1.08)
Mexico: Baja California Sur[1]	**0.93**	(0.13)	**0.52**	(0.06)	**-1.50**	(0.47)	-1.34	(0.87)
Mexico: Campeche[1]	**0.57**	(0.17)	**0.52**	(0.06)	-0.75	(0.72)	-0.19	(0.35)
Mexico: Chihuahua[1]	**0.96**	(0.20)	**0.75**	(0.10)	-1.51	(0.93)	0.25	(1.05)
Mexico: Colima[1]	**0.92**	(0.18)	**0.48**	(0.05)	-0.42	(0.69)	0.32	(1.71)
Mexico: Coahuila[1]	**1.20**	(0.18)	**0.66**	(0.11)	-1.02	(1.80)	0.48	(0.88)
Mexico: Chiapas[1]	**0.55**	(0.15)	**0.43**	(0.06)	**-1.31**	(0.50)	**-0.65**	(0.25)
Mexico: Distrito Federal[1]	**0.46**	(0.19)	**0.56**	(0.14)	0.05	(0.94)	-0.77	(0.96)
Mexico: Durango[1]	**0.80**	(0.13)	**0.53**	(0.08)	**-14.71**	(1.42)	0.86	(0.52)
Mexico: Guerrero[1]	**0.61**	(0.19)	**0.57**	(0.09)	-0.30	(0.70)	0.75	(0.43)
Mexico: Guanajuato[1]	**0.66**	(0.12)	**0.90**	(0.05)	-1.30	(1.47)	0.47	(1.84)
Mexico: Hidalgo[1]	**0.86**	(0.18)	**0.55**	(0.09)	-1.38	(0.77)	**-0.58**	(0.29)
Mexico: Jalisco[1]	**0.77**	(0.13)	**0.64**	(0.08)	-1.19	(1.59)	-0.25	(0.61)
Mexico: Michoacán[1]	**0.60**	(0.16)	**0.50**	(0.06)	**-14.18**	(0.77)	1.74	(1.29)
Mexico: Morelos[1]	**0.87**	(0.20)	**0.62**	(0.08)	-1.17	(0.63)	**14.21**	(1.17)
Mexico: Mexico[1]	**1.01**	(0.17)	**0.56**	(0.07)	-0.86	(0.55)	0.32	(0.59)
Mexico: Nayarit[1]	**0.74**	(0.27)	**0.45**	(0.07)	**-2.04**	(0.83)	-0.42	(1.14)
Mexico: Nuevo León[1]	**0.69**	(0.18)	**0.82**	(0.12)	0.48	(0.38)	**13.51**	(1.19)
Mexico: Oaxaca[1]	**0.62**	(0.14)	**0.45**	(0.09)	-0.86	(0.80)	0.10	(0.38)
Mexico: Puebla[1]	**0.83**	(0.17)	**0.55**	(0.08)	-1.24	(1.19)	-0.94	(1.14)
Mexico: Quintana Roo[1]	**0.58**	(0.16)	**0.76**	(0.07)	-0.85	(0.47)	-0.04	(0.43)
Mexico: Querétaro[1]	**0.64**	(0.15)	**0.78**	(0.08)	0.26	(0.48)	**2.39**	(0.24)
Mexico: Sinaloa[1]	**0.71**	(0.11)	**0.52**	(0.06)	-2.15	(1.36)	**-12.73**	(1.41)
Mexico: San Luis Potosí[1]	**0.53**	(0.22)	**0.61**	(0.08)	-0.87	(0.78)	0.39	(0.41)
Mexico: Sonora[1]	**0.89**	(0.11)	**0.56**	(0.08)	-0.68	(0.92)	0.57	(0.63)
Mexico: Tamaulipas[1]	**1.32**	(0.15)	**0.60**	(0.04)	**-1.89**	(0.82)	**-13.45**	(1.43)
Mexico: Tabasco[1]	**0.65**	(0.12)	**0.34**	(0.11)	**-1.55**	(0.63)	0.45	(0.59)
Mexico: Tlaxcala[1]	**0.90**	(0.13)	**0.65**	(0.08)	**-2.39**	(1.05)	**13.03**	(1.40)
Mexico: Veracruz[1]	**0.68**	(0.09)	**0.65**	(0.12)	-0.75	(0.63)	0.62	(0.43)
Mexico: Yucatán[1]	**0.62**	(0.16)	**0.54**	(0.06)	-0.36	(0.63)	-0.40	(0.29)
Mexico: Zacatecas[1]	**0.98**	(0.22)	**0.59**	(0.10)	0.74	(1.39)	-0.15	(0.89)

Notes: Estimates from a logistic regression model including student background characteristics. Marks are standardised at the country level and interaction terms. Reading and mathematics scores are scaled so that one unit represents 100 score points.

Estimates statistically significantly different from 0 (zero) at a 95% confidence level are highlighted in bold.

1. Macao-China, Mexico and New Zealand distributed, in the Educational Career questionnaire, the alternative question on whether students received a passing or failing mark. Results for these countries and economies are thus based on a dichotomous variable that does not capture the full variability of marks received by students. Estimates for these countries and economies are probably underestimated.

StatLink http://dx.doi.org/10.1787/888932734286

[Part 1/1]

Table B3.6 Relationship between students' background characteristics, performance and programme, and their expectation of completing a university degree

	Information about students' own performance						Student background characteristics							
	Reading performance		Mathematics performance		Non-academic programme		Student is a girl		*PISA index of economic, social and cultural status*		Student has an immigrant background		Student speaks another language at home	
	Coeff.	S.E.	Coeff.	S.E.	Coeff.	S.E.	Coeff.	S.E.	Coeff.	S.E.	Coeff.	S.E.	Coeff.	S.E.
Countries and economies														
Austria	0.07	(0.15)	**1.13**	(0.13)	**-1.36**	(0.20)	**0.47**	(0.14)	**0.69**	(0.07)	**1.16**	(0.21)	0.08	(0.25)
Belgium (Flemish Community)	**0.45**	(0.15)	**1.42**	(0.14)	**-0.99**	(0.36)	**0.43**	(0.12)	**0.66**	(0.06)	**1.43**	(0.28)	-0.03	(0.11)
Croatia	**1.11**	(0.12)	**0.56**	(0.12)	**-2.01**	(0.21)	**0.43**	(0.13)	**0.74**	(0.06)	0.24	(0.15)	0.59	(0.36)
Hungary	**1.10**	(0.18)	**0.55**	(0.14)	**-1.31**	(0.20)	**0.53**	(0.10)	**0.83**	(0.05)	-0.36	(0.30)	0.72	(0.72)
Iceland	**0.61**	(0.10)	**0.35**	(0.10)	c	c	**0.36**	(0.08)	**0.88**	(0.06)	**1.41**	(0.42)	0.28	(0.34)
Ireland	**0.37**	(0.12)	**0.62**	(0.12)	0.00	(0.11)	**0.41**	(0.10)	**0.58**	(0.06)	0.12	(0.15)	0.21	(0.20)
Italy	**0.84**	(0.06)	**0.16**	(0.06)	**-1.85**	(0.25)	**0.45**	(0.06)	**0.61**	(0.02)	0.00	(0.12)	-0.15	(0.08)
Latvia	**0.90**	(0.19)	0.20	(0.18)	**-12.28**	(1.02)	0.25	(0.14)	**0.66**	(0.06)	0.09	(0.20)	-0.09	(0.19)
Macao-China[1]	**1.01**	(0.08)	0.14	(0.07)	-0.46	(0.26)	-0.13	(0.07)	**0.50**	(0.04)	-0.03	(0.07)	**0.40**	(0.12)
Mexico[1]	**0.38**	(0.06)	**0.75**	(0.07)	**-0.64**	(0.09)	**0.80**	(0.04)	**0.39**	(0.02)	-0.14	(0.16)	**0.64**	(0.15)
New Zealand[1]	**1.11**	(0.11)	**-0.23**	(0.11)	c	c	**0.31**	(0.08)	**0.49**	(0.06)	**0.68**	(0.10)	**0.67**	(0.11)
Poland	0.06	(0.12)	**1.11**	(0.10)	**12.79**	(1.61)	**1.15**	(0.10)	**0.88**	(0.05)	**-12.80**	(1.64)	-0.09	(0.53)
Portugal: ISCED2	**1.03**	(0.19)	**0.51**	(0.16)	**-0.90**	(0.24)	**0.78**	(0.15)	**0.67**	(0.06)	0.19	(0.21)	0.30	(0.46)
Portugal: ISCED3	**0.38**	(0.15)	**0.56**	(0.13)	**-1.45**	(0.26)	**0.74**	(0.12)	**0.50**	(0.06)	0.11	(0.21)	-0.03	(0.83)
Serbia	**0.35**	(0.13)	**1.02**	(0.10)	**-1.24**	(0.14)	**0.91**	(0.10)	**0.72**	(0.05)	0.12	(0.12)	0.13	(0.27)
Singapore	**2.13**	(0.93)	0.50	(0.56)	c	c	-0.68	(0.59)	0.71	(0.41)	0.86	(0.86)	0.56	(1.06)
Slovak Republic	**0.62**	(0.17)	**0.98**	(0.15)	**-2.24**	(0.44)	**0.62**	(0.13)	**0.66**	(0.07)	0.70	(0.51)	0.00	(0.23)
Trinidad and Tobago	**0.41**	(0.11)	**0.35**	(0.12)	-0.06	(0.14)	**0.75**	(0.09)	**0.36**	(0.06)	-0.47	(0.32)	0.20	(0.28)
Regions														
Italy: Abruzzo	**1.06**	(0.17)	0.25	(0.15)	0.61	(1.68)	**0.42**	(0.17)	**0.51**	(0.08)	0.33	(0.40)	-0.37	(0.30)
Italy: Basilicata	**0.75**	(0.18)	**0.66**	(0.19)	0.00	(0.00)	**0.96**	(0.21)	**0.53**	(0.08)	-0.07	(0.88)	-0.02	(0.29)
Italy: Bolzano	**0.55**	(0.17)	**0.48**	(0.18)	**-1.21**	(0.20)	0.25	(0.15)	**0.61**	(0.08)	-0.01	(0.34)	**-0.93**	(0.15)
Italy: Calabria	**1.06**	(0.17)	0.27	(0.20)	0.00	(0.00)	**0.54**	(0.18)	**0.66**	(0.12)	-0.18	(0.74)	-0.35	(0.25)
Italy: Campania	**0.76**	(0.19)	**0.51**	(0.21)	0.00	(0.00)	**0.69**	(0.22)	**0.58**	(0.09)	0.56	(0.39)	**-0.61**	(0.22)
Italy: Emilia Romagna	**0.50**	(0.18)	**0.77**	(0.17)	0.06	(0.27)	**0.49**	(0.20)	**0.63**	(0.07)	0.11	(0.32)	0.28	(0.22)
Italy: Friuli Venezia Giulia	**1.33**	(0.21)	0.20	(0.20)	**-13.26**	(0.28)	**0.55**	(0.20)	**0.75**	(0.10)	0.48	(0.31)	-0.23	(0.22)
Italy: Lazio	**0.98**	(0.13)	0.03	(0.17)	**-0.83**	(0.32)	**0.77**	(0.18)	**0.57**	(0.11)	0.27	(0.48)	0.35	(0.31)
Italy: Liguria	**0.67**	(0.22)	**0.87**	(0.18)	-0.76	(1.88)	**0.58**	(0.17)	**0.60**	(0.10)	**0.87**	(0.37)	-0.22	(0.38)
Italy: Lombardia	**1.03**	(0.27)	0.36	(0.25)	-1.27	(1.14)	0.18	(0.23)	**0.67**	(0.07)	0.04	(0.34)	-0.10	(0.42)
Italy: Marche	**1.09**	(0.26)	0.10	(0.26)	0.00	(0.00)	0.37	(0.23)	**0.71**	(0.10)	0.29	(0.44)	-0.22	(0.33)
Italy: Molise	**0.55**	(0.24)	**0.93**	(0.23)	**-9.92**	(1.45)	**0.86**	(0.24)	**0.45**	(0.11)	-0.05	(0.73)	**-0.95**	(0.25)
Italy: Piemonte	**0.86**	(0.25)	**0.41**	(0.20)	**-1.88**	(0.86)	0.46	(0.25)	**0.83**	(0.10)	-0.04	(0.46)	0.40	(0.47)
Italy: Puglia	**1.52**	(0.23)	-0.27	(0.22)	0.00	(0.00)	**0.46**	(0.20)	**0.57**	(0.08)	0.08	(0.82)	-0.35	(0.31)
Italy: Sardegna	**0.68**	(0.26)	**0.75**	(0.29)	0.00	(0.00)	**0.60**	(0.20)	**0.52**	(0.11)	-1.07	(1.19)	-0.38	(0.27)
Italy: Sicilia	**0.81**	(0.22)	**0.60**	(0.17)	**-12.59**	(0.99)	**0.53**	(0.23)	**0.63**	(0.05)	**-12.94**	(1.03)	0.13	(0.30)
Italy: Toscana	**1.04**	(0.21)	0.05	(0.20)	0.00	(0.00)	**0.57**	(0.19)	**0.68**	(0.10)	0.31	(0.40)	0.33	(0.42)
Italy: Trento	**1.17**	(0.32)	0.07	(0.28)	**-1.77**	(0.32)	**0.46**	(0.20)	**0.56**	(0.11)	**0.99**	(0.33)	-0.26	(0.18)
Italy: Umbria	**1.13**	(0.20)	0.23	(0.20)	**-1.24**	(0.36)	**0.45**	(0.20)	**0.70**	(0.09)	**0.64**	(0.30)	-0.36	(0.21)
Italy: Valle d'Aosta	**1.09**	(0.27)	0.15	(0.26)	**-14.36**	(0.19)	0.27	(0.22)	**0.71**	(0.12)	**1.04**	(0.42)	-0.03	(0.24)
Italy: Veneto	**0.86**	(0.26)	0.43	(0.24)	**-1.33**	(0.29)	**0.45**	(0.16)	**0.77**	(0.11)	**1.09**	(0.34)	-0.20	(0.18)
Mexico: Aguascalientes[1]	0.33	(0.24)	0.53	(0.29)	**-0.80**	(0.21)	**0.69**	(0.15)	**0.48**	(0.08)	1.07	(0.87)	-0.01	(0.94)
Mexico: Baja California[1]	**0.83**	(0.27)	0.54	(0.31)	**0.39**	(0.12)	**0.81**	(0.25)	**0.32**	(0.09)	0.17	(0.36)	1.22	(0.98)
Mexico: Baja California Sur[1]	**0.47**	(0.19)	**0.63**	(0.27)	-0.42	(0.33)	**0.95**	(0.13)	**0.39**	(0.06)	-0.71	(0.56)	**-1.68**	(0.78)
Mexico: Campeche[1]	0.34	(0.26)	**1.19**	(0.27)	**-1.73**	(0.17)	**0.66**	(0.19)	**0.38**	(0.07)	0.11	(0.57)	-0.23	(0.31)
Mexico: Chihuahua[1]	0.53	(0.28)	0.47	(0.29)	-0.56	(0.42)	**0.95**	(0.23)	**0.53**	(0.10)	-0.62	(0.96)	0.90	(1.08)
Mexico: Colima[1]	0.19	(0.26)	**0.91**	(0.30)	-0.08	(0.33)	**1.01**	(0.22)	**0.31**	(0.06)	0.19	(0.70)	0.79	(1.79)
Mexico: Coahuila[1]	0.30	(0.25)	**0.68**	(0.28)	-0.26	(0.27)	**1.24**	(0.29)	**0.53**	(0.13)	-0.68	(1.36)	0.49	(0.99)
Mexico: Chiapas[1]	**1.05**	(0.21)	0.06	(0.18)	**-0.59**	(0.11)	**0.39**	(0.16)	**0.31**	(0.04)	-0.88	(0.48)	0.14	(0.24)
Mexico: Distrito Federal[1]	0.35	(0.31)	**0.92**	(0.32)	**-0.49**	(0.20)	**0.65**	(0.22)	**0.31**	(0.11)	0.18	(0.90)	-0.03	(0.96)
Mexico: Durango[1]	0.44	(0.25)	**0.68**	(0.25)	**-0.81**	(0.16)	**0.90**	(0.19)	**0.37**	(0.08)	**-14.93**	(1.17)	**2.04**	(0.50)
Mexico: Guerrero[1]	**0.86**	(0.36)	0.11	(0.36)	-0.16	(0.15)	0.44	(0.27)	**0.46**	(0.10)	0.35	(0.71)	**1.26**	(0.43)
Mexico: Guanajuato[1]	**0.62**	(0.22)	**0.73**	(0.24)	**-0.35**	(0.13)	**0.65**	(0.18)	**0.66**	(0.07)	-0.64	(1.26)	0.46	(2.63)
Mexico: Hidalgo[1]	0.27	(0.19)	**0.64**	(0.22)	**-1.19**	(0.15)	**0.87**	(0.24)	**0.33**	(0.10)	-0.71	(0.89)	-0.30	(0.39)
Mexico: Jalisco[1]	0.47	(0.26)	0.43	(0.26)	-0.86	(0.61)	**0.67**	(0.18)	**0.49**	(0.07)	-0.16	(1.48)	0.39	(0.49)
Mexico: Michoacán[1]	**0.68**	(0.29)	**0.61**	(0.26)	**-0.86**	(0.24)	**0.78**	(0.20)	**0.27**	(0.06)	**-13.34**	(0.92)	1.49	(1.28)
Mexico: Morelos[1]	-0.34	(0.32)	**1.39**	(0.27)	**-1.02**	(0.35)	**1.16**	(0.25)	**0.51**	(0.08)	0.18	(0.66)	**14.35**	(0.99)
Mexico: Mexico[1]	**0.44**	(0.18)	**0.80**	(0.23)	**-0.70**	(0.25)	**1.02**	(0.15)	**0.38**	(0.07)	0.19	(0.52)	1.03	(0.57)
Mexico: Nayarit[1]	**0.77**	(0.31)	0.42	(0.32)	-0.29	(0.41)	0.64	(0.35)	**0.33**	(0.07)	-1.60	(0.83)	-0.31	(1.31)
Mexico: Nuevo León[1]	-0.12	(0.37)	**1.50**	(0.41)	**-0.92**	(0.19)	**0.94**	(0.19)	**0.51**	(0.11)	**1.47**	(0.43)	**14.77**	(1.95)
Mexico: Oaxaca[1]	0.15	(0.22)	**0.93**	(0.34)	-0.25	(0.26)	**0.67**	(0.16)	**0.43**	(0.18)	-0.29	(0.75)	0.66	(0.37)
Mexico: Puebla[1]	0.19	(0.32)	**1.05**	(0.26)	**-0.84**	(0.16)	**1.05**	(0.20)	**0.38**	(0.08)	-0.50	(1.36)	-1.12	(1.02)
Mexico: Quintana Roo[1]	0.14	(0.19)	**0.97**	(0.21)	0.27	(0.33)	**0.75**	(0.19)	**0.55**	(0.07)	0.21	(0.34)	0.15	(0.38)
Mexico: Querétaro[1]	**0.75**	(0.22)	0.46	(0.32)	**-1.11**	(0.14)	**0.60**	(0.18)	**0.53**	(0.08)	**1.33**	(0.47)	**1.84**	(0.23)
Mexico: Sinaloa[1]	0.34	(0.25)	0.59	(0.31)	-0.02	(0.24)	**0.74**	(0.15)	**0.38**	(0.07)	-1.52	(1.44)	**-12.95**	(1.42)
Mexico: San Luis Potosí[1]	0.01	(0.25)	**1.17**	(0.23)	**-2.01**	(0.16)	**0.67**	(0.27)	**0.44**	(0.08)	0.24	(0.77)	0.56	(0.51)
Mexico: Sonora[1]	**0.58**	(0.23)	0.51	(0.30)	-0.60	(0.49)	**0.73**	(0.13)	**0.38**	(0.09)	0.20	(0.94)	0.83	(0.61)
Mexico: Tamaulipas[1]	0.33	(0.22)	**0.90**	(0.27)	-0.18	(0.22)	**1.49**	(0.20)	**0.46**	(0.07)	-1.17	(0.79)	**-13.67**	(1.46)
Mexico: Tabasco[1]	0.19	(0.21)	**1.13**	(0.20)	**-0.91**	(0.10)	**0.73**	(0.15)	**0.20**	(0.10)	-0.85	(0.68)	0.83	(0.65)
Mexico: Tlaxcala[1]	**0.49**	(0.17)	**0.77**	(0.15)	0.00	(0.17)	**1.01**	(0.15)	**0.53**	(0.08)	-1.56	(1.12)	**13.45**	(1.40)
Mexico: Veracruz[1]	-0.12	(0.28)	**1.38**	(0.31)	**-1.21**	(0.11)	**1.05**	(0.13)	**0.53**	(0.11)	-0.30	(0.66)	**0.76**	(0.36)
Mexico: Yucatán[1]	**0.48**	(0.21)	**0.81**	(0.24)	0.20	(0.12)	**0.72**	(0.20)	**0.31**	(0.06)	0.45	(0.53)	-0.02	(0.26)
Mexico: Zacatecas[1]	0.12	(0.30)	**0.75**	(0.18)	**-0.52**	(0.10)	**1.09**	(0.23)	**0.49**	(0.09)	1.32	(1.41)	-0.07	(0.88)

Notes: Estimates from a logistic regression model including student marks, PISA reading and maths scores and background characteristics. Marks are standardised at the country level and interaction terms. Reading and mathematics scores are scaled so that one unit represents 100 score points.

Estimates statistically significantly different from 0 (zero) at a 95% confidence level are highlighted in bold.

1. Macao-China, Mexico and New Zealand distributed, in the Educational Career questionnaire, the alternative question on whether students received a passing or failing mark. Results for these countries and economies are thus based on a dichotomous variable that does not capture the full variability of marks received by students. Estimates for these countries and economies are probably underestimated.

StatLink http://dx.doi.org/10.1787/888932734305

[Part 1/1]

Table B3.7 Relationship between students' marks, background characteristics and their expectation of completing a university degree

	Information about students' own performance and prospects		Student background characteristics							
	Student marks		Student is a girl		*PISA index of economic, social and cultural status*		Student has an immigrant background		Student speaks another language at home	
	Coeff.	S.E.	Coeff.	S.E.	Coeff.	S.E.	Coeff.	S.E.	Coeff.	S.E.
Countries and economies										
Austria	**0.31**	(0.04)	**0.21**	(0.10)	**1.13**	(0.06)	**0.72**	(0.18)	0.12	(0.24)
Belgium (Flemish Community)	**0.34**	(0.06)	0.19	(0.10)	**1.02**	(0.06)	0.41	(0.31)	-0.01	(0.14)
Croatia	**0.86**	(0.06)	**0.49**	(0.10)	**1.05**	(0.06)	0.09	(0.13)	0.36	(0.35)
Hungary	**0.88**	(0.06)	**0.40**	(0.09)	**1.18**	(0.05)	-0.18	(0.28)	0.25	(0.56)
Iceland	**0.61**	(0.05)	**0.41**	(0.07)	**0.92**	(0.06)	**1.11**	(0.37)	0.02	(0.33)
Ireland	**0.42**	(0.06)	**0.35**	(0.09)	**0.78**	(0.06)	0.02	(0.15)	0.05	(0.22)
Italy	**0.47**	(0.02)	**0.53**	(0.06)	**0.74**	(0.02)	**-0.28**	(0.11)	**-0.40**	(0.08)
Latvia	**0.54**	(0.04)	**0.25**	(0.10)	**0.80**	(0.06)	0.00	(0.20)	-0.22	(0.20)
Macao-China[1]	**0.26**	(0.04)	0.11	(0.06)	**0.61**	(0.04)	0.02	(0.06)	-0.13	(0.10)
Mexico[1]	**0.14**	(0.02)	**0.73**	(0.03)	**0.58**	(0.02)	**-0.86**	(0.15)	0.18	(0.13)
New Zealand[1]	**0.26**	(0.03)	**0.67**	(0.06)	**0.79**	(0.05)	**0.64**	(0.10)	**0.24**	(0.10)
Poland	**0.96**	(0.05)	**0.46**	(0.09)	**0.95**	(0.05)	**-9.94**	(1.42)	-0.04	(0.62)
Portugal: ISCED2	**0.77**	(0.06)	**0.66**	(0.11)	**0.87**	(0.06)	0.09	(0.19)	0.27	(0.44)
Portugal: ISCED3	**0.45**	(0.06)	**0.58**	(0.09)	**0.69**	(0.06)	0.11	(0.19)	-0.18	(0.54)
Serbia	**0.80**	(0.06)	**0.59**	(0.08)	**0.93**	(0.05)	**0.25**	(0.12)	-0.10	(0.28)
Singapore	**0.19**	(0.04)	**0.34**	(0.09)	**0.77**	(0.06)	**0.58**	(0.14)	**-0.30**	(0.09)
Slovak Republic	**0.91**	(0.07)	**0.29**	(0.08)	**0.90**	(0.06)	0.33	(0.53)	-0.25	(0.27)
Trinidad and Tobago	**0.22**	(0.05)	**0.83**	(0.08)	**0.52**	(0.05)	-0.53	(0.33)	-0.20	(0.29)
Regions										
Italy: Abruzzo	**0.62**	(0.08)	**0.50**	(0.16)	**0.68**	(0.07)	0.12	(0.42)	-0.68	(0.36)
Italy: Basilicata	**0.70**	(0.10)	**0.77**	(0.17)	**0.70**	(0.09)	0.73	(0.89)	-0.23	(0.30)
Italy: Bolzano	**0.50**	(0.09)	**0.24**	(0.11)	**0.85**	(0.08)	-0.59	(0.43)	**-1.12**	(0.18)
Italy: Calabria	**0.51**	(0.05)	**0.70**	(0.17)	**0.81**	(0.10)	-0.63	(0.85)	**-0.43**	(0.22)
Italy: Campania	**0.43**	(0.10)	**0.58**	(0.20)	**0.72**	(0.09)	0.15	(0.77)	**-0.75**	(0.23)
Italy: Emilia Romagna	**0.43**	(0.07)	0.13	(0.14)	**0.83**	(0.07)	-0.41	(0.28)	-0.16	(0.21)
Italy: Friuli Venezia Giulia	**0.51**	(0.07)	**0.82**	(0.17)	**0.89**	(0.11)	-0.10	(0.31)	-0.29	(0.22)
Italy: Lazio	**0.47**	(0.09)	**0.84**	(0.15)	**0.69**	(0.09)	0.08	(0.39)	-0.17	(0.34)
Italy: Liguria	**0.46**	(0.09)	**0.41**	(0.18)	**0.73**	(0.13)	0.38	(0.36)	-0.53	(0.42)
Italy: Lombardia	**0.49**	(0.09)	0.33	(0.21)	**0.82**	(0.07)	-0.39	(0.30)	-0.52	(0.35)
Italy: Marche	**0.47**	(0.09)	**0.57**	(0.15)	**0.80**	(0.09)	-0.04	(0.41)	-0.41	(0.33)
Italy: Molise	**0.62**	(0.11)	**0.58**	(0.17)	**0.63**	(0.09)	-0.10	(0.63)	**-1.17**	(0.27)
Italy: Piemonte	**0.46**	(0.08)	**0.50**	(0.22)	**1.03**	(0.10)	-0.44	(0.39)	-0.04	(0.42)
Italy: Puglia	**0.82**	(0.08)	**0.77**	(0.15)	**0.70**	(0.09)	-1.06	(0.95)	-0.30	(0.29)
Italy: Sardegna	**0.61**	(0.12)	**0.52**	(0.13)	**0.65**	(0.09)	-2.23	(1.44)	-0.33	(0.36)
Italy: Sicilia	**0.55**	(0.09)	**0.41**	(0.17)	**0.75**	(0.06)	**-13.37**	(0.79)	-0.09	(0.29)
Italy: Toscana	**0.53**	(0.10)	**0.70**	(0.17)	**0.76**	(0.10)	0.12	(0.34)	0.15	(0.35)
Italy: Trento	**0.40**	(0.08)	**0.68**	(0.18)	**0.76**	(0.11)	0.15	(0.27)	**-0.50**	(0.18)
Italy: Umbria	**0.61**	(0.09)	**0.51**	(0.15)	**0.85**	(0.09)	0.22	(0.31)	**-0.56**	(0.19)
Italy: Valle d'Aosta	**0.23**	(0.10)	**0.36**	(0.16)	**0.86**	(0.11)	0.36	(0.38)	-0.20	(0.24)
Italy: Veneto	**0.51**	(0.07)	**0.48**	(0.21)	**0.90**	(0.12)	0.55	(0.31)	**-0.45**	(0.21)
Mexico: Aguascalientes[1]	0.08	(0.07)	**0.70**	(0.14)	**0.63**	(0.07)	0.49	(0.98)	0.20	(1.08)
Mexico: Baja California[1]	**0.12**	(0.05)	**0.87**	(0.14)	**0.51**	(0.07)	**-0.94**	(0.35)	0.50	(1.03)
Mexico: Baja California Sur[1]	0.14	(0.09)	**0.94**	(0.13)	**0.52**	(0.06)	**-1.54**	(0.47)	-1.25	(0.83)
Mexico: Campeche[1]	**0.19**	(0.07)	**0.55**	(0.17)	**0.53**	(0.06)	-0.74	(0.75)	-0.14	(0.34)
Mexico: Chihuahua[1]	0.09	(0.08)	**0.96**	(0.20)	**0.75**	(0.10)	-1.50	(0.95)	0.21	(1.04)
Mexico: Colima[1]	**0.24**	(0.07)	**0.91**	(0.17)	**0.48**	(0.04)	-0.45	(0.70)	0.28	(1.71)
Mexico: Coahuila[1]	-0.07	(0.07)	**1.21**	(0.18)	**0.67**	(0.11)	-1.00	(1.80)	0.44	(0.86)
Mexico: Chiapas[1]	0.08	(0.11)	**0.55**	(0.15)	**0.43**	(0.06)	**-1.30**	(0.50)	**-0.65**	(0.24)
Mexico: Distrito Federal[1]	**0.18**	(0.07)	**0.46**	(0.20)	**0.56**	(0.14)	0.14	(1.01)	-0.89	(0.93)
Mexico: Durango[1]	**0.27**	(0.10)	**0.82**	(0.14)	**0.53**	(0.08)	**-14.63**	(1.40)	0.79	(0.52)
Mexico: Guerrero[1]	**0.24**	(0.07)	**0.60**	(0.19)	**0.58**	(0.09)	-0.25	(0.68)	0.70	(0.43)
Mexico: Guanajuato[1]	0.01	(0.05)	**0.66**	(0.12)	**0.90**	(0.05)	-1.31	(1.47)	0.47	(1.83)
Mexico: Hidalgo[1]	**0.20**	(0.06)	**0.85**	(0.18)	**0.56**	(0.09)	-1.39	(0.74)	**-0.59**	(0.30)
Mexico: Jalisco[1]	**0.28**	(0.06)	**0.73**	(0.15)	**0.62**	(0.08)	-1.00	(1.30)	-0.16	(0.64)
Mexico: Michoacán[1]	0.05	(0.09)	**0.60**	(0.15)	**0.50**	(0.06)	**-14.19**	(0.78)	1.73	(1.29)
Mexico: Morelos[1]	**0.20**	(0.08)	**0.86**	(0.19)	**0.63**	(0.09)	-1.06	(0.57)	**14.15**	(1.17)
Mexico: Mexico[1]	**0.22**	(0.08)	**0.98**	(0.17)	**0.56**	(0.07)	-0.93	(0.55)	0.54	(0.50)
Mexico: Nayarit[1]	0.09	(0.11)	**0.75**	(0.27)	**0.45**	(0.07)	**-2.06**	(0.83)	-0.44	(1.14)
Mexico: Nuevo León[1]	0.09	(0.05)	**0.69**	(0.17)	**0.82**	(0.12)	0.44	(0.38)	**13.47**	(1.19)
Mexico: Oaxaca[1]	**0.28**	(0.08)	**0.62**	(0.14)	**0.47**	(0.09)	-0.91	(0.80)	0.10	(0.37)
Mexico: Puebla[1]	0.06	(0.06)	**0.83**	(0.17)	**0.55**	(0.09)	-1.20	(1.20)	-0.96	(1.14)
Mexico: Quintana Roo[1]	0.03	(0.07)	**0.57**	(0.16)	**0.76**	(0.07)	-0.85	(0.47)	-0.03	(0.43)
Mexico: Querétaro[1]	-0.01	(0.08)	**0.64**	(0.15)	**0.78**	(0.08)	0.26	(0.47)	**2.39**	(0.24)
Mexico: Sinaloa[1]	**0.15**	(0.05)	**0.69**	(0.12)	**0.52**	(0.06)	-2.20	(1.37)	**-12.77**	(1.41)
Mexico: San Luis Potosí[1]	0.03	(0.07)	**0.52**	(0.22)	**0.61**	(0.08)	-0.85	(0.79)	0.39	(0.41)
Mexico: Sonora[1]	**0.19**	(0.07)	**0.88**	(0.11)	**0.57**	(0.09)	-0.63	(0.94)	0.58	(0.64)
Mexico: Tamaulipas[1]	**0.23**	(0.10)	**1.32**	(0.15)	**0.59**	(0.05)	**-1.91**	(0.87)	**-13.51**	(1.43)
Mexico: Tabasco[1]	0.02	(0.08)	**0.65**	(0.12)	**0.34**	(0.12)	**-1.54**	(0.64)	0.45	(0.58)
Mexico: Tlaxcala[1]	0.14	(0.08)	**0.90**	(0.13)	**0.64**	(0.08)	**-2.45**	(1.04)	**12.95**	(1.40)
Mexico: Veracruz[1]	0.10	(0.08)	**0.67**	(0.09)	**0.64**	(0.12)	-0.76	(0.62)	0.60	(0.42)
Mexico: Yucatán[1]	**0.18**	(0.06)	**0.60**	(0.17)	**0.54**	(0.06)	-0.22	(0.62)	-0.41	(0.29)
Mexico: Zacatecas[1]	0.08	(0.12)	**0.97**	(0.22)	**0.60**	(0.10)	0.91	(1.48)	-0.15	(0.96)

Notes: Estimates from a logistic regression model including student marks and background characteristics. Marks are standardised at the country level and interaction terms. Reading and mathematics scores are scaled so that one unit represents 100 score points.

Estimates statistically significantly different from 0 (zero) at a 95% confidence level are highlighted in bold.

1. Macao-China, Mexico and New Zealand distributed, in the Educational Career questionnaire, the alternative question on whether students received a passing or failing mark. Results for these countries and economies are thus based on a dichotomous variable that does not capture the full variability of marks received by students. Estimates for these countries and economies are probably underestimated.

StatLink http://dx.doi.org/10.1787/888932734324

[Part 1/1]

Table B3.8 Relationship between students' background characteristics, information about their performance and prospects, and their expectation of completing a university degree

	Marks		Information about students' own performance and prospects						Student background							
			Reading performance		Mathematics performance		Non-academic programme		Student is a girl		*PISA index of economic, social and cultural status*		Student has an immigrant background		Student speaks another language at home	
	Coeff.	S.E.	Coeff.	S.E.	Coeff.	S.E.	Coeff.	S.E.	Coeff.	S.E.	Coeff.	S.E.	Coeff.	S.E.	Coeff.	S.E.
Countries and economies																
Austria	**0.24**	(0.05)	0.00	(0.16)	**1.12**	(0.13)	**-1.48**	(0.21)	**0.41**	(0.15)	**0.67**	(0.07)	**1.14**	(0.21)	0.14	(0.26)
Belgium (Flemish Community)	**0.29**	(0.06)	**0.34**	(0.15)	**1.46**	(0.14)	**-1.20**	(0.36)	**0.39**	(0.12)	**0.66**	(0.07)	**1.48**	(0.28)	-0.01	(0.12)
Croatia	**0.46**	(0.06)	**0.98**	(0.13)	**0.49**	(0.12)	**-1.93**	(0.21)	**0.28**	(0.13)	**0.77**	(0.07)	0.25	(0.15)	0.53	(0.36)
Hungary	**0.52**	(0.06)	**0.90**	(0.18)	**0.49**	(0.14)	**-1.32**	(0.20)	**0.38**	(0.11)	**0.80**	(0.05)	-0.36	(0.30)	0.75	(0.74)
Iceland	**0.40**	(0.05)	**0.55**	(0.11)	**0.24**	(0.10)	c	c	**0.29**	(0.08)	**0.85**	(0.06)	**1.42**	(0.41)	0.25	(0.35)
Ireland	**0.32**	(0.06)	**0.28**	(0.11)	**0.65**	(0.12)	-0.13	(0.10)	**0.39**	(0.10)	**0.54**	(0.06)	0.13	(0.16)	0.19	(0.21)
Italy	**0.28**	(0.03)	**0.76**	(0.06)	**0.13**	(0.06)	**-2.02**	(0.26)	**0.38**	(0.06)	**0.60**	(0.02)	0.01	(0.12)	-0.17	(0.09)
Latvia	**0.28**	(0.04)	**0.80**	(0.20)	0.11	(0.18)	**-12.39**	(1.13)	0.12	(0.14)	**0.64**	(0.06)	0.02	(0.20)	-0.11	(0.19)
Macao-China[1]	**0.12**	(0.04)	**0.98**	(0.08)	0.13	(0.08)	-0.47	(0.27)	**-0.15**	(0.07)	**0.49**	(0.04)	-0.04	(0.07)	**0.41**	(0.12)
Mexico[1]	**0.10**	(0.02)	**0.38**	(0.06)	**0.75**	(0.07)	**-0.65**	(0.09)	**0.80**	(0.04)	**0.40**	(0.02)	-0.14	(0.16)	**0.63**	(0.15)
New Zealand[1]	**0.14**	(0.04)	**1.09**	(0.11)	**-0.23**	(0.11)	c	c	**0.29**	(0.08)	**0.48**	(0.06)	**0.67**	(0.10)	**0.69**	(0.11)
Poland	**0.69**	(0.06)	-0.16	(0.12)	**0.96**	(0.11)	**13.54**	(1.69)	**0.82**	(0.11)	**0.81**	(0.05)	**-13.34**	(1.72)	-0.08	(0.60)
Portugal: ISCED2	**0.55**	(0.07)	**0.82**	(0.19)	**0.39**	(0.16)	**-1.27**	(0.26)	**0.66**	(0.16)	**0.67**	(0.06)	0.14	(0.21)	0.27	(0.50)
Portugal: ISCED3	**0.44**	(0.08)	0.20	(0.16)	**0.43**	(0.13)	**-1.72**	(0.30)	**0.58**	(0.12)	**0.48**	(0.06)	0.14	(0.22)	-0.04	(0.76)
Serbia	**0.56**	(0.05)	0.15	(0.13)	**0.98**	(0.10)	**-1.28**	(0.14)	**0.81**	(0.11)	**0.70**	(0.05)	0.09	(0.12)	0.14	(0.27)
Singapore	**0.77**	(0.31)	**1.58**	(0.80)	1.01	(0.57)	c	c	-0.56	(0.55)	0.63	(0.45)	0.78	(0.69)	1.18	(1.04)
Slovak Republic	**0.52**	(0.07)	**0.48**	(0.17)	**0.84**	(0.16)	**-2.33**	(0.42)	**0.38**	(0.13)	**0.62**	(0.07)	0.58	(0.54)	0.01	(0.24)
Trinidad and Tobago	**0.12**	(0.05)	**0.40**	(0.12)	**0.34**	(0.12)	-0.09	(0.14)	**0.73**	(0.09)	**0.35**	(0.06)	-0.49	(0.33)	0.19	(0.28)
Regions																
Italy: Abruzzo	**0.35**	(0.09)	**0.93**	(0.19)	0.22	(0.16)	0.62	(1.67)	0.30	(0.17)	**0.51**	(0.08)	0.43	(0.41)	-0.39	(0.32)
Italy: Basilicata	**0.39**	(0.10)	**0.57**	(0.18)	**0.64**	(0.20)	0.00	(0.00)	**0.89**	(0.21)	**0.52**	(0.08)	0.30	(0.88)	-0.04	(0.29)
Italy: Bolzano	**0.28**	(0.09)	**0.47**	(0.18)	**0.42**	(0.19)	**-1.31**	(0.22)	0.13	(0.16)	**0.61**	(0.08)	-0.06	(0.42)	**-1.02**	(0.17)
Italy: Calabria	**0.22**	(0.07)	**0.97**	(0.18)	0.27	(0.20)	0.00	(0.00)	**0.48**	(0.18)	**0.65**	(0.11)	-0.23	(0.75)	-0.36	(0.25)
Italy: Campania	**0.25**	(0.10)	**0.73**	(0.20)	**0.49**	(0.22)	0.00	(0.00)	**0.61**	(0.22)	**0.57**	(0.09)	0.63	(0.43)	**-0.58**	(0.21)
Italy: Emilia Romagna	**0.17**	(0.07)	**0.43**	(0.17)	**0.76**	(0.17)	-0.09	(0.27)	**0.43**	(0.21)	**0.63**	(0.07)	0.14	(0.31)	0.27	(0.22)
Italy: Friuli Venezia Giulia	**0.21**	(0.08)	**1.27**	(0.21)	0.16	(0.20)	**-13.35**	(0.28)	**0.51**	(0.20)	**0.74**	(0.10)	0.47	(0.31)	-0.21	(0.22)
Italy: Lazio	**0.28**	(0.08)	**0.88**	(0.13)	0.04	(0.17)	-0.52	(0.60)	**0.70**	(0.18)	**0.55**	(0.10)	0.29	(0.48)	0.29	(0.32)
Italy: Liguria	**0.24**	(0.10)	**0.60**	(0.23)	**0.86**	(0.19)	-0.76	(1.77)	**0.54**	(0.17)	**0.61**	(0.11)	**0.95**	(0.37)	-0.29	(0.41)
Italy: Lombardia	**0.28**	(0.09)	**0.96**	(0.27)	0.34	(0.26)	-1.42	(1.15)	0.11	(0.24)	**0.66**	(0.07)	0.10	(0.34)	-0.15	(0.42)
Italy: Marche	**0.25**	(0.10)	**1.04**	(0.26)	0.05	(0.26)	0.00	(0.00)	0.27	(0.23)	**0.69**	(0.09)	0.29	(0.44)	-0.22	(0.32)
Italy: Molise	**0.30**	(0.11)	0.43	(0.24)	**0.90**	(0.23)	**-10.29**	(1.46)	**0.79**	(0.24)	**0.45**	(0.11)	0.04	(0.71)	**-0.92**	(0.25)
Italy: Piemonte	**0.24**	(0.07)	**0.77**	(0.25)	**0.42**	(0.21)	**-2.01**	(0.90)	0.42	(0.25)	**0.83**	(0.10)	-0.07	(0.46)	0.40	(0.48)
Italy: Puglia	**0.60**	(0.09)	**1.33**	(0.25)	-0.31	(0.23)	0.00	(0.00)	0.36	(0.22)	**0.55**	(0.09)	-0.05	(0.90)	-0.30	(0.31)
Italy: Sardegna	**0.38**	(0.11)	**0.54**	(0.26)	**0.71**	(0.30)	0.00	(0.00)	**0.54**	(0.19)	**0.51**	(0.10)	-1.40	(1.35)	-0.26	(0.31)
Italy: Sicilia	**0.29**	(0.09)	**0.75**	(0.22)	**0.55**	(0.19)	**-12.90**	(1.03)	**0.45**	(0.22)	**0.60**	(0.05)	**-13.10**	(1.07)	0.09	(0.30)
Italy: Toscana	**0.29**	(0.11)	**0.93**	(0.22)	0.06	(0.21)	0.00	(0.00)	**0.50**	(0.20)	**0.68**	(0.10)	0.34	(0.39)	0.33	(0.42)
Italy: Trento	0.14	(0.09)	**1.13**	(0.32)	0.06	(0.28)	**-1.81**	(0.33)	**0.42**	(0.20)	**0.55**	(0.11)	**0.98**	(0.34)	-0.29	(0.19)
Italy: Umbria	**0.38**	(0.08)	**1.03**	(0.19)	0.20	(0.19)	**-1.59**	(0.40)	0.37	(0.21)	**0.66**	(0.09)	**0.65**	(0.32)	-0.38	(0.21)
Italy: Valle d'Aosta	0.00	(0.12)	**1.09**	(0.29)	0.16	(0.26)	**-14.37**	(0.26)	0.27	(0.22)	**0.71**	(0.12)	**1.04**	(0.42)	-0.03	(0.25)
Italy: Veneto	**0.34**	(0.10)	**0.76**	(0.25)	0.39	(0.24)	**-1.67**	(0.32)	**0.34**	(0.17)	**0.76**	(0.11)	**1.11**	(0.34)	-0.21	(0.18)
Mexico: Aguascalientes[1]	0.00	(0.08)	0.33	(0.24)	0.53	(0.29)	**-0.80**	(0.21)	**0.69**	(0.15)	**0.48**	(0.08)	1.07	(0.87)	-0.01	(0.94)
Mexico: Baja California[1]	0.03	(0.05)	**0.83**	(0.27)	0.54	(0.31)	**0.38**	(0.12)	**0.81**	(0.25)	**0.32**	(0.09)	0.17	(0.36)	1.22	(0.97)
Mexico: Baja California Sur[1]	0.05	(0.09)	**0.48**	(0.18)	**0.62**	(0.27)	-0.42	(0.33)	**0.95**	(0.13)	**0.39**	(0.06)	-0.73	(0.55)	**-1.65**	(0.78)
Mexico: Campeche[1]	0.05	(0.07)	0.34	(0.26)	**1.17**	(0.26)	**-1.73**	(0.17)	**0.65**	(0.19)	**0.38**	(0.07)	0.11	(0.58)	-0.22	(0.31)
Mexico: Chihuahua[1]	0.00	(0.08)	0.53	(0.28)	0.47	(0.29)	-0.56	(0.42)	**0.95**	(0.23)	**0.53**	(0.10)	-0.62	(0.96)	0.90	(1.07)
Mexico: Colima[1]	**0.16**	(0.08)	0.19	(0.26)	**0.89**	(0.30)	-0.10	(0.33)	**1.00**	(0.22)	**0.31**	(0.06)	0.16	(0.70)	0.75	(1.79)
Mexico: Coahuila[1]	**-0.13**	(0.06)	0.29	(0.25)	**0.71**	(0.28)	-0.22	(0.28)	**1.27**	(0.29)	**0.53**	(0.13)	-0.63	(1.36)	0.38	(0.95)
Mexico: Chiapas[1]	0.04	(0.12)	**1.05**	(0.21)	0.06	(0.18)	**-0.60**	(0.12)	**0.39**	(0.16)	**0.31**	(0.05)	-0.88	(0.48)	0.13	(0.24)
Mexico: Distrito Federal[1]	0.15	(0.08)	0.30	(0.32)	**0.94**	(0.32)	**-0.53**	(0.22)	**0.66**	(0.23)	**0.32**	(0.11)	0.23	(0.95)	-0.13	(0.94)
Mexico: Durango[1]	**0.18**	(0.09)	0.42	(0.25)	**0.66**	(0.24)	**-0.85**	(0.15)	**0.90**	(0.19)	**0.38**	(0.08)	**-14.94**	(1.14)	**1.95**	(0.49)
Mexico: Guerrero[1]	**0.18**	(0.07)	**0.85**	(0.36)	0.10	(0.36)	-0.12	(0.15)	0.43	(0.27)	**0.47**	(0.09)	0.37	(0.70)	**1.20**	(0.43)
Mexico: Guanajuato[1]	0.01	(0.05)	**0.62**	(0.22)	**0.72**	(0.24)	**-0.35**	(0.12)	**0.64**	(0.17)	**0.66**	(0.07)	-0.64	(1.26)	0.45	(2.63)
Mexico: Hidalgo[1]	**0.18**	(0.06)	0.31	(0.20)	**0.59**	(0.23)	**-1.24**	(0.15)	**0.85**	(0.25)	**0.34**	(0.10)	-0.73	(0.86)	-0.30	(0.40)
Mexico: Jalisco[1]	**0.24**	(0.06)	0.44	(0.27)	0.42	(0.26)	-0.92	(0.60)	**0.64**	(0.19)	**0.48**	(0.07)	-0.06	(1.26)	0.43	(0.53)
Mexico: Michoacán[1]	0.02	(0.10)	**0.69**	(0.29)	**0.61**	(0.25)	**-0.86**	(0.24)	**0.78**	(0.20)	0.27	(0.06)	**-13.35**	(0.93)	1.48	(1.28)
Mexico: Morelos[1]	0.15	(0.08)	-0.35	(0.31)	**1.38**	(0.27)	**-1.05**	(0.35)	**1.15**	(0.25)	**0.52**	(0.09)	0.23	(0.64)	**14.31**	(0.99)
Mexico: Mexico[1]	**0.16**	(0.07)	**0.46**	(0.18)	**0.76**	(0.24)	**-0.74**	(0.25)	**0.99**	(0.15)	**0.38**	(0.07)	0.12	(0.52)	**1.17**	(0.54)
Mexico: Nayarit[1]	0.04	(0.11)	**0.76**	(0.31)	0.43	(0.32)	-0.29	(0.41)	0.64	(0.34)	**0.34**	(0.07)	-1.62	(0.83)	-0.32	(1.31)
Mexico: Nuevo León[1]	0.10	(0.05)	-0.11	(0.37)	**1.49**	(0.40)	**-0.95**	(0.18)	**0.94**	(0.19)	**0.51**	(0.10)	**1.43**	(0.43)	**14.73**	(1.96)
Mexico: Oaxaca[1]	**0.21**	(0.10)	0.17	(0.22)	**0.89**	(0.36)	-0.25	(0.25)	**0.66**	(0.17)	**0.45**	(0.18)	-0.33	(0.74)	0.65	(0.37)
Mexico: Puebla[1]	0.04	(0.06)	0.18	(0.32)	**1.06**	(0.26)	**-0.85**	(0.16)	**1.05**	(0.20)	**0.38**	(0.08)	-0.48	(1.37)	-1.13	(1.02)
Mexico: Quintana Roo[1]	0.00	(0.07)	0.14	(0.21)	**0.97**	(0.22)	0.27	(0.33)	**0.75**	(0.19)	**0.55**	(0.07)	0.21	(0.34)	0.15	(0.38)
Mexico: Querétaro[1]	-0.04	(0.08)	**0.75**	(0.22)	0.46	(0.32)	**-1.10**	(0.13)	**0.60**	(0.18)	**0.53**	(0.08)	**1.33**	(0.46)	**1.84**	(0.23)
Mexico: Sinaloa[1]	**0.09**	(0.04)	0.32	(0.25)	0.60	(0.30)	-0.05	(0.23)	**0.73**	(0.15)	**0.39**	(0.07)	-1.55	(1.45)	**-12.98**	(1.42)
Mexico: San Luis Potosí[1]	0.02	(0.09)	0.00	(0.26)	**1.17**	(0.25)	**-2.01**	(0.16)	**0.66**	(0.26)	**0.44**	(0.09)	0.26	(0.76)	0.55	(0.52)
Mexico: Sonora[1]	**0.21**	(0.07)	**0.56**	(0.23)	0.55	(0.31)	-0.60	(0.51)	**0.74**	(0.13)	**0.39**	(0.09)	0.24	(0.97)	0.81	(0.60)
Mexico: Tamaulipas[1]	0.15	(0.11)	0.31	(0.21)	**0.89**	(0.27)	-0.18	(0.22)	**1.50**	(0.20)	**0.46**	(0.07)	-1.20	(0.82)	**-13.70**	(1.45)
Mexico: Tabasco[1]	0.01	(0.08)	0.19	(0.21)	**1.14**	(0.20)	**-0.90**	(0.10)	**0.73**	(0.15)	**0.20**	(0.10)	-0.84	(0.69)	0.83	(0.65)
Mexico: Tlaxcala[1]	0.06	(0.08)	**0.48**	(0.17)	**0.76**	(0.16)	-0.01	(0.17)	**1.01**	(0.15)	**0.53**	(0.08)	-1.59	(1.11)	**13.42**	(1.41)
Mexico: Veracruz[1]	0.05	(0.08)	-0.13	(0.27)	**1.38**	(0.30)	**-1.22**	(0.11)	**1.04**	(0.13)	**0.53**	(0.11)	-0.30	(0.65)	**0.75**	(0.36)
Mexico: Yucatán[1]	**0.14**	(0.04)	**0.47**	(0.21)	**0.80**	(0.24)	0.19	(0.12)	**0.71**	(0.21)	**0.31**	(0.06)	0.56	(0.53)	-0.03	(0.26)
Mexico: Zacatecas[1]	0.02	(0.11)	0.12	(0.30)	**0.75**	(0.18)	**-0.52**	(0.10)	**1.09**	(0.23)	**0.49**	(0.08)	1.36	(1.41)	-0.06	(0.91)

Notes: Estimates from a logistic regression model including student marks and background characteristics. Marks are standardised at the country level and interaction terms. Reading and mathematics scores are scaled so that one unit represents 100 score points.

Estimates statistically significantly different from 0 (zero) at a 95% confidence level are highlighted in bold.

1. Macao-China, Mexico and New Zealand distributed, in the Educational Career questionnaire, the alternative question on whether students received a passing or failing mark. Results for these countries and economies are thus based on a dichotomous variable that does not capture the full variability of marks received by students. Estimates for these countries and economies are probably underestimated.

StatLink http://dx.doi.org/10.1787/888932734343

ORGANISATION FOR ECONOMIC CO-OPERATION AND DEVELOPMENT

The OECD is a unique forum where governments work together to address the economic, social and environmental challenges of globalisation. The OECD is also at the forefront of efforts to understand and to help governments respond to new developments and concerns, such as corporate governance, the information economy and the challenges of an ageing population. The Organisation provides a setting where governments can compare policy experiences, seek answers to common problems, identify good practice and work to co-ordinate domestic and international policies.

The OECD member countries are: Australia, Austria, Belgium, Canada, Chile, the Czech Republic, Denmark, Estonia, Finland, France, Germany, Greece, Hungary, Iceland, Ireland, Israel, Italy, Japan, Korea, Luxembourg, Mexico, the Netherlands, New Zealand, Norway, Poland, Portugal, the Slovak Republic, Slovenia, Spain, Sweden, Switzerland, Turkey, the United Kingdom and the United States. The European Commission takes part in the work of the OECD.

OECD Publishing disseminates widely the results of the Organisation's statistics gathering and research on economic, social and environmental issues, as well as the conventions, guidelines and standards agreed by its members.

OECD PUBLISHING, 2, rue André-Pascal, 75775 PARIS CEDEX 16
(98 2012 09 1P) ISBN 978-92-64-18750-4 – No. 60403 2012-04